Frommer's

Complete Hostel Vacation

Guide to

England, Wales & Scotland

Kristina Cordero

MACMILLAN • USA

About the Author

Kristina Cordero was born and raised in New York City. Before receiving her B.A. in Romance Languages from Harvard, she lived in Spain for a year and wrote for *Let's Go: Spain and Portugal* and *Let's Go: Europe*. Since then she has contributed to *Condé Nast Traveler*. She is also a literary translator; recently she completed the translation of a best-selling Chilean novel, to be published by St. Martin's in 1997. She is currently at work on her second translation. This is her first complete travel guide.

Macmillan Travel

A Simon & Schuster Macmillan Company
1633 Broadway
New York, NY 10019

Find us online at **http://www.mgr.com/travel** or on America Online at **Keyword: Frommer's**

ISBN 0-02-860701-5

Editors: Blythe Grossberg and Ron Boudreau
Design by Nick Anderson
Digital Cartography by Ortelius Design
Maps copyright © by Simon & Schuster, Inc.
Front cover photo: England's Lake District
Back cover photos: Kirkby Stephen, Yorkshire (top);
    Ambleside, the Lake District (bottom)

Special Sales

Bulk purchases (10+ copies) of Frommer's travel guides are available to corporations at special discounts. The Special Sales Department can produce custom editions to be used as premiums and/or for sales promotion to suit individual needs. Existing editions can be produced with custom cover imprints such as coprorate logos. For more information write to: Special Sales, Simon & Schuster, 1633 Broadway, New York, NY 10019.

Manufactured in the United States of America

CONTENTS

4   The Best Hostels in Wales 248

5   The Best Hostels in Scotland 281

LIST OF MAPS

Acknowledgments

Fond wishes and many thanks to Maggie and Tracey at HI, Sue at YHA, Carole and Bill at SYHA, and the Campbell brothers. Thanks also to my family and Jim. I also gratefully acknowledge the kind assistance of HI-AYH, Virgin Atlantic Airlines, BritRail Travel International, National Express, Global Village Communications, and the Chippewa Shoe Company.

Invitation to Readers

In researching this book, I've come across many fine establishments, the best of which I've included here. I'm sure that many of you will also come across recommendable hostels, restaurants, shops, and attractions. Please don't keep them to yourself. Share your experiences, especially if you want to comment on places that I've covered in this edition that have changed for the worse. You can address your letters to:

Kristina Cordero
Frommer's Complete Hostel Vacation Guide to England, Wales & Scotland
c/o Macmillan Travel
1633 Broadway
New York, NY 10019

A Disclaimer

Readers are advised that prices fluctuate in the course of time and travel information changes under the impact of the varied and volatile factors that affect the travel industry. The author and publisher cannot be held responsible for the experiences of readers while traveling. Readers are invited to write to the publisher with ideas, comments, and suggestions for future editions.

1 PLANNING A HOSTEL TRIP

This first-ever guide to hostels in England, Wales, and Scotland features inexpensive accommodations that range from a simple former flax mill tucked into England's South Downs to a £2 million converted warehouse on the quayside of Bristol's historic harbor. Some hostels have small rooms and special facilities that attract families; others have field-study rooms for school groups. Some are stocked with bar-hopping tips for 20-something rucksackers, while others are former shepherds' bothies on lonely footpaths. With candid advice about the best hostels in Britain, this guide is a versatile trip-planning tool to enable you to customize your own vacation using this wonderful network of safe, historic, and budget-priced accommodations.

The Birth of Hosteling

In 1909, a teacher named Richard Schirrman was working at a public school in a congested, smoky coal-mining region of Germany. Concerned about the health and welfare of his students, he began taking them on weekend field trips into the neighboring countryside, where the children could walk on forest footpaths, play in open fields, and experience the nature not found in their urban surroundings. School buildings, empty on weekends, were used for overnight accommodations. Schirrman's country field trips were the beginning of the grassroots Youth Hostel movement.

The nascent association grew more quickly than even its own members could have predicted, and word spread at an astonishing rate. The total number of hostels burgeoned to more than 2,000 in Germany and mushroomed in other European countries as well. Switzerland, Poland, the Netherlands, Britain, France, and Belgium quickly followed suit, adding more than 600 hostels to the fold and more than three million members by the end of the 1920s. In 1932, the International Youth Hostelling Federation (IYHF), a nonprofit organization, was christened at an informal hostelers' meeting in Amsterdam, and soon after satellite organizations were set up in the United States, Australia, and New Zealand.

Political tensions during World War II didn't dampen enthusiasm for hosteling. While some hostels were temporarily used by national governments for defense purposes, more than half continued to operate and almost all were reinstated when peace was reestablished.

When the war ended, the adolescent association came of age. The IYHF embraced a new generation of hostelers as legions of independent-minded, intrepid, and adventuresome young travelers caught on to the infectious spirit and began to use the Youth Hostels for a new purpose. Hostels slowly but surely became a mecca for solo travelers looking to bed down in a simple but comfortable and welcoming place where they could exchange information and friendly words

Hostels in England & Wales

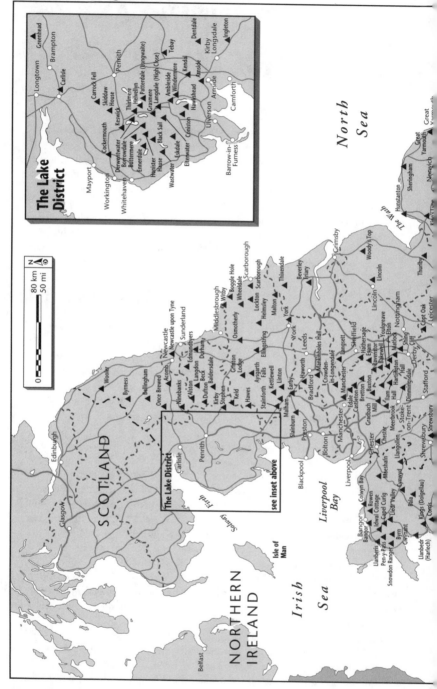

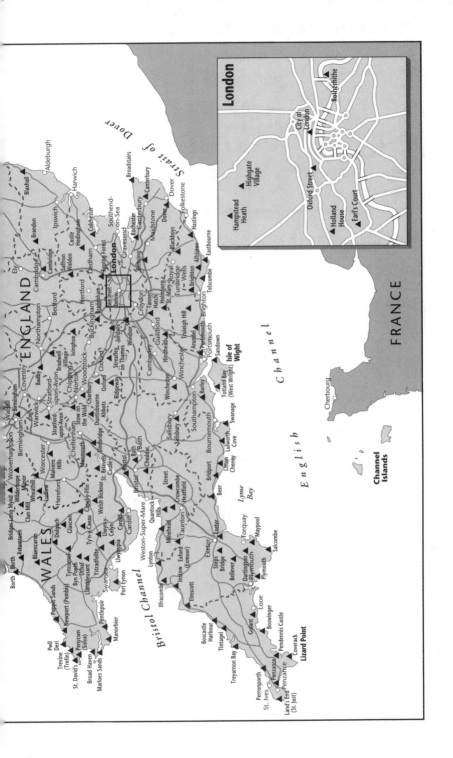

Hostels & Train Routes in Scotland

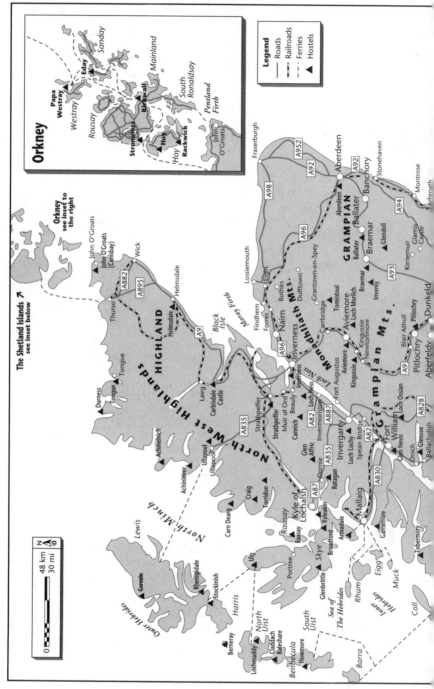

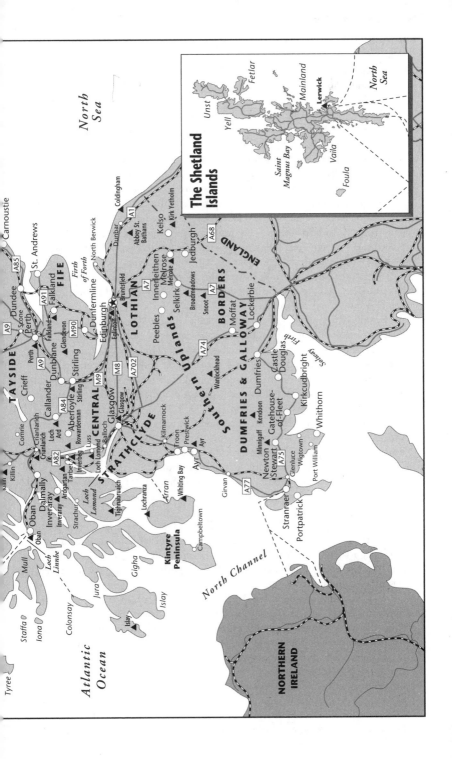

The Shetland Islands

North Sea

Unst
Fetlar
Yell
Mainland
Lerwick
Saint Magnus Bay
Vaila
Foula

North Sea

North Sea

Carnoustie
Dundee
St. Andrews
FIFE
Falkland
Firth of Forth
North Berwick
Dunfermline
Edinburgh
Coldingham
Dunbar
A1
Abbey St. Bathans
Kelso
Kirk Yetholm
Jedburgh
A68
ENGLAND
A85
A9
A9
TAYSIDE
Scone
Perth
Perth
Crieff
Comrie
Callander
Dunblane
Glendevon
M90
Stirling
Stirling
A91
Falkland
Dunblane
Aberfoyle
A84
Rowardennan
Balloch
Loch Ard
Crianlarich
Crianlarich
Killin
Killin
CENTRAL
Glasgow
M9
M8
A702
Bruntsfield
Edinburgh
LOTHIAN
A7
Innerleithen
Peebles
Melrose
Selkirk
Melrose
Broadmeadows
Snoot
BORDERS
Moffat
Lockerbie
A74
Southern Uplands
Wanlockhead
DUMFRIES & GALLOWAY
Dumfries
Castle Douglas
Kirkcudbright
Solway Firth
Whithorn
Kilmarnock
Troon
Prestwick
Ayr
Ayr
STRATHCLYDE
Loch Lomond
Luss
Inverbeg
Tarbet
A82
Ardgartan
Inveraray
Inveraray
Strachur
Dalmally
Oban
Oban
Loch Limnhe
Mull
Staffa
Iona
Colonsay
Jura
Islay
Islay
Gigha
Campbeltown
Kintyre Peninsula
Lochranza
Whiting Bay
Arran
Tighnabruaich
Girvan
A77
Newton Stewart
Minnigaff
Kirdoon
Glenluce
A75
Gatehouse-of-Fleet
Wigtown
Port William
Stranraer
Portpatrick
North Channel
NORTHERN IRELAND
Atlantic Ocean
Tyree

with fellow hostelers. The association responded, placing a premium on the specific needs of its members: shelter, safety, and fun—all at a reasonable price.

In the 1950s, the European and North American organizations grew by leaps and bounds and membership climbed to more than four million. A small collection of hostels began to flourish in Asia, Africa, and South America as more isolated communities struggled to find their way onto IYHF's international gazetteer. As student and youth travel grew in the 1960s and 1970s, the quality of the hostels dramatically improved and additional facilities were added. High standards of cleanliness and security were established, improving the overall quality of the hosteling experience. Today, Hostelling International (HI), as the IYHF is now known, has a membership of about four million hostelers throughout the world.

In Great Britain, hosteling has a special significance. The Youth Hostels Association in England and Wales (YHA) was established in 1930 with the following mission: "To help all, especially young people of limited means, to a greater knowledge, love and care of the countryside." The Scottish Youth Hostels Association (SYHA) began a year later, declaring that "young folks are not wealthy" and so "the surest, the safest, the most human and enjoyable mode of progression is on foot. On foot, and through the most delectable regions of our well-favoured country, they must be encouraged to wander at will."

Because of the hosteling association's origins in the 1930s as a student organization, millions of older folks in Britain have especially fond memories of these places. CEOs, doctors, writers, garbage collectors, lawyers, plumbers, and sculptors alike can remember the days when they went hosteling; the tradition is venerable in this part of the world. Veteran hostelers (and their numbers remain constant) still recall the days when cars were forbidden and beds were granted only to those whose feet were their only form of transportation.

Things have changed over the last 60-odd years. Hostelling International has expanded in order to keep up with its growing membership. As airfares, train tickets, and food prices have crept up, the YHA and SYHA have become a home away from home for a seemingly incongruous combination of travelers: solo backpackers from all over the world, young families driving around Britain and Continental Europe, long-distance cyclists, and long-distance walkers traversing Britain's ancient pathways—to name a few.

Both the England and Wales and the Scotland associations have managed to keep their rates down, and hostels are renovated and refurbished on a rotating schedule, providing comfortable, simple furnishings. Every so often, though, you can find a recently redecorated hostel that's surprisingly elegant and sometimes downright sumptuous.

With its centuries-old history, Britain has an abundance of historic buildings: mansions, country estates, farmhouses, water mills, vicarages, rectories, and castles. This rich architectural heritage has provided the hosteling association with some incredible properties. Some buildings are bequeathed, while others are bought after they have fallen into near-ruin from years of disuse. All are renovated to provide mostly dorm-style bedrooms with hall bathrooms, although sometimes you'll find a double or quad with a private bath. Some hostels offer meal service, and almost all have self-catering kitchens so you can cook your own meals.

Lots of longtime members continue to use hostels even though they could afford more luxurious accommodations. They keep coming back for the convivial, adventuresome, restless spirit that seems to pervade even the busiest, most impersonal city hostel. The hostels in relaxed countryside settings are renowned for their warmth and cozy atmosphere that goes along with the hiking boots, rucksacks, and water bottles that hostelers bring with them.

A gold mine for the budget traveler, British hostels are so much more than mere pound-stretchers. Of course you save tons of money by staying in Youth Hostels. But when you buy your HI card, you also open yourself up to a worldwide network of travel secrets, underground advice, hosteling discounts, and up-to-date news on must-see sights as well as forgettable tourist traps to avoid. And you don't need to wait in line at a tourist office or pay a travel agent to tell you about these things: If the info isn't prominently displayed at the hostel, your bunkmates are likely to clue you in. Of course, not every single hostel experience will bring this, but time and again the prevailing spirit is that of shared experiences among a global village of travelers.

Hostels shouldn't be confused with bed-and-breakfasts (B&Bs). Most hostels have large dorms (4 to 14 beds in a room), hall bathrooms, and certain guidelines hostelers must follow. To check in, you must be a card-carrying member of HI or pay a small surcharge that's applied toward membership. While all hostels provide sheets (free in England and Wales; 60p in Scotland) and most have a small shop selling groceries and toiletries, hostelers are expected to be somewhat self-sufficient. You'll be asked to clean up after yourself, make your own bed, pick up your garbage, and wipe the sink when you're done with the restroom.

All hostels listed in this book are staffed, but many are run single-handedly. They've abolished the chore that was formerly required before morning departure, but cleaning up after dinner or vacuuming the carpet is usually appreciated in the smaller countryside hostels. Many of the city hostels border on budget hotels and you won't be expected to do a thing. Filled with international travelers, urban hostels have lots of staffers on duty throughout the day, smaller rooms with daytime access, banks of lockers, currency exchanges, and tons of travel advice. The more rural hostels have less help, so they tend to be closed during the day and have curfews at night. Generally, though, countryside hostels tend to have a very individual character: You're likely to find home-baked bread, the manager's rock collection, or a pet cat along with larger dorms and more Spartan surroundings.

How This Book Is Organized

Because this is the first travel guide devoted exclusively to hosteling in Britain, the aim was to provide a wide breadth of hostels, all accessible to independent backpackers traveling by train, bus, bike, car, foot, or whatever means they can. The research here is entirely original: If I've said a hostel is up a hill, it's because I walked it. If I've said a hostel manager kicks you out at 9:30am sharp, it's because I was booted out along with the rest of the guests. If I think a hostel isn't really worth your time, I've said that too. The 80 hostels reviewed here were all chosen for some special reason: a luxuriously refurbished landmark building; a serene mountaintop, countryside, or waterfront setting; a traditional cottage, unchanged by the passage of time.

In the rest of this chapter I've given you a list of names, addresses, and phone numbers vital for planning a hosteling trip. There's a list of hosteling associations in different English-speaking countries, as well as regional offices throughout Britain. In addition, I've included a list of organizations and clubs that might be helpful as you plan your trip. Then you'll find a summary of the modes of travel available in Britain: buses, trains, ferries, bikes, ride shares, and feet.

Chapter 2 goes into more detail on the hosteling experience: You'll see how the hosteling association works in your own country and learn how to become a member. The international and local booking systems are explained. Then I've given a rundown of what you'll need to bring and the facilities you can expect to find at most hostels. A variety of basic topics are covered: prices, safety and security, hostel rules, meals at the hostels, advice for women and solo travelers, advice for hostelers with disabilities, hosteling with children, camping, and more.

The remainder of the book covers the hostels themselves. England, Wales, and Scotland have been split into distinct regions with an introduction to each region and a list of the hostels that fall within its boundaries. Each hostel has its own write-up, beginning with a short intro to the **nearest town or village,** including historic information along with news on what's been happening since the days of castles and cobblestones. Whether the destination is a mountain-climbers' mecca, an idyllic island getaway, or an urban wasteland, I've given my honest impression of the place. After that, I've supplied **hostel information:** From prices to room sizes to mealtimes to bathroom quality to lockers, I've tried to give you detailed practical information for each hostel, including information on how to arrive at the hostel, no matter how hidden it is. I have also tried to paint a brief portrait of each hostel's atmosphere. Is smoked mackerel on the breakfast menu? Does the staff offer white-water rafting instruction? Are medieval banquets held on Saturday nights? Do the managers wake hostelers up at the crack of dawn? Are archaeological discovery weekends offered? If a hostel provides some unusual, unexpected, newfangled (or old-world) service, it's listed here. And, surprisingly enough, almost every hostel has something that falls into this category, making each one idiosyncratic despite the common features of bed sheets, muesli, and map-clad walls.

Following the write-up of the hostel itself, you'll find a couple of nearby restaurants plus a grocery store listed in the **Cheap Eats Nearby** section. With the budget traveler in mind, I usually chose friendly cafes and restaurants, usually independently owned, as opposed to the ubiquitous Beefeater pub. Whenever possible, I followed suggestions from people I met along the way: hostel staffers, local bus drivers, fellow hostelers. The result is a mix of places: Mexican restaurants in Scotland, local mountain-climbers' hangouts in Snowdonia and the Lake District, a vegetarian nirvana in Glasgow, plus a (not-so) healthy selection of traditional pubs and restaurants. Atmosphere, value, and good food were my guidelines. Almost always, the whole foods/vegetarian crowd can find things to eat in these places.

Following this, the **Experiences** section gives you an idea of the activities in the closest town, village, and surrounding area, always with an eye for inspired ways to have fun without paying a fortune. This could mean walking the white cliffs of Dover, cycling through the sandstone villages of the Cotswolds, attending a cattle auction in the Yorkshire Dales, visiting a local artists' cooperative in Cardiff, going badger watching just outside Glasgow, or using Hadrian's Wall as a balance beam.

I've included countless other activities similar to these, but keep in mind that you're likely to hit upon some of your best experiences serendipitously in your own travels.

Every town, village, and city has a section called **The Basics,** where you'll find the name, address, phone number, hours, and directions of the nearest tourist office, post office, bank or currency-exchange center, and bike rental shop. The **Getting There** section gives you the lowdown on transportation, telling you whether trains, buses, cars, feet, or bikes are your best bet to arrive at the hostel and how to get transportation schedules by phone. Last, under **What's Next** you'll get an idea of the other nearby hostels and where you can venture next and how to get there. Lots of hostels in Britain are within miles of one another, and this section is where you can read about interhostel walking routes, many of which wind around hills, lakes, coasts, and mountains.

In the **Directory** of this book, you'll find a complete listing of all the hostels in England, Wales, and Scotland.

Budget Travel Organizations

There's an astonishing number of companies and organizations devoted to student, youth, and adventure travel concerns. They all publish information and claim to offer discount prices on plane tickets, special tour packages, and other special services. Some can be useful for planning your trip, some cannot. Most publish loads of freebie leaflets, magazines, and promotional material and can be a good source of information—whether or not you decide to use their products or services. It's always a good idea to stick with a reputable worldwide network that'll stand behind its products. Listed below are some of the best.

The **Council on International Educational Exchange (CIEE)** is a nonprofit organization bridging the fields of educational exchange and student travel. With secondary school, undergraduate, and graduate-level exchange and work exchange programs, they're one of the best sources for anyone looking to spend an extended period abroad. They also issue the International Student Identity Card (ISIC), the International Teacher Identity Card (ITIC), and the International Youth Card (IYC). Their travel subsidiaries, **Council Travel** and **Council Charter,** offer good discounts on international flights, railpasses, and travel insurance. In Canada, **Travel CUTS** serves the same purpose as Council Travel. **STA Travel** is also an international organization, but it's focused primarily on flights and tour packages, railpasses, identification cards, and other travel basics.

Council on International Educational Exchange (CIEE). Offices in New York and Paris: 205 E. 42 St., New York, N.Y., 10017. Tel: 212/661-1414. 49, rue Pierre Charron, 75008 Paris. Tel: 01/43 59 23 69.

Council Travel. Offices around the world, including New York, London, Paris, and other cities: 205 E. 42 St., New York, NY, 10017. Tel: 212/661-1450. 28a Poland St., London W1V 3DB, England. Tel: 0171/437 7767. 49, rue Pierre Charron, 75008 Paris. Tel: 01/45 63 19 87.

Council Charter. Offices in New York and Paris: 205 E. 42 St., New York, NY 10017. Tel: 212/661-1450 or 800/800-8222. 49, rue Pierre Charron, 75008 Paris. Tel: 01/43 59 23 69.

Travel CUTS. Offices in Toronto and London: 187 College St., Toronto, Ontario M5T 2Y1. Tel: 416/979-2406. Fax: 416/979-8167. 295A Regent St., London W1R 7YA. Tel: 0171/637 3161.

STA Travel. Offices in New York, Los Angeles, London, Auckland, Melbourne, and other cities worldwide: 48 E. 11 St., New York, NY 10003. Tel: 212/ 477-7166. 5900 Wilshire Blvd., Suite 2110, Los Angeles, CA 90036. Tel: 800/ 777-0112. 86 Old Brompton Rd., SW7 3LQ. Tel: 0171/937 9921. 10 High St., Auckland 1. Tel: 09/398-9995. 22 Faraday St., Melbourne, Victoria 3053. Tel: 03/349-2411.

BritRail International & BritRail Passes

Nonresidents of Britain are entitled to purchase a bevy of railpasses from British Rail's outpost, BritRail International. Offering a significant discount over point-to-point tickets, these passes come in a variety of denominations. If you've ever used an InterRail or a Eurailpass, you know the deal.

They come in two versions: the basic pass or the Flexipass. The standard BritRail pass gives you unlimited travel in England, Scotland, and Wales (not in Northern Ireland or the Republic of Ireland) over a fixed period of consecutive days. Passes are sold for eight days (adults $230; seniors $209; youths 16 to 25 $189); 15 days (adults $355; seniors $320; youths 16 to 25 $280); 22 days (adults $445; seniors $399; youths 16 to 25 $355); or a full month (adults $520; seniors $465; youths 16 to 25 $415).

These are a good bet if you'll be traveling to a new place every day. Otherwise, try the Flexipass. You get the flexibility of any four days of rail travel within one month (adults $195; seniors $175; youths 16 to 25 $160); any eight days within one month (adults $275; seniors $250; youths 16 to 25 $225); any 15 days within one month (adults $405; seniors $365). Those between 16 and 25 qualify for the Youth Flexipass, good for any 15 days within two months of rail travel ($319). All prices above are for standard-class travel. In 1996, BritRail plans to introduce the Youth Flexipass plus Eurostar, offering any four days within three months, plus a voucher for a single or return ticket on the Eurostar train that crosses the Channel Tunnel to Paris.

BritRail International also sells individual tickets for all British Rail train routes (including the Eurostar); an England and Wales Flexipass; a Freedom of Scotland pass; a ScotRail Rover; and a BritRail Drive pass that combines rail travel and car rental. If you plan on taking more than three train trips of considerable distance (London–Lake District; London–Edinburgh; London–York), the railpass is worth your while.

One nifty thing about BritRail is that you can purchase Channel Tunnel tickets before arriving in Britain. High-speed (up to 185 mph) trains go from London Waterloo to Paris, Calais (right on the Channel), Brussels, or Lille. The price list is divided into a mess of categories and classes, but for a standard-class single (one-way) ticket you can expect to pay $75 to $125 to Paris, $50 to $90 to Calais; $75 to $125 to Brussels; $65 to $105 to Lille. This goes for InterRail and Eurailpass holders, too: Nobody goes for free on this multimillion-dollar train—there may be a slight discount, but not much. BritRail also offers a BritFrance, a BritGerman, and a BritIreland pass.

The passes and the advance purchase of tickets comes in handy; it's just one less thing to shell out money for when you're on the road. This is an excellent option. Train tickets are pricey in Britain, so if you'll be doing a lot of point-to-point trips in areas covered by the British Rail routes, this is a very worthwhile investment. Be aware that BritRail tickets can only be purchased outside of Britain, so once you're over there, there's no turning back. In North America, BritRail's main office is in New York City; Canadian residents can call a toll-free number for information. In Australia and New Zealand, Thomas Cook Travel handles BritRail products.

BritRail. In North America: BritRail British Travel Shop. 551 Fifth Ave., New York, NY 10176. Tel: 212/575-2667. Toll-free numbers: in the United States, 800/677-8585; from Canada, 800/555-2748. Open Monday to Friday from 10am to 6pm. Phone orders accepted.

In Australia: Thomas Cook. Level 8, 321 Kent St., Sydney 2001, NSW Australia. Tel: 02/248 6100. Fax: 02/248 6200.

In New Zealand: Thomas Cook Holidays. 96–98 Anzac Ave., Freepost 262, P.O. Box 24, Auckland 1, New Zealand. Tel: 09/379 6800. Fax: 09/303 0266. Also, Eurolynx in Auckland reserves British Rail tours: 09/379 9716.

Other Travel-Related Organizations

The organizations, commissions, associations, and clubs below can be useful for hostelers by providing detailed information on the specific interests they represent. If you write in advance, they're likely to furnish you with pamphlets, leaflets, brochures, itineraries, and whatever else they publish for visitors.

The National Trust. 36 Queen Anne's Gate, London SW1H 9AS. Tel: 0171/222 9251. Fax: 0171/222 5096. In Scotland: The National Trust for Scotland. 5 Charlotte Square, Edinburgh EH2 4DU. Tel: 0131/226 5922. Fax: 0131/243 9501. A registered charity that oversees and maintains most of Britain's historic buildings, which includes castles, cathedrals, abbeys, stately mansions, and other buildings of historic interest. It also cares for and protects areas of natural beauty, footpaths, bridleways, and bicycle routes throughout Britain.

The Countryside Commission. John Dower House, Crescent Place, Cheltenham, Gloucester. Tel: 01242/521381. Fax: 01242/584270. Another public service organization, the Countryside Commission works on the preservation and maintenance of the 10 national parks in England and Wales, as well as the bikeways, footpaths, and bridleways that pass through them. Its charter, along with its pamphlet entitled *Out in the Country*, explain where you can go and what you can and cannot do in the English countryside. Write to The Countryside Commission Postal Sales, P.O. Box 124, Walgrave, Northampton NN6 9TL.

The Scottish Natural Heritage. 12 Hope Terrace, Edinburgh, EH9 2AS. Tel: 0131/447 4784. The Countryside Commission of Scotland, this organization designates nature reserves and national scenic areas. It also publishes a free informational leaflet on access to the Scottish countryside.

The Ramblers' Association. 1/5 Wandsworth Rd., London SW8 2XX. Tel: 0171/582 6878. Fax: 0171/587 3799. This fellowship of walkers has a huge membership and branches in many towns, cities, and villages. They're particularly concerned with walkers' rights and are devoted to keeping the country's many ancient

Train Routes in England & Wales

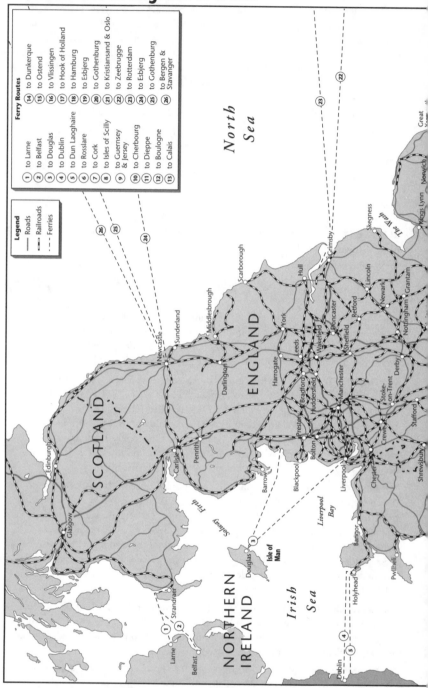

Legend
- Roads
- Railroads
- Ferries

Ferry Routes

1 to Larne
2 to Belfast
3 to Douglas
4 to Dublin
5 to Dun Laoghaire
6 to Rosslare
7 to Cork
8 to Isles of Scilly
9 to Guernsey & Jersey
10 to Cherbourg
11 to Dieppe
12 to Boulogne
13 to Calais
14 to Dunkerque
15 to Ostend
16 to Vlissingen
17 to Hook of Holland
18 to Hamburg
19 to Esbjerg
20 to Gothenburg
21 to Kristiansand & Oslo
22 to Zeebrugge
23 to Rotterdam
24 to Esbjerg
25 to Gothenburg
26 to Bergen & Stavanger

North Sea

Irish Sea

Liverpool Bay

Solway Firth

SCOTLAND

ENGLAND

NORTHERN IRELAND

Isle of Man

The Wash

Belfast
Larne
Strandraer
Glasgow
Edinburgh
Carlisle
Penrith
Newcastle
Sunderland
Middlesbrough
Darlington
Scarborough
Barrow
Blackpool
Douglas
Bangor
Pwllheli
Holyhead
Dublin
Preston
Bolton
Liverpool
Chester
Shrewsbury
Stafford
Crewe
Stoke-on-Trent
Manchester
Huddersfield
Bradford
Harrogate
Leeds
Wakefield
Sheffield
Doncaster
Retford
York
Hull
Grimsby
Skegness
Lincoln
Newark
Nottingham
Grantham
Derby
Kings Lynn
Norwich
Great

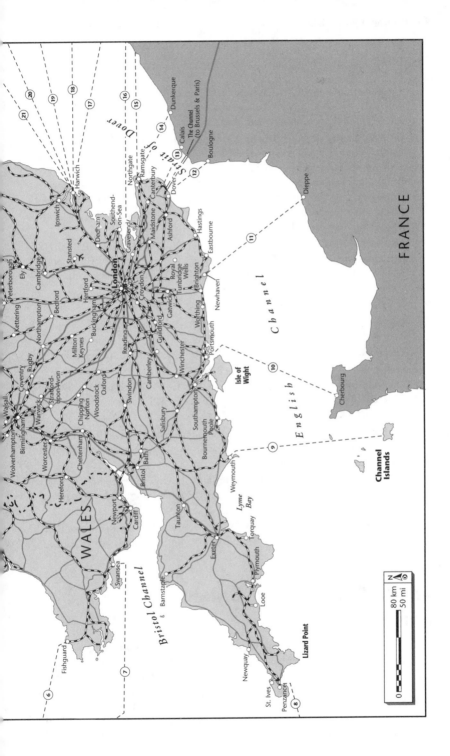

footpaths open to the public. They sponsor walks and are a good source of information on the laws governing rules, regulations, and rights of way pertaining to Ramblers.

The Forest Enterprise. 231 Corstorphine Rd., Edinburgh EH12 7AT. Tel: 0131/334 0303. Fax: 0131/334 3047. They oversee the forest land in England, Scotland, and Wales and sponsor walks, talks, and special events.

Cyclists' Touring Club. 69 Meadrow, Godalming, Surrey GU7 3HS. Tel: 01483/417217. Fax: 01483/426994. Britain's largest national bicycling association, this club promotes bicycling and the protection of cyclists' interests. It provides detailed information about bicycling routes and itineraries, a handbook listing repair shops all over the country, a bimonthly magazine, and a mail-order service for maps, books, clothing and bike equipment. Membership is £25 for adults and £12.50 for those under 18.

Ordnance Survey. Romsey Road, Southampton SO9 4DH. Tel: 01703/792912. The cartographer's choice of maps in England, Scotland, and Wales: No mountaineer, hill walker, or cyclist is without his or her Ordnance Survey maps, which come in varying degrees of magnification.

Postbus Guides. The Post Office. Old Street, 3rd Floor, London ECV 9PQ.

English Heritage. P.O. Box 1BB, London W1A 1BB. Tel: 0171/973 3400. Along with the National Trust, English Heritage preserves the castles, monuments, and historic buildings of England. It publishes lots of detailed informational leaflets, broken down by region, on the sites.

Historic Scotland. Longmore House, Salisbury Place, Edinburgh EH9 1SH. Tel: 0131/668 8800. Fax: 0131/668 6688. Same duties as Historic England, only in Scotland.

Scottish Sports Council. Caledonia House, South Gyle, Edinburgh EH12 9DG. Tel: 0131/317 7200. Fax: 0131/317 7202. This organization disseminates information on climbing in Scotland.

Trekking and Riding Society of Scotland. Boreland, Fearnan, Aberfeldy. PH15 2PG. Tel: 01887/830274. Fax: 01887/830606. Information for horseback riders.

Cadw: Welsh Historic Monuments. Brunel House, 2 Fitzalan Rd., Cardiff CF2 1UY. Tel: 01222/465511. Preserves historic monuments, castles, stately homes in Wales. Publications about historical sites available.

Getting Around Great Britain

BY TRAIN

The most hassle-free way to travel in England by far is with a **BritRail** pass. It must be purchased outside of Britain, so it's one more expense you need not worry about once here (see "BritRail International and BritRail Passes" earlier in this chapter). Passes are good in England, Scotland, and Wales but not in the Republic of Ireland or Northern Ireland. Be aware that Eurailpasses are not valid in Britain.

British Rail is the country's rail network, with regional train systems under the nationalized superstructure. Service varies slightly from region to region, and the most noticeable difference is the separate red-and-blue logo of independent-minded ScotRail. All regional trains link up at their junctures, and service is generally smooth and on time. The intercity routes tend to be the swiftest, linking major cities, and from there, branch lines cover almost the entire country.

Even if you don't have a railpass, there are a few discounts available—handy since British Rail isn't an inexpensive way to travel. Generally, you can expect train fares to be between 25% and 50% higher than coach fares. For £16, those between 16 and 23 (bring passport or birth certificate) can get a **Young Person's Railcard,** which offers up to 33% off standard-class train tickets and some good discounts on ferry rides. The only catch is that you can't travel before 10am. For information, go to any major British Rail station that has a British Rail Travel Centre. Senior citizens (60 and over) can purchase a **Senior Railcard,** which offers similar discounts.

In addition, many of Britain's regional train divisions offer some sort of discount ticket, which comes in handy if you'll be doing a lot of travel in one area. The **Network Card,** offered in 1995, cost £14 (Young Person's Railcard holders £10) and offered 33% off train routes in London, the Thames and Chiltern Valleys, East Anglia, and the Southeast. It was available for travelers of all ages, and the only caveat was that you had to travel after 10am on weekdays. It also included a £3 surcharge for upgrading to First Class. There is also a Cornish Rover, a Devon Rover, a Freedom of Southwest Rover (Southwest England and Wales), and a Severn, Avon, and Wessex Rover. It's always worthwhile to ask at the ticket window if there's a discount card on offer. The train can get expensive if you pay as you go.

In Scotland, you've got a choice of discount tickets. The **Freedom of Scotland Travelpass** gives you unlimited travel on all scheduled ScotRail and Strathclyde PTE trains, unlimited travel on the Glasgow Underground, and unlimited travel on Caledonian MacBrayne ferries on the Firth of Clyde (except Raasay and Scalpay). All other ferry routes (CalMac on the Kyles of Bute and smaller isles; P&O from Scrabster to Stromness and Aberdeen to Orkney; Stena Sealink from Stranraer to Larne) are available at a discount. It's sort of a BritRail pass for Scotland, but you don't have to buy it before you get here. It's offered in denominations of eight consecutive days (£99); 15 consecutive days (£139), and a Flexipass of any eight out of 15 consecutive days (£110). The **ScotRail Rover** gives you flexible travel on any of ScotRail's trains, except for Intercity lines and trains scheduled to arrive between 7 and 9:30am weekdays. It provides travel on any four out of eight consecutive days (£60) or 12 out of 15 consecutive days (£115), and they also offer a straight eight-day pass (£88). Regional rovers, including the **West Highland Rover** and the **North Highland Rover,** give you any four out of eight consecutive days of travel for £39. The **Festival Cities Rover** covers three out of seven consecutive days (£21). You can buy any of the Scottish travel passes at most staffed train stations and at British Rail Travel Centres in England and Wales as well.

In England, the only areas where train service is sketchy is in the Cotswolds, the north coasts of Devon and Cornwall, and certain parts of the Lake District. Mid Wales and the mountains of Snowdonia aren't easily reachable by train, either. In Scotland, the rail system covers most of the main tourist spots, with excellent service to Glasgow, the Strathclyde region, and the West Highlands. Trains also speed from London to Edinburgh and through the Grampians and Cairngorms in the northeast, heading up to Inverness. North of Inverness, there is one lone train line, which goes to Thurso and Wick, where ferries embark for Orkney and Shetland

Britain's Best Train Routes

Britain's railway heritage stretches from the days of steam trains, and there are some historic train routes that are arguably some of the loveliest you'll find anywhere. In Scotland, the **Highland Chieftain** goes from London to Edinburgh and Inverness, passing through the blue Cairngorm and Grampian mountain ranges. The **Royal Scotsman** on the West Highland route from Mallaig to Fort William passes by coastal lochs and winds around 3,000-foot hills as it works its way down Scotland's west coast.

In England, the Settle-Carlisle train line chugs its way up the Yorkshire Dales, passing through viaducts and valleys to the hilltop station of Dent, which, at 1,150 feet above sea level, is the station with the highest altitude in all Britain. The route that heads out from Shrewsbury in the Welsh Borders to Aberystwyth on the coast is another gem, passing through thousands of acres of nature reserves, where wildfowl, birds, and peat bogs coexist in the misty marshland.

Islands. To the northwest, you're on your own. If you have one place to rent a car, the far north of Scotland is where you'd want to do it; public transportation is close to nonexistent.

BY COACH/BUS

In Britain, long-distance buses are referred to as coaches, while local services are called buses. Coach and bus transportation come in a variety of packages. The first and most logical is Britain's largest national bus company, **National Express/Scottish Citylink.** Providing service to all major cities in England, Scotland, and Wales, it also offers connections to small towns via local carriers. It's efficient and as timely as traffic allows, and coaches are usually spanking clean and comfortable. For those traveling from the Continent, National Express links up with Eurolines buses to Paris, Amsterdam, and other major cities, and there is good shuttle service to and from most airports and ferry terminals. Ticket prices are usually about 25% to 50% less than the corresponding train fares, and often coaches and buses go where trains don't, whereas the reverse isn't as likely.

National Express also offers travel passes. The **Tourist Trail Pass** resembles a BritRail Flexipass: It gives you any five days of unlimited travel within a fixed period of 10 consecutive days (£79; £65 for students, youths, and seniors); eight days within a 16-day period (£119; £95 for students, youths, and seniors); or 15 days within a 30-day period (£179; £145 for students, youths, and seniors). The **Young Person's Coachcard** guarantees you a 30% discount on coach fares and is available to those between 16 and 25. Senior citizens can get the same deal with the **Senior Coachcard,** and students get the **Student Coachcard.** The cost is £7—a good value if you're using coaches a lot.

The second form of bus travel is via local buses. Britain is divided up regionally, and within each region, there is usually some sort of local bus operator that links up at major cities or transportation hubs to take you out to smaller towns and villages. If you're traveling short distances within one region, you'll probably use these services. **Stagecoach** is one coach company that generally covers all the regional routes that National Express doesn't. The South Coast of England and the Lake District are especially well connected by the comfortable, reliable Stagecoaches, and every bus route has its own nickname. Even if you're using trains as your main source of transportation, you'll probably end up taking at least a few buses, since hostels can be somewhat removed from major transport links.

Many of these local bus services (there are too many to mention here; see "Getting There," under each hostel entry in later chapters) offer **Rover** or **Explorer** tickets, which are good for unlimited travel within a fixed period of time. For example, Stagecoach offers a Rover ticket covering all Lake District bus routes (day Rover £5.50; week Rover £13.80), South Coast bus routes, and much more. Although it travels all over the country, Stagecoach is decentralized, so you'll find out about these fares and passes when you arrive in the area.

In Scotland, **Lowland Omnibus** offers day and weeklong Rover passes for the Borders and Dumfries and Galloway regions. In Wales, bus service is dominated by **Crosville Cymru,** which operates the main TrawsCambria service from Cardiff up the west coast to Aberystwyth and Caernarfon and on to Bangor. Once you get up into Snowdonia, there is a pretty comprehensive network of independent bus operators, but service is woefully skimpy to the tinier mountaintop and lakeside villages. Some buses will drop you off right at the Youth Hostels. The local county council in Gwynedd (where Snowdonia is located) offers a daylong Red Rover ticket for £4 (children £2), available on the buses. The Rover tickets listed here are only a sampling; always ask around.

If you're stuck in an unfamiliar rural town or village and there doesn't seem to be any regular bus service (not uncommon in the Yorkshire Dales and Moors and some parts of the Peak District), you might luck out at around three or four in the afternoon, when **school buses** carry kids home to their mums and dads. Fares are usually cheap and drivers tend to be sympathetic and helpful (friendly, polite) to backpackers.

Getting hold of bus timetables can be difficult sometimes, though: Some towns and villages don't have central bus stations. When that's the case, the train station (if there is one) doubles as a bus info center, or else head for the tourist office. Sometimes the local post office or cafe next door to the bus stop distributes bus information. In the "Getting There" section under each hostel entry, you'll find this info for the hostel/town, as well as phone numbers for local bus operators.

When there's no National Express stop in sight, you've missed the last school bus, and the closest train station is 20 miles away, you'll probably be seeing red. The hallmark of mail delivery in Britain are the red-and-yellow **Postbuses** that also carry fare-paying passengers to remote towns all over England, Wales, and Scotland. Service comes usually once or twice a day and only to specific regions, but these buses are the backpacker's equivalent of striking gold. If there is any postbus service in a specific area, the hostel will likely list it on it's transportation bulletin board. Otherwise, just ask at the nearest pub, grocery store, or (obviously) post office.

The last form of bus transportation is a little different and a definite favorite among hostelers. Saving you the hassle of schlepping your rucksack from train and bus stations out to hostels (which can be a trek), the **Slow Coach** offers door-to-door bus service on a circuit of Youth Hostels. For £89, you get a one-way circuit starting at the Earl's Court Youth Hostel in London and going on to Windsor,

Bath, Stratford-upon-Avon, The Lake District (Ambleside), Edinburgh, York, Cambridge, and ending back in London. There's no time limit on the ticket, so you can stay as long as you please at each stop. Since they don't operate a daily bus schedule, you have to make sure you have enough time to see what you want to see and still coincide with the arrival and departure times of their service. They advise passengers on vacancies at hostels, too. The Slow Coach Edinburgh stop links up with the **Go Blue Banana** bus tour of Scotland.

Haggis Backpackers, run by the Brothers Campbell (Alastair, Neil, and Donald), seems to have cornered the hosteling market in Scotland with their jump-on, jump-off hostel-to-hostel circuit, which begins and ends in Edinburgh. The Campbells are Scotsmen who know their territory. The bus ride is usually accompanied by music, tea and coffee (free), candy bars (on the honor code), book exchange, and loads of travel advice. The drivers (usually one of the brothers or one of their friends recruited for the job) always opt for back roads whenever possible and know loads of Scottish history to boot. This is the most popular, easiest, and probably the most entertaining way to hostel through Scotland. It's a relaxed crowd, and they often are cheerfully behind schedule. They offer six-days-a-week service to the hostels on their route. For £65, you get a one-way circuit starting in Edinburgh (they stop at both hostels), Perth, Pitlochry, Aviemore, Inverness, Loch Ness, Kyleakin (Skye), Oban, Glen Nevis, Glencoe, Inveraray, Loch Lomond, Glasgow, and Edinburgh. Haggis also has a backpackers' center in Edinburgh with hosteling and good insider travel info, and they'll reserve overnights for you at the hostels. They also operate a currency-exchange service, sell ferry tickets (P&O, Stena Sealink), and can organize discount car rental. And they sell discounted tickets for Guide Friday bus tours of Edinburgh (£4.50 instead of the usual £6) and organize walking tours of Edinburgh. For those headed to Ireland, they sell tickets for backpackers' tours of Ireland as well.

The options for bus travel are plentiful in Britain. Generally speaking, the fare is cheaper, the ride is longer, and the leg room limited. Buses do save you lots of money, though, and can be something of an adventure.

National Express. Victoria Coach Station, 164 Buckingham Palace Rd., London SW1W 0SH. Tel: 0171/730 0202.

Scottish Citylink Coaches/National Express. St. Andrew Square Bus Station, Edinburgh EH1 3DU. Tel: 0131/557 5717. Also at Buchanan Street Bus Station, Killermont Street, Glasgow G2 3NP. Tel: 0141/332 9191.

Crosville Cymru. Cardiff Bus Station, Wood Street, Cardiff. Tel: 01222/398700 or 01222/371331. In Aberystwyth tel: 01970/617951. In Bangor tel: 01248/370295.

Bus Gwynedd. Gwynedd County Council, County Offices, Caernarfon, Gwynedd LL55 1SH. Central Information Line: 01286/679535. Bus Gwynedd publishes a very useful detailed map of all bus services in Snowdonia, with an exhaustive listing of timetables.

Royal Mail Postbus Guides. The Post Office, 3rd Floor, London ECV 9PQ. Royal Mail Public Relations Unit, West Port House, 102 West Port, Edinburgh EH3 9HS. Tel: 0131/228 7407.

The Slow Coach. Earl's Court Youth Hostel, 38 Bolton Gardens, Earl's Court, London SW5 0AQ. Tel: 0171/373 7083. Ask about their routes through Ireland, the West Country, and Scotland.

Haggis Backpackers. The Backpackers Centre. 7–9 Blackfriars St., Edinburgh EH1 1NB. Tel: 0131/557 9393. Fax: 0131/558 1177. Open daily 9am–7pm. Buses leave Edinburgh at 8am. Credit cards: VA, MC, Access. Scotland circuit £65.

BY FERRY

For those traveling to Ireland, around the western isles of Scotland, or to the Isle of Man, there are a few major ferry companies that can get you where you want to go. From Wales to Ireland, there are two companies: B&I Ferries and Stena Sealink. **B&I** runs from Pembroke Dock, South Wales, to Rosslare, Ireland (two per day; three hours; adults £20, children £20, cars £199). **Stena Sealink** runs from Fishguard Harbour, South Wales, to Rosslare, Ireland (two per day; 3¹/₂ hours; adults £20, children under 15 £9, cars £104). From the tip of North Wales, you can catch B&I ferries going from Holyhead to Dublin (two per day; four hours; £25) or Stena Sealink to Dun Laoghaire (April to December only; four per day; four hours; £19 to £26). From lonely Stranraer, Scotland, Stena Sealink runs boats out to Larne, Northern Ireland (eight per day; 2¹/₂ hours; £20). **Seacat** runs to Belfast (four per day; 1¹/₂ hours; £20 to £22) in Northern Ireland.

Ferries out to the Isle of Man travel from Ardrossan Harbour, Scotland, via **Caledonian MacBrayne's** seven-hour ride across the Irish Sea (May to September only; one per day; passengers £28, cars £65 to £87; dogs £4). Otherwise, the **Isle of Man Steam Packet Company** operates between Liverpool, England, and Douglas.

For travel around Scotland, Caledonian MacBrayne covers 23 of Scotland's Western Isles. Harris, Lewis, North Uist, South Uist, Skye, Tiree, Mull, Islay, Arran, and other small islands are reachable from a lineup of ferry ports on Scotland's Western Coast: Ullapool, Kyle of Lochalsh, Armadale, Mallaig, Oban, Kennacraig, Ardrossan, and others. All ferry ports are well equipped with ticket windows and helpful information desks.

For those doing island hopping, Caledonian MacBrayne offers a few special tickets: the **Island Hopscotch** gives a discount for cars and passengers on a number of predesignated ferry routes and are good for three months. **Island Rovers** offer 8- and 15-day tickets for rides on almost all their ferry routes, except those to the smaller islands. **Western Ferries** operate between Islay and Jura. In the north of Scotland, P&O Ferries sail from Thurso and Aberdeen, to Orkney and Shetland, and **Thomas and Bews** operate a passenger service between John O'Groats and Burwick (Orkney).

B&I Ferries. In London, call 0171/734 4681. For advance bookings, go to 16 Westmoreland St., Dublin 2. Tel: 01/679 7977.

Stena Sealink. 12 Westmoreland St., Dublin 2. Tel: 353/1 280 8844. In Holyhead: 01407/766765. In Stranraer: 01776/702262.

Seacat Hoverspeed. Stranraer, Scotland. Tel: 01766/702255.

Isle of Man Steam Packet Company. Douglas, Isle of Man. Tel: 01624/661661.

Caledonian MacBrayne Ferries. Head Office: The Ferry Terminal, Gourock PA19 1QP. Tel: 01475/650100. Fax: 01475/637607. General inquiries: 01475/650100. Car Ferry reservations: 01475/650000.

Western Ferries. Head Office: 16 Woodside Crescent, Glasgow G3 7UT. Tel: 0141/332 9766. Fax: 0141/332 0267.

P&O Scottish Ferries. P.O. Box 5, Jamieson's Quay, Aberdeen AB9 8DL. Tel: 01224/572615. Fax: 01244/574411.

BY CAR

If you have the foresight to book ahead or the money once you get there, traveling around Britain by car can be a lot of fun, especially for Americans and Canadians who've mastered the left-side-of-the-road thing. By far, the best idea is to organize a rental back home; once you get over here, the rates skyrocket. From home, you can get a two-week deal for what would cover three days if you were to pay on the spot. Britain's got **Hertz, Avis, Budget, Europcar** (known as National Car Rental in the United States and Canada), and other car rental (or "hire" in Britain) agencies. Most can be found in major cities, usually located near the railway and bus stations. Some agencies have a "one-way" option, allowing you to rent at one office and drop off at another. If you're making arrangements in advance, give Budget a try: Their bottom-of-the-line Ford Fiestas and Vauxhall Corsas are shiny and new, and they have offices as far north as Inverness in Scotland.

The rules vary from agency to agency, but most have a lower age limit of 25. Budget and Avis will rent to those over 21, as always, with a major credit card. There is also an upper limit, usually 70 to 75 years old. Some car rental agencies have vehicles for drivers with disabilities; call ahead to check. For all drivers, vehicle rental companies require a current driving license. Unless you plan on using a car for more than three months, a license from your own country (with an English translation if in a foreign language) should be fine. If you'll be driving for more than three months at a time, it's a good idea to get an **International Driving Permit (IDP)** before you leave home. In the United States, you must be over 18 and have had a valid license for at least one year. Any branch of the **American Automobile Association (AAA)** can issue one to you. Their main office is AAA Florida, Travel Agency Services Department, 1000 AAA Dr., Heathrow, FL 32746-5080. Tel: 407/444-4245 or 800/222-4357. Fax: 407/444-7823. In Canada, the **Canadian Automobile Association (CAA)** issues the IDP: CAA Toronto, 60 Commerce Valley Dr. East, Thornhill, Ontario L3T 7P9. Tel: 905/771-3000. Fax: 905/771-3046. Be sure to bring both your license and the IDP with you when you travel.

The major disadvantage of driving in Britain is that gas/diesel/petrol costs a fortune (up to £2.50 per gallon), so don't forget to factor that into your price. Other than that, it can be fun. Americans and Canadians and Western Europeans should watch out: It takes at least a couple of days to get used to the driving on the left-hand side of the road, and roundabouts (rotaries) can be deadly.

England and Wales are set up with **motorways** ("M" roads), **dual carriageways** ("A" roads), and a network of single carriageways and secondary roads. Motorway interchanges and road junctions usually converge upon a roundabout (rotary), which can be difficult for inexperienced drivers. Cars and trucks barrel around them, so be sure to give way to traffic on the right. In the north of Scotland, single-track roads dominate the roadscape: When you see a car coming, pull over into the next passing place (on the left), and wait. Always pass on the right. Speed limits are 70mph (112km/h) for motorways and dual carriageways; 60mph (96km/h) for single carriageways; and 30mph (48km/h) for busy, built-up areas. On the motorway, there is always a hard shoulder where you can stop your car, and emergency phone boxes are spread out along the motorway.

Alamo Rent A Car. 7–23 Bryanston St., London W1. (Tube: Marble Arch). Tel: 0171/408 1255. Also at Heathrow Airport, terminals 1, 2, 3, 4. Tel: 0181/759 6200. United Kingdom and European reservations tel: 0800/272300. Branches in Bristol, Cardiff, Edinburgh, Manchester, and Newcastle. Vauxhall Corsa £39 per day.

Avis. 8 Balderton St., London W1. (Tube: Bond Street). Tel: 0171/917 6700. In the United States and Canada: 800/331-2112. Central reservations United Kingdom and worldwide: 0181/848 8733. Fax: 0181/561 2275.

Budget Rent-a-Car. 89 Wigmore St., London W1. (Tube: Marble Arch). Tel: 0171/723 8038. In the United States and Canada, call: 800/472-3325. Ford fiesta £35 per day, including insurance.

Hertz. 35 Edgware Rd., London W1. (Tube: Marble Arch). Tel: 0171/402 4242. At Edinburgh Waverley rail station. Tel: 0131/557 5272. At Glasgow rail station: 0141/248 7736. In the United States and Canada, call 800/654-3001.

BY RIDE SHARING

Freewheelers is an agency that links up drivers with passengers and provides a safe alternative to hitchhiking. A membership fee is charged (£5 per passenger), and for each matchup it costs an additional £1. A security system ensures the identities of drivers and passengers, but ultimately you are responsible for your own safety. Freewheelers isn't liable and doesn't run background checks on members, so beware. They suggest you contribute 5p per mile, but the driver and passenger are free to haggle it out. Freewheelers is at 25 Low Friar St., Newcastle-upon-Tyne, NE1 5UE. Tel: 0191/222 0900.

BY BIKE

Almost every hostel sees at least a few exhausted cyclists stagger in just before dinnertime, especially in the spring and summer. Britain is known for its long-distance bike routes, which run from 50 to 350 miles long. It's a great way to see the countryside but can also be exhausting, since there are so many hills and valleys dotted throughout the land. Before you come, it's wise to make sure you've got the energy to do it and the strength to tote your luggage along with you on the road.

A good place to start is **Mountaineers Books,** 1011 Klickitat Way, Suite 107, Seattle, WA 98134. Tel: 800/553-4453. It publishes a series of books with detailed bike tours, which can be useful. Also, the British Tourist Authority publishes loads of booklets, pamphlets, and leaflets on biking. Its *Britain: Cycling* guide covers just about everything: laws regarding cycling; national cycling clubs in Britain; repair shops; bike rental; tour operators that offer bike tours of Britain; and mountain biking in Britain.

Before you travel, it's a good idea to contact the **Cyclists' Touring Club.** It's Britain's largest national cycling network, with branches all over the country; it's the best organization to turn to with questions and requests for information. It can be found at 69 Meadrow, Godalming, Surrey GU7 3HS. Tel: 01483/417217. Fax 01483/426994.

If you're thinking of bringing your bike with you, think twice. Lots of airlines charge extra to tote a bike if you exceed the space limit (usually 62 inches for luggage), and it may be cheaper to buy a bike in Britain and either resell it there or bring it home to resell. If you leave Britain with a new bike, you'll be charged a tax; used bikes are not charged. Whatever you buy, make sure your bike meets the requirements of British laws. All bikes must have efficient brakes, and if you plan to do any nighttime riding, your bike must have front and rear lights and a rear reflector (no flashing lights). Cyclists must not stop their bikes at pedestrian crossings and may not ride on sidewalks. If you follow the same rules as drivers, you'll be safe. Helmets are not required by law, but long-distance cyclists generally wear them.

If you plan on taking your bike on a train, contact the nearest **British Rail** station first. Most trains accommodate bikes but some have very limited space, so companions often can't travel together. Some train routes require a reservation and charge a small fee. As British Rail may become privatized in the coming years, the rules and regulations may change, so call ahead.

Different types of roads and tracks offer different biking conditions. On the main roads where traffic is heavy, biking can be difficult. You aren't allowed to cycle on motorways (such as M1 or M6), and cyclists are told to avoid the main trunk roads between cities, especially in the high season. These roads are indicated by a "(T)" following the road name. For example, A1 (T). Generally, "A" roads don't have bike paths or a hard shoulder, and maps don't indicate this. Whenever possible, always avoid them if there is an alternative. "B" roads link smaller towns. They are generally less busy and offer some nice bicycling. Roads with four digits (such as B3153) tend to be even quieter and better for cyclists. However, a lot of this is trial and error. If there's only an "A" road linking two places, you don't have much of a choice, and in more rural areas, "A" roads may be quite tranquil and good for biking.

Unclassified roads (without numbers) are really the best for biking: They tend to be narrow, winding, and little used by motorists. This is where you're likely to stumble upon flower beds, farmlands, and lost villages. Off-road biking can be even better. In Britain, cyclists are allowed onto tracks and "unmade roads," which are Public Rights of Way. "Byways open to all traffic" ("boats") and "Roads used as public paths" ("rupps") are also fair game. Cyclists are also permitted on bridleways but must give way to those on foot and on horseback. Footpaths are not accessible to cyclists; look for a circular white sign with a red border and black bike symbol inside, which means no bikes.

In Scotland, the access rules are slightly more complex and maps show no distinction between public and private footpaths. Generally speaking, many of the tracks and paths used by walkers and drivers are open to cyclists. Inquire locally. Remember that track conditions vary wildly in Britain; a squiggly line on a map could be a newly paved road or a muddy, mucky trail of mush, and the weather will often determine the road quality.

There are lots of **National Trails** in Britain, most of which, unfortunately, are open to bicyclists only within specific sections. Only the South Downs Way is open to cyclists for its entire 106-mile stretch from Eastbourne to Winchester. The North Downs Way (in Kent and Surrey), the Ridgeway Path (Buckinghamshire/Wiltshire), Offa's Dyke Path (Welsh Borders), and the West Highland Way

(Scotland) are examples of paths only partially open to cyclists. An increasing number of disused railway lines are being converted into bike paths and offer flat, easy rides. The Tissington and High Peak Trails (Derbyshire) and the Downs Link (Surrey and Sussex) are just a few. Many canal towpaths are also open to bicyclists. The Grand Union Canal (London to Birmingham) and parts of the Kennet and Avon Canal (Reading to Bristol) are good ones. The **Forest Enterprise** welcomes cyclists on many paths, as well. The official long-distance bike routes include the Taff Trail (Cardiff to Brecon in South Wales); the Scottish Border Trail; the Glasgow to Loch Lomond route; the Sea to Sea from Whitehaven in Cumbria to Newcastle-upon-Tyne.

Before you hit the road, make sure you've got all your gear in order. **Ordnance Survey** maps are de rigueur for serious cyclists. Their OS Travelmaster (1:250,000 scale; 1 in. = 4 mi./1cm = $2^1/_2$km) shows all roads, except for a few tiny country lanes. They're good for those on a lengthy tour (Land's End-John O'Groats, for example) who don't want to be loaded with local maps. The OS Landranger series (1:50,000 scale; $1^1/_4$in. = 1 mi./2cm = 1km) cover about 25 miles (40km) per map, and there are 204 in all. These maps show all roads plus public rights of way, such as bridleways that may be used by cyclists. These maps are better for exploring one specific area in depth. The next series, the OS Pathfinder and Outdoor Leisure (1:25,000 scale; $2^1/_2$ in. = 1 mi./4cm = 1km) are really for walkers. Other necessary equipment includes logical stuff: nonequestrian panniers, a strong U-lock, and a very good waterproof poncho. Always label your bike before setting out, and make sure your water bottle is full up.

ON FOOT

There's a huge network of ancient footpaths throughout England. **National Trails,** waymarked by an easy-to-recognize acorn symbol, comprise ancient trackways, public walkways, farm paths, and bridleways. You can follow in the footsteps of the Roman legions in Northumbria, walk through the moorlands that inspired *Lorna Doone*, or re-create the mystery in the bleak moorlands of the Brontë novels. The routes can be split up into manageable, walkable sections, and many hostels lurk nearby, so it's possible to link up your walking routes with hostels that lie on or near these footpaths.

The rules in the British countryside are no surprise. The **Countryside Commission,** the **National Trust,** the **Forestry Commission,** and other outdoor concerns take special care of their land and ask all walkers to respect that. Many of these ancient footpaths traverse farms, estates, and other private property. Because of the historic nature of these footpaths, walkers are allowed on them, as long as they stick to a few simple rules. The main one is that if a public footpath crosses through private property, walkers may not deviate from the footpath and must leave livestock, farm machinery, and crops alone. Many of the trails are bounded by walls and hedges, and walkers should use the gates and stiles provided to cross them. You are asked to close all gates and farm doors behind you, pick up all litter, and do all the other things you learned in kindergarten. These simple rules are taken seriously, and most walkers abide by them, making for a relatively peaceful coexistence between ramblers and property owners.

Before setting out, you'll want to invest in a good pair of lightweight hiking boots, a canteen, and a hat. The sun does come out, and it can be murder on

Take a Hike!

Many of England's official and unofficial National Trails have at least a few Youth Hostels along the way. The **North Downs Way** covers 153 miles, passing by much of the ancient pilgrims' route from Winchester to Canterbury. The **South Downs Way** passes right near the hostels at Eastbourne, Alfriston, Brighton, Arundel. The 598-mile **South West Coast Path** goes through Dorset, Devon, Cornwall, and Somerset, passing by hostels at Exeter, Plymouth, Falmouth (Pendennis Castle), Land's End, Ilfracombe, Lynton, and Minehead.

To the north, the 81-mile-long **Dales Way** runs from the Yorkshire Dales to Lake Windermere in the Lake District. The **Herriot Way** is another footpath that works its way through the Yorkshire Dales, linked up by the Youth Hostels in Wensleydale and Swaledale. The **Pennine Way**, one of England's oldest paths, begins in the Peak District town of Edale and works its way 256 miles north to the most remote part of upland Britain in Northumberland. Passing by the hostels at Haworth, Stainforth, Hawes, Keld, Langdon Beck, Once Brewed, it finishes off at Kirk Yetholm in Scotland. The **Coast-to-Coast Path** is another popular one in England, starting out in St. Bee's Head in Cumbria, passing through three national parks (Lake District, North York Moors, and Yorkshire Dales), countless Youth Hostels, and ending up in Robin Hood's Bay just north of Scarborough and Whitby on England's northeast coast.

In Wales, **Offa's Dyke Path** is a 177-mile route following the English/Welsh border from Chepstow (near St. Briavel's Castle) to the Wye Valley (near Welsh Bicknor hostel), the Shropshire Hills, and ending on the North Wales coast at Prestatyn. Other walks abound all over Snowdonia in North Wales.

In Scotland, there are loads of minor footpaths, but the big three are the **Southern Upland Way**, the **West Highland Way**, and the **Speyside Way**. The Southern Upland Way, 212 miles long, is also known as the Scottish Coast to Coast, starting out in Portpatrick, near Stranraer on Scotland's west coast and working through the hilly Borderlands to its finale at Cockburnspath on the east coast. The West Highland Way, beginning in Glasgow, is a 95-mile extravaganza of lochs, forests, and mountains. The highest peak in Britain, Ben Nevis, is right on this route, as are a number of hostels, including Loch Lomond, Rowardennan, Crianlarich, and Glen Nevis. Finally, the Speyside Way tackles the east of Scotland, heading north from Aviemore through the Cairngorms and up the Moray Firth.

Almost anybody can manage at least a couple of miles of these footpaths: they come in all shapes, sizes, and levels, for serious hikers and Sunday strollers alike. The British Tourist Authority publishes a map/leaflet entitled *Britain for Walkers*, which is useful in figuring out which routes you want to attempt.

walkers, especially on a hot day. Make sure you can sustain your backpack for the intended length of your walk; there's nothing worse than stopping midway on a rocky, desolate footpath and realizing you can't make it the whole way across. Arm yourself with an **Ordnance Survey** Pathfinder or Outdoor Leisure map (1:25,000 scale; $2^1/_2$ in. = 1 mi./4cm = 1km). The Pathfinder maps cover an area of about $12^1/_2$ miles (20km) by 6 miles (10km), and the Outdoor Leisure maps cover about 17 miles (27km) by 12 miles (19km).

2

THE HOSTELING EXPERIENCE

Becoming a Member of Hostelling International (HI)

Hostelling **International (HI), formerly the**
International Youth Hostel Federation (IYHF), serves as the umbrella organization for the national hosteling associations in over 70 countries. It has around four million members and about 5,000 hostels worldwide comprising a constantly growing network. Once you get an HI card from your home country, you'll have access to all HI hostels around the world. It's always a good idea to join HI before you start traveling to take advantage of the particular offerings of your own country's national hosteling association.

To become a member, contact the national association in your home country or the regional association nearest you (see below). Membership is valid for one year from the date of purchase, and your membership fee gets you a Hostelling International ID card, an international hosteling map, a semiannual newsletter (if your country has one), plus discount vouchers, promotional offers, and general budget travel/hosteling information. Make sure you apply for a card at least eight weeks before your departure to allow time for processing and mailing.

If you arrive in Britain without an HI card, you can become a "guest member" by paying an extra £1.50 per night for your first six nights. This way, you're effectively paying the same £9 British residents pay to become members, only in installments, which gives you the flexibility of sampling the hostels before you decide to become a full member. The disadvantage, though, is that you won't get on the mailing list of your home country's association and won't receive your national newsletter, promotions, discount vouchers, and other goodies that come with membership.

When you become a member in your own country, you'll have access to HI's International Booking Network (IBN), which allows you to book your bed up to six months in advance by giving a credit card number (Visa, MasterCard) over the phone. Payment is made in full in your own currency and in your own language; prices are based on the U.S. dollar. The IBN service usually carries a booking fee that varies from country to country. Cancellations made at least three days in advance are refundable, minus a nominal cancellation fee.

Generally, you'll need to present a receipt or voucher for confirmation when you arrive at the hostel, so unless you have access to a fax these reservations should be made well in advance to allow time for mailing the receipt. Most hostel associations recommend that hostelers make IBN reservations in person. Selected hostels are on the system, and by doing it in person you can pay by cash, check, or credit card and walk out with a hostel reservation and receipt in hand for presentation once you arrive in Britain.

Once you're in Britain, you don't need to use IBN. Within England and Wales, the Book-a-Bed-Ahead (BABA) system is used, and in Scotland it's called the Fax-a-Bed-Ahead (FABA) system. These services will be explained later in this chapter. For details on how to become a member, look for your own country in the sections below.

Hostelling International. 9 Guessens Rd., Welwyn Garden City, Hertfordshire, England AL8 6QW. Tel: 01707/324170. Fax: 01707/323980.

BECOMING A MEMBER IN THE UNITED STATES

Hostelling International-American Youth Hostels (HI-AYH). 733 15th St. NW, P.O. Box 37613, Washington, DC 20013-7613. Tel: 202/783-6161. Fax: 202/783-6171. Open for phone orders Monday through Friday from 8am to 6pm, eastern standard time. The toll-free number for domestic reservations is 800/444-6111; open daily from 9am to 9pm, eastern standard time. Overseas IBN reservations tel: 202/783-6161. HI-AYH accepts Visa, MasterCard, and Discover cards, as well as personal checks and money orders. You can become a member at any one of the hostels (over 150) in the United States. Otherwise, enrollment can be done over the phone or by mail. Allow three weeks for delivery. Membership prices, 1995: adults $25; youths (under 18) $10; family (parent or parents with children under 16) $35; senior citizens (over 54) $15; lifetime $250. Nonprofit groups and organizations receive free membership and should call for more information.

With your membership card, you'll receive a hostel map of the United States, discount vouchers and tickets, and a free subscription to the newsletter published by your regional AYH council (twice yearly or quarterly; varies from region to region). The North American hosteling directory, *Hostelling North America*, is free upon request.

In the United States, IBN reservations can be made over the phone with a credit card; call the toll-free number above. Alternatively, you can make international reservations in person at any hostel on the IBN system. In the United States, the following hostels are on IBN: Boston, Los Angeles, Martha's Vineyard, Miami Beach, New York, San Diego, San Francisco, Sausalito, Seattle, and Washington, D.C. There's a $5 booking fee and a $2 cancellation fee.

BECOMING A MEMBER IN CANADA

Hostelling International-Canada (HI-C). 400-205 Catherine St., Ottawa, Ontario, Canada K2P 1C3. Tel: 613/237-7884. Fax: 613/237-7868. Toll-free IBN reservations tel: 800/663-5777. HI-C accepts Visa and MasterCard, as well as personal checks and money orders. You can become a member by going into any one of the hostels. Otherwise, enrollment can be done over the phone or by mail. Allow three weeks for delivery. Membership prices, 1995: adult one-year membership Can$25; adult two-year membership Can$35; juniors (under 18) Can$12; groups Can$40. There's no family membership per se, but when parents (singles or couples) pay the regular adult price, children under 18 receive free membership.

With your membership card, you'll receive a hostel map of Canada, discount vouchers and tickets, and a free subscription to the newsletter published by your regional office. You'll also automatically get a Globafon calling card account, which you can use for international calls (you still have to pay for the calls you make on the card).

In Canada, IBN reservations can be made over the phone by calling the toll-free number above. Phone orders must be paid by credit card. You can also make IBN reservations in person at the following hostels: Banff, Calgary, Edmonton, Halifax, Jasper, Montreal, Ottawa, Quebec, Toronto, Vancouver. Cash or credit cards are accepted as payment for IBN reservations made in person. The booking fee is Can$5, and if you cancel it'll cost Can$6.50. Regional HI-C offices are in St. John's, Newfoundland; Halifax, Nova Scotia; Charlottetown, Prince Edward Island; Fredericton, New Brunswick; Montreal, Quebec; Ottawa, Ontario; Toronto, Ontario; Winnipeg, Manitoba; Regina, Saskatchewan; Edmonton, Alberta; Calgary, Alberta; and Vancouver, British Columbia.

BECOMING A MEMBER IN AUSTRALIA

Australian Youth Hostels Association (AYHA). Executive Office, Level 3, 10 Mallett St., Camperdown NSW 2050, Australia. Tel: 02/565 1699. Fax: 02/565 1325. IBN telephone reservations: 02/261 1111.

The Youth Hostels Association of New South Wales, Inc. State Office, 422 Kent St., Sydney 2000, GPO Box 5276, Sydney NSW 2001. Tel: 02/261 1111. Fax: 02/261 1969.

The Youth Hostels Association of Northern Territory, Inc. Administration and Membership Office, Darwin City Hostel. 69 Mitchell St., Darwin 0800. Tel: 089/816344. Fax: 089/816674. Travel Office: 089/812560.

Youth Hostels Association of Queensland. YHA Membership Office and YHA Travel, 154 Roma St., Brisbane, QLD 4000. Tel: 07/236 1680. Fax: 07/236 1702.

The Youth Hostels Association of South Australia, Inc. State Office, 38 Sturt St., Adelaide, SA 5000. Tel: 08/231 5583. Fax: 08/231 4219.

The Youth Hostels Association of Tasmania, Inc. State Office, 1st Floor, 28 Criterion St., Hobart, TAS 7000. GPO Box 174B, Hobart, TAS 7001. Tel: 002/349617. Fax: 002/347422.

The Youth Hostels Association of Victoria. State Office, 205 King St., Melbourne, VIC 3000. GPO Box 4793, Melbourne, VIC 3001. Tel: 03/670 9611 or 03/670 7991. Fax: 03/670 9840.

The Youth Hostels Association of Western Australia, Inc. State Office, Membership and Travel Centre, 236 William St., Perth, WA 6003. Tel: 09/227 5122. Fax: 09/227 5123.

To become a member, contact your state's association or go into any AYHA hostel. The cost of membership is the same throughout the country. AYHA accepts Visa, MasterCard, Bankcard, and JCB, as well as personal checks and money orders. Membership prices, 1995: adult one-year membership A$42 and A$26 to renew each year thereafter; adult two-year membership A$68 and A$52 to renew each two-year period thereafter; adult three-year membership A$96 and A$78 to renew each three-year period thereafter; children A$13; groups A$42. There's no family membership per se, but when parents (singles or couples) pay the regular adult price, children under 18 receive free membership. Those who have been members for two years or more become eligible for a lifetime membership for A$260.

With your membership card, you'll receive a hostel handbook and map of Australia and discount vouchers. In Australia, IBN reservations can be made by phone; call the reservations line in Sydney: 02/261 1111. Phone orders must be paid for by credit card. You can also make IBN reservations in person at the following hostels: Adelaide, Brisbane, Melbourne, Perth, Sydney. Cash or credit cards are accepted as payment for IBN reservations made in person. The booking fee is A$2.80, and if you cancel, the fee is A$2.80.

BECOMING A MEMBER IN NEW ZEALAND

Youth Hostels Association of New Zealand (YHA-NZ). National Office, P.O. Box 436, Christchurch. Tel: 03/379 9970. Fax: 09/365 4476. For IBN reservations, call the YHA-NZ Holiday Shops in Auckland at 09/379 4224 or Christchurch at 03/379 8046. The holiday shops are open Monday through Friday from 9am to 5pm and Saturday from 9am to 12pm. YHA-NZ accepts Visa, MasterCard, Bankcard, JCB, Diners Club, and American Express, as well as personal checks. You can become a member at the holiday shops or in the hostels themselves. Otherwise, enrollment can be done over the phone or by mail. Allow three weeks for delivery. Membership prices, 1995: adults $NZ34; youths (under 18) $NZ12; groups $NZ34. There is no family membership per se, but when parents (singles or couples) pay the regular adult membership price, all children under 15 get free membership.

With your membership card, you'll receive a hostel map and general travel information for New Zealand, along with some discount coupons. In New Zealand, IBN reservations can be made over the phone with a credit card; call either of the two numbers listed above. Alternatively, you can make international reservations in person at any hostel on the IBN system and pay by cash or credit card. In New Zealand, the following hostels are IBN booking centers: Auckland (three hostels) Christchurch (two hostels), and Wellington. There is a booking fee of $NZ3.50 and a cancellation fee of $NZ3.50.

BECOMING A MEMBER IN ENGLAND & WALES

Youth Hostels Association (England and Wales) (YHA). National Office, Trevelyan House, 8 St. Stephen's Hill, St. Albans, Hertfordshire AL1 2DY. Tel: 01727/855215. Fax: 01727/844126. For IBN reservations (overseas bookings only) the YHA has two Central Bookings Offices/YHA Adventure Shops. One is at 14 Southampton St., Covent Garden, London. Tel: 0171/436 1036. Fax: 0171/836 6372. The other is at 52 Grosvenor Gardens, Victoria, London. Tel: 0171/730 5769. Fax: 0171/ 730 5779. The YHA accepts Visa, MasterCard, Access, Switch, and personal checks. You can become a member at any hostel, at one of the Central Bookings Offices in London, and through the national office by phone or post. Switch cards can only be used in person. Membership prices for 1996: adults £9.30; under 18 £3.20; groups £10; two-parent families £18.60; one-parent families £9.30; lifetime membership £125.

With your membership, you'll receive regular copies of YHA's Triangle magazine, the YHA directory, a Members Discount Book. In addition, all YHA

(England and Wales) members receive a 10% discount on most goods at the YHA Adventure Shops. Student members 18 to 25 (not traveling in a group) receive £1 off the overnight price. Adult members who can prove they receive low-income benefits will be charged the under-18 rate for their overnight stay.

The YHA also publishes a ton of brochures advertising their Great Escapes program, which are outdoor activity weekend and weeklong adventures, usually focusing on one or two sports. Hill walking, horseback riding, abseiling, paragliding, canoeing, kayaking, mountain climbing, orienteering, and other activities are on offer. Two activity centers are fully staffed with instructors and run these programs virtually year-round. One is at Edale in the Peak District, and the other is at Llangollen in Wales. Pen-y-Pass has a number of activities in Snowdonia, and many other hostels offer one or two specialty weekends, as well.

Those wishing to make international reservations will find IBN centers at the Central Bookings Office and at a selection of England's Youth Hostels, including the following: all London hostels, Ambleside, Bath, Bristol, Cambridge, Canterbury, Cardiff, Dover, Newcastle, Oxford, Stratford-upon-Avon, Oxford, Windsor, York. The IBN booking fee is £1.40; the cancellation fee is £1.40.

The staff at England's regional offices can be helpful to hostelers with specific questions about a particular area. These offices are as follows:

YHA Northern England. P.O. Box 11, Matlock, Derbyshire DE4 2XA. Tel: 01629/825850. Fax: 01629/824571.

YHA South England. 11B York Rd., Salisbury, Wiltshire SP2 7AP. Tel: 01722/337515. Fax: 01722/414027.

YHA Wales. 4th Floor, 1 Cathedral Rd., Cardiff CF1 9HA. Tel: 01222/396766. Fax: 01222/237817.

YHA Cities Division. Trevelyan House, 8 St. Stephen's Hill, St. Albans, Hertfordshire AL1 2DY. Tel: 01727/855215. Fax: 01727/844126.

BECOMING A MEMBER IN SCOTLAND

Scottish Youth Hostels Association (SYHA). 7 Glebe Crescent, Stirling FK8 2JA. Tel: 01786/451181. Fax: 01786/450198. For IBN reservations tel. (overseas bookings only): 0141/332 3004. The SYHA accepts Visa, MasterCard, Access, Switch, and personal checks. You can become a member at most hostels or by post through the national or District offices. Switch cards can only be used in person. Membership prices for 1996 are as follows: adults £6.15; ages five to 17 £2.75; groups £6.15; lifetime £60. There's no family membership per se, but parents with SYHA memberships receive free membership for children aged five to 17.

The national office publishes a number of leaflets on activities at or near SYHA hostels. Skiing, cycling, field studies, and other outdoor adventures can be organized through the main office here. The SYHA also has district shops where you can buy outdoor clothing, maps, insect repellent, camping equipment, and other hostelers' gear; national members receive a 10% discount. Members can also contact the national office to receive vouchers for two guests to try hosteling without taking out a full membership. Finally, the SYHA offers two travel passes: The Scottish Wayfarer combines unlimited rail and ferry travel, discounted coach fares, and hostel accommodation vouchers (1995 prices: 8-day pass £165; 15-day pass

£265). The Explore Scotland ticket offers a seven-day travel pass on Scottish Citylink coaches and seven overnight vouchers (1995 price: £120).

To make international reservations, Scotland has the following hostels on the IBN: Edinburgh (Eglinton and Bruntsfield), Glasgow, Carbisdale Castle, Inverness, Stirling. The IBN booking fee is £1.50; the cancellation fee is £1.50.

The following is a list of Scotland's district offices and district shops:

Aberdeen District Office and Shop. 11 Ashvale Place, Aberdeen AB1 6QD. Tel: 01224/588156.

Dundee District Office and Shop. 8 Bell Place, Dundee DD1 1JG. Tel: 01382/ 322150.

Edinburgh District Office and Shop. 161 Warrender Park Rd., Edinburgh EH9 1EQ. Tel: 0131/229 8660.

Glasgow District Office and Shop: 12 Renfield St., Glasgow, G2 5AL. Tel: 0141/226 3976.

Planning a Hosteling Trip: IBN, BABA & FABA

If you want to plan your itinerary in advance, the International Booking System (IBN) allows you to make reservations from your home country. With IBN, you can reserve only at specific hostels linked to this computerized network. These usually tend to be busy city hostels (see listing below) that accommodate lots of international travelers, so they fill up fast.

Reservations can be made up to six months in advance; it's a good idea to book at least three weeks ahead. Simply call the IBN reservations line in your own country (see "Becoming a Member" earlier in this chapter for the number in your country) or go into an IBN reservations center (usually a city hostel) in your home country. You'll pay the full price for the overnight, plus a booking fee, and then you'll receive a receipt. Bring the receipt with you; it'll be used as verification when you check in. This is an excellent way to ensure yourself a bed, at least for your first few nights in Britain.

If you're trying to structure a longer trip, IBN can be useful for spacing out overnight reservations in large cities, and then you can fill in the gaps on your itinerary with smaller hostels at which you can reserve a bed once in Britain. In England and Wales, the hostels currently on the IBN system include these: all London hostels, Ambleside, Bath, Bristol, Cambridge, Canterbury, Cardiff, Dover, Newcastle, Oxford, Stratford-upon-Avon, Windsor, and York. In Scotland, they are the following: Edinburgh, Glasgow, Carbisdale Castle, Inverness, and Stirling.

Once you're in Britain, you can reserve an overnight through the Book-a-Bed-Ahead (BABA) system in England and the Fax-a-Bed-Ahead (FABA) system in Scotland. Both work the same way: Suppose you're in Hawes and you want to go Kirkby Stephen. You go the hostel reception desk and tell them where you want to book ahead. They fax Kirkby Stephen, and then you wait around for the price (since prices vary from hostel to hostel) and for confirmation that they have bed space. If the answer is yes, you'll pay the full price at Hawes and receive a voucher to present when you arrive at Kirkby Stephen. This way, you can ensure that you'll have a bed waiting when you arrive. Of course, you can do it yourself by phone, but if you don't have a form of payment, they can hold the bed for you only until 6pm, and if transportation is slow and you arrive late you may be out of a bed. In England, there's no charge for this service, and BABA can be used to book ahead at a Scottish hostel as well. In Scotland, the Fax-a-Bed-Ahead system works the same way, even though it's under a different name. You can also reserve in England through the Fax-a-Bed-Ahead system in Scotland. This service saves you a lot of hassle and worry, but it does lock you into the hostel for which you've paid.

Prices

Prices range anywhere from £5.50 to £19.75 for overnights at hostels in England and Wales. Hostels are priced according to a sliding scale, with small rural hostels costing less than slick big-city centers. The lowest price is £5.50 and the highest is £10.90 (adult prices). The exception to this rule is London where the hostels are considerably more expensive, ranging from £12.25 to £19.75 (some including breakfast).

In Scotland, the prices are generally a pound or two lower. Scottish hostels are classified into four categories. Big-city hostels with all-day access and extended hours are considered high standard, and prices range from £6.20 to £8.75. Smaller city and busy rural hostels with all-day access fall into standard, costing £5.70 per night. Small country hostels with limited daytime access are categorized as standard (L) and cost £5.25 per night. Small hostels with only the most basic amenities are classified as simple and cost £4. In both England and Scotland, prices for youths under 18 are usually about £1.75 to £3 less than adult prices. Under each hostel entry, you'll find the 1995 prices for adults and under 18, and for all Scottish hostels, you'll get the classification listing.

Prices listed in this guide can be used as general guidelines for what to expect, but are never absolutely guaranteed. Generally, the higher the price, the busier the hostel. Low prices never mean a dip in quality or service; all hostels have to meet the exacting standards of their national organizations as well as HI. Use the service information listings under each hostel entry; you'll see that in general, cheaper hostels may lack a game room or laundry facilities, but the basic facilities are there. In Scotland, the lower prices generally mean that hostels are slightly more basic.

What to Expect at the Hostels

The 240-odd hostels in England and Wales form one organization, YHA England and Wales. While the hostels are not entirely uniform and each is idiosyncratic, there are certain things you can expect across the board. This section deals with what to expect when you check in.

If you've made a reservation and paid in advance, all you'll need to do is give your name and hand over your reservation (IBN or BABA) receipt and HI card. Your HI card is held for the duration of your stay and handed back to you when you check out.

Hostels generally open at around 7 or 8am, but if you're booking in for the first time, your bed may not be ready until 1 to 3pm in city hostels and 5pm in countryside hostels. Almost all hostels will allow you to store your gear until check-in time.

If you've arrived early, most hostel managers don't mind if you hang out for a while; city hostels are often open all day, so you shouldn't be too rushed to get there. Country hostels tend to be closed for cleaning during the day, so if you arrive in the morning, you'll probably have to leave by around 10am and can check in when they reopen at 5pm.

Accommodation is almost always in bunk-bedded rooms. In England and Wales, the overnight price includes a YHA sleep sheet (which you should put on your bed right away) and soft comforter quilts. In Scotland, they throw in the quilt, but you're allowed to use your own sleep sheet. For 60p you can rent a sheet for the duration of your stay. Both the YHA and the SYHA prohibit the use of sleeping bags for sanitary reasons. You'll need to bring your own towel and toiletries, and slippers are definitely worth the space in your rucksack. Hostel bathrooms are always kept pretty neat and clean, but even the most perfectly scrubbed shower stalls get grimy, especially after a team of long-distance cyclists has booked in for the night.

In general, the hostels are kept scrupulously clean, thanks to the exacting standards of HI. Some hostels are older than others, though, and the wear and tear shows. Almost all chores have been officially abolished at the SYHA and YHA hostels, with the exception of after-dinner cleanup at some of the country hostels. Nevertheless, hostelers are asked to pick up after themselves; the staff is usually kept to a minimum, and they appreciate hostelers who don't leave a trail of garbage behind. This is especially true in the countryside hostels.

All hostels have at least one sitting room or lounge, depending on the building and size of the hostel. Some hostels have separate games rooms, TV rooms, field-study rooms, and conference rooms. Hostels that were once mansions often boast faded but beautiful drawing rooms and parlors, now cozy common rooms. Some common rooms have fireplaces, and all have a bookshelf full of hosteling magazines and literature, as well as books left behind by guests, which are yours for the reading. The games can be anything from Monopoly to Pac-Man to pool tables to foosball—it varies from hostel to hostel. The reception desk usually hangs on to a bunch of board games for hostelers to use; sometimes you have to rent them, while sometimes they're free.

All hostels have drying rooms for wet clothes, and many have washers, dryers, and laundry detergent. The cost usually hovers around £1.50 for a wash and 80p to dry a small load, and it's all self-service. You'll also find a small shop at the reception desk in the front, where you can buy canned goods, toiletries, and sometimes small souvenirs; again, this varies from hostel to hostel. All hostels will hold mail sent to hostelers, and most will send and receive faxes for you for a small fee.

When you're ready to check out, don't forget to return your key and sleep sheet to the front desk. Check-out time is usually from 7 to 10am in England and Wales and 7 to 9am in Scotland.

Hostel Rules

In England, Scotland, and Wales, smoking isn't permitted in the bedrooms, dining rooms, bathrooms, or hallways. Where space allows, there's a separate room set aside for smokers; otherwise, light up on the patio outside the building. Hostelers should be advised to leave their dice, drugs, and loaded weapons at home; they are prohibited at hostels and these rules are taken seriously.

Alcohol is another subject entirely. Some hostels have a table license, which allows them to sell beer and wine at meal times and only to accompany a meal. However, you're not supposed to bring in your own stuff, and underage drinking is uniformly prohibited. In England, some managers turn a blind eye if you bring in a bottle of wine and conscientious adults usually don't have to be concerned about getting busted. Anyone who brings booze in on the sly, however, with the intention of having a late-night rave is probably in for disappointment and trouble. Remember, you may be sleeping in a 14-bed room full of young children, senior citizens, or long-distance cyclists (usually a combination of the three), none of whom will have any qualms about getting the hostel manager to boot you out if you're tossing back tequila shots after lights out. In Scottish Youth Hostels, alcohol is strictly prohibited and no exceptions are made. Throughout England, Scotland, and Wales, pets are prohibited at all hostels as well.

Curfews are usually around 11 or 11:30pm in small rural hostels, and some have late closings at 2am. In the country hostels, "quiet time" is usually between 11pm and 7am out of respect for the dead-tired. The earliest you can check out is usually 7am, but if you need to catch an early morning bus or train, they'll usually accommodate you if you ask in advance.

Many city hostels have 24-hour access, with some sort of security system to let you in after the reception desk has closed, and "quiet time" prevails here, too. Check-in and check-out times tend to be more flexible in big-city hostels, since their high turnover requires faster service.

Kitchens & Meal Service

With the exception of some city hostels, all hostels have a self-catering kitchen where you can play house, cook, and clean up. The facilities vary from hostel to hostel, but you can always expect a grill/range of some sort, a refrigerator and cubbies to store your supplies, cutlery, plates, pots, and pans. Some hostels are extremely basic in this respect; others have microwaves and regular ovens. Label your food in the refrigerator and don't forget to take it when you leave.

In Scotland, most hostels don't offer meal service at all, so the kitchens tend to be cleaner, larger, and better equipped than their counterparts in England and Wales. Hostelers using these facilities are expected to clean up after themselves; there's nothing worse than the rank fumes emanating from a dirty self-catering kitchen. Self-catering kitchens are usually open from 7 to 10am and 5 to 11pm. Hostels with all-day access may leave the kitchen open all day.

In England and Wales, all the hostels listed offer meal service. With the exception of London, where breakfast is included at some hostels, meals aren't included in the overnight price. The meals vary widely; if a hostel warden has the time, the staff, and the desire, the meals might be quite tasty and home-cooked; otherwise (and this is always true in large-city hostels), the food is bland and unexciting.

Breakfast is good for those who want serious energy in the morning: For £2.80, you get unlimited coffee, tea, and toast, plus two courses. The first course is either fruit juice or cereal (muesli, cornflakes, Weetabix). You can usually choose the second course from a few options: Usually some sort of a continental croissant-and-fruit affair; a "healthy" yogurt and roll combo; and the traditional English breakfast consisting of eggs, tomato, sausage, and beans. Vegetarian English breakfasts are always offered, and sometimes you'll get regional specialties, such as smoked mackerel in Devon and Cornwall. Packed breakfasts are usually available; ask the night before.

Some large-city hostels stay open during the day and serve a cafeteria-style à la carte lunch, but the majority of the hostels offer packed lunches only. Unless you're hankering for the old days or going to be doing some intense walking and won't be near a pub, the packed lunches aren't much more than you would have gotten in elementary school. They generally come in two sizes, and you get either one or two sandwiches, potato chips, a couple of sweets, and a piece of fruit. The price is £2.35 for a standard lunch and £3.10 for a large one.

Dinner is usually a three-course extravaganza starting with fruit juice or soup, followed by a main course (you'll get a choice) and then dessert and coffee. At £4.10, it's a reasonable deal, and sometimes the food is quite good. Most hostelers, however, head out to pubs and local restaurants.

In Scotland, there aren't as many hostels with meal service, and those that do have it only offer it seasonally. Breakfast is usually coffee, tea, toast, and cereal (£1.80), but some hostels offer the full two-course breakfast offered by hostels in England and Wales (£2.90). The packed lunch is £1.95, and three-course dinner is £3.90. Remember, there's almost always a pub nearby to supplement bland victuals.

Safety & Security

One of the nicest things about staying at an HI hostel is the sense of safety you'll feel inside. The rules and regulations can be a drag sometimes, but they make the hostels secure for everybody, which is especially nice for those traveling alone. There's the feeling that you're being protected by the capable warden, the officious security guard, and even the pimply teenager at the reception desk.

In England, the bedrooms in the larger city hostels all have locks on the doors, for which you'll be given a key. All beds come equipped with individual lockers, but they're really just big cubbies. You'll need to bring your own padlock or buy one at the reception desk (usually £2.50). Most city hostels also have a bank of coin-operated lockers and/or a locked luggage-storage room.

The country hostels often have no locks at all on the bedroom doors and very little in the way of luggage storage. Because the hostels are locked during the day, there isn't usually much danger of anything happening to your stuff, since the only people inside are the one or two staffers cleaning the place. If you're seriously worried about leaving something in the rooms, hostel staff are usually glad to stash your things behind the counter, where they're generally safe. However, if you do leave things in the hostel, it is at your own risk. Anything that falls into the category of I'm-screwed-if-I-lose-this shouldn't be left alone anyway. A camera can be a pain to carry, but leaving it alone can invite theft.

In Scotland, the hostels have been slower in installing good security. Be especially careful in the big cities: The Edinburgh hostel accommodates many transients, which makes it especially ripe for thieves. The hostels are open during the day and in the past lacked adequate security, inviting crime, albeit unwittingly. Also, don't expect your bunkmates to be as virtuous as you. Every once in a blue moon, thieves have been known to stay the night and make their heists on the way out in the morning.

Though theft has been a problem in the past at Scottish hostels, the situation is slowly improving. The SYHA is putting coin-operated lockers in the city hostels, as well as video cameras and secret passwords at the entrance of some of the busier hostels. Remember that ultimately you're the only one responsible for your safety and security, and it's always better to err on the side of safety, even if you risk offending a newfound friend. Your fellow hostelers usually understand, since they're in the same vulnerable position. And everybody sleeps snuggled up with their belt wallets, so you might as well, too.

Women & Solo Travelers

Women and solo travelers should be especially careful: It's always safer to travel in a group. Be especially vigilant about observing the curfew and the rules. Many hostels are situated outside town and city centers, and late-night walks can turn into creepy experiences, especially from lonely train and bus stations half a mile out of town. Since stores and pubs close on the early side, there's not too many places to run if you've got a mile to walk and are concerned for your safety.

The hostels themselves aren't a safety problem. The wisest approach is to avoid situations where you'll be alone in sketchy neighborhoods, and always make sure you've got a phone card or loose change to make a phone call. Keep the hostel phone number on you at all times.

Hostelers with Disabilities

Because so many hostels are in historic buildings, there's little that can be changed in the existing structures. Only a precious few hostels are truly wheelchair accessible. Hostels being built nowadays are designed with the travelers with disabilities in mind, and you're likely to see more ramps, elevators, and special bathrooms and bedrooms in the future.

For the time being, though, hostels make do with what they have. Under the service information listing for each hostel, you'll find whether or not the hostel is wheelchair accessible. The majority in the YHA and SYHA aren't officially sanctioned as accessible to people with disabilities, but hostel managers are pretty sensitive to their needs. While many hostels aren't really equipped for guests with disabilities, it's always a good idea to call ahead and check. Depending on the hostel layout and on your particular need, the hostel may be able to accommodate you. If the bedrooms are up a flight of winding stairs or if the bathroom space is impossibly cramped, the hostels are unable to accommodate guests with disabilities. They can usually suggest another hostel that fits the bill.

Troubleshooting: The Hostel Warden

All the hostels have a manager (warden) who runs the show, keeps the staff in order, and oversees any special activities the hostel offers. In the countryside, they seem to prefer the title "warden," the tradition title for hosteling head honchos. In the cities, where hostels are more like budget hotels, you'll find name tags and a more polished appearance; wardens will frostily tell you they're "managers."

Most hostelers, however, won't really have to deal with the warden unless there's a problem—and 9 times out of 10 it has something to do with the school groups. Lots of the hostels load up with these groups (British schoolchildren in spring and fall; international groups in summer), which can sometimes create friction, since they're often noisy and take up a lot of space. Often, just because of their numbers they'll dominate the atmosphere, rendering what was once a tranquil countryside enclave a juvenile roadhouse. Don't be surprised if you encounter surly French schoolchildren smoking out on the patio, hyperactive English tots working on field-study projects outside, or teenage boys fighting over the TV in the common room. At night, you'll catch the reflection of braces and other orthodontic contraptions bouncing off the mirrors, and there's often a wait for showers, especially in the morning. You may want to bring earplugs if you're an early sleeper, since the youngsters can get noisy.

Most hostel managers make a fairly honest effort to keep school groups relatively peaceful; small groups tend to be pretty calm. If you think the kids will drive you nuts, then when you make your reservation over the phone it's a good idea to ask if they'll be at the hostel. Hostels, however, really do belong to all the members, not just backpackers. If the thought of little tots running around really bothers you, then hosteling might not be right for you. Part of the package is a live-and-let-live attitude that works only if everyone is considerate of everyone else. When all hostelers respect one another's rights to use these buildings, peace and friendliness tend to prevail.

Hosteling with Children

Hostels are trying to become more and more accommodating to couples who travel with children. Kids under 16 receive free hostel memberships if their parents are members, and you'll see lots of small families at the hostels in Britain. The YHA in England and Wales has a lower age limit of three, and in Scotland it's five, though the rules may be bent at the manager/warden's discretion.

In England and Wales, there are three possibilities for families. Family annexes are fully equipped self-contained buildings usually right behind the main hostel building. They've usually got self-catering facilities and keys for all-day access and are usually booked for seven-day periods at a weekly rate, which ranges from £70 to £175 for the week. Write to the YHA national office in England for a list of hostels with family annexes.

Some hostels have designated family rooms, which may have private baths and always come with a key for daytime access. Prices are charged per room per night and go up according to the number of beds. Two-bedded rooms range from £15 to

£19.50 (£25 to £35 in London); three- and four-bed rooms range from £22 to £39 (£36 to £70 in London). Five- and six-bed rooms range from £32 to £58 (£62 to £100 in London). Finally, hostels that don't have official family rooms will reserve small dormitories to accommodate families; the prices are per bed per night.

In Scotland, three hostels (Cannich, Perth, and Whiting Bay) have self-contained family units, intended for families with at least one child under five. The nightly charge is the equivalent of two adult and two junior overnights. Other than that, there are no specially designated rooms or annexes for families, but families will be accommodated in smaller dormitories. Normal overnight charges apply.

The family annexes in England and Wales and the family units in Scotland are fully equipped. However, you'll be expected to bring your own towels. Sheets are provided free of charge in England and Wales and for a small fee in Scotland.

Camping Barns

The YHA in England and Wales has four networks of camping barns: North Yorkshire; the North Pennines; the Forest of Bowland; and Exmoor, Dartmoor, and Tarka country. Sometimes they're little more than farm buildings owned and operated by farmers. They provide basic accommodations: wooden sleeping platforms, tables and benches, cold water, and a flush toilet. These "stone tents" usually aren't heated, so it's essential you bring warm clothing and a good sleeping bag. Prices start at about £2.75 per person per night. For more information, contact the YHA (England and Wales) head office for a brochure.

In Scotland, the SHYA has access to a number of simple croft houses, which are the most basic type of accommodation and are similar to camping barns. Charitable organizations like the Gatliff Hebridean Hostels Trust and Orkney Island Council Department of Education, as well as private property owners, have donated these unused buildings to the members of the hosteling community. Advance bookings often are not accepted and hostelers are expected to make do with only the most basic of amenities.

Certain hostels offer camping in the front or back yard areas, but this varies from season to season and from hostel to hostel. In general, the YHA and the SYHA aren't set up for camping, since the facilities inside (bathrooms, dining room, common areas) are intended to accommodate the number of bed spaces. Nevertheless, it's up to the warden in many cases, so it's a good idea to call ahead and check. In England and Wales, campers are always advised to book in advance, since managers may have to restrict their numbers during busy times. The charge for camping in England and Wales is half the normal overnight fee, and no discounts are available. Hostel equipment may not be brought out to the tents, but campers can use the self-catering kitchens, baths, and common rooms.

3 THE BEST HOSTELS IN ENGLAND

London Area

It would be impossible to mention every single sight, restaurant, and event or to capture entirely the distinctly English yet international atmosphere that lures more than 350,000 hostelers every year to London. Banish your preconceived notions of bobbies on horseback, red-jacketed phone booths, and high tea. Sure, you can find them, but there's so much more happening here and most hostelers are anxious to find the real London lurking under the surface.

Luckily, you can easily explore the real London, from the Victoria and Albert Museum, the National Gallery, and the British Museum to the endless contemporary art galleries; from Camden Town, Bermondsey Market, and Brixton Market to proper storefront shopping in Sloane Square, Knightsbridge, and New Bond Street; from the historical heavyweights Westminster Abbey, Buckingham Palace, the Tower of London, and St. Paul's Cathedral to emerging neighborhoods along London's Docklands; from the straitlaced City of London to such easily walkable neighborhoods as Chelsea, Islington, Bloomsbury, and Covent Garden. Parks and gardens peep out at you everywhere you go.

And that's only central London: Head out a few zones on the Underground and you'll find a jumble of smaller, slightly suburban neighborhoods like Golders Green, Highgate Village, and Hampstead Heath. Just a bit farther out on the tube lies the incredibly rural village of Epping, with its own forest.

Clearly, there's never a lack of things to do here and luckily there isn't a lack of hostels either. Each of the hostels in London is accessible by the comprehensive color-coded Underground, and each presides over its own little corner of the city. The hostels provide distinct experiences in distinct parts of London, and all are great bases from which to explore the surroundings. The variety of hostels reflects the eclecticism of the city itself: You can stay at an old choirboy's dormitory across the street from St. Paul's Cathedral; a fancy old mansion in the middle of Kensington's Holland Park; a small Georgian house in a "village" just north of the city center; or a mammoth, gleaming skylit conference center in the Dockland.

All London hostels meet stringent safety standards: They're well protected against theft with security guards, locks on all doors, and beds that come with individual lockers.

As you'd expect, these hostels tend to fill up quickly, especially in spring and summer, so book by phone at least two to three weeks in advance; the **Central Reservations office** (tel. 0171/248 6547; fax 0171/236 7681) takes care of all London's hostels, making booking efficient and easy. There are a number of YHA Adventure Shops in London that sell outdoor gear and travel accessories and provide hostel information; the YHA distributes a coupon book filled with discounts for sights and attractions (see "London Basics" later in this chapter).

To find out about the latest happenings, pick up *Time Out*, on sale at every newsagent. Don't, however, underestimate the flourishing hostel grapevine: Fellow bunkmates often have the best (and most up-to-date) reports on what to see and do here. Most hostels are staffed with a mix of life-long Londoners and experienced backpackers, who can also be a great source of insider advice on what to do, where to go, and how much to pay in a city that can be a bit overwhelming at first glance.

CITY OF LONDON

Home to the Bank of England, Lloyd's of London, innumerable investment houses, and other financial concerns, the city of London is an impressive neighborhood in which to spend a few days. The Youth Hostel here is practically across the street from the massive domed St. Paul's Cathedral and its pleasant churchyard, which provide a spiritual air to this otherwise no-nonsense neighborhood that shuts down at about 6pm.

Just off the Central Line tube, the hostel is especially well situated for serious sightseeing. To the west, the Strand, Fleet Street, Trafalgar Square, Covent Garden, and Leicester Square are all within walking distance. To the east, the Tower of London presides over the River Thames, also a short walk away. The 60 acres of the Barbican Theatre provide a wealth of culture just to the north.

The hostel accommodates loads of international tourists, a fair number of school groups, and even a few families. There's a good bit of mixing and mingling, with a spirited air of camaraderie among the hostelers, who are eager to get out and see the sights.

❀ City of London Youth Hostel

36 Carter Lane
London EC4V 5AD
Tel: 0171/236 4965. Fax: 0171/236 7681.
Central Reservations tel: 0171/248 6547; Central Reservations fax: 0171/236 7681.
Tube: St. Paul's or Blackfriars

Boasting a choice location a block from St. Paul's Cathedral and a few steps farther from the centrally located Central Line tube stop, this hostel is a great favorite among the international travelers who come here for hard-core sightseeing. Not surprisingly, the City of London hostel is often packed solid, especially in summer when backpackers attack.

The hostel itself is one of the neighborhood's big-time sights. For 850 years, it was the school and dormitory of the St. Paul's choirboys. Little remnants of bygone days lurk in unexpected nooks: Check out the sober inscription along the outside of the building. Inside the hostel, lovingly framed black-and-white photos with images from yesteryear are mounted on the walls. The cafeteria was once the choirboys' refectory, the lounge was a study hall, and the conference room was a chapel.

These touching mementos aside, the hostel is a fairly modern affair. The bedrooms are spanking clean, as are the bathrooms, and some rooms have private baths and TVs. Rooms are priced accordingly: Those with 10 to 15 beds are "economy," five- to eight-bed dorms are "standard," and one- to four-bed dorms are "premium."

Downstairs, the games room, conference room, and dining room are all equally functional, modern, and anything but cozy. Formica dominates the interior design, lending the hostel a slightly antiseptic appearance, but the generally friendly young staff softens the effect. The reception area is filled with leaflets and tube maps, the walls covered with helpful hints on everything from music to markets to favorite restaurants. The Choristers Restaurant (which doubles as a hangout/TV lounge at night) is a madhouse during breakfast hours; don't even try to sneak anything past the watchful food wardens. Lunch and dinner here are forgettable; most hostelers head to the West End for meals.

Since the immediate neighborhood is a business district, it isn't especially interesting if you're looking for local color: gray (the buildings) and blue (the suits) dominate the cityscape. At night, the few shops and pubs close, transforming the area into an eerie ghost town; you'll have to head out of the neighborhood for signs of life. Nevertheless, this is a popular hostel, so, as always, call well in advance to book a bed.

Services

🚆 From any of London's eight British Rail stations, take the Central Line tube to St. Paul's. Exit the station and take a sharp left; walk past St. Paul's Cathedral churchyard. At the zebra crossing, cross Ludgate Hill and turn right down Dean's Court. The hostel is on the right at the corner of Carter Lane. The entrance is on Carter Lane.

🚌 From London's Victoria Station, take the Circle or District Line tube to Blackfriars. From there, walk up New Bridge Street, away from the river. When you reach Ludgate Circus, turn right onto Ludgate Hill and walk toward St. Paul's Cathedral; turn right onto Dean's Court. The hostel is at the end of the street, at the corner of Carter Lane. Enter on Carter Lane.

🚗 From the **south**, head for the A23, A215, or A2 toward The Borough, on the south side of the River Thames. Get onto Blackfriars Road, which leads over Blackfriars Bridge. Turn right on Ludgate Hill and head toward St. Paul's Cathedral. When you reach the cathedral, turn right on Dean's Court; the hostel is at the end of the road, on the corner of Carter Lane. Enter on Carter Lane.

From the **north** of London and the M25, the most effective way to cut through London is to get off the M25 at Junction 25 and take the A10 south toward the city, past Edmonton, Tottenham, and Islington. At the end of the A10 (Kingsland Road),

turn right onto Old Street, pass the Old Street tube station, and turn left onto Aldersgate. Go past the Museum of London, and at the roundabout head straight onto St. Martin's Le Grand, toward St. Paul's Cathedral. Drive around the back of the cathedral on New Change, then turn right onto St. Paul's Churchyard/Ludgate Hill. Turn left on Dean's Court. The hostel is at the end of the street, at the corner of Carter Lane. Enter on Carter Lane.

▦ Open all year. IBN/BABA: both.

🕐 Open 24 hours. Reception staffed 7am–11pm. Security guard on the desk at night. No curfew.

🛏 191 beds. 1-, 2-, 3-, 4-, 5-, 6-, 7-, 8-, 10-, and 15-bed rooms. Some have private bathrooms and can be reserved for families.

£ Members—economy room: adults £14.10; under 18 £11.10. Standard room: adults £19.10; under 18 £16. Premium room: adults £19.70; under 18 £16.70. Super-duper premium room (with TV): adults £22.20; under 18 £18.70. Breakfast included in all prices.

🍴 Meals served continuously 7am–8pm in the Choristers Restaurant. No self-catering kitchen facilities. Breakfast: 7:30–9:30am; included in overnight price. Lunch: à la carte; served throughout the day. Dinner: à la carte or set dinner served from 6:30–8pm.

I Table license.

📦 All beds have individual lockers; bring a padlock or buy one at reception (£2.50). Luggage storage £1.50 per 24 hours.

◎ Washers £1.50; dryers are a bottomless pit of 20p coins; drying room.

P During the week, don't even try parking here. National Car Park £22 per day. On weekends, street parking is free; check the signs carefully.

📄 Shop at the hostel sells National Express and Slow Coach tickets; postcards; Travelcards for the London Underground (Zones 1–2); stamps; Hacky Sacks (£1.50); *London A to Z*; souvenir police helmets (£2.50); film. Soda and candy machines.

📺 Common room; TV lounge/smoking den.

🚬 In TV lounge and upper dining area only.

♿ Not wheelchair accessible.

💱 Travelex currency exchange.

⚫ Bike shed; booking service for theaters and some tours; direct-dial AT&T phone; chapel/boardroom; classroom.

Cheap Eats Nearby

Food for Thought
This vegetarian's paradise is in a green corner of Covent Garden. Nearby, you can prowl through natural foods stores and herbal pharmacies. Rotating hot dishes £3 to £4. Yummy pastas and vegetarian bakes £3.

31 Neal St., WC2. Tel: 0171/836 0239. Tube: Covent Garden. Open: Mon–Sat 9:30am–8pm, Sun 10:30am–4:30pm. Cash only. From the tube, walk up Endell Street, turn left onto Shelton, then turn right on Neal Street.

Wagamama
Deceptively upscale, this spare postmodern dining room with long wooden tables is filled with students gobbling up reasonably priced noodles. Loads of underfed university boys make for good people-watching. There's usually a line, but the turnover is fast. Use the space-age ordering system to be served soba, ramen, udon, and every other noodle known to Japan. Entrées £4 to £6.

4 Streatham St., WC1A. Tel: 0171/323 9223. Tube: Tottenham Court Road. Open: Mon–Sat noon–2:30pm and 6pm–midnight; Sun 12:30–3pm and 6–10pm. From the tube, walk up New Oxford Street to Bloomsbury; turn left and Streatham is your first left. The restaurant is on the left.

Grocery store: Shepherd Food and Wine. Ludgate Circus, EC4. Open: Mon–Fri 7:30am–9pm; Sat 9am–6pm; Sun 10am–4pm.

Experiences

With so many attractions within easy walking distance of the hostel, it's hard to decide where to start sightseeing. The hostel is right across from **St. Paul's Cathedral.** Winston Churchill's funeral was held here; Charles and Diana got married here (the hostel rooftop was used as a royal stakeout); and Martin Luther was officially condemned here. With a 365-foot domed tower, Christopher Wren's Gothic/Baroque masterpiece (completed 1710) is actually the third cathedral to have stood on the site. In 1940, more than 50 firebombs landed on the cathedral during the Nazi blitz, but the brave St. Paul's fire brigade saved most of the cathedral from the blaze, with the exception of the north transept, now covered in glass.

Some interesting sights include the Henry Moore sculpture *Mother and Child;* the Painter's Corner, containing the tombs of Joshua Reynolds and J. M. W. Turner; the memorials to John Constable, William Blake, George Washington, and Lawrence of Arabia; and the Whispering Gallery on the interior base of the dome. The churchyard is a nice grassy spot for a picnic.

North and up the street from St. Peter's is the **Priory Church of St. Bartholomew's,** where scruffy English hunk Hugh Grant attended one of the four weddings in *Four Weddings and a Funeral.* The church has a soothing choral evensong Sundays at 6:30pm and lunchtime recitals during the week. The sweet garden is a peaceful resting spot; from here, you can look out onto the **St. Bartholomew's Hospital,** which, dating from 1123, is the oldest official hospital in the world.

Nearby, Aldersgate Street leads you straight north to the **Barbican,** one of London's many cultural/arts/theater centers. Under one modern roof you can listen to Liszt, inspect a Pissarro, experience Shakespeare, peer at a photography exhibit or two, catch a flick, and even stop for a bite to eat. Built in 1972, this mammoth multilevel complex is an impressive, if slightly unattractive, example of postwar architecture. Covering 60 acres of urban soil, it's home to the **Royal Shakespeare Company,** the **London Symphony Orchestra,** the **Barbican Art Gallery,** the **Barbican Cinema,** and the **Museum of London,** as well as a private girl's school and a local church. The cultural offerings here are plentiful and ever-changing.

A short walk away from the hostel to the east is the **Tower of London,** the home of the Crown Jewels and Europe's oldest, coldest, bloodiest fortress, built by William the Conqueror in 1066. It has been a royal residence, a storage house, an armory, and, most famously, the grim prison of many a royal. Sir Thomas More, Anne Boleyn, Lady Jane Grey, the Little Princes (Edward and Richard), and a host of unfortunate others had their heads chopped off here.

Moving west back in the direction of the hostel, you'll enter the heart of the **city of London,** the financial district. The area around the Bank of England and Lloyd's heaves in the early morning with city highflyers, a stern-looking corps of three-piece suits rushing to the bank. As you walk past them, you'll move onto **Ludgate Hill;** the **Strand;** and **Fleet Street,** formerly the main artery of London's healthy journalistic heart. The *Telegraph,* the *Sun,* the *Daily Express,* and the *Times* all used to churn out their copy around here, although they're now long gone. Heading down the Strand, you'll pass the **Royal Courts of Justice** and the **London School of Economics.** At the far end lies the **Courtauld Institute,** which houses an excellent gallery showcasing impressionist, postimpressionist, Italian, Flemish, and modern works. Among the collection are works by Cézanne, Degas, Gauguin, Seurat, Renoir, van Gogh, Rubens, Breughel, and Modigliani.

Just north of the Strand, the cafes, coffeehouses, bookshops, and style-conscious shops of **Covent Garden** provide a respite for museum-goers. Once the parcel of land on which the monks of Westminster Abbey grew vegetables, Covent Garden became the first planned square in London. In the early 1600s, it became a covered market with colorful stalls selling fruit, vegetables, and flowers. Nowadays, you're more likely to find espresso, arts and crafts, and jewelry stalls, but street performers and outdoor cafes make the area a friendly and fun place to hang out.

Farther into the West End lie **Chinatown,** where cheap food, souvenirs, and fresh fish lie in wait; and **Leicester Square,** London's legendary theater district. Before your feet fall off, note that you're just a few blocks from the **National**

Gallery, where masterpieces by van Eyck, Leonardo, Raphael, Botticelli, Rembrandt, El Greco, and Titian will distract you from your corns and calluses. **Trafalgar Square, Pall Mall, Regent Street,** and other famous avenues are just beyond. Follow the Thames as it curves south, and a 15-minute walk will get you to **Westminster Abbey, St. James's Park,** and **Buckingham Palace.**

Back up by the hostel, the **Brick Lane Market** is an interesting break from the tourist trail. Here you can shop to the sounds of Indian music while you scan the stalls filled with crafts, fabrics, rugs, incense, as well as spices and sweets from Asia. A few blocks away on **Petticoat Lane,** clothes, housewares, linens, and doodads line the streets on Sunday mornings.

St. Paul's Cathedral. Ludgate Hill, EC4. Tel: 0171/236 0792. Tube: St. Paul's. Open: daily 8:30am–4pm; galleries daily 10am–4:15pm; crypt daily 8:45am–4pm. Tape-recorded tours: adults £2.50; students £2. Guided supertours: adults £3; students £2; children £1.

The Priory Church of St. Bartholomew-the-Great. West Smithfield, EC1. Tel: 0171/606 5171. Tube: St. Paul's or Barbican. Open: Mon–Fri 8:30am–4pm; Sat 10am–3pm; Sun 2–6pm.

Barbican Theatre: Royal Shakespeare Company, The Pit, The Young Vic, London Symphony Orchestra. Silk Street, EC2. General Box Office tel: 0171/638 8891. 24-hour information line tel: 0171/628 2295. Tube: Barbican or Moorgate. Box office open: daily 9am–8pm. Ticket prices: Royal Shakespeare Company, £9–£22; The Pit, £10–£16; The Young Vic, £12–£18; London Symphony, £5–£25. Discounts available, starting one hour before performance time; all unsold tickets go on sale.

Barbican Cinema. Silk Street, EC2. Tel: 0171/638 8891 or 0171/382 7000. Tube: Barbican or Moorgate. Admission: adults £6; children and seniors £4.

Barbican Art Gallery. Silk Street, EC2. Tel: 0171/588 9023 or 0171/382 7105. Tube: Barbican or Moorgate. Open: Mon, Wed–Sat 10am–6:45pm; Tues 10am–5:45pm; Sun noon–6:45pm. Admission: adults £4.50; concessions £2.50.

Museum of London. London Wall, EC2. Tel: 0171/600 3699. Tube: Barbican or St. Paul's. 24-hour information line tel: 0171/600 0807. Open: Tues–Sat 10am–5:30pm; Sun noon–5:30pm. Admission: adults £3; concessions £1.50.

Tower of London. Tower Hill, EC3. Tel: 0171/709 0765. Tube: Tower Hill. Open: Mar–Oct: Mon–Sat 9am–6pm; Sun 10am–6pm. Nov–Feb: Mon–Sat 9am–5pm; Sun 10am–5pm. Admission: adults £7.95; students and seniors £5.95. Group concessions available.

Courtauld Institute. Somerset House, The Strand, WC2. Tel: 0171/873 2549. Tube: Temple. Open: Mon–Sat 10am–6pm; Sun 2–6pm. Admission: adults £3; concessions £1.50.

National Gallery. Trafalgar Square, WC2. Tel: 0171/389 1785. Tube: Charing Cross. Open: Mon–Sat 10am–6pm; Sun 2–6pm. Admission: free.

Brick Lane Market. Brick Lane, E1. Tube: Aldgate. Open: Sun 6am–2pm.

Petticoat Lane Market. Petticoat Lane, E1. Tube: Aldgate East or Liverpool Street. Open: Sun 9am–1pm.

See "London Basics" and "What's Next After London" later in this chapter.

EARL'S COURT

For a long time, the neighborhood around Earl's Court was a haven for London's gays, but in the last few years a huge influx of travelers in search of cheap digs has transformed this into something of a tourist zone. Just below Kensington and bordering Chelsea, Earl's Court is a lively mix of restaurants, B&Bs, pubs, coffee shops, and wine bars. In summer, Australians and New Zealanders take over the rooming houses and B&Bs.

The neighborhood is within reach of all the major sights by tube, and the green expanses of Kensington Gardens and Hyde Park are a short walk to the north. Earl's Court, just west of Kensington, Knightsbridge, and Chelsea, is an excellent spot for shopping: The well-trafficked thoroughfares of King's Road, Old Brompton Road, and Sloane Street are all within walking distance. Knightsbridge is also home to a collection of museums: Nearby lie the Victoria and Albert, the Natural History, and the Science Museums. At night, the pubs, clubs, and coffee shops cater to the gay crowd. It's a pretty happening place any hour of day.

✸ Earl's Court Youth Hostel

38 Bolton Gardens
London SW5 0AQ
Tel.: 0171/373 7083. Fax: 0171/835 2034.
Central Reservations tel.: 0171/248 6547. Central Reservations fax: 0171/236 7681.
Tube: Earl's Court

The hostel at Earl's Court offers a special attraction for the independent backpacker: No school groups are accepted, unlike at all other London hostels. The place is thankfully devoid of the hectic, agitated atmosphere and trash trail that harried teachers and hyperactive youngsters seem to bring with them. It's a busy hostel nonetheless, with lots of mixing and mingling among international bunkmates, many of whom are Aussies and Kiwis.

The hostel tends to attract independent travelers who can take care of themselves, but that doesn't mean the facilities or services are paltry. This former Victorian residence was redone recently but still has a fairly strong old-world feeling. The rooms still have old-fashioned locks, and the wooden floors, antique wallpaper, and fresh paint job make it feel comfortably lived in and well cared for. The common room, with major mirroring, has a bay window overlooking the town houses on Bolton Gardens, and there's even a little library. The bedrooms and dining room are concessions to modern practicality: Dormitories have triple-decker bunks and clean hall baths. The dining room, with a two-tone mauve motif, would fit right in at the Holiday Inn, and framed movie stills hang on the walls. Outside is a small garden where barbecues are held in summer. Downstairs, the self-catering kitchen is convenient for do-it-yourself cooking.

The reception area is loaded with tourist information and also lists availability at the other London hostels—handy if you arrive without a reservation on busy summer nights. The Slow Coach has a desk here, which is a convenient service for those heading out on bus tours of England. The Slow Coach is the original 'Round-Britain Budget Bus, offering a totally flexible jump off/jump on service that takes the slog out of backpacking. As always, wise wayfarers book well in advance: The location and atmosphere make this one of London's more popular hostels.

Services

From any of London's eight British Rail stations, take the Piccadilly or District Line to Earl's Court. From the station, turn right onto Earl's Court Road and walk past Barkston Gardens and Bramham Gardens before reaching Bolton Gardens. Turn left; the hostel is on the right.

From Victoria Station, take the Circle or District Line two stops to Earl's Court. From the station, follow directions from the train, given above.

From the **south**, take the A3 (via Wimbledon) to the A219, following signs for Putney Bridge. Cross the river and take Fulham High Street up to Fulham Road, following it as it becomes Fulham Broadway and passing Brompton Cemetery on the left. Turn left onto Redcliffe Gardens and go past Redcliffe Square. Cross Old Brompton Road and you'll be on Earl's Court Road. Bolton Gardens will come up on the right. The hostel is on the right.

From the **north**, take the M41 headed south, following signs to Holland Park and Kensington. When you reach Shepherd's Bush (to the west of Holland Park and Kensington), cross the roundabout and head straight down Holland Road. At Kensington High Street, turn right. After about six blocks, turn right on Earl's Court Road and cross Cromwell Road; from there, Bolton Gardens is the 11th road on the left. The hostel is on the right.

Open all year. IBN/BABA: both.

Open 24 hours. Reception open 7:30am–10:30pm; security guards 10:30pm–7:30am. No curfew.

154 beds. 2-, 3-, 4-, 7-, 12-, 14-, and 26-bed rooms.

£ Members: adults £17.10; under 18 £15.10. All prices include breakfast.

The Academy Restaurant serves meals. Self-catering kitchen facilities open all day and night. Breakfast: 7:30–9:30am; breakfast included in price. Lunch: cafeteria open for lunch noon–5pm. Packed lunches should be ordered the night before. Dinner: 5–8pm. Set meal £4 or à la carte (veggie burger or cheeseburger £3.40).

No table license.

Individual lockers in bedrooms (BYOL—bring your own lock—or buy one at reception for £2.50); locker bank downstairs also requires padlocks.

Washers £1.60; dryers take 20p coins.

P None; cars are a nightmarish prospect in this neighborhood.

Shop at hostel sells National Express and Slow Coach tickets; Travelcards for London Underground (Zones 1 & 2); towels; stamps; film. Vending machines.

 TV room; quiet room.

Allowed in common room only.

Not wheelchair accessible.

Travelex currency exchange.

Bike shed.

Cheap Eats Nearby

Chelsea Kitchen

You get a bird's-eye view of Sloane Square with your filling portion of fettucine Alfredo, chicken Kiev, or potato-mushroom bake (£2.50). Inexpensive and fun, this restaurant caters to King's Road shoppers, artists, musicians, and the usual London melting pot with cozy booths and an inspired, varied menu.

98 King's Rd., SW3. Tel: 0171/589 1330. Tube: Sloane Square. Open: Mon–Sat 8am–11:30pm; Sun 11:30am–11:30pm. From the tube, walk straight up King's Road.

Troubadour Coffee House

Bob Dylan hung out and played tunes in this legendary hippie haunt. Musical instruments and kitchenware dangle from the ceilings. Soups £1.50 to £3. Sandwiches £2 to £3. The place brims over with cappuccinos.

265 Old Brompton Rd., SW5. Tel: 0171/370 1434. Tube: Earl's Court. Open: daily 9:30am–11pm. Cash only. From the tube, walk down Earl's Court Road to Brompton Road. It's on the corner.

Grocery Store: Earl's Court Food and Wine/Costcutter Supermarkets. 304 Earl's Court Rd., SW5. Open: Mon–Sat 9am–11pm.

Experiences

Starting in Knightsbridge, stop by the collection of museums before heading into the boutique-infested zone around Sloane Street and King's Road. The grandmother of London museums is right on Cromwell Road: the **Victoria and Albert,** founded in 1899 by Queen Victoria, has more than 10 acres' worth of gallery space. Beginning in the traditional Renaissance and Medieval galleries, a walk through the labyrinthine corridors will take you through an amazingly exhaustive melange of art: Italian Renaissance sculptures; the Frank Lloyd Wright gallery; centuries' worth of Chinese art; Japanese lacquerwork and sculpture; a clothing collection (from chest-crunching corsets of the 1700s to ankle-busting platform shoes of the 1990s); and a stable of beloved Brits, including John Constable, Beatrix Potter, Charles Rennie Mackintosh, and others. And there's more. Much more. You could easily spend a few days here.

Smaller, though also interesting, museums nearby include the **Accademia Italiani delle Arti,** which sponsors offbeat modern design, costume, and sculpture exhibits as well as retrospectives of classical Italian masters. And the **Commonwealth Institute** has amassed an unusual collection of art from former British colonies. Musical instruments from Africa, rugs from India, and ink drawings and films from the Far East offer a neat history lesson. Evening performances are held here as well.

Shopping in the area is a mix: Quirky shops and antique dealers dot the area just north of here, especially on Kensington Church Street, a great place to ooh and aah over fancy stuff. For antiques priced in the realm of mere mortals, **Alfie's Antique Market** is farther away but heaves with more than 300 stalls of funky finds.

Sloane Street is a parade of designers: Armani, Fendi, Ungaro, and other big names have their boutiques on this leggy street. When it curves around Sloane Square, **King's Road** intersects it with a frenzy of trendy (and not-so-trendy) boutiques. If you head all the way down King's Road, you'll eventually reach the **Chelsea Antique Market,** which is slightly touristy but has some interesting finds, including old books. Up the street at no. 430 is where Vivienne Westwood and Malcolm McLaren started up their "youthquake" in the 1960s when they opened up a bunch of boutiques that institutionalized the underground fashion that rumbled through the times. The Sex Pistols came of age here, too.

Moving away from King's Road, you can have a shot of Stuart England at Christopher Wren's **Royal Hospital,** on the banks of the river. It was built in the late

1600s to house army veterans and still does; they don't seem to mind if people wander through the pretty buildings and grassy grounds. The pleasant, leafy **Ranelagh Gardens** spill out from the hospital and are open until sundown. They're the home of the ever-popular **Chelsea Flower Show,** which blossoms at the end of May.

Up the street is the turn-of-the-century triumvirate of trend: **Cheyne Walk, Tite Street,** and **Cheyne Row.** This area was the lifeblood of Chelsea's artist colony for a long time, but inexorably, rents were raised, buildings were restored, and the "beautiful people" arrived. It's now an upper-crust residential area. Little blue plaques on the buildings tell you what it was like Way Back When. It was at 34 Tite St. that Oscar Wilde sowed his "wilde" oats; Bertrand Russell, James Whistler, and John Singer Sargent also lived on the block. Cheyne Walk was home to J. M. W. Turner, Dante Gabriel Rossetti, and Edgar Allan Poe. In the 1960s, 48 Cheyne Walk was home to Mick Jagger and Keith Richards (Richards still lives around here).

At the end of Cheyne Walk lies the **Chelsea Old Church.** Built in part by Sir Thomas More, it was the site of the marriage between Henry VIII and his third wife, Jane Seymour. At 24 Cheyne Row, Chelsea's favorite son, Thomas Carlyle, penned his magical prose; **Carlyle House** still contains the writer's personal effects, furniture, and paintings almost unchanged from when he lived here.

Victoria and Albert Museum. Cromwell Road, SW7. Tel: 0171/938 8500. Tube: Knightsbridge. Open: Mon noon–5:50pm; Tues–Sun 10am–5:50pm. Admission: free.

Accademia Italiani delle Arti. 24 Rutland Gate, SW7. Tube: Knightsbridge. Open: Tues, Thurs–Sat 10am–5:30pm; Wed 10am–8pm; Sun noon–5:30pm. Admission: adults £5; concessions £2.50; children £1.

Commonwealth Institute. Kensington High Street, W8. Tel: 0171/603 4535. Tube: High Street Kensington. Open: Mon–Sat 10am–5pm; Sun 2–5pm. Admission: adults £1; concessions 50p.

Alfie's Antiques Market. 13–25 Church St., NW8. Tube: Marylebone or Edgware Road. Open: Tues–Sat 10am–6pm.

Chelsea Antique Market. 253 King's Rd., SW3. Tube: Sloane Square. Open: Mon–Sat 10am–6pm.

Royal Hospital and Ranelagh Gardens. Royal Hospital Road, SW3. Tube: Sloane Square. Open: Mon–Sat 10am–noon and 2–4pm; Sun 2–4pm. Admission: free.

Chelsea Flower Show. For information, contact the Royal Horticultural Society, Vincent Square, London SW1P 2PE. Tel: 0171/630 7422.

Chelsea Old Church. Old Church Street, SW3. Tube: Sloane Square. Open: daily 10am–1pm and 2–5pm.

Carlyle House. 24 Cheyne Row, SW3. Tel: 0171/352 7087. Tube: Sloane Square. Open: Apr–Oct: Wed–Sun 11am–5pm. Admission: adults £2.75; children £1.50.

See "London Basics" and "What's Next After London" later in this chapter.

HAMPSTEAD HEATH

Tucked away above the congested city center, the grassy splendor of Hampstead Heath straddles the neighborhoods of Hampstead, Golders Green, and Highgate Village to the north of Regent's Park. Hampstead was once an artists' enclave, peaceful and removed, but the high and mighty got a taste of the good life up here and turned the once-unassuming village into a chichi neighborhood where luxury cars queue up on the cobbled streets.

Today palatial Georgian town houses are hidden behind scrupulously pruned bushes and high brick walls. In the town, too-precious shops sell such worthwhile items as designer baby clothes, expensive jewelry and trinkets, overpriced crafts, and dried flower arrangements. Even the local McDonald's is slick. Nevertheless, there are some good cafes and restaurants, and the elegant sprawling estates certainly make it a pleasant place to stay while in London.

The hostel is at the top edge of the Heath, somewhat removed from luxurious Hampstead. Closer by is Golders Green, the heart of London's Jewish community, which imparts an ethnic flavor to the area just north of the hostel. It's a refreshing break from the sometimes stifling swankiness of Hampstead. This hostel is a good choice for those who'd rather see central London by day and return to a quieter, more natural setting at night.

❀ Hampstead Heath Youth Hostel

4 Wellgarth Rd.
London NW11 7HR
Tel: 0181/458 9054. Fax: 0181/209 0546. Central Reservations tel: 0171/248 6547. Central Reservations fax: 0171/236 7681.
Tube: Golders Green

Set up on the hills inside the mammoth parkland of northern London, Hampstead Heath is a special hostel, urban in location but not citylike at all in character. The tube stop is Golders Green, a friendly residential neighborhood. The hostel's namesake village, however, is a walk in the other direction through the park and down the hill.

Located in the middle of the park, the hostel has its own prim-and-proper history: It served as a former training center for pediatric nurses. Walking up to the building, you'll pass by potted plants, flowers, and fragrant pine bushes, lending it a tidy, picturesque air. Inside, the reception area is loaded with copies of *New Zealand News* and Australian newspapers. The dining room, called The Grapevine, has Impressionist posters on the wall and is outfitted in sturdy plastic and Formica, which stand up remarkably well, given the many school groups that bang their silverware on the tables and shove one another around in here.

To escape the youngsters (they're everywhere), head out to the courtyard; a covered patio with an atrium lies just outside of the common room and restaurant. There's a lovely brick wall with—you guessed it—a creeping grapevine. (One year, the maintenance staff here actually made wine from the stuff.) Barbecues are sometimes held in the garden.

The common room has video games, a pool table, and loads of brochures on the area. Sports fans also come here since Wembley Stadium is only about

3 miles away and easily accessible by bus. Like all London hostels, Hampstead Heath gets booked up fast, so call well in advance. International teen tours and school groups seem to converge here, so prepare yourself for the crowds.

🚆 If you're coming from any one of London's British Rail stations, take the Northern Line tube one stop beyond Hampstead to Golders Green. If you take it to Hampstead, you'll have a 30-minute walk uphill. From the tube station, go past the National Express ticket office and turn left at onto North End Road, away from the center of Golders Green. After about five minutes, you'll come across Wellgarth Road on your left. Turn left at the blue YHA sign and the hostel will be on your right.

🚌 From central London, take the no. 28 bus from Kensington High Street, which also stops at the Golders Green tube stop. From the Highgate Village Youth Hostel, take bus no. 210 (70p); it's a 15-minute ride.

From Victoria Coach station, take the Circle or District Line to Embankment, and switch there for the Northern Line. Get off at Golders Green and follow the directions from the train, given above.

🚗 Arriving in Hampstead from the **north,** take the M1/A1, and switch to the A41, following signs for Hampstead Heath and Golders Green. Just before the Brent Cross tube station, turn left (east) onto the North Circular Road (A406) and take it to Golders Green Road. Take Golders Green Road through the center and continue on North End Road, then turn left onto Wellgarth Road. The hostel is on the right.

From the **south,** follow signs through London to Camden Town, Kentish Town, and Hampstead. Take the A1 to Archway and Highgate Village and curve up past Highgate High Street and onto Hampstead Lane, skirting the north edge of the Heath. Follow Hampstead Lane, bearing left as it turns into Spaniards Road (B519). At the end of Spaniards Road, turn right onto North End Way (A502). Continue up and out of the park and turn right onto Wellgarth Road. The hostel is on the right.

▦ Open all year. IBN/BABA: both.

🕐 Open 24 hours. No curfew.

🛏 198 beds. 2-, 3-, 4-, 5-, 6-, 7-, and 12-bed rooms available.

£ Members: adults £14; under 18 £11.90.

🍴 Grapevine Restaurant. Self-catering kitchen facilities. Breakfast: 7:30–9:30am; not included in overnight price. Lunch: packed lunch only; should be ordered the night before. Dinner: 5–8pm; three-course dinner £4 or à la carte burgers, chili, and the like.

⊺ Table license.

🛄 Individual lockers, one per bed; padlock required (can be bought at reception for £2.50). Luggage room with individual lockers (£1 per day; £5 key deposit required).

▣ Washers £1.50; dryers take 20p coins.

P Ample and free of charge.

🗋 Shop at hostel sells National Express and Eurolines bus tickets; toiletries, T-shirts; Travelcards for London Underground (Zones 1–4).

🛋 Two TV rooms; garden; games room.

🚭 In common room only.

♿ Limited wheelchair accessibility; bedrooms are upstairs. They try to accommodate people in wheelchairs if possible.

💱 Travelex currency exchange.

🔺 Bike shed; booking service for theater and some sights.

Cheap Eats Nearby

Jack Straw's Castle

Set in the middle of Hampstead Heath, this a convenient and cute spot for hostelers. Nests with flowers adorn this ivory shingled house. Bay windows overlook the park, and comfy cushions soothe sore butts. Sausage, baked beans, and chips £2.95. Rolls filled with ham, turkey, and the like £2.95. Salads (£3 to £5) are especially good in summer.

North End Way, NW11. Tel: 0181/435 8885. Tube: Golders Green or Hampstead Heath. Open: Mon–Sat noon–3pm and 6–10pm; Sun noon–10pm. From the Hampstead tube, walk up hilly Heath Street into the park; Jack Straw's is up on the left. From Golders Green, walk down North End Road, past the hostel and into the Heath. Continue downhill on North End Way; the restaurant is on the right, at the intersection with Heath and Spaniards Roads.

Le Petit Prince

This sweet restaurant is a shrine to Antoine de Saint-Exupéry: The walls bring *The Little Prince* alive with lovingly painted depictions of the fictional character against a soothing purple background. The food is French/Algerian, and all entreés come with couscous and consommé. Vegetable couscous is £5; crepes £5 to £6; lamb dishes £6 to £7 and up. The restaurant is worth the price.

5 Holmes Rd., NW5. Tel: 0171/267 0752. Tube: Kentish Town. Open: daily noon–3pm and 7–11:30pm. Cash only. From the tube, walk down Kentish Town Road; Holmes Road is the second road on the right.

Grocery store: Sainsburys. Finchley Road, Golders Green NW11.

Experiences

A great place to start exploring the area is the Heath itself, stretching over 785 acres of wild parkland. It's easy to get lost amid the green pastures and leafy cradle of trees where John Constable and John Keats found solace from urban London. If you do get lost, just make sure it's during the day; like all parks, Hampstead Heath can be risky at night.

If the sun is shining, the **Kenwood Ladies' Pond, Highgate Men's Pond,** and **Mixed Bathing Pond** are nice spots for sunbathing; free souls who want to go topless should go to the Ladies' Pond. **Kenwood House,** an 18th-century mansion and country estate, overlooks the Heath and is open to visitors. It also houses the **Iveagh Bequest,** an impressive collection of British portraits, furniture, some splendid Rembrandts, a Vermeer, and other works of the Dutch Renaissance.

At the southern end of the heath is **Whitestone Pond,** where Percy Bysshe Shelley used to sail paper boats and fly kites with his young children. **Parliament Hill,** at the far southeastern tip of the heath, has some staggering views of central London. The hill has an interesting historical legend: buried plague victims are said to lurk underground, forming the lump of the hill.

Down in Hampstead, **Keats House** is the lovingly preserved home of the Romantic poet; his manuscripts and letters remain in the house, still furnished as it was in his time. Other artistic haunts include John Constable's house at 40 Well Walk; 1 Elm Row, where D. H. Lawrence lived for a spell; and 26 Church Row, once the home of Lord Alfred Douglas, Oscar Wilde's lover.

In Golders Green, the main street is loaded with Jewish delis. Way up the road at the **Golders Green Crematorium** lie the ashes of Sigmund Freud and Bram Stoker, as well as the founder of Marks and Spencer.

Kenwood House and Iveagh Bequest. Hampstead Lane, Hampstead Heath, NW3. Tel: 0181/348 1286. Tube: Golders Green or Archway. Open: May–Oct: daily 10am–6pm; Nov–Apr: daily 10am–4pm. Admission: free.

Keats House. Keats Grove, Hampstead NW3. Tel: 0181/435 2062. Tube: Hampstead. Open: Apr–Oct: Mon–Fri 10am–1pm and 2–6pm; Sat 10am–1pm and 2–5pm; Sun 2–5pm. Nov–Mar: Mon–Fri 1–5pm; Sat 10am–1pm and 2–5pm; Sun 2–5pm. Admission: free; donation suggested.

Golders Green Crematorium. Hoop Lane Road, Golders Green NW11. Tel: 0181/455 2374. Tube: Golders Green. Open: daily 8am–7pm.

See "London Basics" and "What's Next After London" later in this chapter.

HIGHGATE VILLAGE

A short walk to the east of Hampstead Heath, Highgate Village is lined with genteel 16th- and 17th-century mansions. The area is as prosperous as it was back in the old days, with construction workers hammering out finishing touches on the palatial homes of London's elite.

It's not surprising that luminaries like Sting, Annie Lennox, and George Michael live here. Highgate has an exceedingly elegant patina but hasn't lost traces of its bohemian past. Small cottages, tea rooms, and antique shops dot the streets, and the revolutionary bones of Karl Marx rest in the rubble of Highgate Cemetery. Nearby sights include Hampstead Heath; Keats House; and Fenton House, a stately mansion inside the park; in addition, the Freud Museum isn't far away.

Highgate Village also has a great collection of old pubs, but start drinking early: There's a midnight curfew at the hostel here. In a sweet old building, the hostel is a trifle more laid-back and less spiffy than the other hostels in London, but it's a pleasant environment for those looking to get away from the city center's bustle.

Highgate Village Youth Hostel

84 Highgate West Hill
London N6 6LU
Tel: 0181/340 1831. Fax: 0181/341 0376.
Central Reservations tel: 0171/248 6547. Central Reservations fax: 0171/236 7681.
Tube: Archway

The people at the Highgate Village claim to make the best hot chocolate in town; the stuff is dispensed free every morning from 7 to 9am. This Georgian house in the swanky neighborhood of Highgate is comfortable, relaxed, and friendly—and it's also London's least expensive hostel.

While the facilities are fairly basic and it's a bit of a ride on the tube, the hostel does have its rewards. Unlike its more businesslike counterparts in central London, Highgate Village Hostel has a distinct personality. Though there's no dining service here, the smell of granola and herbal tea wafts through the air. The staff sports Doc Martens, and you may spot a few poetry books or socialist manifestoes behind the reception desk.

The common room and reception area are littered with flyers advertising all sorts of alternative activities, from vegetarian holidays to barefoot boogie night at the local community center. The common room and bedrooms are slightly run-down; don't expect anything supermodern or state-of-the-art. Hostelers are a mix of international backpackers and school groups, and large groups seem to like it here. Call ahead to find out what's available.

Services

From any of London's eight British Rail stations, take the Northern Line tube to Archway (Zone 2). From there, take bus no. 210 or 217 to Highgate Village. Turn left at South Grove, just off Highgate Hill. The hostel is 400 yards to the left, past the Angel Pub.

Take bus no. 210, 214, or 271 from London King's Cross to Highgate Village. Bus no. 214 passes directly in front of the hostel; nos. 210 and 217 go to Highgate Village. From there, follow directions from the train, given above.

From London's Victoria Station, take the Circle or District Line tube to Embankment, then the Northern Line to Archway (Zone 2). From there, take bus no. 210 or 217 to Highgate Village. Then follow directions from the Highgate Village, given above.

From the **north,** take the A1 straight into Archway. When you reach the tube station, take a sharp right onto Highgate Hill Road, which turns into Highgate High Street. Turn left onto Highgate West Hill Road; the hostel is on the left, past the Angel Pub.

From the **south,** follow signs to Camden Town, Kentish Town, and Hampstead Heath. Take the A1 or A400 straight into Archway and bear left onto Highgate Hill Road, which turns into Highgate High Street. From here, follow directions from the north, given above.

Open all year. IBN and BABA.

Reception open 8:30am–11pm. Curfew midnight.

71 beds. 2-, 3-, 4-, 8-, 10-, 12-, and 16-bed rooms.

£ Members: adults £11.85; under 18 £7.90.

No meals. Self-catering kitchen facilities include oven, stove, microwave, and toaster.

No alcohol allowed.

Individual lockers in bedrooms; bring a padlock or buy one here (£2.50). Luggage storage room kept under lock and key.

Drying room only.

P Street parking; easy to find spots.

Shop at hostel sells National Express and Eurolines bus tickets; London Underground Travelcards (Zones 1–2, 1–6, 1–4); groceries; and toiletries. They rent hair dryers, irons, and board games (£5 deposit).

TV lounge.

In common room only.

No wheelchair access.

Travelex currency exchange.

Bike shed; booking service for some sights; theater tickets.

Cheap Eats Nearby

The Flask

Not far from the hostel, this is the oldest pub in Highgate Village. Karl Marx, William Hogarth, and other late luminaries hung out here. Gray Lady, the house ghost, still does. Quiz night on Tuesday and jazz on Wednesday bring in a good crowd. Outside tables are a nice spot for drinking; the hot mulled wine (£2.10 per glass) is tasty on cold nights. The traditional pub fare includes shepherd's pie (£4) and steak-and-ale pie (£4.25). Prices go up at night.

77 Highgate Hill, N6. Tel: 0181/340 7260. Tube: Archway. Open: Mon–Sat 11am–11pm; Sun noon–3pm and 7–10:30pm. Cash only. From the tube stop, walk straight up Highgate Hill Road; the restaurant is on the left, where Highgate Hill turns into South Grove.

The Raj Tea Room

This place has wooden floors and tables stuffed to the gills with Bach Flower Remedies, books, and doodads of all sorts. Karl Marx would've been at home among the black-turtlenecked patrons. The menu lists "intuitive home-spun cuisine." Alternative breakfasts and vegan meals £2–£5. Potato-spinach bake £2. Cheese and ratatouille on toast £4. Stop by for music on weekend evenings and afternoon tea any day.

67 Highgate High St., N6. Tel: 0181/348 8760. Tube: Archway. Open: Sun–Thurs 9:30am–6pm; Fri–Sat 9:30am–2am. Cash only. From the Archway tube, walk up Highgate Hill to Highgate High Street; the restaurant is on the left, upstairs from a clothing store.

Grocery Store: Europa Foods. Look for the big yellow sign on Highgate High Street. Open: Mon–Sat 8am–10pm; Sun 9am–10pm.

Experiences

The hostel's communal camaraderie is partially inspired by the socialist spirit wafting down from the tomb of **Highgate Cemetery**'s most illustrious resident. Just south of the hostel, Karl Marx lies underneath a tombstone bearing his unforgettable declaration: "Workers of the world unite." It's unclear as to whether this has come true in ritzy Highgate, but the cemetery is nevertheless worth a visit. Marx's huge monument makes a curious statement, since almost all the other tombs in this Victorian cemetery are snazzy marble pall palaces. George Eliot is also interred here.

Just north of the cemetery, **Waterlow Park** is a pleasant place to reflect on the bourgeois quality of 20th-century life. The beautiful grounds offer excellent views of foggy London down below.

If you head up **Highgate Hill,** you'll pass by Dick Whittington's Stone. As the legend goes, Whittington heard the Higher Power speak to him, telling him to return to London and become mayor. He did, and he did. His dead cat still presides over the historic spot. Once you get up the hill, the views of London, more than 400 feet below, are staggering.

Outside the neighborhood, you can head out to Finchley, where you'll find the three-story **Freud Museum,** a lonely red-brick building. Inside, you can take a look at the home where Sigmund Freud lived after escaping Nazi Vienna; his library is still there, as are his couch and a smattering of letters, manuscripts, and mementos belonging to him and his daughter.

The **Camden Markets** are kind of a shopper's rite of passage in London, especially for first-time visitors. The markets are only a short walk down from the Archway tube station. As long as you guard your belongings carefully, exploring the collection of T-shirts, leather jackets, Singapore noodles, Lycra microminis, vintage clothes, nose rings, bootleg tapes, and Adidas high-tops makes for an amusing outing, even if the market's reputation has slightly faded since its glorious past. Back in the direction of Highgate, Hampstead Heath is a choice place to rest and relax after a day's shopping and sightseeing.

Highgate Cemetery. Swains Lane, N6. Tube: Highgate. Eastern Cemetery open: Mon–Fri 10am–4:45pm; Sat–Sun 11am–4:45pm. Western Cemetery open for guided tours only. Tours offered Mon–Fri at noon, 2pm, 4pm; Sat–Sun on the hour, 11am–4pm. Admission: £2. Camera permit £1.

Freud Museum. 20 Maresfield Gardens, NW3. Tel: 0171/435 2002. Tube: Finchley Road. Open: Wed–Sun noon–5pm. Admission: adults £2.50; children under 12 free.

Camden Markets. Camden High Street, NW2. Tube: Camden Town. Fri–Sun 8:30am–sundown.

See "London Basics" and "What's Next After London" later in this chapter.

HOLLAND PARK

The area in and around Holland Park falls into the Royal Borough of Kensington and Chelsea, home to shops in Knightsbridge and on Kensington High Street, museums in South Kensington, and teenage fashion slaves along King's Road and Sloane Square. Just to the north, ethnic eateries and cool coffeehouses form a nucleus around Notting Hill; to the west, Kensington Gardens and Hyde Park give way to Green Park, St. James's Park, and Buckingham Palace.

Holland Park, like many neighborhoods in London, has an ambience all its own. Lined with towering, elegant homes, this stylish residential neighborhood has its own park with loads of things to do: summer theater; arts exhibition space; a children's playground; an ecology center; a wildlife pond; formal gardens; and a sports center with golf, tennis, squash, and cricket.

Less opulent than its surroundings, the hostel is in the restored eastern wing of Holland House. It's often loaded with school groups frolicking on the grassy gardens. If you don't mind crowds, this isn't a bad spot. The Jacobean mansion manages to blend country and city. Centrally located by tube, it's nonetheless relatively unbothered by the noise, traffic, and congestion of inner London.

❀ Holland House Youth Hostel (King George VI Memorial Youth Hostel)

Holland House, Holland Walk
Kensington, London W8 7QU
Tel: 0171/937 0748. Fax: 0171/376 0667.
Central Reservations tel.: 0171/237 2919. Central Reservations fax: 0171/236 7681.
Tube: High Street Kensington

It doesn't seem improbable that Holland House, ensconced in the leafy shade of Kensington's Holland Park, was once the home of a wealthy nobleman who was Chancellor of the Exchequer to James I. It also doesn't seem improbable that it's one of the few remaining Jacobean mansions in inner London. What does seem improbable is that it has been converted into a Youth Hostel.

Built in the 1600s, Holland House was meant to be a private home, but during the English Civil War the house was confiscated by Oliver Cromwell, who was said to have held secret meetings here with General Treton. In the 18th century, the baroness of Holland played hostess to literary types such as Lord Byron, William Wordsworth, and Charles Dickens in the mansion's many salons. Sadly, during World War II the house was damaged by bombing and fell into disrepair until the local council did a bang-up repair job on the whole complex. The east wing was refashioned: Luxury salons were subdivided, oil paintings came down as YHA posters were tacked up, chaise lounges were replaced by bunk beds, and the place eventually became the King George VI Memorial Youth Hostel.

A 200-bed megahostel, it's in the least spectacular wing of Holland House. Brown leatherette chairs greet you as you enter a hall resembling a second-class car on the Network SouthCentral train to Brighton. A few phones and some vending machines do nothing to enliven the dispirited decor. The bedrooms are standard-issue YHA; All have hall bathrooms. The dining room, aka the Garden Restaurant, is a busy cafeteria serving such incongruous offerings as pork schnitzel (£2.50), samosas (£2.40), and veggie burgers (£2.40). The slightly smoky common room is filled with games, and a sliding door opens onto the green lawn courtyard outside.

The hostel hosts lots of school groups. They tend to dominate the place, especially the cafeteria. The capable staff is used to the young guests, though. A slightly jaded bunch, the staff runs the place as if it were an efficient elementary school.

The hostel's location is its main selling point, and you're not likely to spend too much time inside: London sights are close at hand and nearby Holland Park bursts with activity—recreational, cultural, and horticultural. For urban rucksackers pining for grassy knolls, lagoons, and nature, Holland House offers a tranquil park right in the city center.

Services

From any of London's eight British Rail stations, take the Circle Line tube to Kensington High Street. From the tube, walk along High Street Kensington toward the entrance to Holland Park. Turn right and walk up Holland Walk. The hostel will come up on the left. You can also take the Central Line to Holland Park on the tube, but the walk from Kensington High Street is safer, especially at night.

From Victoria coach station, take the Circle Line tube to High Street Kensington. From here, follow directions from the train, given above. Alternatively, take bus no. 52 from Victoria Station to Kensington High Street.

From the **north,** take the M41 (the West Cross Route) into London, following signs to Holland Park, Hammersmith, and Kensington. When you reach Shepherd's Bush, continue down Holland Road, turning left onto Kensington High Street. After about six blocks, turn left onto Phillimore Gardens, which leads into the park. The hostel is on the left, at the corner of Duchess of Bedford's Walk.

From the **south,** take the A306 up to Hammersmith Bridge and cross the Thames. Follow Hammersmith Bridge Road up to Hammersmith Broadway (where the tube stop is located). Turn right onto Hammersmith Road and follow it as it turns into Kensington High Street. Cross Warwick Road, and after about six blocks turn left onto Phillimore Gardens, which leads into the park. The hostel is on the left, at the corner of Duchess of Bedford's Walk.

▦ Open all year. IBN/BABA: both.

🕐 Open 24 hours. Reception staffed 7am–11:30pm. Security guards 11:30pm–7am. No curfew.

🛏 201 beds. 2-, 3-, 4-, 6-, 8-, 12-, 13-, and 20-bed rooms.

£ Members: adults £17.10; under 18 £15. Prices include breakfast.

🍴 The Garden Restaurant. Self-catering kitchen facilities. Breakfast: 7:30–9:30am. Breakfast included in overnight price. Packed lunch only; should be ordered the night before. Dinner: 5–8pm. Three-course meal £4 or order from à la carte menu.

🍸 No table license.

💼 Individual lockers in bedrooms; bring your own padlock or buy one for £2.50. Lockers bank downstairs £1.50 per day.

⊙ Washers £1.50; dryers take 20p coins.

P No parking on hostel grounds; the closest parking is on Warwick Road.

📖 Shop at Hostel sells National Express and Eurolines bus tickets; towels; candy; toiletries; stamps; postcards.

📺 TV/dining room; quiet room.

🚬 In common room only.

♿ Not wheelchair accessible.

 Travelex currency exchange.

🔺 Bike shed; booking service for theater and some attractions.

Cheap Eats Nearby

Café Pasta

This is a cool, airy, and sophisticated Italian restaurant in Kensington. Though it's part of a chain, it has hanging plants, blond-wood tables, and good music playing. It attracts a healthy crowd of people-watchers and food-lovers. Fusilli with Gorgonzola £5.75. Three-course dinner £6.95. Pizzas £5 to £6.

229–231 Kensington High St., W8. Tel.: 0171/937 6314. Tube: High Street Kensington. Open: Mon–Sat 11am–11:30pm; Sun 11am–11pm. Credit cards: AE, VA, MC, EC, Access, Switch. From the tube, turn left onto Kensington High Street; the cafe is on the left.

Khan's

One of London's many Indian eateries, Khan's is actually busy and has a thoughtful menu with explanations. Locals gobble down a wide selection of tikkas, baltis, kormas, and curries in the big dining room. When they say spicy, they mean it. Chicken tikka £3.50. Vegetable balti £3. Nan £1.

13–15 Westbourne Grove, W2. Tel: 0171/727 5240. Tube: Bayswater. Open: daily noon–3pm and 6pm–midnight. Cash only. From the tube station, walk up Queensway to Westbourne Grove. Turn left; Khan's is on the left.

Grocery Store: Safeway. Kensington High Street, W8. Open: Mon–Thurs and Sat 8am–8pm; Fri 8am–9pm; Sun 10am–4pm.

Experiences

It's worth spending a good afternoon exploring Holland House and Holland Park as a nice break from pounding the urban pavement. The front terrace of Holland

House is home to the **Holland Park Theatre,** which hosts open-air plays, concerts, operas, and ballets in summer—and for a pretty penny, they offer restaurant/ theater tickets. The former **Orangery** is now an arts exhibition space displaying innovative sculpture.

Around the corner, the mansion's old **Ice House** is now a tiny exhibition space, showcasing ceramics, crafts, watercolors, and oil paintings. Just beyond are the serene **Iris Garden** and **Kyoto Garden.** Holland House's **Formal Gardens** feature geometrically arranged flower beds bordered by box hedges, baby ponds, and stone fountains. The park also offers loads of **sports,** including a small driving range, tennis courts (lessons available), squash courts, cricket fields, and a children's adventure playground.

A short jaunt directly east of Holland Park takes you to **Kensington Gardens,** which team up here with **Hyde Park** to create the most unbroken stretch of green space in central London. Covering over 630 acres, the gardens house **Kensington Palace,** where you can check out Princess Diana's wedding dress or watch toy sailboats float on the **Round Pond** on summer weekends. The **Serpentine** is an artificial lake with a Henry Moore sculpture at one end and an interesting **Serpentine Gallery,** which hosts traveling art exhibitions as well as art lectures, symposia, and other events.

If you head north, you'll go toward Notting Hill, where the cool kids of London mix and mingle amid various ethnic communities. The legendary **Portobello Road** is just up the street from the Notting Hill Gate tube stop. The market here is crowded and vaguely dangerous but does have decent deals on incense, bootleg tapes, used clothing, and trendy curios. A London institution, it's worth investigating. At the north end, you'll find antiques and produce. Guard your valuables with your life.

Those looking for thinner crowds and less of a scene can head out to Islington, where **Camden Passage** (not Camden Town) has a huge collection of antiques, prints, and drawings. Also in Islington, **Chapel Market** is a potpourri of the same stuff you'll find in Portobello, but it's less chaotic.

Holland Park Theatre. Holland Park, W8. Tel: 0171/602 7856. Tube: Holland Park or High Street Kensington. Box office open: May–Aug only; Mon–Sat 11am– 8pm. Tickets: adults £18; students, seniors, and children £12.

The Orangery and the Ice House. Holland Park, off Kensington High Street, W8. Tel: 0171/603 1123. Tube: Holland Park or High Street Kensington. Open: daily 11am–7pm.

Holland Park Sports Booking Office. Holland Park, W8. Tel: 0171/602 2226. Tube: Holland Park or High Street Kensington. Tennis courts (per hour): adults £4.20; children £1.70; racket hire £1 (£10 deposit); ball hire £1.55 for three balls. Squash courts (per hour): adults £3.60; children £1.85. Cricket (May–Aug only): reserved match pitch £39.50; practice session £16. Golf driving nets (per half hour): adults £1; children 75p.

Kensington Palace and Gardens. Kensington Gardens, W8. Tel: 0171/937 9561. Tube: High Street Kensington. Palace open: Mon–Sat 9am–5:30pm; Sun 11am– 5:30pm. Admission: adults £3.75; students and seniors £3; children £2.50. Gardens open: summer: Mon–Fri 10am–6pm; Sat–Sun 10am–7pm. Winter: Mon– Fri 10am–sundown; Sat–Sun 10am–4pm.

Serpentine Gallery. Kensington Gardens, W8. Tel: 0171/402 6075. Tube: High Street Kensington. Open: daily 10am–6pm.

Portobello Road. W11. Tube: Notting Hill Gate. Antiques: Sat 7am–5pm. Clothing, etc.: Fri–Sat 8am–3pm.

Camden Passage. Islington High Street, N1. Tube: Angel. Wed and Sat 8:30am–3pm.

Chapel Market. Off Liverpool Road, N1. Tube: Angel. Tues–Wed and Fri–Sat 8am–6:30pm; Thurs and Sun 8am–12:30pm.

See "London Basics" and "What's Next After London" later in this chapter.

OXFORD STREET

Shoe stores and electronics shops peep out from between Marks and Spencer, Selfridges, Top Shop, Next, and other mainstream multiple stores on Oxford Street, one of London's most famous thoroughfares. Leaflets are thrust into the hands of harried passersby and cars try to squeeze through Oxford Street's clogged arteries.

This is one of the main hubs of tourist activity, mainly because it's such a luscious spot for sightseeing. Within easy walking distance are Bloomsbury and the British Museum, Soho, Chinatown, the National Gallery, Buckingham Palace, Green Park, St. James's Park, the Wallace Collection, Hyde Park and Kensington Gardens, and many other attractions.

The wayfarers who stay in the no-frills hostel on Noel Street are mainly dawn-to-dusk sightseers. There's little space inside the cramped third-floor quarters to hang out, and most people here seem to use the hostel for a (brief) night's sleep and little more. Because of its prime location, the hostel's price is unsurprisingly high. As usual, you'll need to be supervigilant of your belongings and your person in this commercial zone: The area is teeming with tourists, and unsuspecting hostelers often feel tugs at their bum bags, belt wallets, and camera straps. Welcome to London.

Oxford Street Youth Hostel

14 Noel St.
London W1V 3PD
Tel: 0171/734 1618. Fax: 0171/734 1657.
Central Reservations tel: 0171/237 2919. Central Reservations fax: 0171/236 7681.
Tube: Oxford Circus

Oxford Street is known the world over, as is Oxford Street Youth Hostel. Legions of international tourists make reservations here months in advance, insisting on staying at the Youth Hostel, sight unseen, that bears this famous name. If they saw the place beforehand, maybe they'd think twice. Squashed onto the third floor of a building, the hostel is a no-frills outfit sandwiched between the Oxford Circus and Tottenham Court Road tube stations. It certainly doesn't feel like Christmas here on Noel Street: The quarters are cramped, the surroundings noisy, and the facilities spartan. Still, that doesn't stop hordes from keeping this place booked solid almost year-round.

As you walk up the stairs, you're greeted by posters of other, prettier hostels. This place doesn't beg to be photographed. Boring brown leatherette couches, a bulletin board, and walls with ever-popular movie stills render the decor haggard and half-hearted. The lounge has a vending machine and TV, and the small rooms have cramped bunks. The staff is efficient and friendly, though, and most of the hostelers don't seem bothered by the uninspiring interior.

Featuring doubles and quads, this is the perfect place for those traveling in twos and threes. If you aren't too finicky about atmosphere, the reward of this hostel is its central location. The price may seem high for such simplicity, but the quantity of hostelers that book in make it London's most popular. Reserve at least three weeks in advance.

Services

From any of London's eight British Rail stations, take the Bakerloo, Central, or Victoria Line tube to Oxford Circus. From there, walk down Oxford Street toward Marks and Spencer. After about five blocks, turn right on Poland Street and left on Noel. The hostel is across the street on the right.

From London's Victoria Station, take the Victoria Line directly to Oxford Circus. Follow above directions from the train.

From the **west,** take the A40 into London down Harrow Road, past the Edgware Road tube stop, and onto Marylebone Road. When you reach the Regent's Park tube stop, turn right onto the Park Crescent and bear right onto Portland Place. Pass through Langham Place and continue straight onto Regent Street. When you reach Oxford Street, turn left toward Marks and Spencer. After you pass five roads, turn right onto Poland Street and then left onto Noel Street; the hostel is on the right.

From the **north,** take the A1 into London. At the Angel tube stop, bear right onto St. John. Then bear right again onto Rosebery Avenue (A401), which becomes Theobalds Road. As you pass through Bloomsbury, it becomes New Oxford Street (A40) and then Oxford Street. Pass the Tottenham Court Road tube station and continue on Oxford Street. Just before Marks and Spencer,

turn left onto Poland Street. Noel Street is your first left; the hostel is on the right.

Open all year. IBN/BABA: both.

Open 24 hours. Reception open 7am–11pm. Security guards 11pm–7am.

84 beds. 2-, 3-, and 4-bed rooms.

£ Members: adults £16.70; under 18 £13.60.

No meals served. Self-catering kitchen facilities.

No table license.

Individual lockers in all bedrooms; bring a padlock or buy one here (£2.50).

No laundry facilities.

P No parking anywhere near hostel; parking down Poland Street £24 per day.

Shop at hostel sells Travelcards for London Underground (Zones 1 and 2); local maps; stamps. Loads of other stores just outside hostel.

TV lounge.

Allowed in TV lounge only.

Not accessible to wheelchairs.

Travelex currency exchange.

Theater booking service.

Cheap Eats Nearby

Mandeer

Animal lovers will rejoice at this all-vegetarian Indian restaurant in Soho. Samosas and bhajis are light and crispy, (£2 to £3), as are the interesting bean dishes. The management takes a sort of a holistic approach to food and cares about your health, and there's a science to the preparation of their food. Vegetable masala £4.50. Other entrées can be pricier.

21 Hanway Place, W1. Tel: 0171/323 0660. Tube: Tottenham Court Road. Open: Mon–Sat noon–3pm and 5:30–10pm. Credit cards: VA, MC, EC. From the tube stop, walk up Tottenham Court Road and turn left onto Hanley Place.

Wong Kei

This three-story Asian pleasure palace has a waterfall, a cavernous basement dining room, a spacious upstairs, and ground-floor seating. It's nonetheless always packed, and the humorless waiters routinely put strangers at the same table. Many patrons behave like death-row prisoners at their last meal; the food is cheap, plentiful, and good. Pork fried noodles £2.50. Mushrooms, vegetables, and rice £2.90. Singapore noodles £2.70.

41–43 Wardour St., W1. Tel: 0171/437 3071. Tube: Oxford Street or Tottenham Court Road. Open: daily noon–11pm. Cash only. From the tube, walk down Oxford Street; Wardour Street is halfway between Tottenham Court Road and Oxford Circus.

Grocery Stores: Marks and Spencer. Oxford Street, W1. Open: Mon–Fri 8:30am–7pm; Sat 9:30am–7pm. Gateway Supermarkets. Peter Street, W1. Open: Mon–Sat 8am–8pm; Sun 11am–6pm. On Berwick Street, the market has stalls with food, groceries, flowers, records, and CDs.

Experiences

If you've paid good money to stay here on Oxford Street, chances are you want to do some power sightseeing. A gentle place to start is **Bloomsbury,** where the **British Museum** holds court along with the University of London and an appropriately intellectual air still pervades. The museum, chronicling the rise and fall of the Empire, houses archaeology, coin, print, and drawing collections. The adjoining **British Library** has piles of manuscripts, including the Gutenberg Bible, the Magna Carta, the *Canterbury Tales,* as well as works by a pantheon of more contemporary British writers.

While in the neighborhood, check out no. 20 Bloomsbury Square. Gertrude Stein lived here before heading off to Paris. No. 46 Gordon Square is the former home of economist and Bloomsbury boy John Maynard Keynes. The Bloomsbury Group read, wrote, nested, and lusted here on many an afternoon. At 82 Gower St. you can see the very first branch of **Dillon's,** the chain bookstore started by Una Dillon in 1937 and now found all over Britain.

If you head down across New Oxford Street, you'll reach the **Soho/Covent Garden/Leicester Square** area. Once the territory of sex shops, peep shows, and sleazy bars, Soho has gone through a rebirth. Now artists, writers, and media types lounge around in the cafes, and Old Compton Street has become a mainstay of London's gay community.

Hands-down, **Berwick Street Market,** by Wardour Street, has the area's best, biggest, and cheapest selection of produce, as well as a burgeoning clothing and appliance mart. **Covent Garden,** the grateful recipient of many pounds' worth of urban redevelopment, is now the perfectly lovely home of loads of smart cafes, upscale shops, and a smattering of bookstores. **Neal's Yard** is London's herbal/homeopathic/health-food nook, and vegetarian restaurants are plentiful here.

Just like New York's Times Square, **Leicester Square** is clogged with massive cineplexes and theaters and is jammed with tourists all day and all night. Those in search of theater should head straight to the **Leicester Square Ticket Booth,** where half-price tickets for shows in the Barbican, National Theater, and West End are available on performance days. You can't be choosy, though, so some people prefer to head straight to the box offices of the particular show they want to see so they can look at a seating plan.

Walking down Whitehall and past the Houses of Parliament will get you to **Westminster Abbey,** and a short walk farther brings you to **Buckingham Palace.** The lines are long, the crowds fierce, and the prices high, but even the most jaded travelers fork over the money for these sights.

Heading down into the direction of Pimlico will get you to the **Tate Gallery,** where a world-class, eye-popping collection of great artists lies under one roof. Exhaustive and exhausting: Gainsborough, Reynolds, Turner, Constable, Rodin, Matisse, Dalí, Modigliani, Rothko, and a host of others have tourists oohing and aahing from opening to closing time.

British Museum and Library. Great Russell Street, WC1. Tel: 0171/636 1555. Tube: Russell Square or Goodge Street. Open: Mon–Sat 10am–5pm; Sun 2:30–6pm. Admission: free, except for special exhibitions.

Dillon's. 82 Gower St., WC1. Tel: 0171/636 1577. Tube: Goodge Street. Open: Mon–Fri 9:30am–7pm; Sat 9:30am–6pm.

Berwick Street Market. Berwick Street, W1. Tube: Oxford Circus or Tottenham Court Road. Open: Mon–Sat 9am–6pm.

Leicester Square Ticket Booth. Leicester Square, W1. Tube: Leicester Square. Open: Mon–Sat noon–2pm and 2:30–6pm. Cash only. Four-ticket maximum per person.

Westminster Abbey. Broad Sanctuary, SW1. Tel: 0171/222 7110. Tube: Westminster or St. James's Park. Open: Mon–Fri 9:20am–4pm; Sat 9:30am–2pm and 3:45–5pm. Admission to Abbey: free. Admission to Royal Chapels, Royal Tombs, Coronation Chair, Henry VIII Chapel: adults £4; children £1. Guided Supertours (1 1/2 hours): £7.

Buckingham Palace and Gardens. Tel: 0171/930 4832. Tube: St. James's Park or Green Park. State apartments and picture galleries only. Open: Aug–Sept only at the whim of the Queen. Admission: adults £8; seniors £5.50; children £4. Changing of the Guard 11:30am.

Tate Gallery. Millbank, SW1. Tel: 0171/887 8000 or 0171/821 1313. Tube: Pimlico. Open: Mon–Sat 10am–5:50pm; Sun 2–5:50pm. Admission: free.

See "London Basics" and "What's Next After London" later in this chapter.

ROTHERHITHE

The port of London has been operating since Roman times and has seen its share of seafaring action. In the 20th century, it has had its ups and downs. London's docks were pelted with bombs during World War II. After the war, the entire area from Tower Hill to Greenwich sank into the doldrums, weighed down by a depressed economy. Surrey Quays, Wapping, and Rotherhithe became synonymous with derelict docks, abandoned streets, and boarded-up warehouses.

In the last 10 years, the area has been rejuvenated with the birth of the London Docklands (capital *L*, capital *D*). Public funding and serious corporate bucks have changed the face of this once-deserted area, and sparkling space-age buildings are replacing the decayed structures. With the redevelopment of Canary Wharf, banks and hotels are moving into the former ghost town, and an alternative Fleet Street has sprung up as many businesses move their digs to these up-and-coming addresses. Luckily, this development has also showered some attention on nearby funky-but-forgotten neighborhoods, where markets and street life flourish on the other side of the Thames.

Rotherhithe YHA
& Conference Centre

Salter Road, Rotherhithe
London SE16 1PP
Tel: 017/232 2114. Fax: 0171/237 2919.
Central Reservations tel: 0171/237 2919. Central Reservations fax: 0171/236 7681.
Tube: Rotherhithe

The Youth Hostels Association has contributed to the renewal of the Docklands by putting up a megaslick monolith of a hostel in the middle of Salter Road. The jewel in the crown of the London hostel network, it has a whopping 320 beds in its chrome-and-glass palace. An easy walk from the Rotherhithe tube station (be careful at night), the hostel is impossible to miss.

An atrium opens up the huge reception area, where the comfortable modern Pilgrim's Lounge has a tiny bar area serving soft drinks. The coffee tables are piled with painstaking sourcebooks on London's sights and attractions. Conference facilities hold up to 100 and have all sorts of audiovisual equipment. The Mayflower Restaurant, the hostel cafeteria, has a fairly extensive menu of bland but filling food, and it's a pleasant, if plastic, setting. Upstairs, all the rooms have their own bathrooms. The rooms are divided into categories: "Economy" rooms are in large dorms, "superior" rooms have four beds, and "premium" rooms are doubles with color TVs.

A huge number of school groups come here, so prepare yourself for the pitter-patter of little feet and a corresponding superefficient, businesslike attitude among the staff. The hostel is modern and well equipped, but it lacks coziness because it's so huge. The perfectly well-trained and pleasant staff are busy with the crowds, so don't expect personal attention. Despite the rosy future of the Docklands, the present reality is that the area is still lonely at night. As always, don't wander around alone, and if you park your car don't leave anything inside.

Services

🚇 From any of London's eight British Rail stations, take the Underground to Liverpool Street (which is both a tube stop and a British Rail station). Take the East London line to Rotherhithe; from the station, turn left onto Salter Road. The hostel is a brisk five-minute walk up the street.

🚌 From Victoria Coach station, take the Circle or District Line tube to Whitechapel. Switch to the East London line and get off at Rotherhithe. Follow directions from the train, above.

🚗 Rotherhithe is in East London on the south side of the River Thames. From the **north,** get to the A10 or A11 and follow signs to Tower Bridge; cross the bridge and exit onto Jamaica Road (the A200) with the river to your left. Continue on as Jamaica Road becomes Brunel Road, which then becomes Salter Road. The hostel will come up on the left.

From the **south,** get to the M102/A102 and follow signs to Tower Bridge, but don't cross it; instead, turn right onto the Jamaica Road (the A200), which becomes Brunel Road, which then becomes Salter Road. The hostel is a large glass-and-steel structure; you can't miss it.

▦ Open all year. IBN/BABA: both.

🕐 Open 24 hours. Manned reception 7am–11:30pm; security guard 11:30pm–7am.

🛏 320 beds. 2-, 4-, 6-, and 10-bed rooms, all with private bathrooms. Small rooms can be used as family rooms.

£ Members—economy rooms: adults £14; under 18 £11. Standard/superior rooms: adults £19.10–19.50; under 18 £16–£16.50. Premium rooms: adults £22; under 18 £18.50. Prices include breakfast.

🍴 Mayflower Restaurant. Self-catering kitchen facilities. Breakfast: 7:30–9:30am; breakfast includes five items from buffet and is covered in overnight price. À la carte lunch: noon–2pm. Packed lunches available; order the night before. Dinner: 5:30–8:30pm.

🍸 Table license.

🧳 Individual lockers attached to each bed; bring your own lock or buy one at reception (£2.50). Luggage storage room downstairs under video surveillance.

🌀 Washers £1.50; dryers take 20p coins; ironing facilities.

P Parking on street only; limited. Coaches and large vans must go to nearby car park.

🛍 Shop at Hostel sells National Express tickets; stamps; toiletries; cute souvenirs like miniature buses; padlocks. Vending machines for candy and hot and cold drinks.

🛋 Games room with board games; TV lounge.

🚬 In Pilgrim's Lounge.

♿ All areas are wheelchair accessible, including bathrooms, bedrooms, and elevators.

💱 Travelex currency exchange.

🔺 Bike shed; bookings service for theater and some excursions; three meeting rooms; VIP lounge.

Cheap Eats Nearby

Bloom's

Here you'll find pastrami sandwiches, latkes, and tzimmes just like Bubby made them. It's a tough choice deciding between the matzo ball soup and cabbage borscht, but make up your mind—London's best Jewish deli doesn't have time for dilly-dallying. Takeout available. Soups and appetizers £2 to £3.50. Sandwiches and main courses £3–£8.50. Bloom's isn't far from Rotherhithe and the Docklands.

9 Whitechapel High St., E1. Tel: 0171/247 6001. Tube: Aldgate East. Open: Sun–Thurs 11:30am–9:30pm; Fri 11:30am–3pm. Credit cards: AE, MC, VA, DC, EC, Access. From the tube, turn down Whitechapel High Street toward the Aldgate tube stop. Bloom's also has a branch at 130 Golders Green Rd., Golders Green, NW11.

The Rogue's Kitchen

This is a good place to splurge in London's Docklands. Creole and Cajun food are served in an adorably homey wooden restaurant filled with sepia tints, old newspaper clippings, wicker, and inviting aromas. Starters include jerk fish kebabs £4. Chicken-and-sausage gumbo £11. Jambalaya is a specialty. Blackened redfish £11.

St. Mary Church Street, SE16. Tel: 0171/237 7452. Tube: Rotherhithe. Open: Tues–Fri 8–11pm; Sat 7–11pm. Reservations accepted. Credit cards: MC, VA, Access, Switch. From the Rotherhithe tube stop, it's a five-minute walk. Turn left onto Railway Avenue and then left onto St. Mary Church Street. It's at the corner of Tunnel Road and St. Mary Church Street.

Experiences

Via its convenient tube stop, Rotherhithe is within easy reach of lots of London's major sights. If you're here already, however, it's worth staying around to explore this underappreciated developing neighborhood. The **Docklands Light Railway (DLR)** transports you through the area easily, and Travelcards are valid on all DLR trains (make sure you've got the right zones). Riding on the elevated automatic rail line is a sort of futuristic experience. The **London Docklands Visitor Centre** is a good place to start: They hand out the (free) *DLR Tourist Guide* and have a large exhibition devoted to Docklands history and architecture. Maps, prints, and photos are used to illustrate the story.

In the 1800s, the peninsula in the Thames known as the Isle of Dogs had a plethora of docks and factories that churned endlessly in response to the demands of the Industrial Revolution. The area fell into decline during the 1900s. Enter **Canary Wharf**—a slick, sexy skyscraper. Architect Cesar Pelli capped off the building with a pyramid dome (not unlike his World Financial Center in New York City), making it not only the tallest in all of Britain but also a suave addition to the London skyline. Canary Wharf has shops, restaurants, a concert venue, and a visitors' center underneath the endless floors of offices.

Back in the other direction is a smattering of sights worth seeing in East London. The **Museum of the Moving Image,** in a spectacular building on London's South Bank, has a fun exhibit on the use of light in the development of the modern moving image. The mainly interactive exhibits are especially good for kids; one allows you to participate in your own TV news show.

The **Whitechapel Art Gallery,** a couple of tube stops to the north of Rotherhithe, has some of the most experimental exhibitions you'll find in London. They're just as likely to have an exhibit on German postexpressionism as Latin American art. Not far away, the **New Caledonian Market** (aka Bermondsey Market) is an antique dealers' market that specializes in silver and silver-plated items, accompanied by the usual mishmash of merchandise. It gets going at about 5am, and regulars sometimes bring torches to see their way through the dawn darkness. The **Brixton Market** livens up Electric (Eddie Grant) Avenue in SW9. The market reflects the neighborhood, where Caribbean and African cultures blend together. You're likely to catch a whiff of sizzling steaks and perfume oils as well as the heady air of radicalism: the neighborhood is a mecca for budding Buddhas, British Bolsheviks, and Rastafarians. Food, clothes, hair accessories, and music are among the offerings here.

The village of **Greenwich** is also worth a visit. After Charles II founded an observatory here in 1675, his scientists honed their navigational and astronomical skills to such a degree that the prime meridian was established here in 1884. Modern-day Greenwich still retains its villagelike charm, and little markets here have stalls heaped with goodies, usually at decent prices. Summer Sundays see the **Greenwich Market** blossom with bargains on clothes, music, leather, jewelry, and more. Down the street, the **Greenwich Antiques Market** on Burney Street sells doodads, old books, and furniture. The park there, the burial ground of 14th-century plague victims, is a nice place for a frolic, and you might even spy some wild deer. In the center of the park is the **Royal Observatory,** inside the **National Maritime Museum.** In this beautifully restored building, you can straddle the spot where the **prime meridian** is marked off by a brass pointer. Set your watch to Greenwich mean time, displayed on the century-old clock. To get to Greenwich, you can take the Docklands Light Railway, a British Rail train, or walk under the foot tunnel beneath the Thames (when you emerge from the depths you'll have reached Greenwich).

Docklands Visitors Centre. 3 Limeharbour, Isle of Dogs, E14. Tel: 0171/512 1111. DLR: Crossharbour. Open: Mon–Fri 8:30am–6pm; Sat–Sun 10am 4:30pm.

Canary Wharf. Isle of Dogs, E14. DLR: Canary Wharf. Open: Mon–Sat 10am–6pm.

Museum of the Moving Image. South Bank Centre, SE1. Tel: 0171/928 3232. Tube: Waterloo. Open: daily 10am–6pm. Admission: adults £5.50; students £4.70; people with disabilities and children £4.

Whitechapel Art Gallery. Whitechapel High Street, E1. Tel: 0171/377 0107. Tube: Whitechapel. Open: Tues and Thurs–Sun 11am–5pm; Wed 11am–7pm. Admission: free.

New Caledonian Market. Bermondsey Square, SE1. Tube: Bermondsey. Open: Fri 5am–noon.

Brixton Market. Electric Avenue, Brixton Station Road, SW2 and SW9. Tube: Brixton. Open: Mon–Tues and Thurs–Fri 8am–6pm; Wed 8am–1pm.

Greenwich Market. Greenwich Church Street and College Approach. Summer: Sat–Sun 9am–6pm. Winter: 9am–5pm.

Greenwich Antiques Market. Burney Street, Greenwich. Sat–Sun 8am–4pm.

Old Royal Observatory and National Maritime Museum. Romney Road, Greenwich. Tel: 0181/858 4422. Open: Apr–Sept: Mon–Sat 10am–6pm; Sun noon–6pm. Oct–Mar: Mon–Sat 10am–5pm; Sun 2–5pm. Admission: adults £3.95; students, seniors, and children £2.95.

See "London Basics" and "What's Next After London" later in this chapter.

LONDON BASICS

Tourist Office: British Travel Centre. 12 Lower Regent St., Piccadilly Circus, SW1. Tube: Piccadilly Circus. Open: Mon–Fri 9am–6:30pm; Sat–Sun 10am–6pm. Each desk has its own phone line. Main information tel.: 0181/846 9000. Theater desk tel.: 0171/839 3952. Ireland desk tel.: 0171/839 8416. Wales desk tel.: 0171/409 0969. The Scottish Centre is down the street at 19 Cockspur St., SW1. Tel.:0171/ 930 8661. Tube: Piccadilly Circus. Open: Mon–Fri 9:30am–5:30pm.

Student Travel Agency: Council Travel. 28a Poland St., W1. Tel: 0171/287 3337. Tube: Oxford Circus. Open: Mon–Fri 9am–6pm (Thurs until 7pm); Sat 10am–5pm. YHA London Information Office and Adventure Shop: 14 Southampton St., WC2. Tel: 0171/836 1036. Tube: Covent Garden. Open: Mon–Wed 10am–6pm; Thurs–Fri 10am–7pm; Sat 9am–6:30pm.

Transportation Information: London Regional Transport (LRT) operates both the Underground and the buses. The **Underground** (tube) isn't cheap, but it's comprehensive, faster than the bus, and less expensive than cabs. A series of concentric circles divides the city into travel zones (1–6); Zones 1 and 2 cover most of Central London. Before boarding the tube, make sure you've purchased a ticket that covers all the zones you're going through. It's usually worth purchasing one of LRT's Travelcards, which can be bought for one day (restrictions apply), one week, or one month of unlimited tube travel within the zones you specify. Passport-size photos are needed to buy the week and month Travelcards. All manned booths in the Underground have printed information. A one-day Travelcard for Zones 1 and 2 costs £2.70; one-week Travelcards cost £13. Beware that the tube shuts down at midnight.

Buses aren't bad if you've got time to ride and to figure out the maze of stops and routes. On most buses, pay the driver when you board; exact change is required. **Night buses** (N routes) run from 11am–6pm with fairly frequent service. All buses go through Trafalgar Square. For Underground or bus information, call 0171/222 1234.

Post Office: There are post offices and subpost offices all over London. The London Chief Office is at King Edward Street, EC1A 1AA. Tel: 0171/239 5047. Tube: St. Paul's. Open: Mon–Tues and Thurs–Fri 8:30am–6:30pm; Wed 9am–6:30pm. Trafalgar Square Post Office, 24–28 William IV St., London WC2N 4DL. Tel: 0171/930 9580. Tube: Charing Cross. Open: Mon–Sat 8am–8pm.

Currency Exchange: American Express. 6 Haymarket, SW1. Tel: 0171/930 4411 or 0171/839 2179. Foreign exchange services: Mon–Fri 9am–5:30pm; Sat 9am–6pm; Sun 10am–6pm. Travel services: Mon–Fri 9am–5:30pm; Sat 9am–4pm. Other American Express branches: Victoria Station, 147 Victoria St., SW1; tel.: 0171/828 7411. Knightsbridge, 78 Brompton Rd., SW3; tel.: 0171/584 6182. Cannon Street, 54 Cannon St., EC4; tel.: 0171/248 2671.

Thomas Cook. 15 Shaftesbury Ave., WC2. Tube: Piccadilly Circus. Marks and Spencer. 458 Oxford St., W1. Tel: 0171/935 7954. Tube: Oxford Circus. Open: Mon–Fri 8:30am–7pm; Sat 9:30am–7pm. All London hostels have Travelex currency exchange (except Epping Forest).

Telephone Code: 0171 and 0181.

Bike Rental: Brixton Cycles Co-op. 435 Coldharbour Lane, SW9. Tel: 0171/733 6055. Tube: Brixton. Open: Mon–Sat 9am–6pm.

Mountain Bike and Ski. 18 Gillingham St., SW1. Tel: 0171/834 8933. Tube: Victoria. Open: Mon–Thurs 8:30am–5pm; Fri 8:30am–7:30pm; Sat 8:30am–4pm. Full-day rental £8; weekend rental £14. Insurance not included. £50 deposit required.

Bike Park. 14¹/₂ Stukeley St., WC2. Tel: 0171/430 0083 or 0171/373 3657. Tube: Covent Garden. £10 for first day; £5 for second day; £3 per day thereafter.

Getting to London: By train: London is accessible by eight centrally located British Rail stations, all connected to the London Underground. Different stations serve different routes. **King's Cross** connects with Scotland and the Northeast, and **St. Pancras** goes through Hertfordshire to the East and the Midlands. **Liverpool Street** connects with East Anglia. **Charing Cross** connects with South East and South Central England. **Waterloo** goes to the South and Southeast. **Victoria Station** connects to Gatwick Airport, the South, and the Southeast. **Paddington Station** connects to Wales and the Southwest. **Euston Station** heads out to Stafford and the Northwest.

For information about East Anglia, Essex, the South, and Southeast, call 0171/928 5100. For the West of England and South Wales, call 0171/262 6767. For the West Midlands, Northwest, and Scotland, call 0171/387 7070. For the Northeast and Scotland, call 0171/278 2477.

Destinations serviced by train include the following (fares are one way): **Gatwick Airport** (56 per day; 30 minutes; £8.50); **Bath** (25 per day; 1¹/₄ hours; £24); **Cambridge** (31 per day; one hour; £15); **Oxford** (35 per day; one hour; £9); **Brighton** (35 per day; one hour; £9); **Penzance** (five per day; five hours; £50); **Cardiff** (21 per day; 1³/₄ hours; £30); **York** (27 per day; two hours; £35); **Windermere** (six per day; 3³/₄ hours; £37); **Edinburgh** (17 per day; four hours; £49); **Glasgow** (eight per day; five hours; £49).

By bus: The main bus station is London's Victoria Coach station, from which **National Express** operates its far-flung service. The coaches go to cities large and small throughout Britain, and where they leave off competing bus companies pick up. Some routes overlap, but prices don't vary very much. National Express is reliable, superclean, and smoke-free. It's cheaper than the train, but generally buses take longer. At Victoria Station, you can buy a Tourist Trail Ticket (£39–£179) for unlimited coach travel within a fixed time period; students, youths, and seniors can get 30% off if they buy a Discount Coach Card for £7. For National Express information, call 0171/730 0202 or 0990/808080.

Destinations serviced by bus include the following (fares are one way): **Cardiff** (3¹/₄ hours; £19); **Exeter** (3³/₄ hours; £27); **Oxford** (1¹/₄ hours; £5.50); **Stratford-upon-Avon** (2³/₄ hours; £11.75); **York** (four hours; £29.50); **Edinburgh** (7³/₄ hours; £29.50).

By car: Motorways emanate from London like so many arms from an octopus. The **M25/M20** connects Dover and the Southeast; the **M23** connects the South Coast; the **M3** goes to Southampton; the **M4** connects Bristol, Bath, Cardiff, and heads on to the West Country (via the M5). To points north, the **M11** goes to Cambridge and the **M1** heads straight north to York and Newcastle-upon-Tyne; from there, the **A66/A68** continues to Edinburgh and the east of Scotland. The **M1/M6** gets you to Birmingham, Manchester, and the Lake District; from there, the **M74** goes up to Glasgow.

From the airports: From **Heathrow,** the easiest thing is to get right on the tube. The Piccadilly Line connects Central London to the airport's four terminals, all in Zone 6. It's about a 45-minute ride. By bus, you can take the London Regional Transport's Airbus, which runs from Heathrow to different points in London, including Earl's Court, Holland Park, and London Victoria, among other stops. The buses run daily, every half hour from 8:30am–8pm, and the ride costs £5, £3 for children. Call 0171/222 1234 for information.

From **Gatwick Airport,** take the British Rail Gatwick Express into London's Victoria Station. Trains run every half hour during the day and every hour from midnight–4am. The ride takes 35 minutes and costs £8.50. National Express also runs coaches between Gatwick and London's Victoria Station for £7.50.

From **Stansted** Airport, take British Rail's Stansted Express into London's Liverpool Street station. The ride is about 40 minutes and costs £10 for adults, £5 for children.

WHAT'S NEXT AFTER LONDON

From London, the whole of Britain is at your doorstep. It depends on what you want, how long you're here, and how much money you have. For those looking for a rural escape outside London, the hostels of **Alfriston** and **Arundel,** picturesque little villages on England's South Coast, are about an hour's train ride and a world away from London in spirit.

To the north, the village of **Streatley-on-Thames** is so precious and pictureperfect that more than a few Londoners have traded in their town houses for farms here. Only 40 miles from London, the area retains an air of the quintessential English countryside: winding, hilly lanes; grassy pastures dotted with wildflowers; riverside resting spots; and a sugary-sweet village with a couple of tea rooms and antique shops.

The university towns of **Cambridge** (56 miles away) and **Oxford** (64 miles away) and the royal town of **Windsor** (21 miles away) are all within an hour of London. The trio of **Bath** (107 miles away), **Bristol** (119 miles away), and **Cardiff** (155 miles away) lie to the west. Each offers something different. Bath, a city with Georgian architecture and Roman baths, was traditionally a spa/vacation town for wealthy Londoners; Bristol boasts a university, swanky shopping, and a tremendous seafaring and railway history. Cardiff, the capital of Wales, has a castle and loads of museums with exhibits on Welsh folklore and legends, as well as a gritty industrial heritage that has given way to a lively underground arts scene.

To the north, the cathedral city of **York** beckons most whirlwind travelers. To the west, **Manchester** is an underappreciated gem of a city: from the ashes of postindustrial gloom, it rose to become a mecca for musicians. Its waterfront is undergoing major urban renewal. Bars, nightclubs, and counterculture are flourishing here.

To the northwest, the **Lake District** brims with hostelers in the summertime, but you can find hidden lagoons and untrodden hills if you have a good pair of hiking boots. Way up north (each 400 miles away) are the feisty, rivalrous cities of Scotland: **Edinburgh** is the classic cathedral/castle city that comes alive during its yearly festival in August. **Glasgow,** while less popular and less touristed than Edinburgh (thanks to its working-class reputation), has come into its own in the last 20 to 30 years. With a luscious park, excellent museums, and an active arts/ music/nightclub scene, it's a friendly, fashionable city up in the northern reaches of Britain.

East Anglia

Deriving its name from the Anglo-Saxon kingdom once ruled by the Danes, East Anglia comprises the four present-day counties of Essex, Suffolk, Norfolk, and Cambridgeshire. While the region as a whole isn't exactly a hotbed of activity, interesting little pockets lurk in its marshy corners, cathedral towns, and bucolic pastures.

In the 1100s, the cloth industry brought people and prosperity to the region, giving rise to the profusion of churches dotting the countryside. Nowadays, Cambridgeshire sees the most tourist action, thanks to its university town. With dazzling Gothic buildings, stone passageways, riverside gardens, and carefully clipped greens, Cambridge attracts tourists by the busload. The town is a paradigm of English university life: students ride bikes through the cobbled alleyways, cafes and pubs bubble over with activity, rare volumes gather dust on the shelves of centuries-old bookshops, and world-class museums (many free) stand at attention, waiting to inspire budding Byrons. Farther down the river Cam, punters propel their way to pastoral countryside villages. The pleasant Cambridge hostel is conveniently located and open all day.

South of Cambridge, the market town of Colchester can trace its origins back to Roman times. Ancient city walls still protect the city, and William the Conqueror's Norman Castle still stands in defiance to the Saxon rule he overthrew.

These days, there's little strife in this pleasant city. An old Dutch quarter is testament to the woolen trade that once thrived here, and the surrounding countryside offers the real-life version of a Constable oil painting.

CAMBRIDGE

It was 1209 when a group of students broke away from Oxford and made their way 92 miles across Buckinghamshire and Bedfordshire to establish their own school at the small village by the River Cam. More than 700 years later, they're still pouring in. The likes of John Milton, Erasmus of Rotterdam, Lord Byron, Prince Charles, Stephen Hawking, and countless others have marked time in this city, where ancient university buildings stand side by side with coffeehouses, clothing stores, and dusty bookshops.

Much smaller than its big brother, Oxford, Cambridge fulfills every typical image of traditional collegiate life: Bicycles weave through cobbled streets; rowers struggle against the curving River Cam; great lawns and flower gardens pepper the colleges; and spires and stained-glass Gothic chapels scrape the sky. It's also home to world-class museums, endless literary haunts, and excellent bike routes out to the quiet hamlets along the River Granta.

The hostel, conveniently next door to a bike rental shop, is only a block from the train station and a 10-minute walk from the city center. The friendly, knowledgeable staff makes Cambridge accessible and enjoyable, even to the nonacademic.

Cambridge Youth Hostel

97 Tenison Rd.
Cambridge, Cambridgeshire CB1 2DN
Tel: 01223/354601. Fax: 01223/312780.

The Youth Hostel in Cambridge has every amenity you'd expect at an international city hostel. It's open 24 hours; there's no curfew; it has small bedrooms and clean bathrooms; a currency exchange is available; and tourist leaflets, maps, and travel advice are offered aplenty. The place is run professionally, and the common rooms are spotless. There's only one thing out of place: The staff, a cheery mix of wandering souls and professional hostel honchos, blends genuine warmth with punctilious efficiency. Most city hostels suffer from business-as-usual malaise, leaving charm and friendliness to their less polished counterparts in the countryside and mountaintop hostels, but Cambridge thankfully breaks the mold.

The staff's charm seems to be working. Guests tend to linger for a while, and anyone planning to stay here should call well in advance to reserve a spot. The fairly diverse group of guests includes backpackers arriving on the trains and the Slow Coach, school groups, families, and even a few older folks cycling through the area.

The hostel is comfortable enough—not grand, but cozy and warm. With a courtyard garden in front and a pleasant dining room where beer and wine are served along with cafeteria food, the hostel is a welcoming place to come home to after a day out. Hostelers don't hang out for very long, though: The bike store next door offers three-speeds for rent, and the center of Cambridge is only about 10 minutes by foot. Most hostelers park their bags (in lockers) and head out.

Services

Exit Cambridge Station onto Station Road and take the first right onto Tenison Road. Walk one block; the hostel is at the corner of Devonshire Road on the right. It's a three- to five-minute walk.

Exit the coach station, turn left onto Drummer Street, and follow it as it turns into Parker Street then Parkside (walk past the park) then Mill Road. Once you reach Mill Road, Tenison Road is the fourth road on the right; turn right onto Tenison and the Youth Hostel will come up on the left, after the intersection with Lyndewode Road. It's a 15-minute walk.

From the A603, A1134, and A1303, follow signs to the railway station. Turn onto Hills Road (a continuation of Regent Street, away from the city center); after seven blocks, bear left onto Station Road. Turn left onto Tenison Road and the hostel is at the corner of Tenison and Devonshire Roads.

Open year-round. IBN/BABA: both.

Reception open 24 hours.

102 beds. 2-, 4-, 5-, 6-, and 8-bed rooms. Family rooms available.

£ Members: adults £9.70; under 18 £6.55.

Self-catering kitchen facilities. Breakfast: 7:30–9:30am. Lunch: packed lunch only; should be ordered the night before. Dinner: 6–7:30pm.

Table license. Beer and wine served.

Most bedrooms have lockers; otherwise, there's a bank of lockers downstairs. Bring your own padlock or buy one for £2.50.

Washer £1.25; dryer takes 30p tokens (available at reception).

P Very limited (2 spots); parking at 2-hour meters on the street.

Shop at hostel sells sweets, toiletries, maps, stamps, and laundry detergent.

TV room; games room; smoking lounge.

In games room only.

Not wheelchair accessible. Upstairs dormitories only.

Travelex currency exchange.

Bike shed; meeting room; Slow Coach tickets for sale at reception.

Cheap Eats Nearby

The Bun Shop

This pub/tapas bar/blues music venue/restaurant serves the best Spanish food in town. Raciones £4 to £6. Try the Spanish-style tortilla with eggs and potatoes.

1 King St., Cambridge. Tel: 01223/366866. Open: daily 6pm–midnight. Credit cards: VA, MC, Access. From the hostel, exit and walk left onto Tenison Road. Turn right on Station Road and right at Hills Road, following it into Regent Street, St. Andrew's Street, and Sidney Street (pedestrianized). Bear right onto Hobson Street and follow it around to the right; it becomes King Street. The restaurant is on the left. It's about a 25-minute walk.

Clown's Café

This cafe has wood floors, wood stools, and—surprise—clowns on the wall. Sandwich maker, pizza spinner, and baguette baker, owner Raffaello keeps students wired with his jolting java. Café latte £1.20. Homemade quiche with salad £3.10. Sweets galore.

54 King St., Cambridge. Tel: 01223/355711. Open: daily 9am–midnight. Cash only. Exit the hostel and walk left onto Tenison Road. Turn right on Station Road and then right at Hills Road, following it into Regent Street, St. Andrew's Street, and Sidney Street (pedestrianized). Bear right onto Hobson Street and follow it around to the right; it becomes King Street. The cafe is on the right. It's a 15-minute walk from the hostel.

Grocery store: Marks and Spencer. Sidney Street, Cambridge. Open: Mon–Tues 9:30am–5:30pm; Wed 9am–7:30pm; Thurs 9am–5:30pm; Fri 9am–6pm; Sat 8:30am–6pm.

Experiences

Even if you're not on a tight schedule, it's worth £6 per day to rent a bike—you'll see a lot more of the city and countryside. In Cambridge, the **colleges** are a good place to start. **Kings College,** at the heart of the city on King's Parade, has a painstakingly clipped grassy green (don't walk on it or else) and a cathedral-like chapel with some big buttresses and an excellent choral evensong daily at 5:30pm. **Trinity College,** Cambridge's largest, has the university's largest courtyard and an appropriately enormous library designed by Christopher Wren, whose buildings are scattered all over Cambridge. **Clare College** boasts beautiful riverside gardens for picnicking philosophers. Beyond the Third Court of **St. John's College,** you can walk out to the Kitchen Bridge and catch a glimpse of the **Bridge of Sighs,** modeled after the one in Venice. All the colleges dotting the river and Trumpington Street/King's Parade/Trinity Street/St. John Street are equally impressive/awe-inspiring/intimidating. If you walk down **The Backs** (the backs of the colleges), you'll find the roads are free of shops and buildings and offer less obstructed views of these big beautiful structures.

Another way to see the colleges is by boat: **Punts** can be rented at the shack in front of Trinity College or across from Magdalene College. Working your way south along the river (or along the riverside footpath/bridleway), you'll eventually get to **Grantchester;** here the river changes its name to the Granta. This quiet countryside village is dotted with farmhouses (one of which belongs to author Jeffrey Archer), a couple of pubs, and some beautiful riverside resting spots.

Back in Cambridge, the **Fitzwilliam Museum** boasts works by Titian, Rubens, Hals, Courbet, Delacroix, Leonardo, and Rembrandt. The substantial bunch of British artists in its collection include Hogarth, Reynolds, Gainsborough, Stubbs, Turner, and Constable. On top of that, they have antiquities, coins and medals, Asian art, Egyptian art, and special exhibitions. It's one of England's best museums; even the most unaesthetic tend to drag themselves here. Up Castle Street is **Kettle's Yard,** the former home of the Tate Gallery's curator. Housing 20th-century art and sculpture, the museum hosts talks, lunchtime concerts, workshops, and other special events.

At night, the **Corn Exchange** is the local concert venue, and **The ADC Theatre** hosts classic theater, poetry readings, and experimental dance. **The Boat Race** features a democratic assortment of music: metal, jazz, Latin rhythms, mandolin quartets, and Irish alternative sounds can all be heard here.

Cambridge Colleges. King's College: 01223/331100. Trinity College: 01223/338400. St. John's College: 01223/338600. Some have an admission charge.

Punting on the Cam. Trinity Punts: £5.60 per hour. £25 deposit required. Scudamore's Boatyards. Quayside (across from Magdalene College). Tel: 01223/359750. Punts: £8 per hour; £4 per half hour. £30 deposit.

Fitzwilliam Museum. Trumpington Street, Cambridge. Tel: 01223/332900. Open: Lower Galleries Tues–Fri 10am–2pm; Upper Galleries Tues–Fri 2pm–5pm; Adeane Gallery (Temporary Exhibitions) Tues–Fri 10am–5pm, Sat 10am–5pm, Sun 2:15–5pm. Admission: free.

Kettle's Yard. Castle Street, Cambridge. Tel: 01223/352124. House open: Tues–Sun 2–4pm. Gallery open: Tues–Sat 12:30–5:30pm; Sun 2–5:30pm. Admission: free.

Corn Exchange. Wheeler Street, Cambridge. Tel: 01223/357851.

ADC Theatre. Park Street, Cambridge. Tel: 01223/352001. Ticket prices: adults £2.50–£6; concessions £2.50–£4.

The Boat Race. East Road, Cambridge. Tel: 01223/570063. Cover: £3–£8.

The Basics

Tourist Office: Cambridge T.I.C. The Old Library, Wheeler Street, Cambridge. Tel: 01223/322640. Open: Easter–June and Oct–Easter: Mon–Fri 9am–6pm; Sat 9am–5pm; Sun 10:30am–3:30pm. July–Sept: Mon–Fri 9am–7pm; Sat 9am–5pm; Sun 10:30am–3:30pm. Exit the hostel and go left on Tenison Road. Turn right on Station Road and right at Hills Road, following it into Regent Street and up St. Andrew's Street. Turn left on Downing Street then right on Corn Exchange Street. From the intersection with Wheeler Street, it's straight ahead. It's a 15-minute walk from the hostel.

Post Office: Cambridge Post Office. 9–11 St. Andrew's St., Cambridge. Open: Mon–Fri 9am–5:30pm; Sat 9am–7pm. Exit the hostel and go left on Tenison Road. Turn right on Station Road and right at Hills Road, following it into Regent Street and up St. Andrew's Street. The post office is on the left.

Currency Exchange: American Express. 25 Sidney St., Cambridge. Tel: 01223/351636. Open: Mon–Fri 9am–5:30pm (Wed 9:30am opening); Sat 9am–5pm. You can also exchange money at the hostel and the post office.

Telephone Code: 01223.

Bike Rental: Geoff's Bike Shop. 65 Devonshire Rd., Cambridge (next door to the hostel). Tel: 01223/365629. Open: Apr–Oct: daily 9am–6pm. Nov–Mar: Mon–Sat 9am–5:30pm. £6 per day. Geoff also runs bike tours of the area around the area to Anglesey Abbey, Ely Cathedral, and Wimpole Hall.

Getting There: Cambridge is easy to get to by **train** from the following places: **London King's Cross** (6–8 per day; 1 hour); **Norwich** (8 per day; 1½ hours); **Colchester** (12 per day; 2 hours). For train information, call 01223/311999.

By **coach,** there's hourly service from London's **Victoria** station via National Express (2 hours) and frequent service from **Oxford** (5 per day; 3 hours) and other cities. For bus information, call 01223/423554.

By **car,** take the M11 north from London and at Junction 12 take the A603 into Cambridge. From the north, get the A1 south to Huntingdon; there, switch for the A14 headed east to Cambridge.

What's Next

From here, it's only 55 miles down to **London,** where there are seven city hostels to choose from; most are in central locations, and all are accessible by the Underground. If you head southeast from Cambridge you'll reach **Colchester,** the first recorded town in Roman England. The Norman keep, Saxon church, and Roman wall will keep historians happy. If you're heading north, the next major tourist city is **York,** 151 miles away. **Oxford** is 55 miles west.

COLCHESTER

The local tourist brochure brazenly asserts that "all roads lead to Colchester," something of an overstatement in 20th-century England. (Colchester is 62 miles north of London and 48 miles east of Cambridge.) In the first century A.D., however, it was another story. When London was nothing more than a puny trading post, suave, sophisticated Colchester was a city to be reckoned with—it was the capital of Roman Britannia after Claudius's ruthless conquest. On the banks of the River Colne, Colchester had ready access to the sea (20 miles away) and good inland roads, so it grew to be an important trading town. City walls were erected but provided protection only for so long: William the Conqueror's armies stormed through in the late 11th century and built a sturdy castle atop the razed Roman settlement.

As the years passed, continental commerce flourished and a community of Flemish weavers who were Protestant refugees emigrated here. Their Dutch quarter still stands next to the Roman walls and Norman castle. The result is a town that provides a pleasant riverside backdrop for a serious lesson in British history.

John Constable was especially enamored of the city and environs. Bicycle tours, walking paths, and bridleways trace his journeys through the region, making Colchester palatable to outdoorsy types as well. The hostel, a simple, large Georgian house at the east end of town, is only steps away from the undulating Colne.

❀ Colchester Youth Hostel

East Bay House
18 East Bay
Colchester, Essex CO1 2UE
Tel: 01206/867982. Fax: 01206/868628.

The hostel, a breezy Georgian structure, is a residence from the days of Colchester's active mercantile life. Now it's got the YHA patina all over it: sturdy brick outside and sturdy, serviceable accommodations inside. The dining room has an unfortunately bricked-in fireplace and long wooden tables, lending it the air of an old-fashioned elementary school (which isn't so hard to imagine when you sit down to your morning muesli with a group of fidgeting schoolchildren). The meals here are tasty and mainly vegetarian, though with advance warning they'll accommodate most special requests.

The clientele is an even spread of HI cardholders. Small bedrooms make this an ideal destination for families (call ahead to ensure a private room), and cyclists and walkers tend to pass through as well. Bay windows in the dining room and lounge make the hostel a comfortable spot to rest, and the staff is cheery and efficient. You must obey the rules, but the staff is sympathetic to the overloaded backpacker who arrives during lockout time: If they're in, you can drop your rucksack and head out.

Services

🚆 The hostel is 2 miles from the train station. From the Colchester North station, take bus no. 2B, pass through the town, and the hostel is on the right. It's a 5-minute ride.

🚌 From the bus station, come out onto East Hill, turn right, and go down the hill. The hostel is on the right past the traffic lights and first roundabout but before the bridge. It's about a 10-minute walk.

🚗 From the A12, take the town bypass past the Sports Centre and follow the road until reaching a roundabout. Take the right-hand exit, curve around to the right, and cross the river onto East Hill. The hostel is on the left.

▦ Mar–Dec 15. Closed Sun–Mon in Mar, Sept–Oct. Weekends only Nov–Dec. BABA only. No hostel rental available except for groups when hostel is closed.

🕐 Reception open 8–10am and 5–10:30pm. Curfew 10:30pm.

🛏 52 beds. 2-, 4-, 6-, 8-, and 10-bed rooms.

£ Members: adults £7.20; under 18 £4.85

🍴 Self-catering kitchen facilities; nice bay window. Breakfast: 8am. Lunch: packed lunch only; should be ordered by the night before. Dinner: 7pm.

Ⅹ No table license.

🧳 Lockers downstairs; bring a padlock or buy one here (£2.50).

◻ Drying room only.

P In front of hostel; free.

🛍 Shop at hostel sells sweets and crisps.

TV lounge.

In smoking lounge only.

Not wheelchair accessible.

See "Currency Exchange" under "The Basics" in Colchester.

Bike shed; classroom for groups and meetings.

Cheap Eats Nearby

The Siege House

Bullet holes from the English Civil War and Colchester memorabilia on the walls make for an interesting atmosphere in which to chow down on Greek chicken kebabs (£4.25), sausage and chips (£3.70), or vegetable pasta (£4.10). It's part of the Beefeater chain, but you'd never guess it. Ask about the ghost.

75 East St., Colchester. Tel: 01206/867121. Open: Mon–Thurs noon–2:30pm and 6–10:30pm; Fri noon–2:30pm and 6–11pm; Sat noon–2:30 and 5:30–11pm; Sun noon–10:30pm. Credit cards: AE, VA, MC, EC, Delta, Access, Switch. From the hostel, turn right onto East Street and cross the bridge. It's on your left—a five-minute walk from the hostel.

Toto's

If the Romans hadn't been banished from Colchester, Toto's could certainly have provided tasty thin-crust pizzas (£4 to £5) for the soldiers. Hanging plants make it cheerful. Lunchtime pizza and pasta specials only £2.95.

5–7 Museum St., Colchester. Tel: 01206/762000. Open: Mon–Sat 10am–11pm. Reservations for large parties. Credit cards: VA, MC, EC, Switch. From the hostel, turn left on East Hill and follow it to High Street. Turn left onto Museum Street; Toto's is on the left. It's 10 minutes by foot.

Grocery Store: Marks and Spencer. High Street, Colchester.

Experiences

Colchester is a living history lesson and most visitors start at the beginning: the **Roman walls** (built A.D. 50) snake for 1¹/₂ miles around the city, and the most substantial remnants are at Balkerne Way, Park Folley, and Priory Street. The **Colchester Castle,** built with 12-foot-thick walls, sits atop the vaults of the Roman Temple of Claudius. Its gigantic dimensions make it about half the size of the Tower of London's White Tower. It's now a museum with one of the largest collections of Roman remains in England. Across the way is the **Colchester Natural History Museum,** which follows the development of the natural environment from the Ice Age to the Computer Age; it's especially enjoyable for children. **Walking tours** of the city are a good and relatively inexpensive option because they go into some detail about local history, especially in the Dutch quarter and the Hynde, Colchester's still-active port.

The **Bourne Mill,** a 16th-century fishing lodge that was converted into a mill, sits just outside town. Much of the machinery remains intact, and a four-acre mill pond makes a pleasant escape.

For forays farther afield, the **"Colchester's Countryside"** leaflet lists all sorts of walks, talks, and activities in the city and in the local country parks (Cudmore Grove and High Woods). Cyclists can head out toward Ipswich and Sudbury, where John Constable and Thomas Gainsborough found countryside inspiration to paint their oily English landscapes.

Market days in Colchester are Friday and Saturday. Follow your nose toward the smell of incense and you'll find other scent sensations, as well as rugs, jewelry, sweets, and loads more at the open-air stalls on Pelhams Lane.

Colchester Castle and Museum. Castle Park, Colchester. Tel: 01206/712931. Open: Mar–Nov: Mon–Sat 10am–5pm; Sun 2–5pm. Nov–Mar: Mon–Sat 10am–5pm. Admission: adults £2.50; concessions and children £1.50. Excellent tours (including vaults) take 45 minutes and run hourly: adults £1; children 50p.

Colchester Natural History Museum. High Street, Colchester. Tel: 01206/282937. Open: Tues–Sat 10am–1pm and 2–5pm. Admission: free.

Colchester walking tours. Book at the tourist office: Colchester T.I.C. 1 Queen St., Colchester. Tel: 01206/712920. June–Sept only: Mon–Sat at 2pm; Sun at 11am. 1^1/$_2$-hour tours: adults £1.50; children and concessions 75p.

Bourne Mill. Colchester. Tel: 01206/572422. Open: July–Aug only: Tues and Sun 2–5:30pm. Admission: adults £1.30; children 65p.

Colchester's Countryside. Leaflets available at the tourist office (see "Tourist Office" under "The Basics" in Colchester).

The Basics

Tourist Office: Colchester T.I.C. 1 Queen St., Colchester. Tel: 01206/712920. Open: Mon–Tues and Thurs–Fri 9am–5pm; Wed and Sat 10am–5pm. From the hostel, turn left on East Hill and follow the street for about two blocks; it's on the left, a 10-minute walk from the hostel.

Post Office: Colchester Post Office. 56 East Hill, Colchester. Tel: 01206/867765. Open: Mon–Fri 9am–5:30pm (Thurs 1pm closing); Sat 9am–12:30pm. From the hostel, turn left onto East Hill. The post office is across the street. It take five minutes on foot from the hostel.

Currency Exchange: Thomas Cook. 124 High St., Colchester. Tel: 01206/471411. Open: Mon–Sat 9am–5:30pm (Wed 10am opening).

Telephone Code: 01206.

Bike Rental: Anglian Cycle Hire. Unit 7, Peartree Road, Colchester. Tel: 01206/563377. Open: Mon–Sat 8:30am–5:30pm. Full-day rentals £4. Book ahead.

Getting There: Colchester North station is right on the London–Ipswich route. **Trains** leave London's **Liverpool Street** station for Colchester every 40 minutes and take 50 minutes. You can also take a train to Colchester from the following places: **Cambridge** (14 per day; 1^1/$_3$ hours); Norwich (18 per day; 1 hour). For rail information, call 01206/564777.

By **coach,** there's service into Colchester from London **Victoria** (3 per day; 1^1/$_2$ hours); **Cambridge** (2 per day; 1^1/$_2$ hours); and **Norwich** (every hour; 2 hours). For other cities and general bus information, call 01206/571451. For local buses, call 01206/764029.

By **car,** take the A12 northeast from London. From Cambridge, take the A1307 southeast to its end and continue on the A604, which goes directly into Colchester.

What's Next

From Colchester, it's only 48 miles to the quintessentially collegiate town of **Cambridge:** punt on the River Cam, visit the impressive Fitzwilliam Collection, walk through the colleges, peruse the dusty bookshops, and soak in the scholarly atmosphere. The hostel is convenient, friendly, and right next door to a bike rental shop. Heading south, **Central London** is only 62 miles away, and there are seven hostels in the city center to suit a variety of tastes. The **Epping Forest** hostel, just north of the city, is in a supremely quiet rural location, but it's conveniently only a bus ride away from a stop on the Underground.

Southern England

Border crossings, beach resorts, naval harbors, cathedral towns, farming villages, and even a tranquil island come together in the southern counties of Kent, Sussex, Hampshire, and Wiltshire. Only about 70 miles from London lies the small city of Canterbury, dominated by its world-famous cathedral. Home to the shrine to English martyr Thomas à Becket, the cathedral receives hundreds of tired pilgrims, many of whom travel far distances to visit the altar where he was brutally killed.

About 14 miles away, tough, stony-faced Dover guards the English Channel. Dating from the days of William the Conqueror, the immense Dover Castle stands as a menacing reminder of the country's impenetrable imperial past. Nowadays the city, a shade of its former self, is used mainly as an overnight stop for those hopping on and off the Calais ferry to the Continent. The hostel here is perfectly fine for a stay of a night or two.

If you head into Sussex, you'll encounter the seaside resort towns of Hastings and Brighton. Both have overcrowded pedestrianized streets and shopping precincts filled with multiples—a far cry from the genteel spas that were here in the Victorian era. Nevertheless, the hostels are outside of the town centers and surprisingly peaceful: The hostels have countryside pastures and trails spilling out from their front doors.

Away from the coast lie the tiny riverside villages of Alfriston and Arundel. The last time Alfriston saw any action was back in 1815, when the Duke of Wellington housed his soldiers in the Waterloo Cottages. The village, full of stone houses and flower gardens, is a cultured pearl on the necklace of South Coast hamlets. Arundel, home of a castle, a cathedral, antique shops, and tearooms, is also a gem. Both towns have homey, traditional hostels as well as some spicy smuggling lore: in the 1600s, boats filled with contraband snaked up the silent rivers in this part of England.

Only a few miles from Portsmouth is Winchester, home to a cathedral, a menagerie of military museums, and the remnants of a castle holding the Round Table of King Arthur. The simple, traditional hostel here is housed in a former water mill. Farther up the road, Salisbury and its cathedral preside over Wiltshire, located down the hill from a grass-covered Iron Age fort and only 9 miles from Stonehenge.

The entire south of England is extremely easy to get around via public transportation. Rail service is comprehensive, though east-west trips involve changing trains. Buses scoot up the coastal road through Kent and Sussex, providing a pleasant sea view to accompany the ride. Roads can get congested down here. Most of the hostels have ample parking, but the towns are often difficult to navigate, especially in summer.

CANTERBURY

Geoffrey Chaucer must be turning over in his grave from the shameless appropriation of his name and work by Canterbury's enterprising tourist hawkers, who milk him for all his medieval worth. Unlike many other cities in southern England, though, Canterbury has sufficient history and folklore, not to mention a cathedral that witnessed a real-life martyrization, to forgive its descent to crass commercialism.

Surrounded by a stone wall dating from Roman times, Canterbury is the Cornish pasty of English cities—it's crusty on the outside, tender on the inside. Modern-day Canterbury is undaunted by the specter of its former glory: Chaucer, Thomas à Becket, Christopher Marlowe, and Charles Dickens all left their mark on the city, but Canterbury leaves its chilling history in its museums and monuments and offers a young, lively street life that both locals and visitors enjoy.

Once you've visited the city's triumvirate of religious monuments (Canterbury Cathedral, St. Augustine's Abbey, and St. Martin's Church), you can hit the main pedestrian street in the center of town and see how the once-forbidding Norman city has turned into a homey enclave for cafe goers, street musicians, and antiques shoppers. In fall, the city fills with visitors to the annual Canterbury Festival and withcyclists and walkers following the Pilgrim's Route laid out in Chaucer's *Canterbury Tales*.

Despite its small size, Canterbury offers a surprisingly wide spectrum of things to do. The Youth Hostel, not surprisingly, attracts myriad wayfarers. It lies just outside the center, near St. Augustine's Abbey and St. Martin's Church, about a 10-minute walk from Canterbury's main shopping and sightseeing area. It's perennially busy, so make your reservations in advance, especially during festivals and summer.

Canterbury Youth Hostel

Ellersie
54 New Dover Rd.
Canterbury, Kent CT1 3DT
Tel: 01227/462911. Fax: 01227/470752.

The Canterbury Youth Hostel has the mixed blessing of being a busy hostel in a busy city. You're best off if you use it as a place to park your pack while you roam the inviting streets of Canterbury.

This Victorian villa somehow manages to squeeze in 81 beds with just barely enough bathroom space for its guests (don't forget those bath slippers!). Nevertheless, the city itself, as well as the hostel's proximity to St. Augustine's famous abbey and St. Martin's Church (the oldest one in England), make up for the sometimes hectic atmosphere inside the hostel. The staff manages to cater to 20-something travelers following the Pilgrims' Way, school groups arriving by the busload, and small families making do in the many-bed dormitory rooms. Somehow, the staff still finds time to prepare especially good home-cooked meals, with an emphasis on tasty vegetarian options—don't be surprised if something as sophisticated as cannelloni verdi finds its way onto your cafeteria tray. They're equally adept at steering you in the right direction if you're looking for the area's best pubs and restaurants; just remember to find your way back by 11pm—don't mess around with Sue's curfew!

Services

Canterbury has two stations: East and West. If possible, plan to arrive at the Canterbury East station; otherwise you'll be forced to fight through the crowds on High Street with your backpack and will endure a longer trek to the hostel.

From the Canterbury East station: Allow a good 20 minutes to walk because of the slight incline. Exit the station and turn right onto Station Road East; pass through the roundabout onto Upper Bridge Street. At the next roundabout, turn right onto St. George's Place, where there's an MGM theater. This will eventually turn into New Dover Street, where you'll huff and puff past Blockbuster Video and a row of B&Bs till you reach the green YHA sign. The hostel is on your right.

From Canterbury West: Turn right as you exit the station, and at the main road (High Street) turn left, go through the arch, and continue up High Street till you hit McDonald's. Go through the underground tunnel. When you get out, the MGM Cinema will be on your right. From here, follow directions from Canterbury East station, given above.

Exit the bus station, turn right, go under the roundabout, and come out at the MGM Cinema. Follow St. George's Place as it becomes New Dover Street, and the hostel is past the Blockbuster Video and the lineup of B&Bs. It's on your right.

From points **north,** take the A2/M2 motorway. From Dover, go straight up the A2, and from Ramsgate, take the A290 into the A28; look for signs to Canterbury.

Open Feb–Dec. They can sometimes accommodate groups in winter when the hostel is normally closed. IBN/BABA: both.

Reception open 7–10am and 1–11pm. Curfew 11pm.

81 beds. 2-, 6-, 8-, and 12-bed rooms. Mar–Sept, 10 extra beds are crammed in.

£ Adults £8.80; under 18 £5.95. £1 key deposit, returned when you check out.

Self-catering kitchen facilities. Breakfast: 7:45–8:45am. Packed breakfasts available as well; order the night before. Lunch: packed lunch only, small or large; order the night before. Dinner: 6:30pm.

No table license.

Individual key-operated lockers free with a £5 returnable key deposit. Large lockers £1 per day.

Washer and dryer downstairs.

P Room for one minibus and up to eight cars.

Shop at hostel sells candy; stamps; postcards; National Express and Eurolines bus tickets.

Small but sweet. No TV.

Not permitted.

Not wheelchair accessible.

They only buy foreign currency.

Bike shed.

Cheap Eats Nearby

Beau's Creperie
Nestled just behind the cathedral, this dainty pink-and-white-flowered place serves not only crepes but also salads and omelets that range from £3 to £6. Big windows allow patrons at two lucky tables to look out onto the street as Canterbury's cool crowd strolls by.

59 Palace St. Tel: 01227/464285. Open: Mon–Fri 10:30am–10pm; Sat 9am–10pm; Sun 10am–10pm. Credit cards: VA, MC, Switch, Access, Eurocard. Reservations accepted.

Fungus Mungus

Just 10 steps from the ancient West Gate in Canterbury, this plant-filled trellised restaurant serves up a huge variety of vegetarian and vegan food. Pick from the endless lists on the chalkboards behind the bar. In warm weather, there's outdoor seating, perfect for people-watching on St. Peter's Street. The tropical-motif restaurant has two-tone green walls that match the parquet floors, and the bar stools are larger-than-life-size red-and-white mushrooms. The walls groan with cheerful murals depicting exotic birds and blue skies, and the friendly staff dart around, dodging the hanging plants and vines dangling here and there. French-bread pizza goes for £2.95; spinach curry with coconut rice costs £5.95.

34 St. Peter's St. Tel: 01227/781922. Open: Mon–Sat 9am–11pm; Sun 10am–10:30pm. Cash only. From the hostel, turn left on New Dover Street, follow it as it turns into St. George's Place. At the roundabout, turn at McDonald's onto St. George's Street, which turns into High Street, which turns into St. Peter's Street. The restaurant is on your left just before West Gate.

Grocery Store: Safeway, on the Safeway Precinct off St. George's Place. It also has a pharmacy. Open: Mon–Thurs 9am–8pm; Fri 9am–9pm; Sat 9am–7pm. From the hostel, take New Dover Street to Blockbuster Video. The store is across the street on your right.

Experiences

Even for those who shun traditional visits to castles and cathedrals, the **Canterbury Cathedral** is worth a stop. Under its huge arches, flying buttresses, and kaleidoscopic stained-glass windows, Thomas Becket, one-time Archbishop of Canterbury, was killed in 1170 (and thereby made a martyr) by four butt-kissing knights who thought the king wanted him dead. Sad for the king (Becket was a close friend) but not bad for the city. Canterbury has since been believed to have been the site of a miracle or two. It's not surprising since the tomb of the tempestuous **St. Augustine** lies only blocks away near the abbey named for him. About a block away is **St. Martin's Church,** the oldest in England. If you wish to undertake a serious religious journey, the Canterbury City Council publishes a leaflet illustrating a cycle tour of the area churches, as well as athletic activities for noneclesiastical purposes.

At the nearby **Roman Museum,** you can trace the town's ancient history, which local builders discovered when digging the foundation of a shopping arcade. Those interested in brushing up on medieval literature can travel back to 14th-century England at **The Canterbury Tales.** For £4.50, you can put on headphones and enjoy a simulation of some of Chaucer's stories. Medieval odors are included in the 45-minute tour. Of course it's nothing short of blatant tourist commercialism, but it beats reading 400 pages of Middle English!

Those in search of 20th-century street life can pop out onto High Street, where English grunge boys play the harmonica for adoring female fans. Under an archway, an old Victrola churns out 1930s music from a quirky little storefront by the name of the **Canterbury Rastro,** an antique-book and vintage-clothing shop in a converted 17th-century barn. The gregarious owner, Paula, is happy to hang out and tell you about the history of the place. She knows a lot of hidden corners in this city. They're not too hard to find on your own, though. **Waterstone's** bookstore holds regular poetry and fiction readings at its huge store (with a cafe upstairs) on St. Margaret's Street, and nearby **Marlowe Theatre** shows everything from ballet to first-run drama straight from London.

Canterbury Cathedral. 11 The Precincts, Canterbury. Open: Easter–Oct, Mon–Sat 8:45am–7pm; Nov–Easter, Mon–Sat 8:45–5pm. Choral evensong Monday evenings. Guided tours available.

Roman Museum. Tel: 01227/785575. Open: Mon–Sat 10am–5pm (last entry 4pm); open Sun 1:30–5pm Jul–Aug only. Admission: adults £1.60; concessions £1; children 80p; families £3.70.

The Canterbury Tales. St. Margaret's Street, Canterbury. Tel: 01227/454888. Open: all year except Christmas daily 9:30am–5:30pm. Admission: adults £4.50; children 4–14: £3.25; senior citizens and students £3.75; families £14.

Canterbury Rastro. 44a High St., Canterbury. Open: daily 10am–5pm.

Waterstone's. 20/21 St. Margaret's St., Canterbury. Tel: 01227/456343. Open: Mon–Sat 9am–7pm; Sun 11am–5pm. Café open: Mon–Sat 9am–4:45pm.

Marlowe Theatre. The Friars, Canterbury. Tel: 01227/781802 or 01227/787787. Box office open: Mon–Sat 10am–8pm; nonperformance days 10am–6pm.

The Basics

Tourist Office: Canterbury T.I.C. 34 St. Margaret's St., Canterbury. Tel: 01227/766567. Open: Mon–Sat 9:30am–5:30pm. Services include currency exchange; ticket sales for cathedral recitals; and guided city tours. They also sell bus, ferry, and Hovercraft tickets. From the hostel, turn left onto New Dover, which turns into St. George's Place until you reach McDonald's. Go down High Street and take the second left onto St. Margaret's Street. The office is on the right.

Post Office: 31 High St. Open: Mon–Fri 9am–5:30pm; Sat 9am–12:30pm. Exit the hostel and turn left onto New Dover. Follow it till you reach McDonald's, and the post office is on your left next door to American Express.

Currency Exchange: at the Youth Hostel. You can also exchange money at American Express, 29 High St. Tel: 01227/784865. Open: Mon–Sat 9am–5pm.

Telephone Code: 01227.

Bike Rental: Canterbury Cycle Mart. Lower Bridge Street. Tel: 01227/761488. Open for bike rental: Easter–Oct: Mon–Sat 8:30am–5pm; Sun noon–4pm. HI members get a discount. Prices begin at £15 per day, £50 per week. £90 deposit.

Taxi: tel. 01227/464232.

Getting There: Canterbury has two **train** stations: East and West. Canterbury East is on the line that terminates at Dover Priory, and West is on the line that goes down to the coast. Trains leave from **London** twice hourly (1¹/₂ hours; £12.50–£14.50. For information, call British Rail's main information line at 01722/770111. **Buses** leave **London** frequently and Dover seven times daily (45 minutes; £2.70). For bus information, call the Canterbury Bus Station at 01227/472082. Their ticket window hours are Mon–Sat 8:15am–5pm.

What's Next

Canterbury is a good base from which to begin exploring the area south of London. The next stops for cyclists on their way to the Continent are **Dover** and the entire southern coast: **Brighton** is an easy hop on the coastal bus route down the A259, and **Hastings** is reachable by train (frequent service; 1 hour; £8.70–£9.20) or bus.

DOVER

Mainly a stopover for people either going to or coming from France via the Dover-Calais ferry, Dover has the unfortunate ambience of a border crossing but is worth an overnight if you're in the vicinity for its immense fortress castle. Built in the 1100s, this mass of bricks later proved invaluable when Winston Churchill planted his naval intelligence headquarters here in World War II. It's said still to be used for top-secret defense strategy, and with its maze of tunnels, turrets, and garrets it could sure come in handy guarding the hotly contested English coastline.

In the town center is a Victorian gaol (jail) just up the street from the old Victorian hostel, but you aren't likely to confuse the two. Both are on the main street, both have entertained overnight visitors, and both have centuries of history. But only one has a deluxe coffee machine in its cafeteria.

✸ Dover Youth Hostel

306 London Rd.
Dover, Kent CT17 0SY
Tel: 01304/201314. Fax: 01304/202236.

The uninspiring town of Dover may lack the charm of other English historic cities and the sophistication of its Continental neighbors to the south, but there's much more than meets the eye at the hostel on London Road (and the annex on Goodwyne Road). The managers-cum-historians of this Georgian town house can tell you the bittersweet story of the place, which may just inspire you to stay an extra few days, whether you're here for the white cliffs, the Castle, or the next ferry to France.

The hostel is the former home of Dr. Reginald Koetelitz, the chief medical surgeon on Captain Scott's ill-fated trip to the Arctic. The captain died before reaching the North Pole, but "Dr. K" returned with a husky named Nell. The hostel manager can verify this since he discovered her grave marker one day while digging a garden in the backyard. The tree towering above the tomb is in honor of the dog, who couldn't adjust to the mild (ha!) British weather. The manager uncovered more history while he was planting a flower bed and dug into what he discovered was a dry pond. He learned that a German V-2 "Doodlebug" bomb had landed across the street and cracked the little pleasure pool. He fixed it and refilled it with water.

Inside, there are a greenhouse full of cacti and an elegant little dining room with stained-glass French doors that lead onto an indoor patio overlooking the garden. In winter, tasty meals and a tidy self-catering kitchen bring hostelers together. The lounge, also a gathering spot, has a TV and a very serious looking collection of leather-bound volumes.

The large dormitories upstairs often host large groups of Continental school-children on spring and summer holiday. The hostel consists of two buildings. The annex on Goodwyne Road (about two blocks away) has rooms with private bathrooms and is usually used by small groups or families. All newcomers report to London Road for their room assignments.

🚆 The hostel is a 10-minute walk from the train station. Exit the station, pass Dover College on your left, go through the roundabout, and turn left onto the main street—London Road. Walk about four blocks until you reach the Eagle Pub on your left. The hostel is a bit farther up on your left.

🚌 With your back to the park, turn left and go to the end of Pencester Road. Turn right onto London Road until you reach the Eagle Pub. The hostel is a bit farther up on your left.

🚗 From **London,** take the M25 to the M20. When you reach Dover, the road becomes a dual carriageway. You'll pass through a series of roundabouts; turn left at the fourth one. At the next roundabout, go straight across through two sets of traffic lights, which will put you on London Road. Continue up London Road until you see the Eagle Pub; the hostel is a bit farther up on the left.

▦ Open year-round. IBN/BABA: both. Groups larger than 50 can rent the entire building for exclusive use; contact the manager.

🕐 Reception open 7–10am and 1–11pm, but there's usually staff around to direct you to the luggage storage if you arrive early. Curfew 11pm.

🛏 110 beds. 2-, 4-, 6-, 8-, and 10-bed rooms. The annex on Godwyn Road has small rooms with private bathrooms.

£ Members adult £8.80; under 18 £5.95. For family rooms en suite, prices range from £9.75 (double room) to £19.75 (single room with bath).

🍴 Self-catering kitchen facilities: small but sweet. Breakfast: 7–9am. Packed breakfasts available as well; order by 11pm the night before. Lunch: packed lunch only; order by 10pm the night before. Dinner: 7pm; limited "call-order" menu is available if you order an hour ahead.

🍸 No table license.

💼 Individual lockers in the game room £1 per day.

🔲 No laundry facilities.

P None.

🛍 Shop at hostel sells candy; stamps; and National Express tickets.

🛋 Lounge with usual board games, video games, and pool table.

🚬 In games room only.

♿ Not wheelchair accessible.

💱 Currency exchange with flat rate of £2.50

🔺 Bike shed; hostel also sells tickets for tours of the White Cliffs.

Cheap Eats Nearby

Pig-Casso's

You'll pass this little hog heaven if you arrive at the hostel from the train or bus station. A menagerie of ceramic, rubber, and stuffed piggies sits on top of the counter, but the food is more varied than the name might suggest. At this cheerful little cafe

Services

with wooden benches and dainty flowered tablecloths, you can order food to stay or take out. English breakfast £1.50; other breakfast platters up to £3. Savory cottage pie £1.99. Some vegetarian options.

89 High St. Tel: 01304/213086. Open: Mon–Fri 7:30am–3pm; Sat 7:30am–2pm. It's about three minutes by foot from the hostel. Turn right onto London Road, cross Towerhamlets Road, and it's just ahead on your right.

Tower Kebab

Around the corner from the hostel, this teensy little kitchen touts itself as "Dover's award-winning kebab house." It's convenient, tasty, and economical, but you can get takeout only. Kebabs are served with pita bread and salad. Kofte kebabs £2.20; deluxe mixed kebabs £4.80. Veg-burger £1.70.

12 Towerhamlets Rd., Dover. Tel: 01304/242170. Open: Mon–Sat noon–2am; Sun and bank holidays 4pm–2am. Cash only. From the hostel, turn right onto London Road, then turn right at the corner. This place is on your right. It's a five-minute walk.

Grocery Store: Ed's, High Street. Open: Mon–Thurs 9am–6pm; Fri 9am–6pm; Sat 9am–6pm. From the hostel, turn right on London Road and continue as it turns into High Street. Ed's is about three blocks down across the street on your left.

Experiences

Eight-hundred-year old monuments are a dime a dozen in England, but **Dover Castle** is likely to impress even the most jaded fortress-goer. Despite its crusty old age, Dover Castle still protects the southeastern tip of England. In Hellfire Corner, underneath the castle and within the white cliffs themselves, you can explore the maze of underground passageways from which Winston Churchill supervised the British forces during World War II. A more-than-adequate tour complete with film and newsreel takes you through this amazing structure.

If you want to visit just the cliffs but not the castle, the **White Cliffs Countryside Commission** offers guided tours of the great White Cliffs; you can purchase tickets at the Youth Hostel. This small local organization is extremely knowledgeable about their territory. Both daytime and evening walking tours are available and wind up at a local pub.

From Dover, many people begin **bicycle tours** of the southern coast, heading west to sandier, less forbidding shores such as Brighton, Eastbourne, and the Isle of Wight. In the Dover area, though, there's one beach you can actually walk on—if you don't mind pebbles. A brisk $3^1/_2$-mile walk over the top of the cliffs from Dover, **St. Margaret's Bay** is the closest place for water sports. It's worth the walk for the panoramic views of the cliffs. This slightly strenuous walk is rewarded by a nice beach and an even nicer beach pub, aptly named the Coastguard. Finally, prison-history buffs can go to the **Dover Old Town Gaol,** where a guided tour simulates the experience of condemned prisoners with a Victorian court scene and jailing. Like Dover itself, it's not for the weak-spirited.

Dover Castle. Dover. Tel: 01304/201268. Open: Apr–Sept: daily 10am–6pm. Oct–Mar: 10am–4pm. Admission: adults £5.50; concessions £4.10; children £2.80.

The White Cliffs Countryside Commission. Contact Stan at the Dover Youth Hostel. Tel: 01304/201314.

Dover Old Town Gaol. Biggin Street, Dover. Tel: 01304/ 201200. Open: May–Sept: Mon–Sat 10am–4:30pm; Sun 2–4:30pm. Oct–May: Wed–Sat 10am–4:30pm; Sun 2–4:30pm. Guided tours.

The Basics

Tourist Office: Dover T.I.C. Townwall Street, Dover. Tel: 01304/205108. Open: July–Aug: daily 9am–7:30pm. Sept–June: daily 9am–6pm. From the Youth Hostel, it's a five-minute walk. Turn right onto London Road, which turns into High Street, then bear left onto Biggin Street. When you reach Market Square, turn right onto Bench Street. At the end of Bench Street, turn left. It's on the corner of Townwall Road.

Post Office: Dover Post Office. 65/66 Biggin St., Dover. Open: Mon–Fri 9am–5:30pm; Sat 9am–12:30pm. From the hostel, turn right onto London Road, which becomes High Street, then bear left onto Biggin Street. It's on the right.

Currency Exchange: At the Youth Hostel.

Telephone Code: 01304.

Bike Rental: Canterbury Cycle Mart. London Road. Tel: 01304/225063. Open: Mon–Sat 9:30am–5:30pm. Sunday hires can be arranged.

Taxi: tel. 01304/225522.

Getting There: Southeast England is easy to get around by **train,** and Dover Priory station is at the end of the South Eastern train line. Trains leave frequently (four per hour) from London's **Victoria** and **Charing Cross** stations. For information, call British Rail's main information line at 01722/770111. **Coaches** leave London hourly (2¹/₂ hours; £10.50) and **Canterbury** every two hours (45 minutes; £2.80). For bus information, call Stagecoach Bus Company at 01304/240024.

Ferries connect Dover to Calais 24 hours a day. Two companies offer hourly departures: P&O Ferries (tel.: 01304/203388) and Sealink (tel.: 01233/647047). Either will get you to France in 1¹/₂ hours. Hovercrafts, which take 35 minutes, leave from the Hoverport off the Prince of Wales Pier next to the Western Docks. For Hovercraft information, call 01304/204241.

If you're coming from London by **car,** take the M25 and switch to the M20 at Swanley. Take it to Folkestone; there the A20 runs straight to Dover.

What's Next

Dover is a great place from which to begin a tour of the southern coast of England. There's hourly train service between Dover and the beach town of **Hastings** (1¹/₂ hours; £9.60), and every other hour, trains leave from **Canterbury** (15 to 30 minutes; £3.70). Bus service takes a bit longer but is considerably cheaper: Canterbury is yours for £2.80 and a ticket to Hastings costs £5.40 if you purchase the day-long Explorer ticket offered by Stagecoach—it gives you a full day of bus travel. The advantage of the bus is that it takes you along the A259, the coastal highway, and lets you take in the landscape while deciding which beach town to settle on. Hastings and **Brighton** are on this bus's path, and each offers a tranquil Youth Hostel within easy reach. For those looking for sun and surf, Hastings is a good bet, and those looking for nature trails, countryside footpaths, and a gay little beach town can head for Brighton.

HASTINGS

Almost every tourist brochure on Hastings is sure to remind you (as if you don't already know) that you're in "1066 country." The town's name has been immortalized thanks to the historical battle (which actually took place in the nearby town of Battle) led by William the Conqueror that effectively changed the course of British history by introducing Norman rule to the formerly Anglo-Saxon kingdom.

Unfortunately, modern-day Hastings, 63 miles southeast of London, no longer evokes knights in shining armor. Hastings does boast a castle and a quaint old quarter, but the overall mood in the town is more *Baywatch* than Bayeux Tapestry: Postcard shops, beach bums, and a strip of hotels fill the town's main drag along the beach. Hastings gets as much mileage as possible out of its prime beachside spot and proximity to London (only two hours away), so those seeking a quiet coastal enclave will probably be only too happy to take the 20-minute bus ride to Guestling House, the local Youth Hostel.

The words *Battle of Hastings* gain new meaning when you drag yourself and your backpack (pack light!) through the Lycra-clad crowds to the bus stop, but it's worth the trip to the hostel. Five miles outside of town, Guestling House lets you enjoy Hastings from a distance—you'll heave a sigh of relief when you return home to sleep on the comfy bunk beds and soft pillows.

Hastings Youth Hostel Guestling Hall

Rye Road
Guestling, Hastings
East Sussex TN35 4LP
Tel: 01424/812373. Fax: 01424/814273.

Despite the in-your-face atmosphere of Hastings proper, the scenery begins to change as you cruise down the A259 toward Rye: The noise levels off, the highway smooths out, and the car (or bus no. 711) speeds up. All of a sudden, you magically start to see farms, goats, grazing sheep, and the general countryside beauty you tend to get used to in Southern England.

At about the time the knots have unfolded in your shoulders (approximately 15 minutes), you'll reach the Youth Hostel, smack in the middle of what appears to be the set of a Merchant-Ivory movie. If it weren't for the green YHA sign, you might suspect you were visiting the country home of a British nobleman. Melanie, Emma, and the staff treat hostelers as if they were old friends, so don't be surprised if they greet you by name as you make your way up the driveway. They can also point you to the best place to relax on the wooded grounds behind the building.

Guestling Hall, the former manor home of a tea merchant, is a huge rambling house set on four acres of woods with a small lake in the backyard and endless little paths that snake through a thicket of trees, bushes, and wildflowers. There are lots of places to run and play outside, weather permitting. Your hostel mates are likely to be a mixed bag of English schoolchildren, cyclists winding their way across the coast, and solo travelers from the Continent in search of sun and surf.

The dining room is intimate, so if you plan on eating here you're more than likely to make a few new friends over a shared meal. The dining room is outfitted with a TV and a small selection of videos. If you decide to prepare your own meals, note that there are few stores or pubs in the immediate vicinity, so pick up provisions in Hastings. The self-catering facilities are spartan, but the staff will accommodate you as best they can. You may be asked to assist with some light cleanup.

🚆 Take bus no. 347 from the Hastings train station or bus no. 711 from the oceanfront bus stop on Pelham Arcade in front of the Iceland supermarket (both run hourly, £1.10). It's about a 20-minute ride out to Guestling Hill; tell the driver to stop at the Youth Hostel. When you get off, you'll see a pub called the White Hart to your left. Follow the foot/bike path that runs alongside it; the hostel is on your left. A long driveway curves to your left.

🚌 When you exit the bus station, turn right up Station Road and head up to the train station to catch bus no. 346 or 711 out to Guestling Hill. See directions from train, given above.

🚗 From points **west,** take the A259 into Hastings. From **London** and the **north,** take the A21 into Hastings. Guestling Hill lies approximately 6 miles to the east of the town center.

📅 Open Feb–Nov. The hostel also can be made available for groups in December and January; contact the manager. BABA only.

🕐 Reception open 7:30–10am and 5–11pm. Curfew: 11pm.

🛏 57 beds. 4-, 5-, 6-, 10-, and 12-bed rooms.

£ Members: adults £7.20; under 18 £4.85.

🍴 Small self-catering kitchen. Breakfast: 8am. Lunch: packed lunch only; should be ordered by the night before. Dinner: 7pm.

🍸 No table license.

💼 None.

🌀 Drying room only. They'll do your laundry for a small fee.

P Carpark on hostel grounds; free.

🛍 Shop at hostel sells candy, toiletries, and canned foods.

🛋 Games, couches, and table tennis.

🚬 In common room only.

♿ Not wheelchair accessible.

💱 See "Currency Exchange" under "The Basics" in Hastings.

🔺 TV with videos in dining room; bike shed; outdoor toilet.

Cheap Eats Nearby

Café Metro

Right on the oceanfront esplanade, this airy little French-style cafe serves up sandwiches, salads, and pastries to stay or take out. Sit by the windows for a while and you'll see the full gamut of Hastings's beach crowd. Sandwiches on white or whole wheat bread start at £1.60. Hot dishes include cottage pie (£2.65) and tagliatelle niçoise (£2.75). Good vegetarian options.

37 d/e Robertson St., Hastings. Tel: 01424/437640. Open: Mon–Sat 10am–5:30pm. Cash only. From the hostel, take bus no. 711 (about a 20-minute ride) from across the street and get off in Hastings town center. It's at the corner of Robertson Street and the Esplanade, about two blocks away from the tourist office.

The George Hotel

Only 9 miles down the A259 in the nearby cobblestoned town of Rye, the elegant old-world George Hotel is an ideal spot to enjoy cider or a nouvelle-English meal. Built in 1575, it's smack in the middle of the High Street and blocks away from an abundance of crafts shops and other crusty old buildings. Light bar food is served in the pub or treat yourself to a beautifully prepared three-course meal in the interior restaurant. The menu changes daily but might include vegetable risotto with spicy tomato sauce or smoked mackerel filet. Three-course meal £15.95.

High Street, Rye. Tel: 01797/222114. Open: Mon–Thurs 12:30–2pm and 7–9pm; Fri–Sat noon–2:30pm and 7–9:30pm. Bar snacks available throughout the day. Reservations accepted for dinner. Credit cards: AE, VA, MC, EC, Switch, Access. From the hostel, take Stagecoach bus no. 711 into Rye, about a 20-minute ride.

Grocery Store: Marks and Spencer, Queens Road, Hastings. Open: Mon–Tues 9:30am–5:30pm; Wed–Fri 9am–5:30pm; Sat 8:30am–5:30pm. Exit the train station, turn left on Queens Road, and pass the Town Hall. It's on your left. It's a 20-minute bus ride from the hostel.

Experiences

After fighting your way through the crowds on the main streets of Hastings to the **Esplanade,** you're rewarded for your efforts, especially on a clear day. Evoking the grandeur of a turn-of-the-century beachside resort, the Esplanade is lined with faded but grand hotels from yesteryear. Facing the water, the old town stretches up to your left. You can walk up the winding streets with crumbling old houses overflowing with flowers and peer into the antiques and rare-book shops.

Budding botanists won't want to miss the **Flower Makers Museum** on High Street, which chronicles the history of artificial flower making since the turn of the century. In the town hall, you'll find the **Hastings Embroidery,** a newfangled Bayeux Tapestry sewn in 1966 to commemorate the 900th anniversary of you-know-what.

The **Hastings Castle** also chronicles the events of 1066 with a modern audio-visual extravaganza. The equally high-tech **Smuggler's Adventure** leads you on a tour through the underground tunnels used by medieval bad boys who smuggled contraband into England.

For those in search of authentic old stuff, nearby **Battle** is the town where the Battle of Hastings actually took place and the home of the spectacular **Battle Abbey,** which William the Conqueror built to rub in the face of the defeated Saxon King Harold. Built directly over the spot of the battle, what remains today is a huge, peaceful, green courtyard and some great examples of monastic architecture.

If none of these things is high on your list, next door to the hostel is a farm with grazing horses and tomato plants and wildflowers for sale. And across the street is a great vantage point with views of the nearby towns. Nine miles to the east lies the market town of **Rye,** where you'll find red-brick Queen Anne–style houses, shops selling lace pillows and New Age books, and cobbled alleyways.

Flower Makers Museum. 58a High St., Old Town, Hastings. Tel: 01424/427793. Open: Mon–Fri 9:30am–4:30pm; Sat 11am–5pm; Sun by appointment. Admission: £1 for everyone.

Hastings Embroidery. Town Hall, Queens Road, Hastings. Tel: 01424/781166. Open: May–Sept: Mon–Fri 10am–4:30pm. Oct–Apr: Mon–Fri 11:30am–3pm. Admission: adults £1.25; students, seniors, children 75p. Disabled access.

Hastings Castle. Castle Hill Road, West Hill, Hastings. Tel: 01424/422964. Open: Easter–Sept: daily 10am–5pm. Oct–Easter: daily 11am–3:30pm. Closed Jan–Feb. Admission: adults £2.50; children £1.75; seniors £2; families £7.50.

Smuggler's Adventure. St. Clements Caves, West Hill, Hastings. Tel: 01424/422964. Open: Easter–Sept: daily 10am–5pm. Oct–Easter: daily 11am–4:30pm. Admission: adults £3.80; children £2.50; families £10.95.

Battle Abbey. High Street, Battle. Tel: 01424/773792. Open: May–Sept: daily 10am–6pm. Oct–Apr: Daily 10am–4pm. Admission: £1.70.

The Basics

Tourist Office: Hastings T.I.C. 4 Robertson Terrace, Hastings. Tel: 01424/781111. Open: Sept–June, Mon–Sat 10am–5pm; July–Aug, daily 10am–6pm. From the hostel, take bus no. 711 into town; get off on the beachfront. Walk past Harold Place, continuing onto Denmark Place and Carlisle Parade. Turn right onto Robertson Street. It's on the Esplanade, facing the water. The ride from the hostel takes 30 minutes.

Post Office: Hastings Post Office. 16 Cambridge Rd., Hastings. Tel: 01424/223344. From the hostel, take bus no. 711 to town; get off at Harold Place. Walk up Harold Place, turning left on Cambridge Road. It's on the right. The ride from the hostel takes 30 minutes.

Currency Exchange: Thomas Cook, 209 Queens Rd., Hastings. Tel: 01424/722360. Open: Mon–Sat 9am–5:30pm (Wed 9:30am opening).

Telephone Code: 01424.

Bike Rental: Romney Marsh Cycle Tours. Rye, 9 miles away. Tel: 01303/875296.

Taxi: tel. 01424/422386 (24 hours); tel. 01424/424557.

Getting There: Hastings is easy to reach by rail, whether you're coming from London and other points north or from any part of the southern coast. Connections are usually necessary (Ashford or Tonbridge), but service is efficient and frequent in the area. **Trains** arrive from **Arundel** (30 minutes; £3.95) and **Brighton** every hour (1 hour; £7.70). The ticket booth is open 24 hours. For train information, call 01732/770111.

Buses stop at all different points in the town, and the main station is on Queens Road. National Express buses come in from London **Victoria** regularly, and service is frequent from nearby **Canterbury** (3 hours; £4); Dover (3 hours; £5.50) and London as well. Day-long Explorer tickets are valid on these buses. For information, call South Coast Buses (tel. 01345/581457).

By **car** from London, take the M25 south; at Sevenoaks, switch to the A225 leading to the A21, which takes you the rest of the way down to Hastings. From Eastbourne and Brighton, take the coastal road (A259) east to Hastings.

What's Next

If you want to continue on the coastal path down the A259, a number of hostels await you west of Hastings. To the west lie the busy beach town of **Brighton** and the tranquil bayside hostel at Totland Bay on the **Isle of Wight.** To the nearby north lie the castle and abbey of **Canterbury,** three hours by train (five per day, £4). To the east, it's also a three-hour hop by train to the border/castle town of **Dover** (six per day, £5.50).

ALFRISTON

Afriston oozes history. Recorded in the Domesday Book as "Alvriceston," it was originally a Saxon settlement and received village status in 1085. Since then, it's had its ups and downs. In 1349, the bubonic plague swept through the area, destroying the little civilization that existed here. In 1396, a strange thing happened: when the prior of the local abbey planned the reconstruction of Alfriston's church, he moved a set of stones to the field known as Seven Crofts. Mysteriously—supernaturally, some think—the stones were hurled to another field called the Tye. The prior saw this as a providential sign. Not wanting to play with fate, he built the church there, bestowing tiny Alfriston with relatively good luck ever since.

The Cuckmere Valley later saw fame as the South Coast capital of smuggling. The silent, twisting river was ideal for great wooden ships smuggling tea, brandy, and other contraband ashore. The local inn was the home of Alfriston's most notorious smuggler, who was sent to the Colonies for seven years of penal servitude, but even he couldn't resist this peach of a town and returned before long.

Lots of people from the former colonies have followed in his footsteps and wander through the antiques shops; the local Clergy House; and the so-called Waterloo Cottages in town, which housed Wellington's armies. Nearby, the South Downs Way attracts walkers heading out to Beachy Head and beyond.

The hostel, an old Sussex farmhouse nestled in the valley about a mile out of town, is every bit as pristine and picture-perfect as it was hundreds of years ago. Attracting school groups, walkers, and cyclists, the village is a diversion for an afternoon or two between walks through the bucolic river valley of this ancient settlement.

Alfriston Youth Hostel

Frog Firle
Alfriston, Polegate
East Sussex BN26 5TT
Tel: 01323/870423. Fax: 01323/870615.

About half a mile south of the village, this little hostel, named Frog Firle, sits tucked away in the heart of the Cuckmere Valley. The local hills, dappled with oak trees, and the frogs from the Cuckmere River gave this house its name back in the 16th century.

The old stone building, originally a farm, is a traditional Sussex flint-and-tile house. It's one of the few hostels, however, that hasn't lost its charm inside: rather than being gutted, the interior has been painstakingly preserved, and it feels as if you're staying in an old farmer's cottage. The exposed beams in the tiny common room date to 1530, and oak-timbered walls line the room. A wood-burning fireplace lends a warm glow on cold nights. Another sitting room has beautiful little lanterns and a country-style green-and-white motif.

Upstairs, the facilities bow to the standard hostel decorating scheme of creaky beds and crowded dormitories, but the bathrooms and showers are clean and pleasant. Downstairs in the dining room, the homemade food shows a spark of creativity: this may be the only hostel that has served carrot lasagna for dinner and smoked mackerel for breakfast. Vegetarians are well cared for here.

Guests here tend to be a no-nonsense crowd: Cylists working their way across the South Downs, couples and families savoring English village life, and solo backpackers looking for a break from the concrete jungles of the nearby South Coast seaside towns. The inevitable school groups can make the place feel cramped, but the accommodating staff, surrounding scenery, and stunning interior make up for the close quarters.

The closest train station is in Seaford, 3 miles away. Take bus no. 713 (every 2 hours) to Alfriston. The driver will let you off either at the hostel or in the village, which is half a mile farther down the road. Alternatively, taxis from Seaford cost about £3.50.

The closest major coach station is in Eastbourne, about 8 miles away. From there, catch bus no. 713 to Alfriston. The driver will let you off either at the hostel or in the village, which is a half mile farther down the road. Alternatively, taxis from Seaford cost about £3.50.

Follow signs to Alfriston village from the A27. Go straight through the village; the hostel is ³/₄ mile farther south, on the left.

Open Feb–Dec. Closed Sun in Feb–Jun and Sept–Nov. Nov–Dec open only Fri–Sat. BABA only.

Reception open 8:30–10am and 5–10:30pm. Curfew 11pm.

68 beds. 2-, 4-, 6-, 8-, and 10-bed rooms.

£ Members: adults £8; under 18 £5.35.

Self-catering kitchen facilities. Breakfast: 8am. Lunch: packed lunch only; order by 10pm the night before. Dinner: 6:30pm.

No table license.

None.

Drying room only.

P Ample and free of charge.

Shop at hostel sells candy; canned goods; and souvenirs, often froggy in nature.

Two common rooms: one for smokers, one nonsmoking.

In common room only.

Not wheelchair accessible.

See "Currency Exchange" under "The Basics" in Alfriston.

Bike shed; classroom available.

Services

Cheap Eats Nearby

The Star Inn

Built in the 1200s, this restaurant was once a hostelry for religious pilgrims and mendicant friars. Nowadays, contemporary British fare is carefully prepared in the busy kitchen. Wooden sanctuary posts still stand in the bar area. Sandwiches £2 to £4.25. Avocado salad £4.50. Jacket potatoes £2 to £3. Chalkboard specials include duck with sauce (£6.50).

High Street, Alfriston. Tel: 01323/870495. Open: Mon–Sat 11am–2:30pm and 6–11pm; Sun noon–2:30pm and 7–10:30pm. Credit cards: AE, VA, MC, EC, Access. From the hostel, turn right and walk ¼ mile into the village. You'll go straight onto the High Street. The restaurant is on the left; it's a 45-minute walk.

Ye Olde Smuggler's Inne

A homey little spot popular among walkers, this inn has a beer garden out back. Cozy booths by the window look onto the Market Square. Double-decker sandwiches and chips £3.45. Countryman's lunch: French bread, cheese, apple, and salad £2.95. Huntsman's lunch: French bread, pâté, and salad £2.95. Albert's sausages £3.95.

Market Cross, Alfriston. Tel: 01323/870241. Open: Mon–Fri noon–2pm and 7:30–9pm; Sat–Sun noon–2pm and 7–9pm. Cash only. Exit the hostel and turn right; walk 1¼ miles into the village. You'll enter onto the High Street. It's on the left at the Market Square; the walk takes 45 minutes.

Grocery Store: Alfriston Village Store and Post Office, Waterloo Square, Alfriston. Open: Mon–Fri 9am–1pm and 2–5:30pm; Sat 9am–5pm; Sun 11am–4pm.

Experiences

Most tourists—and there are many, especially in summer—come here for the "ye olde village experience," and Alfriston certainly satisfies in this regard. The local **Candy Cottage,** which was a glove factory in Napoleonic times, has an interesting history display upstairs where you can learn about the smugglers who hid out in the nearby Market Cross Inn. There's also the story of the soldiers who lived in the Waterloo Cottages, which were set up when the Duke of Wellington stationed his troops in Alfriston. Down the street, the **Clergy House** is a traditional 14th-century thatched cottage. The very first building acquired by the National Trust, it has a tiny medieval hall, an exhibition room, and a sweet flower garden.

Walk down Cuckmere Valley (about two miles from the hostel) and you'll reach the **Seven Sisters Country Park,** with over 700 acres of grassy farmland, a winding river, and dramatic chalk cliffs. Canoe instruction is available on the river. Cycle paths and walking routes wend their way around the park, and you can rent bikes here. The park's paths lead to nearby **Friston Forest.** The nearby beaches are nice for walks, and the white cliffs of Beachy Head are only about eight miles away. The shore is generally rocky or pebbly in the area around Cuckmere Haven; seashell collectors will be in heaven, but sun worshipers won't.

Candy Cottage. Alfriston. Open: daily 10am–5:30pm. Admission: free.

Alfriston Clergy House. Alfriston. Tel: 01323/870001. Open: Apr–Oct only: daily 10:30am–5pm; last entry 4:30pm. Admission: adults £2; children £1.

Seven Sisters Country Park. On the A259, 3 miles from Alfriston. Tel: 01323/870280. Canoe instruction tel.: 01273/643761. Bike rental tel.: 01323/870310.

Friston Forest. Contact the Forestry Commission. Tel: 01323/870911.

The Basics

Tourist Office: The nearest T.I.C. is in Seaford, 3 miles away. Seaford T.I.C. Station Approach, Seaford. Tel: 01323/879426. Open: Apr–Sept: Mon–Fri 9am–5pm;

Sat 10am–5pm; Sun 11am–2pm. Oct–Mar: Mon–Fri 9am–5pm. From the hostel, take bus no. 713 to Seaford; it's on your right as you walk from the train station.

Post Office: Alfriston Village Store and Post Office. Waterloo Square, Alfriston. Tel: 01323/870201. Open: Mon, Tues, Thurs, and Fri 9am–1pm and 2–5:30pm; Wed and Sat 9am–12:30pm. From the hostel, turn right and walk about a mile into the village. Continue up High Street until you reach the Market Cross. It's on the left.

Currency Exchange: The nearest place is in Seaford, 3 miles away. National Westminster Bank. Clinton Place, Seaford. Open: Mon–Fri 9am–4:30pm (Wed 9:30am opening).

Telephone Code: 01323.

Bike Rental: Cuckmere Cycle Co./Forest Cycle Centre. Seven Sisters Country Park. Tel: 01323/870310. Open: Apr–Sept: daily 9am–6pm. Oct–Mar: Tues–Sun 9am–6pm. Full-day rentals £12–£15; half-day rentals £7–£8.

Getting There: Those coming by **train** are best off going to **Seaford** (3 miles away), which is a small branch line emanating from Lewes on the London-Eastbourne route. If you're coming from far away, the train has decent service from South Coast towns, **London,** and **Gatwick airport.** For train info, call 01273/206755.

If you're already on the South Coast, it's easier (and prettier) to take local **buses,** which zip along the A259 coastal road, going from **Hastings, Eastbourne, Seaford, Brighton,** and even as far as **Arundel.** For information, call South Coast Buses at 01273/474441. For those coming from London and beyond, the nearest National Express coach stop is in **Eastbourne,** where you switch for a local bus the last 8 miles out to Alfriston. For National Express information, call 01323/416416.

By **car** from **London,** take the ring road (aka the M25) east; at East Grinstead, switch to the A26 south to Lewes. From Lewes, take the A27 to Alfriston; follow the signs.

What's Next

From Alfriston, it's only a local bus ride to the small traditional hostel above the chalk cliffs of **Beachy Head.** Eighteen miles to the west of Eastborne lies the university town and faded seaside resort of **Brighton,** with its garish "Hindoo" Royal Pavilion, lively nightlife, active gay scene, cafes, and restaurants. The South Downs Way meanders right in front of the hostel, about 4 miles from the congested town center.

BRIGHTON

More than 30 trains per day make the 1½-hour trip from London's Victoria Station to Brighton, 52 miles away on England's South Coast. One of the country's first real seaside resorts, Brighton (aka Brighthelmstone) was originally a puny fishing village, but in the late 1700s the Prince of Wales starting hanging out here. In addition, prominent doctors declared the healthy effects of bathing and drinking sea water, so Londoners began flocking here. They haven't stopped.

The remains of old Brighton are a mishmash of Georgian, Regency, and Victorian architecture punctuated by modern shops, endless cafes and restaurants, and quirky pubs and clubs. At the far end of the center, the oriental-style Royal Pavilion sits by the beach. At once bulbous, spiked, turreted, and trellised, King George IV's pleasure palace is a fitting testament to the extravagance of 19th-century life here.

Day-trippers galore spill out of the trains from London, lending a harsh commercial air to the city center. The University of Sussex, on the outskirts of Brighton, brings in a huge student population, and with them come alternative cafes, pubs, clubs, and a "youthquakey" atmosphere on the side streets and narrow alleys away from the central shopping zone. At night, "London-by-the-Sea" lights up with good music, dance clubs, and an active gay scene, and there's a surprisingly varied mix of things to, especially if the sun isn't shining.

The Youth Hostel is in the nearby suburb of Patcham, a short bus ride away. Only steps from the amazingly quiet footpaths and bridleways that wind through grassy fields and open coastline, the hostel here is thoughtfully situated. Sun worshipers and long-distance walkers aren't far from their haunts and seem to coexist quite nicely when they come back to bed down at Patcham Place.

Brighton Youth Hostel

Patcham Place, London Road
Patcham, Brighton BH1 8YD
Tel: 01273/556196. Fax: 01273/509366.

In a 17th-century house, the Youth Hostel in Patcham has long felt like a home. Once the domain of a captain in the British Armed Forces, it retains a feeling of military efficiency with just an added dash of Youth Hostel friendliness.

As one of the busier hostels on the South Coast, it caters to an especially wide range of travelers, which is no easy task. School groups often share digs with cyclists and solo travelers, but the hostel staff welcomes everyone. A lounge with foosball and video games allows kiddies to run around, while more sedate types can curl up on the chairs in the warm TV room. Meals are fairly good here, and the evening selection is posted up on the board as you enter.

Nevertheless, bear in mind that Brighton is the kind of place hostelers visit for no more than two or three nights, so it lacks the homey atmosphere of some of the slower, quieter hostels. The 11pm curfew can make club hopping difficult, so night owls and late sleepers might want to think twice before coming here.

Services

🚂 Exit the train station and immediately turn left and go downhill on Trafalgar Street. When you reach York Place/London Street, catch bus no. 5 or 5a going left in the direction of Patcham. Get off at Patcham Place and follow the sign to the hostel. It's a 20-minute walk.

🚌 From the bus station at Old Steine, walk away from the water up Old Steine until you reach the Royal Pavilion, a Taj Mahal–esque building. From the bus stop in front of the building, take bus no. 5 or 5a in the direction of Patcham. Get off at Patcham Place and follow the sign to the hostel. The walk takes 20 minutes. If you're coming by National Express from, tell the driver to stop at the hostel.

🚗 The hostel is on the west side of the main London Road, the A23, close to the junction with the A27. It's opposite the Black Lion Hotel, 4 miles north of Brighton.

🎟 Open year-round. BABA only.

⏰ Reception open May–Aug: 7–10am and 1–11pm. Sept–Apr: 7–10am and 5–11pm. Curfew 11pm year-round.

🛏 84 beds. 6-, 8-, 10-, and 12-bed rooms.

£ Members: adults £8.80; under 18 £5.95.

🍴 Self-catering kitchen facilities. Breakfast: 8–9am. Lunch: packed lunch only; order by the night before. Dinner: 7pm.

🍸 Table license.

🧳 Individual lockers downstairs 50p.

🔲 Washer, dryer, and drying room.

P Ample and free of charge.

🛍 Shop at hostel sells candy and toiletries.

🛋 Games room with TV, video games, and foosball.

🚭 Not permitted inside hostel.

♿ Not wheelchair accessible, but there's a ground-floor room.

💱 See "Currency Exchange" under "The Basics" in Brighton.

🚲 Bike shed.

Cheap Eats Nearby

Food for Friends

A cheery whole foods heaven in the center of Brighton, this cafeteria-style place has yellow walls and comfy wood tables. Onion-and-pepper quiche £1.85. Bean-and-mushroom stroganoff £2. Vegetable stir-fry with rice £3.45. Vegan specials.

Flat 18, Prince Albert Street, The Lanes, Brighton. Tel: 01273/736236. Open: Mon–Sat 8am–10pm; Sun 9:30am–10pm. Cash only. From the hostel, take bus no. 5 or 5a into town. From North Street, walk past the clock tower, turn onto Ship Street (the post office is on the left), and then bear left onto Prince Albert Street. It's on the left. The walk from the hostel takes 20 minutes.

The Sanctuary

The vintage-clothing and Lennon-spec set hang out here. Brightly colored walls, a big old chandelier, and jars full of coffee beans provide appropriately alternative decorations, and the window seat is piled high with flyers of local goings-on. Pasta with garlic £4.75. Lemon cake £2.45. Coffee £2. At night, listen to funk music in the basement.

51–55 Brunswick St. East, Hove, Brighton. Tel: 01273/770002. Open: Mon 12:30–11:30pm; Tues–Sun 10am–11:30pm. Cash only. From the hostel, take the bus into the town center, and walk away from Churchill Square about 20 minutes down Western Road to the area of Hove. Turn left onto Brunswick Street East; look for the flag. It's on the left.

Grocery Store: Patcham Coop. Old London Road, in a building called The Elms. Look for the sign. Open: Mon–Thurs 8:30am–6pm; Fri 8:30am–7pm; Sat 8am–6pm.

Experiences

Modern-day Brighton doesn't live up to its former glory as a sumptuous, privileged seaside resort, but a few vestiges of the olden days remain. **The Lanes,** a maze of narrow streets between North and Prince Albert streets, are the former haunt of Brighthelmstone fishermen. They lie in a still-friendly small-town zone with restaurants, shops, and a mix of wandering minstrels and curious tourists.

Down the road, the pebbly beach stretches out with a number of tired mansions languishing in the post-1980s real estate doldrums along the water. At the far end, however, the flamboyant facade of the **Royal Pavilion** stands out from the rest. It's hard to imagine, but it was once a modest farmhouse—that is, before George VI had a series of architects and designers add exotic, Hershey's kiss–shaped domes; Moorish latticework on the patios; and spires, spikes, and fancy tiles everywhere. Inside, it's smothered by Chinese decorations: A silver dragon tops off the chandelier in the Banqueting Room; lotus-shaped gasoliers lurk in the Music Room; and gold-leaf and chinoiserie cover every available inch of wall and floor space. Outside, green gardens surround the opulent structure.

Those looking for more natural settings might want to head out onto the **North Brighton Countryside Trail,** which begins just a few yards north of the hostel. An ocean of green tumbles out from the farmhouses here, and sheep, horses, and cows graze lazily in the pastures. From Patcham, there are circular walks ranging from three to nine miles. The sights along the way include the twin "Jack and Jill" windmills, crematory stones, and a monument to Indian soldiers from World War I. The setting is bucolic and unspoiled, and on cloudy days the heaving skies rush over the farmland, spilling shade and light in every direction.

Back in town, entertainment comes in all shapes and sizes. The **Brighton Poets** hold readings and workshops at the Sanctuary Café, and some are free. The **University of Sussex (USSU)** is a treasure trove of world music, funk, acid jazz, and other sounds; they also present theatrical and other performances. The local **Duke of York Cinema** offers European, Japanese, Australian, and classic films. For dancing, **The Zap** keeps ravers happy at the King's Road Arches, and **The Jazz Rooms** on West Street fire up Cuban, Brazilian, African, and acid jazz music. Every year, the **Brighton Festival** brings everything from Israeli puppets to *Don Giovanni* to Irish drama to town during May.

Royal Pavilion. Brighton. Tel: 01273/603005. Open: June–Sept: daily 10am–6pm. Oct–May: daily 10am–5pm. Admission: adults £3.75; seniors and students £2.75; children £2.10.

The North Brighton Countryside Trail. The hostel and tourist office (see "Tourist Office" under "The Basics" in Brighton) should have leaflets with maps; otherwise, contact The Countryside Service, Brighton Borough Council, Bartholomew House, Bartholomew Square, Brighton BN1 1JP. Tel: 01273/710000.

Brighton Poets. Readings are held at the Sanctuary Cafe, 51–55 Brunswick St. East. Tel: 01273/770002. Their offices are at 2 Freshfield Place, Brighton. Tel: 01273/688676. Admission: free–£3.50.

University of Sussex (USSU). Box office information tel.: 01273/678230.

Duke of York Cinema. Preston Circus, Brighton. Tel: 01273/626261, 24 hours. Evening shows: £3.50. Shows before 6pm: adults £2.70; concessions £2.

The Brighton Festival. Box Office: The Dome Box Office, 29 New Rd., Brighton. Tel: 01273/709709.

The Basics

Tourist Office: Brighton T.I.C. Bartholomew Square, Brighton. Tel: 01272/323755. Open: Mon–Fri 9am–5pm; Sat 10am–5pm; Sun 10am–4pm. From the hostel, take bus no. 5 or 5a into town to the Royal Pavilion. From there, walk down Old Steine and turn right onto North Street. Turn left onto Market Street and walk down to the intersection with Prince Albert Street. It's across the street. It takes 20 minutes by bus and on foot.

Post Office: Brighton Post Office. 51 Ship St., Brighton. Tel: 01273/573209. Open: Mon–Fri 9am–5:30pm; Sat 9am–12:30pm. From the hostel, take bus no. 5 or 5a into town to the Royal Pavilion. Walk down Old Steine, turning right on North Street. The post office is on the left, after four blocks. It takes 20 minutes by bus and on foot.

Currency Exchange: American Express. 66 Churchill Square, Brighton. Tel: 01273/ 321242. Open: Mon–Fri 9am–5:30pm (Wed 9:30am opening); Sat 9am–5pm. Thomas Cook. 58 North St., Brighton. Tel: 01273/328154.

Telephone Code: 01273.

Bike Rental: Harmon Leisure Hire. 21–24 Montpelier Rd. Tel: 01273/205206. Open: Mon–Fri 9am–5pm; Sat 9am–2pm.

Getting There: Brighton is well connected by **train** on the London-Gatwick-Brighton line. Two trains per hour come in from **London,** and service is frequent from other locations on the South Coast. **Dover, Eastbourne,** and **Hastings** to the east are no more than a couple of hours away. The same is true for towns to the west: **Portsmouth** and **Arundel** are about each 1½ hours away. For schedules and fare information, call 01273/206755.

By **bus,** National Express comes in from London about seven to eight times per day. Local buses from **Eastbourne, Hastings,** and **Portsmouth** come up and down the coast road every half hour. For bus information, call 01273/206666.

By **car,** take the A23/M23 south from **London,** which goes directly into Brighton. From **Hastings** and **Eastbourne,** take the coastal road (A259) straight into Brighton.

What's Next

The teeny-tiny, picture-perfect village of **Alfriston**, a welcome respite from the busy South Coast resort towns, is only 18 miles from here. The hostel, a traditional Sussex flint house nestled in the Cuckmere Valley with views over the river, is one of the best-preserved old hostels. A local museum and loads of local walking routes make it a favorite among veteran English hostelers.

Twenty miles to the west lies the sweet town of **Arundel,** by the South Downs Way. A pleasant little river gurgles by the town. A morning's walk takes you to **Littlehampton,** home of international chain The Body Shop, where a tour reveals everything you ever wanted to know about serious skin care.

ARUNDEL

Home of poet Philip Larkin, Arundel is sufficiently picturesque and historical to inspire even the most illiterate to burst into babbling verse on the banks of the River Arun. Antique shops, pleasant tea rooms, and a friendly feeling fill this perfectly cute Sussex village only 58 miles south of London and 21 miles west of Brighton.

The town prides itself on its history. Arundel Castle (home of the dukes of Norfolk) and the Cathedral of Our Lady and St. Philip Howard provide the usual dose of historical English streets and buildings. The town can get congested with bus tours in spring and summer, but Arundel is nevertheless a refreshing break from the overrated, overpopulated, and over-fish-and-chipped towns lining the South Coast. Set farther inland, it manages to remain relatively unsullied by the hordes of tourists that descend upon the area in midsummer. The hostel, about 1¼ miles from the town, is inside a Georgian house at the edge of the South Downs Way. It's relatively popular among students, walkers, and cyclists.

Arundel Youth Hostel

Warningcamp
Arundel, West Sussex BN18 9QY
Tel: 01903/882204. Fax: 01903/882776.

You can hear the trains whiz by at night here, but don't be fooled: The hostel is a hearty walk from the nearest means of public transport. Getting to this hostel in Warningcamp, 1¼ miles from the town of Arundel, is a bit of a pain. If you're willing to shell out £2 for a cab or endure a (mostly flat) walk, however, the hostel provides a nice base from which to see the area.

The hostel attracts lots of walkers on the South Downs way, so it's kind of a quiet crowd. (That is, unless you happen to be sharing a dining room with a school group in the middle of a burping contest, which has been known to happen here.) Even when filled with school groups, the hostel seems to be able to accommodate everyone. The nice covered patio is great, especially in the late afternoon sun, and there's lots of space in the front yard for tossing Frisbees.

The building, a former private residence, served as a school before becoming a hostel, and the oldest part dates to 1720. From May to mid-July, the hostel is loaded with school groups of all ages, and from July to September, families and independent backpackers descend. The beaches and South Downs Way are each only about 4 miles away, so walkers and cyclists find their way off the paths and into the hostel as well.

Services

The train station in Arundel is 1¼ miles from the hostel. A taxi costs approximately £2. Alternatively, exit the station, turn right onto The Causeway, and go over the railroad bridge. When you reach the intersection, turn left in the direction of Warningcamp. Follow the road for about 1 mile; look for the sign for the Youth Hostel on the left; the hostel is at the end of the driveway. The walk takes about half an hour.

Buses coming in from Brighton will drop you off at the railway station in Arundel. Follow directions from there, given above.

From the **east,** come down toward Arundel on the A27 (look for the castle). Turn right three-quarters of the way down the hill, following the sign for the Youth Hostel. From there, turn right at intersection, going in the direction of Warningcamp. The hostel is approximately 1 mile up the road on the left.

From the **west,** come toward Arundel on the A27; pass through the town center (or by the town bypass). Take The Causeway past the railway station; when you reach the intersection, turn left in the direction of Warningcamp; the hostel is approximately 1 mile up the road on the left.

▦ Open Apr–Dec. Closed Sun from Apr–June 30. Closed Sun–Mon from Sept–Oct. BABA.

🕐 Reception open 7:30–10am and 5–11pm. Curfew 11:30pm.

🛏 60 beds. 4-, 6-, 8-, 12-, and 16-bed rooms. Some with locks for daytime access.

£ Members: adults £7.20; under 18 £4.85.

🍴 Self-catering kitchen facilities. Breakfast: 8:15am. Lunch: packed lunch only; order the night before. Dinner: 7pm.

I No table license.

💼 No luggage storage.

🗑 Drying room only.

P Ample and free of charge. No coaches.

🛍 Shop at hostel sells candy, canned goods.

🛋 Conservatory, games room, reception area (with TV).

🚬 In designated areas only.

♿ Not wheelchair accessible.

💱 See "Currency Exchange" under "The Basics" in Arundel.

🔺 Bike shed.

Cheap Eats Nearby

The Country Life

Once a 17th-century candle factory, this place has wooden armoires, local artwork on the walls, and exposed beams. Homemade vegetarian and whole food meals are served with a smile. Shepherd's pie £3.45; lentil au gratin £3.45; quiche £1.95; toasted sandwiches £1.50–£1.75.

1 Tarrant Square, Arundel. Tel: 01903/883456. Open: daily 10am–5pm. Cash only. From the hostel, turn left out of the driveway and right at the intersection. Walk straight up the road into town, 1¼ miles away. Walk up The Causeway, then Queen Street, and onto High Street. Turn left on Tarrant Street; it's on your right, in the square. It's a 45-minute walk.

Hemingway's American Bistro

At Hemingway's, you'll find brick walls, movie posters, a big dead animal's head mounted on the wall, and good food. Burgers £4.95 to £7.55. Vegetarian specials: broccoli and cream cheese bake £5.75; nut cutlets £5.75. Salads £5–£6.

33 High St., Arundel. Tel: 01903/883378. Open: Mon–Fri noon–2:30pm and 6:30–10pm; Sat noon–2:30pm and 6:30–10:30pm; Sun noon–4pm and 6:30–9:30pm. Credit cards: AE, VA, MC, EC, DC, Switch. From the hostel, turn left out of the driveway and right at the intersection. Walk straight up the road into town, 1¼ miles away. Walk up The Causeway, then Queen Street, and onto High Street. It's on the left.

Grocery Store: Alldays. Queen Street, Arundel. Open: daily 8am–11pm.

Experiences

If you're not into castles, old buildings, and walking, then you might get bored here. A riverside walk takes you from the hostel into the town. Mentioned in the 1086 Domesday Survey, Arundel is a pile of historical houses, mostly dating from the 18th and 19th centuries. Upon closer inspection, some reveal traces of timber, hinting at medieval or Tudor origins. There are also traces of Roman buildings in the area, as well as ancient earthworks in Arundel Park.

Arundel Castle is the major sight in town. Built in the 11th century by Roger de Montgomery, first Earl of Arundel, it has stayed in the family ever since. Overlooking the River Arun, it has a huge collection of furniture, tapestries, clocks, as well as paintings by Gainsborough, Van Dyck, Reynolds, and others. A great hall with vaulted ceilings, Gothic archways, marble staircases, and a 1,000-acre park are a few highlights here. In the town, **Arundel Cathedral** stands at the highest spot in Arundel and has some serious Sussex wrought ironwork inside.

Four miles away in Littlehampton, the tour of **The Body Shop,** an international bath products chain, explains how products are tested, what they do with their industrial waste, and how they cull ingredients from indigenous peoples. A step above the usual museum tour, it's worth the trip out of town.

Walking out of the hostel leads directly onto **The South Downs Way.** Within about two miles, you'll find panoramic views of the area, sometimes out to the Isle of Wight.

Arundel Castle. Arundel. Tel: 01903/883136. Open: Apr–Oct only: Sun–Fri noon–5pm; last entry 4pm. Admission: adults £4.50; children £3.50.

Arundel Cathedral. London Road, Arundel. Tel: 01903/882297. Open: June–Sept: daily 9am–6pm. Oct–May: daily 9am–dusk. Admission: free.

The Body Shop. Watersmead, Littlehampton. Tel: 01903/31500. Open: Mon, Wed, and Thurs 9:20am–3:20pm; Tues and Fri 10:20am–3:20pm. Tours last one hour; advance booking is essential. Admission: adults £3.20; children £2.

The Basics

Tourist Office: Arundel T.I.C. 61 High St., Arundel. Tel: 01903/882268. Open: May–Sept: Mon–Fri 9am–5pm; Sat–Sun 10am–5pm. Oct–Easter: Mon–Fri 9am–3:30pm; Sat–Sun 10am–3:30pm. From the hostel, turn left out of the driveway and turn right at the intersection. Walk into the town up The Causeway, up Queen Street, over the bridge, and onto High Street. It's on the left. The walk from the hostel takes about 45 minutes.

Post Office: Arundel Post Office. 234 High St., Arundel. Tel: 01903/882113. Open: Mon–Fri 9am–5:30pm; Sat 9am–12:30pm. From the hostel, turn left out of the driveway and turn right at the intersection. Walk into the town, up The Causeway, up Queen Street, and over the bridge. It's at the corner of High Street and Mill Road, by the river. It's about a 45-minute walk.

Currency Exchange: Lloyds Bank. High Street, Arundel. Tel: 01903/717221. Open: Mon–Fri 9:30am–4:30pm.

Telephone Code: 01903.

Bike Rental: Arundel Cycle Hire. 4 School Lane, Arundel. Tel: 01903/883712. Mountain bikes: half-day rental £6; full-day rental £10.

Getting There: Arundel is relatively easy to get to by **train.** Those coming from **London Victoria**, **Charing Cross,** or **Waterloo** have a direct line (about 1 hour and 40 minutes) into Arundel, which is an unmanned station. Otherwise, those coming from **Brighton** and points east or **Portsmouth** and points west will likely have to change at Barnham, but service is frequent. For schedule information, call the Brighton station at 01273/721032.

The closest major **bus** station is in Brighton. National Express coaches come in from **London** (7–8 per day) and other cities. In **Brighton**, take Brighton and Hove Bus no. 77 or Coastline bus no. X27 to get to Arundel. For National Express schedules, call 01273/206666, and for local bus schedules call 01273/886200 or 01903/237661.

What's Next

Twenty miles to the east is the coastal town of **Brighton,** a faded summer resort and university town with a pounding club scene; pebbly beaches; and a bulbous, Oriental-style palace from the bygone days of luxury and grandeur. Now Brighton is filled with Lycra and grunge, but it's a fun town. The hostel is just off some beautiful footpaths through farmland and open downs.

TOTLAND BAY (ISLE OF WIGHT)

The Beatles sang about this idyllic dreamscape back in 1967, and maybe when you're 64 you too can get your own little piece of this island paradise. Until then, though, the Youth Hostel at Totland Bay accommodates hostelers in search of rest and relaxation.

After taking a half-hour ferry ride and a couple of Southern Vectis bus connections and plunking down a mere £8.80 a night (in high season), the joys of laid-back island living can be yours. Think *Cocktail.* Think Beach Boys. On a sunny summer day, it's hard to believe this enchanted isle actually belongs to a country that sees more than 300 days per year of rainfall: The waters here are bluer, the leaves greener, and the sunsets more shades of lavender than in a Monet.

Whether you come here to see the beach and its famous Needles, ride old steam trains, or visit the castle and summer home of Queen Victoria, you'll have a friendly place to go home to at night in Totland Bay. John Ledwood and his wife (themselves experienced travelers) run an airy, homey hostel with a relaxed touch. This place is legendary among England's hostelers-in-the-know, especially those who are on the Jimi Hendrix–Bob Dylan historical-concert-venue warpath.

Totland Bay is anywhere from 15 minutes to an hour by bus from the ferry ports (depending on where you arrive), so be sure to reserve a room in advance. You wouldn't want to break your reverie by arriving without a reservation and getting shut out. The island is deceptively tiny on maps of the British Isles, so allow extra time for bus travel once you're on it. There's no need to be concerned, however, if you come without a car: Southern Vectis runs a comprehensive network of buses (get the map when you arrive from the ferry) which run frequently, making for easy sightseeing and beach-hopping.

Totland Bay Youth Hostel (West Wight)

Hurst Hill
Totland Bay, Isle of Wight PO39 0HD
Tel: 01983/752165. Fax: 01983/756443.

The hostel is on a hilltop in West Wight, which has been designated an Area of Outstanding Natural Beauty. Downs, seashore, chalk cliffs, and a host of twisty footpaths and bridleways await you right at the doorstep.

A rambling Victorian mansion, the hostel was once the summer home of a wealthy English nobleman. Now its master is John Ledwood, who manages to keep it homey and welcoming despite the huge volume of visitors who come here. Each bedroom door bears a hand-painted wooden plaque with a name on it, so you instantly feel you're a guest in his home rather than another sleeping-bag overnighter. No matter how long the line is to get in, the staff always greet weary backpackers with a smile and kind word.

A sunny reception room loaded with games and books invites you to while away the afternoon writing postcards or reading books from the sizable library. In the dining room, lace curtains sway in the breeze coming through the picture windows. Look around and you'll find that your hosts are seasoned travelers themselves: The dining room boasts one or two mementos from the Ledwoods' six trips to China.

This hostel is not your big-city tourist center. There isn't much in the way of modern conveniences—bring provisions if you don't plan on eating here, and change money before arriving because Totland Bay is on a rather secluded corner of the island. Once you've stayed here for a night, though, you wouldn't have it any other way.

Services

🚌 Once you get on the island, your best bet is to catch one of the Southern Vectis buses (no. 7, 7a, or 7b) heading out to Totland Bay. Service is frequent, and the ride should take about an hour from the Ryde Esplanade and about 15 minutes from Yarmouth. When you get off the bus, go past the roundabout in the town center, bearing left past the garage up Weston Road. Take the second left up Hurst Hill, and the hostel is at the top of the short hill on the left.

🚗 The two car ferries in operation are the Lymington-Yarmouth and Portsmouth-Fishbourne. From Yarmouth, turn right as you exit the ferry carpark. It's 3 miles to Totland Bay. Once you get to the roundabout at the Broadway Inn, head up past the garage to Hurst Hill, your second left; the hostel is at the top of the short hill on your left.

📅 Open Feb–Nov. Schedule varies slightly from year to year, so call ahead to check during winter. BABA.

🕐 Reception open 7–10am and 5–10pm. There's limited daytime access for new arrivals, and on busy days they may open earlier. Call ahead to check.

🛏️ 78 beds. 4-, 5-, 6-, 8-, 12-, and 14-bed rooms, including family rooms with locks on doors for daytime access.

£ Sept–June: adults £8, under 18 £5.35. Jul–Aug: adults £8.80; under 18 £5.95.

🍴 Self-catering kitchen facilities. Breakfast: 8am. Packed breakfasts available as well; order the night before. Lunch: packed lunch only, small or large; order by 8:30pm the night before. Dinner: 6:30pm.

🍸 No table license.

🎒 No lockers.

⬚ Speak to manager.

P Limited; free of charge.

🏪 Shop at hostel sells candy, tea bags, and jams.

🛋️ Games room and TV lounge.

🚭 Not permitted.

♿ Not wheelchair accessible.

💱 See "Currency Exchange" under "The Basics" in Totland Bay (Isle of Wight).

🔺 Bike shed.

Cheap Eats Nearby

The Broadway Inn

When you get off bus no. 7 at the roundabout in the center of Totland Bay's main street, you can hear the laughter and music coming out of The Broadway Inn, a favorite spot among locals. Lunch and dinner are served in the dark pub inside and in the beer garden out back (weather permitting). Traditional pub food includes chili for £3.95 and a children's menu. Vegetarians can dig into a broccoli-and-tomato bake (£2.50), the secret recipe of the owner's mother. If you come on a Saturday night, you're likely to hear the sounds of local bands; otherwise shoot some pool with the regulars.

The Broadway. Tel: 01983/752453. Open: Mon–Sat 11am–11pm, Sun noon–3pm and 7–10:30pm. Cash only. From the hostel, it's a three-minute walk down Hurst Hill and across the roundabout.

Totland Pier Café

For a beachfront bite that won't break your wallet, head down to this cafeteria/snack bar on the Totland Pier. When the place gets busy, you can stare out at the water or play video games in their miniarcade. Prawn and crab sandwiches £1.50 to £1.95. Vegetarians can choose between jacket potatoes from £2.50 and a variety of specials. Seafood platter £3.90.

Totland Pier. Tel: 01983/756677. Open: daily 11am–sunset. From the hostel, head down to the roundabout and turn left at the Broadway Inn onto Madeira Road. Follow the signs down the hill to the pier; it's straight ahead on the beach.

Grocery Stores: Thresher's Food and Wine, Union Street up from the Ryde Esplanade. Open: Mon–Sat 9am–10pm; Sun noon–3pm and 7–10pm. Holland and Barrett (health food), 1 High St., off the Ryde Esplanade. Open: Mon–Sat 9am–5:30pm. It's best to stock up before heading out to Totland Bay, especially if you don't have a car.

Experiences

Many people come to the Isle of Wight just to see the colored sands of nearby Alum Bay and the **Needles,** a series of rocks that go out to sea, best viewed by chairlift above the cliffy beach. From the **Needles Battery,** a clifftop fort open to the public, innumerable walking paths branch out along the coast, the downs, and ancient railway tracks. The tourist office provides detailed routes for cyclists and walkers. The hostel has a great three-hour walking route that goes straight from the hostel down to Alum Bay, where Marconi made his famous first radio transmissions.

If you continue to Freshwater Bay, you can spiritually relive the famous music festival of 1962. There's some good **fishing** here too—plaice, flounder, mullet, eels, and other creepy crawlies can be caught off the coast and in the River Medina.

Those in search of island history can head out to the **Isle of Wight Steam Railway,** at the old Smallbrook Junction station (two stops away from the Ryde Esplanade). The painstakingly restored vintage cars recall the days when steam trains were once the main form of transportation on the island. You can take a 10-minute ride to the Havenstreet Station, which houses an old museum and loads of train memorabilia for sale. Hop off at Wootton and hop aboard the **Victorian Coach,** a 1949 Bedford Coach that takes you around the island.

If you get off at **Osborne House,** you can visit Queen Victoria's summer home, where her nine children learned how to cook and clean like the little people in their very own miniature mansion known as the Swiss Cottage. Nearby **Carisbrooke Castle** is also worth a visit for the donkeys-in-residence and the surprisingly simple Bernini memorial to Charles I, who was imprisoned here during the Civil War.

Needles and Needles Battery. Tel: 01983/754772. Open: July–Aug: daily 10:30am–5pm; last admission 4:30pm. Mar–June and Sept–Nov: Mon–Thurs 10:30am–5pm;, last admission 4:30pm. Admission: adults £2.40; children £1.20; families £6. Chairlift information tel.: 01983/752401.

Isle of Wight Steam Railway. Havenstreet Station. Tel: 01983/884343 or 01983/882204. Operates Mar–May and Oct–Nov on selected weekends and with frequent service Jun–Sept. Admission for third-class seats: adults £5.50; children 5–15 £3.50; families £17.

Victorian Coach. John Woodhams Vintage Tours. Tel: 01983/565082. Operates June–Sept 17 and on selected weekends Apr–May. Call ahead. Admission: adults £2.75; children £1.25; families £8. Fares for partial journeys available.

Osborne House. York Avenue, East Cowes. Tel: 01983/200022. Open: Apr–Oct 3: daily 10am–5pm. Admission: adults £5.80; concessions £5.40; children £2.90.

Carisbrooke Castle. Newport. Tel: 01983/522107. Open: Apr–Sept: daily 10am–6pm. Nov–Mar: daily 10am–4pm. Admission: adults £3.50; concessions £2.50; children £1.80.

The Basics

Tourist Office: Western Esplanade, 81/83 Union St., Ryde, Isle of Wight. Tel: 01983/521548. Open: daily in summer 9:15am–5:45pm. If you're coming from the Ryde Esplanade, turn right; it's at the corner of the Western Esplanade and Union Street. Other offices: Yarmouth, The Quay. Tel: 01983/760015, Sandown Esplanade. Tel: 01983/403886. Ventnor, 34 High St. Tel: 01983/853625. Shanklin, 67 High St. Tel: 01983/862942. Shanklin handles inquiries for the West Wight area in winter.

Post Office: at the Forbuoys newsagents. 47/48 Union St. Open: Mon–Fri 9am–5:30pm; Sat 9am–12:30pm.

Currency Exchange: Freshwater Bank, The Broadway, about a mile away from the hostel.

Telephone Code: 01983.

Bike Rental: Forge Bikes. The Forge, Nettlestone Hill. Tel: 01983/811743. Mountain bikes for half-day (£5), full-day (£8), and week-long (£40) rentals. Family discounts available.

Bus Service: Southern Vectis runs regular service throughout the island. Day Rover tickets are a good deal at £4.50. Tel: 01983/522456 or 01983/826826.

Getting There: Passengers and cars can get out to the island from various points of departure on the mainland. Situated opposite Southampton Water, the closest (and most scenic) **catamaran ride** is the Lymington (on the mainland)-Yarmouth route, operated by Wightlink. It takes 30 minutes and carries both cars and solo passengers. **Ferries** run hourly and the **bus** ride to Totland Bay from Lymington Pier takes 15 minutes. The other car/passenger ferry line is Portsmouth-Fishbourne, and the no. 7B bus can take you from there to Totland Bay. Otherwise, take the no. 1 and change for the no. 7 at Newport.

Solo passengers (no cars) coming from Portsmouth and Southsea can also take the Wightlink catamaran directly from the Portsmouth train station to the Ryde Esplanade. When you get off at the end of the pier, take the Island Line train (BritRail passes are valid) one stop to the Ryde Esplanade, and pick up Southern Vectis bus no. 7, 7a, or 7b to Totland Bay. For Wightlink information, call 01705/827744 or 01705/751751. For Island Line information, call 01983/562492.

What's Next

When you're ready to return to reality, head back up to the Ryde Esplanade to catch the ferry to Portsmouth, where you have a number of hostels within easy reach by train or bus. Farther north is the town of **Winchester,** where you can stay in a hostel that was once a working wheat mill and is now a precious historic building cared for by England's National Trust. Trains run from Lymington to Winchester via Brockenhurst (1 hour, about £8). But if you're still hoping to stay near the briny breezes of the South Coast, rail links will keep you connected to **Brighton** and **Hastings** to the east. For train information, call British Rail in Southampton at 01703/229393.

WINCHESTER

Straddling the River Itchen, the city of Winchester (72 miles southwest of London) is the stuff of legend. Once the capital of Wessex and of England itself way back when, this cathedral town got its real start in 878, when Alfred the Great fortified it against the invading Danish armies. Rough, tough Winchester withstood their brutish advances and held strong, eventually becoming important enough for William the Conqueror to be crowned here. Later, he built a castle and cathedral for the city.

Strange things have happened here. The town's patron saint, St. Swithun, was said to have miraculously restored a basket of broken eggs when they fell from the clutches of a maiden crossing the bridge. Long after he died, the townspeople moved his coffin from an outdoor graveyard, despite his wishes to rest in the open air. Torrential rains came down that day, and ever since they say that when it rains on St. Swithun's Day (July 15), you can expect showers for 40 days and 40 nights.

The legendary King Arthur's Round Table sits in the Great Hall, an imposing structure with a timber roof and supporting columns of pure marble. Nearby, a plethora of military museums line the castle property. Farther into the city is a pedestrianized shopping district with guitar players strumming away underneath the arcade archways. A bit farther is the river Itchen and a 900-year-old water mill, now home to a quaint museum and the local Youth Hostel. Most of the visitors here seem to be in town for a reason: the cathedral, the King Arthur connection, and the bike routes following the path of the rushing river.

❀ Winchester Youth Hostel

The City Mill
1 Water Lane
Winchester, Hampshire SO23 0ER
Tel/fax: 01962/853723.

This hostel, a carefully preserved watermill, sits astride the River Itchen, which rushes 30 miles down the length of Hampshire from Winchester to Southampton. Years ago, hostelers had no choice but to dunk themselves in the frigid waters to bathe themselves with nothing but a flimsy sheet separating the men from the women.

Times have changed since then, but not too much. Walking downstairs, you'll find the mill race nestled underneath the building. The water wheels are still in place, even though the place stopped functioning as a corn mill over 70 years ago. The National Trust organization now owns the building, which means the hostel shares its digs with an exhibition/museum space detailing the structure of the old mill and a chichi gift shop. Between the two is an old-fashioned common area with barn ceilings, brick walls, and exposed beams. This is where the hostel's meals are served in a rustic setting overlooking the river. A working piano livens up the evenings when brave hostelers pound the ivories, but otherwise this is a quiet, simple place.

Outside, there's a walled-in garden on a small stump of earth that juts out from the mill, surrounded by water. Just beyond the garden, a weeping willow dangles its melancholic branches over the rushing rapids, and footpaths extend farther back. Cyclists coming up from Arundel, Portsmouth, and over from Stonehenge and Salisbury stop here precisely because the hostel is refreshingly simple, homey, and different from many others in the area. Walkers on their way to Canterbury via the Pilgrims Way as well as South Downs walkers stop here as well. The hostel has only two large dormitories, but given the chance to stay in such an unusual location, most visitors don't mind sacrificing the comforts of home.

Services

🚆 The train station is on the northwest end of town. Turn right on Station Road and follow the curve. Bear left onto Upper High Street and continue down High Street and Broadway, past King Alfred's statue. Go over the bridge, turn left on Water Lane, and it's on the left. It's a 20-minute walk.

🚌 The bus station is just off Broadway. Exit, turn left on Broadway (Guildhall is opposite), and walk past King Alfred's statue. Go over the bridge, turn left on Water Lane, and it's on the left. It's a 10-minute walk.

🚗 From the M3, exit at the sign for Winnall Industrial Estate. Continue on the road past the First In, Last Out Pub, and The Ship Inn. Turn left before the bridge onto Water Lane. The hostel is at the end of the road to the right.

▦ Open mid-Mar to Oct. Rent-a-hostel available. BABA only.

🕐 Reception open 7–10am and 5–10:30pm. Curfew 11pm.

🛏 31 beds. 9- and 18-bed rooms.

£ Members: adults £7.20 (Jul–Aug £8); under 18 £4.85 (July–Aug £5.35).

🍴 Limited self-catering kitchen facilities. Breakfast: 8am. Lunch: packed lunch only; should be ordered by 9pm the night before. Dinner: 7pm.

🚫 No table license.

💼 No lockers.

⊙ No facilities.

P No parking. Car park on Chesil Street £1.60 per day.

🛍 Shop at hostel sells breakfast items.

🛋 One main common area/dining room.

⤴ Not allowed inside building.

♿ Not wheelchair accessible.

💱 See "Currency Exchange" under "The Basics" in Winchester.

🔺 Bike shed.

Cheap Eats Nearby

The Eclipse Inn

Regulars hang their mugs on the wall of this tiny pub, and the chalkboards conveniently list the alcohol content of the cask ales on offer here. Vegetarian pie £3.50. Ploughman's platter £3 to £3.50.

25 The Square, Winchester. Tel: 01962/865676. Open: Mon–Sat noon–3pm and 6–9pm; Sun noon–3pm. Cash only. From the hostel, turn right, cross the bridge, and pass the Guildhall. Continue up the Broadway and turn left at the Butter Cross monument. It's around the corner from the cathedral, a 10-minute walk from the hostel.

The Minstrels

The plants in the window and the soothing music that wafts down to the street are what attract people here. Inside, it's a warm, comfortable, and airy lunch/tea room. Quiche £2.75. Jacket potatoes £2.50. Muffins 85p.

Little Minster Street, Winchester. Tel: 01962/867212. Open: Mon–Sat 9:30am–5pm; Sun noon–4:30pm. From the hostel, turn right, cross the bridge, and pass the Guildhall. Continue up the Broadway and turn left at the Butter Cross monument. It's to your right, up a narrow alley. From the hostel, it's a 10-minute walk.

Grocery Store: Marks and Spencer. High Street, Winchester. Open: Mon–Tues 9:30am–5:30pm; Wed–Thurs 9am–6pm; Fri 9am–5pm; Sat 8:30am–6pm.

Experiences

The first thing to do here is get a look at the infamous table inside the **Great Hall,** conveniently located near the train station. Featuring a rather dapper depiction of King Arthur in the middle, it bears the solemn inscription: "This is the round table of Arthur with twenty-four of his named knights." It looks a lot like a giant green-and-red zodiac. The Great Hall itself is worth a prowl: its huge timbered ceilings and marble pillars are a sight in themselves.

Up the street is a cluster of military museums. Most notable is **The Ghurka Museum,** which reveals the unusual history of the highly respected Nepalese soldiers who've traditionally fought for the English crown. Aside from being incredibly interesting and beautifully presented, the museum offers a smattering of lectures, slide shows, and discussions on topics like weaving in Nepal.

Down the street is the **Winchester Cathedral,** which dates to 1079. Among its treasures is the Winchester Bible; only die-hard cathedral buffs will want to stop in.

Just off the North Walls on Park Avenue is the **Winchester Gallery at Winchester School of Art.** The gallery is a wonderfully roomy, whitewashed exhibition space featuring a constantly rotating program of contemporary art, crafts, and design.

Located at the hostel itself, the museum inside the **City Mill** is worth a look. The exhibition on the mill's history is quite detailed, and on display are traditional corn dollies, decorative crafts of woven corn silk, and an important part of harvest mythology.

Those here for cycling and walking have a good selection of routes: **The South Downs Way** stretches for 99 miles from Winchester to Eastbourne on the South Coast; **The Clarendon Way** links Winchester with Salisbury for a stretch of 24 miles; and **The Itchen Way** follows the path of the river down to its source in Southampton. The terrain here is mainly downland and chalk streams. It never gets too hilly, so the paths can be followed their full length or in bits and pieces for relaxing days out.

The Great Hall of Winchester. High Street, Winchester. Tel: 01962/846476. Open: Apr–Oct: 10am–5pm. Nov–Mar: 10am–4pm. Admission: free.

The Ghurka Museum. Peninsula Barracks, Romsey Road, Winchester. Tel: 01962/842832. Open: Tues–Sat 10am–5pm. Admission: free.

Winchester Cathedral and Visitors' Centre. The Close, Winchester. Tel: 01962/853137. Open: daily 7:15am–5:30pm. Visitors' Centre open: daily 9:30am–5pm. Disabled access. "Expected donation": £2.

Winchester Gallery at Winchester School of Art. Park Avenue, Winchester. Tel: 01962/852664. Open: Tues–Fri 10am–4:30pm. Admission: free.

Winchester City Mill. Bridge Street, Winchester. Tel: 01962/870057. Open: Apr–Sept: daily 11am–4:45pm. Mar and Oct: Sat–Sun noon–4pm. Admission: adults 90p; children 45p.

The Basics

Tourist Office: Winchester T.I.C. Guildhall, Broadway. Winchester. Tel: 01962/840500. Open: June–Sept: Mon–Sat 10am–6pm; Sun 11am–2pm. Oct–May: Mon–Sat 10am–5pm. From the hostel, turn right and cross the bridge. It's just past the King Alfred's Statue, on the left. From the hostel, it's a five-minute walk.

Post Office: Winchester Post Office. Middle Brook Street, Winchester. Tel: 01962/854004. Open: Mon–Fri 9am–5:30pm; Sat 9am–7pm. From the hostel, it's a 10-minute walk across the bridge and up Broadway past the Guildhall; turn right on Middle Brook Street. It's on the right past King's Walk.

Currency Exchange: Thomas Cook. 30 High St., Winchester. Tel: 01962/849427. Open: Mon–Sat 9am–5:30pm (Wed 10am opening).

Telephone Code: 01962.

Bike Rental: Mike's Bikes. Winchester. Tel: 01962/885651.

Getting There: Winchester is easily reached; it's a stop on the route between London and Southampton. There is hourly **train** service from **London**, with frequent service as well from **Windsor, Salisbury, Exeter,** and **Southampton.** From the South Coast or the West Country, you'll need to make at least one or two connections, but service is frequent. For information, call 01256/464966. By **coach,** Winchester is served by National Express, which has connections from **London** and all major cities. For information, call 01329/230023. From the South Coast, Stagecoach buses run the show. Call 01256/464501.

By **car,** Winchester lies on or near the major southern routes. The M3 comes in from **London** and the M27 connects **Portsmouth** and the south coast. From the West Country, head for the A303, which brings you to Winchester.

What's Next

Salisbury (24 miles away), home to another illustrious cathedral and a (heavy) stone's throw from Stonehenge, is an easy trip by train or bus. A comfortable 200-year-old house on secluded grounds, the hostel is a nice base for visits out to the Salisbury Plain, and the city is pleasant enough.

SALISBURY

Salisbury has come a long way. Who would ever have guessed that this Iron Age hill fort would grow into a bustling market city with a cathedral, a lineup of specialty shops, and a bevy of pubs serving beer for as little as £1 a pop? By the 1200s, the settlement of Old Sarum was no longer needed as a fort, so its inhabitants decided to move 2 miles down the road, leaving their buildings and cathedral behind. Their goal: to take advantage of the River Avon and obtain the proper water supply needed for farming.

Thus began the town of New Sarum, whose name was eventually slurred into Salisbury. The folks promptly got to work on their cathedral and finished fast: It's one of the most unified cathedrals in all Britain and dates mainly from the 13th century. People in the 20th century tend to come here to see the church, a few historic buildings, and the open-air markets in town.

Salisbury is only nine miles from Stonehenge, which draws people with high hopes of catching some Stone Age vibes. Unfortunately, the rocks are surrounded by an electrified fence, but they make their point nonetheless. In addition, the original settlement of Old Sarum, covered over in grass, is still two miles north on the Salisbury Plain, so there's enough to keep budding archeologists busy here for a day or so. About 90 miles southwest of London and 50 miles west of Bristol, Salisbury is a good location for those wanting to launch into Bath, Bristol, the West Country, or Wales.

✸ Salisbury Youth Hostel Milford Hill House

Milford Hill
Salisbury, Wiltshire SP1 2QW
Tel: 01722/327572. Fax: 01722/330446.

Just outside the center of town, the Salisbury Youth Hostel is a 200-year-old listed building. Its main selling point is a humongous 150-year-old Cedar of Lebanon hovering over the front yard. Inside, the entrance is slightly disappointing. Nonetheless, the staff is friendly, and you'll find a bulletin board loaded with information on what to do in the area. The bedrooms are the usual 10-to-a-room scenario, but they have decent bathrooms.

Downstairs is a spiritless but comfortable sitting room with a toasty radiator for those cold nights on the Plains. The patio outside is a nice spot to listen to the birds chirping away on the rare sunny day. Just beyond, the hostel's garden extends for two acres, much to the delight of the many families and schoolchildren that come here. Salisbury sees a pretty good cross section of travelers, but with Stonehenge, Old Sarum, and Avebury nearby, it does load up with the training-bra-and-night-brace

Services

set. It's small enough that hostelers either mix and mingle or head out to the bars to avoid the crowds. Either way, it's a friendly, relaxed place.

The train station is on South Western Road on the east side of town. From here, walk down Fisherton Street and follow it as it becomes Bridge Street. Turn right onto High Street and then left onto New Canal. Pass the movie theater on your right and continue as it becomes Milford Street. Walk down Milford, go through the underpass, and the hostel is on Milford Hill, up on the left. It's a 20-minute walk.

The bus station is on Endless Street, which you won't have to take forever. Turn left onto Endless and continue one block until Milford Street comes up on the left. Turn left on Milford Street and follow it down. Go through the underpass, and the hostel is on Milford Hill up on the left. It's a 20-minute walk to the hostel.

Avoid the city center and take the ring road. Traveling from **London** on the A30 south, enter the dual carriageway at St. Mark's roundabout, following signs for the A36 and Southampton. Bear left for the city center service traffic and follow the signs to the hostel. Coming north on the A36, as you enter Salisbury turn right onto Tollgate Road to the traffic lights, and turn right onto Milford Hill.

Open year-round. IBN/BABA: both.

Reception open 7:30–10am and 1–11:30pm. Curfew 11:30pm.

74 beds. 4-, 6-, 7-, 8-, 10-, and 12-bed rooms.

£ Members: adults £8.80; under 18 £5.95.

Self-catering kitchen facilities. Breakfast: 8am. Lunch: packed lunch only; should be ordered by the night before. Dinner: 7pm.

Table license for wine and beer.

No lockers, but the staff guards valuables behind the desk.

Washers £1; dryers take 20p coins. Detergent 20p.

P In driveway.

Shop at hostel sells confectionery and canned goods.

TV room downstairs; lounge.

In TV lounge only.

Not wheelchair accessible.

Currency exchange

Bike shed.

Cheap Eats Nearby

The Oddfellows Arms

This tiny watering hole, which features an astonishing collection of international currency taped on its walls and a caseful of menacing sabers, has been a pub since the 1500s. Cottage pie, roast chicken, and steak-and-kidney pie are all £3.90 and come with vegetables. Tasty homemade faggots.

Milford Street, Salisbury. Tel: 01722/334633. Open: Mon–Sat noon–2:30pm and 6–8:30pm; Sun noon–3pm. Cash only. From the hostel, turn right, go down Milford Hill, and pass through the underpass onto Milford Street. It's about three blocks ahead on the left.

Sunflowers Vegetarian Restaurant

The simple, clean interior has—you guessed it—a sunflower motif. The menu changes daily and features vegan specials and gluten-free food. Shepherdess pie, the pride of the chef, has lentils, vegetables, cheese, and mashed potatoes (£4). Lunch meals £4 to £5. Dinner £6 to £7.

2/4 Ivy St., Salisbury. Tel: 01722/333948. Open: Mon–Wed 10am–3pm; Thurs–Sat 10am–3pm and 6:30–9:30pm. Reservations accepted. No smoking. Credit cards: VA, MC, EC, Access. From the hostel, turn right, go down Milford Hill, and pass through the underpass onto Milford Street. Walk three blocks and turn left onto Brown Street and then right on Ivy Street. It's on the left, across the street. It's a 15-minute walk from the hostel.

Grocery Store: Salisbury Health Foods, 15 Queen St., Salisbury. Open: Mon–Sat 9am–5:30pm.

Experiences

Of all the medieval cathedrals in England, **Salisbury Cathedral** distinguishes itself from the rest by being the only one of an entirely uniform Early English style. Built in one fell swoop in the 1220s, it's silver-gray limestone exterior and 400-foot spire (the tallest in England) are worth a visit for their perfectly consistent, unified beauty. Spiral staircases lead up to the base of the tower, from which there are excellent views of Old Sarum. Inside the cathedral's **Chapter House** is one of the original four copies of the Magna Carta.

The spiritual air of Salisbury continues nine miles outside of town, where **Stonehenge** sits surrounded by its protective fence. Its main axis (by the entrance) is aligned with the rising of the midsummer sun, leading some to think it was used as a temple; others believe it was an astronomical observatory, while yet others believe it was a sanctuary for sun worshipers. Nowadays we can only speculate as to why these two- to four-ton stones were hauled all the way from southwest Wales. At sunrise it is at its eeriest (and least crowded) as the light shines down on the Heel Stone at its center. Local buses can take you there.

Down the A36 and only two miles from Salisbury, the vast earthworks of an Iron Age hill fort and the abandoned remains of a Norman Castle are what's left of the ancient settlement of **Old Sarum.** Stretching over 56 acres of stony ruins covered over by grass and dotted with trees, it makes for a nice outing: There are some excellent views from the ramparts and loads of room for picnicking.

Back in town, the five-screen **Odeon Theatre** shows first-run, foreign, and unusual films in a former banquet hall. Each theater has its own personality with tapestries, chandeliers, and elegant upholstery; it's worth a visit even if you don't want to see a movie. Up the street, stalls fill the Market Square on Saturdays and Tuesdays with arts, crafts, linens, and the usual fare. For two weeks beginning in mid-May, the **Salisbury Festival** takes over the town. Comedians, musicians, poets, performance artists, and others entertain the townsfolk and tourists, and there are some good events for children as well.

Salisbury Cathedral and Chapter House. Cathedral Close, Salisbury. Tel: 01722/328726. Open: May–Aug: daily 8am–8:15pm. Sept–Apr: daily 8am–6:30pm. Chapter House admission: £1.

Stonehenge. 9 miles away, at the junction of the A303 and the A344/360 (bus no. 3). Tel: 01980/634715. Open: Apr–Oct: daily 10am–6pm. Nov–Mar: daily 10am–4pm. Admission: adults £2.85; concessions £2.15; children £1.40.

Old Sarum. 2 miles away, off the A345 (bus no. 3, 5, or X96 from Salisbury). Tel: 01722/335398. Open: Apr–Oct: daily 10am–6pm. Nov–Mar: daily 10am–4pm. Admission: adults £1.35; concessions £1; children 65p.

Odeon Theatre. Milford Street, Salisbury. Tel: 01722/335924. Tickets: £4.50. Half price on Mon. Special film series on Thurs.

Salisbury Festival. Festival Box Office, Salisbury Playhouse, Malthouse Lane, Salisbury. Tel: 01722/320333. Open: Mon–Sat 10am–6pm. During the Festival, Mon–Sat 10am–8pm; Sun 10am–4pm. Ticket prices vary. Readings £5–£9. Concerts £3–£9. Walks and talks £1.50–£4.

The Basics

Tourist Office: Salisbury T.I.C. Fish Row (behind the Guildhall), Salisbury. Tel: 01722/334956. Open: Mon–Sat 9:30am–5pm. Extended hours on Sun in summer. From the hostel, turn right onto Milford Hill and go through the underpass onto Milford Street. Walk up Milford Street and turn right after four blocks onto Queen Street/Catherine Street. The office is on the left as you approach the Market Square. It's a 15-minute walk.

Post Office: Salisbury Post Office. 24 Castle St., Salisbury. Tel: 01722/413051. Open: Mon–Fri 9am–5:30pm; Sat 9am–7pm. From the hostel, turn right onto Milford Hill and go through the underpass onto Milford Street. Walk up Milford Street and turn right onto Queen Street/Catherine Street, passing the Market Square. Continue one block farther along the same street and turn left onto Chipper Street. The Post Office is at the corner of Chipper and Castle. It's a 15-minute walk.

Currency Exchange: Thomas Cook. 18/19 Queen St., Salisbury. Tel: 01722/412787. Open: Mon–Sat 9am–5:30pm (Wed 10am opening).

Telephone Code: 01722.

Bike Rental: Hayball. 30 Winchester St., Salisbury. Tel: 01722/411378. Open: Mon–Sat 9am–5:30pm. One-day rental £7.50. £25 deposit required.

Getting There: Salisbury is pretty easy to get to because it's a juncture on the London-Southampton and London-Exeter lines. Those coming from the West Country and the South Coast will have no problem getting here. From **Bath** and **Bristol,** service is frequent, and the ride takes just about an hour. Trains from **Exeter** come once every two hours and take hours; train come from **Portsmouth** hourly. For train information, call 01703/229393. By **coach,** there's service from **Oxford** (2$^{1}/_{2}$ hours; switch at Basingstoke), **Exeter,** and **London.** Local buses can deliver you from **Bath** and **Bristol** (2 hours). For bus information, call 01722/336855.

By **car,** Salisbury is reachable via the A36 north from **Southampton.** From **London,** get to the M3 going west through Basingstoke, and at exit 8 switch for the A303, following signs for the A30. Get onto the A30 going west, which takes you straight into Salisbury.

What's Next

Only 39 miles away lies the bubbling cauldron of steamy green water in the elegant Georgian/Roman city of **Bath.** Graceful colonnades, honey-colored buildings, and a handful of museums and monuments make it one of the most popular spots for those on the sightseeing trail. Fifty miles away, **Bristol** is a lively university town and a real underrated gem. With open-air bars, a huge covered market, and a sophisticated artsy element based in its two cultural centers, it's less crowded than Bath and has a real personality of its own since tourism isn't its main business.

Southwest England

There's something so alluring about the West Country. Maybe it's the cliffside farms and rolling hills of South Devon. Maybe it's the salty air and purple moorland of North Devon and Exmoor. Maybe it's the swirling waters of the Gulf Stream and the spirit of Basil Fawlty. Whatever it is, this part of the country has the English people hooked. Mention Devon, Cornwall, Exmoor, or Dartmoor in even the grittiest biker bar in East London, and you'll elicit wistful sighs.

Jutting out of England's westernmost peninsula, the duchy of Cornwall has a geography and history distinct from that of the rest of England. Historically, its inhabitants have kept to themselves and still consider themselves a breed apart: They're Cornish first and English second. Weather-beaten cliffs battered by the foamy waters of the Channel contrast sharply with the tidal estuaries and small islands where strange subtropical vegetation flourishes. The Cornish have a language all their own (though it's used less and less these days) and a distant Celtic-Iberian heritage evident in the oddly Mediterranean-style fishing villages lining both the north and south coasts. Legends of King Arthur are taken seriously here. He and his knights are said to have roamed around Tintagel and Boscastle along the north coast in the days of magic and mist.

The hamlet of Golant is a teensy speck on the River Fowey, and the heavenly hostel here is sandwiched between the coast and the rugged countryside of the Bodmin Moor just to the north. Moving down the coastal road, you'll reach Falmouth, where twin castles—Pendennis and St. Mawes—tower above Falmouth Bay. The Youth Hostel is on the grounds of Pendennis Castle, where floodlights illuminate the medieval fortress against the night sky.

Up the road, Penzance is but a minor blight on the landscape. Trains come charging down, dispensing passengers on their way to visit the sights at Land's End. You can visit the Isles of Scilly here or take day trips out to the artist colonies of St. Ives and Mousehole. In foggy St. Just, a farmhouse turned hostel sits in a forgotten field, only miles away from Land's End. You can experience the amusement-park fanfare of Land's End; watch a performance at the Minack Theatre, Cornwall's dramatic oceanfront amphitheater; or explore the hundreds of stone circles and other prehistoric Celtic ruins lying in the Cornish countryside.

Up on the northern coast, Treyarnon Bay sits in its sandy nook, oblivious to everything but white crescent beaches, turbulent Atlantic waters, and the hippie surfers that ride the waves all summer long. Up the coast and into North Devon, the cliffside village of Lynton (and its twin coastal village Lynmouth) forms the largest settlement inside the 200-plus miles of combes, cliffs, heaths, and vales comprising Exmoor National Park. R. D. Blackmore was inspired here to pen *Lorna Doone;* most hostelers are likewise awed by the landscape. The entire West Country retains a mystical, magical, slightly mysterious air.

Not surprisingly, it can be tricky to get around here without a car. Plymouth, Penzance, and Newquay are central rail hubs, and local buses cut into the area from these points. Just don't expect quick service; buses dodder through the region, and North Devon and Cornwall are notoriously frustrating for those without a car. The unsullied landscapes and natural wonders, however, are usually found in the most inaccessible corners. After a shower and a nap, most hostelers who trek to these remote spots grudgingly attest that it was worth the hassle.

GOLANT

Only 35 miles into Cornwall and about halfway between Plymouth and Falmouth lies the sleepy hamlet of Golant, lost in the brush of the local farmland and swallowed up by the imposing, craggy peaks on the bleak Bodmin Moor 12 miles to the north. Despite its capricious weather, Golant attracts those who want to experience the true Cornish landscape—minus the crowds, the amusement parks, and surf scene of some of the larger towns.

Gentle hills, overgrown country lanes, and rich farmlands surround the hostel and the area along the rivers and inland. Four miles down on the coast, the landscape changes dramatically into rugged cliffs and rocky coastal paths. Fishing on the nearby River Fowey (pronounced "foy") and watersports on the Siblyback Lake in Bodmin Moor are on offer, and bridleways and footpaths abound. There's really no semblance of village life here, so bring provisions with you. Getting here is no picnic, but those who persevere are rewarded with an elegant hostel overlooking the wooded river valley—a truly peaceful escape.

❀ Golant Youth Hostel Penquite House

Golant, Fowey
Cornwall PL23 1LA
Tel: 01726/833507. Fax: 01726/832947.

Penquite House, a Georgian-style country home, is straight out of Daphne du Maurier's Cornwall. It's surprising that some enterprising hotelier hasn't snatched this place up for romantic summer weddings: China plates carefully mounted on the walls, delicate watercolors, and exceptionally pretty wooded grounds give this hostel the feel of a romantic country inn.

The dining room, with its 18th-century moldings, flowered wallpaper, and soft lighting, can really help get your romance going. Meals are all home-cooked and the dining options are better than the standard three-course set meal at most hostels. A short-order menu is available, as is an extensive wine list.

The bedrooms, mainly with two to six beds per room, are a thankful break from the usual boot-camp dorms of country hostels. One large dormitory boasts exposed pine beams. Downstairs, a sitting room with a crackling log fire looks out onto the river and trees below, and the reception area doubles as an elegant (but bargain-priced) gift shop.

The manager, Sandra, grows flowers in the hothouse on the hostel grounds, and her husband, Mike, keeps the bushes pruned, the gift shop stocked, and the staff cheerful. Somehow, he also manages to find time to prepare smoked mackerel, a local specialty he serves for breakfast. If you'd rather not be wined and dined by your hosts, they'll sell you what you need to cook in the totally modern self-catering kitchen, which looks as if it belonged in a private ski house in Switzerland.

The hostel, with fully equipped classrooms, tends to attract a fair amount of school groups on field trips, but you're just as likely to see young families and solo backpackers. They all seem to coexist harmoniously for the most part. For those who want to spend time outside, there are tons of walking paths that sprout out from the hostel, and the managers can tell you where to go and how to find your way around.

🚆 The closest train station is Par, 3 miles away on the London-Penzance rail line. Get off and exit up the path leading out to Eastcliffe Road. At the top of the road there is a bus stop. Take Western National bus no. 24 to the Castle Dore crossroads; it runs every half hour until 11pm during the week and every hour until 6pm on Sunday. When the bus drops you off at the Castle Dore stop, follow the sign to the Youth Hostel. About halfway, you'll see another green sign. Walk down the long drive until you reach a fork in the road, where another sign pointing right leads you to Penquite House; the hostel is at the end of this road to the left. For anyone with a backpack, it's a hike.

🚌 The London-Penzance National Express passes through St. Austell, 9 miles away. From St. Austell, catch the Western National bus no. 24 and take it to Castle Dore crossroads. Follow the directions from the train, given above.

🚐 From the East, pass through Lostwithiel on the A390. Turn left onto the B3269 pointing to Fowey. After $2^1/_2$ miles turn left, and there is a sign pointing to Golant. The hostel is on your left after half a mile.

▦ Open Feb–Oct. For group bookings in winter, call the manager. It's sometimes open during the Christmas and New Year's holiday. BABA.

🕐 Reception open 7–10am and 5–11pm. Curfew 11pm.

🛏 94 beds. 2-, 3-, 4-, 6-, 10- and 21-bed rooms available. Family rooms (not en suite) are available with keys for daytime access.

£ Members: adults £8.80; under 18 £5.95. Field study rates are available for groups larger than 10 on full board using the two classrooms.

🍴 Self-catering kitchen facilities: Very well-stocked kitchen with gas ranges and a grill. The hostel has a supply of bread, milk, and other basic provisions. Breakfast: 8am. Lunch: packed lunches (including tasty Cornish pasties); should be ordered by 10pm the night before. Dinner: 7pm. Food is also served outside of normal meal hours from a short-order menu.

🍷 They have a table license, an extensive wine list from clarets to muscadet, and a selection of beers and cider.

🛄 No lockers.

⬜ Washers (£1), dryers (take 20p), and drying room.

P Ample and free of charge.

🛍 Shop at hostel is a gift shop with the best prices around: toiletries; candy; maps; teas; local gift items. Map hire available.

🛋 TV lounge with extensive library and board games; reception area; games room with pool table and video games.

🚬 In TV lounge and games room only.

♿ Not wheelchair accessible.

🔁 See "Currency Exchange" under "The Basics" in Golant.

🔺 Bike shed; two classrooms available for groups, one with reference library for environmental studies.

Cheap Eats Nearby

Imperial Palace Chinese Restaurant

This is one of a precious few restaurants in the area. You can take out your order or eat here. King prawns with mushrooms £3.80. Curried mixed vegetables £2.50. Three-course dinner for two £14.

115 Par Green, Par (3 miles away). Tel: 01726/816199. Open: daily 5:30–11:30pm. Cash only. From the hostel, walk up the driveway and back to the Castle Dore Crossroads, then pick up the bus into Par. From the Par train station, turn right onto Eastcliffe Road. Follow the road past Spar and turn right at the green. It's on the right. The ride/walk from the hostel takes one hour.

Grocery Store: Spar, on Eastcliffe Road, Par (3 miles away). Open: Mon–Sat 8am–10pm.

Experiences

Golant can be a tricky place for those without their own transportation, but it's far from impossible to navigate. As long as you can tackle a few hills, the scenery is worth your trouble. For **horseback riding,** Trill Farm in nearby Par (three miles away) isn't too far. The terrain isn't dangerous or terribly rocky: It's mostly farmlands and wooded lanes. For slightly more experienced riders, there is pony trekking on the barren Bodmin Moor, 12 miles north of the hostel. Bodmin Moor lures fearless mountain bikers as well. It offers rugged terrain, peaks that reach up to 1,400 feet, and a desolate moorland down below.

Walking paths and **water sports** (windsurfing boards, dinghies, canoes, kayaks, and wetsuits available) are plentiful on Siblyback Lake, about eight miles farther into the moorland. Closer to the hostel is the unspoiled riverside village of Fowey, only four miles south. Here you can take **guided boat rides** or rent your own sailboat, dinghy, or motorboat. Some of the boat trips go as far as Polperro, about 8 miles east along the rugged coastline.

Fishing trips are also a possibility: Mackerel and "wreck" fishing produce good results around here, and you can cook up the day's catch back at the hostel. In the area around Fowey, there are also many walking paths, and there are some healthy, blood-pumping circuits to go around the coast.

Nearby Charlestown makes for a nice day visit too. Built in the 1790s, it's still a busy port and has a **Shipwreck and Heritage Museum** with lots of juicy history on smuggling, shipwrecks, and sailing lore.

Horseback Riding. Trill Farm, Par. Tel 01726/812071. Little Barton Riding Centre. Bodmin Moor. St. Cleer, Liskeard. Tel: 01579/342444.

Peninsula Watersports Centres. Siblyback Lake, Bodmin Moor. Tel: 01579/346522. Courses in windsurfing, kayaking, canoeing.

Fowey Marine Services. 21/27 Station Rd., Fowey (4 miles away). Tel: 01726/833236. Half-day mirror dinghy £13; 15-foot motorboat £20; fishing trips from £50.

Fishing and boat trips in Fowey. Contact the hostel manager; he's got locals lined up. He can also advise you about walking routes around Fowey.

Charlestown Shipwreck and Heritage Museum. Charlestown, St. Austell (9 miles away). Tel: 01726/67526. Open: daily Mar 31–Oct 10am–5pm.

The Basics

Tourist Office: 4 Custom House Hill, Fowey (4 miles away). Tel: 01726/833616. Open: Mon–Fri 9am–5pm; Sat 9am–12:30pm. Summer: Mon–Sat 9am–5pm.

Post Office: 4 Custom House Hill, Fowey (4 miles away). Tel: 01726/833616. Open: Mon–Fri 9am–5pm; Sat 9am–12:30pm. Summer: Mon–Sat 9am–5pm. In Par (3 miles away): Par Post Office. 31 Par Green, Par. Tel: 01726/812838. Open: Mon–Thurs 9am–1pm and 2–5:30pm; Fri 9am–1pm; Sat 9am–12:30pm.

Currency Exchange: You should exchange money before arriving here. Fowey (4 miles away) has three banks and a cash machine. In Plymouth, there's a Thomas Cook and American Express. 63 Cornwall St., Plymouth. Tel: 01752/601352. Open: Mon–Sat 9am–5:30pm (Thurs 10am opening).

Telephone Code: 01726.

Bike Rental: Contact the hostel manager; rentals can be arranged locally.

Getting There: Be aware that the closest local bus stop is about two miles away at the Castle Dore crossroads. Those arriving from other cities by train or coach can pick up Western National bus no. 24 in the village of Par to get to Castle Dore. Don't come out here unless you're prepared to walk; it's not uphill, but the weather is very unpredictable and there aren't very many cars driving around to pick up worn-out backpackers. Call Western National ahead to double-check their schedule. They're in Plymouth at 01752/222666; they are open Mon–Sat 7:30am–7pm, Sun 8am–2:20pm.

The nearest **train** station is three miles away in Par, which is on the line running between Penzance and Plymouth. Service is frequent out from **London, Exeter, Plymouth**, **Penzance**, and **Land's End.** The station is unmanned, so call 01872/76244 or 01752/221300 for information.

The closest major **bus** station is in Bodmin (about 15 miles away); National Express buses come in from **London** and other major cities. From Bodmin, local buses run by Western National connect you to Golant. For National Express, call 0990/808080. For Western National information, call 01208/79898 or 01209/719988.

By **car** from **London,** take the M4 to Bristol and then the M5 south to Exeter. From **Exeter,** take the A38 through Plymouth to Liskeard. There, switch to the A390 heading for Lostwithiel, and about three miles past Lostwithiel, turn onto the B3269 south for Golant.

What's Next

From Golant, there's a lineup of hostels along the Par-Penzance train route. In **Falmouth,** the Youth Hostel is inside the old army barracks of Pendennis Castle, which overlooks Falmouth Bay on its jutting peninsula. Farther along, the port town of **Penzance** isn't far from some popular fishing villages and art colonies, and the town itself is a friendly, bustling center with shops and a waterfront promenade, as well as bars and meaderies to keep you busy by night. About eight miles farther west lies St. Just Youth Hostel, in a sleepy village that's a few miles from the hordes of camera-snappers crowding into the amusement park at **Land's End.** Isolated and dreamlike, the hostel has some great water views. Coastal paths lead out to stone ruins, an outdoor theater, and the other towns on the western tip of Cornwall.

FALMOUTH (PENDENNIS CASTLE)

This area, home of not one but two ancient castles, has long since shed its stony, Dark Age image and has opened itself up to the more modern torture device of crass commercialism. Tourists are now chained to surf shops, Italian wine bars, and beachfront stalls selling multicolored candles and Anthrax T-shirts. Nobody said Falmouth was Cornwall's most picturesque village, but visitors are lured here for other reasons.

Staying at the hostel here, located in the fortified army barracks of a Tudor castle, is one such reason. In the 16th century, Henry VIII recognized the strategic importance of this harbor, the third-deepest in the world. The tiny peninsulas of Falmouth and St. Mawes needed protection against the Spanish and French, so Henry promptly built two castles, Pendennis and St. Mawes, one on each side of the harbor. Both castles saw action through World War I and World War II, and one is now home to the local Youth Hostel.

With its beautiful weather and choice location in the sunniest spot in England, Falmouth has come into its own as a summer resort. It has attracted the likes of Roger Moore and Pete Townsend to its unusually sandy beaches, swanky yacht club scene, and lively nightlife. There's a burgeoning arts scene here as well with a local arts college, some traditional galleries, and an cultural center featuring alternative films and cutting-edge creative work. Despite the hordes of tourists, the locals tend to be a bit wary of visitors and will vociferously assert their fiery Cornish (not English, mind you) temperaments—so beware.

✹ Pendennis Castle Youth Hostel
Pendennis Castle

Falmouth, Cornwall TR11 4LP
Tel: 01326/311435. Fax: 01326/315473.

The mazelike hostel is not actually inside the castle but in the old Victorian-era army barracks behind it. Accordingly, there are lots of things here that are sturdy, reliable, and standard-issue: The service, the common rooms, the kitchen, and the spare classroom are all regulation Youth Hostel. Although the building is spiritless and dark compared its next-door neighbor, the nighttime views more than make up for the chilly air here. The breathtaking castle glows under the floodlights, lighting up the night sky.

Also breathtaking is the mile-long trek up to the castle from the train station; it's a hearty uphill climb. Hostelers usually stop grumbling and start gushing about three-quarters of the way here, once the towering castle comes into full view. Most visitors come for the fortress experience since this is the only hostel in England on castle property—but beware: the hostel falls under the scrutiny of the English Heritage watchdoglike guards who patrol the area. Nevertheless, it's worth staying here a night or two to take in some of the local scenery and snap some beautiful photos from this craggy perch high above Falmouth harbor.

🚆 The train station closest to the town is Falmouth Town, but the station closer to the hostel is Falmouth Docks. From the Falmouth Docks station, turn left and follow the brown signs to Pendennis Castle. You'll reach the seaside Castle Drive, and the castle is visible from there, to your left. It's a 15-minute walk uphill.

🚌 Buses arrive at the Moor. Walk up the main shopping street (which is called High Street, then Market Street, then Arwenack Street) with the docks to your left until you reach a sign for Pendennis Castle, which will lead you to Castle Drive; from there, the castle is visible up on the peninsula. It's a 30-minute walk.

🚗 Follow the signs on the A39 to Falmouth. When you reach the main roundabout before coming into town, head straight, with the water on your left. Follow the brown signs to Pendennis Castle, with the water to your right.

▦ Open Feb–Nov 25. Call ahead; schedule varies from year to year. BABA.

🕐 Reception open 8:30–10am and 5–10:30pm. Hostel is open at 7am but doesn't staff reception during breakfast hours. Curfew 11pm.

🛏 72 beds; 18-bed dormitory added in July–Aug. 2-, 4-, and 6-bed dormitories available.

£ Members: adults £8; under 18 £5.35.

🍴 Small self-catering kitchen facilities. Breakfast: 8–8:30am. Lunch: packed lunch only; order by 9pm the night before. Dinner: 7pm.

🍸 No table license.

💼 No lockers.

⊡ Washers £1.50; dryers 60p (tokens available at reception).

P Parking outside the castle gates during the night; during the day, cars must go to public car parks by the beaches down Castle Drive and Cliff Road.

🛍 Shop at hostel sells candy and canned goods.

🛋 TV lounge with a huge mural of Cornwall on the wall; small smoking lounge.

🚬 In smoking room next to TV lounge.

♿ Not wheelchair accessible.

💱 See "Currency Exchange" under "The Basics" in Falmouth.

⚠ Bike shed. Hostelers get free admission to the castle during summer from 5–6pm.

Cheap Eats Nearby

The Bank Café

In the center of town, this cafe has an appropriately beachy motif: aqua-colored walls, tablecloths, and chairs and hanging flower prints. Cream cheese and walnut sandwiches £2.60. Special sandwiches £1.95 to £3. Roast ham salad £3.75. Chicken curry and rice £3.75.

4 Killigrew St., Falmouth. Tel: 01326/312991. Open: Mon–Sat 10am–4pm. From the hostel, walk down the hill into Falmouth town onto Market Street and bear left onto Killigrew. It's on the left; the walk takes 25 minutes.

Bedruthen Café

This simple beachfront lunch spot lies on the main road between the castle and Falmouth town. Tables outside overlook the bay. Bacon baps £1.65. Steak-and-kidney pie £2.35. Pasty and chips £2.45.

49 Castle Dr., Falmouth. No phone. Open: Easter–autumn: daily 11am–6pm. Cash only. From the hostel, walk down the hill. It'll be on your right after about five minutes.

Grocery Store: Marks and Spencer, on Market Street, Falmouth. Open: Mon–Wed 9:30am–5pm; Thurs–Fri 9am–5pm; Sat 8:30am–5pm.

Experiences

Hostelers lucky enough to come here in summer get into the castle for free on weekdays between 5 and 6pm. Overlooking Carrick Roads, the estuary of the River Fal, **Pendennis Castle** has a Tudor battle exhibition in the old gun room, uniforms from the two World Wars, and artifacts from its 450 years of warring history. On some weekends, they hold cannon exhibitions and other special events. In isolation atop Pendennis Point, it's truly spectacular.

Across the estuary from Pendennis Castle, you can see **St. Mawes Castle,** which is reachable by **ferry** from Falmouth and is just as impressive as Pendennis. Surrounded by luscious subtropical gardens, the castle was constructed in a cloverleaf design with gun ports covering every possible angle of approach. From here, you can savor your lunch along with some excellent views of Falmouth and Pendennis Castle. Across the bay on the other side of St. Mawes lies the even tinier peninsula of **Place,** which has some beautiful coastal walks passing by a lighthouse, skinny creeks, barren cliffs, and flocks of frolicking seabirds.

In Falmouth itself, the **Falmouth Arts Centre** presents independent, foreign, and first-run movies; concerts; dance performances; theater; and visual arts. Subjects range from the music of Tibetan Monks to the paintings of Cornwall. A small children's workshop is offered as well. The nearby **Falmouth Art Gallery** is more traditional and features thoughtfully presented local art exhibitions.

Farther down from the town, a few lovely sandy **beaches** stretch down the coast. Castle Beach, Gyllingvase Beach, Swanpool, and Maenporth are all subject to the ever-changing tides but are beautiful spots for walking, exploring, and sunbathing.

Pendennis Castle. Pendennis Point, Falmouth. Tel: 01326/316594. Open: Apr–Sept: daily 10am–6pm; Oct–Mar: daily 10am–4pm. Admission: adults £2.20; concessions £1.70; children £1.10. Hostelers staying at Pendennis get free admission from 5–6pm in summer.

St. Mawes Castle. St. Mawes. Tel: 01326/270526. Open: Apr–Sept: daily 10am–6pm; Oct: daily 10am–4pm. Nov–Mar: Wed–Sun 10am–4pm. Admission: adults £1.50; concessions £1.10; children 80p.

Ferries to St. Mawes. St. Mawes Ferry Company. Prince of Wales Pier, Falmouth. Tel: 01326/313234.

Ferries from St. Mawes to Place. Balcomb Boats, St. Mawes. Tel: 01209/214901. May–Sept only: Mon–Sat half-hourly departures 10am–4:30pm. Tickets for adults: single £1; return £1.50. Children: single 50p; return £1; bikes 50p.

Falmouth Arts Centre. Church Street, Falmouth. Tel: 01326/212300. Box office open: Mon–Sat 10am–1pm and one hour prior to scheduled events. Movie tickets: adults £3.50; concessions £2.50. Theater, music, and dance tickets: £4–£6. Student standby tickets £2.

Falmouth Art Gallery. Municipal Buildings, The Moor. Falmouth, Cornwall. Tel: 01326/313863. Open: Mon–Fri 10am–4:30pm; Sat 10am–1pm. Admission: free.

The Basics

Tourist Office: Falmouth T.I.C. 28 Killigrew St., Falmouth. Tel: 01326/312300. Open: Mon–Thurs 8:45am–5:15pm; Fri 8:45am–4:45pm; Sat 9am–5pm. In July–Aug, open Sun 9am–5pm. From the hostel, follow Castle Drive along the coast until it forks. Bear right, going toward the train station, and turn left onto Melvill Road. Continue as Melvill turns into Lansdowne Road and turn right on Avenue Road. When you reach the Port Pendennis Development, turn left onto Grove Place, which turns into the main shopping streets of Arwenack, Church, and Market. Follow it until you reach Killigrew Street, which opens onto the Moor, where all the buses are. The tourist office is on your left.

Post Office: Falmouth Post Office. The Moor, Falmouth. Tel: 01326/312525. Open: Mon–Fri 9am–5:30pm; Sat 9am–12:30pm. To get to the Moor, follow directions to the tourist office, given above. The post office is on your right, just past the library.

Currency Exchange: Falmouth Post Office. The Moor, Falmouth. Tel: 01326/312525. Open: Mon–Fri 9am–5:30pm; Sat 9am–12:30pm. Also, NatWest Bank. 29 Market Street, Falmouth. Tel: 01326/212020. Open: Mon–Tues 9am–5pm; Wed 9:30am–5pm; Thurs–Fri 9am–5pm. NatWest can only convert foreign currency into pounds, not the other way around.

Telephone Code: 01326.

Bike Rental: Alldridge Cycles. 1 Swanpool St., Falmouth. Tel: 01326/318600. Open: Mon–Sat 9am–1pm and 2–5pm; Wed open half day only. Mountain bikes £4 per day, £20 deposit.

Getting There: By **train**, Falmouth is reachable via the London-Penzance route; change at Truro for Falmouth. There are two stops: Falmouth Docks brings you closer to the hostel, but Falmouth Town leaves you near the shops, bars, and restaurants. Service is hourly from **London**, and trains from **Bristol** and **Bath** also come in frequently. For information, call 01872/76244.

There's no central **bus** station in Falmouth, but Western National provides good service from **Camborne** and **Newquay** (for those coming from Northern Cornwall), as well as **Truro, Penzance, Land's End,** and **Plymouth**. For information, call 01752/222666 or 01209/7199888.

By **car:** From **London**, take the M4 to Bristol, where you switch for the M5, heading for Exeter. From **Exeter**, take the A30 west, following signs for Truro; switch to the A39, which takes you into Truro, and continue about 10 miles farther into Falmouth.

What's Next

Once you're in Cornwall, it's hard to resist checking out the town Gilbert and Sullivan made famous: 24 miles away, the port town of **Penzance** is slightly congested but has a lively nightlife in its bars and meaderies. It's close to some Cornish artist colonies and fishing villages and is only a ferry ride away from the Isles of Scilly, where the warm breezes of the Gulf Stream swirl around this subtropical archipelago. Thirty miles from Falmouth lies the **Land's End** Youth Hostel, in a delightfully sleepy Cornish village about four miles from the amusements at the westernmost tip of England. From the hostel, there are views of the beach, and public footpaths lead you to the coast and to an impressive outdoor theater. Western National has a good local bus network to take you to either spot, and after the dark gloom of the Pendennis Castle, the lively scene on the streets of these two towns might be a welcome change.

PENZANCE

Gilbert and Sullivan may have been the only two people who thought anything of this seaside town 280 miles south of London. Even the hostel warden here admits there's not much to see or do in Penzance itself, but the attractions just outside town make it a worthwhile stay, especially if you're compelled by Celtic anthropology, rock formations, or cliffside walking routes to nearby Land's End.

While it's short on museums and doesn't have a big theme park like Land's End, Penzance is a lively, happy little town. After parking your pack at the Youth Hostel, head back down to the town center, where ferries are ready to whisk you away to the legendary island of St. Michael's Mount or farther into the Atlantic to the Isles of Scilly, warmed by the Gulf Stream.

For those who can't bear to be away from a museum, farther up the coast in the town of St. Ives is the highly respected outpost of London's Tate Gallery, where many local artists show their stuff. In Penzance itself are hippie stores selling antiques, used records, rare books, and tie-dyed clothing. Proper Cornish pasties pop out of bakery windows. The subtropical Morrab Gardens beckon picnickers, and the seaside promenade makes for a nice afternoon walk. And when the sun goes down, watch out—modern-day pirates of Penzance prowl the local meaderies and nightclubs looking for their wenches.

❂ Penzance Youth Hostel

Castle Horneck, Alverton
Penzance, Cornwall TR20 8TF
Tel: 01736/62666. Fax: 01736/62663.

On the outskirts of Penzance, this hostel is between Penzance and the fishing town of Newlynn. It's called Castle Horneck but don't be fooled: It's really just the site of an ancient fortification. The wardens believe that the slabs in the basement are more than 600 years old, though from the current state of affairs here you'd never guess it. One of the best-preserved old buildings in the area, this place has been known to receive visits from the Cornish Home Society as well as archaeologists, who like to poke around downstairs.

A huge 250-year-old Monterey pine tree towers above the hostel. There's an attractive light-green-and-white motif in the hall, and the manager boasts that he has the finest Georgian staircase in all Cornwall. The hallway leading to it is adorned with old sepia tints of the house at the turn of the century.

History pervades the house: In the 1740s, Methodist evangelist John Wesley was imprisoned here for heresy (in the kitchen, according to the managers) by the Penzance magistrate who owned the house. Outside, a 200-year-old mineral grotto displays minerals collected from local tin mines. There's also a babbling brook just outside the hostel grounds, formerly part of the home's arboretum. The expansive, well-maintained grounds offer views of the Lizard Peninsula and of St. Michael's Mount in the distance. Upstairs, some of the bedrooms have sea glimpses as well.

As for the food, Paul the warden doesn't settle for standard hostel grub. In the dining room, a chalkboard lists the à la carte dishes, which range from vegetarian curry with nan bread to Spicy Pirate Pizza (pepperoni, onion, pepper, herbs, chili, and tomato sauce) for £3.95. They also have a separate dessert menu featuring Cornish clotted cream and regular dairy ice cream.

The crowds that come here tend to be a mix of school groups on field trips and solo travelers curious about the legendary town. The hostel is large enough to accommodate everyone and friendly enough to keep most visitors happy.

Services

🚆 Exit the train station and walk up Market Jew Street through Market Place. Go straight up Alverton Street, then Alverton Road. Pass the YMCA and the turnoff is on the right. Go up Castle Horneck Road and follow the signs. It's a 30-minute walk. Alternately, exit the train station, cross the street, and pick up Western National bus no. 10b, 5, or B to the Pirate Pub. Cross over to Castle Horneck Road and the hostel is straight ahead. Those arriving late can call a **taxi** at 01736/66626; it'll take you to the hostel for £1.80.

🚌 Exit the bus station and walk up Market Jew Street through Market Place. Go straight up Alverton Street, then Alverton Road. Pass the YMCA and the turnoff is on the right. Go up Castle Horneck Road and follow the signs. It's a 30-minute walk. Alternately, cross the street from the bus station and pick up Western National bus no. 10b, 5, or B to the Pirate Pub. Follow directions from the train, given above.

🚗 From the A30, look for signs to Castle Horneck. Don't go into Penzance. Follow the signs and turn onto Castle Horneck Street. From the direction of London, turn right. From the direction of Land's End, turn left.

🗓 Open Feb–Dec; schedule varies, so call ahead for winter openings. BABA.

🕐 Reception open 8:30–10am and 5–10:30pm. Curfew 11pm.

🛏 84 beds. 4-, 6-, 8-, 10-, and 14-bed rooms.

£ Members: adults £8.80; under 18 £5.95.

🍴 Standard self-catering kitchen facilities. Breakfast: 7:45–8:30am; packed breakfasts should be ordered by 10pm the night before. Lunch: packed lunch only; should be ordered by 10pm the night before. Dinner: 5:30–7:45pm.

🍸 No table license.

🧳 Lockers in hallway. 30p plus £5 key deposit.

⊡ Washers £1.50; dryers take 20p coins.

P Out front; accommodates up to 25 cars.

🛍 Shop at hostel open 5–10pm but closed during busy hours; sells candy and food.

 TV lounge.

🚬 In downstairs lounge only.

♿ Not wheelchair accessible.

💱 See "Currency Exchange" under "The Basics" in Penzance.

🔺 Harry Safari offers tours in the Cornwall area that leave straight from the hostel, and he'll tailor them to what you want to see. Call 01736/711427. Penzance is also a stop on the Slow Coach's West Country route, which operates in summer. Bike shed.

Cheap Eats Nearby

Baytree Restaurant

This cavernous, light-filled pizza-and-pasta spot is popular with locals. It's connected to a furniture/batik clothing store next door. Pizzas £4 to £5. Cannelloni £5. Vegetarian specials. Afternoon tea, scones, and pastries.

8/9 Causeway Head, Penzance. Tel: 01736/68383. Open: Mon–Sat 10am–4pm and 6:30–9pm. Credit cards: VA, MC, EC, Access. £1 surcharge for AE. From the hostel, turn right onto Castle Horneck, left onto Alverton Road, and follow it onto Alverton Street. Just before the Market Square, bear left onto Causeway Head. Look for the sign; through the alley. It's 30 minutes by foot, 10 minutes by bus.

Brown's Vegetarian Café

Stone walls, brightly flowered tablecloths, and postcards featuring local artists make this a warm, comfortable hangout. Hummus and pita £2.25. Provençale pasta bake £3.35 and a wide variety of vegan food as well. Sweets 80p to 90p. The friendly waitresses are a great source of local information.

Bread Street, Penzance. Tel: 01736/51320. Open: Mon–Sat 10am–4pm. Cash only. From the hostel, turn right onto Castle Horneck, left onto Alverton Road, and follow it onto Alverton Street. Just before the Market Square, bear left onto Bread Street. To the right, downstairs from the Betowski Gallery; look for the sign. It's a 30-minute walk or a 10-minute bus ride.

Grocery Store: Lo-Cost Foodstore. Market Jew Street, Penzance. Open: Mon–Thurs 8:30am–6pm; Fri 8:30am–7pm.

Experiences

The town of Penzance combines a seaside shopping district with cobblestone streets and alleyways. It's characterized by an artsy-craftsy atmosphere verging on grunge. Tattoos, old records, and antique-clothing stores are mixed in with surf-and-sweatshirt shops on the streets radiating off the main drag, Market Jew Street.

On the other side of the shopping district, Morrab Road leads you to the quiet **Morrab Gardens,** where tulips and lily ponds blend in with palm and coconut trees and provide an unusual backdrop for an English picnic. Churches, quiet pubs, art-supply stores, and second-hand bookshops line the strangely serene streets in this area. A block down, the Western Promenade provides a beachfront walkway along Mount's Bay.

Three miles away, the castle at **St. Michael's Mount** towers 250 feet above the sea. Reachable by causeway during low tide and by ferry during high tide, it has always been considered a magical little island. Dedicated to the archangel St. Michael, who appeared to a group of Cornish fishermen in the year 495, the mount has long been a pilgrimage site. The castle, originally a Benedictine priory, contains paintings, armor, furniture, and weapons, all belonging to the family that has lived here since the 1600s.

For those with extra money, a round-trip ferry ride out to the **Isles of Scilly** can be done in a day. Warmed by the Gulf Stream, these thinly populated islands have exotic plants and wildflowers, ancient cairns, and white-sand beaches only 28 miles from the tip of Land's End. The ferry ride is expensive but a very unusual spectacle.

The alternative, black-turtleneck crowd heads for St. Ives (10 miles away) and Mousehole (three miles away). Once mere fishing villages, they've become active and well-touristed artist colonies. The **Tate Gallery** now has an outpost on Portmeor Beach in St. Ives, and **The Barbara Hepworth Museum and Garden** is the former studio of local sculptress Barbara Hepworth, who died in 1975.

Back in Penzance, the annual **Glowan Festival** (Feast of St. John) attracts Breton pipers, dancers from the Baltic states, and Celts from all over the world. The weeklong celebration takes place in mid-June. With live music, fireworks, and processions, it's a fun, fascinating peek into the somewhat mysterious, far-flung influence of the Celtic peoples.

St. Michael's Mount. Mount's Bay. Tel: 01736/710507. Open: Apr–Oct: Mon–Fri 10:30am–4:45pm; Nov–Mar Mon, Wed, Fri by conducted tour only. Admission: adults £3.20; children £1.60. Call ahead to find out the causeway situation, which tends to change with the weather; bus nos. 20, 21, and 22 head out from Penzance.

Ferry to Isles of Scilly. Isles of Scilly Steamship Company, Ltd. The Weighbridge, Penzance. Tel: 01736/62009. Day trips: adults £29; students (ID required) £20; children (2–16) £15; infants (under 2) £2; dogs £7. Trip lasts about one hour and 40 minutes.

The Tate Gallery. Portmeor Beach, St. Ives (10 miles away; buses from Penzance). Tel: 01736/796226. Open: Sept–May: Tues 11am–7pm; Wed–Sat 11am–5pm; Sun 1–5pm. Jun–Aug: Mon, Wed, Fri, Sat 11am–7pm; Tues and Thurs 11am–9pm; Sun 1–7pm. Admission: adults £2.50; seniors, students, and children £1.50; includes entrance to the Barbara Hepworth Museum and Garden.

Barbara Hepworth Museum and Garden. Barnoon Hill, St. Ives. Tel: 01736/796226. Open: Apr–Oct: Mon, Wed, Fri, Sat 11am–7pm; Tues and Thurs 11am–9pm. Nov–Mar: Tues–Sat 11am–5pm; Sun 1–5pm. Admission included in Tate Gallery admission.

Glowan Festival. Contact the Penzance T.I.C. Station Road, Penzance. Tel: 01736/62207. Open: Mon–Sat 9am–5pm; Sat 10am–1pm. July–Aug, also open Sun 10am–1pm.

The Basics

Tourist Office: Penzance T.I.C. Station Road, Penzance. Tel: 01736/62207. Open: Mon–Sat 9am–5pm; Sat 10am–1pm. Jul–Aug, also open Sun 10am–1pm. From the hostel, turn right down Castle Horneck and left on Alverton Road. Follow it as it becomes Alverton Street. At Market Place, walk down Market Jew Street toward the train station. It's on the right, just before the station. It's a 30-minute walk or a 10-minute bus ride.

Post Office: Penzance Post Office. 113 Market Jew St., Penzance. Tel: 01736/63284. Open: Mon–Fri 9am–5:30pm; Sat 9am–12:30pm. From the hostel, follow directions to the tourist office, given above. Walk down Market Jew Street and you'll find it on the right. It's a 30-minute walk or a 10-minute bus ride.

Currency Exchange: Penzance Post Office. 113 Market Jew St., Penzance. Tel: 01736/63284. Open: Mon–Fri 9am–5:30pm; Sat 9am–12:30pm.

Telephone Code: 01736.

Bike Rental: The Cycle Centre. Bread Street, Penzance. Tel: 01736/51671. Open: Mon–Sat 9am–5:30pm. Full-day rental £7–£10. £20 deposit required.

Getting There: Penzance is at the end of the London-Penzance line, departing from London Paddington and taking five hours. **Train** service is excellent and fast from **Plymouth** (40 minutes) and good from **Salisbury, Falmouth, Bath, Bristol,** and **Cardiff**. For information, call 01872/76244. National Express **coaches** arrive from London **Victoria** (eight hours) and from **Cardiff, Bristol, Bath,** and other major cities. For information, call 0171/730 0202 or 0990/808080. Western National provides local service within Cornwall: Those coming from Land's End, Camborne, Bodmin, Falmouth, and other towns in Cornwall can call 01209/719988 for local timetables. Those coming by **car** should take the M4 to Bristol and then the M5 from Bristol to Exeter. From there, the A30 covers the last 110 miles straight into Penzance.

What's Next

A mere eight miles away lies the misty village of St. Just, on the far side of the Cornish peninsula. The hostel closest to **Land's End,** this traditional house offers sublimely simple lodgings in a secluded, overgrown spot looking out on the Cot Valley, far from the obnoxious throngs at the amusement park down the road. With nighttime log fires, water views, and a large selection of local literature, it's a relaxing hideaway. Twenty-four miles in the other direction in **Falmouth,** impressive Pendennis Castle is the setting for the Youth Hostel on Pendennis Point. Housed in Victorian army barracks behind the castle, the hostel towers over Falmouth Bay below. A short ferry ride across the estuary takes you to St. Mawes, where another castle shares guard duty over the harbor, and cliffside walks lead to some nice sandy beaches.

LAND'S END (ST. JUST)

In the farthest reaches of Cornwall, St. Just (288 miles from London and eight miles from Penzance) is a lonely little village in the most westerly corner of England. An ethereal town shrouded in Celtic legend, St. Just has more charm and mystery than Land's End, its much ballyhooed neighbor five miles down the road. Surrounded by Celtic stone relics, the mist that seems to hang over this town even on sunny days, and the legend that the locals here possess strange powers, this little never-never land has a mystical, timeless mood.

Visitors will certainly get a taste of true Cornwall at the local pubs and pastry shops, on the coastal footpaths to Land's End and Cape Cornwall, and in the deserted tin and copper mines nearby. The Land's End peninsula has a high concentration of ancient Celtic ruins: stone circles, quoits, holed stones, and holy wells dot the rugged landscape and offer an unusual glimpse into the spiritual and ceremonial life of the ancient Cornish people. The Minack Theatre, a seafront amphitheater, is a blustery walk along the beach from the town.

The hostel, run by a friendly young family, is a small, traditional house with log fires and views of the surf. St. Just makes for an interesting journey into authentic Cornwall, especially if you want to avoid the commercialism of Land's End and the hustle-bustle of nearby Penzance.

Land's End Youth Hostel

Letcha Vean
Cot Valley, St. Just
Penzance, Cornwall TR19 7NT
Tel: 01736/788437. Fax: 01736/787337.

Definitely off the beaten path, this place is just outside the town of St. Just, about five miles away from Land's End (four miles if you go by coastal footpath). To get here, you must walk down a rocky little drive and through cow pastures. Overlooking the Cot Valley and the crashing waves of the Atlantic, it's quiet country hosteling at its best.

Although cycling isn't permitted on the South West Coast Footpaths, you're in just the right place to begin the long-distance Land's End–John O'Groats bike ride. The muscled manager, Rob, has done it and can tell you all about it, as well as about other bike rides around here.

The hostel itself is warm and welcoming. The dining and living rooms form one common area, and the wood-burning fireplace warms up both rooms on cold Cornish nights. Outside is a glassed-in conservatory that looks out onto the glistening blue sea, making for Kodak moments and brilliant sunset views. The rooms upstairs look down onto the fields and walking paths that wind around the area.

The hostel has a detailed photo display of the mysterious ancient Celtic stone circles—quoits—in the area. For those who want an in-depth lesson, the wardens also offer autumn walking weekends around the old ruins (£45) and also have a tin-mining weekend (£55) on the Atlantic mining coast. The packages include two nights' accommodation, full board, bus fares, and entry to local museums. The crowds that come here are a nice blend of school groups and solo travelers. The small hostel has a familiar, cozy atmosphere that many large, busy hostels lack.

Services

🚆 The closest train station is Penzance (eight miles away). From the station, cross the road to the Western National bus station and get on bus no. 10, 10a, or 10b. They run every 20 minutes from 7am to 5pm and hourly until 11pm; less frequently on Sundays. For information, call Camborne at 01209/719988. From the St. Just bus stop, turn left. The library in front of you has a map in the window that shows the route to the hostel. Turn left at the library, then left again at the T junction. Pass the Methodist Church on your right and the modern houses, and as the road bends around to the left, keep right and follow it to the end. The hostel is reached by turning right down a rough and rocky track. Keep left at the bottom as you pass some houses. A rushing stream runs to your right; look for the brown Youth Hostel sign ahead. The hostel is straight ahead. From the St. Just bus stop, it's one mile (a 20-minute walk).

🚌 The closest major bus station is Penzance. From the bus station, get on bus no. 10, 10a, or 10b. See directions from the train station, given above.

🚗 Take the A3071 from Penzance to St. Just. Before getting into St. Just, turn left on the B3306, which has a signpost directing you to the hostel. After about a mile, turn right at Kelynack; the hostel is about half a mile down the road, straight ahead.

▦ Open Apr–Oct. Groups larger than 10 can call to book during winter. BABA.

🕐 Reception open 8:30–10am and 5–10:30pm. Daytime access for the common room, dining room, and self-catering kitchen. No curfew.

🛏 45 beds. 8- and 9-bed rooms, one 20-bed room in an annex.

£ Members: adults £7.20 (£8 July–Aug); under 18 £4.85 (£5.35 Jul–Aug).

🍴 Self-catering kitchen facilities, including gas cooker and oven. Breakfast: 8am. Lunch: packed lunch; order by 10pm the night before. Dinner: 6–8pm; until 9pm for desserts and drinks. There's a good variety of homemade meals such as lasagne, shepherd pie, quiche; ice cream sundaes are a specialty.

I No table license.

▥ No lockers.

☐ Drying room only.

P Out front.

🛍 Shop at Hostel sells candy, suntan lotion, soap, canned items.

🛋 One common room.

🚬 In conservatory only.

♿ Not wheelchair accessible.

⬤ Bike shed; bike and binocular rental. The Slow Coach stops here on its West Country route, which operates in summer.

Cheap Eats Nearby

The King's Arms

This friendly place is the other St. Just hangout. Supposedly the oldest pub in town, it was built in the 1400s to go along with the church next door. Locals here can tell you secrets of Celtic history over a glass of the local cask ales, which are pumped to you right from the wood. Food here is standard English pub grub with a fishy twist: Ploughman's lunch with smoked mackerel (£3.50); fresh crab sandwiches (£2), and Cornish pasties (£2.60) are a house specialty.

Market Square, St. Just. Tel: 01736/788545. Open: Mon–Sat 11am–11pm; Sun noon–3pm and 7–10:30pm. Cash only. From the hostel, go back into town, pass the library on your left, and it's straight ahead in the middle of Market Square. It's a 25-minute walk.

The Star Inn

Reckoned to be the oldest inn in St. Just, this dark little cavern has a room set aside for card games next to its small bar area. On Monday and Friday nights local bands play. They fire up a good selection of bar food. A welcoming little fireplace crackles away. Cheese melty £3.20. Vegetable curry £3.70. An array of sandwiches.

1 Fore St., St. Just. Tel: 01736/788789. Open: Mon–Sat noon–2pm and 6–9pm for food, 11am–11pm for drinks; Sun noon–2pm and 6–9pm. Cash only. From the hostel, go back into the town, pass the library on your left, and turn right at Market Square. Turn right onto Fore Street and it's on your left. It's a 25-minute walk.

Grocery Store: Stop & Shop, Market Square, St. Just. Open: Mon–Sat 8:30am–8pm; Sun 10am–4pm.

Experiences

The Land's End peninsula, or West Penwith, is a bulky chunk of granite separated from the rest of Cornwall by the Hayle River. Within its 87 miles lie 800 **archaeological sites,** mostly on the high moors. Because of their isolation, they're in excellent condition and fall into four categories: quoits (chamber tombs) and entrance graves from the Neolithic era; stone circles and menhirs of the Bronze Age; hill forts and villages of the Iron Age; and crosses and holy wells from the Christian Era. The stone circle of Men-an-Tol, for example, has sat on the West Penwith moors for around 4,000 years. The Lanyon Quoit, a nearby prehistoric Stonehenge-like structure, has had a similarly long history. The Youth Hostel has tons of information on these eerie, dramatic structures; many are only a walk away.

Tin and copper mining also have played an important part in the peninsula's history, going as far back as the Middle Ages. There are a few museums several miles north of the town that detail this history. A good 13-mile walking route called **The Tinners Way** runs from Cape Cornwall to St. Ives, covering the path from which tin and copper were transported from St. Ives to St. Just long ago. The hostel wardens have a book and lots of information on this, and the local Ramblers walk The Tinners Way at midnight in the summertime when the full moon is out.

A five-minute walk from the hostel to the coast takes you straight onto the **South West Coast Path.** From here, it's one mile to Cape Cornwall in the north and four miles south to Land's End. The walk to Land's End is full of rocky cliffs and crashing waves as well as the occasional dolphin and seal. Just before Land's End is the sweet village of Sennen, where tea rooms abound and quiet coves dot the coastline. The **Sennen Surfing Centre** offers classes as well as good advice on surfing in the area.

You can also take a rather strenuous daylong hike along the South West Coast Path to St. Ives, about 18 miles away along the northern coast. In St. Ives, the **Tate Gallery** and **Barbara Hepworth Museum** both offer excellent painting and sculpture exhibitions.

About halfway between St. Just and Penzance, the open-air **Minack Theatre** in Porthcurno is a breathtaking spot to enjoy Shakespeare plays, Mozart recitals, or Rodgers and Hammerstein musicals. Operating in summer only, it provides a stony setting and blustery backdrop, day or night. Matinees can be hot, evenings can get chilly, and performances are canceled only in extreme conditions. Bring a raincoat and cushion or rent from them.

Archeological Sites. Ask at the hostel.

Tinners Way and South West Coast Path. Either ask at the hostel or contact the South West Coast Path Association. 1 Orchard Dr., Kingskerswell, Newton Abbot, Devon, TQ12 5DG. Tel: 01803/873061.

Sennen Surfing Centre. 4 Trevilley Farm Cottages. Sennen, Land's End. Tel: 01736/871404; 01736/871458 after 6:30pm. Open: daily 10am–6:30pm. Rentals from £15.

The Tate Gallery and Barbara Hepworth Museum and Garden. See "Experiences" under "Penzance" earlier in this chapter.

The Minack Theatre and Exhibition Centre. Porthcurno (5 miles away), Cornwall. Tel: 01736/810181 or 01736/810471. Box office open: May–Sept: Mon–Sat 10am–8pm; Sat–Sun 10am–5pm. Shows go on from May–Sept; bring a cushion. Out of season, write to The Minack Theatre (Party Bookings), Porthcurno, Penzance TR19 6JU. Include SASE (self-addressed stamped envelope).

The Basics

Tourist Office: The closest T.I.C. is in Penzance, eight miles away. Penzance T.I.C. Station Road, Penzance. Tel: 01736/62207. Open: Mon–Sat 9am–5pm; Sat 10am–1pm. In Jul–Aug, also open Sun 10am–1pm. From the hostel, walk into St. Just and catch bus no. 10, 10a, or 10b into Penzance. The office is next door to the bus station. It takes one hour from the St. Just hostel.

Post Office: St. Just Post Office. Center Square, St. Just. Tel: 01736/788432. Open: Mon–Wed 9am–1pm and 2–5:30pm; Thurs 9am–1pm; Fri 9am–1pm and 2–5:30pm; Sat 9am–12:30pm. From the hostel, walk up the track and into St. Just. Pass the bus stop on the right, and head up the street. It's on the right; a 20-minute walk.

Currency Exchange: The nearest place is in Penzance, 8 miles away. Penzance Post Office. 113 Market Jew St., Penzance. Tel: 01736/63284. Open: Mon–Fri 9am–5:30pm; Sat 9am–12:30pm.

Telephone Code: 01736.

Bike Rental: At the Youth Hostel. £7 per day; £25 deposit. Comes with a map and lock.

Taxi: tel. 01736/810751.

Getting There: The closest **train** station is in Penzance (eight miles away), which is at the end of the London-Penzance line; trains come in from London **Paddington** (10 per day; 5 hours), and there are easy connections from **Cardiff, Bath, Bristol, Salisbury,** and **Plymouth.** From **Penzance,** local buses leave every 20 minutes for St. Just. For train information, call 01872/76244.

Long-distance **coaches** come as close as **Penzance,** and local buses take you the extra eight miles to St. Just. National Express coaches come out from London **Victoria** (eight hours), and service from **Cardiff, Bristol, Bath,** and other major cities is decent. For information, call 0171/730 0202 or 0990/808080. For local bus timetables, call Western National at 01209/719988. Those coming by **car** should take the M4 to Bristol and then the M5 from Bristol to Exeter. From there, the A30 covers the 110 miles into Penzance. From there, take the A3071 into St. Just.

What's Next

Penzance, eight miles away, offers more of a town life than St. Just, so those in search of nightlife, cobbled shopping streets, and an oceanfront esplanade may want to head there. Nearby, St. Michael's Mount, connected by causeway and ferryboat (depending on the tides), has a castle and gardens worth visiting. A Celtic Festival livens things up in mid-June, and the hostel is another bright spot, with a friendly staff and a fairly high standard of hosteling. Farther east, the hostel on the grounds of Pendennis Castle is your one chance in England to stay within spitting distance of a medieval coastal fortress. Overlooking the town and bay of **Falmouth,** the grounds are stony and spectacular, especially when the floodlit castle glows in the midnight sky. The town is a beach resort with a few interesting art galleries and a lineup of shops. Across the straits sits the cloverleaf St. Mawes Castle, which shares guard duty over this once-strategic military zone on the south Cornish coast.

TREYARNON BAY

Treyarnon Bay and its corresponding "village," 10 miles north of Newquay and 40 miles west of Plymouth, sit in splendid isolation on the sandy, peaceful shores of Constantine Bay. Placid blue waters are all that's visible from this coastal hideaway.

Treyarnon Bay proves the general rule that a hostel's quality is inversely proportional to the length and difficulty of the public transportation connections necessary to arrive. If coming by public transport, expect to take a combination of buses and trains and who knows what else to get here. Once you've arrived, you'll be rewarded by beautiful beaches, unspoiled nature paths, a hotel pub with live music on Saturday nights, and surfboards for rent only a few hundred yards from the hostel.

With the beach at the doorstep, the hostel is as remote and peaceful as you could ask for, and because of its location Treyarnon Bay is one of the warmer spots in England. Fishing, surfing, body bronzing, and boogie boarding are all readily available here. It also makes a good spot for walking along the north Cornish coast. Be careful, though: Outside of a hotel, a caravan park, and a hostel, there's not much of anything here. Even the bus drivers tend to get confused, so it's helpful to bring a map along with your bathing suit, wetsuit, and surfboard.

Treyarnon Bay Youth Hostel

Tregonnan, Treyarnon
Padstow, Cornwall PL34 0DW
Tel: 01841/520322. Fax: 01841/520322.

The hostel sitting on Treyarnon Bay looking out onto the Atlantic Ocean is the former holiday home of a lucky Londoner who came here at the turn of the century to escape urban life. What he left behind was a peaceful beachfront cottage that is one of the most popular hostels among veteran hostelers in the south of England.

In a friendly, laid-back atmosphere, the staff keeps the place in fine shape for the adrenaline-pumped cyclists who stop here as they work their way up the Land's End–John O'Groats route. Quarters are somewhat cramped inside, so the grassy front yard and garden (with picnic tables for evening meals) provide nice spots for bunkmates to exchange information and hang out.

There's nothing particularly stunning about the hostel building except for the unbroken sea view from the front door and the ticklish sea breezes that waft through the common room. Things are a little more old-fashioned here than in most other hostels. Meals are cooked on a coal-burning Aga, and the common area/dining room gets its heat from a coal fireplace, which is lit up on breezy nights. In summer, hostelers sometimes request to be put in the one giant 14-bed room. Its water views compensate for the cramped quarters and make for a wonderful wake-up call.

Services

The closest major train station is in Newquay, 10 miles away. From there, walk into the town center and pick up Western National bus no. 56 headed for Padstow. Tell the driver to drop you at Constantine (the stop before St. Merryn, on the way to Padstow). The bus drops you off at the local shop. Follow the road straight, heading for the caravan park. Go through the gate and walk diagonally through the caravan park until you reach the Treyarnon Bay Hotel on the left. From there, turn right onto the oceanfront road, and the hostel is about 300 yards up on the right. The bus ride from Newquay takes about one hour.

The closest major bus station is in Newquay. From there, pick up Western National bus no. 56 headed for Padstow. Follow directions from the train, given above.

From the A30 (Exeter-Penzance road), follow signs for Bodmin, but turn off at the exit to Padstow (look for the white sign). After about five miles, you'll reach the town of Padstow. Go straight past the town, following signs to St. Merryn. Go through the village of St. Merryn until you reach a brown sign that says Constantine (by the village hall). Follow this road for about two miles. When you reach Constantine Stores, continue straight, pass the campsite, and follow the road around. Then follow the signs to the Youth Hostel, around the coastal road. The hostel is up on your left.

Open Apr–Oct. Closed Fri from Apr–June and Sept–Nov 4. BABA. Rent-a-hostel: Jan–Mar; Nov–Dec.

Reception open 8–10am and 5–11pm. Curfew 11pm.

42 beds. 4-, 6-, 8-, 12-, and 14-bed rooms.

£ Members: adults £7.20; under 18 £4.85; July–Aug: adults £8; under 18 £5.35.

Self-catering kitchen facilities. Breakfast: 7:30am or 8:30am. Lunch: packed lunch only; should be ordered by the night before. Dinner: 7pm.

No table license.

No lockers.

Drying room only. Launderette at nearby caravan site.

P Ample and free of charge.

Shop at hostel sells candy, canned goods.

One common/dining room.

No smoking.

Not wheelchair accessible.

See "Currency Exchange" under "The Basics" in Treyarnon Bay.

Bike shed.

Cheap Eats Nearby

The Treyarnon Bay Hotel

With a wood-burning stove, a pool table, and Saturday-night entertainment, this is the most happening—and only—spot in town for nightlife and good food. Burgers are £2.95 to £3.95. Fish and chips £4.25 to £4.75. Vegetarian specials, including lasagne; veggieburger; macaroni and cheese, £3.95 to £4.50.

Treyarnon Bay, near Padstow. Tel: 01841/520235. Open: May–Sept: daily 8am–9:30pm. Oct–Apr:
daily 8am–3pm and 6–9pm. Credit cards: VA, MC, EC, Access, Switch. From the hostel, it's a three-
minute walk: Turn left and pass the beachfront shop—it's straight ahead.

Treyarnon Bay Takeaway

Next door to the hotel, this little beachfront kitchen has video games, T-shirts
and suntan lotion on display, and a rack of wetsuits for decoration (and rent
too). Chow down on burgers (£1.45 to £2.30), pizza (£1.30), pasties (£1.30), and
jacket potatoes (£1.25 to £2.24) on the little tables out front. Real coffee is 60p
a mug.

Treyarnon Bay, near Padstow. Tel: 01841/520983. Open: Easter–Sept: daily 9:30am–7:30pm, but
hours tend to fluctuate. Cash only. From the hostel, turn left, and pass the beachfront shop.
It's straight ahead, in front of the Treyarnon Bay Hotel.

Grocery Store: Constantine Bay Stores. Tel: 01841/520573. Open: summer: daily
8am–6pm; hours vary out of season.

Experiences

A random sampling of hostelers reveals that hanging out on the beach is the preferred activity on Treyarnon Bay. You don't need to go very far—there are a pub, a
shop, and a cafe right on the beach. Surfboards, boogie boards, and wetsuits are
all available for rent from the **Treyarnon Bay Takeaway.** The north side of this
narrow, sandy beach is rocky but has a large natural swimming pool washed clean
by high tides.

For slightly more active pursuits, head over to the **Treyarnon Bay Angling
Centre,** where local legend Ed Schliffke (seen on British TV) offers shore fishing
trips as well as bait, tackle, and supplies for those with their own rods. He knows
these waters well, and his trips usually reap mackerel, bass, and plaice. He operates all
year long, even though he says the best time for fishing is from July to Christmas.

Less than a mile away sits the lonely **Trevose Lighthouse,** which is one of the
area's last remaining manually operated lighthouses. No longer operational, it's now
open to the public. You can climb to the top for some unobstructed sea views.

A coastal walk for about mile south of Treyarnon leads you to Porthcothan Bay,
where there are a few coastal caves to prowl around. Another mile farther down is
Port Mear, a tiny, rocky bay where footpaths take you to the **Bedruthen Steps.**
Bedruthen is a legendary giant, and the steps actually are the rocky islands dotting
the beach.

The Camel Trail, so called because it follows the Camel Estuary, is an excellent
bike path that goes up Trevose Head and around the coast to Padstow before
heading inland to Bodmin. The path covers a total of 30 miles, but it can be cut
short at various points. Its attractions include its coastal stretches and its basically
flat terrain.

Treyarnon Bay Takeaway. Treyarnon Bay. Tel: 01841/520983. Open: Easter–Sept:
daily 9:30am–7:30pm. Rentals: wetsuits £4; surfboards £5; boogie boards £5;
windbreakers £1.

Treyarnon Bay Angling Centre. Treyarnon Bay Hotel. Tel: 01841/521157.
Ed Schliffke runs three-hour fishing trips for £10, including tackle and bait.

Bedruthen Steps and Camel Trail. Near Padstow. For information, contact the Padstow T.I.C. (see "Tourist Office" under "The Basics" in Treyarnon Bay).

The Basics

Tourist Office: Padstow T.I.C. Red Brick Building, North Quay, Padstow (2¹/₂ miles away). Tel: 01841/533449. Open: Apr–July 20: Mon–Fri 10am–5pm; Sat 1–4pm; Sun 11am–4:30pm. July 21–Sept: Mon–Fri 10am–7pm; Sat 1–4pm; Sun 11am–4:30pm. Oct: Mon–Fri 10am–5pm; Sat 1–4pm. From the hostel, take bus no. 55 or 56 into Constantine. Also, Newquay T.I.C. Marcus Hill, Newquay (12¹/₂ miles away). Tel: 01637/871343.

Post Office: St. Merryn Post Office. St. Merryn, Padstow (1 mile up the road). Tel: 01841/520284. Open: May–Sept: Mon–Tues and Thurs–Fri 9am–5:30pm; Wed and Sat 9am–12:30pm. From the hostel, turn left and walk toward the hotel. Turn left and walk through the caravan park. Either wait for bus no. 55 or 56 into St. Merryn or walk 1 mile toward Padstow. It's on the left.

Currency Exchange: Padstow T.I.C. See "Tourist Office" under "The Basics" in Treyarnon Bay.

Telephone Code: 01841.

Bike Rental: Glyn Davis Cycle Hire. South Quay, Padstow (2¹/₂ miles away). Tel: 01841/532594.

Getting There: The closest **train** station is 12 miles away in Newquay. Newquay is at the end of a branch line off the Exeter-Penzance route, so you'll need to switch at Par to get there. For information, call 01872/76244 or 01752/221300.

The closest **bus** station is in Newquay. Western National operates buses all around Devon and Cornwall, and service to Newquay is decent from **Penzance, Land's End, Plymouth,** and **Exeter.** Once you arrive in Newquay, local buses head out four times daily to Treyarnon Bay on the Newquay-Constantine route. Be sure to tell the driver it is the stop just before St. Merryn on the way to Padstow. For bus information, call 01208/79898 or 01752/222666.

By **car,** take the A30 from Penzance heading north. At Three Burrows, switch for the A3075 north, heading for Newquay. At Newquay, take the B3276 about 12¹/₂ miles out to Constantine; when you get to Constantine, follow signs for Treyarnon Bay.

What's Next

After the peace and quiet of this happy beach community, you can head south to the slightly congested town of **Penzance,** where the Youth Hostel is reputed to have a smuggler's tunnel beneath its foundations. The city itself is unremarkable except for a few charming shopping streets and some good meaderies that see lots of action at night. Close by are the strangely tropical Isles of Scilly, which make a great day trip by ferry. Farther along (50 miles away, but accessible by train and bus) is the sleepy town of St. Just, which serves as the **Land's End** Youth Hostel. A few miles from the end itself, this hostel is in a tiny village shrouded in the Cornish mist—a world away from the boisterous carnival at Land's End. Set on three acres in the quiet Cot Valley, the hostel is a real traditional treat, with log fires, a good selection of local literature, and some pretty sea views to soothe nerves rattled by the amusement park up the road.

LYNTON

One wrong move in Lynton will send you careening down a 500-foot drop to the Bristol Channel. This precarious perch at the very tip-top edge of North Devon, 60 miles north of Exeter and 205 miles west of London, isn't easy to reach. Formed around the swirling, wooded river valleys of East and West Lyn, this lofty little village is set in a swath of countryside so idyllic that the Victorian summer crowds dubbed it "little Switzerland."

To the north, a vertical railway on a rocky cliff leads down to Lynton's twin village, Lynmouth, which has its own harbor and summertime crowds. To the south, walking paths and bike trails take you into Exmoor National Park. Covering 267 square miles in Devon and Somerset, it's one of England's smaller parks but has a surprising breadth of landscapes. Rocky cliffs, wooded combes, colorful heaths, and wild-grass moors foster all sorts of flora and fauna.

Lynton and Lynmouth, with a combined population of 1,700, form the largest settlement in the park. The National Park Authority allows for only a limited amount of development, which makes both places refreshingly free of shopping strips and fast-food restaurants. Because they saw an influx of summer tourists in the late 1800s, both villages have their fair share of pubs, tea rooms, and small shops, but their presence is relatively unobtrusive compared to the spectacular sea below and the open, wild vistas of the national park.

The Youth Hostel is in Lynton, where there are staggering views and staggering hostelers. Set above the town, the hostel is up a pretty steep hill. Most hostelers think the setting makes it worth the climb. Visitors here tend to stop into the towns for refueling and some quick shopping but mainly come for the breathtaking view of the sea, the stony gorges, and expansive moorland jutting beyond.

Lynton Youth Hostel

Lynbridge, Lynton
Devon EX35 6AZ
Tel: 01598/753237. Fax: 01598/753305.

Bring your allergy medicine along with your hiking boots. The trek up here is no mean feat, even for the hardiest of backpackers, and the fragrant blossoms by the side of the road quickly become menacing pollen producers after a few steep paces. Once they reach the top of the hill, grumbling hostelers grudgingly admit the setting is pretty amazing. The cute, airy bedrooms inside are all adorned with little name plates listing a color, and each bedroom is appropriately outfitted in its signature shade. Downstairs, the common room has a well-worn cabinet piano and a cluster of comfortable chairs.

As in many hostels, lots of school groups come here from April through June, so booking ahead is essential. There is also a sizable crowd of walkers, cyclists, and young families that regularly checks in here in summer, so spots go quickly. The West Country Slow Coach stops here in the summer, keeping things even busier and making Lynton more convenient for those hostelers without their own transportation.

Services

🚂 The closest train station is Barnstaple, 20 miles away. From there, walk into the town and take Red Bus no. 310 to Lynton. Once in Lynton, walk down Lee Road and turn right onto Queen Street. Go down a slight hill and then up steep Sinai Hill. When you reach Lynway (the sign resembles a public footpath sign), turn left. Walk along for about five minutes, and the hostel will come up on your right. It's another steep climb up the driveway.

🚌 The closest major bus/coach station is Barnstaple, 20 miles away. From there, walk into the town and take Red Bus no. 310 to Lynton. From there, follow directions from the train, given above.

🚗 From **Barnstaple,** take the A39. Then take the B3234, following signs to Lynbridge. Once you reach the Ye Olde Cottage Inn, you'll fine the hostel driveway directly opposite up a steep hill.

▦ Open Feb–Dec 21. Open Fri–Sat only during Nov, Dec, and Feb. Closed Sun–Mon in Mar. Closed Sun in Apr–June. Closed Sun–Mon in Sept–Oct. BABA.

🕐 Reception open 7:30–10am and 5–11pm. Curfew 11pm.

🛏 38 beds. 2-, 4-, and 6-bed rooms; some have showers en suite.

£ Members: adults £7.20; under 18 £4.85. Jul–Aug: adults £8.80, under 18 £5.95.

🍴 Self-catering kitchen facilities. Breakfast: 8am. Lunch: packed lunch only; order the night before. Dinner: 7pm.

🍸 No table license.

💼 No lockers.

◻ Washer and drying room.

P Ample and free of charge.

🛍 Shop at hostel sells candy.

🛋 One living room.

🚭 No smoking.

♿ Not wheelchair accessible.

💱 See "Currency Exchange" under "The Basics" in Lynton.

🔺 Bike shed.

Cheap Eats Nearby

The Greenhouse Restaurant

With a waterwheel at its bar and a subtly maritime motif, this airy dining room feels like an English Charthouse. The homemade fare includes a good selection of vegetarian dishes: Lasagne, moussaka, and curries are £5.50 to £6.75. Fish dishes run £7.25 to £9; jacket potatoes £2.35 to £3.75.

6 Lee Rd., Lynton. Tel: 01598/753358. Open: Mar–Oct: Sun–Thurs, Sat 9:30am–10pm. Credit cards: VA, MC, EC, Access, Switch. From the hostel, turn left and walk down Lynway until reaching Sinai Hill. Turn right onto Sinai Hill, follow it into Queen Street, and turn left onto Lee Road. It's on the left. It's a 20-minute walk.

The Old Bank Café

This was—guess what?—a bank back in 1885, but now it's a friendly little coffeehouse with exposed wooden beams. The photo-filled menu helps you envision the sausage and chips, cod and chips, and broccoli-cheese bake (main dishes £3.50 to £5.75). Sandwiches are £1.60 to £2.50; salads £3.75 to £5.95.

Church Steps, Lynton. Tel: 01598/753500. Open: Mar–June: Mon–Sat 10am–5pm. July–Sept 15: daily 10am–8pm. Sept 15–Nov: Mon–Sat 10am–5pm. Cash only. From the hostel, turn left and walk down Lynway for about 10 minutes. At Sinai Hill, turn right and continue onto Queen Street. The cafe is on the right, just up the steps. It's a 20-minute walk.

Grocery Store: Londis. Lee Road, Lynton. Open: Mon–Sat 8:30am–7pm; Sun 10am–7pm.

Experiences

A good way to get acquainted with the area is to hop on the **Lynton Cliff Railway,** which takes you on a three-minute ride from Lynton down to Lynmouth via a hydro-powered chairlift. When it opened in 1890, it was the steepest railway in the world; the two carriages are mounted over 700-gallon water tanks and connect to one another by cables and pulleys. While it's a seemingly primitive way to travel, there has never once been a derailment in its entire history.

The railway takes you to the cute little seaside village of Lynmouth, which is slightly touristy but has some excellent views of the Bristol Channel. By the waterside are a small 18-hole **golf course** and **public tennis courts** with rackets for rent.

Along the Lyn River Valley is an easy 3¹/₂-mile stroll. Beginning at the Lynmouth Esplanade, you walk down undulating river banks and cross stone bridges over rocky streams. Eventually you reach Watersmeet, where deep gorges are formed by the constant rising and falling of the water levels; a circular path takes you over and back to Lynmouth.

Heading out from Lynton, the **Valley of the Rocks** is a well-known local landmark; there's a good circular walk out to the valley that takes about 1¹/₂ to two hours to complete. Walking on the cliffside North Walk along the bay, it takes about an hour to get to the valley. Said to be the site of a Dark Age castle whose inhabitants were plagued by the devil, Castle Rock is a motley pileup of rocks on a promontory overlooking Wringcliff Bay. Among the other rock formations in the valley is the Devil's Cheesewring, a rocky tor that resembles a cheese press used for making cider. It's mentioned in R. D. Blackmore's *Lorna Doone*. The walk back involves a steep ascent up Hollerday Hill, the overgrown former estate of a wealthy London publisher. You can extend the walk by about two miles by going back via Southcliff, which offers more of the same coastal views. You're likely to see Cheviot goats wandering around, as well as seabirds such as guillemots, razorbills, and kittiwakes.

Back in Lynton, satisfy the folks back home by shopping for bargains at the weekly **Craft Fayre** that takes place every Sunday in the Town Hall. The **Antiques Collectors Fair** goes on every Monday.

Lynton Cliff Railway. Open: Mon–Sat 8am–7pm; Sun 10am–7pm.

Golf and tennis. Lynmouth Council, Lynmouth. Tel: 01598/752384. Open: Easter–Oct only; call for opening times. 18 holes of golf: adults £1.20; children 80p. Tennis: £3 per hour for up to four people; includes racket and balls.

Walks from Lynton and Lynmouth. Leaflets as well as guided walks are available. Contact the Lynton T.I.C. (see "Tourist Office" under "The Basics" in Lynton). Walks under four hours: £1; walks over four hours: £2.

Craft Fayre. Lynton Town Hall, Lynton. Tel: 01598/752332. June–Sept: Sun 10am–4pm.

Antiques Collectors Fair. Lynton Town Hall, Lynton. Tel: 01271/882006. May–Sept: Mon 10am–3pm.

The Basics

Tourist Office: Lynton T.I.C. Town Hall, Lee Road, Lynton. Tel: 01598/752225. Open: Easter–Oct: daily 9am–6pm. Nov–Easter: Mon–Sat 9:30am–1pm. From the hostel, turn left on Lynway. At Sinai Hill, turn right and follow it into Queen Street. Turn left onto Lee Road. It's on the left and a 30-minute walk.

Post Office: Lynton Post Office. Lee Road, Lynton. Tel: 01598/753313. Open: Mon–Fri 9am–5:30pm; Sat 9am–12:30pm. From the hostel, turn left on Lynway. At Sinai Hill, turn right, and follow it onto Queen Street. When you reach Lee Road, turn left. It's on the left and a 30-minute walk.

Currency Exchange: Lynton T.I.C. See "Tourist Office" under "The Basics" in Lynton.

Telephone Code: 01598.

Bike Rental: Berry's. Castle Hill. Tel: 01598/752463. Tarka Trail Cycle Hire. British Rail Station, Barnstaple (20 miles away). Tel: 01271/24202. Open: May–Oct only: daily 9am–5pm.

Getting There: Getting to Lynton can be tricky: the closest **train** station is in Barnstaple, which is 20 miles away; it's at the end of a branch line from Exeter. From there, local bus no. 310 takes you into Lynton. The Taunton railway station, also about 20 miles from here, is more conveniently located on the line between Exeter and Bristol, but connecting bus service is less frequent. For local bus information, call 01271/45444. For bus information from Taunton, call 01598/752470. Long-distance **coaches** don't come into Lynton, either, but National Express buses head into **Plymouth** and **Exeter** from other major cities. There is good service into **Barnstaple** from there, and from Barnstaple, you can get local buses into Lynton. For National Express information, call 0990/808080. For local bus information, call Red Express at 01271/45444.

By **car,** take the M44 west from **London** to the junction of the M5, and then head south. At Junction 23, switch to the A38, continue for about four miles, and then switch for the A39 toward Minehead and Lynton.

Central England & the Cotswolds

Delineated by the Thames Valley to the east, the hills of Warwickshire to the north, the Bristol Channel and the Welsh borderlands to the west, and with Oxford and the Cotswolds somewhere in the middle of it all, Central England fulfills storybook images of fabled cities, traditional villages, and pastoral countryside. Only 23 miles west of London, the royal city of Windsor gleams. It's a fastidious place where nothing seems out of place: The unabashedly grand castle with meticulously clipped grounds; the freshly lacquered look of the train station and city center; prim, patrician Eton College; the rowers gliding up the Thames; and when the queen's in, the tripled crowds on the high street.

The pristine village of Streatley lies 25 miles farther along the banks of the same river. Nestled between the Chiltern Hills and Berkshire Downs, it's a blessedly bucolic setting especially good for gentle hill walking. Streatley's elegant hostel, set up on a hill, is a favorite among long-distance walkers working the ancient Ridgeway Path.

Continue up the A329 and you'll reach Oxford, where tightly packed streets wind through the university's ancient colleges. Green grass and leafy gardens lurk within the colleges, but traffic is heavy, commercial action is intense, and the hostel is out of town. Continuing up the A329, you'll hit Stratford-upon-Avon, where William Shakespeare is remembered in every coffee shop, gas station, and shoe store—and, of course, in the endless houses, museums, and theaters dedicated to him. The hostel there is a rambling old mansion outside the city.

In the Cotswolds, just south of Stratford, you'll find deep valleys belted by a series of exquisite sandstone villages shaded by beech trees. Since the Middle Ages, the area has built its prosperity on the local wool trade, and sheep grazing in roadside pastures are a common sight. Stow-on-the-Wold is just the sort of town you may have read about in an English cozy but with a twist: The traditional pubs, tea rooms, and antique shops are joined by a few specialty health-food shops and a contemporary bookstore. Farther south in the Cotswold countryside lies the isolated village of Slimbridge, where wildfowl, birds, and fish are allowed to roam free on the nature reserve.

From the Cotswolds, it's only 25 miles to the historic town of Bristol, made famous by architect/engineer Isambord Kingdom Brunel. In the 1800s, he put Bristol on the map when he built the Clifton Suspension Bridge, masterminded the broad-gauge Great Western Railway line, and designed the steamship that still sits in the harbor. Today's Bristol boasts an eclectic mix of art galleries, open-air markets, snazzy shops, hip restaurants, and a lively university scene. The absolutely fabulous hostel sits right on the harbor.

For at least 100,000 years, hot springs have emanated from the fertile ground at Bath, about 14 miles from Bristol. The water continues to bubble away inside the Roman temple in the center of town. Georgian architecture blossomed here in the 1800s, and what remains is a city full of crescents, colonnades, parks, and perfectly symmetrical designs on the sandstone buildings. Travelers pour into the city, lured by the healing waters, and the hostel sits amid luscious vegetation up a hill in a genteel residential neighborhood.

As you travel north, you'll reach the town of Ludlow on the Welsh Borderlands. Ludlow is a fine example of a planned Norman town, and the castle there is one of a lineup of fortresses built in the 1200s to protect the area from the threatening Welsh across the hills.

Central England can be a dream or a nightmare when it comes to transportation. Busy towns like Windsor, Oxford, Stratford, Bath, and Bristol are well connected by buses and trains; Ludlow is accessible mainly by train. The Cotswolds, however, are trickier, and you'll have to take a combination of local buses to get around; the area is not particularly easy to hitchhike around, either, so build extra time in if you don't come with a car.

WINDSOR

Who wouldn't be merry in Windsor? The people, the sights, and even the train stations have a royal twinkle about them. Clearly, the ever-vigilant Queen Elizabeth wouldn't have it any other way for her hometown. Whether or not she's in residence (you can tell by the Royal Standard hanging from the castle), the town is first and foremost a tribute to her and her brooding bunch. Every day at 11am (every other day in winter), there's a ceremonial changing of the guard to remind you just who wears the pants in her family and in her kingdom.

Despite the high-strung personalities that battle it out behind the castle gates, Windsor is a chipper little hamlet with much more to offer than just the wealthiest landowner in the western world. With gems such as the Windsor Great Park, Eton College, and the legendary Ascot Racetrack nearby, as well as the proximity of London, Henley-on-Thames, and Heathrow, it's no wonder hordes of English and international visitors descend upon the town. It has been said that there's nothing more awe-inspiring than Windsor on a sunny day, but rain or shine, it's worth a visit.

The cheery hostel here is nestled about a mile away in the village of Clewer. It attracts a mix of hostelers: foreigners sampling London in small doses, student groups from all over, and solo travelers on their way in or out of England.

✸ Windsor Youth Hostel Edgeworth House

Mill Lane, Clewer
Windsor, Berkshire SL4 5JE
Tel: 01753/861710. Fax: 01753/832100.

The Youth Hostel, in nearby Clewer village, is a Queen Anne–style residence that served as a home for wayward women at the turn of the century. It was converted to a hostel in 1944. As to the current staff, however, you won't find a floozy in the bunch; they all keep the place running in top condition. Their two information books are bibles for travelers just arriving in Windsor. They provide you with everything you'd ever want to know about Windsor and environs, including exhaustive transport information.

The lodgings are comfortable, and the Holly Hobbie blue patchwork quilts in the bedroom make you feel as if you were staying in a life-size dollhouse. Downstairs, you can mingle with fellow hostelers over a game of pool in the huge dining room overlooking the garden. There are two lounges at your disposal: a quiet non-smoking room for serious readers and postcard writers as well as a "vice room" with video games, a TV, and a deluxe coffee machine. The latter is where the action is, especially if you're here during school vacation; in spring and summer, this place fills up with teenagers faster than you can say "long live the queen." To escape your bunkmates, you can hire a bike from the bike shop down the road and escape to lively Windsor or tranquil Eton town.

Services

🚆 You'll arrive at one of two stations: Windsor and Eton Central or Windsor and Eton Riverside. Those coming from Oxford, London Paddington, and points north will arrive at Central. Those coming from the south will likely arrive at Riverside. From Central, drool over the fancy cafe before heading out to Thames Street and bear up for the 30-minute walk. Facing the castle, turn left and follow Thames Street to the river. Turn left at The Old Trout Inn onto Barry Avenue, with the river to your right and Alexandra Gardens to your left. Follow this road until you reach the train bridge and go through the archway. You'll pass a Leisure Centre on your right. Go down into the underpass, turn left when you get out, and follow the road as it curves to the right. A church is to the left. Turn left and the hostel is up the road to the left. Brown signs lead you all the way from Windsor Centre; follow those rather than street names.

From the Riverside station, turn right onto Datchet Road, follow it until it turns into Thames Avenue, and turn right onto Barry Avenue at the Old Trout Inn. From there, follow the directions given above from Central station.

To catch a bus to the hostel, travelers from both stations can head up Thames Street (not Avenue) as it turns into High Street and pick up bus no. 50b, 51b, or 52b in front of Barclays Bank and get off at the Mobil station on Maidenhead Road. The hostel is around the corner to your right.

🚌 There's no official bus station in Windsor, but coaches coming from Heathrow and London Victoria stop at the Castle Hotel on High Street. Catch bus no. 50b, 51b, or 52b from Barclays Bank and get out at the Mobil Station on Maidenhead Road, then turn right; the hostel is on your right. To walk, get yourself to the Old Trout Inn by walking down High Street as it turns into Thames Street and turn left just before the river. Follow the directions from the train station, given above.

🚗 From **London,** take the M4 motorway to Junction 6. Follow signs to Slough, then to Windsor, and get on the A355. Get to the roundabout at the bottom and take the third right from the roundabout. You'll then reach a smaller roundabout. Follow signs to the Youth Hostel.

▦ Open Jan 4–Dec 23. IBN and BABA.

🕐 Reception open 7–10am and 1–10pm. Curfew 11pm. 24-hour opening is said to be imminent.

🛏 82 beds. 2-, 6-, 8-, 10-, and 22-bed rooms.

£ Members: adults £8.80; under 18 £5.95.

🍴 Self-catering kitchen facilities. Breakfast: 7:45–8:30am. Lunch: packed lunch only, small or large; order by 8pm the night before. Dinner 7pm. Children's menu available, only for families.

⊥ No table license.

🔒 Lockers in common room; key is at reception. Staff will guard valuables behind desk.

🔲 Washers £1; tokens at reception. Dryers 20p.

P In car park; free. Gates close at 11pm.

🗋 Shop at hostel sells candy, soaps, stamps.

📺 Quiet room; TV lounge with video games.

🚬 In TV lounge only.

♿ Not wheelchair accessible.

💱 Fexco Currency exchange.

🔺 Bike shed.

Cheap Eats Nearby

Nürnbergers

After taking the 15-minute walk into the quintessentially English school town of Eton, take a load off in this artsy little cafe, a hangout for Eton boys and their teachers. You can peruse the books and magazines in the old armoire and admire the artwork on the walls painted by the daughter of owner Sandra. Homemade cakes, tasty sandwiches, and tea are the bill of fare here. Soup specials £2.75. Hot cross buns and tea £2.75. Vegetarian specials.

3 Barnes Pool, High Street, Eton. Tel: 01753/831811. Open: Mon–Fri 11am–6pm; Sat–Sun noon–6pm. From the Youth Hostel, take Barry Avenue to Windsor Bridge, turn left and go over the bridge. Follow High Street past the post office and library; it's on your left.

The Vansittart Arms

Just you try to squeeze past the crowds here on a Sunday afternoon. This is a traditional English pub with a Laura Ashley influence—yellow-flowered wallpaper surrounds ale-drinking grandfathers and young kids feeding the "fruit machines." The bar staff efficiently pumps out pints of Guinness for the convivial crowd as Annie Lennox belts it out on the stereo. Ploughman's lunch with Brie £2.95. Hefty steak, kidney, and Guinness pie fills the tummy for £4.25. Daily specials, and a children's menu as well.

Vansittart Road, Clewer. Tel: 01753/865988. Open: Mon–Sat noon–2:30pm and 7–9:30pm; Sun noon–2:30pm. A 10-minute walk: From the hostel, turn left, and at the roundabout take another left. When you reach the large roundabout, go straight across and turn right at the traffic lights. Walk up a bit and it's on your right. There are a few other pubs in the area as well.

Grocery Store: Tesco, in the King Edward Court Shopping Centre. Tel: 01753/855577. Open: Mon–Tues 8:30am–6pm; Wed–Thurs 8:30am–8pm; Fri 8:30am–9pm; Sat 8:30am–6pm.

Experiences

If you arrive in Windsor anytime around 11am, it's worth hanging out for the Changing of the Guard at **Windsor Castle** before trekking up to the hostel to dump your sack. Otherwise allow for at least a couple of hours to gawk at the blinding stained glass in St. George's Chapel and awesome state apartments of the queen's humble home. You decide if it's worth the £8 admission.

The Long Walk (no cycling, please) leading down from the castle makes for real Kodak moments. It leads you directly into the 4,000-plus acres of **Windsor Great Park,** where you can cycle around to your heart's content in the grassy green fields. In **Savill Garden,** an explosion of rhododendrons, camellias, magnolias, and other flora will astound even the most sophisticated horticulturist. This is what picnic lunches were made for.

Take a five-minute bike ride over to nearby **Eton** and watch young English lads struggle to come of age in their pinstriped trousers and tails. Eton College and its picturesque town, lined with painfully adorable shops and pubs, are well worth a visit, especially for the chapel and main campus. For more ambitious **bike routes** into the Chiltern Hills, Peter at the bike shop can point you in the right direction. For those in search of a romantic ride up the Thames, **motorboats** and **rowboats** can be hired on the stretch of river between Windsor Bridge and the Youth Hostel. For entertainment, the old **Theatre Royal** puts on Agatha Christie plays as well as contemporary dramatic works, and the **Windsor Arts Centre** offers exhibitions and New Age art fairs.

Windsor Castle. Tel: 01753/831118 or 01753/868286. Open: daily 10am–5pm; last entrance 4pm. Admission: adults £8; under 17s £4; seniors £5.50.

Savill Garden. The Great Park, Windsor. Tel 01753/860222. Admission: adults £3.30; children under 16 free; seniors £2.80; reduced rates for groups.

Eton College. High Street, Eton. Tel: 01753/671177 or 01753/671000. Chapel, cloister, school yard, and natural history museum open: daily 2–5pm. Call for bookings.

Gamble and Logie Motorboats. Barry Avenue, Windsor. Tel: 01753/863160 or 01753/861064. Motorboats: £12 per half hour and £22 per hour. Rowboats: £5 per half hour and £9 per hour.

Windsor Cycle Hire. 50 The Arches, Alma Road, Windsor. Tel: 01753/830220. Half-day rental £5; full day £10. Includes handy messenger bag. Trikes available for tots; also traditional 12-speeds and tandem bikes.

Theatre Royal. Thames Street, Windsor. Ticket office tel.: 01753/853888.

Windsor Arts Centre. St. Leonard's Road, Windsor. Tel: 01753/859336.

The Basics

Tourist Office: Royal Windsor Visitor Information Centre, 24 High St. Tel: 01753/852010 or 01753/831164 for currency exchange. Open: Mon–Fri 9:30am–5pm; Sat 9:30am–6pm; Sun 10am–4pm. Services include currency exchange, bus ticket reservations, stamp and phonecard sales. From the hostel, walk along Barry Avenue to Windsor Centre. Turn right onto River Street, then right on Thames Street, which turns into High Street. It's on your right; a 20- to 30-minute walk.

Post Office: 38/39 Peascod St. Tel: 01753/861451. Open: Mon–Fri 9:30am–5:30pm; Sat 9am–1pm. Currency exchange available. From the hostel, walk up Barry Avenue and cut through the King Edward Court Shopping Centre. Go left onto Peascod Street and it's on your right.

Currency Exchange: At the hostel, tourist office, and post office (see "Tourist Office" and "Post Office" under "The Basics" in Windsor).

Telephone Code: 01753.

Taxi: tel. 01753/677677 or 01753/858888.

Getting There: Windsor is extremely accessible by **train;** get a copy of the London Connections rail map; most trains hook you up either at Slough or Richmond. There is twice-hourly service to the Central Station from London **Paddington** (via Slough), and to Riverside from London **Waterloo** (both £5.50). From **Oxford,** trains also come in twice hourly (also via Slough, £9.50). For information, call London Waterloo at 0171/928 5100. Central station ticket office open: Mon–Sat 7am–8pm; Sun 8:30am–5pm. Riverside station ticket office open: Mon–Sat 6:35am–8:10pm; Sun 8:55am–6:25pm. By **bus,** Green Line Travel Line no. 700 and no. 702 run from London **Victoria** hourly (one hour, £5.50). For information, call 0181/668 7261. Bee Line Buses run regular service to and from **Heathrow;** pick up bus no. 192.

What's Next

Just a few stops on the Windsor-Slough-Oxford train route is calm, flower-filled **Streatley-on-Thames,** which shares a train station with its sister town of Goring-on-Thames just over the bridge. The gleaming little hostel there is a favorite among cyclists making their way through the Chiltern Valley and walkers on the Ridgeway Trail, which winds its way around the town and beyond. Trains go hourly from Windsor (45 minutes; £6.30). Crusty old **Oxford** is just a few stops farther, and trains run twice hourly from Windsor Central (change at Slough; £9.50). If you're hot on the path of ye olde English history, Oxford in all its academic glory is an obvious next stop. The quiet Youth Hostel at Jordans (Beaconsfield) is only 13 miles away and slightly tough to reach (change at Slough), but it's well suited to those in search of countryside comfort only a stone's throw from London.

STREATLEY-ON-THAMES

Tucked away between the Chiltern Hills and the Berkshire Downs, Streatley is but a tiny speck on the Thames Trains route connecting Windsor and Oxford. Not big enough to get its own train station, it shares one with the equally tiny, equally quaint town of Goring-on-Thames across the river. And if you ask for the bus station, you might get a chuckle out of the locals: "A bus station? In *Streatley?*"

Don't make the faux pas of even calling it a town: This is a village, and the locals like it that way, especially those tooling around in their brand-new hunter green Range Rovers. Only about an hour away from London, this picturesque town on the banks of the Thames has an interesting local crowd: Little old ladies riding their bikes around town tip their hats to the well-dressed professional types on their way to London for the day's work.

There's also a core community of amateur naturalists, since Streatley-on-Thames is on the cusp of the Ridgeway Path and Lardon Chase, two of many beautiful walking routes in the Thames Valley. Both are protected by the National Trust and the Countryside Commission. Thanks to these preservation societies, you can be sure of unspoiled (but well-signed) walking paths, meadows filled with chirping birds and wildflowers, and spectacular views of the towns and river below. The result is a harmonious blend of local wealth and countryside charm, with a little environmental awareness thrown in.

Housed in a stately Victorian home, the Youth Hostel is as elegant as the town. It serves as a way station for many walkers, young and old, making their way around the Ridgeway.

Streatley-on-Thames Youth Hostel

Hill House
Streatley, Reading, Berkshire RG8 9JJ
Tel: 01491/872278. Fax: 01491/873056.

There's something in the air at the Streatley-on-Thames Youth Hostel—and it's not dirty socks. An unmistakably noble character is evident the minute you walk into this well-preserved Victorian house on the hill above the Oxford-Reading Road. In the 1800s, the Reisses, the London tea merchants that lived in Hill House, opened their doors to young boys from the depressed Bermondsey area in London, allowing them to camp out in the meadow behind the house. The family's descendants eventually donated the building to the Youth Hostel Association.

In the elegant lounge, red velvet curtains frame the huge picture windows looking out on the hill. Carefully tended dried flowers sit in the fireplace, and commemorative plaques recount the family's history—just in case you were wondering how in the world this swanky place could actually house a hostel.

Outside this room, however, history is left behind: The bulletin boards in the hallway are loaded with useful information about land conservation, recycling, and British Telecom's annual Environment Week. The hostel also posts local walking paths, carefully laid out on maps for Ridgeway rookies. The rooms upstairs, though, might entice you to stay in bed all day: Cherry blossoms blow their petals just outside your window, and comfy pink quilts keep your toes warm at night.

The dining room serves breakfast and evening meals. It's a great place to trade stories with other guests, who tend to be a broad cross section of independent travelers, including lots of cute couples on weekend breaks from big-city life, as well as backpackers en route to Oxford and Windsor.

Services

Turn left out of the train station; make another left at the bridge going over the railroad tracks. Go up High Street, passing the post office. Bear right at the next fork and go over the two bridges that cross the Thames. You'll reach a traffic light; the Bull Pub will be across the street. Turn left; the Hostel is across the road on your right.

There's no bus station in Streatley, but the village's main bus stop is right on Reading Road in front of the Bull Pub. The bus connecting Reading to Wallingford (where you can change for Oxford) runs right down this road (the A259). When you get off at the Bull Pub, go up the road with the pub on your right and the hostel is just ahead on the right.

Get onto the M4, take Junction 12, and follow signs for the A329 to Pangbourne. Look for signs to Child Beale Wildlife Park. Keep on the A329 through Pangbourne and the hostel comes up on your left. Look for the Youth Hostel sign.

Open Feb to mid-Dec.

Reception open 7–10am and 5–10:30pm. Curfew 11:15pm.

53 beds. 4-, 5-, 6-, 7-, and 10-bed rooms. Family rooms with keys for daytime access.

£ Members: adults £8; under 18 £5.35.

Breakfast: 7:45–8:45am. Continental breakfast 7:15–9:15am. Children's breakfast £1.50. Packed breakfast available; order by 10:30pm the night before. Lunch: packed lunch only, small or large; order by 10pm the night before. Dinner 7pm; book by 6pm. "Mr. Muncher's evening meals" available for children, £2.

In bike shed; at your own risk.

No laundry facilities.

P In car park; free of charge.

Shop at hostel sells canned goods and toiletries. Rents towels for 50p per day; hair dryers for 50p per half hour; iron 50p per half hour (hair dryer and iron £1 deposit).

Lounge with TV and books resembles grandmother's living room.

In TV lounge only.

Not wheelchair accessible.

See "Currency Exchange" under "The Basics" in Streatley.

Bike shed out back.

Cheap Eats Nearby

The Bull Pub

In the days of stagecoaches and scarlet letters, this place was a hotbed of Streatley scandal. In 1440, a nun and priest were convicted of "misconduct" and together met their unfortunate demise in the garden. A yew tree was planted in their memory above their graves. The mood here, however, is anything but somber—gaming machines and a burning fireplace make for a warm atmosphere as you dig in to daily specials like fisherman's pie (£4.50) and vegetable tikka masala (£4.15). Lunch special (£10) for two includes starter, main course, and coffee or tea.

Reading Road, Streatley. Tel: 01491/872392. Open: Mon–Sat noon–2:30pm and 7–9:30pm; Sun noon–2:30pm. Credit cards: AE, VA, MC, DC, Switch, Access. From the hostel, turn left and it's right on your left, a two-minute walk.

Riverside Tea Rooms & Café

This quaint skylit tea room is a three-minute walk across the Thames, right on the main street of Goring. This busy little spot sells adorable postcards as well as locally bottled sweet wines and attracts locals for cream tea (£3.25) in the afternoon. Full lunches are also available; you can fill up on pasties (from £3.50), omelets (from £2.25), or delicious homemade blackberry pie (£4.95). Children's and vegetarian specials as well.

High Street, Goring-on-Thames. Tel: 01491/872243. Open: daily 10am–5pm; July–Aug until 6pm. Cash only. From the hostel, turn left onto Reading Road and turn right at the traffic light. Go over the two bridges and it's on your left. A five-minute walk.

Grocery Store: W. H. Napper and Son. High Street, Goring-on-Thames. Open: Mon–Sat 8:30am–5:30pm. From the hostel, turn left onto Reading Road and right at the traffic light. Go over the bridge and up the High Street of Goring. On your left.

Experiences

Two famous walking routes join at Streatley and Goring: the ancient **Ridgeway Path** and the old trading route **Ickfield Way.** Signs can set you on your way and the hostel offers lots of helpful info. If you want a short route, take a left up the steep hill road behind the Bull Pub and climb up to Lardon Chase, where wild-flowers and green fields offer a great little picnic spot high above the Thames. For ambitious walkers, the hostel provides a detailed route through the Ashampstead Circuit, a five- to six-hour hike through the rolling wooded terrain south of the hostel. For other outdoor activities, **Adventure Dolphin** offers orienteering, climbing, and water-sports excursions.

More sedentary attractions include the nearby **Didcot Railway Centre,** where you can ride the old steam railway that ran through the area in the mid-1800s. The railway center has a fascinating relics display that chronicles the rail heritage so central to this area's history. **Warren Farm,** two miles up the road, is an organic farm that teaches agricultural techniques to Ugandan farmers. Run by the Kulika Trust, it's also open to the public. Finally, the **Mapledurham House** has a working watermill and a beautiful Elizabethan mansion on the north bank of the Thames near Reading, only six miles away.

Ridgeway Path. Ridgeway Officer, Countryside service, Holton, Oxford. Tel: 01865/810244.

Didcot Railway Centre. Didcot, Oxfordshire. Tel: 01235/817200. Open: Apr–Sept 24 daily 11am–5pm, and on weekends throughout the rest of the year. Admission: adults £4.50–£5; children £3.50–£4; families £13.50–£15. Prices vary depending on events.

Warren Farm. Rectory Road, Streatley-on-Thames. Tel: 01491/872149. Appointments should be made by phone; arrangements can be made to meet arrivals at the Goring/Streatley railway station.

Mapledurham House. Tel: 01734/723350.

The Basics

Tourist Office: Goring and Streatley Information Office. The Old School House, Station Road, Goring-on-Thames. Tel: 01491/873565. Open: Mon–Sat 10am–12pm. Doubles as the town community center. From the hostel, turn right at the Bull Pub and cross the bridges onto High Street in Goring. Turn right just before the Goring post office and then turn left. It's a brick-and-stone building on your left.

Post Office: High Street, Goring-on-Thames. Open: Mon–Tues 9am–1pm and 2–5:30pm; Wed 9am–1pm; Thurs–Fri 9am–1pm and 2–5:30pm; Sat 9am–12:30pm. Inside the Forbuoys stationery store. From the hostel, turn right at the Bull Pub, cross the bridges onto High Street in Goring, and it's on your right.

Currency Exchange: The closest place is at the Pangbourne Post Office, 16 Reading Rd., Pangbourne.

Telephone Code: 01491.

Getting There: Trains come into Goring/Streatley frequently from the Windsor-Oxford line; they arrive every half hour from **Windsor** (45 minutes; £7.30) and **Oxford** (30 minutes; £5.40). From **London,** change at Reading (every hour, £9.20), and you're here in an hour. The ticket office is open Mon–Thurs 6:30am–1am; Fri 6:30am–midnight; Sat 7am–12:45am. For information call 01734/595911. The only **buses** come in from the Wallingford-Reading line; bus no. 105, with a connection in Oxford, stops outside the Bull Pub near the hostel. For information, call 01865/711312.

By **car** from London, take the M4 headed west, following the signs to Reading; at junction 10, switch to the A329, which takes you directly to Streatley, about 18 miles from the turnoff. From Oxford, take the A34 south to Didcot. Then switch for the A4130 headed east toward Wallingford. After about 15 miles look for the A329 headed south. This takes you directly to Streatley.

What's Next

After a countryside break in this idyllic riverside town, **Oxford** is a logical next stop, with its ancient university and huge meadow. It's reachable by train or bus. **Windsor** is also a stone's throw away. Its royal castle and gardens make for a nice stopover for travelers headed in the direction of London and Heathrow.

OXFORD

In the early 1800s, John Keats smugly claimed that "this Oxford, I have no doubt, is the finest city in the world." Add about a hundred years, a few million cars, thousands of students, and a healthy layer of soot, and you may have your doubts. Crammed into less than a square mile is a mother lode of colleges, chapels, quadrangles, libraries, and all sorts of university haunts, making this a prime target for academic and literary pilgrims from all over the world and causing the city to roil with modern unpleasantness such as pollution, traffic, stressed-out students, and the inevitable aura of conspicuous consumption.

Nevertheless, underneath the grime, the city is still a resplendent tribute to academia and the buildings are nothing less than awe-inspiring. Best appreciated from the relative tranquillity of a secluded college quad, the city does make a good overall impression. For over 800 years, it has been the Rosetta Stone of higher education, schooling philosophers, scientists, poets, and scholars of all sorts. Oxford the city is almost entirely dominated by the university: it has the usual juxtaposition of modern and ancient characteristic of English college towns. Once you get past Carfax Tower, the colleges, and the other big sights, though, there is life after graduation. To the west of the city center, the neighborhood of Jericho offers alternative cinemas and some offbeat shops. From here, you can escape the throngs on St. Aldate's and Cornmarket Street to an expansive, hidden farmland.

A curious mix of the urban and bucolic, Oxford is a many-layered (soot notwithstanding) city. A trip here is worth at least a couple of days. The hostel, outside the center, is about a 15-minute bus ride. While you're here, think of the money you're saving and think of it as a bed—and not much more.

Oxford Youth Hostel

32 Jack Straw's Lane
Oxford OX3 0DW
Tel: 01865/62997. Fax: 01865/69402.

The Oxford Youth Hostel was formerly a big, ugly pimple on the otherwise fair complexion of the English hosteling association. Recently it underwent the hosteling equivalent of Retin-A treatment and it's looking better. The YHA scrubbed it clean, hung some new curtains, and fixed the plumbing. They now assure hostelers of "plentiful hot water," which is a comfort to the many sore-shouldered sightseers that pile in here. Nothing can help that this is a crumbling old building that got lost in the "in" box of hostel bureaucracy for many years, but things are looking better on Jack Straw's Lane. If you can find it, that is. Outside the city, across the Magdalene Bridge over the Thames, and a mile (partially uphill) from there, it's a good 45-minute walk from Cerfax in the center of Oxford. The bus is a better option for those with heavy packs. Prepare yourself: The atmosphere here can get chaotic, with international student groups and a load of independent hostelers. As always, take care of your belongings; this 112-bed hostel is often packed solid, so security is a big issue. The bedrooms do have keys, and some rooms even have individual lockers, but it's strictly bring your own padlock for the lockers in the downstairs area, where most people end up throwing their gear. Especially because it's removed from the main part of town, you're best off getting provisions (the self-catering kitchen is pretty good) before coming out. It's best to use the place to park your things, take a shower in the suprisingly clean bathrooms, and head out. The manager and staff all seem to work triple-time trying to keep the hostel together, and somehow they actually manage to be nice about it.

🚆 The train station is off Park End Street, west of the city. Walk down Park End Street, follow it onto New Road and Queen Street. When you reach St. Aldate's (look for the Carfax Tower), turn right and look for the bus stop in front of the Post

Office. Take no. 13 or 14 out to the Youth Hostel stop on Marston Road, in a residential neighborhood. From there, turn right onto Jack Straw's Lane. The hostel is up the hill on the right. The whole trip will take about 40 minutes.

🚌 The bus station is on George Street. From there, turn left and walk along George Street. When you reach Cornmarket Street, turn right and follow it as it turns into St. Aldate's. From there, follow directions from the train, given above.

🚗 From the A40, get on to ring road around Oxford, and follow signs to the city center. After about a mile, turn right at the traffic lights by the White Horse pub and continue until you reach Staunton Road on the left. Turn left and continue as it becomes Jack Straw's Lane. The hostel is on the left.

🗓 Open year-round. Occasional two- to three-week closing in winter. Call to check. IBN and BABA.

🕐 Reception open 7:30–10am and 1–11pm. No curfew; security guard lets you in at night.

🛏 112 beds. 2-, 4-, 6-, 8-, 10-, and 12-bed rooms.

£ Members: adults £8.80; under 18 £5.95.

🍴 Self-catering kitchen facilities: open all day except 10:30am–noon. Breakfast: 8–9am. Lunch: packed lunch only; should be ordered by 6pm the night before.

Dinner: 5:30–7:30pm.

🍸 No table license.

🧳 Precious few lockers in bedrooms; more downstairs. Bike shed serves as luggage storage. Bring a padlock or buy one (£2.70).

🧺 Washers £1.50; dryers 50p. Detergent for sale at reception.

P Ample and free of charge.

🏪 Shop at hostel sells maps, canned food.

🛋 Games room with pool table, books, video games.

🚬 Not encouraged; allowed outside.

♿ Not wheelchair accessible.

💱 Travelex currency exchange.

🔺 Bike shed.

Cheap Eats Nearby

Chang Mai Kitchen

New-fangled Thai food is served in this 360-year-old former police station, a standard first-date restaurant for young scholars. Lilies decorate the tables and wood carvings adorn the walls: This place is lovely and worth the expense. Prawns with fresh chili £5.10. Vegetarian specials £2.90 to £4.50. Pad thai £4.80.

Kemp Hall Passage, 130a High St., Oxford. Tel: 01865/202233. Open: Mon–Sat noon–2:30pm and 6–11pm. Reservations accepted. Credit cards: AE, VA, MC, EC, DC. From the hostel, walk down to Marston Road and take the bus to St. Aldate's (20 minutes). From Carfax, head down High Street. It's on your right, down a small alleyway.

Heroes

The classic Oxford eatery: newspapers on a rack, wooden stools, and glassy-eyed overworked students chowing down in this tiny sandwich bar. Sandwiches on a variety of breads with a variety of fillings served with salad and coleslaw £1.80 to £2.95. Hot specials include BLTs, chicken and cheese (£2.70). Soups, bagels, and pastries. They take phone orders.

8 Ship St., Oxford. Tel: 01865/723459. Open: Mon–Fri 8am–7pm; Sat 8:30am–5pm; Sun 10am–5pm. From the hostel, walk down to Marston Road and take the bus to St. Aldate's (20 minutes). From Carfax, walk up Cornmarket Street, and turn right onto Ship Street. It's on the left.

Grocery store: Coop Supermarket, Cornmarket Street. Open: Mon–Fri 8am–7pm; Sat 8am–7pm.

Experiences

The logical place to start any walking tour of Oxford is at **Carfax Tower,** the structure dominating the city from its vantage point at the juncture of St. Aldate's, Queen, Cornmarket, and High streets. From there, it's up to you. Walk up Cornmarket and you'll head for the famous Covered Market. A few blocks up the street sit the cloistered Canterbury Quad, winding paths, and shady gardens of **St. John's College.** Down St. Aldate's is **Christ Church College,** where you can set your Swatch to the bells of Tom Tower. Ever since the student curfew was set at 9:05pm, Tom has faithfully clanged 101 times (for 101 original students) nightly at precisely that hour. There is also a dreamy flower garden, and the chapel at Christ Church doubles as Oxford's official cathedral.

Magdalene College (pronounced "maudlin"), at the far end of High Street, has an enormous deer park and a water meadow that glows purple in May from the snake's-head fritillaries in bloom. **New College** has an El Greco and a chapel full of treasures a bit farther away. Walk through any of the colleges in the center of the city and you'll see secluded quads, gargoyled facades, imposing towers, and elaborately carved entrances. They say guests are to pay an entrance fee, but if you were a guard at a school with 40 colleges and more than 12,000 students, would you stop every single person at the entrance gate and check IDs? They don't.

Other sights worth a peek in Oxford include the **University Museum,** a Victorian Gothic building with the remains of a dodo inside, as well as a huge natural history museum. Visiting sadists flock to the **Pitt Rivers Museum** behind it, which has an impressive anthropology collection, most notably a section devoted to punishment and instruments of torture.

Moving away from the university and down St. Giles is the **Eagle and Child,** C. S. Lewis's old hangout and still a lively pub. Down Little Clarendon Street, you'll find trendy clothing shops, a few crafts stores, and the **George and Davis** ice-cream parlor. Complete with little cows at the entrance, it is a well-loved local landmark.

Moving onto Walton Street takes you into the neighborhood of Jericho: All of a sudden, the noise level drops, bicycles don't careen into pedestrians, and you can take a deep breath. The tremendous, imposing home of **Oxford University Press** resides back here with a beautiful lawn out front. The **Phoenix Picture House** up the road is a great place to watch foreign and independent films.

At the far end of Walton Street is the entrance to Oxford's **Port Meadow.** Horses gallop, geese roam, and little streams wind their way through this open farmland. If you walk through the meadow and cross the river, you'll reach a cute pub called The Perch, which leads to a narrow driveway and eventually to a graveyard by St. Margaret's Church. Outside, there's a well that Princess Ffrediswyde built in the Middle Ages in gratitude to St. Mags for restoring sight to her lover's eyes, which had been struck by lightning. The church has always been (and still is) a special place to come to for inspiration and healing, especially after a harried day of sight-seeing in Oxford.

Carfax Tower. Oxford. Tel: 01865/726871. Open: Mar–Nov: daily 10am–6pm. Admission: adults £1; children 80p.

University Museum and Pitt Rivers Museum. Parks Road, Oxford. Tel: 01865/ 270949. University Museum open: Mon–Sat noon–5pm. Pitt Rivers Museum open: Mon–Sat 1–4:30pm. Admission: free for both.

Phoenix Picture House. 57 Walton St., Oxford. Tel: 01865/54909 or 01865/ 512526. Evening films: £3.80. Matinees: adults £2.80; concessions £2.20.

The Basics

Tourist Office: Oxford T.I.C. The Old School, Oxford. Tel: 01865/726871. Open: Mon–Sat 9:30am–5pm; Sun 10am–3:30pm. From the hostel, walk to Marston Road and get bus no. 12 or 13 into the city center. From Carfax, walk up Cornmarket and Magdalen streets and turn left on George Street. On your right, you'll see a green square, Gloucester Green. It's at the far end, 45 minutes from the hostel.

Post Office: Oxford Post Office. 102/104 St. Aldate's, Oxford. Tel: 01865/814785. Open: Mon–Fri 9am–5:30pm; Sat 9am–7pm. From the hostel, walk to Marston Road and get bus no. 12 or 13 into the city center. It's just beyond Carfax, where the bus stops.

Currency Exchange: American Express. 4 Queen St., Oxford. Tel: 01865/792033. Open: Mon–Sat 9am–5:30pm. Thomas Cook. 5 Queen St., Oxford. Tel: 01865/ 728604. Open: Mon–Sat 9am–5:30pm.

Telephone Code: 01865.

Bike Rental: Pennyfarthing Cycle Centre. 5 George St., Oxford. Tel: 01865/249368. Open: Mon–Sat 8:30am–5:30pm. One-day rental £5; one-week rental £9. £25 deposit required.

Getting There: Hourly **train** service from London **Paddington** makes it a snap to get here (one hour), and there's also good service from **Bath, Bristol** (change at Didcot Parkway for both), and **Stratford-upon-Avon.** For information, call 01865/ 722333 or 0121/643 2711. **Coach** service from **London** runs every 20 minutes via The Oxford Tube, which runs from Victoria Station, picking up passengers at Marble Arch, Notting Hill Gate, and Shepherd's Bush on the way to London. For info, call 01865/772250. National Express has connections from **London, Bristol, Bath, Salisbury,** and most other major cities. Those coming from **Cambridge** or **Stansted Airport** can take the Inter Varsity Link. For info, call 01223/236333. For bus information, call 01865/791579. By **car,** take the A40/M40 from **London,** which comes directly into Oxford.

What's Next

Only 30 miles away is the sugar-coated Shakespearean city **Stratford-upon-Avon,** lying on the banks of the river. It's everything you'd expect of Shakespeare's birth-place, chock-full of museums, monuments, and a wide variety of sights devoted to the Bard. The hostel is about two miles out of town, but it's nice enough, friendly enough, and big enough to hold school groups, solo backpackers, and young families alike together under one roof. The tiny town of **Streatley-on-Thames,** only 19 miles east, is a lovely little spot just off the Reading-Oxford line and a stone's throw from the Ridgeway Path. With gentle hills, the winding Thames River, and a sweet twin town across the bridge, it's nice for relaxing, easy hill walking, or even commuting into London for day-trips—that's what most of the townsfolk do in this well-to-do country enclave.

STRATFORD-UPON-AVON

What woe to be William Shakespeare. He certainly has suffered the slings and arrows of Stratford's outrageous fortune-hunters: his name summarily slapped on everything from bakeries to auto shops; his bashful gaze photocopied ad nauseum on everything from movie schedules to restaurant menus; his plays rotated regularly, like so many *Partridge Family* reruns; his life and times chronicled blow by blow in the tenderly preserved historic buildings where he lived, loved, lusted, and liquored up during his lifetime.

He will live on forever—or at least as long as Stratford (91 miles northwest of London and 45 miles north of Oxford) remains England's number-two tourist town. That seems likely: Even cynical, postmodern, black-turtleneck-clad, Camel-smoking types tend to wax sentimental about The Man, and the city certainly serves him up on a silver platter.

It doesn't take more than a couple of days to see everything. If you tire of William worship, you can rent rowboats, canoes, and motorboats on the banks of the river, and some alternative theater does exist. The area has some decent walking and cycling routes, which come in handy since the "Stratford" hostel is set in the idyllic village of Alveston, $2^1/_2$ miles away. A lovely rambling house, it's a pleasant spot accessible by public transport but an anticlimax for those who want to fully experience Shakespeare's Stratford.

Stratford-upon-Avon International YHA Centre

Hemmingford House
Alveston, Stratford-upon-Avon
Warwickshire CV37 7RG
Tel: 01789/297093. Fax: 01789/205513.

Set on sprawling grounds, this Georgian mansion is 200 years old, though you might not guess its age from the semimodern mauve-and-green motif in the entrance hall. Don't worry: The spirit of you-know-who lurks in Alveston too. Just beyond the entrance is the Shakespeare Room, a conference/class room with a portrait of The Man on the wall, and the stairway leading upstairs heaves with still shots of other famous thespians.

The dining room is called the "Encore Café," and the food does get pretty good reviews; they offer individual entrées and snacks in addition to the usual £4 set meal. The games room, with a slot machine, pool table, and video games, gets endless use from the under-15 crowd. There's also a quieter sitting room for grownups, with tapestries on the wall and blue damask draperies on the picture window. Up the stairs, past the huge dormitories, is a new skylit wing with small bedrooms, squeaky clean private baths, and alluring views of the cherry blossoms and picnic tables outside.

One of the busier hostels, this place hosts a huge cross section of travelers. Lots of school groups come for the classroom facilities, families come for the private rooms, and backpackers pour off the Slow Coach. The staff, which makes a valiant attempt to stay cheery despite the hectic atmosphere, strongly recommends that hostelers call in advance to book their rooms. There's nothing worse than trekking the two miles out of town to discover they're booked, which happens often.

🚆 Exit the station and turn right onto Wood Street. Follow it onto Bridge Street and take bus no. 18 (£1) from the stop in front of Marks and Spencer. It's a 10-minute ride. Alternatively, walk across the Clopton Bridge, turn and left onto Tiddington Road (B4086); it's 2 miles to the hostel.

🚌 Intercity buses stop right in front of Marks and Spencer. From there, take bus no. 18 (£1), a 10-minute ride. Alternatively, walk across the Clopton Bridge and turn left onto Tiddington Road (B4086); it's 2 miles to the hostel.

🚗 From Stratford, pass Marks and Spencer and head for the river. Go over the Clopton Bridge and follow Tiddington Road (B4086) to the Youth Hostel, 2 miles away.

▦ Open Jan 4–Dec 18. Opening and closing dates can vary slightly; call ahead. IBN and BABA.

🕐 24-hour access to hostel; check in from 12pm. Doors lock at midnight; from then on, the night porter will let you in.

🛏 152 beds. 2-, 4-, 6-, 8-, 10-, and 12-bed rooms. Some bedrooms with private bath (£1 extra).

£ Members: adults £12.20; under 18 £9.05. All prices include breakfast.

🍴 Self-catering kitchen facilities; open all day. Breakfast: 7:30–9am; included in price. Lunch: packed lunch only; should be ordered by 10pm the night before. Dinner: 5–7:45pm.

🍸 No table license.

🧳 In locked closet by reception. Valuables can be stored in hostel safe.

▢ Drying room only. They'll wash for £1.50 a load.

P Ample and free of charge.

🛍 Shop at hostel sells canned goods; candy; miniature Shakespearean houses; *As You Like It* T-shirts.

🛋 Games room with pool, slot machine; TV/sitting room.

📞 In TV lounge only.

♿ Not wheelchair accessible.

💱 Travelex currency exchange.

🔺 Bike shed; classroom with slide projector and equipment; Slow Coach tickets for sale; hair dryers 10p a blow.

Cheap Eats Nearby

Hathaway Tea Rooms

The local bailiff lived here in the 1600s. Now it's a sweet cafe with a fudge shop/bakery in front and a proper tea room in back serving much more than scones and jam. Pasties £1. Sausage rolls 85p. Welsh rarebit £3.90. Bangers and beans on toast £2.95.

19 High St., Stratford. Tel: 01789/292404. Open: daily 9am–5:30pm. Cash only. From the hostel, take bus no. 18 into town (10-minute ride) and walk up Bridge Street away from the river. Turn left onto High Street. It's on the left.

Lamb's

Two bay trees greet you outside this polished but unpretentious restaurant with flowers on the wooden trencher tables and a log fireplace. Pastas and salads £5.50 to £6.75 are the most economical choices. Scrumpy sausage plate £5.50. Lamb-and-apricot pie £7.

12 Sheep St., Stratford. Tel: 01789/292554. Open: Mon–Sat 12–2:30pm and 5:30–11pm; Sun 6:30–11pm. Reservations accepted. Credit cards: AE, MC, VA, Access, Switch. From the hostel, take bus no. 18 into town (10-minute ride) and walk along the waterside. Pass the World of Shakespeare on your right and turn right onto Sheep Street. It's on the left.

Grocery store: Safeway, Alcester Road. Open: Mon–Thurs 8am–8pm; Fri 8am–9pm; Sat 8am–8pm; Sun 10am–4pm.

Experiences

It all depends on your degree of Shakespeare fever, but most hostelers seem to linger in Stratford for two to three days, which is enough time to do the Shakespeare trail (all his and his family's houses), a little river activity (rent a rowboat, motorboat, or canoe), and maybe some theater. **Shakespeare's Birthplace** is a half-timbered house with a garden full of the flowers, plants, and trees mentioned in his works. At **New Place/Nash's House,** you can visit the local history museum and walk through the site of his family home; the only remnants are the garden and two water wells. Finally, **Hall's Croft** is the home of Shakespeare's daughter Susanna and her husband, a doctor. It was also his office and dispensary, and there's an interesting exhibition on Tudor medicine.

Nearby, **Harvard House** is a fine example of a 16th-century town house. It once belonged to the local butcher whose ambitious son emigrated to the United States and became the benefactor of the university that now bears his name.

Outside, **rowboats and motorboats** can be rented between Clopton and Tramway bridges along the duck-dappled River Avon, which gets busy in summer. An **open-air market** takes place here every Tuesday, with clothes, food, and music at the intersection of Greenhill, Rother, Wood, and Windsor Streets. The **Greenway,** a former railway track, leads you out of town 2 1/2 miles to the Milcote Picnic area or farther along into the countryside toward Long Marston.

Back in town, theater is on offer at a number of venues: the **Royal Shakespeare Company** (strictly Shakespeare); **The Swan** (Shakespeare and some classics) and **The Other Place** (everything else: Golden Age theater, modern adaptations, alternative theater). Bear in mind that Stratford's popularity means things can get expensive, especially in the high season, so watch out.

Shakespeare's Birthplace. Henley Street, Stratford. Tel: 01789/204016. Open: summer: Mon–Sat 9am–5:30pm; Sun 9:30am–5:30pm. Winter: Mon–Sat 9:30am–4pm; Sun 10am–5:30pm. Admission: adults £2.75; children £1.30.

New Place/Nash's House. Chapel Street, Stratford. Tel: 01789/292325. Open: summer: Mon–Sat 9:30am–5pm; Sun 10am–5pm. Winter: Mon–Sat 10am–4pm; Sun 10:30am–4pm. Admission: adults £1.90; children 90p.

Hall's Croft. Old Town, Stratford. Tel: 01789/204016. Open: summer: 9:30am–5pm; Sun 10am–5pm. Winter: Mon–Sat 10am–4pm; Sun 10:30am–4pm. Admission: adults £1.90; children 90p.

Shakespeare's Town Heritage Trail. Combined admission to the three places listed above. Admission: adults £5.50; seniors and students £5; children £2.50.

Harvard House. High Street, Stratford. Tel: 01789/292325. Open: May–Sept only: daily 10am–4pm. Admission: adults £1; children 50p.

Stratford Marina. Next to the Moat House Hotel and Wharf, Stratford. Tel: 01789/269669. Open: Mar–Oct: daily 10am–dusk. Rowboats: £4 per hour. Motorboats: £5 per half hour.

The Greenway. Leaflet available at the tourist office (see "Tourist Office" under "The Basics" in Stratford-upon-Avon).

Royal Shakespeare Theatre. Waterside, Stratford. Tel: 01789/205301. Bookings for RSC, The Other Place, and The Swan Theatre can be done here. Phone bookings: 01789/295623. Fax bookings: 01789/261974. Box office hours: Mon–Sat 9am–8pm (6pm when theaters are closed). Balcony seats £4.50–£15. Stalls and Circle seats £10.50–£34. Superseats £25–£42.

The Basics

Tourist Office: Stratford-upon-Avon T.I.C. Bridgefoot, Stratford. Tel: 01789/293127. Open: Mon–Sat 9am–6pm; Sun 11am–5pm. From the hostel, take bus no. 18 into town (10-minute ride). From Marks and Spencer, walk toward the river. It's on the left just before Clopton Bridge.

Post Office: Stratford-upon-Avon Post Office. 2–3 Henley St., Stratford. Tel: 01789/414939. Open: Mon–Fri 9am–5:30pm; Sat 9am–7pm. Take bus no. 18 from the hostel (10-minute ride). From Marks and Spencer, walk up Bridge Street away from the river, and the post office is at the corner of Henley and Union streets.

Currency Exchange: American Express, in the Stratford T.I.C. Bridgefoot, Stratford. Tel: 01789/293127. Open: Mon–Sat 9am–6pm; Sun 11am–5pm.

Telephone Code: 01789.

Bike Rental: Clarke's Stratford Cycle Shop. Guild Street, Stratford. Tel: 01789/205057. Tourers, roadsters, mountain bikes from £6 and up per day.

Getting There: Stratford is easy as pie on public transport. **Trains** come in from London **Paddington** at least six times a day (2¹/₂ hours). From **Oxford,** it's a 1¹/₂-hour ride, and service is frequent as well. For info, call 01203/555211. **Coaches** come in thrice daily from London **Victoria** (a few pounds cheaper than the train) and take about three hours. Buses from **Bath** (3 hours), **Oxford** (1¹/₂ hours), and **Cheltenham** (1 hour) come in twice daily. For bus information, call 0121/6224373.

By **car** from **London,** take the M40 northwest. At Junction 15, exit to Wellesbourne. Follow signs to Stratford, and just before you hit the town turn left onto Bridgeway, go over the Clopton Bridge, and take the B4086 out to Alveston. From **Oxford,** take the A34 and follow the same directions as above.

What's Next

From Stratford, you can try to make your way into the Cotswolds. The buses are slightly infrequent, but brave souls try their thumbs with good results. **Stow-on-the-Wold,** a precious, pristine, perfect limestone village 20 miles away, makes a great base for exploring all the other towns in these hilly environs. Those looking for signs of city life can head down to **Oxford** (45 miles away); the bubbling university with its legendary colleges and churches, Rhodes Scholars, and busy streets are nothing less than inspiring for those who can look past the ramshackle Youth Hostel outside town. Otherwise, head for the gentle Georgian architecture and Roman spa waters in **Bath,** three hours to the south. The hilltop hostel is in a palatial home, and the friendly, extremely helpful staff strike a nice balance between big-city efficiency and small-town warmth and hospitality.

STOW-ON-THE-WOLD

Cots means "sheepfold." *Wold* means "uncultivated land, downs, or woods." Put together, the Cotswolds comprise the legendary hills stretching from Bath in Somerset up to Chipping Campden in Gloucestershire. Deriving its name from the ancient Anglo-Saxon language, the area was settled by Cistercian monks who first came here with their furry flocks in the 13th century. The wool trade has flourished here ever since.

The tiny villages and market towns, intersected by straight Roman roads, bear the unmistakable Cotswold stamp: limestone. The hills are actually formed from a single slab of the stuff, providing the area with almost all of its building material and creating a warm, rich landscape of honey-colored buildings.

Set against a backdrop of gently rolling hills, slowly winding rivers, and mist-covered fields, Stow-on-the-Wold is typical of the Cotswolds. If you had an English granny, you'd expect her to live here, 20 miles south of Stratford and 30 miles west of Oxford. The town's narrow alleyways were originally carved out so farmers could count their sheep as they ran into the market square, and the architecture has remained unchanged since the 1400s.

Amid this perfectly proper English picture, however, runs a curiously country-bohemian streak: The town has two organic shops (one with an arts-and-crafts annex), loads of tea rooms, an excellent local bookstore, and some high-quality antiques shops. An unusual blend of travelers—shoppers, history buffs, mystery-book lovers, and outdoor types—all seem to enjoy it here.

The area around the town is legendary for its quintessentially English country lanes, gentle bike paths, and stunning, unspoiled scenery. The weather is capricious. At 800 feet above sea level, Stow is the highest town in the Cotswolds.

The Youth Hostel, in the center of Stow, is a truly harmonious part of the townscape. Nestled in an old merchant's home, it's as lovely as the rest of this wooly wonderland.

❊ Stow-on-the-Wold Youth Hostel

Stow-on-the-Wold
Cheltenham, Gloucestershire GL54 1AF
Tel: 01451/830497. Fax: 01451/870102.

Joanna Trollope would do well to set her next book in this 16th-century brew-house-turned-hostel. Situated in the cobbled Market Square in the center of town, it feels like a cross between a country inn and mountain refuge. Certain features are unmistakeably "hostelian": the dormitory rooms, the communal bathrooms, the daytime lockout. The amenities, however, make you feel downright pampered: A winding staircase leads to a top-floor room complete with a barn ceiling, stone walls, and comfy quilts. Some bedrooms even have skylights.

Downstairs, the dining room is picture-perfect with yellow and white flowers and wooden tables and chairs that look like they belong in an old English inn. In the sitting room downstairs, a "countryside folder" and bulletin board are full of helpful information on what to do in the area. Jane, the manager, can point you in the right direction, as can many of your fellow guests.

The people who come here are a mixed bag: families on a weekend vacation, Continental backpackers walking their way through England and Wales, and English cyclists, who are often quite knowledgeable about the area.

Early risers are in for a wonderful wake-up call. The singsong of the birds in the nearby hills and the view from the bedroom windows present the Cotswolds at their best: A blanket of mist envelops the farmlands at this time of day, lending a dreamlike, timeless quality to both the hostel and the town.

Services

🚆 The closest train station is in Moreton-in-Marsh, 4 miles away. From there, take Pulhams Bus into Stow; the hostel is in the center of the village.

🚌 The bus stop is in the center of town; the hostel is behind the Town Hall on the High Street.

🚗 Stow is directly down the A429 (Fosseway), 20 miles south of Stratford-upon-Avon and 30 miles northwest of Oxford on the A436.

🎛 May–Aug: open daily. Mar–Apr and Sept–Oct: open Mon–Sat. Feb, Nov, Dec: open weekends only. BABA.

🕐 Reception open 7–10am and 5–11pm. Curfew 11pm.

🛏 60 beds. 8-, 10-, 12-, 14-, and 18-bed rooms.

£ Members: adults £6.55; under 18 £4.45.

🍴 Self-catering kitchen facilities. Breakfast: 8:30am. Lunch: packed lunch only; order by the night before. Dinner: 5:30–7:30pm.

🍸 No table license.

📦 No lockers.

📋 Drying room only. They will do laundry for a nominal fee.

P Limited; free. Parking in town from 4pm–11am; free and easy to find.

🛍 Shop at hostel sells canned food; candy; cute emblems of the hostel.

🛋 TV in dining room; games room.

🚬 In smoking lounge only.

♿ Not wheelchair accessible.

💱 See "Currency Exchange" under "The Basics" in Stow-on-the-Wold.

🔺 Bike shed.

Cheap Eats Nearby

St. Edwards Café
You'll find wooden tables and benches and a country cupboard full of hearty jams and jellies in this tiny tea room, a former wool merchant's home. Quiche and jacket potato £3.50. Chicken curry, Yorkshire pudding, mincemeat pie all around £4 to £5. Generous cream teas £3.

The Square, Stow-on-the-Wold. Tel: 01451/830351. Open: Mon–Sat 9am–5pm; Sun 10am–5pm. From the hostel, turn left and walk around the town hall. It's straight ahead.

The White Hart

Home of the Stow-on-the-Wold Rotary Club, this friendly pub has beer mugs hanging from the ceiling and an intriguing collection of brass horns on the wall. Locals love it here. Tudor chicken pie £4.95. Corn, egg, and cheese bake £4.85. Pizzas £5 to £6.

The Square, Stow-on-the-Wold. Tel: 01451/830674. Open: Mon–Sat noon–3pm and 6–10pm; Sun noon–2:30pm and 7–10pm. Reservations accepted. Cash only. From the hostel, turn left. It's next door.

Grocery store: The Organic Shop. The Square, Stow-on-the-Wold. Open: daily 9:30am–5:30pm. There's also an 8 to 8 shop on the High Street.

Experiences

In ancient times, the local lode of oolite limestone provided Neolithic humans with ideal farming country in the Cotswolds. The land serves modern humans equally well by offering cycling tracks, footpaths, and bridleways. Stow is an excellent base for exploring the entire Cotswolds region. Pedestrians, cyclists, and pony trekkers will be grateful of one thing: The hills hover in the 600- to 800-foot range, making trails and cycleways gentle on backpackers' strained muscles. In addition, a decent bus service picks up where you leave off.

The eight-mile circular walk to **Upper and Lower Slaughter, Bourton-on-Water,** and back to Stow is an excellent way to start exploring the area. Bourton, standing astride the River Windrush, is typically charming with a sweet "model village" and an old stone bridge. The Slaughters, linked by a series of skinny bridges, have a few old churches, an old mill, and loads of sandy stone cottages with flower beds. Some excellent cycle routes fan out from Stow north toward Don-nington, Longbourough, Moreton-in-Marsh, and some other picturesque villages. Heading south takes you to Bourton-on-Water, Naunton, and other villages along the River Windrush. **Pony trekking** can be arranged at the stables in Bourton-on-Water as well.

The town of Stow radiates warmth, despite its moniker "Stow on the Wold where the winds blow cold." Shops with names such as The Borzoi Bookshop, The Powder Puff, In the Pink, and The Curiosity Shop lend it a special quaintness, as do the arts, crafts, and antiques fairs held in **St. Edwards Hall** in the main square.

Cirencester, about 18 miles away, holds the biweekly **Cotswold Craft Market** in its Corn Hall; it features crochet, patchwork, woodwork, Danish embroidery, and loads of other items. Near Cirencester is **The Butts Farm,** offering "rare farm animals and the sunrising stud of Welsh Mountain Ponies." It's especially nice for children, with goat milking, pig feeding, horse cart rides, and "cuddle time."

For more arts and crafts, head for **Moreton-in-Marsh,** a former linen-weaving town and yet another limestone village (bring your camera) about four miles away. The open-air market on Tuesday is especially known for its cane work and has pottery, flowers, food, and jewelry, among other items.

About a nine-mile walk away is **Chipping Campden,** which some say is the most beautiful Cotswolds town: with 14th-century inns, a 15th-century grammar school, a 17th-century almshouse, and an 18th-century town hall, it's one of the area's best-preserved towns.

Bear in mind that the better-known towns like Bourton and the Slaughters can get busy on summer weekends, so if you're looking for picturesque scenes and spiritual renewal, come in the off-season or in the middle of the week. The "Cotswold Events" leaflet available at the tourist office can give you a good idea of what's going on in the area.

Pony trekking. Court Hayes Farm Stables. Wyck Beacon (4 miles away). Tel: 01451/820524.

St. Edwards Hall Craft Fairs. St. Edwards Hall, Stow-on-the-Wold. Tel: 01367/ 860411. Dates vary; call ahead to check.

Cotswold Craft Market. The Corn Hall, Cirencester (20 miles away). Tel: 01684/ 296995. Second and fourth Saturdays of every month. 10am–4:30pm. Admission: free.

The Butts Farm. Near South Cerney, Cirencester (20 miles away). Tel: 01285/ 862205. Open: Easter–Sept: Wed–Sun 11am–5pm.

Moreton-in-Marsh (4 miles away). Open-air market in the Town Square. Tues 7:30am–5pm.

The Basics

Tourist Office: Stow-on-the-Wold T.I.C. Hollis House, The Square, Stow-on-the-Wold. Tel: 01451/831082. Open: Easter–Oct: Mon–Sat 10am–5:30pm; Sun 10:30am–4pm. Nov–Easter: Mon–Sat 10am–5:30pm. From the hostel turn left. It's on the left.

Post Office: Stow-on-the-Wold Post Office. Sheep Street, Stow-on-the-Wold. Tel: 01451/830415. Open: Mon–Tues and Thurs–Fri 9am–1pm and 2–5:30pm. Wed and Sat 9am–1pm. From the hostel, turn left onto The Square and then right onto Church Street. It's on the right; a three-minute walk.

Currency Exchange: Lloyds Bank. The Square, Stow-on-the-Wold. Tel: 01451/ 830135. Open: Mon–Fri 9:30am–4:30pm.

Bike Rental: B. D. Jeffrey. The Toy Shop, Moreton-in-Marsh, 4 miles away. Tel: 01608/650756.

Telephone Code: 01451.

Getting There: Stow is not easy to get to, especially by public transportation. The closest **train** station is 4 miles away in Moreton-in-Marsh, which is on the London-Oxford-Worcester line. From there, hitchhiking or Pulhams Bus will get you out to the hostel. For train information, call 01452/529501. For local **bus** information, call Pulhams at 01451/820369. For destinations beyond the local Cotswold bus links, the closest bus station is in Cheltenham, about 20 miles away. National Express coaches from **London, Oxford, Cambridge,** and beyond come into Cheltenham, where you can get connecting buses out to Stow. For National Express info, call 01242/584111 or 0121/626 6226. **By car,** Stow is 20 miles south of Stratford-upon-Avon on the A429. From **London,** take the M40 past Beaconsfield and High Wycombe, following signs for Oxford. Just before Oxford, exit at Junction 8 (which is about 30 miles from Stow), and switch to the A40, following signs for Witney and Burford. At Burford, head north on the A424, which takes you directly into Stow.

What's Next

Those with young children or a strong interest in wildfowl may want to head south to **Slimbridge.** The main attraction in this part of the Cotswolds is the Wildfowl and Wetlands Trust, a nature reserve and museum. In the other direction, **Oxford** is just 30 miles away by bus (to Moreton) and then train. With its fabled university, soot-stained Carfax Tower, and wide expanse of park just outside the city center, it's a common stop for those doing the city circuit. **Bath** and **Bristol,** about two hours to the south, are also easy train rides from Stow. The former, one of England's celebrated Georgian cities, is modeled on the seven hills of Rome. The latter is a much-underrated, sophisticated university city with elegant neighborhoods, a swanky riverside hostel, hopping nightlife, and a good arts/music scene.

BATH

For two millennia, mysterious hot springs have lured wayfarers to Bath (115 miles west of London and 13 miles southeast of Bristol) in search of the healing properties said to emanate from the steaming baths. The sick, the dying, and the wealthy have traditionally come here. Since the Youth Hostel has been around, the sleep-sack and backpack brigade has gravitated here as well.

The Roman goddess Sulis was believed to be the force behind the city's potent pools—thus the original name of the city, Aquae Sulis. Although the water isn't swimmable or drinkable (a teenage girl in the 1970s died of meningitis from drinking it), this urban oasis still seems to radiate good vibes. One of the best-preserved 18th-century cities in the world, Bath has some of the most spectacular Roman remains in all Britain, plus a dizzying number of museums and historic homes built of golden-hued limestone in the Georgian style.

It takes at least a day just to walk around and drink in the scenery. Elegant terraces, sweeping colonnades, and royal gardens on the banks of the Bristol Avon make this a genteel city, despite the fair amount of tourist traffic. Bathe yourself in the nightlife here too. The city has an intense pub and club scene down by Walton Street, where jazz, blues, alternative, and all sorts of bands with unmentionable names turn up their amps.

The Youth Hostel is on top of it all. Literally. Situated in the elegant neighborhood of Bathwick Hill, Bath Youth Hostel is a well-kept Italianate villa with verandas and gardens. A relaxing and friendly spot, it's a great place to rest from sightseeing and hang out with other hostelers. The staff is chock-full of information on what to do in this pleasant, accessible, and inviting city.

✪ Bath Youth Hostel

Bathwick Hill
Bath, Avon BA2 6JZ
Tel: 01225/475674. Fax: 01225/482947.

Like the fair city itself, the Youth Hostel is a vision of loveliness. Seemingly a mirage in the eyes of those unlucky souls climbing Bathwick Hill, it's an imposing Italianate villa tucked away behind a lush, leafy driveway. It's worthy of much more than a one-night stopover.

The entrance hall and reception area, with comfy couches, welcome hostelers warmly. Chalkboards galore have information about walks, boat trips, historic tours, arts cinemas, and museums, many offering discounts for hostelers. The hostel itself is an architectural gem. Even the moldings are beautiful. The dining room has an Victorian-era chandelier showering light on the hostel grub.

Upstairs, the rooms are no less impressive, especially if you luck into one of the two Tower Rooms, which have their own bathroom and windows that open out onto the trees and city below. One even has a baby balcony. The dormitory rooms are more crowded but livable; nobody seems to spend much time in them anyway.

Hostelers hang out by the video games in the hallway, on the veranda out back, and on the lawn out front. Since the hostel has no curfew, you can really luxuriate in Bath at your leisure. The staff is a lively bunch of 20-somethings who know every last pub, rave club, dive bar, and vegetarian restaurant in the city. The hostel also offers a Historic Bath weekend package, which includes two overnights, two evening meals, two breakfasts, a combined ticket for museums, and a Guide Friday tour (adults £36; under 18 £28).

From the Bath Spa Train Station, catch Badgerline bus no. 18 (the University bus; 80p) and tell the driver to let you off at the Youth Hostel.

Alternatively, exit the station, go up Manvers Street, turn right onto North Parade Road, and cross over the river. Turn left onto Pulteney Road. When you reach the roundabout at Laura Place, turn right up Bathwick Hill. The hostel is up the hill on your left. This is not recommended: The walk takes 30 minutes, while the ride takes 10 minutes and is worth every penny.

The bus station is on Manvers Street. From there, take Badgerline bus no. 18 (see directions from train, given above).

The A36 is the main ring road that circles Bath (leading out to Bristol); take that out to the Sydney Gardens roundabout and follow the signs to the Youth Hostel up Bathwick Hill. The hostel is on your left, halfway up the hill. Beware that there's no parking at the hostel; you must find parking on the hill.

Open year-round. IBN and BABA.

Reception open 7:30am–11pm; early reservation and check-in is advised. No curfew. You can use a key code if you come back after 11pm.

125 beds. 2-, 4-, 5-, 6-, 8-, 12-, and 14-bed rooms. There's an annex with 4-bed rooms. Two twin Tower Rooms have sinks and amazing views.

£ Members: adults £8 (Jun–Aug £8.80); under 18 £5.35 (Jul–Aug £5.95). Bath also offers a family bed and breakfast discount, which is cheaper than the usual family price.

Fiesole Café serves meals. Self-catering kitchen facilities: a gleaming kitchen with microwave and full oven. Breakfast: 8–9am. Packed breakfast available; order in advance. Lunch: packed lunch only; should be ordered by 8pm the night before. Dinner: 5:30–7:30pm. Weekly menu is on the reception desk.

No table license.

Almost all rooms have lockers; valuables can also be stored in locked closet, and the staff will keep valuables behind desk.

Washers £1.50 per load; dryer 60p–80p.

P No parking at Youth Hostel; cars must find a spot on Bathwick Hill, which isn't difficult.

Services

⬛ Shop at Hostel sells postcards; toiletries; very cute and useful foldout maps; candy; Slow Coach tickets.

🛋 No separate common room; dining room doubles as a TV and postcard-writing room.

🚭 Not allowed, except on veranda.

♿ Not wheelchair accessible.

💱 Travelex currency exchange.

🔺 Bike shed; Turners Tickets (inexpensive bus tickets to London); Guide Friday tour bus tickets; combined ticket for Roman Baths and Costume Museum (Hostelling International discount).

Cheap Eats Nearby

Café Retro

Retro is definitely the name for this chic little spot with old-world ceilings, creaky wooden floors. and major mirrors. The chairs in this place are old church pews, but the bold and beautiful of Bath don't seem to mind squishing into them. A bulletin board bursts with flyers advertising everything from hip-hop music to aromatherapy. Burgers (£4.20–£5.20), sandwiches (£2.50–£3), and salads (£3–£5).

18 York St. Tel: 01225/339347. Open: Mon–Thurs 10am–6pm; Fri–Sat 10am–late; Sun 10am–6pm. Credit cards: AE, VA, MC, EC, DC, Access. From the hostel, go down Bathwick Hill and cross Pulteney Bridge. Take a left onto Grand Parade, and when you reach the far side of Orange Grove, turn right onto York Street. It's on your right; a 10- to 15-minute walk from the hostel.

Demuth's Coffee House & Restaurant

Tucked away on a side street behind the Abbey, this place is anything but medieval and somber. Pale-yellow walls decorated with modern art and plants give this vegetarian restaurant a relaxed, young atmosphere despite the ancient location. It has the Vegetarian Society's official stamp of approval. Pesto toast (£4.25), mozzarella salad (£3.65), and whole wheat pizza (£4.25). Vegan specials and yummy desserts. Also open for breakfast.

2 North Parade Passage, Bath. Tel: 01225/446059. Open: Mon–Fri 9:30am–10pm; Sat 9am–10pm; Sun 10am–9pm. Credit cards: VA, MC, EC, Access, Delta. From the hostel, go down Bathwick Hill to the Laura Place roundabout and cross Pulteney Bridge. Turn left on Grand Parade, left around the Orange Grove roundabout, and go around the abbey. Turn right on York Street and then left at North Abbey Passage. It's on your left, just off the green; a 15- to 20-minute walk from the hostel.

Grocery store: Waitrose, on Northgate Street, opposite the central post office. Open: Mon–Fri 9am–6pm; Sat 9am–5pm.

Experiences

There are so many sights in Bath that upon arrival it's wise to take a walk around the city to view the Royal Crescent, Queen's Parade, Queen Square, the river, and Royal Victoria Park (especially pretty during the annual flower show in late April). Peek into the **Roman Baths,** where steaming green waters bubble and boil in the middle of an impressive mazelike Roman building that was excavated only last century. Just outside is the formidable **Bath Abbey,** a 15th-century anachronism on the Roman/Georgian landscape but pleasantly peaceful and surprisingly educational; there are more than 50 stained-glass windows offering a quick and colorful history lesson on Jesus's life and times.

The Bath Abbey Music Society organizes organ recitals, Christmas concerts, and other events throughout the year, usually at a reasonable price.

Among the museums, the most celebrated (and worth the entrance fee) is probably the **Victoria Art Gallery,** displaying old masters, contemporary painters, and sculptors and a good collection of decorative arts as well. Bath is home to the headquarters of **The Royal Photographic Society** and has a regular schedule of internationally renowned photography exhibitions.

For outdoor pursuits, **The Avon Valley Cycleway** winds its way from Bath to Bristol, and **The Cotswold Way** is a 100-mile footpath from Bath north through the western Cotswolds, ending up in Chipping Campden. **Canal** and **river trips** are also available here and are pretty popular in summer. For alternative cafes, recording studios, and second-hand clothes shops, head to Walcot Street. **Bath Reclamation,** an old warehouse and open yard, is now a repository for old architectural remnants, and there's a stonemason and glassblowing workshop there, too.

Before going out after dark, first consult the *Venue,* a magazine (£1.50) that covers the arts/entertainment scene in Bath and Bristol, and then ask the ravers at the hostel reception desk. The Bell Pub is known for jazz, blues, and funk. For a wilder scene, the Hat and Feathers is for ravers; it's a stopover before heading out to clubs such as The Hub (on The Paragon) and Mole's (on George Street), both of which are right near The Bell. The hostel has a special deal with the Hub, and hostelers can get a discount with their Hostelling International card.

Festivals seem to pop up all year long here. They include the International Literature Festival (Feb) and the International Music Festival (May–June), which has a Festival Fringe that attracts jazz players, performance artists, jugglers, musicians, and the like.

The Roman Baths Museum. Bath. Tel: 01225/461111. Open: Apr–July and Sept: daily 9am–6pm. Aug: daily 9am–6pm and 8–10pm. Oct–Mar: Mon–Sat 9:30am–5pm; Sun 10:30am–5pm. Admission: adults £5; children £3. Combined ticket for Baths, Assembly Rooms, and Costume Museum for £6.60; the hostel offers this ticket at a discount.

Bath Abbey. Orange Grove, Bath. Tel: 01225/422462. Open: Apr–Oct: Mon–Sat 9am–6pm; Sun 1–2:30pm and 4:30–5:30pm. Nov–Mar: Mon–Sat 9am–4:30pm; Sun 1–2:30pm and 4:30–5:30pm. Heritage vaults open: Mon–Sat 10am–4pm. Admission: free.

Bath Abbey Music Society. Bath Abbey. Orange Grove, Bath. Tel: 01225/422462 or 01225/767317. Lunchtime recitals (£2.50–£3.50) and evening performances (£3.50–£8). Call for schedule.

Victoria Art Gallery. Bridge Street, Bath. Tel: 01225/461111. Open: Mon–Fri 10am–5:30pm; Sat 10am–5pm. Admission: free.

Royal Photographic Society. Milsom Street, Bath. Tel: 01225/462841. Open: daily 9:30am–5:30pm. Admission: adults £3; concessions £1.75; children and people with disabilities free.

Avon Valley Cycleway. Contact Avon Valley Cyclery. Arch 37, Bath Spa Station, Bath. Tel: 01225/461880. Bike rentals available.

The Cotswold Way. Contact The Cotswold Warden Service. County Planning Department, Gloucestershire County Council, Shire Hall, Gloucester GL1 2TN. Tel: 01452/425674.

Canal and river trips. Pulteney Princess. Pulteney Bridge. Tel: 01453/836639. Easter–Oct: daily departures on the half hour 10:30am–4:30pm; evening departures subject to demand.

Bath Festivals Booking Office/Bath Festivals Trust. Linley House, Pierrepoint Place, Bath. Tel: 01225/463362.

The Basics

Bath Tourist Office: Abbey Chambers, Abbey Churchyard. Tel: 01225/462831. Open: June 15–Sept 15: Mon–Sat 9:30am–6pm; Sun 10am–4pm. Sept 16–June 14: Mon–Sat 9:30am–5pm. From the hostel, take Bathwick Hill down to Laura Place, follow the street, and cross Pulteney Bridge. Turn left onto Grand Parade; the Abbey is in the far corner, near the Roman Baths. The office is behind the Abbey.

Post Office: Bathwick Hill Post Office. 2 George's Place. Tel: 01225/461771. Open: Mon–Fri 9am–1pm and 2–5pm; Sat 9am–12:30pm. From the hostel, go down Bathwick Hill, and it's on your right; a five-minute walk.

Currency Exchange: Travelex Currency Exchange at the hostel. American Express. 5 Bridge St. Tel: 01225/444747. Open: Mon–Fri 9am–5:30pm (Wed open at 9:30am); Sat 9am–5pm.

Telephone Code: 01225.

Bike Rental: Avon Valley Cyclery. Arch 37, by the Bath Spa Station (British Rail). Tel: 01225/461880. Full-day rental: city riders £10.50; cruisers £14.50; mountain bikes £22; rickshaws £25; tandems £20–28. Hourly and weekly rates available.

Getting There: Bath Spa is serviced by hourly Intercity **train** service from London **Paddington** (2 hours), **Oxford** (1½ hours), and **Cardiff** (1¼ hours). Trains to **Bristol** run every 20 minutes (15 minutes), and there is good service to **Exeter** and **Plymouth.** For information, call 0117/929 4255. **Coaches** leave from London **Victoria** every two hours (3 hours), **Bristol** every 15 minutes, and other cities as well. Turners Coachways (tel. 01272/555333) have a special deal, with convenient stops in London (including Earl's Court). For general bus information, call 01225/464446. By **car,** take the M4 motorway west from **London** (and east from Cardiff) to Junction 18. There, switch to the A46 south, which goes directly into Bath.

What's Next

Bristol is so close and yet so very far away. Bristol has a rough, tough reputation, probably from its ashy industrial heritage, and many hostelers think of it as a missable city. Only 14 miles away, Bristol is somewhat overshadowed by Bath's immense popularity: It's nevertheless one of Britain's most wonderful forgotten cities. Bristol is now a genteel cathedral and university city with a luxurious riverside hostel, an excellent alternative arts and music scene, and trendy restaurants and nightlife. Beyond Bristol and over the Severn Road Bridge lies **Cardiff,** the capital of Wales and another interesting, undiscovered gem. It has an ornate castle, a good smattering of Welsh museums, and a monstrous park. For countryside pursuits, head for the Cotswolds: **Slimbridge** is only 30 miles away from Bath and has a wildfowl nature reserve that's especially nice for children and families and nature lovers.

BRISTOL

Right across the Bristol Channel from Wales, Bristol (121 miles west of London and 14 miles northwest of Bath) is the largest city in England's West Country. Home to just over 400,000 souls, including a sizable university population, it's a sprawling, elegant city with a river and "floating harbor" winding around its relatively uncrowded streets.

Curiously enough, it has more Georgian architecture than Bath but a fraction of the tourists. In medieval days, Bristol was a trading center, thanks to its close proximity to the water. In the 1800s, it grew prosperous, benefiting from the brains of visionary engineer Isambord Brunel. He was the mastermind behind Bristol's Clifton Suspension Bridge, the steamship *Great Britain,* and the meticulously planned broad-gauge Great Western Railway, which has its terminus here at the Bristol Temple Meads station. All these accomplishments are living landmarks in modern Bristol.

Nevertheless, Bristol isn't content resting on its laurels. One of England's most progressive cities, it boasts a thriving contemporary arts and cinema scene at Arnolfini, Watershed, and a host of other cultural centers. The Bristol Old Vic, along with other drama venues, lives up to the city's reputation for theater and performance art. Boats sail by the riverside cafes, and shoppers wander in and out of chic boutiques and covered markets. On the main street by the university, bookstores, bars, trendy restaurants, and nightclubs keep students—and hostelers— entertained. The upscale neighborhood of Clifton, with a cathedral in its center, is perfect for meandering up its surprisingly hilly cityscape on sunny afternoons.

Bristol International YHA

64 Prince St.
Bristol BS1 4HU
Tel: 0117/922 1659. Fax: 0117/927 3789.

A converted grain warehouse right on the waterfront, this Youth Hostel should be filed under "T" for "too fancy to be a Youth Hostel." Wearing blue plastic nametags and guarding the reception with an official air, the efficient, professional staff seems ready to catapult their hostel headlong into a more upscale range of accommodations.

The basics are still here, though: There are communal bathrooms and dormitories, and the unmistakable aroma of freshly thawed steak pies sitting under heatlamps wafts up from the second-floor Harborside Restaurant. Nevertheless, this is one of the shinier, swankier, cooler hostels, and the restaurant actually serves meals to lots of nonhostelers who come here for the food.

Slated as a converted warehouse, the hostel has actually recently undergone a total overhaul worth at least a couple million pounds. It strikes a neat balance between retaining its original character (stone walls, pillars, sepia tints on the walls) and providing modern amenities (locks on all doors and a postmodern art-gallery ambience). An excellent book in the ground-floor hallway lists what to do in Bristol from A to Z; it's infinitely better than anything you could ask for in the tourist office. The nametag posse clearly knows what's going on in the area.

Right outside the hostel is the waterfront, and the annual regatta in July goes right past. Don't expect Warden Wendy's Flapjacks or home-baked bread here—this isn't a country hostel with homey touches. It's an International YHA: The building is impressive and the service professional—pretty much what you'd expect in this sophisticated city.

Services

🚆 Exit the station, turn right, and follow the signs to the city center and Youth Hostel. Once you reach the waterfront, bear left and follow Prince Street around; the hostel entrance is on the waterfront, so walk past the newsagent and turn left onto Farrs Lane and left again onto Narrow Quay. The entrance is on your left. It's a 15-minute walk. Alternately, take bus no. 9 to St. Augustine's Parade. From there, walk onto Prince Street and turn left onto Farrs Lane, which takes you to the waterfront; the hostel is on your left. If you get lost, ask for the Arnolfini.

🚌 Exit the Marlborough Street bus station in the same direction as the buses. Follow the road around to the left; pass the White Hart Pub on your left, which brings you to an intersection. When you reach the Artichoke Pub on your right, cross the street, and walk straight down until you reach St. Augustine's Parade. From there, walk straight until you reach the waterfront, passing the Hippodrome Theatre. Walk down the waterfront for about five minutes, and the hostel will come up on your left.

🚗 Follow signs to the city center, following the one-way system. From the M32, turn onto the M4, which brings you to Newfoundland Road. Turn right at the Broadmead Shopping Centre, and follow the road straight, following signs to the center. Pass through the center, and take Prince Street, which will come up on your left. The hostel is on your right, just past Jurys Hotel.

▦ Open Jan–Dec 20. IBN and BABA.

🕐 Reception open 7:30am–10:30pm. Curfew 2am.

🛏 130 beds. 2-, 4-, 5-, 6-, and 10-bed rooms. Some 4-bed rooms with bathrooms en suite. All rooms with locks on doors.

£ Members: adults £10.60; under 18 £7.20.

🍴 Wayfarer Café serves meals. Self-catering kitchen facilities. Breakfast: 7:45–9:15am. Lunch: noon–3pm. Dinner: 6–7:45pm. Snack menu available continuously until 7:45pm.

🍸 Table license.

▯ Lockers in bedrooms for use with padlocks. Padlocks for sale at reception (£2.50).

⊡ Washers, dryers, and drying room.

P None, except from 6pm–8am and on Sundays. Limited street parking nearby. Car park at nearby hotel.

🛍 Shop at hostel sells toiletries. Attractions leaflet with vouchers for local museums.

🎮 Games room, TV lounge (non-smoking).

🚬 In smoking section of cafeteria; in games room.

♿ Wheelchair accessible: large bedrooms; showers not en suite; elevator.

💱 Travelex currency exchange.

⚑ Bike room; three conference rooms with TV, overhead projectors, VCR, slide projectors.

Cheap Eats Nearby

The Bristol Coffee Company

Claiming it brews the best cappuccino in town, this pleasant natural-food cafe has a vintage atmosphere, with old armoires lying around and creaky wooden floors.

Good music on the airwaves. Soups £1.50 to £2.50. Interesting sandwiches £3 to £5. Bagels 50p. Specials £2.50 to £3.

39–41 St. Nicholas St., Bristol. Tel: 0117/925 0656. Open: Mon–Fri 7:30am–6pm; Sat 8am–5pm. Cash only. From the hostel, turn right onto Narrow Quay, right onto Farrs Lane, and left when you reach Prince Street. Pass the roundabout, and walk up Broad Quay, past the Hippodrome. Turn right onto Corn Street and right again on St. Nicholas Street. It's on the right; a 20-minute walk.

Rocinante's Café and Tapas Bar

The sophisticated young customers in this hip Mediterranean-style restaurant relax with drinks on the front patio on sunny days. Tapas galore. Patatas bravas, tortilla española, garlic mushrooms £1.95 to £4.95. Small dishes such as grilled fish, chicken and rice, ceviche £5 to £7. Seafood variada £8.

8 Whiteladies Rd. Tel: 0117/973 4482. Open: Mon–Sat 9am–11pm; Sun 10am–10:30pm. Reservations accepted. Credit cards: VA, MC, EC, Access, Switch. From the hostel, a 25-minute walk. Turn right onto Narrow Quay, right onto Farrs Lane, and left onto Prince Street. At the roundabout, bear left up Broad Quay, and just before the Hippodrome, cross the river and start walking up Park Street. Follow it up past the Wills Memorial Building, the City Museum and Art Gallery, and bear left onto Queen's Road. At the end of Queen's Road, pass Victoria Rooms and walk up Whiteladies Road. This place is on the right. The walk is worth it, I promise.

Grocery store: Asda. Coronation Road, Bristol. Open: Mon–Tues 9am–9pm; Wed–Fri 9am–10pm; Sat 8:30am–9pm; Sun 10:30am–4pm. Also, St. Nicholas Markets, off St. Nicholas Street, sells fruit, vegetables, cheese, meat, and other staples. Open: Mon–Fri 9am–4pm; Sat 9am–5pm.

Experiences

Bristol follows the mold of most English cities: Once you get past the congested area right around the Hippodrome, the city fans out. To the east is the **Bristol Old Vic,** which is still the preeminent local theatre and drama school. Here, performances of Gilbert and Sullivan and Arthur Miller run concurrently with the New Vic, which presents performances by visiting groups.

Up the street, **St. Nicholas Market** spans a couple of city blocks and sells everything from groceries to baby's clothes, comic books, and model trains under its canopy. To the west lie Bristol University, the Roman Catholic Cathedral, and the civilized enclave of Clifton, where tree-lined streets hide impressive houses and cool parks.

On Jacob Wells's Road is the **QEH Theatre,** where alternative drama and performance art compete with children's opera, classical music recitals, and a collection of offbeat offerings. To the north is Whiteladies Road, the main drag with all the usual university haunts: record stores, clothing shops, bookstores, and a relaxed 20-something scene at the outdoor patios of the trendy restaurants and pubs.

Near the lower end of Whiteladies Road, Queen's Road leads to the **City Museum and Art Gallery,** a massive building with a fairly impressive collection of modern art, old masters, and a comprehensive natural sciences wing. A bit farther down the road is the **Watershed Media Centre,** a cultural mecca with "world cinema" and two galleries' worth of painting, photography, and sculpture exhibitions. Upstairs, the lights go down at night when the bar, an airy, domed affair, fills up with Bristol's beautiful people admiring the river rushing below.

Back by the hostel, the **Arnolfini** is the other, and probably the better known, arts complex in town. With visual arts, dance, theater, music, film, and a bookshop, it keeps the other side of the river on the cutting edge of culture.

For less cerebral pursuits, there are **boat trips** around the city and even as far as Bath, and you can rent rowboats as well. The city, slightly eccentrically laid out, has enough to keep urban hostelers busy for at least a couple of days, so bring a map and expect to get a good workout walking around.

Bristol Old Vic. King Street, Bristol. Tel: 0117/987 7877. Box office open: Mon–Sat 10am–8pm (Thurs 10am opening) on performance days. Nonperformance days, box office closes at 5:30pm. Evening performances: adults £5–£17; concessions £3–£14. Matinees: adults £4–£11; concessions £2–£8. Bookings taken for New Vic performances as well.

St Nicholas Market. St. Nicholas Street, Bristol. Mon–Sat 9:30am–5pm.

QEH Theatre. Jacob's Wells Road, Bristol. Tel: 0117/925 0551.

City Museum and Art Gallery. Queen's Road, Bristol. Tel: 0117/922 3571. Open: daily 10am–5pm. Admission: adults £2; seniors £1; students free.

Watershed Media Centre. 1 Canon's Rd., Bristol. Tel: 0117/925 3845. Box office open: daily 11am–5:45pm. Access for people with disabilities. Films: adults £4; concessions £2.50. Photography gallery open: daily 11am–7pm. Admission: free.

Arnolfini. 16 Narrow Quay, Bristol. Tel: 0117/929 9191. Galleries open: Mon–Sat 10am–7pm; Sun noon–6pm. Admission: free. Cinema: times and prices vary. Access for people with disabilities.

Boat Trips. The Bristol Packet. Wapping Wharf, Gas Ferry Road, Bristol. Tel: 0117/926 8157. Apr–Oct. One-hour city docks tour: adults £2.90; seniors £2.15; children £1.85. Evening tour of dockside pubs: adults £6. Day trip to Bath: adults £9.50; seniors £8.50; children £6.50.

The Basics

Tourist Office: Bristol T.I.C. St. Nicholas Church, St. Nicholas Street, Bristol. Tel: 0117/926 0767. Open: daily 9:30am–5:30pm. From the hostel, turn right on Narrow Quay, right on Farrs Lane, and left on Prince Street. At the roundabout, go straight up Broad Quay, and turn right on Baldwin Street. Follow the signs and turn left up the steps. The entrance is on St. Nicholas Street; a 15-minute walk.

Post Office: The Post Office. Prince Street, Bristol. Tel: 0117/929 3348. Open: Mon–Thurs 9am–5:30pm; Fri 9:30am–5:30pm; Sat 9am–12:30pm. From the hostel, turn right on Narrow Quay, right on Farrs Lane, and left on Prince Street. The post office is three blocks ahead, at the corner of Queen Street; a 5- to 10-minute walk.

Currency Exchange: At the hostel. Also, American Express. 74 Queen's Rd., Clifton, Bristol. Tel: 0117/975 7001. Open: Mon–Fri 9am–5:30pm (Tues 9:30am opening); Sat 9am–5pm. Thomas Cook. Alliance House, 12 Baldwin St., Bristol. Tel: 0117/929 3621. Open: Mon–Thurs 9am–5:30pm; Fri 9:30am–5:30pm; Sat 9am–7pm.

Telephone Code: 0117.

Bike Rental: Mud Docks Cycleworks and Café. Tel: 0117/929 2151.

Getting There: Bristol is served by the Great Western Railways, linking it **by train** to London **Paddington** (hourly service), **Cardiff** (hourly service), **Bath** (every 15 minutes), as well as **Taunton, Plymouth,** and **Penzance.** For fare and schedule information, call 0117/929 4255. By **coach,** Bristol is serviced by National Express to London **Victoria** (2 ¹/₂ hours), **Bath,** and other cities in Southern England. For information, call 0117/954 1022. By **car,** Bristol is reachable from **London** via the M4. At Junction 19, switch to the M32 going south, straight into Bristol. From **Bath,** it's a straight zip up the A4, only 15 miles.

What's Next

The fabled city of **Bath,** with its healing waters; soothing, symmetrical Georgian architecture; wide colonnades; and sumptuous gardens, draws in just about anyone within a 40-mile radius. The hostel there, set up high on a hill, is a friendly scene with a young staff keeping the villa in ship-shape order and the hostelers happy. In the other direction, **Cardiff** is about an hour's train ride away. It's a nice introduction to Wales: With a lively arts scene, a ridiculously garish castle, some excellent museums on Welsh life, and a park or two, it's a good place from which to begin a trip into Celtic Country. Go south to **Salisbury** and you've got a mammoth cathedral and a mysterious bunch of rocks to ask you to ponder the questions that loom larger than the usual, "I wonder how long the walk is from the train station." It's a standard hostel in a standard cathedral city, but Stonehenge is hard to resist, and it's only a bus or bike ride from the town center.

LUDLOW

With 500 listed bulidings, Ludlow (pop. 8,000) is known for being the most beautiful small town in England. A gentle riverside town in the turbulent Shropshire countryside, near the border of England and Wales, Ludlow has been around since Domesday times, when Henry VIII built a clifftop castle here to protect the area against the invading Welsh. Ludlow's Georgian architecture belies the town's medieval roots. Sadly, the only vestiges of medieval architecture here are the castle and Broad Gate, which has now been painted over in white.

Nevertheless, there's an unusual confluence of ancient and modern here. The cobbled streets are well trodden on Market Day (check out the cattle market on Station Drive), and antique shops litter the main shopping streets leading up to the castle. Deviate a block from Broad Street and Mill Street might surprise you with its contemporary art installations and creative theater, cannily disguised on the very proper, very Georgian Broad Street.

In July, the Ludlow Festival comes to life with music, art, and one selected Shakespeare production staged in the inner bailey of the castle courtyard, complete with flying bats, whipping winds, and dramatic night skies as set design. For anyone traveling down to Wales from the north or traveling north from Cardiff, Ludlow makes a pleasant, restful stop. While there's not that much to do here, you might as well do nothing in a pretty setting.

Ludlow Youth Hostel
Ludford Lodge

Ludford, Ludlow
Shropshire SY8 1PJ
Tel: 01584/872472. Fax: 01584/872095.

On the banks of the River Teme, overlooking medieval Ludlow, the hostel is technically in the village of Ludford, even though it's right across the river from the town. The bulding is a few hundred years old and has been a Youth Hostel ever since the war.

It's easy to get to: Just walk through the pleasant town, cross the river, and there you are. A lovely little garden greets you out front. Elevated ever so slightly above the riverbank, it's on its own little perch from which you can sometimes spot herons, kingfishers, and dippers. The hostel is clean and quiet inside. It accommodates lots of cyclists, couples, and families who all come here for the Shropshire serenity. School groups also come around a lot, and the hostel is small, so be prepared: You may have to line up with a rowdy bunch of under-eights for the few showers. The warden, Linda, is a flexible, easygoing woman, and during festival time, she's willing to let hostelers in later so they can enjoy the local revelry.

Services

🚆 Turn right and walk down Station Road. Turn left onto Corve Street. Turn right onto King Street, then left onto Broad Street; follow it down through the archway, Broad Gate (at the bottom of the hill), then over Ludford Bridge (watch out for the traffic). The hostel is the first building past the bridge, on the left side; a 10-minute walk.

🚌 Buses leave you on Corve Street. From there, follow directions from train, given above.

🚗 From the A49 (the main north-south route from Shrewsbury-Hereford), follow signs to the town center of Ludlow. Those coming from the **south** will not pass through the town; the hostel is on the right just before Ludford Bridge. Those coming from the **north** will enter the town via Corve Street. Continue through Bull Ring and Old Street, following it all the way down to the river (keeping to the right). You will reach Ludford Bridge; cross it, and the hostel is the first building on the left, on the riverbank.

📅 Open Feb–Oct. Opening dates may vary and there are some closed periods. Call ahead to check. BABA.

🕐 Reception open 7–10am and 5–11pm. Curfew 11pm.

🛏 50 beds. 4-, 6-, and 8-bed rooms. Some with keys for daytime access.

£ Members: adults £6.55; under 18 £4.45.

🍴 Self-catering kitchen facilities. Breakfast: 8am. Lunch: packed lunch only; order by 10pm the night before. Dinner: 7pm.

🍸 No table license.

💼 No lockers.

⚪ Drying room only.

P Limited but free of charge. Free parking in the town.

🛍 Shop at hostel sells candy and canned goods.

🛋 One quiet room; one TV room.

🚬 In common room only.

♿ Not wheelchair accessible.

 See "Currency Exchange" under "The Basics" in Ludlow.

🔺 Bike shed.

Cheap Eats Nearby

Aragon Restaurant

Named for the queen whose marriage to Henry VIII was annulled up the street, this is a friendly, efficient little place. The decor follows the familiar, comfortable red-velvet-and-banquette motif, and the food is vaguely Italian: homemade pizzas sizzle at £2.75 to £4. Pastas are £4 to £6; omelets £1.95 to £3.75.

5 Church St., Ludlow. Tel: 01584/873282. Open: Sun–Thurs 8am–7pm; Fri–Sat 8am–10pm. During festival, open daily 8am–10pm. Credit cards: AE, VA, MC, EC, DC, Access. A 10-minute walk from the hostel: Turn right, cross the bridge, and walk up Broad Street. Turn left at Castle Street. When you reach Woolworth's, it's right across the street.

The Olive Branch

Whole foods are served with a smile in this airy light-wood cafeteria. Cauliflower-and-leek bake, celery-mushroom crumble, vegetarian chili among other delectables range from £4 to £5. Traditional English fare like steak-and-Guinness pie, pasties, and other gut-busting goodies also on offer (£4 to £5).

24 Old St., Ludlow. Tel: 01584/874314. Open: Mon–Fri 10am–3pm; Sat–Sun 10am–4pm. Cash only. A 10-minute walk from the hostel: Turn right, cross the bridge, and walk up Broad Street. Turn right at Brand Lane, and left onto Old Street. It's just ahead on the left.

Grocery store: Somerfield. Off Tower Street, Ludlow. Open: Mon–Fri 8:30am–8pm; Sat 8:30am–6pm; Sun 10am–4pm.

Experiences

Ludlow, with its medieval castle, cobbled streets, and more than 500 listed build-ings, is a sight in and of itself, especially on Market Monday. The architecture ranges from medieval to Elizabethan to Georgian, and together they compose a picturesque, soothing townscape. In 1065, Roger DeLacy built the castle and then laid out the town, so the very wide main streets have a convenient service road, making Ludlow a paradigm of the planned Norman town.

The town's eight bookshops and numerous antique shops can be lots of fun to prowl through, especially on the not-so-odd rainy day. The **Castle** is worth a visit and won't break the bank; it's especially nice during festival season when Shakespeare is performed at night in the inner courtyard.

The town's tourist office contains the small **Ludlow Museum,** with displays on the social and geological history of the area. The **Ludlow Assembly Rooms** are the heart of the local arts and music scene; they serve as a venue for bands and as exhibition space for local artists. Their cinema offers first-run movies.

Not far from the hostel, right on the banks of the River Teme, is the **Whitcliffe Common.** Townspeople used it for centuries as sheep-grazing land. A verdant open area for quiet riverside recreation and contemplation, it's still open to the public.

The Forestry Commission at nearby **Mortimer Forest** (one-half mile away) provides well-signed footpaths through this unspoiled woodland for walkers of all levels (some for the wheelchair-bound, too). There are excellent trails for watching deer and other wildlife. Geologists will find the local rock formations on the geol-ogy trail intriguing.

Festivals and open-air markets abound in Ludlow: Market Square, just outside the castle, hums on Mondays, Fridays, and Saturdays all year-round and on Wednes-day in summer. The **Ludlow Festival,** held during the last week in June and first week in July, offers theater, music, arts, and lots of "fringe," with street theater, bands, and other entertainers.

Ludlow Castle. Ludlow. Tel: 01584/873947. Open: Feb–Apr: daily 10:30am–4pm. May–Sept: daily 10:30am–5pm. Oct–Dec: 10:30am–4pm. Admission: adults £2.50; seniors £2; children £1.50.

Ludlow Museum. Ludlow T.I.C. Castle Street, Ludlow. Tel: 01584/875053. Open: Easter–Oct: Mon–Sat 10am–5pm; Sun 10:30am–5pm. Nov–Easter: Mon–Fri 10am–5pm; Sat 10am–4pm. Admission: adults £1; children 50p.

Ludlow Assembly Rooms. 1 Mill St., Ludlow. Tel: 01584/878141. Cinema: adults £2.50–£3; students and seniors £2–£2.50; children £1.50–£2. Crafts, arts, music, dance workshops £3–£5. Musical performances £3–£10. Get a copy of their *Events Diary* for current activities.

Mortimer Forest. Tel: 01584/874542. The Forestry Commission offers talks, walks, drives, and bike rides. Call for details.

Ludlow Festival. Late June to early July. Contact Ludlow's T.I.C. or the Festival Box Office, Castle Square, Ludlow, Shropshire, SY8 1AY. Tel: 01584/872150.

The Basics

Tourist Office: Ludlow T.I.C. Castle Street, Ludlow. Tel: 01584/875053. Open: Easter–Oct: Mon–Sat 10am–5pm; Sun 10:30am–5pm. Nov–Easter: Mon–Fri 10am–5pm; Sat 10am–4pm. From the hostel, a 10-minute walk: turn right, cross the bridge, and walk up Broad Street. Turn left onto Market Street, which turns into Castle Street after one block. It's on the left.

Post Office: Ludlow Post Office. 7 Corve St., Ludlow. Tel: 01854/872356. Open: Mon–Fri 9am–5:30pm; Sat 9am–12:30pm. From the hostel, turn right and cross the bridge. Turn right when you reach King Street, and turn left onto Corve Street. It's on the left; a 10-minute walk.

Currency Exchange: Barclays Bank. 3 King St., Ludlow. Tel: 01584/872484. Open: Mon 9am–5pm; Tues 10am–4:30pm; Wed–Fri 9am–4:30pm.

Telephone Code: 01584.

Bike Rental: Wheely Wonderful Cycling. Petchfield Farm, Elton (5 miles from Ludlow; will deliver). Tel: 01568/770755. Adult bikes: £10–£12 per day; £2–£3 per hour. Children's bikes: £6 per day; £2 per hour.

Getting There: Getting to Ludlow is easy by **train,** since it is right on the Cardiff-Manchester line, skirting the Welsh Borders. The cute little ticket hut at the station can be reached at 01584/877090, or else call Shrewsbury at 01743/364041 for info. By **coach,** it's not too hard, even though there isn't a real bus station in town. Midland Red West buses go to **Hereford, Cardiff,** and **Birmingham.** For information, call 01905/763888. By **car,** Ludlow is just off the A49, running between Hereford and Shrewsbury. From **London,** take the M4 west; cross the Severn Road Bridge into Chepstow. At Junction 22, change for the A466 going north in the direction of Monmouth. Just before King's Thorn, the A466 turns into the A49, which will take you up to Ludlow.

What's Next

There are a few other hostels nestled in the Welsh Borderland on either side of the boundary. North lies the walled cathedral city of **Chester,** a decidedly English settlement on the borderline between the two regions. Its medieval shopping arcades are something of an architectural anomaly: All the buildings were designed with stone stairs leading up to second-floor balconies, which are now peppered with cafes, boutiques, and jewelry stores. To the south, **Ludlow** is only a train ride away from **Cardiff,** the scrappy, workhorse capital city of Wales. Underneath the industrial grit coughed out of the nearby coal mines, the city is surprisingly lovely, with a ridiculously ornate castle, a small but lively arts movement, and a handful of unusual museums.

Manchester & the Peak District

In 1951, the Peak District became Britain's first national park, encompassing 542 square miles in north-central England. Despite the area's name, the hills never get too jagged or the heights too vertigo-causing, but the peaty moors and smooth, slippery limestone present challenging climbing surfaces. Separated by the broad shale valleys of the Wye and Derwent Rivers, the region is divided into two territories: the Dark Peaks and the White Peaks.

The millstone grit moors and precipitous crags of the Dark Peaks are found in the north, west, and east, culminating in the 2,000-foot Kinder Scout in the north. The village of Edale sits amid the somber grit-stone moors beneath Kinder Scout and marks the beginning of the Pennine Way. Just over the hill underneath an old castle and an abundance of caves lies Castleton.

The charming market town of Bakewell, with its honey-colored buildings and open-air stalls, is nestled amid porous rocks and limestone ridges. Farther south, Matlock offers spa waters and a cable-car ride that takes you to dizzying heights above the limestone countryside. The village of Ilam boasts a historic stone mansion and countryside estate that's now home to ducks, birds, flowers, and a splendid Youth Hostel. Although hill walking is the pastime of choice around here, the area has an array of sights: heathered moors, stately homes, historical viaducts belying abandoned railway lines, a plague village, and colorfully "dressed" wells.

The nearest large city is Manchester, to the northwest of the Peaks. The industrial, administrative, and cultural capital of the area, it contains music venues, art exhibitions, and historical museums that chronicle the eclectic history of this once-depressed city. It boasts a revived canalside district and a lively nightlife, as well as a tantalizing selection of shopping. Vintage clothing stalls, purveyors of New Age products, record shops, and commercial stores are all within walking distance of the swanky Youth Hostel. From here, you can hop a train and get to the Peak District within an hour.

Buses shuttle through the Peak District with decent service. You must be patient, however: 10-mile rides can become hour-long odysseys on the winding roads here.

MANCHESTER

The locals in Snowdonia and the Peak District seem to think of Manchester as nothing more than a big industrial eyesore amid their mystical mountaintop enclaves. At first glance, this may seem true: Motorcycle shops, computer stores, and smokestacks do seem to dominate the cityscape. Those who pry beneath the surface, however, are rewarded with a load of museums and galleries, an excellent music scene, tons of cheap shopping, and a recently revamped canalside area where urban renewal is in full swing. The Castlefield area (home to the luxury hostel) boasts a hands-on science museum, canal rides, and a visitors center that touts the neighborhood's electic heritage of Roman history and more recent industrial development.

All over the city, art and commerce make strange but stimulating bedfellows. Ethnic restaurants and open-air bars sit tucked in between factories and warehouses. The Oldham Street area has always been, and continues to be, the place for bar hopping, listening to music, and general hanging out. Markets abound. There's a New Age market at the Corn Exchange, and Affleck Palace is a two-story arcade with biker shops, mod-1960s clothing stores, old record shops, and cool cafes.

The city, a center of liberal politics, has absorbed lots of young English migrants in recent years. It isn't a bad spot for intrepid hostelers as well.

Manchester Youth Hostel

Potato Wharf, Castlefield
Manchester M3 4NB
Tel: 0161/839 9960. Fax: 0161/835 2054.

In March 1995, the Youth Hostel here was built at a cost of £2 million. The hostel is a gleaming brick-and-glass structure sitting right between Liverpool Road and the canal, across from the Science Museum. It's smack in the heart of the city's formerly industrial (now verging on swanky) Castlefield area, the center of the city's recent urban renewal.

What that means for hostelers is a big-city hostel with the sparkle of recent renovation but still at relatively low prices. It's got brand-new everything: squeaky clean rooms (with their own showers and toilets), lounges with framed oil paintings and a monster TV, and a modern cafeteria with a good, varied menu. It's also one of the few hostels completely outfitted with wheelchair-accessible rooms and baths.

Whether you're here for the underground grunge music scene or the rugged hills just outside the city in the Peak District, this is a sumptuous place to rest your bones. Enjoy it while it still glistens and before the school-group circuit finds its way up here.

Services

🚋 From Piccadilly Station, take the MetroLink to G-Mex centre. Take the elevated walkway to Castlefield, go around the canal, and turn left. The YHA is behind the Castlefield hotel. Bus no. 33 also goes directly from the station to Liverpool Road and drops you off across from the Science Museum. Walk up Liverpool Road with the Castlefield Hotel to your left, turn left at Potato Wharf, and the hostel is on the left under the first bridge.

🚌 The bus station is on Cannon Street, by the Arndale Centre. Exit, turn right, and cross Corporation Street. Pass the Corn Exchange, walking down Cateaton Street onto Victoria Street. Follow it as it turns into Deansgate until you reach Liverpool Road (after 5–10 minutes). Turn right onto Liverpool Road, and pass the Castlefield Centre on your left and the Science Museum on the right. The Youth Hostel is about a block up, on the left. Walk through the car park, and it's to your left, on the canal.

🚗 Every motorway coming into Manchester has brown tourist signs pointing to Castlefield and the Museum of Science and Industry. Follow the signs, and once you're on Liverpool Road turn onto Potato Wharf; the hostel is on your left.

▦ Open year-round. IBN and BABA.

🕐 Reception open 24 hours; check in at any time.

🛏 152 beds. Four-bed standard and premium rooms. Six-bed economy rooms. Premium rooms have TVs, kettle for tea/coffee, table. Standard and economy are the same except for number of beds. Rooms for people with disabilities with extra bed for attendant and bathroom en suite. All rooms have bathrooms en suite.

£ Members: adult premium £12; adult standard £10.60; adult economy £9. Under 18 premium £8.40; under 18 standard £7.20; under 18 economy £6.50

The Canalside Restaurant serves meals. Self-catering kitchen facilities including microwave. Breakfast: 7:30–9:30am. Lunch: packed lunch only; order by 11pm the night before. Dinner: 5:30–7:45pm. Set menu only (choices available); £4.

Table license.

All rooms have lockers; bring your own padlock. Coin-operated lockers available as well (coins returned); staff will also guard valuables in the office.

Washers (£1.50), dryers take 20p coins (one load usually takes £1).

Ample; in front of hostel. Free of charge.

Shop at hostel sells National Express tickets, souvenirs, toiletries, and stamps.

Lounge; TV room; games room.

In entrance hall and TV lounge only.

Fully wheelchair accessible; rooms for people with disabilities include bathrooms en suite and extra beds for attendants.

Travelex currency exchange.

Bike shed.

Cheap Eats Nearby

Al-Faisal Tandoori

This is one of a number of inconspicuous, inexpensive Indian luncheonettes in the Tib Street area. Generous portions of fresh food are served at low prices: chicken or lamb tikka £2.60; vegetable curry a steal at £1.60. An especially good location before bar hopping afterward.

58 Thomas St., Manchester. Tel: 0161/834 3266. Open: Mon–Wed 11am–7pm; Thurs–Fri 11am–8pm; Sat 11am–7pm; Sun 11am–4pm. Cash only. From the hostel, turn right on Liverpool Road, left on Deansgate, right on Peter Street. Turn left up Mosley Street, follow the street on the left, and it turns into Tib Street. Go up Tib Street and then left on Thomas Street. It's on your left; a 20-minute walk.

Dry 201 Bar

Don't let the name fool you: All sorts of beverages flow freely here amid the strains of house, funk, and New Order tunes (New Order owns the place). In the front, is a spacious mirrored bar with a hip crowd. Further inside lies brightly painted Tommo's Tasty Tapas, where surprisingly authentic Spanish *comida* is served in snack-size *tapas* (£1.50 to £3) or meal-size *raciones* (£2.50 to £5). Regular entrées are also available (£4 to £6). The Happy Mondays love this place so much they filmed a video upstairs.

28/30 Oldham St., Manchester. Tel: 0161/226 5920. Open: Mon–Sat noon–7pm. Bar open: Mon–Sat noon–11pm. Cash only. From the hostel, turn right on Liverpool Road, left on Deansgate, and right on Peter Street. Go straight up Mosley Street, passing Piccadilly Gardens on your right. Bear right onto Piccadilly then left onto Oldham Road, and the bar is on your right. A 20-minute walk.

Grocery Store: Marks and Spencer, Cross Street. Open: Mon 10am–5pm; Tues–Wed 9am–6pm; Thurs 9am–8pm; Fri 9am–6pm; Sat 8:30am–6pm; Sun 11am–5pm. There's also a fruit-and-vegetable market on Church Street, between Tib and Jones Street, in front of the bus station.

Experiences

With Manchester University, Manchester Metropolitan University, and three other universities here, there's a huge student population that seems to converge on the bars and shops. **Affleck Palace,** with its stalls selling biker togs, used records, furry Lycra and vintage clothes, T-shirts, incense, and jewelry, provides hours of slacker shopping. Just up the road on Corporation Street is the Corn Exchange, where a New Age market holds court upstairs. Downstairs from the Affleck Palace is the Iso Bar, and up the road on Oldham Street, bars such as Dry 201, Night and Day, and others attract local musicians, artists, university students, and anyone else under age 35.

Up Tib Street, tons of Middle Eastern and Indian restaurants quietly serve up inexpensive food. Nearby, Chinatown also offers grub, though it's slightly removed from the cool kids.

There are art galleries all over the city. Cafe/bars, which display art on the walls, mostly lie in the Oldham Street area and on Whitworth Street. Also on Whitworth Street is the **Hacienda,** Manchester's legendary concert venue that has hosted the likes of Erasure, the Violent Femmes, Madonna, and New Order when they were just emerging. It still has house music, gay nights on Wednesdays, jungle nights, and regular concerts that entertain locals and dance/music fans from all over England.

The **Castlefield Gallery,** on the corner of Deansgate and Liverpool Road, features excellent contemporary art installations and is the only artist-run gallery in Northern England. Up-and-coming painters, sculptors, photographers, as well as more recognized artists display their works and give lectures here. Just up the road from the Castlefield Gallery is the **Museum of Science and Industry,** with hot-air engines, waterwheels, and the oldest steam train in England. The **Manchester City Art Galleries,** the People's Museum, and the Jewish Museum round out the cultural sights, making Manchester a much more intriguing place than it would seem on its sooty surface.

Affleck Palace. Affleck's Arcade, Manchester. Open: Mon–Fri 10am–5:15pm; Sat 9:30am–5:30pm.

The Hacienda. 11/13 Whitworth St. West. Tel: 0161/236 5051. Fri–Sat: cover £8–£15.

Castlefield Gallery. 5 Campfield Ave. Arcade, Manchester. Tel: 0161/832 8034. Open: Tues–Fri 10:30am–5pm; Sat–Sun noon–5pm. Admission: free.

Museum of Science and Industry. Liverpool Road, Castlefield, Manchester. Tel: 0161/832 2244. Open: daily 10am–5pm. Admission: adults £4; concessions £2.

Manchester City Art Galleries. Mosley and Princess streets, Manchester. Tel: 0161/236 5244. Open: Mon–Sat 10am–5:45pm; Sun 2–5:45pm. Admission: free.

The Basics

Tourist Office: Manchester Tourist Information Centre. Town Hall Extension, St. Peter's Square, Manchester. Tel: 0161/234 3157. 24-hour information line tel: 0189/171 5533. Open: Mon–Sat 10am–5:30pm; Sun 11am–4pm. From the hostel, turn right on Liverpool Road, left on Deansgate, right on Peter Street. Cross St. Peter's Square, and bear left after the Old Library. It's on your left; 10–15 minutes from the hostel.

Post Office: 26 Spring Gardens, Manchester. Tel: 0161/837 8253 or 0161/839 0697. Open: Mon–Fri 8:30am–6pm; Sat 8:30am–7pm. From the hostel, turn right and walk down Liverpool Road. Turn left onto Deansgate and walk about

10 minutes until you reach King Street; turn right and follow King Street to Spring Gardens. It's across the street.

Currency Exchange: at the hostel. Also at Thomas Cook. 2 Oxford St. Tel: 0161/ 236 8575. Open: Mon–Fri 9am–5:30pm; Sat 9am–5pm.

Telephone Code: 0161.

Bike Rental: in Withington (3 miles away). Withington Cycles. Burton Road. Tel: 0161/445 3492. Open: Mon–Sat 9am–6pm. £5–10 per day, plus deposit.

Getting There: Manchester is well connected by **train;** Piccadilly is the main station in town; it's on the main line from London-Carlisle and Glasgow and on the line that connects Liverpool-Hull to the east. For information, call 0161/832 8353. National Express **coaches** come into Chorlton Street Bus Station from major cities in England. For information, call 0161/228 3881. Coming by **car,** take the M1 from **London** to Birmingham and then pick up the M6 north to Junction 19. Switching to the A556 north and then the M56 into Manchester. Follow the signs to the hostel.

What's Next

Manchester is an excellent place to start a tour of the Peak District. **Edale,** at the start of the Pennine Way and in the heart of the Dark Peaks, is only 50 miles southeast of Manchester via an easy train ride. With the dramatic ridge of Kinder Scout right behind the hostel, it's a great spot for climbing, abseiling, and other adventure sports. The hostel there is one of the YHA's Activity Centres, offering weekend packages in a variety of different sports, from canoeing to hang gliding to caving. Only two miles farther is the pristine town of **Castleton,** with its quarries and show caves. Beyond lies the market town of **Bakewell,** famous for its local tart and some more rigorous hill walking to work it off.

EDALE

It's hard to believe Edale is only 50 miles away from smoky, industrial Manchester. Pull out your regional railways map and there it is, in black, white, and magenta, about halfway down the Manchester-Sheffield rail line that zips through the farmland and rolling hills of Derbyshire.

One of the central villages in the Peak District National Park, Edale is little more than a two-pub, one-store town that sees most of its action on the marshy bogs, grassy highlands, and riverside paths that comprise this Area of Outstanding Natural Beauty. People from all over England come here armed with their Wellies to wander through the gentle (often muddy) hills and hike through the peaceful (often muddy) moors and bogs that seem to turn up at every mountain pass. Rocky paths offer a good challenge to mountain bikers and equestrians who trot their way through the local bridlepaths.

At the starting point for the Pennine Way, Edale is a gateway to northern England. Even if you don't have the time or inclination to make the 250-mile trek, you can take full advantage of the great outdoors here. The area is full of short paths, and the hostel doubles as a YHA Activity Centre that plans weekend courses for those who want a bit of structure. Among the sports on offer are abseiling, caving, kayaking, and hill walking, all taught by a host of extremely capable (and extremely cute) professionals. Otherwise, the hills, dales, and vales are yours to enjoy, no entrance fee required.

Edale Youth Hostel & Activity Centre

Rowland Cote
Edale, Derbyshire S30 2ZH
Tel: 01433/670302. Fax: 01433/670243.

The 18th century marks the beginning of this former country mansion's recorded history. September 1732 was when Joshua Hardy tearfully sold his beloved home to John Tym of Castleton, who kept the place in his family for years and years, to the chagrin of its original owner. In October 1986 Joe Hardy returned to the home of his namesake. With a family in tow and the ardent memory of his ancestors fresh in his heart, he whipped the place into shape, eventually turning it into one of the premier hostels in Northern England. In 1987, he officiated the inauguration of the Edale Activity Centre, created to offer weekend and week-long courses for unfortunate souls not as muscle bound and fit as he.

In 1995, it was still booming with, yes, activity. A sizable stable of pumped-up young adults, all with mile-long lists of athletic accomplishments, teach courses in this heavenly setting. The hostel itself is pretty cute too. The bedrooms are named after hills in the surrounding landscape: Mam Tor, Back Tor, Seal Edge. This adds the slight feel of an elementary school to the place, which isn't surprising, since squawking schoolchildren can be both seen and heard from as far away as the bottom of the hostel drive.

The dining room downstairs is full of light and a nice place to gulp down your meal before heading off to the more peaceful sitting rooms, where books, board games, and a television provide evening entertainment. The guest list here is diverse: Student groups, English walkers, international backpackers, and special-interest groups using the hostel's conference facilities make for a potpourri of interesting conversationalists and can be good hunting ground for walking/climbing companions.

Services

🚆 The Youth Hostel is 1¹/₂ miles from the Edale train station on the Manchester-Sheffield line. From the station, exit, turn right and you'll reach a junction with Youth Hostel signs. Turn left there and follow the road for about 1¹/₂ miles. The Youth Hostel will come up on your left. There's a slight hill toward the end. It's about a 40-minute walk. If you're arriving for an activity weekend, a van will meet the afternoon train and drive you up to the hostel.

🚌 Buses do come into Edale *very* infrequently from Hope and Castleton, but when they do, they stop at the bottom of the hostel drive.

🚗 Coming from the **east,** follow signs to Hope. The road opposite the church has a sign pointing to Edale. The sign takes you directly to the hostel, which will come up on your right. From the **west,** follow signs to Chapel-en-le-Frith. Once there, follow the A625 as far as Man Tor, and look for the Edale sign on your left. You will suddenly come to the top of a hill; follow this road down the valley. The hostel will come up on your left.

🗓 Open year-round, with the exception of two weeks in Dec. Call ahead to check. BABA.

🕐 Reception open 7am–10:30pm. Curfew 11:30pm.

🛏 141 beds. 2-, 3-, 4-, 6-, 7-, 8-, and 12-bed rooms available in three separate buildings. Some rooms en suite with keys for daytime access.

£ Members: adults £8.80; under 18 £5.95.

🍴 Self-catering kitchen facilities. Breakfast: 7:30–8:30am. Lunch: packed lunch only; order the night before. Dinner: 5:30–7:15pm. Set menu only (minimum of three choices).

🍸 Table license.

💼 No lockers. All rooms have locks.

⬜ Washers (£1.50) and dryers 50p. Drying room.

P Out front; ample and free of charge.

🛍 Shop at hostel sells very limited selection of candy and canned foods.

Souvenirs and the much-coveted YHA polo shirt for sale here (£11.99). Maps, walking guides available.

🛋 Lounge; games room with pool, video games, and TV.

🚬 Definitely.

♿ Not wheelchair accessible.

💱 See "Currency Exchange" under "The Basics" in Edale.

🔺 Bike shed; study rooms with overhead projecters, flip charts; activity center with organized outdoor activities.

Cheap Eats Nearby

The Old Nag's Head

The local hiker's bar, this place is at the very start of the Pennine Way and atop a rocky stream. All your usual bar food. Soup £1.35. Cornish pasty with jumbo sausage £4.75. Cod fillet £4.50. Yorkshire pudding with stew £4.95.

Edale. Tel: 01433/670291. Open: Apr–Oct: daily 11:30am–11pm. Nov–Mar: daily noon–3pm and 7–11pm. Credit cards: VA, MC, EC, DC, Access. From the hostel, walk down the driveway and turn right. It's 1¹/₂ miles down the footpath, in the direction of the railway station; a 40-minute walk.

The Rambler Inn

A friendly little joint with the same-old-same-old. Steak-and-kidney pie £4.95; veggie burger £1.75; lasagne £4.95.

Edale. Tel: 01433/670268. open: Apr–Sept: Mon–Sat 11am–11pm; Sun noon–10:30pm. Oct–Mar: Wed–Sat noon–3pm and 7–11pm. Cash only. From the hostel, a 45-minute walk. Turn right out of the hostel. Follow the road until you reach a car park. Turn right and it's on your left as you approach the railway station.

Experiences

Because of Edale's choice location in the middle of a national park, you can pick from a number of organized outdoor sports activities. You can also have a great time here without spending much money. **Mountain biking** up the paths that crawl behind the hostel is possible on your own or with a guide. **Pony trekking** is available right at the bottom of the hostel driveway. Hang gliding, in the capable hands of the **Peak School of Hang Gliding,** can be practiced in the local hills. Water sports are a possibility but are about 30 miles away in **Rother Valley County Park** (accessible by public transport).

Walking trails abound high above the local valley. **Kinder Scout** is a steep hill just behind the hostel. It offers panoramic vistas of the valley, including the two-car Manchester-Sheffield train that zips through the countryside. It traverses peat bogs and marshy farmland, so be careful of the weather. It's extremely easy to get extremely lost around here, so in addition to good hiking boots and a water bottle, pack a good Ordnance Survey map before taking off. Nearby, **Mam Tor** ("Mother Hill") is also a popular hill to climb. It's the peak that separates the Edale Valley from Castleton with the creepy, slimy caverns lurking under the hills. The **Pennine Way** begins at the Old Nags Head pub in Edale village, and walkers from all over England embark on the journey from there. It's designed as a walking route, so mountain bikers must use an alternate route.

A great way to hook up with other travelers is to go on one of the **Activity Centre's** weekend packages, but this requires advance planning and advance payment. Participants, in addition to full board, get taken to local pubs at night if the staff are so inclined, which makes it kind of casual and fun.

For information on local goings-on, check out the Parish newsletter, *Ringing Roger*. The dates for the annual Harvest Festival (late October), the Firework and Bonfire Party, and Horticultural Show are all in there; the festivals are a neat way to spend a couple of days here.

Mountain bikes. The hostel make arrangemens for you (call in advance), and they'll deliver the bike to the hostel. Alternatively, you can arrange rentals yourself: Mode. Tel: 01836/291740. David Buckingham. Tel: 0161/447 7346.

Lady Boothe Pony Trekking. Edale. Tel: 01433/670205. £12 per day. Call 3–4 days in advance. A two-minute walk from the hostel.

Peak School of Hang Gliding. Sheffield. Tel: 01335/312357. Based in Sheffield, but they offer classes in the hills about 5–6 miles from the hostel.

Peak Paragliding. Tel: 0114/274 8796. Operates in the hills 5–6 miles away from the hostel.

Watersports at Rother Valley Country Park. Rother Valley (30 miles away). Tel: 0114/247 1453. Canoeing, sailing, and windsurfing.

Edale Activity Centre. Edale Youth Hostel, Rowland Cote, Edale. Tel: 01433/670302. Week-long and weekend activity courses available in parasailing, hang gliding, kayaking, canoeing, abseiling/rock climbing, mountain biking, walking. Packages from around £80 include accommodations, full board, all transportation and equipment, as well as pickup from the Edale train station.

The Basics

Tourist Office: Peak National Park Information Centre. Edale. Tel: 01433/670207. Open: daily 9am–5:30pm. Maps, books, and a cute display on the national park. From the Youth Hostel, go straight down the road into town; it's on your right past the train station.

Post Office: Edale Post Office. High Street, Edale. Tel: 01433/670220. Open: Mon–Tues 9am–1pm and 2–5:30pm; Wed 9am–midnight; Thurs–Sat 9am–1pm and 2–5:30pm. From the hostel, walk down the driveway, turn right, and head straight into town. From the train station, it's up the road and to the left.

Currency Exchange: The closest place is in Hathersage, 10 miles away. National Westminster Bank. High Street, Hathersage. Open: Mon–Fri 9am–4:30pm.

Telephone Code: 01433.

Bike Rental: can be done through the Edale Youth Hostel; call in advance.

Taxi: tel: 01433/620732 or 01433/620221.

Getting There: Trains are the main way to get here; Edale is about midway on the Manchester-Sheffield train line, and trains dart out of both places almost hourly. The hostel itself is 1$\frac{1}{2}$ miles from the station, so you can walk it or get there by taxi. Forget about **buses** when it comes to Edale. Buses run very infrequently from Hope and Castleton (on Sundays and bank holidays in the summer), so you're best bet is the train. By **car,** Edale is reachable by the M1 from **London,** the A6 from **Manchester,** and the M1 from York.

What's Next

For those who want city life, clubs, music, and a grunge shopping arcade, **Manchester** is a mere 50 miles—and a whole world—away; it's an easy hop on the train. For intrepid hostelers unlikely to be capsized by cumbersome rucksacks, the hostelling association publishes a leaflet entitled *Peak District Inter-Hostel Walking Routes.* You can take your pick from these routes. An easy one to start out with is the Edale-Castleton hop; it's only about four miles, less if you go through the farm path. Just make sure you do it in the morning before the sun gets too high. There is one steep, rocky area, so those without walking/hiking boots should take special care. **Castleton** is known for its caving, and there are a few interesting caves dripping with muck sure to delight spelunkers of all ages.

CASTLETON

Castleton is a happy little village. Why shouldn't it be? Tourists can't get enough of this place: Smack in the middle of the Peak district, Castleton has an old castle, stone houses, quaint gift shops, and four (heavily promoted) caves.

The limestone of the White Peak district and the gritstone of the Dark Peaks come together in Castleton, a village that saw its heyday as a tin- and lead-mining town in Norman times. The castle was built to ensure Norman control over the area, and the ruins of this fort are a short walk up from the village center.

Walkers trekking through the White Peak Way (a 90-mile walk from Youth Hostel to Youth Hostel) and day-trippers from nearby Manchester and Sheffield stop here for the bucolic small-village setting. Budding geologists and spelunkers are lured by the gooey prehistoric drippings in the local caves, where they can see stalactites and stalagmites taking shape in the dark caverns. The caves lurk underneath Mam Tor, also known as the "Shivering Mountain." Every so often, crumbling layers of her gritstone and shale tumble down the hill, causing land slips. That's the most excitement this place seems to get outside of Garland Day, the ancient annual fertility festival held here in May.

The village, with its lovingly restored country-home-turned-hostel, is a charming place to stay for a night or two. If you're not a cave enthusiast or a devoted walker, however, you may be hard-pressed for activity in this hamlet.

✸ Castleton Youth Hostel

Castleton Hall
Castleton, Sheffield S30 2WG
Tel: 01433/620235. Fax: 01433/621764.

Ahh, Alistair! The local tourist brochure reads, "Look at Castleton," but some travelers might just prefer to look at wonder warden Alistair in action—he's much cuter. He and his staff run a most unusual hostel. Bordering on sumptuous, it was recently (but sensitively) renovated, and it shows. Alistair and his staff seem to really care about about the village, the guests, and the hostel. A little leather-bound menu lists the varied dining choices, and French, Chilean, and other wines are on offer.

Castleton Hall was originally a family home; later it was converted into a tithe barn where people would come to pay their church taxes. Various families owned it; the last owners made their fortune in cutlery, and the house was quite luxurious. Rooms 1 and 2 housed the family's crystal collection. Rooms 12, 14, and 16 comprised the family dining room. In addition, this building has what was the first flushing toilet in Castleton.

The vicarage next door functions as annex. It has lots of old fireplaces and nooks for special mountain moments. Christmas is an especially fun time here: Alistair organizes walks on Christmas Eve (you can watch him come running up Mam Tor dressed as Santa Claus), and there might also be caving and climbing depending on the weather. Whatever the season, however, Alistair and staff (especially Alistair!) won't disappoint.

Services

🚆 Hope is the closest train station, 2 miles away (on the Manchester-Sheffield line). Exit the station, turn right, and walk up the main road. When you get into the village, turn left onto Castle Street; the hostel is on your right, just across the street from the church. Alternately, take the no. 272 bus right into the village. From the bus stop, turn right, pass the post office, and left onto the main road. Turn left at the Castle Pub and the hostel is up the road on your right.

🚌 The local bus stop is on How Street, just up from the post office. When you get off, turn right, pass the post office, and turn left onto the main road. Turn left again at the Castle Pub, and the hostel is up the road on your right.

🚗 From the **west,** look for signs to Castleton Caverns, which will bring you into the village. At the Castle Pub, turn right; the hostel is on your right, across from the church in the center of the market place. From **Sheffield,** head straight up the A625, which takes you directly into town. Turn left at the Castle Pub, and the hostel is up the road on your right, just across the street from the church.

🗓 Open Feb–Jan 1. The hostel is closed for two weeks in January; it varies from year to year, so call ahead to check. Rent-a-hostel: available when the hostel is closed. BABA.

🕐 Reception open 7am–11pm. Curfew 11pm.

🛏 145 beds in the main building, barn, and vicarage. 2-, 4-, 6-, 8-, and 10-bed rooms available. All rooms have keys for daytime access.

£ Members: adults £8; under 18 £5.35.

🍴 Self-catering kitchen facilities. Breakfast: 7:30–8:30am. Lunch: packed lunch only; should be ordered by the evening before. Dinner: 6, 6:30, or 7pm.

🍸 Table license.

🎒 No lockers, but all rooms lock; the staff will guard valuables on request.

🧺 No laundry facilities; staff will do laundry for a nominal fee.

P Parking nearby; free of charge and ample.

🛍 Shop at hostel sells canned goods, candy, souvenirs.

🛋 Quiet room with good nature library; games room with video games, pool, Ping-Pong, foosball.

🚬 In games room and common room only.

♿ The barn and vicarage (annexes) have wheelchair-accessible rooms with wheelchair-accessible bathrooms.

💱 See "Currency Exchange" under "The Basics" in Castleton.

🔺 Bike shed; small classroom with overhead and slide projector and TV/video.

Cheap Eats Nearby

Hilary Beth's Tea Room

This old stone building has whitewashed walls, lace tablecloths, and shining china. There's seating on the patio when weather permits. Toasted sandwiches £1.60 to £1.75. Ploughman's lunch £2.25. Scones with jam and cream 90p.

1 Laburnum Market Place, Castleton. Tel: 01433/620397. Open: Jan–June: Fri–Mon, Wed noon–5pm. July–Sept; Dec: daily 11am–6pm. Closed: Oct–Nov. Cash only. From the hostel, turn right and walk to the marketplace. It's on the right.

The Peak Hotel

Those ubiquitous red-velvet banquettes, a pool table, and an array of ales make this the general favorite among local climbers. Vegetarian dishes include veggie burger and spinach cannelloni (£3.50 to £4.95). Grilled trout and fried haddock £5 to £6. Sunday is quiz night.

How Lane, Castleton. Tel: 01433/620247. Open: daily noon–2:30pm and 6:30–9pm. Cash only. From the hostel, a five-minute walk: turn left and walk to the main road. Turn right, and walk around the bend until reaching How Lane on the right. It's just ahead on the right.

Grocery store: Peveril Store. How Street, Castleton. Open: Sun–Thurs 6:45am–6pm; Fri–Sat 6:45am–7pm.

Experiences

Those here for hill walking should head out to the **Ladybower Reservoir** (three or six miles away, depending on your route), an exquisitely somber place. In the 1940s, the towns of Derwent and Ashopton were completely razed—even the houses, the church, and graves in the town churchyard—to make room for the big reservoir. A bike ride around the reservoir offers beautiful, if creepy, views of the pool, full of ghosts of Derwent past. **Bike rentals** are available here.

Mam Tor is another good walk. From the hostel, you can follow the Castleton skyline, going around Hollins Cross and up to Mam Tor, the site of an Iron Age fort. From Mam Tor, you come around the caverns and **Winnet's Pass** and over to **Cavedale** (a cave that collapsed a few hundred years ago and which has since become a steep dale). You travel back toward the village via **Peveril Castle,** which overlooks it from behind.

Castleton is also known for its shadowy, dank caves, of which there are four you can visit in the area. The original village of Castleton was nestled within the walls of **Peak Caverns,** right under the castle, before the town grew too big for those boundaries. Prisoners from Peveril Castle were thrown in here in the Middle Ages. The other caverns in town include the **Blue John Cavern** on the shoulder of Mam Tor, named after the "Blue John" mineral that has been mined here for generations in very high, very colorful chambers. **Treak Cliff Cavern** was discovered by local spar miners at the earlier part of the century and is best known for its stalactites and stalagmites. **Speedwell Cavern** is a short trip away but novel because it has an underground canal boat ride. All four are "show caves," and tours are led by guides.

At the top of Winnet's Pass lurks **Giant's Hole Cave,** one of the deepest cave systems in England. This is a real cave for real caving, and to get in all you have to do is ask permission of the farmer who owns it. The **Castleton Village Museum,** housed in the Methodist church, gives a charming display of the town's local lore.

Ladybower Reservoir (and cycle hire). Fairholmes Visitors Centre. Tel: 01433/651261.

Peveril Castle. Castleton. Tel: 01433/620613. Open: Apr–Oct: daily 10am–6pm. Nov–Mar: daily 10am–4pm. Admission: adults £1.25; concessions 95p; children 60p.

Peak Cavern. Castleton. Tel: 01433/620285. Open: Apr–Oct: 10am–5pm.

Blue John Cavern. Castleton. Tel: 01433/620638. Open: daily 9:30am–sunset. Admission: adults £4; children £2; seniors £2.50.

Treak Cliff Cavern. Castleton. Tel: 01433/620571. Open: Mar–Oct: daily 9:30am–5:30pm. Nov–Feb: daily 10am–4pm. Tours last about 40 minutes. Admission: adults £3.95; children £1.95; seniors and HI cardholders £3.

Speedwell Cavern. Castleton. Tel: 01433/620512. Open: daily 9:30am–5:30pm (4:30pm in winter). Admission: adults £4.50; children £2.75.

Giant's Hole Cave. Ask Alistair, the hostel warden, or the hostel staff about getting permission to go caving there.

Castleton Village Museum. Inside the Methodist Church, Buxton Road, Castleton. Tel: 01433/620518.Open: Easter and bank holiday weekends: 2–5pm. May, Sept–Oct: Sun 2–5pm. June–July: Sun, Wed 2–5pm. Aug: Sun, Tues–Thurs 2–5pm. Admission: adults 40p; children 20p.

The Basics

Tourist Office: Peak National Park Information Centre. Castle Street, Castleton. Tel: 01433/620679. Open: Easter–Oct: daily 10am–1pm and 2–5:30pm. Nov–Mar: Sat–Sun 10am–1pm and 2–5pm. From the hostel, turn left. It's up the road on the right. A two-minute walk.

Post Office: Castleton Post Office. How Lane, Castleton. Tel: 01433/620241. Open: Mon–Tues 9am–1pm and 2–5pm; Wed 9am–1pm; Thurs–Fri 9am–1pm and 2–5pm; Sat 9am–12:30pm

Currency Exchange: The closest place is in Hathersage, 6 miles away. National Westminster Bank. High Street, Hathersage. Open: Mon–Fri 9am–4:30pm.

Telephone Code: 01433.

Bike Rental: The hostel can arrange local bike rental. Call in advance and bikes will be delivered to the hostel. Prices start at around £10 per day.

Getting There: Trains pop through nearby **Hope,** 2 miles away form Castleton on the Manchester-Sheffield line; there's frequent service. For train information, call the Sheffield Rail Station at 0114/272 6411. This is one stop farther than Edale on the same line (although you can take a 3-mile walk over the Hollins Cross to get here from Edale). **Buses** dawdle a bit through the Peaks. Service isn't terribly frequent, but it is reliable. You can connect into **Hope, Bradwell, Bakewell,** and **Buxton,** all of which make for nice day-trips. For information, call Derbyshire Bus Lines at 01332/292200. Those coming by **car** should take the A6 south from **Manchester** (or north from Buxton). At Chapel-en-le-Frith, switch to the A625; Castleton is about 8 miles to the east.

What's Next

Edale, the official starting point of the Pennine Way long-distance footpath, is only three miles; from Castleton, it's a nice walk over a rocky stream and up a substantial hill. The hostel doubles as a YHA Activity Centre, and weekend activity breaks are available, including canoeing, sailing, kayaking, hiking, biking, and other sports, all taught by their instructors. In the other direction lies the bustling, beautiful sandstone market town of **Bakewell** (home of the eponymous pudding). Perched on a hill overlooking the Wye Valley, the hostel is right in the town, so it's a little less isolated and a little more lively than its northern brothers. North of here, the hostels at **Castleton** and **Edale** are in small villages like Hathersage, but the hostels themselves are quite spectacular: Castleton (six miles away) is a former mansion with small bedrooms, a good dinner menu, and even a wine list. Edale (10 miles away) is a fully outfitted Activity Centre, offering weekend and weeklong courses in a panoply of sports, from pony trekking to kayaking to hang gliding and more.

BAKEWELL

Situated at a dramatic crossroads, the town of Bakewell is an excellent spot to enjoy a variety of Peak pleasures. To the north, the peat soil characteristic of the Dark Peaks produces lonely moorlands, a stark contrast with the limestone dales and White Peaks to the south. A number of gentle hills, a disgarded railway line, and loads of country paths provide endless walking routes of all levels.

The real local claim to fame is Bakewell Pudding. A pastry shell with almond and jam filling, it was actually a baker's accident served to some homeless wayfarers in the 1700s. It became so popular that they just kept baking it. Every last bakery, souvenir shop, grocery store, and outdoor stall in town sells the creation, making it difficult to ignore.

Aside from candy, though, there are lots of things to savor here. The 700-year-old weekly market still held every Monday sells everything from laces to livestock in the Market Square. At the beginning of July, Bakewell's five wells are decorated with artistically arranged flowers, usually centered around a theme. Bakewell Carnival follows closely after, with raft racing, football, cricket, and other competitions. It culminates with a final parade of trucks, bedecked with flowers, hurtling down the High Street. Every village around the Peak District has well dressings and carnivals, but the one in Bakewell is the biggest and most popular.

Bakewell's atmosphere is pleasant and convivial. The uniformly light limestone architecture is a soothing presence in town, so even on a rainy day, it's a pretty pleasant place to be.

Bakewell Youth Hostel

Fly Hill
Bakewell, Derbyshire DE4 1DN
Tel: 01629/812313. Fax: 01629/812313.

School groups, solo backpackers, and families all gravitate to the hostel in Bakewell, an excellent place from which to launch into the Peak District. Built in the 1960s, this "purpose-built" hostel overlooks the Wye Valley from its repose on Fly Hill, just steps from the town.

In May (and sometimes September), the hostel offers Introduction to Carriage Driving, an all-inclusive weekend package that includes two nights' accommodation, full board, and instruction on how to drive a "turnout," which is a two-wheeled vehicle pulled by a horse. They also run a Railway Weekend in June in coordination with Peak Rail, which has a line running from Matlock to Darley

Dale. You can fulfill all your childhood fantasies: help fire the locomotive, serve food in the buffet car, or work as a signalman.

At the hostel, you can eat a wholesome, filling dinner as you look out the window out across the Wye Valley. Homemade food is served here: Meat-and-potato pies, chocolate fudge pudding, and surprise lemon pudding are only a few of specialties of the warden Simon.

Services

🚆 The nearest train station is in Matlock (8 miles away). From there, take the Trent bus no. 32 or R1 (a long distance from Nottingham-Manchester) to Bakewell town. From Rutland Square in the center of town, walk up North Church Street toward the Rutland Tavern. Once you reach the tavern, go straight up the hill, and the hostel is the second turn on the right. From Matlock, it's about 30 minutes.

🚌 Buses drop you in the center of town. From Rutland Square in the center of town, walk up North Church Street toward the Rutland Tavern. Once you reach the tavern, go straight up the hill, and the hostel is the second turn on the right. A seven-minute walk.

🚗 From the A6 (from Matlock), head toward Bakewell. From Rutland Square in the center of town, take the Buxton Road exit off the roundabout. Turn left onto North Church Street, heading for the Rutland Tavern. Once you reach the tavern, go straight up the hill, and the hostel is the second turn on the right.

📅 Open Feb–Easter weekends only. Easter–Nov 30 open every day but Sunday. On holiday weekends, open Sun, closed Mon. Call to check. BABA.

🕐 Reception open 7:15–10am. 5–10:30pm. Curfew 11pm.

🛏 36 beds. 6- and 12-bed dormitories.

£ Members: adults £6.55; under 18 £4.45.

🍴 Self-catering kitchen facilities. Breakfast: 8am. Lunch: packed lunch only; should be ordered by 7pm the night before. Dinner: 7pm.

✗ No table license.

🔒 No lockers.

▢ No laundry facilities; drying room.

P Ample and free of charge.

🛍 Shop at hostel sells candy, souvenirs, canned goods. Maps and guidebooks for hire (50p per day).

🛋 Lounge; smokers' lounge/games room.

🚬 In smokers' lounge only

♿ Not wheelchair accessible.

💱 See "Currency Exchange" under "The Basics" in Bakewell.

🔵 Bike shed; wet-weather shelter.

Cheap Eats Nearby

The Green Apple

Tucked on a little alleyway, this cute restaurant has an outdoor garden as well as indoor seating. There's an excellent bulletin board with local events and shops. Salads are £4.50 to £5. Quiche, lasagne, and other main dishes come with potato or roll and a side salad for £4 to £5. Dinner is slightly pricier: Main courses run £6 to £9, but the food is good here.

Water Street, Bakewell. Tel: 01629/814044. Open: Oct–May: Mon–Sat 11am–5pm; Sun noon–5pm. Jul–Sept: Mon 11am–5pm; Tues–Sat 11am–5pm and 7–10:30pm; Sun noon–5pm. Cash only. From the hostel, turn left down Fly Hill onto North Church Street. When you reach Rutland Square, turn left and then right onto Water Street; it's to the right, in Diamond Court; a five-minute walk.

The Old Original Bakewell Pudding Shop

Downstairs they hawk the local sweet, but upstairs it's a pleasant, if busy, country restaurant, with dried flowers, exposed beams, and baskets everywhere. Main dishes include halibut, stuffed chicken, and steak-and-kidney pie, all £5 to £6. Bakewell pudding £1.50 per slice. Takeout available downstairs.

Rutland Square, Bakewell. Tel: 01629/812193. Open: Easter–Oct: daily 9am–9pm. Nov–Easter: daily 9am–6pm. Credit cards: VA, MC, EC, Access. From the hostel, turn left down Fly Hill to Rutland Square. Turn left and then right onto Water Street; it's on your right; a five-minute walk.

Grocery store: Gateway Foodmarkets. Rutland Square, Bakewell. Open: Mon–Wed 8:30am–5:30pm; Thurs–Fri 8:30am–7:30pm; Sat 8:30am–5:30pm; Sun 10am–4pm.

Experiences

If you're here in July and August, pick up a copy of the *Peakland Post* to see what shows, markets, and festivals are going in Bakewell. The **weekly market** on Mondays is always fun. The agricultural **Bakewell Show** and the **Bakewell Carnival** in August keeps the town stirring during the summer.

A pleasant 3-mile walk out of Bakewell, **Caudwell's Mill** is a flour mill powered by the River Wye. It's still cranking as it did in Victorian days. In fact, it's said that there has been a mill at this site for over 400 years. They offer crafts workshops as well as some exhibitions and models. **Haddon Hall,** only 2 miles away, is an impressive medieval manor house open to visitors: with a 14th-century chapel, wall frescoes, and some beautifully appointed rooms, it's a nice outing. **Chatsworth House** (4 miles away), the home of the duke and duchess of Devonshire, is even more impressive: perfectly clipped green lawns roll out endlessly from this monstrous and elaborately decorated Elizabethan mansion. Fountains spout outside, brass and wood fixtures shine inside; it might be hard to return to the hostel after touring the house.

Cyclists and long-distance walkers might want to check out **The White Peak Way**, an interhostel walking route that stops in Bakewell. The seven hostels on the path aren't too far apart from one another, making it relatively easy.

Caudwell's Mill. Rowsley (3 miles east of Bakewell). Tel: 01629/734374. Open: Apr–Oct: daily 10am–6pm. Nov–Mar: daily 10am–4:30pm. Admission: adults £2; children and seniors £1.

Haddon Hall. Bakewell (2 miles east of the town). Tel: 01629/812855. Open: Apr–June: daily 11am–5:45pm (last entry 5pm). July–Aug: Mon–Sat 11am–5:45pm (last entry 5pm). Sept: daily 11am–5:45pm (last entry 5pm). Admission: adults £4.50; seniors £3.50; children £2.80.

Chatsworth House. Bakewell (about 4 miles east of town). Tel: 01246/582204. Mar–May: House open daily 11am–4:30pm; garden open daily 11am–5pm. June–Aug: House open daily 11am–4:30pm; garden open daily 10:30am–5pm. Oct: House open daily 11am–4:30pm; garden open daily 11am–5pm. House and garden admission: adults £5.75; seniors and students £5; children £3. Garden admission only: adults £3; seniors and students £3; children £1.50.

The White Peak Way. Ask for details at the hostel reception desk.

The Basics

Tourist Office: Bakewell T.I.C. The Old Market, Bakewell. Tel: 01629/813227. Open: Easter–Oct: Mon–Fri 9:30am–5:30pm; Sat–Sun 9:30am–6pm. Oct–Easter: Mon–Wed 9:30am–5:30pm; Thurs 9:30am–1pm; Fri–Sun 9:30am–5:30pm. From the hostel, it takes five minutes: turn left down Fly Hill. At Rutland Square, turn left, and it's straight ahead.

Post Office: Bakewell Post Office. Portland Square, Bakewell. Tel: 01629/814427. Open: Mon–Fri 9am–5:30pm; Sat 9am–12:30pm. From the hostel, it takes five minutes: turn left down Fly Hill. At Rutland Square, turn right down Water Lane. Follow Water Lane and it's around the corner to the left.

Currency Exchange: Royal Bank of Scotland. Rutland Square, Bakewell. Tel: 01629/812055. Open: Mon–Fri 9:15am–4:45pm (Wed 10am opening).

Telephone Code: 01629.

Bike Rental: The closest place is Peak District Cycle Hire in Parsley Hay (7 miles away), on the Tissington Trail near Buxton. Tel: 01298/84493. Open: daily.

Getting There: The closest **train** station is in **Matlock** (8 miles away), which is on a branch line from Derby on the main London-York-Edinburgh line. If you're coming from Manchester and the northwest, the **Buxton** station (12 miles away) is more convenient; it's a branch line off the Manchester-Sheffield line. For train information, call 0114/253 7676. Main **bus** links to and from Bakewell include **Sheffield, Derby,** and **Manchester.** Trent buses (service to Manchester, Nottingham, and Derby) can be reached at 01298/23098 for schedule infor-mation. For service in the direction of Sheffield, call Main Line buses at 0114/256 7000. By **car,** it's a half-hour drive down the A621 from **Sheffield;** switch to the A619 south at Nether End and follow signs for Bakewell. From the direction of **Manchester,** it's an hour's ride down the A6 through Chapel-en-le-Frith and Buxton. From Buxton, Bakewell is about 12 miles.

What's Next

Heading back about 14 miles to the north, you'll reach the luxuriously refurbished **Castleton** Youth Hostel, which sits right on the Market Square of this ancient village, home to four caves. Faurther up the road, the hostel at **Edale** is a fully decked-out Activity Centre with a group of able (and attractive) professionals ready to instruct you in the ways of kayaking, canoeing, mountain climbing, hang glid-ing, and much more on their weekend package deals. Otherwise, take to the peat bogs and marshy moorland yourself: walking trails are available aplenty there, and the Pennine Way has its official start at the pub in the village.

ASHBOURNE (ILAM HALL)

The Ilam Hall Youth Hostel rests in the outskirts of Ashbourne, 20 miles east of Matlock. Aside from a car mechanic, the hostel, and loads of tourists rambling around the hostel property, there's no sign of a "village" here as such. The area is engulfed by the Youth Hostel, officially entitled Ilam Hall and Country Park.

Owned and maintained by the National Trust, the hostel is a ridiculously grand stone mansion that was bequeathed to the YHA in the 1930s. Its 84 acres of wooded grounds (river included) are open to visitors, who come in droves, thanks to Ilam's close proximity to Manchester, Sheffield, Derby, Stoke, and Nottingham.

Located at the very southern tip of the Peak District National Park, the landscape here consists of the light-green limestone of the White Peaks. It could take you a day or two to wander through the hostel property itself.

Nearby are the ever-popular walking routes and a huge amusement park is only 10 miles away. The bus ride out here is lovely, but once you get off, be prepared to walk: The nearest semblance of organized town life is an hour's walk away in Ashbourne, five miles south. City dwellers will be twiddling their thumbs after a day or two here.

❋ Ilam Hall Youth Hostel

Ashbourne
Derbyshire DE6 2AZ
Tel: 01335/350212. Fax: 01335/350350.

Forget for a moment the dense woodlands, the rushing river, the expansive lawns, the geese. The first thing you see as you walk up the driveway is the the sizable lump of limestones that form graceful Ilam Hall. Overlooking Bunster Hill and Thorpe Cloud right at the entrance of Dovedale, this place fulfills even the most unrealistic stereotype image of an English country home. The mansion, with a huge main wing, gardens, and stone walkways, has a central courtyard into which you half expect knights to come rushing.

Beginning in Reformation days, it was a private home for wealthy local families, and in the 1800s it was redecorated according to Gothic standards of grandiosity: soaring towers, formal rooms, ornamental chimneys, and parapets were added. After a brief period as a luxury hotel, it was bought by Rob McDougall (of McDougall flour fame), who then turned it over in 1934 to the National Trust and the YHA for use as a Youth Hostel.

What remains is still pretty impressive. Behind the mansion is a stone terrace with steps and pathways that lead to a rushing river below and a bridge leading to the woodlands beyond. Out back is an old stable that houses a National Trust shop and tearoom, and there's also an old church on the front part of the property.

Naturally, the building has undergone the usual Youth Hostel overhaul to create subdivided, cell-like rooms and communal bathrooms, but Ilam Hall is more elegant than most hostels. Dark woodwork, mammoth picture windows, and "sympathetic" country-house decor (flowered wallpaper, flowered curtains) distinguish this hostel from the bruised-and-battered look of so many others. This is quite surprising, considering the turnover of school groups here. Because of its superior facilities, this is a prime target for attack by the brown-bag brigade. With a classroom, games room (Ping-Pong, video games, jukebox), and disco, the little ones love it here. Prepare yourself.

🚆 The most convenient train station is in Derby, 20 miles away. From there, walk to the bus station and catch Trent bus no. 107 or 109 or Manchester Express no. 201 to Ashbourne. From Ashbourne, change for the no. 441 or 443 to Ilam. The bus drops you off at the foot of the hostel driveway.

🚌 The closest major coach station is in Derby, 20 miles away. From there, walk to the bus station and follow directions from the train station, given above.

🚗 From the M1 (London-Leeds motorway), turn off at the A52, following signs to Derby. From there, stay on the A52 until you reach Ashbourne. Take the

Services

A515 out of Ashbourne in the direction of Buxton. After half a mile, turn left, following signs to Dovedale and Ilam. When you reach the monument in the center of Ilam, turn right, and the hostel is straight ahead, down the long driveway.

▦ Open Jan–Nov 30. BABA.

🕐 Reception open 7am–11pm. Curfew 11pm.

🛏 145 beds. 3-, 4-, 5-, 6-, 8-, 10-, 13-, and 14-bed rooms. Annex has 4- and 6-bed rooms with showers and keys for daytime access.

£ Members: adults £8.80; under 18 £5.95. Brewhouse annex: adults £10.60; under 18 £7.20.

🍴 Self-catering kitchen facilities. Breakfast: 8am. Lunch: packed lunch, only for groups. Dinner: 7pm.

⊥ Table license.

💼 No lockers. The staff will guard valuables behind the desk.

◯ Washers, dryers, and drying room.

P Ample; £1 per day.

🛍 Shop at hostel sells candy, canned goods, and maps. Discount tickets to Alton Towers (£2 off) available.

🛋 Lounge/quiet room; games room.

🚬 In designated area only.

♿ Wheelchair accessible. Bedrooms and bathrooms for people with disabilities.

💱 See "Currency Exchange" under "The Basics" in Ashbourne.

⬤ Bike shed; classroom with overhead projectors.

Cheap Eats Nearby

The Caverns Bistro

Underneath the buildings on Ashbourne's busy marketplace lurks this hidden gem with a cozy atmosphere, white stone walls, and a red carpet. For lunch, toasties and jacket potatoes (£2 to £3) are the most economical choice. At dinner, pizzas are £5.75 to £6.25 and vegetarian dishes (curry, lasagne) are £6 to £6.50.

St. John Street, Ashbourne (5 miles away). Tel: 01335/300305. Open: daily 10am–3pm and 7–9:30pm. Reservations recommended in the evening. Credit cards: VA, MC, AE, EC, Access. From the hostel, take the bus into Ashbourne or walk 5 miles down the road. From the bus stop in Ashbourne, turn left onto Dig Street, then right on St. John Street, and it's on your left. A 5-minute walk from the bus stop.

The Horns Inn

The outside tables of this friendly, busy little restaurant form the nucleus of Ashbourne. Burgers £1.95–£3.50. Salas £4–£6. Gamekeeper's platter (meat, salad, and bread) £4.50.

Victoria Square, Ashbourne (5 miles away). Tel: 01335/300737. Open: daily noon–2:30pm. Sun, Tues–Thurs only: 7–9:30pm. Credit cards: VA, MC, EC, Access. From the hostel, take the bus into Ashbourne or walk 5 miles down the road. From the bus stop, turn left on Dig Street, right on St. John Street, and when you reach the fork, it's on the left. Five minutes from the bus stop.

Grocery Store: Somerfield. Ashbourne (5 miles away). Open: Mon–Fri 8:30am–8pm; Sat 8:30am–7pm; Sun 10am–4pm.

Experiences

The 84 acres of grounds around the hostel are some of the loveliest in the area. Get lost on the winding paths that take you down to the river; on a sunny day, it's a nice spot for a secluded picnic. The church on the hostel property is an attractive example of Peak village architecture.

Hang gliding is available in nearby Ashbourne; it doesn't come cheap, but the terrain is especially good for beginners. Nature, however, need not cost a penny: the **Tissington Trail,** which goes from Ashbourne almost to Buxton, is a great walk or bike route to take from the town of Ashbourne. From the hostel to Ashbourne, it's a wooded 4^1/$_2$-mile walk, a nice alternative to the school bus you'll have to squeeze into otherwise. Even closer is **Dovedale,** a mere ^{3}/$_4$-mile walk from the hostel. Massive, lovely limestone hills tower over either side of a skinny river, and the area is peppered with little spots with names such as Lover's Leap.

Unless you're a fan of theme parks planted in the middle of the wilderness, there's a serious lack of organized activity in the immediate area around Ilam. The school groups that descend upon the place are usually intent upon visiting **Alton Towers,** with its bulbous towers, artificial lakes, and amusements. Log flumes, river rapids, haunted houses, a wax museum, and more can be yours for a day, for one all-inclusive price.

Peak School of Hang Gliding. The Elms, Wetton, Ashbourne (5 miles away). Tel: 01335/310257. Open: all year, by appointment only.

The Tissington Trail. Leaflet available at the hostel or at Ashbourne T.I.C. Tel: 01335/343666.

Alton Towers. Alton, Staffordshire (10 miles away). Tel: 01538/702200. Open: Mar–Nov: daily 10am–5pm; closing time varies throughout the year. Admission: adults £16; children £12.

The Basics

Tourist Office: The nearest T.I.C. is in Ashbourne, 5 miles away. Ashbourne T.I.C. 13 Market Place, Ashbourne. Tel: 01335/343666. Open: Mon–Sat 9am–5pm. From the hostel, take the bus (or walk 5 miles) into Ashbourne. From the bus stop there, turn left onto Dig Street, then right onto St. John Street. At the marketplace, bear left. It's to the left of the car park. Five minutes from the bus stop.

Post Office: The nearest Post Office is in Ashbourne, 5 miles away. Ashbourne Post Office, CMCS-Shawcroft Centre. Dig Street, Ashbourne. Tel: 01335/300117. Open: Mon–Fri 9am–5:30pm; Sat 9am–12:30pm.

Currency Exchange: Barclays Bank. 8 St. John St., Ashbourne (5 miles away). Tel: 01332/363451. Open: Mon–Fri 9:30am–4:30pm (Wed 10am opening).

Telephone Code: 01335.

Bike Rental: Ashbourne Cycle Hire Centre. Mapleton Lane, Ashbourne (5 miles away). Tel: 01335/343156.

Getting There: Coming by **train** isn't too difficult, though you will have to change for (slightly infrequent) local buses. **Derby** is the nearest station, 20 miles away, and from there, local buses (no. 107 or 109) take you to **Ilam.** For train info, call 01332/332051. **Derby** is also the closest station for long-distance **buses.** For information, call National Express at 01602/585317. From there, local buses get you out to Ilam. Trent buses operate from Derby to Ashbourne: call 01332/292200. By **car:** from the south, take the M1 up to **Nottingham.** At Junction 25, switch for the A52 going west. Pass through Derby and continue on the A52 until you reach Ashbourne. From there, follow signs to Ilam, 5 miles farther. From

Manchester and the north, take the A6 south to Buxton. There, change for the A515, and follow signs for Ashbourne. From Ashbourne, follow signs to Ilam 5 miles farther.

What's Next

Head back to the train and bus stations in Derby, and you can easily get out to **Matlock,** where there's a first-rate Youth Hostel in a somewhat tired spa town. About a mile from the town, the dizzying Heights of Abraham are visible from a cablecar ride, and the limestone gorge is a spectacular sight. Farther north is the market town of **Bakewell,** especially festive in summer. A bunch of local festivals and agricultural shows follow the mid-July well dressings, a local tradition of decorating the town's wells as a way of saying thanks for the year's prosperity. Good walks, challenging bike routes, and the tasty Bakewell Pudding are plentiful here.

York & the Yorkshire Dales

One of England's lonelier literary locales, Yorkshire is well known for having inspired novels of Gothic proportions and stories of veterinary tribulations. The moorlands, peat brown in winter and purple heather in summer, provided the setting for the brooding tales of the sisters Brontë in South Yorkshire. The town of Haworth is little more than a shrine to them, with tea rooms, literary walks, and the faithfully preserved vicarage where they grew up. The hostel is a fine Victorian mansion just outside of town.

Moving up the Pennines, Hawes, Dentdale, and Kirkby Stephen all fall within the confines of the Yorkshire Dales National Park, 700 square miles of leafy, sheepy farmland lined by rushing waterways. Hawes, home of smooth, mild Wensleydale cheese, is England's highest market town. The long-distance Pennine Way footpath worms its way up here from Edale, as do the Herriot Way and the Brontë Trail, two literary walks that cover the terrain that inspired famous scribes James Herriot and the Brontës. This is fertile ground for both farmers and walkers as well, and during the summer, Day-Glo backpacks bob up and down the hills and in the valleys.

There's a string of hostels here, all within 10 to 15 miles of one another. From Hawes, it's only about 10 miles to Dent, where a hostel sits in solitude in the valley of the River Dee. Farther north, the market town of Kirkby Stephen boasts a Youth Hostel situated in a former church, and footpaths spill out from there as well. To the east lies the pea-sized village of Aysgarth, where the frothing waters of the River Ure plunge down over a series of rocky steps, creating a small but sweet waterfall.

To the southeast of the Yorkshire Dales is the walled cathedral city of York. Among England's most touristed spots, it has one of the country's most celebrated cathedrals, the York Minster. Museums abound, as do the usual run of ghost tours, city walks, and heritage centers. The remnants of Roman walls form the perimeter of the city, which is best seen on foot. The streets are pristine and the prices high, but that doesn't seem to stop the tourists. It's an excellent place to load up on information about the Yorkshire Dales.

The Leeds-Settle-Carlisle railway line is the best (though not the cheapest) form of transportation in the area; it's also known throughout England as one of the most scenic and unspoiled routes. Speeding through tunnels and ancient viaducts, it offers breathtaking views of the fertile countryside. The station at Dent has the highest elevation of any station in the entire British Rail system. York is on the rail line from London-Edinburgh, and trains connect to Keighley and up into the Dales. Beware, though, that some of the hostels are as far as 6 miles from the nearest rail stop. Post buses crawl through the region as seldom as twice a week, so many travelers take to the open road. Thankfully, locals are very sympathetic to backpackers. Despite the hassles, though, most hostelers think the area is definitely worth it.

YORK

So many ghosts, so little time. The wondrous walled city of York, with its renowned cathedral, cobbled streets, and arched gateways, is a perennial favorite on the hostel circuit. For fans of English history, a trip to York is a worthwhile undertaking because almost every major era is represented here.

Built as a fortress by the Roman Ninth Legion in A.D. 71, Eboracum (as it was then called) was intended to defend the Romans against the Brigantes tribe. When the Vikings came on the scene a few hundred years later, the name of the city was changed to Yorvik and it flourished as a vital trading center. Norman rule later enhanced the city as a nucleus of government, commerce, and religion for northern Britain. By the time the Tudors came in the late 1400s, York was at its peak, with its Minster finally completed and a prosperous economy offering a comfortable way of life. In the 1800s, the city became something of a resort and Georgian architecture emerged, giving it the elegant, privileged air it still retains. The early part of the 20th century saw the railway industry grow here, and the later part has seen tourism take over as the main industry.

York shamelessly bows and scrapes to the crowds of international tourists that come here by the busload, but it's still a beautiful place, set right on the banks of the River Ouse, 207 miles north of London. Thanks to the high volume of visitors, every measure is taken to preserve the strange and eclectic beauty of the buildings, streets, and walls in this buzzing city. Nighttime comes alive when church bells toll, ghost tours start, and the bars fill up with traveling revelers. The Youth Hostel, a converted mansion, is about a mile from the town center in the sedate Clifton area, a bus ride away from the town center.

❂ York International Youth Hostel

Water End, Clifton
York, North Yorkshire YO3 6LT
Tel: 01904/653147. Fax: 01904/651230.

A 20-minute stroll from the city center, this converted mansion is the former home of the Rowntree family, local chocolatiers who sold out to Nestlé when times grew bitter. Overlooking the river Ouse, the hostel is in a nice spot, quiet enough so that it feels restful, but close enough to the city center that it's not too much of a hike.

The place has been restored and outfitted to the highest of hosteling standards, which means staff wears little name tags and has their "welcome host" lines down cold. It offers exactly what you'd expect from a city hostel: nice rooms with bedside lights and sinks, decent bathrooms, two lounges, an ample cafeteria (overlooking the water), and military efficiency.

What the hostel lacks in warmth, it makes up for in other ways: a discount voucher book is available at reception (£1), a good deal for anyone wanting to load up on museums. They also offer a Weekend in York package that includes two nights with half board, a ticket to the Jorvik Viking Centre, a river cruise, and an evening ghost walk.

Loads of international tourists pour in here off the Slow Coach, so this can be an excellent place to meet up with fellow hostelers. The place also, however, attracts a fair number of school groups, so be prepared. Lines outside the cafeteria can stretch halfway up the stairs when they're full, and the peaceful riverside setting can quickly turn into summer camp.

Services

🚆 Exit the train station and turn left onto Station Road. Follow the road until you reach Lendal Bridge over the river; cross the bridge. From there, turn left, go down the steps on the left, and follow the footpath to the first road bridge, Clifton Bridge. Go up; the hostel is right ahead; a 30-minute walk. Alternatively, take bus no. 30 or 31 or any bus going to Clifton Green. York is trafficky and not worth walking though. A taxi runs about £3.

🚌 The bus station is on Rougier Street. From there, turn left, and cross Lendal Bridge over the river. Follow directions from the train station, given above.

🚗 From the A1237 north of the city, follow the A19 towards the city center. When you reach the first set traffic lights you come to on Clifton Green, turn right on Water End, and the hostel is 200 yards up on your right.

▦ Open Jan–Dec 15. Schedule may vary from year to year. Call to check. IBN and BABA.

⏰ 24-hour access. No curfew.

🛏 146 beds. 2-, 4-, 6-, and 8-bed rooms. Some have TV and hot drinks caddy; one room en suite. All rooms have keys.

£ Members: adults £13.10; under 18 £9.70. Breakfast included in prices. Premium rates for deluxe rooms.

🍴 Ebor Restaurant open from 7:30am–10pm. Self-catering kitchen facilities. Breakfast: 7:30–9am. Lunch: packed lunch available; order by 9pm the night before. Dinner: 5:30–7:30pm for set menu; cafeteria open for à la carte until 10pm.

☦ Table license.

🧳 Luggage storage room; key at reception. Locks on all room doors.

◻ Coin-operated washers (£1) and dryers (60p); iron free of charge.

P In front of hostel; free of charge.

◻ Shop at hostel sells candy and limited toiletries. Slow Coach tickets. Tickets for the Ghost Trail; York Pullman Open Top bus tour; York Out and About booklet (£1) contains discount vouchers for museums. Vending machines.

🛋 TV lounge and games room; reception/sitting area.

🚬 In smoker's lounge only.

♿ Limited wheelchair access (rooms, toilet, but no shower).

💱 Travelex currency exchange.

🔺 Bike shed; study rooms.

Cheap Eats Nearby

Café Concerto

Wallpapered in sheet music, this warm country kitchen has suave sounds on the airwaves and savory aromas wafting from the stove. The interesting, sophisticated menu includes pâtés (£3.25 to £4.75), leek-and-Gruyère tart (£4.75), and dauphinoise—a creamy combo of potato, cream, and cheese—(£4.75).

21 High Petergate, York. Tel: 01904/610478. Open: daily 10am–5:30pm, later on some summer evenings; call ahead. Cash only. From the hostel, a 30-minute walk: Turn left, walk down the street to Bootham. Turn right and walk straight through Bootham Bar to High Petergate. It's on your right, just before the west entrance to the Minster.

The Greenhouse Coffee Shop & Restaurant

A bright and airy restaurant, this was the first nonsmoking establishment in York. Good portions for the price. Yorkshire pudding with mince £4.25. Pastas £4 to £4.50. Vegetarian options always available. On Saturday nights there's a line out the door to get in.

12a Church St., York. Tel: 01904/629615. Open: June–Sept: daily 9:30am–9:30pm. Oct–May: Mon–Wed 9:30am–6pm; Thurs–Sat 9:30am–9:30pm. Credit cards: VA, MC, EC, Access. From the hostel, turn left and walk down the street to Bootham. Turn right and walk straight through Bootham Bar to High Petergate, continue through Low Petergate, and then right on Church Street. It's on the left; a 30-minute walk.

Grocery Store: Spar, Bootham. Open: Mon–Sat 9am–9pm.

Experiences

So-called "Historic York" is brimming with activities: art museums, a Viking Museum, a Railway Museum, and countless Ghost Tours. However, the resourceful traveler need not go broke here. Precisely because it's so geared to tourists, there are vouchers that knock prices down, and there are also lots of things to do that don't cost a thing.

The **York Minster** is usually on the list of must-see attractions, and even if you're sick to death of cathedrals, this one is probably worth the trip. There's a somewhat interesting "five sisters window" in the north end, and stained glass spills forth a myriad of colors on a sunny day. Choral evensong, at 5pm every day except Sunday (4pm), is a lovely time to sit in the church and listen to the choir sing.

The immense **city walls** (no admission charge) enclose the three square miles comprising the old city. They are a mixture of Roman and medieval structures punctuated by arched gateways or bars. Monk Bar has a working portcullis for chopping heads off unwelcome visitors, and Walmgate Bar is the only town gate in England that has retained its barbican, a funnel-like structure that forced attackers to bunch together. The walk around makes a tidy history lesson, and the Association of Voluntary Guides can tell you about it in detail; free tours around the city run daily, with evening tours in summertime.

The **York City Art Gallery,** featuring seven centuries of European and British art, also merits a peek. York-born William Etty, a painter of nudes, is well represented here.

The Shambles, one of the narrowest medieval streets, is a neat slice of history. It was the old butcher's row, and you can still see meat hooks hanging from the buildings. Meatcutters would stun the sheep in their shops, and the blood would run down the narrow passageway of the Shambles. Just around the corner along Newgate Street is an outdoor covered market every day from 9am to 5pm; it's fun to prowl through here.

When night falls, check out the *What's On* guide for music listings. There are 365 pubs in York, and live music is plentiful. The Punch Bowl and the White Swan both have bands regularly.

York Minster. York. Tel: 01904/624406. Open: summer: daily 7am–8:30pm. Winter: daily 7am–5pm. Donation requested.

Association of Voluntary Guides to the City of York. De Grey Rooms, Exhibition Square. Tel: 01904/640780. Daily tours: 10:15am. Apr–Oct: additional tours at 2:15pm. Jun–Aug: additional tours at 7pm. Special tours available upon request. Meet outside York City Art Gallery, Exhibition Square.

York City Art Gallery. Exhibition Square, York. Tel: 01904/623839. Open: Mon–Sat 10am–5pm; Sun 2:30–5pm. Last entry: 4:30pm. Admission: free. Access for people with disabilities.

The Basics

Tourist Office: York T.I.C. De Grey Rooms, Exhibition Square, York. Tel: 01904/621756. Open: Sept–June: Mon–Sat 9am–6pm; Sun 10am–6pm. July–Aug: daily 9am–7pm. From the hostel, cross the street, turn right, and go down the steps. Walk alongside the river until you reach Lendal Bridge. Turn left onto Museum Street, then left onto St. Leonard's Place. It's on the right, across from the Museum Garden; a 15-minute walk.

Post Office: York Post Office. 4 Lendal, York. Tel: 01904/617210. Open: Mon–Fri 9am–5:30pm; Sat 9am–12:30pm. From the hostel, cross the street, turn right, and go down the steps. Walk alongside the river until you reach Lendal Bridge. Turn left onto Museum Street, and take the first right onto Lendal. It's on the right; a 15-minute walk.

Currency Exchange: Thomas Cook. 31 Stonegate, York. Tel: 01904/644344. Open: Mon–Sat 10am–5pm. American Express. 6 Stonegate, York. Tel: 01904/611727. Open: Mon–Fri 9am–5:30pm; Sat 9am–5pm. Open Sun in Apr–Oct: 10:30am–4:30pm.

Telephone Code: 01904.

Bike Rental: Time Cycles, Exhibition Square. Tel: 01904/448971. Full day £10; half day £5.

Getting There: By **train,** York is on the main Intercity railway line between London **King's Cross** and **Edinburgh,** so there is frequent service from both cities, as well as a TransPennine link to **Manchester** and **Manchester airport.** For schedule and fare info., call 01904/642155. By **coach,** York is reachable by National Express to and from most major cities in England, including **London, Cambridge, Sheffield, Manchester,** and **Leeds.** For info, call 0990/808080. By **car,** take the A1/M1 south from **Edinburgh** and north from **London.** From **Liverpool** and **Manchester,** the M62 brings you straight into York.

What's Next

From York, there's a vast number of places that are easy to get to; an hour's drive/train ride to the northeast will get you to the coast. Directly to the north lies Yorkshire, where gentle rolling hills and heather covered moorland beckon long-distance walkers and cyclists. A beautiful train ride takes you up into **Wensleydale** and **Swaledale,** where some homey hostels lie in wait. Forty-five miles to the west lies **Haworth,** where the Brontë's bones and bric-a-brac attract tourists from all over the world to a quiet one-street parish town.

HAWORTH

The parish of Haworth, 45 miles west of York, was little more than a small weaving town of 4,600 souls when the Reverend Patrick Brontë and his six children arrived in 1820. A sickly family, they didn't last very long in the bleak, wind-whipped moors of West Yorkshire. One by one, they fell victim to consumption, but not before leaving behind an immense literary legacy. Their name is now synonymous with the forbidding landscape they romanticized in books such as *Jane Eyre* and *Wuthering Heights.*

Times have changed here since the Brontës. Haworth has become the second most popular literary pilgrimage in England (after Stratford-upon-Avon), so the usual curio shops, antique shops, and general Brontëmania have settled over the town like so much heather on an August field. It's not particularly unpleasant, but it does make Haworth a town with a one-track mind; even the local footpaths involve the sisters' favorite haunts and spots of supposed creative inspiration.

Those uninterested in all things Brontë, however, have some good alternatives. Industrial Bradford is only a bus ride away; it has an IMAX theater and an excellent museum of film and photography. Nevertheless, don't come here unless you want a good dose of Emily, Charlotte, Anne, and brother, Branwell. Their spirit is everywhere—in the pub where Branwell drank himself to death, in the pharmacy where Anne shopped for cough medicine, but most of all, on the open moors just behind the church and beyond the confines of their austere parsonage.

Haworth Youth Hostel

Longlands Hall
Longlands Drive
Haworth, West Yorkshire BD22 8RT
Tel: 01535/642234. Fax: 01535/643023.

Built in 1884, this Youth Hostel once belonged to a local mill owner, an extravagant sort out to impress the local gentry. Constructed of the same gritstone found on the main road in Haworth, it still bears the residue of coal from the mining days of the early 1900s. The nouveau riche family here tried to replicate the old English country gentleman's home by installing stained-glass windows, a large upstairs balcony overlooking the entrance hall, and a walled-in garden with a tiny pool and flowers.

Today, all this means that it's a pretty comfortable, spacious hostel. A skylight in the center of the entrance hall showers light into the entire hostel, and a nice sitting room with big windows overlooks the garden on the front side of the house.

You'll be thankful for the generous sizes of the rooms here. Springtime sees the usual round of school groups, and then an avalanche of independent travelers tumbles into town (from as far away as Japan) in July and August for moor brooding and Brontë worshiping.

The closest train station is in Keighley, 8 miles away; from the train station, walk through the town to the bus station. From there, pick up Keighley and District bus no. 663, 664, or 665 (departures every 15–20 minutes) to Haworth Youth Hostel; a 10-minute ride.

From the bus stop on Lees Lane, turn around and make a left on Longlands Drive. The hostel is on the end of the road.

Bradford (8 miles away) is the closest town with links to national bus lines. From

Services

there, follow directions from the train station, given above.

🚗 The town of Haworth is off the main road running between Keighley and Hebden Bridge. From the B6042, turn onto Longlands Drive, and the hostel is at the end of the drive.

🗓 Feb–Nov. BABA.

🕐 Reception open 7:30–10am and 1–11pm. Curfew 11pm.

🛏 90 beds. 2-, 4-, 6-, 8-, 10-, and 15-bed rooms available.

£ Members: adults £8; under 18 £5.35.

🍴 Self-catering kitchen facilities. Breakfast: 8:15am. Lunch: packed lunch only; order by the night before. Dinner: 7pm.

🍸 No table license.

🧳 No lockers. Valuables can be stored in the hostel office.

🔲 Washing machine (£1.50) and drying room.

P Ample and free of charge.

🛍 Shop at hostel sells candy and some canned goods.

🛋 TV lounge and Ping-Pong table.

🚬 In common room only.

♿ Not wheelchair accessible.

💱 See "Currency Exchange" under "The Basics" in Haworth.

🔺 Bike shed; study room.

Cheap Eats Nearby

The Black Bull Hotel

Bramwell Brontë drowned his sorrows in the ale here; his favorite chair is enshrined on a stairwell, and his ghost lingers. Old prints of Haworth line the walls of this cozy pub, and incongruous gaming tables keep the atmosphere lively. Fare includes sandwiches (£2 to £3); traditional English pies (£3 to £4), and daily specials, including roast beef and roast lamb (£4 to £5).

119 Main St., Haworth. Tel: 01535/642249. Open: Mon–Fri 11am–11pm; Sun noon–10:30pm. Credit cards: VA, MC, Access. A 20-minute walk from the hostel. Go down Longlands Drive, right on Mill Hay, and up the cobbled hill onto Main Street. It's on your left, just past the tourist office.

The Cobbled Way Tea Room

This civilized little cafe has watercolors on the wall, lacy tablecloths, and very ladylike little sandwiches (£1.75 and £2.50). Omelets are £2.75 to £3.50. Five-course "country fayre" menu includes roast beef and Yorkshire pudding (£5.95). Vegetarian dishes.

60 Main St. Tel: 01535/642735. Open: Apr–Sept: daily 10:30am–8pm. Oct–Mar: daily 10:30am–4pm. Cash only. A 20-minute walk from the hostel. Go down Longlands Drive, right on Mill Hay, and up the cobbled hill onto Main Street. It's on your right.

Grocery Store: Southam's. Main Street. Open: daily 9am–5:30pm.

Experiences

There's very little point in coming to Haworth unless you want to see the house, church, and environment in which the Brontës lived, loved, suffered, and wrote during their moody and melancholy lives. Their legacy lives on here, but curiously enough, there isn't a single bookshop in town with their complete works. The

Parsonage they lived in is now open to visitors; it's furnished with a load of family relics. The parish church in front contains the family vault.

Fans of *Wuthering Heights* may want to visit **Top Withens,** a ruined farmhouse set in the desolate moorland. It's said to have been the inspiration for Heathcliff's house. It's a relatively easy six-mile circuit, and in summer the grounds are smothered in purple heather. For longer walks, the **Brontë Trail** is a good way to see the moorlands. It links about 40 to 50 miles of Brontëland: where they were born, where they died, where they had tea and scones.

In the village, there are a few shops worth exploring. **The Old Apothecary** is a sad reminder of the tragic story of brother Branwell. The runt of the family and a brilliant ne'er-do-well, he bought the opium that fed his drug habit here. Across the street is his old watering hole. For those uninspired by the moors, the Brontës, and the Victorian melodrama, hop over to nearby Bradford, where there's a **Sony IMAX** theater, a first-rate **photography museum,** and a good arts cinema.

Brontë Parsonage Museum. Haworth, Keighley. Tel: 01535/642323. Open: Apr–Sept: daily 10am–5pm. Oct–Mar: 11am–4:30pm. Admission: adults £3.60; students and seniors £2.60; children £1.10.

The Old Apothecary. 84 Main St., Haworth. Tel: 01535/646830. Open: daily 10:30am–5:30pm.

Pictureville Cinema and Sony IMAX Cinema. Pictureville, Bradford. Tel: 01274/727488. Box office open: daily 10am–8pm. Pictureville Cinema admission: adults £3.80; concessions £2.60. IMAX Cinema admission: adults £3.90; children £2.70.

National Museum of Photography, Film, and Television. Pictureville, Bradford. Tel: 01274/732277. Open: Tues–Sun 10:30am–6pm.

The Basics

Tourist Office: Haworth Tourist Information Centre. 2–4 West Lane, Haworth. Tel: 01535/642329. Open: Apr–Oct: daily 9:30am–5:30pm; Nov–Mar: daily 9:30am–5pm. From the hostel, go down Longlands Drive, turn right on Mill Hay, and walk down the road till you reach Main Street, a cobbled hill on your left. Go up Main Street; the office is straight ahead; a 20-minute walk.

Post Office: 10 Mill Hay, Haworth Brow. Tel: 01535/642242. Open: Mon 9am–1pm and 2–5:30pm; Tues 9am–1pm; Wed–Fri 9am–1pm and 2–5pm; Sat 9am–12:30pm. From the hostel, go down Longlands Drive, and turn right on Mill Hay. It's on your left after about three blocks; a 5-minute walk.

Currency Exchange: The closest place is Bradford, 8 miles away. Thomas Cook. 45/47 Market St., Bradford. Tel: 01274/370263. Open: Mon–Fri 9am–5:30pm.

Telephone Code: 01535.

Bike Rental: The closest place is in Bingley, about 5 miles away. Lambert Keith Cyclesports. 108 Main St., Bingley. Tel: 01274/560605.

Getting There: The **train** station closest to Haworth is **Keighley** (about 5 miles away) on the York-Skipton line. Trains run frequently from **York, Skipton,** and **Leeds.** Once in Keighley, it's a 5-minute walk from the train station to the bus terminal, where bus nos. 663, 664, and 665 depart every 15 minutes to Haworth town and other nearby towns as well. For train information, call 01274/732237.

For local bus connections, call Keighley and District at 01535/602384. **Coaches** from **York, Leeds,** and other cities come straight into the **Keighley** bus terminal, and the local buses will take you into Haworth. The bus ride from Keighley takes about 10 minutes. By **car,** Haworth is reachable from a number of cities on the Midlands. From **Bradford,** take the A650 heading north into Keighley. From there, it's 4 miles south on the A629 to Haworth. From **Halifax,** it's a straight ride north on the A629 to Haworth.

What's Next

From Haworth, the Leeds-Carlisle train line takes you straight into the north Pennines. **Hawes** (alight in Garsdale) boasts a creamery and waterfall; **Dentdale** (alight in Dent) features a precipitous wooded gorge; and **Kirkby Stephen** has one of the more unusual hostels in the area: a converted chapel with pews in the dining room and stained-glass windows in the sitting room. From all these towns, spectacular views can be had on walking paths and cycle routes through the area. The Settle-Carlisle train, however, also offers some of the most panoramic views of all, and many people come here just to ride the train through the Three Peaks, the moorlands, and green farmlands. Traveling through gritstone bridges, endless viaducts, and around some vertiginous passes, it's an excellent way to see the area, although prepare to walk from train station to Youth Hostel. Hawes is six miles, Dent is two miles, and Kirkby Stephen is $1^1/_2$ miles from the nearest respective station.

HAWES

Anyone who's mean to small animals or pushes little old ladies won't feel at home here: It's too sweet. Set amid the hills of gentle, pastoral Upper Wensleydale, Hawes is 64 miles northwest of York and in the center of the 700-square miles that comprise the Yorkshire Dales National Park.

James Herriot was inspired to write his many animal stories in and around this farmland. Much of the British TV series of his *All Creatures Great and Small*, about the trials and tribulations of a Yorkshire veterinarian, was filmed in Hawes.

Off-camera, this little market town won't disappoint you. A local creamery, tea rooms playing soothing New Age music, curio shops, pottery studios, a wood carver, and a bookshop or two make Hawes a popular spot for people winding their way through the dales. There's even a toy shop where you can watch the owner carve wooden mobiles.

The only thing not at all cute about Hawes is the weather, which vacillates between cloudy, windy, and (very occasionally) sunny in summer. So if you're here to walk through some of the sleepy, sheepy Pennines, bring your Wellies and Barbour jacket, and be prepared for the cold winds that tend to whip through the dales even in late spring and summer.

The town's happiness rubs off on visitors: school groups visiting the local cheesemaker, elderly couples walking their terriers, and backpackers starting to walk the Pennine Way. The bucolic meadows, outlined by drystone walls separating the sheep farms, refresh the weary (which you will be after getting here by public transportation) and invigorate the lusty. The Youth Hostel here is every bit as adorable as the town.

Hawes Youth Hostel

Lancaster Terrace
Hawes, North Yorkshire DL8 3LQ
Tel: 01969/667368. Fax: 01969/667368.

Vaguely reminiscent of a nursery school, the hostel at Hawes gets points for being warm and fuzzy. The manager's philosophy is simple: This is his home, and he likes to make it as pleasant as possible for everyone who crosses his doorstep.

Helpful local information and hostel rules are posted on the walls in bubbles emanating from the mouths of furry animals. Oil paintings hang on the wall in the dining room, and more talking animals indicate dining choices on the bulletin board, carefully prepared by Pauline. You get the feeling they see a lot of the 10- and-under crowd here, although walkers and cyclists seem to love it here as well.

The bedrooms are standard YHA bunk rooms, sturdy and with nice quilts for snuggling. Just make sure you tuck in by the curfew: The rules are strictly observed. Guests are asked to do their part in cleaning up after dinner as well. A reward for good hostelers comes in the form of a discount at two local museums: both the Creamery and the Dales Museum offer a two-for-one rate if you show your Hostelling International card.

🚆 The closest train station is Garsdale, 6 miles away. From the station, turn right; when you reach the crossroads, Hawes is to the right, 5³/₄ miles ahead. A minibus runs from here to Hawes twice a week, on Tuesdays and Saturdays, and you must book it by at least the night before by calling 01969/66748. Otherwise, you can try your luck with the kind farm neighbors.

🚌 The closest bus station is in Richmond. From there United bus no. 26 goes to Hawes, on the main street. From there, turn left, go past the garage, and the Youth Hostel is up on the left.

🚗 Hawes is just off the A684, the road running from North Allerton to Kendal. Follow signs to Hawes. Those coming from the **east** will go through the town; the hostel will be on the left past the garage. Those coming from the **west** will approach Hawes and will make a sharp right on the Ingleton Road; the hostel is up on the left.

🗓 Open Feb 15–Dec 28. BABA.

🕐 Reception open 8:45–10am and 5–10:30pm. Curfew 11pm.

🛏 58 beds. 2-, 3-, 4-, 5-, and 8-bed rooms.

£ Members: adults £8; under 18 £5.35.

🍴 Self-catering kitchen facilities. Breakfast: 8am. Lunch: packed lunch only; order by 7pm the night before. Dinner: 7pm.

🍷 No table license.

🧺 No lockers.

🧺 Washers (£1.50); drying room.

P No parking at hostel. The car park next to the fish-and-chips shop on Market Place is free.

🛍 Shop at hostel sells candy, souvenirs, batteries, maps, and guidebooks.

🛋 Games room with pool table and TV.

♿ Not wheelchair accessible.

🚬 In entrance hall only.

 See "Currency Exchange" under "The Basics" in Hawes.

🔺 Bike shed.

Services

Cheap Eats Nearby

The Crown

One of the reasonably priced, reasonably good pubs in town, this place has an elegant sitting area away from the bar action and an outdoor terrace. Salads cost £4 to £5; fish dishes £6 to £7. The manager cooks a great big paella for £9. Vegetarian specials; Theakston's Old Peculier ale (£2.10).

Market Place, Hawes. Tel: 01969/667212. Open: Mon–Sat noon–2:30pm and 6:30–9:30pm; Sun noon–2:30pm and 7–9pm. Credit cards: VA, MC, Access, EC. From the hostel, turn right on Market Place, and it's on your left, after a 3- to 5-minute walk.

Laura's Cottage

The owner has been known to pick up desperate backpackers on lonely country roads on her way to her busy little tea room in the center of Hawes with comfortable green banquettes, posters of Yorkshire, and soothing classical music. Ploughman's lunch (£3 to £4) and lip-smacking lasagne (£4) are offered. Cream teas and homemade tea cakes too.

Market Place, Hawes. Tel: 01969/667325. Open: May–Sept daily 10am–6pm. Closed Oct–Apr. Cash only. From the hostel, turn right on Market Place, and it's just past Barclays Bank on the left side of the street.

Grocery store: Spar. Market Place. Open: Mon–Sat 8am–9pm; Sun 10am–6pm.

Experiences

Some say that apple pie without a slice of Wensleydale cheese is like a kiss without a squeeze. You can find out for yourself if you wander over to the **Wensleydale Creamery** down the road, where gigantic vats bubble with thick pools of the milky stuff. An interesting exhibition walks you through the cheese-making process and explains a bit about local farming history. Samples are offered at the end of the tour. Just beyond the town, the **Dales Countryside Museum** tells about the Dales of old, going all the way back to the Ice Age, when rhinoceroses and hyena roamed the land.

For more athletic pursuits, Hawes is on the paths of both the **Pennine Way** and a few other long-distance footpaths, and you can take lots of short-distance strolls in the area. The circuit to **Hardraw** is a gentle 4$^{1}/_{2}$ miles and takes you to the highest unbroken waterfall in Britain, something of a romantic escape. Another 4-mile walk takes you out to **Semer Water,** the only natural lake in Yorkshire. There was once a village there, but all the townspeople were drowned after a curse was cast by a wandering pilgrim who was denied lodging by the locals. The only thing left in the town is the eerie, haunted Semer Water—not for the faint of heart. For a day of excitement in the Yorkshire Dales (speaking in relative terms), stick around for market day, when the sheep auction takes place and local merchants sell their wares at *baa*-gain prices.

Wensleydale Creamery and Cheese Experience. Gayle Lane, Hawes. Tel: 01969/667664. Open: Mon–Sat 9:30am–5pm; Sun 10am–4:30pm. Admission: adults £2.95; children £1.95; senior citizens £2.70. Discount with Hostelling International card.

Dales Countryside Museum. Station Yard, Hawes. Tel: 01969/667450. Open: Apr–Oct: daily 10am–5pm. Admission: adults £1.50; children and students 75p.

Hardraw Falls. Admission: adults 60p; children 30p. Pay at the Green Dragon Inn.

The Basics

Tourist Office: National Park Centre. Station Yard, Hawes. Tel: 01969/667450. Open: Easter–Oct: daily 10am–5pm. Open some weekends in winter. Call ahead for exact dates. From the hostel, about a 10-minute walk. Go down the road and turn right onto Market Place. Walk all the way through town to the Dales Countryside Museum, about 100 yards farther, on your left. It's inside the museum gift shop.

Post Office: Town Foot, Hawes. Tel: 01969/667201. Open: Mon–Tues and Thurs–Fri 8:30am–midnight and 1–5pm; Wed 8:30am–midnight; Sat 8:30am–midnight. From the hostel, 5 minutes down the road. Exit, turn right, and go through the town. At the fork, bear right; it's on your right.

Currency Exchange: Barclays Bank. Market Place, Hawes. Tel: 01969/667203.

Telephone Code: 01969.

Bike Rental: in Askrigg, 5 miles away. Ian Rawlins. Woodburn Garage, Askrigg. Tel: 01969/650455.

Getting There: Darlington is the closest major **bus** station that has connections to and from large cities, including **Sheffield, York,** and **London.** From the Darlington bus station, you can take the United Bus no. 24 or 25 to Richmond, then the no. 26 from Richmond straight into Hawes. For schedule information, call 01325/355415. For those coming by **train,** Hawes is reachable on the Leeds-Carlisle line, and trains go as far as **Garsdale,** 6 miles away. From there, take the twice weekly bus on Tuesdays and Saturdays, which you must book by at least the night before by calling 01969/66748. You can also try your luck on the road. By **car,** Hawes is reachable by the M6, the Birmingham-Carlisle motorway. Turn off at Junction 37 and head east on the A684, passing through Sedbergh and Garsdale. From Garsdale, Hawes is 6 miles down the road.

What's Next

Nine miles east of Hawes sits the misty village of **Aysgarth,** another stop on the Pennine Way and Coast to Coast Path. Aside from a locally famous waterfall, carriage museum, and homey hostel, there's not much else in the town except for some excellent dale walking. Heading west of Wensleydale gets you to **Dent** (eight miles away), another quiet speck on the Pennine landscape. Drystone walls and sheep farms dot the lonely road between the hostel and the village, which boasts a train station with the highest elevation of any in England. Traveling further south on the Settle-Carlisle train route takes you to **Haworth,** former home of (and current shrine to) the Brontë sisters. The Youth Hostel is about a 15-minute walk from the town, which has dedicated itself lock, stock, and barrel to preserving the memory of its famous sisters and one wayward brother: Charlotte, Anne, Emily, and Branwell Brontë.

DENTDALE

At first glance, the village of Dent seems like not much more than what its name suggests—a tiny dimple in the cheeky hills along the Settle-Carlisle railway line. With little more than a train station, a brewery, and sheep farms, Dent is nestled in the shadows of its juxtaposing landscape.

At the top of this 1,150-foot dale is the precariously perched train station, surrounded by a treeless moorland, dark and barren in winter and heavenly heathered during the summer. Winds whip through here, and locals say it's haunted by Hob the fairy. As you walk down the dale (carefully, please), the landscape turns into a fertile farm land with glades, streams, passes, and public footpaths with names such as Lenny's Leap.

If you're not interested in countryside rambling, you might be better off staying on the train to Carlisle and other points north. There's nothing to do here but walk and cycle, unless you have the money and interest for pony trekking, climbing, and caving, all of which can be pricey. The walk into the microscopic village can be long, and if you're looking for action, look elsewhere. Dent doesn't have it.

❄ Dentdale Youth Hostel

Cowgill, Dent
Sedbergh, Cumbria LA10 5RN
Tel: 015396/25251.

Set on a beautiful patch of land high above Dentdale, this listed building is an old hunting lodge that was converted into a Youth Hostel in 1944. Right on the banks of the river Dee, the hostel has lots of room out back for sitting, relaxing, playing ball, or barbecuing on sunny summer evenings.

Rooms upstairs are named after the three peaks of the Yorkshire Dales: Peny-Ghent, Ingleborough, and Whernside. There's a log fire usually roaring in the common room, which has picture windows that look out onto the garden and the Wensleydale sheep nibbling on the grassy lawn out front.

The simplicity of this hostel is striking: there's no TV and no games room. What you get is a secluded old lodge with some friendly house cats prowling about. The hostel is actually very convenient if you don't mind walking: Once you get down the hill from the Dent station, it's a very flat walk to the hostel on a one-lane road by the side of a sweet little river.

Services

🚆 At Dent train station, walk (carefully) down the steep hill; at the crossroads, turn left (turning right will take you to the village of Dent, 3 1/2 miles in the other direction). Walk about 3/4 mile to the Youth Hostel, which will come up on your right.

🚌 The only bus that comes to Dent is the minibus service that runs through Yorkshire. Rail transportation is the only sensible way to come here (see above).

🚗 Dent is 2 miles off the A684, the Hawes-Ingleton road. From either direction, you'll eventually reach a crossroads with signs to Dent and the YHA. From that junction, it's another 2 miles to the Youth Hostel, which will come up on your left.

🗓 Open Jan–Dec 15. Closed Thurs. BABA.

🕐 Reception open 8–9am and 5–9pm.

🛏 55 beds. 8-, 10-, and 12-bed rooms.

£ Members: adults £7.20; under 18 £4.85.

🍴 Self-catering kitchen facilities. Breakfast: 8:15am. Lunch: packed lunch only; order by 5pm the night before. Dinner:7pm.

⌶ No table license.

🧳 No lockers.

☐ Drying room only.

P Limited but free of charge.

🛍 Shop at hostel sells candy, toiletries, and canned goods.

🔥 One lounge with fireplace.

🚭 Not allowed.

♿ Not wheelchair accessible.

💱 See "Currency Exchange" under "The Basics" in Dent.

▲ Bike shed.

Cheap Eats Nearby

The George & Dragon

Traditional English fare is served in this comfortable bar and restaurant. Brown leather banquettes heave with old folks on Thursdays (over-60s lunch special £3.25). Dent Bitter (£1.40 per pint) and Ram's Bottom (£1.60 per pint and drink slowly) are brewed two miles up the road. Three-course evening meal in the restaurant (£10.50) features T'owd Tup Pie (steak cooked in Dent Brewery's stout). Vegetable curry (£4) and veggie burger (£1.70) for weaker stomachs.

Main Street, Dent. Tel: 015396/25256. Open: daily noon–2pm and 6:30–10pm. From the Youth Hostel, 5 miles down the road. Once you reach Dent, go up the main street. It's on your left.

The Stone Close

You'll find a cast-iron stove, a log fire, and gourmet country cooking at this elegant inn that was once two farmhouses. It's also the conveniently located home of Dent's tourist information point. The inspired menu offers aubergine-and-spinach layer (£4), mushroom-and-herb flan (£4), as well as old favorites like ploughman's lunch, homity pie, and oven-baked potatoes. Small but good wine selection. Delicate craft items for sale too.

Main Street, Dent. Tel: 015396/25231. Open: daily 10:30am–5:30pm. Cash only. From the Youth Hostel, a 2-hour walk: turn left and go 5 miles down the road. Once you reach Dent, go up the main street, and turn right at the Sun Inn. It's down the street to your left.

Grocery store: Dent Stores. Main Street, Dent. Groceries, toiletries, and Julie's Knitwear from up the road. Open: Easter–Christmas: Mon–Fri 8:30am–5:30pm; Sat 9am–5:30pm; Sun 9am–4pm. Christmas–Easter: Mon–Fri 8:30am–5:30pm; Sat 9am–5:30pm. It's 5 miles down the road from the hostel.

Experiences

Those hardy enough to make it out here are rewarded by a treasure trove of virtually untouched landmarks from bygone days. Walking through the town of **Dent,** you will pass through an ancient Celtic kingdom, a Norman church, and an Elizabethan mill. The countless stone-walled farms crammed full with Wensleydale sheep and mooing cows haven't changed too much over the years, either.

The village itself has some interesting history: the open area in front of the churchyard was once the location of the Dent market place, where the town crier would yell out the news and the bailiff would sell off cattle and property confiscated from Quakers who refused to pay the tithe. The fountain in the town center is a one-man memorial to the town's favorite son, Adam Sedgwick, a local wonder boy who later became a pioneer of modern geology.

Caving is fun in nearby Ribblesdale (10 miles away). You can get guided tours of caves or don a body slicker and do some proper caving with a qualified instructor. Most people, however, walk, hike, and bike through Dentdale. The **Three Peaks,** inside the rough triangle between Dent, Horton-in-Ribblesdale, and Ingleton, provide ample challenge even for the physically fit. Lots of people rise to the local challenge of climbing the three monsters in one single day, and those who make it win a certificate.

Another way to see the area is by train: The **Settle-Carlisle** line is one of the most famous in England for its breathtaking ride, passing right through the Three Peaks of Yorkshire and over the quarter-mile viaduct at Ribblehead. The locals have fought to keep the line from being dismantled and are proud of this bit of living history.

Caving courses. Freetime Activities. Sun Lea, Joss Lane, Sedbergh (8 miles away). Tel: 015396/20828. Or contact Clapham National Park Information Centre, Clapham, Lancaster. Tel: 015242/51419. £12 per person.

The Settle and Carlisle Railway Trust. Railway Station, Broughton Road, Skipton. Tel: 01756/796084 or 01132/448133.

The Basics

Tourist Office: An "information point" is in The Stone Close, in Dent village. Main Street, Dent. Tel: 015396/25231. Open: Mar–Oct: daily 10:30am–5:45pm; Nov–Christmas Sat–Sun 10:30am–5:45pm. Also open daily during Christmas Week: 10:30am–5:45pm. From the Youth Hostel, a 2-hour walk: Turn left and go 5 miles down the road. Once you reach Dent, go up the main street, and turn right at the Sun Inn. It's down the street to your left. The closest official tourist office is the National Park Centre in Sedbergh, 5 miles away from Dent. 72 Main Street, Sedbergh. Tel: 015396/20125. Open: Mar 31–Oct: daily 10am–4:30pm. Nov–Mar 30: Wed 10am–12:30pm and 1–4:30pm; Sat 10am–1pm and 1:30–4:30pm.

Post Office: Main Street, Dent. Tel: 015396/25201. Open: Mon–Wed 9am–5:30pm; Thurs 9am–12:30pm; Fri 9am–5:30pm; Sat 9am–12:30pm. From the hostel, a 2-hour walk: turn left and go 5 miles down the road. Once you reach Dent, go up the main street, and turn left at the George and Dragon. It's on your right.

Currency Exchange: The closest bank is in Hawes (8 miles away). Barclays Bank. Market Place, Hawes. Tel: 01969/667203.

Telephone Code: 015396.

Bike Rental: Sedbergh Cycles. Howgill Lane, Sedbergh. Tel: 015396/21000. About 8 miles from the hostel. Guided tours.

Taxi: tel. 015396/20414.

Getting There: Dent is another out-of-the-way town, but **trains** work their way through on the Settle-Carlisle line that connects into **Leeds, York,** and beyond. The Dent station is unmanned, so for information call the station in Leeds at 0113/244 8133. **Buses** can be even trickier: The best idea is to get to Leeds or Settle and take the train to Dent. For bus schedules, call Leeds Bus Station at 0113/245 7676. If you are already in the Yorkshire area, there is infrequent (once or twice weekly) but dependable service from Hawes and Kirkby Stephen in Yorkshire, and Kendal, Keswick, and Windermere in the Lakes District. The Cumbria County Council publishes a brown leaflet *Settle and Carlisle Bus Links* with times. Call ahead to confirm because public transportation can be very capricious here. By phone, call Settle and Carlisle Bus Links at 01228/812812. For those coming by **car** from the east of England, take the A1 or M1, coming across any of the major roads M65, which comes across Manchester. From the south, take the M6, which straddles Yorkshire and the Lake District, past Birmingham and Manchester, and up to Lancaster and Carlisle, following signs pointing north.

What's Next

Along the Settle-Carlisle train line, there are quite a few places to stop for a dose of Dales life. **Hawes** (alight in Garsdale train station on the Settle-Carlisle line) is only 8 miles away. It's a quintessential Wensleydale town with its own creamery and spouting waterfall nearby. **Kirkby Stephen** (23 miles away), also on the awe-inspiring Settle-Carlisle line, has a Youth Hostel that's equally uplifting. In a converted chapel, you'll dine on the pews and play checkers against the backdrop of stained-glass windows in this old market town nestled in the Eden Valley. Or try heading south toward Keighley: the Youth Hostel at **Haworth** welcomes hundreds of Brontë pilgrims every year who look for their own inspiration in the village and surrounding moors.

KIRKBY STEPHEN

There's not much happening in Kirkby Stephen (pop. 1,600)—only a few pubs, a few antiques shops, two bike stores, and a load of tea rooms. This lonely little town mainly sees action from the cross-country walkers who stop here, almost halfway along the 190-mile trail that goes from St. Bees Head on the west coast (on the Irish Sea) to Robin Hood's Bay on the North Sea.

If you end up here, you'll find a strangely inspirational air: There are four churches in town (one of which houses the Youth Hostel). The river Eden snakes through the rolling green hills with nice waterside picnic spots and twisting little bridleways. Other than that, and a few long-distance walking routes, there's really not much to entertain visitors for more than a day or two. The unusual hostel is worth the trip if you're in the area, but otherwise, Kirkby Stephen is just a sleepy, somewhat simple Cumbrian village.

✿ Kirkby Stephen Youth Hostel

Fletcher Hill, Market Street
Kirkby Stephen
Cumbria CA17 4QQ
Tel: 017683/71793. Fax: 017683/71793.

A former Methodist chapel, this hostel has been more sensitively restored than most, retaining many of the building's original features. A stained-glass window showers light onto the common room, overlooking the pews lined up in the dining room. One remaining gravestone sits in the kitchen, serving as a somber warning to those hostelers who try to escape their wash-up duties. It remains a traditional hostel, with no TV to spoil the quiet, pensive atmosphere.

Students of medieval history will delight in studying the small Gothic stained-glass windows in the dining room, and the warden claims that there's a "presence" (no further elaboration) in the building. Guests tend to come to Kirkby Stephen for its convenience to the walking routes, so they're a quiet lot who study their Ordnance Survey maps and write postcards before retiring early.

🚆 From the train station, catch the no. 505 bus to Market Place. From there, turn around and walk to the church across from the Coop supermarket. The hostel is inside the church. Alternatively, exit the station and turn right. The hostel and town are a $1^{1}/_{2}$-mile walk.

Services

🚌 The bus stop is on Market Street. From there, turn around and walk to the church across from the Coop supermarket. The hostel is inside the church.

🚗 On the M6, take Junction 38 at Brough. Follow the road marked Kirkby Stephen, 12 miles away. When you come in to the town, the hostel will come up on your right if you are arriving from the south and on your left if you are arriving from the north.

🗓 Open Mar–Dec 15. BABA.

🕐 Reception open 7–10am and 5–9:30pm.

🛏 44 beds. 2-, 4-, 6-, and 8-bed rooms. One family room en suite with daytime access.

£ Members: adults £7.20; under 18 £4.85.

🍴 Self-catering kitchen facilities. Breakfast: 8am. Lunch: packed lunch only; should be ordered by 9:30pm the night before. Dinner: 7pm.

🍸 No table license.

🗄 No lockers.

⊙ Drying room only.

P None.

🛍 Shop at hostel sells hand-knitted caps, souvenirs, and candy.

🛋 Common area in a balcony upstairs from dining room.

🚭 Verboten.

♿ Not wheelchair accessible.

💱 See "Currency Exchange" under "The Basics" in Kirkby Stephen.

🅰 Bike shed.

Cheap Eats Nearby

Lonsdale's Tea Room

Good value and lip-smacking sausage sandwiches are offered at this busy little tea room in the center of town. Fare includes soup and roll (£1.10), baked potatoes (£1.30 to £1.70), and a variety of vegetarian specials.

Market Square, Kirkby Stephen. Tel: 017683/71731. Open: Mon–Wed and Fri–Sat 9:30am–5pm; Sun 10am–5pm. Cash only. From the hostel, a 2-minute walk. Exit and turn left onto Market Street. It's on your left.

The Old Forge Bistro

Nouveau country meets French bistro in the middle of nowhere. A wine rack peeps out of the stone walls, and dishes such as red snapper and Roquefort risotto (£5.75), beef in orange sauce (£5.95), and mushroom tagliatelle (£6.50) top the list of specials. Good vegetarian and wholefood dishes.

39 North Rd., Kirkby Stephen. Tel: 017683/71832. Open: Tues–Sun noon–2pm and 6–10pm. Reservations recommended. Credit cards: VA, MC, Access. From the hostel, turn left and it's on your left, about three blocks down; a 5-minute walk.

Grocery store: Walter Wilson. Market Street, Kirkby Stephen. Open: Mon–Sat 8am–10pm; Sun 9am–10pm.

Experiences

Kirkby Stephen is mainly known for its convenient location right on the **Coast to Coast Path** that starts at St. Bees Head in the west and goes to Robin Hood's Bay in the east. It is also on the alternative Pennine Way, the Eden Way, and the Cumbrian Cycleway, so there are lots of well-marked **footpaths** and **bridleways** in the area.

Monday is **Market Day** in Kirkby Stephen, when stalls set up in the Market Square offer farming tools, clothes, fruit, vegetables, and the usual assortment of goodies. Behind Market Square, you can catch the cattle auction, which is held in the early evening. From the Market Square, the narrow, winding passageways lead down to the River Eden. The largest of these alleys is Stoneshot, partially built over tunnels that were dug as shelter for those luckless souls trying to escape the Scottish raids between 1250 and 1550.

Continue down Stoneshot, and you'll cross Frank's Bridge over the river. From there you can take the 10-minute walk up to the little hamlet of Hartley. Lined with cherry blossoms, Georgian houses, and old barns, it's a well-preserved little Cumbrian town with the river running right through it.

Footpaths and bike routes. Contact the Kirkby Stephen T.I.C.

The Basics

Tourist Office: Kirkby Stephen T.I.C. Market Street, Kirkby Stephen. Tel: 017683/71199. Open: Easter–Oct: Mon–Sat 9:30am–5:30pm; Sun 10am–4pm. Nov–Easter: Mon 10am–midnight and 2–4pm; Tues–Sat 10am–midnight. From the hostel, turn left onto Market Street. It's two blocks down on the left; a 2-minute walk.

Post Office: Kirkby Stephen Post Office. Victoria Square, Kirkby Stephen. Tel: 017683/71383. Open: Mon–Fri 9am–5:30pm; Sat 9am–12:30pm. From the hostel, turn right past the freezer shop. Turn left onto Nateby Road. The P.O. is on the right, across from the Temperance Hall.

Currency Exchange: Kirkby Stephen Post Office. See "Post Office" under "The Basics" in Kirkby Stephen.

Telephone Code: 017683.

Bike Rental: H. S. Robinson. The Cycle Shop. 2 Market St., Kirkby Stephen. Tel: 017683/71519. Open: Mon–Tues and Thurs–Sat 9am–5:30pm; Wed 9am–midnight. Full day £10; half day £5.

Getting There: Kirkby Stephen is on the Settle-Carlisle **train** line, which offers frequent service with connections to and from **Newcastle, Edinburgh,** and **Glasgow** via Carlisle. From the south and east, it isn't too hard to get here from York, Leeds, and the Midlands, but you'll have to switch trains. Call 01228/44711 for information. The closest major **bus** station is in **Penrith,** about 20 miles away. From there, local buses connect to Kirkby Stephen. For schedule information, call Stagecoach Buses in Penrith at 01768/65783. Local buses also go as far as Kendal, which is the main town in the South Lakes, and a transport hub for the entire Lake District. For local bus info, call 01228/812812. By **car,** take the M6 motorway south from **Carlisle** and north from **Kendal, Lancaster,** and **Manchester,** following signs for Tebay. At Junction 38, switch to the A685 going east, and Kirkby Stephen is 12 miles from there.

What's Next

Any of the hostels on the Settle-Carlisle train line make nice stops: **Hawes,** 15 miles away, is a traditional Wensleydale market town. With a local history museum as well as a creamery, it offers a real slice of Yorkshire life. **Dent** is an isolated village with an old hunting lodge for a hostel and some excellent hill walking, about 23 miles south of Kirkby Stephen. For those who want out of this pastoral farmland, there are good bus and train connections to **Kendal,** which is the entry point into the Lake District; the hostel is in an old brewery, and the town is a lively spot on the fringes of this much-visited, much-admired corner of England, with shining lakes and craggy fells.

AYSGARTH FALLS

Cascading down from the tip-top of Upper Wensleydale, the village here owes its existence and its name to the foamy waters spouting from their source in the River Ure. In the heart of the Yorkshire Dales 24 miles east of Northallerton, Aysgarth is set amid the mellow sandstone, limestone, and shale that have given this region its delicate scarred hills, hay meadows, and traditional stone walls and farmhouses.

There's not much in the way of tourist activity in this rural community. Hill walkers and romantic types make their way up here to gush over the falls, and students of British history trickle in to inspect the local carriage museum and nearby Bolton Castle, where Mary, Queen of Scots was imprisoned. The village is often shrouded in mist from the annual rainfall of 50 inches, providing the falls with a steady shower and the local farmers with acres of green grass to feed the flocks of sheep that dot this gentle landscape.

Aysgarth Falls Youth Hostel

Aysgarth, Leyburn
North Yorkshire DL8 3SR
Tel: 01969/663260. Fax: 01969/663110.

Only steps away from the falls, this homey little hostel has lots of room, allowing backpackers, hill walkers, and school groups to coexist relatively peacefully. When it starts getting claustrophobic, an excellent pub next door provides a quick escape and good local brews.

Built of mellow sandstone, this house was originally a private school built following the construction of the (now dismantled) railway in the 1870s, and the wardens can tell you all about the local history. Author Alf Wight (aka James Herriot) loved it here, and you can read all about the hostel in James Herriot's Yorkshire, in which he remembers the days of old-fashioned hosteling.

Members are still asked to do their bit. The hardy types who make it here don't seem to mind clearing the table after the tasty evening meal anyway—it only adds to the homey feeling.

Services

The most convenient train station is Darlington, 34 miles away. From there, walk into the town center and take United bus no. 29 to Richmond; change to the no. 26 from Richmond-Hawes and tell the driver to drop you at the Aysgarth Falls Youth Hostel. This could take 1–2 hours, depending on the connections you make. There is also a train station at Northallerton, 24 miles away, but bus service is less frequent from there.

The closest major bus station is in Darlington, 34 miles away. From there, walk into the town center and follow directions from the train station, given above.

From the **north** on the A1, exit at Scotch Corner for Richmond, following signs to Leyburn. From there, take the A684 8 miles to Aysgarth Falls. The hostel will come up on your right. From the **south,** leave the A1 at Beedale. Take the A684 through Leyburn to Aysgarth, and the hostel will come up on your right.

Open Feb–Nov. Weekends only in Feb, Mar, Nov. BABA.

🕐 Reception open 7:30–10am and 5–10:30pm. Curfew 11pm.

🛏 65 beds. 3-, 4-, 6-, and 8-bed rooms.

£ Members: adults £7.20; under 18 £4.85.

🍴 Self-catering kitchen facilities. Breakfast: 8:15am. Lunch: packed lunch only; order the night before. Dinner: 7pm.

🍸 Alcohol prohibited.

👜 No lockers.

🖻 Drying rooms.

P Ample and free of charge.

🛍 Shop at hostel sells canned goods, candy, local maps.

🛋 Common room; TV room; games room with pool table.

🚬 In common room only.

♿ Not wheelchair accessible.

💱 See "Currency Exchange" under "The Basics" in Aysgarth Falls.

🔺 Bike shed.

Cheap Eats Nearby

The George & Dragon Inn

Gleaming copper beer mugs dangle from the ceiling and pencil drawings of local patrons hang on the walls in this popular restaurant. Soup £1.95. Sandwiches are £1.50 to £2.85. Hot dishes include lasagne, vegetable tikka, and mushroom stroganoff, £4 to £6.

Aysgarth. Tel: 01969/663358. Open: Mon–Sat noon–2:30pm and 6–11pm; Sun noon–3pm and 7–10:30pm. Credit cards: VA, MC, EC, Access. From the hostel, turn right onto Dyke Hollins, then right again at the filling station toward the village. It's about 200 yards up on the left; a 10-minute walk.

Palmer Flatt Restaurant

This old coaching inn keeps Aysgarth in its cups with ales from local breweries and provides hearty sustenance by its wood-burning stove in a converted stable. Fish dishes are £4 to £5. Steak pies sell like hotcakes here at £4.95 a pop. A chalkboard lists specials and "promotionales."

Aysgarth. Tel: 01969/663228. Open: daily noon–2pm and 7–9:30pm. Credit cards: VA, MC, EC, Access, Switch. From the hostel, cross the street. It's on the right.

Grocery store: Yoredale House and Tea Rooms. Main Street, Aysgarth.

Experiences

The splashing waters of **Aysgarth Falls,** set in a wooded gorge of the River Ure, are at their most spectacular after a rain. They're tiny in comparison to those of Niagara, but their surging spray gives forth glimmering rainbows when caught at the right angle. Just up the road from the falls is a former mill that now houses a small but lovingly preserved collection of old Victorian coaches.

Only four miles away on the north side of Wensleydale, **Bolton Castle** makes a good day trip. Mary, Queen of Scots was imprisoned here for six months, and her bedchamber remains as its was in the 16th century. Walking paths abound in the area. The hostel is right on the YHA's interhostel **Herriot Way** through the Yorkshire Dales and is only seven miles from the **Coast to Coast Path** and the **Pennine Way.** *Gentle* is the key word here, though: The hills never get too strenuous.

The tiny village of Askrigg, setting of the TV series *All Creatures Great and Small* based on James Herriot's stories, is a languorous six-mile walk. Walk past

Dales farmhouses and underneath limestone cliffs, and then vary the scenery by going gently along the River Ure back to the hostel.

Victorian Carriage Museum. Aysgarth Falls, Aysgarth. Tel: 01969/663399. Open: Easter–Oct: daily 9:30am–8pm. In winter, call for an appointment. Admission: adults £1.50; children 50p; two-for-one discount with Hostelling Interantional card.

Bolton Castle. Wensleydale, North Yorkshire (4 miles away). Tel: 01969/23981. Open: Mar–Nov only: daily 10am–5pm. In winter, call for an appointment. Admission: adults £2.50; children and senior citizens £1.50.

The Basics

Tourist Office: Aysgarth Falls Yorkshire Dales National Park Information Centre. Aysgarth Falls, Aysgarth. Tel: 01969/663424. Open: Apr–Oct only: daily 9:30am–5pm. From the hostel, turn right, cross the bridge, and pass the falls. It's down the road to the left. The closest Tourist Information Centre is in Leyburn (7 miles away). Leyburn T.I.C. Thronborough Hall, Leyburn. Tel: 01969/623069. Open: Apr–Oct: daily 9:30am–5:30pm. Nov–Mar: Mon–Sat 9:30am–4:30pm. From Aysgarth, take bus no. 26 or 142 into Leyburn.

Post Office: Aysgarth Post Office. Main Street, Aysgarth. Tel: 01969/663413. Open: Mon 9am–midnight and 2–5pm; Tues 9am–midnight; Thurs 9am–midnight and 2–5pm; Fri 9am–midnight. From the hostel, a 10-minute walk: turn right up Dyke Hollins, and walk to the filling station. Turn right and walk into Aysgarth. It's on the right.

Currency Exchange: The closest place is in Leyburn (7 miles away). Barclays Bank. Market Place, Leyburn. Tel: 01969/623117.

Telephone Code: 01969.

Bike Rental: Mr. Rawlins, Woodburn Garage, Askrigg (6 miles away). Tel: 01969/650455.

Getting There: Trains come to the area as close as **Northallerton,** 24 miles away, or **Darlington,** 34 miles away; both are stops on the main London-York-Newcastle line. From there, local buses head to Aysgarth. For schedule information, call 0191/232 6262. **Coaches** come into **Darlington** from major cities in England, and from there, you can switch for local buses out to Aysgarth. For coach information, call 01325/468771. By **car,** take the A19 north from **York** toward Thirsk, switching there for the A168 to Northallerton. From Northallerton, it's 24 miles west on the A684, passing through Leyburn before reaching Aysgarth.

What's Next

Once you make it into the Yorkshire Dales, it's easy to get around. Buses shuttle through Swaledale and Wensleydale, making hostel-hopping a piece of cake. **Hawes,** a typically quaint Yorkshire village that is the home of the Wensleydale Creamery, is only 10 miles away. The town of **Dent** is eight miles farther. Cobbled streets and tiny cottages cluster around this 17th-century town in the deep valley of the River Dee; the area provides some good challenges for cyclists and walkers.

The Lake District

Wordsworth said it was heaven, but it's not. The Lake District comprises England's best-known, busiest, and (some say) most beautiful national park. The area was catapulted into geographic superstardom by the pantheon of Lakeland poets: William Wordsworth, Robert Southey, and Samuel Taylor Coleridge, as well as sheep-farmer-turned-storyteller Beatrix Potter, whose *Tales of Peter Rabbit* has taught many a toddler how to read English.

Year-round, the area draws international tourists, who scale the scree of Wast Water; walk along the drystone walls lining the fells; and climb to the top of Scafell Pike, England's highest peak at 3,206 feet. Therein lies the annoying paradox of the Lakes: While the natural setting is every bit as beautiful, breathtaking, and brilliant as you'd imagine, the overwhelming crowds of camera-wielding tourists interfere with the idyllic images the poets wrote about. The most heavily touristed spots include the South Lakes towns of Windermere, Ambleside, and Keswick in the North Lakes.

Kendal, not officially part of the Lake District, serves as a point of entry for those coming from the south. It's a pleasant, historic little town where you can get your bearings and buy outdoors supplies before heading west. Windermere, at the end of the branch-line train, gets heavy tourist traffic, as does its sister village, Bowness, a mile south. The hostel, $1^1/_2$ miles out of town, presides over the lake from its hilltop perch. From there, it's only a short walk to a number of towns. Ambleside, only three miles away, has a superdeluxe hostel sitting on the shores of Lake Windermere. The towns of Grasmere and Hawkshead, on the other side of the lake, comprise the heart of the Lakeland literary shrines.

Farther north lie the more remote, quiet villages of Borrowdale and the tranquil shores of Derwent Water, where two lovely hostels provide country charm. The Derwentwater hostel sits across from its namesake lake and lonely Longthwaite sits in the woods a few miles beyond. To the north, Cockermouth is a picturesque little town on the River Cocker where you'll find a teeny-weeny old watermill which has been converted into a traditional hostel.

For the independent traveler, the beauty of this area is that public transport is extensive (if slightly expensive). Bus service is excellent here, and if time allows it's always worth taking an extra half-hour bus ride to more remote spots like Borrowdale, Buttermere, and the West Lakes. The Lake District hostels are all relatively close to one another. Hostel-to-hostel hikes can be done in a day and wind their way past dewy countryside, shimmering pools, and impressive peaks.

KENDAL

Conveniently situated on the Manchester-Carlisle train line, Kendal lies 264 miles northwest of London on the fringes of the Lake District, which can be both a blessing and a curse. Travelers on the hostel hopscotch often overlook this small town, preferring to head out to the more tantalizing parts of Cumbria— the proper Lake District towns of Ambleside, Windermere, and Grasmere.

While Kendal may not be on a big lake, what it lacks in geographical panache it makes up for in other ways, such as its history. In the 1700s, Kendal became a hotbed of snuff production when tobacco was imported here from the New World. What remains is a well-preserved riverside market town with much less tourist traffic than its neighbors up the A591. This is one of the few towns in the area where there is a real sense of local industry. In addition to tobacco (which lends a spicy aroma to some of the streets here), Kendal is probably best known for its mint cake, first developed by local sweetboilers in the 1800s. A staple of mountain climbers in need of a quick energy fix, this compact little taste treat accompanied Hillary and Tensing all the way to the top of Mount Everest.

Modern-day Kendal is far from stale. Aside from being the commercial center of the Lake District, the town bubbles with activity, thanks to the Brewery, the local cultural center. Offering films, drama, dance performances, live music, arts exhibitions, and a host of festivals throughout the year, it's the cultural nucleus of the South Lakes. The Youth Hostel, which shares an entranceway with the Brewery, sometimes plays host to visiting performers. Additionally, Kendal has a few museums of local interest, and walks and cyclepaths abound in this countryside setting.

❈ Kendal Youth Hostel

118 Highgate
Kendal, Cumbria LA9 4HE
Tel: 01539/724066. Fax: 01539/724906.

In the town center, the building is a Georgian town house, formerly the home of the local brewery owner. Downstairs is a comfortable lounge area, and a curving staircase leads you to the labyrinthine halls where the bedrooms lurk. Recently modernized with a soft touch, this clean hostel has a relaxed, warm atmosphere thanks to the friendly staff and warden Tim. The meals are quite good and might even include local Cumberland sausage or a bean casserole for vegetarians—a cut above the usual hostel fare.

Lots of individual travelers stay here on their way in or out of the Lake District, but with the Brewery next door you never know who you might find. You could share a bunk with anyone from a Russian theater group to a traveling folk band. The Brewery's restaurant and bar often offer live music, a poetry reading, or some other event, providing instant nightlife for weary hostelers.

Services

🚆 Exit, turn right, and follow the signs down Sandes Avenue to the town center. Turn left on Stricklandgate, which turns into Highgate. Go past the tourist office and the hostel is about three blocks up on your right next to the Brewery Arts Centre.

🚌 The bus station is on Blackhall Road. Turn right onto Blackhall Road and take the first right onto Stramongate, which turns into Finkle Street. When you reach the intersection with Highgate, turn left, and the hostel is about four blocks up on your right next to the Brewery Arts Centre.

🚗 The hostel is in the town center; if you're coming from the **south,** get off the M6 at Junction 36 and follow the signs for Kendal. Once in town, follow signs to the Brewery Arts Centre. From the **north,** you have to navigate the one-way traffic system, following signs to Abbot Hall and the Brewery Arts Centre. The hostel is next door to the Arts Centre on Highgate.

▦ Open Feb 15–Jan 5. Oct–Mar closed Sun and Mon. BABA.

🕐 Reception open 7:30–10am and 5–11pm.

🛏 54 beds. 2-, 4-, 6-, and 11-bed rooms. One room has a toilet en suite.

£ Members: adults £8; under 18 £5.35.

🍴 Self-catering kitchen facilities. Breakfast: 8:15am. Lunch: packed lunch only; should be ordered by the night before. Dinner: 7pm.

I No table license.

💼 Locked luggage storage room.

⊡ Drying room only.

P Ample and free overnight (rates apply during the day).

🛍 Shop at hostel sells candy, drinks, and souvenirs.

🛋 Quiet room; common room/reception area.

🚬 In common room.

♿ Not wheelchair accessible.

💱 See "Currency Exchange" under "The Basics" in Kendal.

🔺 Bike shed.

Cheap Eats Nearby

The India Palace Ultimate Tandoori Restaurant
Recommended by locals, this is a step above your average curry joint. A fountain with vines, chandeliers (check out the ladies' room), and dramatically draped cloths from the ceiling. And the food's good too. Vindaloos run £4 to £6; curries £3 to £5. Good vegetarian dishes are £4 to £6. Takeout is available.

8 Stramongate, Kendal. Tel: 01539/723787. Open: Mon–Thurs noon–2pm and 5:30pm–midnight; Fri–Sat noon–2pm and 5:30pm–1am; Sun 5–11:30pm. Credit cards: VA, MC, EC, Access. From the hostel, turn left on Highgate, right on Finkle Street, and cross Kent Street onto Stramongate. On the left; a 5-minute walk.

Pizza Margherita
Plants and flowers hang from the ceiling and cool music plays in this sophisticated eatery. Whole meal and regular pizzas are £4 to £6; pastas £5 to £6; salads £2. Lunch prices are slightly cheaper.

181 Highgate. Tel: 01539/731303. Open: Mon–Thurs 10:30am–10pm; Fri–Sat 10:30am–10:30pm; Sun 11am–10pm. Reservations accepted on weekends. Credit cards: AE, VA, MC, EC, Access. From the hostel, turn right and walk about a block. It's across the street on your left.

Grocery Store: Booth, Highgate. Open: Mon–Wed 8:30am–5:30pm; Thurs–Fri 8:30am–7:30pm; Sat 8:30am–5:30pm.

Experiences

Ten paces from the front door of the Youth Hostel is the **Brewery Arts Centre,** which has a movie theater that shows both first-run films and foreign flicks, a theater with traveling shows, and a small concert venue that hosts bands. In August, they host a **Folk Festival** in the garden behind the hostel with bands playing in the open air. During the **November Jazz Festival,** live music plays nightly for two weeks.

If that isn't enough, Kendal also has its own festival, the **Kendal Gathering,** in late August. More of a local show, it includes the Westmoreland County Show at which local farmers buy and sell their animals. Other events include hound trailing, sheep-dog trials, and a parade that goes right by the hostel on the final night.

Even if you don't hit Kendal during festival time, the town is worth exploring. Many of the old buildings have plaques explaining local history, and the cobbled alleyways lead off the main street to the river Kent, which offers loads of green space and picnic areas. Two especially pretty enclaves include the area right by the Parish Church as well as the Bowling Green and Park, littered with flower beds and a lovely, sprawling lawn.

Students of English history might want to stop at the ruins of **Kendal Castle.** It was the home of the Parr family, whose daughter Katherine was the sixth wife of Henry VIII and one of the only spouses the remorseless regent didn't kill—he died while married to her. Legend says they lived there together. Other sights in town include the **Abbot Hall Art Gallery** and **Museum of Lakeland Life and Industry,** which provides an overview of the area. If you go to the tourist office, pick up a copy of *Off The Beat,* which lists cultural events and gives a good summary of local goings-on in South Lakeland.

The Brewery. Highgate, Kendal. Tel: 01539/725133. Arts Centre open: Mon–Sat 9am–11pm. Box Office: Mon–Sat 10am–8pm. Theatre and concert times vary, as do ticket prices (usually £4–£6). Films are shown at 8pm: adults £3.50; children, students, senior citizens £2.50.

Abbot Hall Art Gallery and Museum of Lakeland Life and Industry. Abbot Hall, Kirkland, Kendal. Tel: 01539/722464. Open: Mon–Sat 10:30am–5pm; Sun 2–5pm. Admission: adults £2.50; children £1.50.

The Basics

Tourist Office: Kendal T.I.C. Town Hall, Highgate, Kendal. Tel: 01539/725758. Open: June–Sept: Mon–Sat 9am–6pm; Sun 10am–5pm. Oct–May: Mon–Sat 9am–5pm; Sun 10am–4pm. From the hostel, turn left, walk about two blocks, and it's on the right.

Post Office: Kendal Post Office. 75 Stricklandgate, Kendal. Tel: 01539/725592. Open: Mon–Fri 9am–5:30pm; Sat 9am–7pm. From the hostel, turn left, and continue down Highgate as it becomes Stricklandgate. On your right; a 10-minute walk.

Currency Exchange: Kendal Post Office. 75 Stricklandgate, Kendal. Tel: 01539/725592. Open: Mon–Fri 9am–5:30pm; Sat 9am–7pm.

Telephone Code: 01539.

Bike Rental: Askew's Cycles. Kent Works, Burnside Road, Kendal. Tel: 01539/728057.

Getting There: Kendal is the first stop on the Oxenholme-Windermere branch line off the London-Glasgow main line **train.** It is only three hours from **London** by train, and service is frequent. Kendal station is unmanned, so call Oxenholme at 01539/720397. Getting here by **bus** is also easy; National Express buses come up from London three times daily. For bus information call 0990/808080. There are local buses aplenty that pertain to the Cumberland Motor Services. Kendal is a hub for them. They service **Ambleside, Windermere, Hawkshead** and **Coniston** (via Ambleside), **Grasmere, Keswick,** and other towns farther afield in the lakes. If you're doing a lot of traveling in the lakes, it may be worthwhile to buy a one-day explorer ticket that gives you unlimited travel for £5.20; for four days, it's £12.99. For local bus information call 01946/63222. To get here by **car,** find your way to the M6. From **London,** take the M40 to Birmingham and then switch to the M6, following signs for Stoke-on-Trent, Lancaster, and Kendal. Take care to bypass Manchester entirely.

What's Next

As the "gateway to the Lakes," Kendal is closest to Windermere (12 miles north), one stop away by train. England's most famous lake, Windermere is one of the most popular spots in the Lake District, and the hostel, about two miles from the town, sits in quiet woods overlooking the water. Also nearby (15 miles away) is Ambleside, which boasts one of England's most shamelessly luxurious hostels, sitting right on Ambleside Pier at the northern end of Lake Windermere. Both Ambleside and Windermere tend to be packed, so call ahead to book. If you don't have luck, Hawkshead is slightly farther (nine miles by ferry) but offers a rambling old mansion in a secluded corner of the Lake District.

WINDERMERE

William Wordsworth, Beatrix Potter, John Keats, and a host of other English literary luminaries have oohed and aahed over the now-legendary Windermere, 274 miles northwest of London and 10 miles north of Kendal. While the lake remains stunning, Windermere the town (along with twin horror Bowness) is another story. The Lake poets brought international renown to the area, giving rise, unfortunately, to some of the most crass commercialism in England. A tourist mecca for travelers the world over, the town is teeming with camera-happy crowds and local merchants pandering to their every whim with saccharine-sweet flower shops, furniture stores, and a few restaurants.

About a mile farther up the road is Bowness, a bustling little village with more action than Windermere. It's got restaurants, a movie theater, and a glossy Beatrix Potter museum. Both towns are a disappointment for anyone looking for peace and solitude. Luckily, the lake is still a spectacular sight in and of itself. While filled almost nonstop with steamers on pleasure trips in summer, it manages to hang on to its breathtaking hallmark beauty.

Thankfully, the hostel sits in wooded solitude in the village of Troutbeck, two miles away and a five-minute bus ride from town. It overlooks the lake in a quiet wooded enclave, and good bus service shuttles back and forth, making it easily accessible. This hostel is a good option for those wishing to sample the sights by day and bed down in calmer surroundings.

Windermere Youth Hostel

High Cross, Bridge Lane
Troutbeck, Windermere
Cumbria LA23 1LA
Tel: 015394/43543. Fax: 025394/47165.

From the bus stop at Troutbeck, it's an uphill hike to the hostel along the wooded, flower-lined driveway. After dropping your pack, you can enjoy the view: this is the Lake District those poets raved about. The whitewashed mansion is set on lushly beautiful grounds evocative of a Greek isle.

A strong presence on Lake Windermere, this former family home (its name is derived from a stone cross on the hostel grounds) is a local landmark boasting three-tiled minarets, a square tower, a dome, and an all-glass roof. Rolling hills resembling a PGA golf course stretch out between the hostel and the water and are dotted with lazy sheep chewing on the grass.

The house is rambling and comfortable; the dining room accompanying the self-catering kitchen looks out onto the lake, as do some of the rooms, making it a grand place to awaken. Despite its perennial popularity, it retains the traditional feel of the simpler hostels in the Lake district. Tucked away above the lake, it revels in its solitude.

Hostelers benefit from a load of local discounts, including 10% off bike rental and 10% off the Windermere Lake Cruises. For the first time in 1995, they began offering free minibus service to the hostel from the Windermere train station in July and August.

Services

🚃 From the train station, take bus W1 or no. 555 to Troutbeck Bridge (5-minute ride); walk up the road past the gas station and turn right at the sign to the Youth Hostel. Walk up the hill (about ³/₄ mile), and the hostel entrance will come up on your left. The walk from the train station takes about 45 minutes: from the station, turn left and walk up the A591 (the Ambleside Road) until you reach the gas station. Turn right at the sign pointing to the Youth Hostel; walk up the hill (about ³/₄ mile), and the hostel entrance will come up on your left. During summer, the hostel operates a free minibus service departing from the rail station at 5:15 and 6:15pm.

🚌 Buses arriving in Windermere come into the railway station. Follow directions from the train station, given above.

🚗 Windermere is right on the A591, on the Ambleside-Kendal road, and the hostel is well signposted from the main road. If you're coming from Ambleside, take the first left before the garage and the hostel is about ³/₄ mile up the road on your left. From Kendal, take the first right after the garage at Troutbeck Bridge and the hostel is about ³/₄ mile up the road on your left.

🖩 Open Jan–Oct. BABA.

🕐 Reception open 8:30–10am and 1–11:30pm. Curfew 11:30pm.

🛏 73 beds. 4-, 6-, 8-, and 16-bed rooms. Family rooms with daytime access available.

£ Members: adults £7.20; under 18 £4.85.

🍴 Self-catering kitchen facilities. Breakfast: 8am. Lunch: packed lunch only; order by 9pm the night before. Dinner: 7pm.

🍸 No table license.

🧳 Locked luggage storage room.

🔲 Washer and drying room.

P Ample and free of charge.

🛍 Shop at hostel sells candy and canned goods.

🛋 Common room in entrance hall.

🚬 In common room only.

♿ Not wheelchair accessible.

💱 See "Currency Exchange" under "The Basics" in Windermere.

🔺 Bike shed.

Cheap Eats Nearby

The Coffee Pot

Outdoor tables on the stone patio are great for watching the passers-by fumble with their cameras and moneybelts. Inside, a sweet tea room hums with activity. Sandwiches cost £1.70 to £2.10; soup and bread £1.35; pita bread with various fillings £1.50 to £3.

15 Main Rd., Windermere. Tel: 01539/488738. Open: Mon–Wed; Fri–Sat 10am–6pm; Sun 1–5pm. Cash only. From the hostel, it takes about half an hour: walk to the bus stop and take bus W1 or no. 555 into Windermere. From the train station, walk past the tourist office, and turn left onto High Street; follow it as it becomes Main Road, and it's on your left.

M & J's Fish Restaurant and Coffee Gallery

Lanterns hang from the ceiling in the front of this resort restaurant. Photos of Ambleside and Windermere of yore hang on the walls. Fish dishes range from £4.95 to £6.95; salads £5 to £6; vegetarian dishes £6. Roast ewe and sow for the adventurous and wealthy is £9.95; children's portion £6.95.

Birch Street, Windermere. Tel: 01539/442522. Open: daily 10:30am–10pm. Credit cards: AE, MC, VA, Access, Switch, Transmedia. From the hostel, about half an hour; walk to the bus stop, and take bus W1 or no. 555 into Windermere. From the train stop, turn left onto High Street, and bear left onto Crescent Road. On the left.

Grocery Store: Booth's. Station Precinct. Open: Mon–Wed 9am–6pm; Thurs 9am–7pm; Fri 9am–8pm; Sat 8:30am–6pm; Sun 10am–4pm.

Experiences

Right from the hostel doorstep, a **footpath** through Troutbeck offering some dandy views of Lake Windermere takes you the four miles to Ambleside. You'll pass through Troutbeck village, which has a 17th-century statesman's house, a crumbling old barn, and a few local folks to help you find your way. About a mile into the walk, you'll reach Dick Johnson's seat, with a bench and a beautiful view. If you take the detour at Jenkyn's Crag farther up, you'll get another romantic lookout. The walk then takes you into Skelghyll Woods, down a few rocky paths leading toward the boats on the pier (and the Ambleside hostel), or into Ambleside itself—a pricey, precious little resort town.

For the robust, Grasmere is a six-mile walk farther along the road. Going through the town of Ambleside, follow the footpath to Rydal Hall and pass through Rydal Park along the back of Rydal Hall, turning right and then left after Rydal Mount. Through woods and fields and past a pond, a footpath will take you up to Alcock Tarn, where there's another excellent lookout; from there, Grasmere is a short walk downhill.

For less strenuous pursuits, **Windermere Lake Cruises** runs steamboats between Ambleside, Bowness (one mile from Windermere), and Haverthwaite at the very south end of the lake. The ride from Ambleside to Windermere lasts about half an hour and is a nice slow chug. You can sit up top: The views are sublime. Rowboats can also be rented inexpensively at Bowness.

Beatrix Potter fans may want to make a visit to the gimmicky but sweet **World of Beatrix Potter Museum,** where Flopsy, Mopsy, and Jemima Puddle Duck pose in their unnatural habitats, lovingly crafted from papier-mâché. The Old Laundry theater next door has traveling shows from September to April and in summer offers arts exhibitions.

Windermere Lake Cruises. Bowness Pier, Bowness-on-Windermere. Tel: 01539/443468. Apr–Nov only: daily 9am–6pm; departures every 20 minutes. Bowness-Ambleside single trip: adults £3.20; children £2.60. Return trip: adults £5; children £2.50. Boat and train single trip: adults £4.80; children £2.65. Return trip: adults £7.60; children £3.90.

Bowness Bay Boating Co. Boat Rentals. Bowness Pier. Tel: 01539/488510. May–Aug only: daily 9am–7pm. £3 per person per hour.

World of Beatrix Potter Museum. The Old Laundry, Bowness-on-Windermere. Tel: 01539/488444. Open: Easter–Sept: daily 10am–6:30pm. Oct–Easter: 10am–4pm. Admission: adults £2.85; children £1.85.

The Basics

Tourist Office: Windermere T.I.C. Victoria Street, Windermere. Tel: 01539/446499. Open: Apr–Oct: daily 9am–6pm. Nov–Apr: daily 9am–5pm. From the hostel, walk to the bus stop and take bus no. 555 or W1 to the Windermere train station. With the station to your left, walk past Booth's supermarket, and it's on your left. The walk takes 20 minutes. For more specific info on walks, nature, and the National Park, go to Bowness (1 mile farther on the bus) to the Lake District National Park Centre. The Glebe, Bowness-on-Windermere. Tel: 01539/442895. Open: Easter–Oct only: daily 9:30am–5:30pm.

Post Office: Windermere Post Office. 21 Crescent Rd., Windermere. Tel: 01539/443245. Open: Mon–Fri 9am–5:30pm; Sat 9am–12:30pm. From the hostel, walk to the bus stop and take no. 555 or W1 to the Windermere train station. Walk past Booth's and the tourist office, and turn left onto High Street. Bear left onto Crescent Road. On your left. The walk takes 30 minutes.

Currency Exchange: Post Office, 21 Crescent Rd., Windermere. Tel: 015394/43245. Open: Mon–Fri 9am–5:30pm; Sat 9am–12:30pm. Also at the tourist offices on Victoria Street and at the Bowness Pier.

Telephone Code: 01539.

Bike Rental: Lakeland Leisure. The Chalets, Station Precinct. Tel: 015394/44786. Receive 10% discount with Hostelling International card.

Getting There: Trains are a snap here: Windermere is at the end of the branch line from Manchester-Oxenholme-Kendal. Service is good, so it's easy to get here from **London, Manchester, Edinburgh,** and most major rail stations. For information, call: 01539/443025. There's a daily National Express **bus** that comes in from **London.** Local buses zip in and out of here from every major town in the south Lakes, including **Ambleside, Grasmere, Hawkshead** (change at Ambleside), **Coniston,** and **Buttermere.** Buses also run regularly to **Kendal,** which has connections to London via National Express. For bus information, call Stagecoach at 01946/63222. By **car,** Windermere is easily reachable off the M6. At the South Kendal turnoff, get onto the A591, which connects from Kendal all the way to Keswick.

What's Next

Ambleside, only three miles away, sits at the north end of Lake Windermere; it has a spectacular lakefront hostel and is a short walk away from the town, busy with shops and restaurants. Bus no. 555 or W1 heads there from Windermere, but the walk from Troutbeck is beautiful and not at all strenuous. Farther along on the tourist trail lies **Grasmere,** home of William Wordsworth and the famous Dove Cottage and a sweet little town. **Hawkshead,** nine miles away on the other side of Lake Windermere, is a slightly less interesting town, but the gem of a hostel sits right across the street from Esthwaite Water, one of the smaller lakes.

AMBLESIDE

Ambleside (278 miles northwest of London and four miles from Windermere) is the hub of the Lake District. As such, it's everything you'd expect a big-time Lake District town to be—and then some. The location, right on the shores of Lake Windermere, is unrivaled. Water-skiers glide over the water as steamboats chug by. People on package tours of England tend to head to this central spot for its natural beauty and for Hilltop, the nearby home of Beatrix Potter. Most local buses pass through here, making for easy day trips to other Lake towns.

Everything you could ever want to do in the water and on the hills is possible here. Ambleside has shops, instructors, and package tours ready to draw you in for all you've got. Pony trekking, waterskiing, hang gliding, mountain biking, and canoeing are all available—for a price. However, armed with a good map and a pair of sneakers or hiking boots, you don't need to spend anything.

Watching the blue mist rise over Lake Windermere at sunset is one of the most beautiful outdoors activities here and comes free of charge at the Ambleside Youth Hostel, where you can sit in the bay windows of the lounge and take in the sight. The pride and joy of the English hosteling association, the hostel is in the center of it all, a 10-minute walk from the town center and steps away from the action on Lake Windermere.

Ambleside Youth Hostel

Waterhead, Ambleside
Cumbria LA22 0EU
Tel: 015394/32304. Fax: 015394/34408.

You could spit into Lake Windermere from the hostel windows. This world-class hostel, with more than 200 beds, is one of the most popular in England. The Slow Coach stops here on its circuit of England, as do thousands of international travelers all year long. Be sure to book in advance, especially during summer.

With a private waterfront and jetty, the hostel is the best equipped in the Lake District. The dining room has exquisite lake views across to Coniston and Langdale fells. The newly renovated sitting rooms downstairs also overlook the pier and lake beyond. Some of the rooms have lake views, but even those that don't aren't too shabby. The hostel is probably your best information center about the area: they have tons of dirt on local activities and the countless walking paths that radiate out from Ambleside.

Getting here is a snap: Take either the bus or the free minibus that runs from Windermere train station evenings in July and August. Your Hostelling International card also gets you 10% off the Windermere Lake Cruises, bike rentals, and pony trekking (weekdays only).

Services

The closest train station is in Windermere. From there, take the W1 or the no. 555 (a 5-minute ride) to Ambleside and get off at Waterhead. The Youth Hostel is to the left of the Windermere Lake Cruises ticket office. In the summer, the hostel operates a minibus service from Windermere railway station daily at 5:15 and 6:15pm.

The bus stop at Waterhead is across the street from the hostel. Cross the road and turn left; the hostel is next to the Windermere Lake Cruises ticket office. From the King Street stop in Ambleside town, it's a 15-minute walk. Turn right at the row of shops where the post office is located and head down the A591 to the pier with the Windermere Lake Cruises ticket office. If you face the lake, you'll find the hostel about 100 yards to the left. National Express buses stop at the Fisherbeck Hotel. From there, walk back down the road to the lake; the hostel is about 100 yards from the Windermere Lake Cruises ticket office.

Ambleside Youth Hostel is right on the A591, which connects Kendal all the way to Keswick. From **Kendal**, go up the A591 through Windermere. Follow signs to Ambleside, and the hostel will come up on your left before you reach the town. Turn left about 100 yards after the Esso station. From **Keswick,** go down the A591 through the town of Ambleside, and when you reach Lake Windermere, turn right into the YHA parking lot.

▦ Open year-round. IBN and BABA.

⏰ Reception open 7:15am–11:30pm. Curfew 11:30pm.

🛏 226 beds. 2-, 3-, 4-, 5-, 6-, and 8-bed rooms. Family rooms available.

£ Members: adults £8.80; under 18 £5.95.

🍴 The Lakeside Restaurant serves meals. Self-catering kitchen facilities. Breakfast: 7:45–9am. Lunch: packed lunches should be ordered by 7pm the night before. Light snacks are available throughout the day in the restaurant.

▦ Dinner: 5:30–7:30pm. Set menu with lots of choices.

🍸 Table license.

🧳 Locked luggage storage room.

◯ Washers (£1.25), dryers (60p), and a drying room.

P Ample and free of charge.

🛍 Shop at hostel sells stuffed animals; Slow Coach tickets; Mountain Goat and Lakes Supertours tickets.

🛋 Three alcoves by reception area; TV/games room; quiet room.

🚭 In TV room only.

♿ Not wheelchair accessible.

💱 See "Currency Exchange" under "The Basics" in Ambleside.

🔺 Bike shed.

Cheap Eats Nearby

The Old Smithy Fish & Chips Restaurant

Order takeout or sit in the cavernous dining room. A wide variety of greasy grub includes fish and chips, £1.50 to £3; vegetable dishes (£2 to £3); sausage, haggis, and chicken pie all come with chips (£1.50 to £3).

The Slack, Ambleside. Tel: 01539/432720. Open: Apr–June: Mon–Thurs 11:30am–2pm and 5–8:30pm; Fri–Sat 11:30am–2pm and 5–10:30pm. July–Sept: daily 11:30am–10:30pm. Oct–Apr: Thurs–Mon noon–2pm and 5–8pm. Cash only. From the hostel, a 15-minute walk: turn left onto the A591 (Lake Road), and left onto The Slack. On the right.

Pippin's Café

This airy, friendly spot has comfortable wooden banquettes and bar seating. Earrings for sale on the wall. Burgers and sandwiches run £1.95 to £3; Peppy pizza baguettes are £2 to £3; soup du jour £1.45.

10 Lake Rd., Ambleside. Tel: 01539/431338. Open: Thurs–Tues 9am–5pm; until midnight on summer weekends. Cash only. From the hostel, a 15-minute walk: turn left onto the A591 (Lake Road) and walk into Ambleside town. On your right.

Grocery Store: Spar. Compston Road, Ambleside. Open: Mon–Fri 8am–10pm.

Experiences

Many people while away their time here just hanging out on the grass by the lake. The more ambitious head a few steps off the hostel grounds over to the pier, where **steamboats** run out to Bowness (Windermere) and Brockhole (National Park Visitor Centre) as well as Lakeside, at the very south end of the lake.

Two Wordsworth landmarks are within easy reach of Ambleside: **Rydal Mount** (his home from 1813 to 1850), and **Dove Cottage** (where he lived from 1799 to 1808). Rydal Mount is only 1 1/2 miles north of Ambleside on the A591. The cottage is full of mementos, books, and furnishings, as is Dove Cottage, which also houses a museum. The especially beautiful walk between the two (about two miles) passes Rydal Water and ends up right by Grasmere. In Rydal, there are a couple of pony trekking centers, but horseback riding can be expensive here.

Hilltop, the former home of Beatrix Potter, is another tremendously popular spot. It gets very crowded, so go early or late and not at midday. It's only a bus ride away in Near Sawrey, on the other side of the lake.

Aside from the museums, Ambleside is primarily a great base for local **fell walking:** Hawkshead and Coniston across the lake (reachable via Coniston Rambler bus no. 505) have some good hills for rock climbing, and the views are gorgeous. The Langdale valley near Elterwater has some good paths as well. There are some excellent hostel-to-hostel walks of varying difficult in the area. The four-mile hike to Windermere is steep at first, but once you get through Skelghyll Woods and Jenkin Crag, the views are beautiful and the hill becomes gentler. The 10-mile walk to the hostel at Hawkshead is more rigorous but leads to a more remote location on the banks of Eskdale Water. When night falls, **Zeffirelli's Cinema** in Ambleside shows first-run movies in its small theater.

Windermere Lake Cruises. Ambleside Pier, Ambleside. Tel: 01539/432225. Apr–Nov only: daily 9am–6pm; departures every 20 minutes. Bowness-Ambleside single trip: adults £3.20; children £2.60. Return trip: adults £5; children £2.50. Boat and train single trip: adults £4.80; children £2.65. Return trip: adults £7.60; children £3.90.

Rydal Mount. Ambleside. Tel: 01539/433002. Open: Mar–Oct: daily 9:30am–5pm. Nov–Feb: Wed–Mon 10am–4pm. Admission: adults £2; children 80p.

Dove Cottage and Wordsworth Museum. Grasmere. Tel: 01539/435544. Open: daily 9:30am–5:30pm (last entry 5pm). Closed: Dec 24–26; Jan. Admission: adults £3.90; children £1.95.

The Lake District Trail Riding Center. Rydal (1¹/₂ miles from Ambleside). Tel: 01539/432765.

Hilltop. Near Sawrey. Tel: 01539/436269. Open: Apr–Oct only: Sat–Wed 11am–5pm (last entry 4:30pm). Admission: £3.30. Take bus W1 or no. 555 to Bowness and the ferry to Hawkshead.

Zeffirelli's Cinema. Compston Road, Ambleside. Tel: 01539/433845. Early evening and matinees: adults £3; seniors and children £2. Main (8:30pm) show: adults £3.50; seniors and children £2.50.

The Basics

Tourist Office: Ambleside T.I.C. Church Street, Ambleside. Tel: 01539/432582. Open: Mar–Oct: daily 9am–5pm. Nov–Feb: Fri–Sun 9am–5pm. From the hostel, turn left onto the A591 (Lake Road) and follow it for about 20 minutes (on foot) into Ambleside town. It's on the left.

Post Office: Ambleside Post Office. Market Place, Ambleside. Tel: 01539/432267. Open: Mon–Fri 9am–5:30pm; Sat 9am–12:30pm. From the hostel, turn left onto the A591 (Lake Road) and follow it for about 20 minutes (on foot) into Ambleside town, to the intersection with Church Street.

Currency Exchange: Ambleside Post Office. Market Place, Ambleside. Tel: 01539/432267. Open: Mon–Fri 9am–5:30pm; Sat 9am–12:30pm.

Telephone Code: 015394.

Bike Rental: Ambleside Mountain Bikes/Ghyllside Cycles. The Slack, Ambleside. Tel: 01539/433592. Full-day rental £11 with Hostelling International card.

Getting There: Ambleside is easily reachable by **train:** get to **Windermere,** which is on a branch line off the London-Glasgow train line, and local buses (W1 and no. 555) go to Ambleside. For train information, call 015394/43025. National Express **coaches** come in twice daily on the London-Keswick route and stop 10 minutes away from the hostel. For schedule information call London at 0171/730 0202. By **car,** take the M6 up to Junction 36 just before Kendal, which puts you on to the A591, the main road connecting the South Lakes area. Follow signs to Ambleside.

What's Next

Windermere is only a four-mile walk away and **Grasmere** only 5^1/$_2$ miles, but for those with time, it's easy enough to head out to the more tranquil parts of the Lake District. Directly around Lake Windermere is **Hawkshead** Youth Hostel, sitting on Eskdale Water in relative calm, and further north lie **Borrowdale** (Longthwaite) and **Derwentwater** hostels in the Central Lakes. Neither hostel is connected to a village, and quiet solitude is the reward you get for taking the plunge into the cool blue waters here.

HAWKSHEAD

When William Wordsworth returned to his hometown of Hawkshead, he was dismayed by the construction of Assembly Hall on his former soccer ground. Assembly Hall is still here, but, unlike Wordsworth, most visitors relish it and the rest of the whitewashed stone buildings in this market town.

Formerly the center of the wool trade in the Lake District, Hawkshead is a pristine three-block affair with a mishmash of historical buildings dating from the 16th, 17th, and 18th centuries. By these standards, the Regency-style hostel, from the early 19th century, is modern. A mile from Hawkshead town, the hostel is a country mansion overlooking Esthwaite Water, a small, serene lake where watersports are strictly prohibited. True lakeside tranquillity is what you will find here.

✺ Hawkshead Youth Hostel

Esthwaite Lodge
Hawkshead, Ambleside
Cumbria LA22 0QD
Tel: 015394/36293. Fax: 015394/36720.

A classic Regency mansion set amid trees and flowers on sprawling grounds, the hostel owes its gentle landscaping to its original owner, Thomas Beck. A handicapped nobleman, Beck designed the building so he could appreciate the panorama of Esthwaite Water below without endangering himself or his wheelchair. When Beck left, the house was rented out to a variety of tenants, the most famous of whom was poet Francis Brett Young; his chum Hugh Walpole is said to have finished a book or two while staying here as a guest.

The house, rambling and grand, has carpeted hallways upstairs leading to lakeview rooms. Japanese lanterns lend a warm glow to the place. In the dining room, prints of Beatrix Potter's warm and fuzzy characters adorn the walls. Dappled with trees, the lawns invite you to spend lazy days picnicking and snoozing, and there's even a patio with benches to enjoy your morning coffee. The annex out back attracts lots of families and school groups, but there's enough space that the hostel is a little less harried than you might expect.

🚆 The closest train station is Windermere: from there, take the no. 555 or W1 to Ambleside and then switch to bus no. 505 to Hawkshead (40 minutes–1¹/₂ hours, depending on the connection). From the bus stop in Hawkshead, turn left and go past the school; the hostel is about a mile up on the right. While walking, Esthwaite Water will be on your left.

🚌 From the bus stop in Hawkshead, follow the directions from the train, given above.

⛴ Take the Bowness car ferry (1 mile down the road from Windermere Station) to Far Sawrey. Head for Near Sawrey, following signs for Hilltop (Beatrix Potter's home). From there, come around the bottom of the lake, and when you reach the junction, turn right and then pass the Trout Farm. The hostel will come on your left after about a mile.

🚗 Take the A591 into Ambleside. From there, follow the signs to Hawkshead/Coniston. When you reach the town, go around the ring road, and when you reach the T junction, get on Newby Bridge Road. The hostel is about a mile down the road on your right.

📅 Open Feb–Christmas. Nov–Dec, the hostel is closed Sundays and Mondays. Opening times in winter tend to vary. Call ahead. BABA.

⏰ Reception open 7:15–10am and 1–10:30pm. Curfew 11pm.

🛏 117 beds. 4-, 6-, 8-, 16-, and 18-bed rooms. Courtyard complex with some en suite family rooms with keys for daytime access.

£ Members: adults £8.80; under 18 £5.95.

🍴 Self-catering kitchen facilities. Breakfast: 8:15am. Lunch: packed lunch only; order by 10:30pm the night before. Dinner: 7pm.

🍷 Table license.

🧳 No lockers.

⚙ Washers (£1) and dryers (30p) and two drying rooms.

P Ample and free of charge.

🛍 Shop at hostel sells candy, canned goods, and souvenirs.

🛋 One common room overlooking grounds and water beyond; TV/pool room.

🚬 In pool room.

♿ Not wheelchair accessible.

💱 See "Currency Exchange" under "The Basics" in Hawkshead.

🔺 Bike shed; two classrooms with overhead projector, blackboards.

Cheap Eats Nearby

Queen's Head Hotel

This little country pub has a traditional bar area as well as a romantic lunchroom adorably adorned with proper paisley curtains and lanterns. A smattering of culinary treats includes prawn cocktail £4.75; vegetable fritters £3.25; vegetable risotto and other main dishes £5.95. Chips and other pub grub as well. Coffees are a specialty.

Main Street, Hawkshead. Tel: 015394/36271. Open: daily noon–2:30pm and 6:15–9:30pm; open all day for drinks. Cash only. From the hostel, turn left and walk 1 mile into town. From the Park Centre, walk up the street, turn right, and it's at the far end of the Market Square.

Whig's

This warm, friendly coffeehouse is home of the locally famous Hawkshead Whig, a yeast bun with caraway seeds. Soothing music wafts through the air as you down your Whigwiches (£3 to £4). Soup with roll is £1.90; scones 85p.

The Square, Hawkshead. Tel: 015394/36614. Open: May–Oct: daily 10:30am–6pm. Nov–Apr: Fri–Sun 10:30am–6pm. Cash only. From the hostel, turn left and walk 1 mile into town. From the Park Centre, walk up the street, and it's on the left side of the Market Square.

Grocery Store: Hawkshead Coop, Hawkshead. Open: Mon–Sat 8am–8pm; Sun 10am–4pm.

Experiences

Comprising a relatively flat part of the Lake District, Hawkshead and its environs provide a restful break for walkers exhausted from hiking the high fells to the north and east. Although water sports are prohibited on Esthwaite Water, **trout fishing** is permitted, and licenses are available in town. The route to Tarn Hows, an artificial lake, is a long but generally unstrenuous eight-mile circuit that passes through the village and churchyard to some gently rolling hills.

Nearby, **Grizedale Forest Centre** (about a mile from the village) has some good marked walks through its wooded grounds and is an especially nice escape on cloudy days, when high hill walking is too dangerous. Red squirrels, badgers, foxes, and deer all meander through this unspoiled reserve. The forestry commission provides talks, walks, and a variety of special events, including a summertime **Theatre in the Forest.** Additionally, the forest is home to more than 50 sculptures by local artists, providing an unusual cultural dimension to the otherwise wild landscape.

For more rigorous activities, head to **Coniston** (4½ miles away and easily reachable by bus): Sailing, waterskiing, canoeing, and other water sports are available on the lake there, and a restored **steam yacht** ferries passengers up and down the lake on pleasure trips. Old Man Coniston is the main hill. A climb of 2,635 feet takes you to the top, which offers views of Esthwaite and Lake Windermere. For more sedentary folks, Hawkshead's local council offers a pleasant **guided tour** covering the history and architecture of this old market town.

Trout Fishing. The Boathouse, Ridding Wood, Hawkshead. Tel: 015394/36541. Licenses (£11) available at the post office. Rod hire and boat hire available at a discount (ask at the hostel for leaflet).

Grizedale Forest Park. Recreation Ranger, Forest Park Visitor Centre. South Lakes Forest District. Tel: 01229/860373. Theatre in the Forest Box Office tel: 01229/860291. Bike rental tel: 01229/860369.

Summitreks Adventure Centre. 14 Yewdale Rd., Coniston (6 miles away). Tel: 015394/41212. Open: Easter–Sept. Kayak hire: half day £9.50; full day £13.50. Windsurfer hire: half day £15.50; full day £23.50. Instruction in canoeing, windsurfing, rock climbing, abseiling, aquseiling, gorge scrambling. Prices range from £13.50–£20. More economical for groups.

Coniston Steam Yacht Gondola. Pier Cottage, Coniston (6 miles away). Tel: 015394/41288. Apr–Nov: 4–5 departures daily. 1-hour round-trip: adults £4.30; children £2.50.

Guided tours of Hawkshead. Opposite the police station, Hawkshead. Tel: 015394/ 36030. Summer only. Adults £2; children under 12 free.

The Basics

Tourist Office: Lake District National Park Information Centre. Main Car Park, Hawkshead. Tel: 015394/36525. Open: July–Sept: daily 9:30am–6pm. Oct–June: daily 9:30am–5pm. From the hostel, a 30-minute walk: turn left and walk 1 mile into town; it's on your right past the car park.

Post Office: Hawkshead Post Office. Main Street, Hawkshead. Tel: 015394/36201. Open: Mon–Fri 9am–5:30pm; Sat 9am–12:30pm. From the hostel, a 30-minute walk: turn left and walk 1 mile into town, past the tourist office. It's on your right past the Queen's Head pub.

Currency Exchange: Lake District National Park Information Centre. Main Car Park, Hawkshead. Tel: 015394/36525. Open: Jul–Sept: daily 9:30am–6pm. Oct–Jun: daily 9:30am–5pm.

Telephone Code: 015394.

Bike Rental: The Croft Mountain Bike Hire/Caravan and Campsite. Hawkshead. Tel: 015394/36374. Full day £11; half day £6; hourly £3.

Getting There: The closest **train** station is in **Windermere,** which is on a branch line off the London-Glasgow train line. From Windermere, it's 9 miles away, and local buses take you out to Hawkshead. For train information, call Windermere at 015394/43025. National Express **coaches** come in twice daily on the London-Keswick route; alight at **Ambleside** for local buses to Hawkshead. For schedule info, call London at 0171/730 0202. By **car,** take the M6 up to Junction 36 just before Kendal, which puts you on to the A591, the main road connecting the South Lakes area. Follow signs to Ambleside, and switch to the B5286 south to Hawkshead.

What's Next

Ambleside and **Windermere** are six and nine miles away, respectively, and offer a glistening mammoth lake and water sports galore. Expect crowds and a resort atmosphere in this, the nucleus of the Lake District. More centrally located than Hawkshead, they also provide good connections to the hostels at **Derwentwater** and **Longthwaite,** which are blessedly free of town life, crowds, and tourist hawkers in their tranquil perch among the trees and fells.

GRASMERE (BUTTERLIP HOW)

Flanked by its eponymous lake to the west and towering Rydal Fell to the east, Grasmere is indebted to William Wordsworth for putting it on the literary map. His "sweet paradise" is now a pleasant shrine to him and his honeysuckle verse. The Wordsworth Museum and Dove Cottage draw visitors from afar, lending the town an incongruously international atmosphere.

Grasmere, like all the Lakes villages, offers rigorous walks of varying lengths. Alfred Wainwright's 192-mile Coast-to-Coast Walk passes the hostel, and literary walks provide an intellectual component to huffing and puffing. There are also a few good hostel-to-hostel walks going along back roads and passing by some otherwise hidden corners of this idyllic enclave.

Wordworth's powerful nature writing was inspired here; if you tote around your complete works, you can spot many of the places mentioned in his poems and prose. Samuel Taylor Coleridge (who lived in Keswick) hung out a lot at Dove Cottage with Wordsworth, and together they produced lyrical ballads. Coleridge fans can also follow his trail here.

Grasmere Youth Hostel (Butterlip How)

Easedale Road
Grasmere, Cumbria LA22 9XQ
Tel: 015394/35316. Fax: 015394/35798.

One of two hostels in Grasmere, this place is situated just behind Butterlip How (hence its name), a small rounded hill that was once a Danish stronghold and later a burial ground of soldiers killed fighting for King Bothar. The grounds are spread out, and it's easy to get lost here. The hostel is only about a block up from the village of Grasmere; you can hop off the bus and scoot right in the door without climbing any major hills.

The Victorian-style building boasts a big plaque with an M on the front: The hostel is believed to have been the site of an old Masonic lodge. Loads of walkers tend to come to Butterlip How because the long-distance Coast-to-Coast Path wends its way right past the hostel. The twin attractions of Wordsworth and Beatrix Potter lure loads of Japanese tourists to the hostel, adding an international tang to the place.

The small, comfortable rooms in this traditional Lakeland mansion make for an especially peaceful rest. There are even a few family rooms with keys for daytime access, but they tend to get snatched up right away. As always, reserve well in advance; it's especially busy here in spring (with school groups) and summer.

Services

The closest train station is Windermere. From there, take bus W1 or no. 555 to Grasmere center, a 30-minute ride past Rydal and Grasmere lakes. From the stop, walk up Easedale road, and the hostel is about 300 yards ahead of you.

The London-Keswick bus stops at the end of Easedale Road. From the stop, walk up Easedale Road, and the hostel is about 300 yards ahead of you.

From the A591, follow signs to Keswick and Grasmere, passing through Windermere and Ambleside on your way. When you reach the village, turn left on Easedale Road, and the hostel is 300 yards ahead of you.

Open year-round. Closed Mon Sept–Mar. BABA.

Reception open 7–9:30am and 1–11:30pm. Curfew 11pm.

104 beds. 2-, 4-, 5-, 8-, and 12-bed rooms. Family rooms with keys for daytime access.

£ Members: adults £8; under 18 £5.35.

Self-catering kitchen facilities. Breakfast: 8am. Lunch: packed lunch only; should be ordered by the night before. Dinner: 7pm.

No table license.

No lockers.

☐ Drying room only.

P Limited; free of charge.

⌂ Shop at hostel sells candy and canned goods only.

🛋 Games room with pool table; lounge.

🚬 In annex only.

♿ Not wheelchair accessible.

💱 See "Currency Exchange" under "The Basics" in Grasmere.

🔺 Bike shed; classroom.

Cheap Eats Nearby

Baldry's
High ceilings, chintz drapes, and old sepia tints on the walls lie in the faded elegance of this old tearoom. Baked potatoes cost £2 to £3; daily soups; roast ham platter £5; soothing teas and lip-smacking sweets.

Red Lion Square, Grasmere. Tel: 015394/35301. Open: Mon–Fri 9am–8pm; Sat–Sun 9am–9pm. From the hostel, go down Easedale Road, cross Broadgate, and continue straight onto College Street; make a right on Red Lion Square. It's on your right.

The Rowan Tree
This serene, refined vegetarian restaurant serves wholefoods a step up from the usual veggie burgers and broccoli bakes. Salads run £4 to £5. A cheese platter is £4.25; vegetable stir-fry £5.50; Mediterranean dishes £5.95 to £6.95.

Church Bridge, Stock Lane, Grasmere. Tel: 015394/35528. Open: daily 10am–5pm and 6–9pm. Reservations essential. Cash only. From the hostel, ease on down Easedale Road to Broadgate. Cross Broadgate to College Street, pass St. Oswald's Church, go over the river, and the restaurant will come up on your left just past the bookshop; 10 minutes on foot.

Grocery Store: Coop. Broadgate, Grasmere.

Experiences

The beauty of beautiful Grasmere is its location: It's practically in the center of the Lake District, so there is a whole cluster of villages around 8 to 10 miles from here, many with Youth Hostels. Ambleside is a five-mile stroll away; Patterdale, Elterwater, Borrowdale, and Langdale are all around eight miles from here over rocky fells and past glistening lakes.

The ever-popular **Fairfield Horseshoe** is a challenging hill walk that starts in Ambleside, hits Grasmere about at its midpoint, and makes a nice thigh-busting day-long walk. It goes to the summit of Fairfield (2,800 ft), which offers great views of Lake Grasmere, Windermere to the east, and Skiddaw to the north. On a (rare) cloudless day, you can see out to Yorkshire to the east, across the Solway Firth to Scotland in the north, and even out to the Irish Sea and the Isle of Man to the west.

Right on Grasmere Lake you can rent your own **rowboats;** for groups, the price is feasible; otherwise, it can get expensive. **Dove Cottage** and the **Wordsworth Museum** are both just a short walk from the hostel, but beware the vicious summer crowds.

Lake Walks. Ask at the hostel for leaflets.

Rowboat rental. Landing stage, Red Bank Road. £10 per hour.

Dove Cottage and Wordsworth Museum. Grasmere. Tel: 01539/435544. Open: daily 9:30am–5:30pm (last entry 5pm). Closed: Dec 24–26; Jan. Admission: adults £3.90; children £1.95.

The Basics

Tourist Office: Grasmere T.I.C. Redbank Road, Grasmere. Tel: 015394/35245. Open: Easter–Oct: daily 9:30am–5:30pm. Nov–Christmas: Sat–Sun 9:30am–5:30pm. From the hostel, walk down Easedale Road and turn right onto Broadgate, bearing left onto Langdale Road. When you reach the end of the road, walk into the Garden Center car park, and it's on the left. The walk is 10 minutes.

Post Office: Grasmere Post Office. Red Lion Square, Grasmere. Tel: 015394/35261. Open: Mon–Wed 9am–1pm and 2–5:30pm; Thurs 9am–midnight; Fri 9am–1pm and 2–5:30pm; Sat 9am–12:30pm. From the hostel, walk down Easedale Road to Broadgate. Cross Broadgate to College Street, and walk down until you reach Red Lion Square on the right. Turn right. It's opposite the Red Lion Hotel.

Currency Exchange: Grasmere T.I.C. Redbank Road, Grasmere. Tel: 015394/35245. Open: Easter–Oct: daily 9:30am–5:30pm. Nov–Christmas: Sat–Sun 9:30am–5:30pm.

Telephone Code: 015394.

Bike Rental: Ambleside Mountain Bikes/Ghyllside Cycles. The Slack, Ambleside. Tel: 01539/433592. Full-day rental £11 with Hostelling International card. They'll deliver to the hostel.

Getting There: The closest **train** station to Grasmere is in **Windermere,** 8^1/$_2$ miles away. Windermere is at the end of the Oxenholme-Windermere branch line off the London-Glasgow route, and service is frequent; for information, call 015394/43025. From there, it's a local bus ride out to Grasmere. The twice-daily National Express **coach** from **London** to Keswick stops right in Grasmere town. For schedule information, call London at 0171/730 0202. By **car,** take the M6 up to Junction 36 just before Kendal, which puts you on to the A591, the main road connecting the South Lakes area. Follow the A591 through Windermere and Ambleside, following signs to Grasmere.

What's Next

For those heading south, **Ambleside** and **Windermere** are perfectly lovely, if slightly overcrowded, towns on the east side of Lake Windermere. Both are a short bus ride away from Grasmere. Windermere's hostel is set away from the town in serene isolation in Troutbeck Village, while Ambleside Youth Hostel is right on the lakefront, only a short walk from the town. Moving north, the quieter hostels of **Derwentwater** and **Borrowdale** (10 to 15 miles away) provide a lot more room for peaceful contemplation against the dramatic backdrop of Derwent Water. They're especially cozy and friendly, and the absence of town life around this part of the Lakes doesn't seem to bother the walkers and cyclists (and school groups) that make it this far.

BORROWDALE (LONGTHWAITE)

A mere seven miles south of Keswick, a small cluster of villages nestles in the misty Borrowdale valley. Snow-capped crags shrouded in a haze tower over the area. Rocky streams run down the valley toward a crystalline lake, and sheep roam free in this sleepy corner of the Lake District.

Borrowdale manages to remain unsullied despite the obvious tourist potential of the lakes and surrounding countryside. It's a peaceful farming community content to go about its business as walkers, hikers, and cyclists work their way across the many footpaths and bridleways that crisscross the hills. A lone road running through the oak woodland leads to the hostel, sitting in splendid solitude. The post office is operated out of a local resident's kitchen, and the only pubs are about a mile away. When the mists descend upon this vale, it's easy to see why William Wordsworth, Hugh Walpole, Samuel Taylor Coleridge, and John Constable flocked to this sheep-speckled land for creative inspiration.

Borrowdale (Longthwaite) Youth Hostel

Longthwaite, Keswick
Cumbria CA12 5XE
Tel: 017687/77257. Fax: 017687/77393.

Built in 1939 to house war evacuees, this red cedar mountain lodge is a welcome sight to weary hill walkers. The dense thicket of Johnny's Wood rises behind the hostel, providing a natural buffer against the imposing presence of Great Gable (2,949 feet) and Scafell Pike (3,162 feet). The Coast-to-Coast and other long-distance walking routes pass right in front of the hostel. The River Derwent runs right in front of the hostel, and there's an little arcadian stone bridge that completes the pastoral picture.

The cheery staff contributes to the laid-back atmosphere, and the hostelers that make it here share a special camaraderie. The upstairs is decorated with dainty flower prints and curtains, and the views from the bedrooms are worthy of a snapshot or two. A glassed-in patio and skylit living room are just right for curling up with a good book (no TV). The resident chef provides homemade bread for breakfast, and the evening meals are reputed to be some of the best in the Lake District: The visitors (including some large school groups) who come here year after year can tell you all about it.

Services

The closest train station is in Windermere. From there, take the no. 555 or W1 bus to Keswick (a 30-minute ride). Change at Keswick for the no. 79 Borrowdale bus, a 20-minute ride. Tell the driver you are going to the Longthwaite Youth Hostel; the bus stops at the end of the hostel driveway.

The nearest bus exchange is in Keswick. From there, take the no. 79 Borrowdale bus to Longthwaite and follow directions from the train, given above.

Take the Borrowdale Road out of Keswick for 7 miles. Then take the second turn on the right at Rosthwaite village. The hostel is at the end of the lane, down a long driveway on your right.

Open Feb–Dec. Nov–Mar closed Mon and Tues. BABA.

Reception open 7:30–10am and 1–10:30pm. Curfew 11pm.

91 beds. 2-, 4-, 6-, 8-, and 12-bed rooms. Family rooms with keys for daytime access available.

£ Members: adults £7.20; under 18 £4.85.

Self-catering kitchen facilities. Breakfast: 8am. Lunch: packed lunch only; order the night before. Dinner: 7pm.

No table license.

No lockers.

Drying room only.

P Ample and free of charge.

Shop at hostel sells candy and canned goods. Items for hire: maps, towels; water bottles; compasses; some waterproof clothing.

One central living room.

In front porch area only.

Not officially wheelchair accessible but has ground-floor bedrooms.

See "Currency Exchange" under "The Basics" in Borrowdale.

Bike shed.

Cheap Eats Nearby

The Langstrath Inn

This airy restaurant inside a cozy country inn serves "anything but pub food": Fresh, healthful food with a gourmet touch is the specialty here. Vegetarian soup (£1.85) is always available. Sandwiches (£1.85 to £4.75) provide fell-walking sustenance. Main courses (£6 to £7) might include fresh Borrowdale trout, wild boar and duckling pie, and Cumberland sausage, all with vegetables. Local "guest" brews are on tap.

Stonethwaite, Borrowdale. Tel: 017687/77239. Open: daily 11:30am–2pm and 6:30–9pm. Credit cards: VA, MC. Reservations recommended. From the hostel, walk down the driveway, cross the road, and follow sign to Stonethwaite. It's on your left; a 30-minute walk.

The Yew Tree Country Restaurant

Hearty, wholesome Cumbrian food is dished out at this restored miner's cottage a mile up the road from the hostel. Jams and jellies for sale. Fell farmer's lunch is £5.45. Hearty soups are £2.10; lamb stew and other hot dishes £5 to £6. Sandwiches are available.

Seatoller (1 mile away). Tel: 017687/77634. Open: Mar–Nov: daily noon–2:30pm; 2:30–5pm (afternoon tea only); 6:30–9pm. Dec–Feb: Tues–Sun noon–2:30; 2:30–5pm (afternoon tea only); 6:30–9pm. Credit cards: VA, MC, Delta, Access. Reservations recommended. From the hostel, turn right onto the B5289 (Borrowdale Road), and head about 1 mile into the village of Seatoller. It's on your left, across from the tourist office.

Grocery Store: Rosthwaite General Store. Rosthwaite, Borrowdale (¹/₂ mile away).

Experiences

There's virtually no organized activity in the immediate vicinity of the hostel, so come prepared with a good compass and an Ordnance Survey map. A pool for river bathing lies just a few hundred yards upstream behind the hostel: take care, since the pool can be cold and deep (although Ian the warden says it's "quite pleasant"). A straight five-mile walk from the hostel will get you to **Derwentwater,** where canoes are available for rent and launches can take you on a circuit around the lake.

There are all sorts of mountain walks of varying levels of difficulty. In general, though, the terrain is rougher, the mountains craggier, and the landscape less pastoral and bucolic as you work your way up Scafell Pike and Great Gable. A less strenuous valley walk to **Seatoller** (one mile away) takes you past oak woodlands and drystone walls to a former quarrying community. There you'll find a National Park Centre with a small exhibit on the area.

Grange (1¹/₂ miles north toward Keswick) is a tiny village established by 13th-century monks as a farm for nearby **Furness Abbey.** On the way there, you'll pass by the legendary Jaws of Borrowdale, where Skiddaw slate meets volcanic rock, forming a natural barrier as the dale narrows. Ice Age melting and falling rocks ground the terrain into a U shape, and glaciers gave way to a lake in the valley bottom, to the delight of 20th-century geologists.

Long-distance walkers should ask at the hostel for interhostel walking paths. Seven and a half miles away is the legendary Black Sail hut, a former shepherd's bothy in remote Ennerdale (not accessible to cars). There, gas light and only the most basic amenities provide a true escape from modern civilization.

Boats on Derwentwater. Keswick Launch on Derwentwater. 29 Manor Park, Keswick. Tel: 017687/72263. Open: Mar–Nov: daily 10am–7:30pm; hourly departures. Dec–Feb: Sat–Sun only; 2 departures. About 4 miles away.

Nichol End Marine. Portinscale, Keswick. Tel: 017687/73082. Open: daily. Windsurfing, boating, and canoeing. Accessible via the Keswick Launch on Derwentwater, 5 miles down the road.

The Basics

Tourist Office: Lake District National Park Information Centre. The Barn, Seatoller (1 mile away). Tel: 017687/77294. Open: Easter–Nov: daily 10am–5pm. From the hostel, turn right onto B5289 (Borrowdale Road). Walk 1 mile into the town of Seatoller. It's on your right. In winter, go to Keswick (9 miles away): Keswick T.I.C. The Moot Hall, Main Street, Keswick. Tel: 017687/72645. Open: Apr–Jun and Sept–Oct: daily 9:30am–5:30pm; Jul–Aug: daily 9:30am–7pm; Nov–Mar: daily 10am–4pm.

Post Office: Ivy Cottage, Stonethwaite. Open: Mon, Wed, Fri, Sat 9:30am–12:30pm; Tues, Thurs 9:30am–noon and 2–5pm.From the hostel, walk out to the B5289 and cross the road in the direction of Stonethwaite, about ¹/₂ mile away. It's on your right, in a private home; look for the Royal Mail sign in the window.

Currency Exchange: The nearest place is in Keswick (9 miles away). Keswick T.I.C. (see "Tourist Office" under "The Basics" in Borrowdale).

Telephone Code: 017687.

Bike Rental: The nearest place in Keswick (9 miles away). Keswick Mountain Sports. 73 Main St., Keswick. Tel: 017687/73843.

Getting There: National Express **coaches** from London come daily to **Keswick,** about 7 miles away. From there, you can catch the local Borrowdale bus (no. 79) out to Longthwaite. For coach schedules, call 0171/730 0202. By **train,** the closest you can get to Borrowdale is the **Windermere** station, at the end of the branch line off the London-Manchester-Glasgow service. Local buses take you from Windermere, about 30 miles away. For train information, call Windermere at 015394/43025.

By **car,** take the M6 up to Junction 36 just before Kendal, which puts you on to the A591 north, the main road connecting the South Lakes area. Follow signs to

Keswick. Once in Keswick, take the B5289 in the direction of Borrowdale and Buttermere; the hostel is 9 miles from there.

What's Next

The five-mile walk (or bus ride) to **Derwentwater** is fast and fruitful. This hostel is a regal old mansion set on top of a lake and boasts a waterfall in its backyard. The tiny hostel at **Cockermouth,** 20 miles away via Keswick, is set on a river just outside a picturesque Lakeland town, it's a quiet, simple place where a guitar in the common room awaits traveling musicians and nearby sights include yet another museum dedicated to William Wordsworth.

DERWENTWATER

Driving the two-mile stretch down here from Keswick, you know you've reached Derwent Water when the souvenir shops begin to disappear, the traffic thins, and huge mountains and a massive lake appear to the right of the skinny, winding road. The hostel here gets its name from the lake that dominates the northern end of the Borrowdale valley.

There's no village to speak of and only a few hotels and a Youth Hostel 5 miles up the road. The lake Derwent Water spills out across the street from the hostel, and despite its relatively secluded location, boats lumber across the lake up to the riverside market town of Keswick, which has banks, post offices, supermarkets, and tourist offices. The tiny cafe up the road from the hostel is a favorite hangout of local outdoorsy types; you can swap stories and information with them and the many walkers, climbers, and bike riders exploring the area. Otherwise, sit back, relax, and pull up a piece of lake.

❂ Derwentwater Youth Hostel

Barrow House
Borrowdale, Keswick
Cumbria CA12 5UR
Tel: 017687/77246. Fax: 017687/77396.

Big blooming rhododendron bushes (in season) greet you as you approach Barrow House from Borrowdale Road. The 200-year-old listed building, one of John Adam's architectural masterpieces, is set on 15 acres of grounds overlooking Derwentwater and has its own 108-foot waterfall out back.

Decorated with a gently hippie touch, the hostel feels more beatnik than baronial. There are tapestries on the walls, plants scattered about, and an easygoing group of young adults keeping order at reception and in the kitchen. Home-baked bread, a specialty, creates a homey aroma, and meals get top marks from visitors.

The sleeping quarters range from 4- to 26-bed dorms. School groups often occupy the latter, so be prepared. One interesting room is the Adam Room, a former ballroom (now dormitory) with a fancy fireplace and beautiful bay windows overlooking the huge flower bushes, mountains, and lake beyond.

Tickets for the Keswick Launch on Derwent Water (the ferry that takes you to Keswick) are available at a discount here. For advice on climbing, go no farther than the intrepid staff, who head for the hills when they're not tending the hostel.

Otherwise, hang out at the hostel for a slice of wildlife. Red squirrels can be spotted bullying the birds; deer, badgers, and foxes can also be spied roaming around the grounds.

The closest train station is in Penrith, 19 miles away. Take bus no. X5 to Keswick, then change for the no. 79 Borrowdale Bus to Derwentwater, 2 miles from Keswick. This bus leaves you right at the driveway to the hostel in Winder-mere, 20 miles away. From there, take the W1 or the no. 555 bus to Keswick (a 25-minute ride). At Keswick, change for the green no. 79 Borrowdale bus, heading for Seatoller. Again, the bus drops you off at the end of the driveway after a 5-minute ride.

The closest bus station is in Keswick, 2 miles away. From there, follow the directions from the train, given above.

The launch service that operates from Keswick lands about 200 yards from the hostel driveway. When you get off, turn right onto Borrowdale road, and look for the hostel sign.

The hostel is 2 miles south of Keswick on the Borrowdale Road, B5289. From Keswick, take this road; the hostel is 100 yards past the left-hand side turnoff to Watendlath.

Open Jan–Nov. BABA.

Reception open 8:30–10am and 1–10pm. Curfew 11pm.

95 beds. 4-, 5-, 6-, 8-, 9-, and 26-bed rooms.

£ Members: adults £8.80; under 18 £5.95.

Self-catering kitchen facilities. Breakfast: 8am. Lunch: packed lunch only; order by 10pm the night before. Dinner: 7pm.

Table license.

No lockers.

Drying room only.

P Ample and free of charge.

Shop at hostel sells candy; canned goods; water bottles; maps; survival bags; socks; compasses.

One common area for smokers; one for nonsmokers; Ping-Pong room.

In smoking room only.

Not wheelchair accessible.

See "Currency Exchange" under "The Basics" in Derwentwater.

Bike shed.

Cheap Eats Nearby

The Riverside Inn

This substantial hotel restaurant has a traditional bar loaded up with Scotch whisky. Sandwiches are £1.60 to £3. Soup of the day with granary roll is £1.40. Main dishes include lasagne (£4.75), Cumberland sausage (£5), steak-and-kidney pie (£5).

Scafell Hotel, Borrowdale. Tel: 017687/77208. Open: daily noon–2pm and 6:30–9pm. Credit cards: VA, MC, Access (£10 minimum for plastic). From the hostel, turn left up the Borrowdale Road. It's 3 miles away, on your left.

Shepherd's Caff

The gregarious, amiable Martin runs the show at this cavernlike sweet shop up the road from the hostel. It's very popular with the rugged mountain-climbing set.

Sandwiches are £2 to £3. Beans on toast, cheese on toast is £1.75 to £2. Martin's wife makes a mean pineapple cheesecake.

High Lodore Farm, Borrowdale. No tel. Open: daily 10am–7. Cash only. From the hostel, turn left and walk about 2 miles up the road. It's on the left.

Grocery Store: Rosthwaite General Store. Borrowdale Road, Borrowdale (3^1/$_2$ miles from the hostel). Open: Mon–Sat 8:30am–6pm; Sun 8:30am–5pm. Very basic.

Experiences

Because of the hostel's choice location on Derwentwater, there are oodles of low-level **walks** in the area, most notably the 10-mile lake loop. High-level walks along the **Cat Bells** ridge offer sights of most of the northern fells: Skiddaw, Blencathra, and others. There is a 10-mph speed limit (and no waterskiing) on Derwentwater, so it's a rather quiet spot. From the pier by the hostel, boats ferry the two miles up to Keswick and all around the lake. Two **marinas** (at the Keswick end of the lake) offer windsurfing, canoeing, and boat rentals.

Experienced rock climbers can head out to **Shepherd's Crag** and **Falcon Crag** for some stomach-wrenching courses. For the inexperienced, the hostel offers activity weekends that have a pretty good local reputation. White-water canoeing, hill climbing, orienteering, mountain scrambling, drawing, and painting weekends are offered on selected dates throughout summer. They're inclusive of accommodations and full board and use local instructors.

The folks at the hostel also recommend the nearby **Whinlatter Forest Park,** at the top of Whinlatter Pass, just outside of Keswick (two miles down the road). Part of the Forest Enterprise, it has a visitor center with exhibits on Lakeland history, geology, wildlife, and nature, as well as some good footpaths up to nearby Lord's Seat and Barf. They offer some courses (including orienteering), and there's even a cafe overlooking Hospital Fell and Grisedale Pike.

Boats on Derwentwater. Keswick Launch on Derwentwater. 29 Manor Park, Keswick. Tel: 017687/72263. Open: Mar–Nov: daily 10am–7:30pm; hourly departures. Dec–Feb: Sat–Sun only; 2 departures.

Nichol End Marina. Portinscale, Keswick. Tel: 017687/73082. Open: daily. Windsurfing, boat rental, and canoeing. Accessible via the Keswick Launch on Derwentwater.

Derwentwater Summer Activity Breaks. Ask at the hostel reception desk.

Whinlatter Forest Park. Visitor Centre, Braithwaite, Keswick. Tel: 017687/78469. Open: daily 10am–5:30pm.

The Basics

Tourist Office: The nearest T.I.C. is in Keswick (2 miles away). Keswick T.I.C. The Moot Hall, Main Street, Keswick. Tel: 017687/72645. Open: Apr–June and Sept–Oct: daily 9:30am–5:30pm. July–Aug: daily 9:30am–7pm. Nov–Mar: daily 10am–4pm.

Post Office: The nearest post office is in Keswick. Keswick Post Office. 48 Main St., Keswick. Tel: 017687/72269. Open: May 31–Sept: Mon–Sat: 8:30am–8pm; Sun 10am–4pm. Oct–May 30: Mon–Sat 8:30am–5:30pm.

Currency Exchange: The nearest place is in Keswick, at the tourist office. See "Tourist Office" under "The Basics" in Derwentwater.

Telephone Code: 017687.

Bike Rental: The nearest place is in Keswick. Keswick Mountain Sports. 73 Main St., Keswick. Tel: 017687/73843.

Getting There: By **boat** from **Keswick,** take the Keswick Launch on Derwentwater. Tel: 017687/73843 (buy ticket at the hostel). For those coming by **train,** either get off at **Penrith** (19 miles away) or **Windermere** (24 miles away). Penrith is right on the main London-Glasgow route, and Windermere is at the end of a branch line off London-Glasgow. Local buses take you the rest of the way. For train information, call 015394/43025. National Express **coaches** come in twice daily on the London-Keswick route, and local buses take you the extra 2 miles to Derwentwater. For schedule info, call London at 0171/730 0202. By **car,** take the M6 up to Junction 36 just before Kendal, which puts you onto the A591, the main road connecting the South Lakes area. Follow signs into Keswick; from there take the B5289 2 miles along Derwentwater to the hostel.

What's Next

The tidy riverside **Cockermouth** Youth Hostel, which lies outside Keswick (2 miles away), is right on the banks of the pulsating river Cocker. A mining museum, brewery, and Wordsworth House provide some activity, but the town, river, and wooded areas are reason enough to make the 15-mile trip out here.

COCKERMOUTH

About 12 miles northeast of Keswick, Cockermouth pulsates at the juncture of the rivers Cocker and Derwent. Contrary to popular legend, it derives its name from its geographical location eight miles from the Irish Sea.

The birthplace of Lakeland wonder boy William Wordsworth, the town is a simple, pleasant hamlet; like most in the Lake area, it sees its fill of weekenders and summer folks, but it's charming nonetheless. Pubs and crafts shops line the streets, and there are a few museums here of interest to bookworms and beer drinkers. Jennings Brewery, is located in town, as is Wordsworth's birthplace. You can tour both places (samples available) and still have time to contemplate life on one of the hills nearby or in relative seclusion at the tiny hostel, a 10-minute walk from the town over the river and through the woods.

❋ Cockermouth Youth Hostel

Double Mills
Cockermouth, Cumbria CA13 0DS
Tel: 01900/822561.

Sitting contentedly on the River Cocker about half a mile out of town, the Youth Hostel here is a lusty blend of country vigor and quiet repose. Doubling as hostel manager and local historian, marvelous mountain man Martin is the one-man show here. According to him, the hostel was built in the 1600s and was a working watermill for grinding corn until about 100 years ago. The two water wheels, both of which are still intact, sit just outside the building, and downstairs you can see the remains of the grindstones that were used to press the corn into flour.

The hostel does feel kind of old on the inside, and it is a bit more basic than some other hostels. It's also less expensive than most in the area, however, and the jolly hostelers here don't seem to mind a bit. Claustrophobics beware: There's only one common room/dining area, but most hostelers seem to head for the pubs at night. Cockermouth seems to attract the carefree guitar-strumming set, and coincidentally, there's a guitar in the common room for those evening singalongs. It's an unusually warm and pleasant place to bed down for the night.

Services

🚆 The most convenient train station is Penrith. From there, take the X5 to Cockermouth. From Main Street, walk up Station Street and pass the war memorial. Turn left into Fern Bank and walk down the gravel track, which leads straight to the hostel; a 15-minute walk.

🚌 From Main Street, follow directions from the train, given above.

🚗 From the A66, turn right into the town and take the second right into Fern Bank. Continue down the gravel track, which leads straight to the hostel.

▦ Open Easter–Oct. Closed Tues–Wed. Closed Wednesday only Jul–Aug. Rent-a-Hostel: available during the closed months.

🕐 Reception open 7–10am and 5–10:30pm. Curfew 11pm.

🛏 28 beds. 6-, 10-, and 12-bed rooms.

£ Members: adults £6.55; under 18 £4.45.

🍴 Self-catering kitchen facilities. Breakfast: 8am. Lunch: packed lunch only; order by 10pm the night before. Dinner: 7pm.

🍸 No table license.

👜 No lockers.

🔲 Drying room only.

P Limited; free of charge.

🛍 Shop at hostel sells candy and canned goods.

🍽 Dining room/common area.

🔥 In basement.

♿ Not wheelchair accessible.

💱 See "Currency Exchange" under "The Basics" in Cockermouth.

🔺 Bike shed.

Cheap Eats Nearby

The Brown Cow

One of a lineup of pubs on the main road, this place has the usual banquettes and fruit machines and an unusually inexpensive menu. Gammon steak, Cumberland sausage, and breaded haddock are £2.50; sandwiches 75p to 95p. Daily lunch specials (steak pie and chips; roast with vegetables) are only £2.50. Jennings Bitter is on tap.

37 Main St., Cockermouth. Tel: 01900/823174. Open: Sun–Thurs 11:30am–2pm and 6:30–9pm; Fri–Sat 6:30–9pm. Cash only. From the hostel, turn left and walk along the river; turn right over the footbridge and walk until you reach the tourist office. From there, turn left onto Main Street. It's to the left, at the corner of Station Street; a 20-minute walk.

Over the Top Café

The decor is English bohemian and the cuisine international crunch. Classical music on the airwaves and art on the walls make this a comfortable hangout in a quiet part of town. Vegetarian food is a specialty. Soups are £1.75 to £2. Curries are £4.25; mushroom-and-chestnut bake £4.50. Melted Brie and mustard with bread (£4) is finger-lickin'.

36 Kirkgate, Cockermouth. Tel: 01900/827016. Open: Tues 10am–4pm; Wed–Sat 10am–4pm and 7:30–9pm. Credit cards: VA, MC, Access. From the hostel, turn left and walk along the river. Turn right over the footbridge and go past the tourist office and onto Church Walk. Follow it around the corner and it's on your left; a 20-minute walk.

Grocery Store: Walter Wilson's. Main Street.

Experiences

Despite the flurry of activity in the town, Martin the hostel manager insists that the main diversion is **walking.** You can take a 12-mile low-level walk circuit to the fells, from which you'll have views of Helvellyn, Skiddaw, Scafell to the south and east. To the west, you can see out to the Isle of Man, and to the north you can even see Scotland. A six-mile circuit to **Watch Hill** takes you northeast, and on a clear day you can catch a glimpse of Scotland and the Buttermere Fells.

The town itself is good for a romantic little stroll. On a wet day, there's a **sports center** with a pool and indoor climbing wall. If you haven't had enough of him already, **William Wordsworth's birthplace** is in town. **Jennings Brewery** bubbles with activity here, providing Cumbria with its local brew. Guided tours finish off with free samples of their frothy concoctions.

Cockermouth Sports Centre. Castle Gate Drive. Tel: 01900/823596. A 10-minute walk from the hostel. Swimming pool, climbing wall, sauna, weight room.

Wordsworth House. Main Street, Cockermouth. Tel: 01900/824805. Open: Apr–June: Mon–Fri 11am–5pm. July–Aug: daily 11am–5pm. Sept–Oct: Mon–Fri 11am–5pm. Last entry 4:30pm. Admission: adults £2.40; children £1.20.

Jennings Brothers Brewery. Castle Brewery, Cockermouth. Tel: 01900/823214. Mar, Oct: Mon–Fri: tours at 11am and 2pm. Apr–Sept: Mon–Fri: tours at 11am and 2pm; Sat tour at 11am. Adults £2.70; children and seniors £1.50.

The Basics

Tourist Office: Cockermouth T.I.C. Town Hall, Cockermouth. Tel: 01900/822634. Apr–June: Mon–Sat 9:30am–4:30pm. July–Sept: Mon–Sat 9:30am–5:30pm; Sun 2–5pm. Oct: Mon–Sat 9:30am–4:30pm. Nov–Mar: Mon–Sat 9:30am–4pm. From the hostel, turn left, and walk along the river for about 10 minutes. Turn right and cross the bridge, which brings you to the back of the T.I.C.; a 15-minute walk.

Post Office: Cockermouth Post Office. 18 Main St., Cockermouth. Tel: 01900/822277. Open: Mon–Sat 9am–5:30pm. From the hostel, turn left and walk along the river for about 10 minutes. Turn right onto Main Street; it's across the street on the left.

Currency Exchange: Cockermouth Post Office. 18 Main St., Cockermouth. Tel: 01900/822277. Open: Mon–Sat 9am–5:30pm.

Telephone Code: 01900.

Bike Rental: Track and Trail Mountain Bike Hire. Cockermouth. Tel: 01900/ 827243. Full day £12; half day £7. They will deliver to the hostel.

Getting There: Coming by **train** can be tricky: The closest station is 8 miles away in **Workington,** a stop on the Barrow-Carlisle line on the west coast. From there, local buses (X5) run to Cockermouth. Those coming from the south and east should head for **Windermere** and catch a local bus to Cockermouth via **Keswick.** For train information, call 015394/43025. By **coach,** there is daily National Express service to **Keswick,** and from Keswick, local bus X5 goes to Cockermouth. For National Express schedule info, call 0171/730 0202. For local bus info., call 01946/ 63222. By **car,** take the M6 up to Junction 36 just before Kendal. From there, take the A591 to Keswick, and then the A66 12 miles west to Cockermouth.

What's Next

The megamarket town of **Keswick,** 12 miles away, can't compete with Cockermouth's small-town cuteness, but it is a major connection for those wishing to travel further south into the Lake district. A transportation hub just north of the mammoth Derwent Water, Keswick has good connections to the south Lakes; Windermere and Ambleside are easy trips from here. From Keswick, buses also head up the B5289 to the more isolated, idyllic **Borrowdale** valley, where two country hostels await in magnificent wooded solitude. The Longthwaite hostel is only about 20 miles from Cockermouth, and **Derwentwater** a mere 15 miles; the trip is especially nice if you forget the bus and hop on the boat across Derwentwater.

Northeast England

Travelers exploring the northernmost boundary of England are confronted with a bleak, tough landscape—a far cry from the idyllic country lanes and flowery gardens of southern England. In A.D. 120, the Roman emperor Hadrian surveyed this rugged, hilly land and decided to build a wall running from the Irish Sea in the west to the North Sea in the east to protect his outpost from the barbarians to the north. Legionnaires set to work and built the $73^1/_2$-mile-long brick wall running roughly between Newcastle and Carlisle. They also built a series of forts along the wall. The bits and pieces of Hadrian's handiwork that remain comprise some of the best Roman ruins outside Rome.

Northumberland, where the oldest traces of the empire sit on hilltops, has an air of antiquity and prehistory about it; it feels more Roman than British. The ancient Pennine Way footpath winds up here. The Youth Hostel at Once Brewed sits in virtual isolation only a short walk away from the wall and one of Hadrian's forts.

To the south, the Yorkshire landscape breaks into bleak moorlands. The Youth Hostel at Osmotherley is in a tranquil wooded setting perfect for summertime heather stomping. Scarborough lies on the Yorkshire coast. This faded seaside town became famous for its "fayre." The countryside and coast are at their prettiest by the hostel, a few miles to the north.

Transportation in the area can be difficult, especially as you go west: Once Brewed is as close to the middle of nowhere as you're likely to get in England. The only reliable form of transport is the Newcastle-Carlisle train line, which drops you off a few miles away. Osmotherley is equally tough. It's lost in the moorlands of North

Yorkshire, and you'll have to change buses a few times (from anywhere) to get here. Newcastle, in comparison, is a snap, thanks to the trains that run there regularly.

ONCE BREWED (BARDON MILL)

Way back around A.D. 120, the Roman emperor Hadrian ordered three legions of soldiers to build a massive wall to run east-west along the rugged land between Newcastle and Bowness-on-Solway. Suspicious of imperial wannabes, he wanted to build a fortification to keep foreign invaders at bay.

Only bits and pieces of the wall remain, but his wishes have been fulfilled: Nobody has invaded the area. Only truly intrepid travelers (and those obsessed with Roman archaeology) seem to make it out here. There's a lot of open land, rugged rocks, bits and pieces of the legendary wall, and not much else. The village (and that's a generous term) of Once Brewed contains the Youth Hostel (of the same name), the information center (of the same name), and a couple of street signs.

Legend has it that during the Jacobite rebellion in 1745, General Wade waited here to fend off the armies of Bonnie Prince Charlie. Since Bonny P.C. came down via Carlisle to the west, General Wade built a road to catch his army and hacked away at a huge section of Hadrian's Wall, excavating a military thoroughfare (aka the B6318). The workers took a break at a nearby inn and were served a beverage so weak that they threw it back and said to brew it again. Hence, the name of the "village" up the street, Twice Brewed.

The Youth Hostel was founded 189 years later. The founder, Lady Trevelyan, declared that no alcohol would be permitted, and she said that the tea and coffee here need only be brewed once. Hence, Once Brewed. What remains is a one-pub town midway between Carlisle and Newcastle: A dot on the bleak landscape of Northumbria.

Once Brewed Youth Hostel Military Road

Bardon Mill, Hexham
Northumberland NE47 7AN
Tel: 01434/344360. Fax: 01434/344045.

There's no escaping the unattractive modern Youth Hostel. Built in 1934, it's one of the few buildings dotting this giant golf course with sheep. This isn't one of the YHA's more attractive "purpose-built" hostels. It feels like a cross between an ugly modern college, an ugly modern public school, and an ugly second-rate nature museum. It is, however, conveniently located next door to a very helpful tourist office.

Despite the unfortunate architecture and lonely landscape (or maybe because of it), the staff here is nice and helpful. They try to make the place more appealing: Vines and hanging plants drape over the flat square windows, and the hostel shop sells some nifty Australian wood knickknacks. A rock display and fish tank grace the hostel's lounge, and there's usually a cup of tea or coffee available for guests upon arrival. Don't come here to hang out inside, however. This is a place to park your stuff, get out, and walk around some wall. The hostel offers a tour service around the wall, mainly for large school parties, but they can also tailor it for smaller groups. Call ahead to book your bed: This is a popular place among the primary-school set.

Services

🚆 From the Bardon Mill train station, turn left as you come out of the station, follow the signs to Once Brewed, 2¹/₂ miles away. No bus service.

🚌 The closest bus stop is in Henshaw, 2 miles to the south. Follow the signs to the hostel.

🚗 The hostel is on the B6318, Military Road. From the A69, turn onto the B6318 following signs to Hadrian's Wall.

▦ Open Feb–Nov. Closed Sun in Nov, Feb, Mar. BABA.

🕐 Reception open 7–10am and 1–11:30pm. Curfew 11pm.

🛏 87 beds. 2-, 3-, 4-, 5-, and 7-bed rooms. Rooms with keys for daytime access.

£ Members: adults £8; under 18 £5.35.

🍴 Self-catering kitchen facilities. Breakfast: 7:45–8:30am. Lunch: packed lunch only; order the night before. Dinner: 6–7pm.

🍸 No table license.

💼 No lockers.

◻ Washers, dryers, and drying room.

P Ample and free of charge.

🛍 Shop at hostel sells candy, canned goods, and little Australian woodcrafts.

🛋 Common room; games room.

🚬 In common room only.

♿ Limited wheelchair accessibility. Ground-floor rooms but no wheelchair bathrooms.

💱 See "Currency Exchange" under "The Basics" in Once Brewed.

🔺 Bike shed.

Cheap Eats Nearby

The Twice Brewed Inn

You'll find lovely lanterns, a log fireplace, and a pool table in this traditional pub/restaurant—the only one for miles around. Dishes include beef-and-ale pie £5.75; cauliflower broccoli mornay £5.45; tuna pasta bake £5.45; sesame chicken £5.50. Daily specials are £3 to £4.

Military Road, Twice Brewed, Hexham. Tel: 01434/344534. Open: Mon–Sat 11am–9pm; Sun noon–3pm and 7–10:30pm. Cash only. From the hostel, walk through the car park, turn right on the footpath, and it's straight ahead; a 5-minute walk.

Grocery Store: Bardon Mill Post Office, Bardon Mill (2¹/₂ miles away). Open: Mon–Fri 8:30am–5:30pm; Sat–Sun 8:30am–12:30pm.

Experiences

Friends, Romans, countrymen, and hostelers alike will find more Roman monuments around Once Brewed than anywhere else outside Rome. Only half a mile from the 80-mile-long **Hadrian's Wall,** the village is an excellent base from which to explore Northumberland National Park and the Northern Pennines. Walkers finishing up the last leg of the **Pennine Way** pass through here, and there are some unforgettable sights along this ancient route. In the Roman days, the wall was home to 40,000 soldiers, and in the first and second centuries the land was fertile enough to grow grapes along the wall. The wall itself is a geological wonder. Standing on the site of a volcanic intrusion, it provides loads of specimens and hours of fun for rock lovers.

From the hostel, an easy three-mile walk following the path of the wall takes you to **Housesteads.** One of Hadrian's many forts, it once housed up to 1,000 soldiers in its self-contained community. Now, Housesteads has a small historical exhibition with artifacts uncovered in the area, and you can wander through the remains of the garrison. **Vindolanda,** just up the road from Housesteads, offers a more substantial museum (also in an old fort) with a turf-and-stone replica of the Wall as the Romans knew it.

A visit here can be more than a Roman holiday, though. Just over the wall is the **Wark Forest,** which leads into **Kielder Forest,** the largest human-made forest in Europe. The forest has some good rock climbing and abseiling on the Peel Crags and Steel Rigg as well as water sports on Kielder Water. Check out the *What's On: Walks and Events in Northumberland* guide (available in the park center) for a listing of special events, including a mix of **ranger-guided walks,** arts lectures and classes, and sport outings in the area.

Housesteads Roman Fort. Near Bardon Mill. Tel: 01434/344363. Open: Apr–Sept: daily 10am–6pm. Oct–Mar: daily 10am–4pm. Admission: adults £2.30; concessions £1.70; children £1.20. Accessible on foot or by local bus.

Vindolanda Fort and Museum. Vindolanda Trust, Near Bardon Mill. Tel: 01434/ 344277. Open: Feb–Nov: daily 10am–4pm. Mar and Oct: daily 10am–5pm. Apr and Sept: daily 10am–5:30pm. May–Jun: daily 10am–6pm. Jul–Aug: daily 10am–6:30pm.

Wark and Kielder Forests. Forest Enterprise, Kielder Forest District, Eals Burn, Bellingham. Tel: 01434/220242. The Park Centre at Once Brewed also has information on the forests.

Ranger-guided walks in Northumberland. Contact the Northumberland National Park Information Centre in Once Brewed. Full-day walks: adults £3, children and seniors £1.50. Half-day walks: adults £1.50; children and seniors 75p.

The Basics

Tourist Office: Northumberland National Park Information Centre. Once Brewed. Tel: 01434/344396. Open: Mar 4–Apr: daily 10am–5pm; May–Oct: daily 10am–6pm; Nov: Sat–Sun 10am–3pm. Closed Dec–Mar 3. Located next door to the hostel.

Post Office: Bardon Mill Post Office. Bardon Mill. Tel: 01434/344231. Open: Mon–Tues and Thurs–Fri 9am–12:30pm and 1:30–5:30pm; Wed and Sat 9am–12:30pm. From the hostel, it's 2½ miles down Military Road, next to the rail station in Bardon Mill. It doubles as a convenience store.

Currency Exchange: The closest place is Hexham, 15 miles away. Callers Pegasus Travel Agency. Tynedale Park, Hexham. Tel: 01434/600023. Open: Mon–Sat 10am–6pm; Sun 11am–5pm.

Telephone Code: 01434.

Bike Rental: Tyne Valley Cycle. 1 Tyne Rd., Haltwhistle. Tel: 01434/322793. Hostelers get a 10% discount.

Getting There: By **train,** Bardon Mill is on the Carlisle-Newcastle route, which connects to the London-Glasgow and London-Edinburgh main line. Bardon Mill is an unmanned stop, so call ahead for schedule information: 01228/44711 or 0191/232 6262. By **bus,** there's only a local service, Hadrian's Wall Bus, that operates between **Carlisle** and **Newcastle.** For information, call 01946/63222. Those coming from farther away can get to either city by National Express. Call 0171/730 0202 for information. By **car,** take the A1/M1 to Newcastle-upon-Tyne; there, switch to the A69, following signs to Hexham and Bardon Mill. From Bardon Mill, it's 2^1/2 miles to Once Brewed.

What's Next

Once Brewed is in something of a no-man's-land, but it's actually quite accessible to both the east coast and the Northern Lakes. To the west, the market town of **Keswick** is a gateway to the Lake District. From here, there's good service to Ambleside, Windermere, Borrowdale, and Grasmere, all of which provide glistening waters, high fells, and literary shrines.

OSMOTHERLEY

Osmotherley, a sleepy village, is but a tiny speck on the vast moorlands of North Yorkshire. It's actually quite centrally located: York is a 45-minute drive to the south, the Yorkshire Dales are about 40 miles from here, and the Yorkshire Coast (Scarborough and Whitby) are about a 50-minute drive away.

The town itself, on its lofty perch on the western side of the North Yorkshire Moors National Park, is as cute as a button. It's an ancient village with traditional stone cottages, a few antiques shops, and a couple of country inns. An old market cross is the lone landmark in the center of town; John Wesley reputedly preached his Methodist sermons to the townsfolk here. Not far away lie a medieval chapel and Carthusian monastery.

The local agricultural show brings locals together in early August, and some say the best time of year here is in late August or early September, when the moorlands are smothered in purple heather. They may be made up mostly of peat bogs and hardy farmland, but the moors aren't nearly as bleak as the Brontës would lead you to imagine. Just ask all the folks toting water bottles and walking sticks. Osmotherley is a stop on the Coast-to-Coast Path (192 miles), The Cleveleand Way (108 miles through the Yorkshire Moors), and the Lyke Wake Walk (40 miles). Those looking for more activity can head a few miles away to the classic market towns of Northallerton and Thirsk, with their open-air markets and too-cute tearooms.

✸ Osmotherley Youth Hostel

Coat Ghyll
Osmotherley, Northallerton
North Yorkshire DL6 3AH
Tel: 01609/883575. Fax: 01609/883715.

A short walk from the village of Osmotherley takes you down a quiet road, over a bridge, and past a few cascading waterfalls on the way to this cheery Youth Hostel. The 200-year-old building was originally a flax mill that generated its power from a stream that still rushes past the hostel. In the war years, the structure was used as a dance hall and then served as a chicken shed in the 1950s and 1960s before falling into disrepair.

In 1980 the hosteling association rescued it and did a bang-up job repairing the place. A cheery entrance hall provides a warm welcome for guests, and a hot cup of tea is always on offer. Loaded with magazines, hanging plants, and comfy chairs, the hall is good spot to trade stories with fellow hostelers (who include lots of walkers and cyclists) and map out the next day's walking route.

The homemade meals are good here, especially the vegetarian options, and snacks are available from the kitchen if you arrive after dinner. The airy dining room has a neat little divider that separates the school groups from the independent travelers, so even when the kiddies are in (and they're in quite often), the hostel manages to be roomy enough for everyone.

The closest train station is Northallerton, 8 miles away. Walk into the town center, and outside the Bull Pub, pick up bus no. 90 (united or Tees and District) in the direction of Middlesbrough and get off at Osmotherley village: a 15-minute ride. From the bus stop, walk up the hill past the Top Shop for about a half mile until you reach the hostel drive, which is signposted. The hostel is at the end of the long drive; a 15-minute walk from the village.

Middlesbrough is the closest large coach station. From there, take bus no. 90 in the direction of Northallerton, and get off at Osmotherley; a 50-minute ride. From the bus stop, follow directions from the train, given above.

From the A19, take the A684 turnoff for Northallerton. Once you reach Northallerton, follow signs for Osmotherley, 8 miles away. Once in Osmotherley, turn left at the cross, and the hostel is about a half mile up the road.

Open Jan 17–Oct. Sept–Oct closed Sun and Mon. BABA.

Reception open 7–10am and 5–11pm. Curfew 11:30pm.

80 beds. 2-, 4-, 6-, 8-, and 10-bed rooms, all with toilets and wash basins. Some have keys for daytime access.

£ Members: adults £7.45; under 18 £5.

Self-catering kitchen facilities. Breakfast: 8am. Lunch: packed lunch only; should be ordered by 10:30pm the night before. Dinner: 7pm.

No table license.

No lockers.

Washer and drying room.

P Ample and free of charge.

Shop at hostel sells candy, canned goods, maps.

Reception area (good reading area); TV room. Dining room has a pool table.

In TV room only.

Not wheelchair accessible.

See "Currency Exchange" under "The Basics" in Osmotherley.

Bike shed; classroom with overhead projector.

Cheap Eats Nearby

The Golden Lion
This local watering hole has Yorkshire brews on tap and serves up hefty hunks of food by its wood-burning stove. Walkers' specials include soup with granary bread

(£1.95), savory mince with giant Yorkshire pudding (£3.50), and an assortment of the usual sandwiches (£2).

6 West End, Osmotherley. Tel: 01609/883526. Open: daily noon–2pm and 6–9pm. Cash only. From the hostel, turn left down the driveway and follow North End into the village. At the Market Cross, turn right. It's on your right past the post office.

Queen Catherine Hotel

Mary and Charlie serve traditional stick-to-your-ribs English fare in this friendly inn in the center of the village. Steak pie, roast beef, broccoli-and-cheese pie all £4.95. Sandwiches are £1.50 to £2.50.

7 West End, Osmotherley. Tel: 01609/883209. Open: Mon–Sat noon–2pm and 6–9:30pm; Sun noon–2pm and 7–9:30pm. From the hostel, turn left down the driveway and follow North End into the village. At the Market Cross, turn right. It's across the street on the left.

Grocery Store: D. T. and S. Burgon Top Shop. North End, Osmotherley. Open: Mon–Sat 8:30am–5:30pm; Sun 9am–5pm.

Experiences

Medieval history and moor walking are the name of the game here. The well-preserved **Mount Grace Priory,** built in 1398, is one of the largest Carthusian monasteries in England; it's 1 1/2 miles west of town. The restored monk's cell with adjoining herb garden is especially interesting. The walk out there along public footpaths traverses a pleasant stretch of farms and fields. Nearby, another footpath goes to **Lady Chapel,** founded in 1515 by Catherine of Aragon, the first of Henry VIII's six wives.

The village of Osmotherley itself also makes a nice, albeit short, historical journey. The Market Cross (where cattle and sheep were once traded) and the Old Methodist Chapel are a tribute to the influence of John Wesley, who is said to have brought Methodism to this part of England.

About three miles from the hostel, **Black Hambleton** is the largest hill in the area, and the vantage point there offers views of the dales and the moors. In the back of the hostel is a reservoir (a 10-minute walk) perfect for picnics; it gives way to open moorland. If you come here on the right day, you might hit Osmotherley's **annual show,** when everything from moorland cattle to gooseberries to baby's clothes are displayed, and prizes are given out to those with the most impressive entries.

Mount Grace Priory and Lady Chapel. Near Saddlebridge, North Yorkshire. Tel: 01609/883494. Open: Apr–Sept: daily 10am–6pm. Oct–Mar: Wed–Sun 10am–4pm. Admission: adults £2.20; concessions £1.70; children £1.10. Walking map available from the grocery store in town.

Annual Fair. Osmotherley and District Horticultural and Agricultural Society. For info, call Mrs. Lowther at tel: 01609/780403. Held in early August. Admission: adults £1.50; children 50p; senior citizens £1.

The Basics

Tourist Office: The closest T.I.C. is in Northallerton (8 miles away). Applegarth Car Park, Northallerton. Tel: 01609/776864. Open: Easter–Oct: daily 10am–5pm. Nov–Easter: Wed–Sat 10am–4pm. From the hostel, walk to the Market Cross and take bus no. 90 into Northallerton. It's behind the Main Street; a 25-minute ride.

Post Office: Osmotherley Post Office, Osmotherley. Tel: 01609/883201. Open: Mon–Tues and Thurs–Fri 9am–5pm; Wed and Sat 9am–midnight. From the hostel, turn left and walk down North End to the Market Cross. It's on the right.

Currency Exchange: The closest place is in Northallerton (8 miles away). Barclays Bank. 193 High St., Northallerton. Tel: 01609/780111. Open: Mon–Fri 9am–5:30pm; Sat 9:30am–midnight.

Telephone Code: 01609.

Bike Rental: North Yorkshire Moors Adventure Centre. Tel: 01609/882571. Also, Bike of Beyond. Grinton Lodge Youth Hostel (31 miles away).

Getting There: The closest **train** station is in **Northallerton** (8 miles away), right on the main line between York and Darlington, so it's easy to connect from eastern England. For schedule information, call 01904/642155. **Coaches** don't come into Osmotherley, only local buses do. The nearest large bus station is in **Middlesbrough,** where good local bus service connects to Osmotherley. For bus information, call 01642/210131. By **car,** head up the A19 from **York,** following signs to Thirsk and Middlesbrough; Osmotherley is about midway between the two.

What's Next

For those heading farther into Yorkshire, there are some beautiful villages to the east. **Aysgarth Falls** is a short ride along the A684. Another tiny dot on the landscape, it offers wooded scenery and a cascading waterfall. A few bus connections (via Northallerton) can get you to the heart of the Yorkshire Dales, where **Hawes** and **Dent** sit in unspoiled farming valleys with drystone walls and picture-perfect villages.

4 THE BEST HOSTELS IN WALES

Wales & the Welsh Borders

Bounded by England to the east and the Atlantic Ocean to the west, the feisty country of Wales is culturally, geographically, and linguistically distinct from England. Once you've crossed the Welsh border, you'll unquestionably know you've entered another country. Although it still pertains to the English throne, the country's independent, spunky nature contrasts sharply with that of its staid imperial neighbor to the east.

The ancient Welsh tongue, Celtic in origin, was recognized in 1284 by Edward I as an official, legal language. Over the years, monarchs alternately rescinded and reinstated his statute. Today the language flourishes. You're more likely to hear it spoken in the north, but throughout the country street signs and tourist information are almost uniformly bilingual. Newspapers and magazines are available in both languages wherever you go, and Channel 4 broadcasts TV programs in Welsh.

If you're coming from the east, you'll approach the country via the English marshlands. In the south, the Royal Forest of Dean creates a natural barrier between Central England and Wales. There stands St. Briavel's Castle, built by the Earl of Hereford in the 1100s. A century later, the castle was converted into a royal hunting lodge, and it's now home to a Youth Hostel. Just to the north, Welsh Bicknor, tucked into the wooded gorges of the Wye Valley, also straddles the Borders. Hostelers paddle their way upriver to spend a night or two at the rectory-turned-hostel here.

South lies the capital city of Cardiff, where a lively arts scene coexists with traditional folk museums. The world's principal coal port at the turn of the century, Cardiff has polished away the soot and is beginning to emerge as a cultural center for all Wales. To the northwest, the coastal town of Borth boasts some beautiful sandy beaches and an abundance of marshlands good for bird watching and beach walking.

Continue up the west coast and you'll reach the spiky peaks of Snowdonia National Park, where mountain climbing is a religion and explorer Edmund Hillary is God. The snow-capped peaks, between 1,000 and 3,500 feet, cluster in the northwest corner of Wales, attracting tourists from Ireland, England, and Continental Europe. The hostels Bryn Gwynant, Snowdon Ranger, and Pen-y-Pass are nestled amid icy lakes and fragrant forests of pine off the narrow roads that wind through the area.

To the north, the city of Bangor is only a short ride from the ferry to Ireland and close enough to the mountains for day trips. A quick train ride east takes you to the cathedral city of Chester on the English side of the borderlands. Inside the Roman walls surrounding the town, history lives on in the shopping arcades. This has been a mercantile community since medieval times, and all the buildings have balconies on which additional shops sit high above the city streets. Modern-day merchants from Jaeger to Warner Brothers peep out of the medieval buildings.

Cradled in the Dee Valley is the small town of Llangollen, where climbers, canoers, and outdoor types attack the luxuriant natural setting. A network of hills, streams, and bike paths covers the area.

On the whole, traveling through Wales isn't easy: Cardiff, Bangor, and Chester serve as rail links, but otherwise the only service is on buses. There's good service in Snowdonia and Llangollen and drivers can be responsive to wandering backpackers, but expect to change buses more than once to get to the more remote areas. Farther down in the Wye Valley, bus service is even sketchier, so plan on waiting and walking.

CARDIFF

Cardiff owes at least some of its international renown to having given birth to hunky Tom Jones, singer and gyrator extraordinaire who was born in a small coal-mining town just outside the city limits. Located 155 miles west of London and 188 miles south of Manchester, Cardiff usually falls into the category of missable cities for those travelers on a tour of picturesque country lanes, traditional pubs, and Victorian frippery—too bad for them.

Once a quiet fishing village, Cardiff boomed in the 1800s when coal was discovered in the nearby Rhondda Valley. From its port, the black gold was shipped all over the world. An orderly Victorian town in the 19th century, with Beaux Arts buildings (one of which is now the Civic Centre) and rolling parklands, it began to decline at the turn of this century and struggled with industrial and financial woes.

Recently, however, prosperity has returned to Cardiff. It has long since shed its layer of soot. About a decade ago, it rose from its ashy grave to become what it is today: a triumphant city with a booming contemporary arts movement, some spruced-up museums, good theater, and a substantial university population to keep the bars, clubs, and pubs humming.

While it's not unlike its postindustrial peers Bristol, Manchester, and Glasgow, the feeling here is unmistakably Welsh. English is the mother tongue spoken in the streets, but signs, leaflets, and even books and magazines are generally bilingual. Granted regional autonomy in 1975 (but still represented in London's Parliament), Wales takes immense pride in its Celtic heritage, its struggle for independence, and the numerous cultural landmarks that distinguish it from its neighbors to the east. A visit to Cardiff will give you a greater appreciation of what is distinctly Welsh and will serve you well if you intend to head farther into the country.

Cardiff Youth Hostel
Hostel IeuenctidCaerdydd

2 Wedal Rd.
Roath Park, Cardiff CF2 5PG
Tel: 01222/462303. Fax: 01222/464571.

At the front entrance of the Cardiff Youth Hostel is a sign declaring it a "Ty croeso" ("welcome house"), and that's the theme here. The staff make an extraspecial effort to make this place cheery and homey. About two miles outside the center of Cardiff, the hostel sits next to Roath Park, which has some beautiful gardens, playing fields, a human-size lake, and tennis courts. The traffic here isn't as noisy, the people don't walk as fast, and it's slightly calmer than it is downtown.

The kindly, soft-spoken warden, Hillary, is used to handling all sorts of questions and problems and keeps the place running like a well-oiled machine with her soothing touch. Each bedroom has its own proper name, thoughtfully provided in both English and Welsh, and the dining room is vaguely reminiscent of an elementary school cafeteria. The food is good. On the chalkboard is a list of the specials, including a tasty vegetarian cottage pie (£3), beef curry with chips (£3), and other homemade meals.

A mixed lot of travelers finds their way here, from school groups (the hostel has a classroom) to individual backpackers to families. In this quiet hostel in a quiet neighborhood, the guests seem to coexist relatively peacefully. Nobody spends much time here anyway—bags are parked, maps are examined, and from there most hostelers are gone until the wee hours of the morning.

Services

From Cardiff Central, catch bus no. 78, 80, or 82 and tell the driver to let you off at the Youth Hostel. When you get off, turn onto Wedal Road and the hostel is on your right. It's a 20-minute ride.

From the bus station, catch bus no. 78, 80, or 82 and follow directions from the train station, given above.

From the **east,** take the M4 to Junction 29. Then take the A48M along to the A470 Junction, which is signed "City Centre." From there, you'll reach a roundabout. Take the first exit off the roundabout, which is Whitchurch Road. Go on Whitchurch for about a quarter of a mile, take left at the Heath Pub, then the first right onto Wedal Road. The hostel is at the bottom of the road on the left. From the **west** take the M4 to Junction 32, then the A470 toward Cardiff to the Cross Inn. Go on to the roundabout behind the Cross Inn. Take the second exit off the roundabout and you'll reach Whitchurch Road. Go on Whitchurch for about one-fourth mile, take left at the Heath Pub, then the first right onto Wedal Road. The hostel is at the bottom of the road on the left.

Open Jan–Nov. Closed Sun in Jan, Feb, and Nov. IBN/BABA.

Reception open 7:30–10am and 3–10:30pm. No curfew (there's a code for the front door), but new arrivals must come before 10:30pm.

68 beds. 4-, 6-, 8-, 14-, and 16-bed rooms available.

£ Members: adults £8.80; under 18 £5.95

Croeso Café serves meals. Self-catering kitchen facilities with separate dining room. Breakfast: 8–8:30am; order by 10pm the night before. Lunch: packed lunch; order by 10pm the night before. Dinner: 6–7pm. No set menu—choices are listed on a blackboard, including the "Cardiff Filler," a special low-priced option.

Table license.

No lockers, but staff will store valuables on request.

Washers £1.50; dryers 60p; drying room.

P Available.

Shop at hostel sells candy; Welsh mementos: stickers, flags, and dolls.

TV lounge with games; nonsmoking sitting rooms next to self-catering kitchen.

In TV lounge only.

Wheelchair accessible.

See "Currency Exchange" under "The Basics" in Cardiff.

Cheap Eats Nearby

Bella Pasta

Close to the castle and to night spots, this upscale pizza-and-pasta chain delivers good, reasonably priced Italian food. Specialties include Margherita pizza £4.65; vegetarian pizza £5.90; pastas £6 to £8; lunch special of pasta with garlic bread £3.95.

6 High St., Cardiff. Tel: 01222/399466. Open: Sun–Thurs 11am–11pm; Fri–Sat 11am–midnight. Reservations accepted. Wheelchair accessible. Credit cards: AE, VA, MC, EC, Access, Switch. Take bus no. 78, 80, or 82 into the city center (20 minutes); from the Castle, walk straight up High Street and it's on the left.

The Celtic Cauldron

Traditional Welsh dishes with a vegetarian flair are served in this homey place with a tangle of plants hanging from the ceiling. Fare includes Welsh faggots £3.70; Anglesey eggs £3.90; vegetarian casserole £1.70; vegetarian lasagne £3.70; omelets £3.50 to £3.70.

47–49 Castle Arcade, Cardiff. Tel: 01222/387185. Open: Mon–Sat 8:30am–6pm; later in summertime. Credit cards: AE, MC, VA, EC, Access. From the hostel, take bus no. 78, 80, or 82 into the city center. It's opposite the main entrance to the Castle; it's about a 20-minute ride.

Grocery Store: Tesco, on Albany Road.

Experiences

There's so much more to Cardiff than meets the eye—literally. Visual arts are big here, as well as photography, crafts, furniture design, and performance art. After you've been to the **National Museum of Wales** and drooled over its collection of French impressionists and after you've seen the garish grandeur of the Norman **Cardiff Castle** (refurbished in the 19th century), head out of town on bus no. 17 or 18 to the **Chapter,** a gallery/theater/alternative cinema. A thriving venue of all sorts of local arts happenings with pubs and cafes, it offers a real little slice of Cardiff life.

Some galleries in town showcasing both local and international artists include **Ffotogallery, Oriel,** and **The Makers' Guild Craft Centre**. **The Old Library Artists** formed a cooperative of sorts, named for the studio space they used to rent in Cardiff's Old Library (before it was renovated into a swanky exhibition hall). This group represents the alter ego of Cardiff's arts scene and is comprised of Welsh-born and English expatriates including comic strip artists, printmakers, photographers, sculptors, a clown, and even a bonsai artist. The Tourist Information Centre can tell you where they are; they welcome visitors to their studios.

For fresh-air aficionados, the **Taff Trail** is a 55-mile bike path that starts out in Cardiff Bay and goes north to the town of Brecon. It offers beautiful views of the upper Wye Valley and the River Usk.

Other must-see sights in Cardiff include the village of **St. Fagans** with its castle and the **Welsh Folk Museum.** Set on 100 acres of parkland outside of the city center, the castle is a nobleman's home. The museum includes a restored Celtic village—a slightly corny, if entertaining, presentation of life in a Welsh industrial community. It's a nice spot to relax.

Cardiff is also rife with festivals and markets. The covered **Cardiff Market** in the center of town sells everything from soup to nuts and bolts under one roof and offers great prices on produce; it's fun to wander through. Festival time runs from May to September, when the city plays host to an international animation festival, the traditional Cardiff Festival and Welsh Proms, an arts festival, and other smaller arts and music events.

Welsh National Museum. Cathays Park, Cardiff. Tel: 01222/397951. Open: Tues–Sat 10am–5pm; Sun 2–5pm. Admission: adults £4.80; seniors £3.60; children £2.40.

Cardiff Castle. Castle Street, Cardiff. Tel: 01222/822083. Open: daily 10am–5pm. Mar–Oct: tours from 10am–12:30pm and 2–4pm. Adults: admission £2.20; admission and tour £3.50. Children: admission £1.10; admission and tour £1.70.

Chapter. Market Road. Canton, Cardiff. Tel: 01222/399666. Box office hours: Mon–Fri 11am–9pm; Sat–Sun 3–9pm. Theater: performance times vary; call ahead. Theater tickets: £4.50–£7.50; concessions available. Art Gallery: open Tues–Sun noon–5pm and 7–10pm. Gallery admission: free. Cinema: show times vary; call ahead. Tickets: adults £3.60; students and seniors £2.60. To get here, take bus no. 17, 18, or 31 from the city center.

Fotogallery. 31 Charles St., Cardiff. Tel: 01222/341667. Open: Tues–Sat 10am–5:30pm. Admission: free.

Oriel. The Friary, Cardiff. Tel: 01222/395548. Open: Mon–Sat 9am–5:30pm. Admission: free.

Old Library Artists and Makers Guild Craft Centre. Trinity Street, The Hayes, Cardiff. Tel: 01222/343941. Open: Mon–Sat 10am–5pm. This information was accurate as of 1995. The Old Library Artists' and Makers Guild new location can be obtained by calling the Cardiff T.I.C. Be sure to ask for the artists group, not the building itself.

Welsh Folk Museum. St. Fagans, Cardiff. Tel: 01222/569441. Open: Apr–Oct: daily 10am–5pm. Nov–Mar: Mon–Sat 10am–5pm. From Cardiff, take bus no. 32 from the bus station to St. Fagan's (a 25-minute ride).

The Basics

Tourist Office: Cardiff T.I.C. 8–14 Bridge St., Cardiff. Tel: 01222/227281. Open: Apr–Sept: Mon–Sat 9am–6:30pm; Sun 10am–4pm. Oct–Mar: Mon–Sat 9am–5:30pm; Sun 10am–4pm. Free tour of Cardiff Bay, a new development. Take bus no. 78, 80, or 82 into the city center (20 minutes). From Cardiff Castle, walk up High Street, continue up St. Mary Street, and turn left on Mill Lane. At the intersection, bear right onto Bridge Street; it's on your right.

Post Office: The Hayes Post Office. Oxford House, 2–4 Hill's St., Cardiff. Tel: 01222/232410. Open: Mon–Fri 9am–5:30pm; Sat 9am–4:30pm. Take bus no. 78, 80, or 82 into the city center (20 minutes). From Cardiff Castle, walk up High Street, and turn left into Royal Arcade. Walk through to The Hayes, then turn right onto Hill's Street. It's on the right.

Currency Exchange: American Express. 3 Queen St., Cardiff. Tel: 01222/665843. Open: Mon–Fri 9am–5:30pm; Sat 9am–5pm. Thomas Cook. 16 Queen St., Cardiff. Tel: 01222/343865. Open: Mon–Thurs 9am–5:30pm; Fri 10am–5:30pm; Sat 9am–5:30pm.

Telephone Code: 01222.

Bike Rental: Freewheel. 9 Castle St., Cardiff. Tel: 01222/667049. Open: Mon–Sat 9am–5:30pm. Full-day rental £7; deposit required. Outside Cardiff: Forest Farm Country Park, Whitchurch. Tel: 01222/751235 or 01222/529108.

Getting There: Cardiff has direct **train** links to and from **Cornwall** (Penzance, Falmouth), **London, Bristol, Bath, Shrewsbury, Manchester,** and **York.** Within Wales, the western line from Cardiff heads west to **Fishguard** (the ferry port to Rosslare). The Heart of Wales line goes through Llangammarch to Llandrinod to Shrewsbury in England and then back into Wales, up to Llandudno and Bangor in the north and Aberystwyth, Harlech, and Holyhead to the west, skirting Snowdonia. For train information, call 01222/228000. **Coaches,** including National Express (to most English and Scottish cities) and TrawsCambria (towns in Wales), leave continuously from the bus exchange in Cardiff. For National Express information, call 01222/344751. For TrawsCambria, call 01222/398700. For local buses in Cardiff, call 01222/396521. By **car,** Cardiff is a straight shot west on the M4 from **London** through Reading and Swindon going over the Severn Road Bridge and bypassing Chepstow and Newport and then heading west to Cardiff. From **Manchester** and the north, take the M6 south to Birmingham, then the M5 south to Junction 15 (just before Bristol), and then the M4 over the Severn Road Bridge, past Newport and Chepstow into Cardiff.

What's Next

The twisty river Wye works its way 135 miles up Wales from the Bristol Channel. With secluded wooded walks in the Forest of Dean, a major long-distance footpath nearby, canoeing, hiking, and abseiling, there's not a lack of things to do at the hostel in **Welsh Bicknor,** a restored priory. A few miles down the road, you can feast at a medieval banquet in the castle-turned-Youth-Hostel at **St. Briavel's.** Formerly King John's hunting lodge, it's worth the trip out to the forest just to stay overnight in an old Norman castle. Otherwise, head north. The TrawsCambria bus will take you on a gut-wrenching ride along the coast to Aberystwyth and into Snowdonia, where a handful of mountain lodges nestle against the tree-clad slopes of Gwynedd's National Park. Before making it out to the mountains, you may want to stop halfway at the village of **Borth.** The Youth Hostel here is 30 meters from the sandy beach and boasts excellent views in all directions; there's also a wildlife preserve just a walk away.

ROSS-ON-WYE (WELSH BICKNOR)

Why Wye? Well, why not? Near Gloucester (19 miles east) and Monmouth (eight miles south), the tiny parish of Welsh Bicknor in the Welsh Borderlands is a veritable needle in the haystack of hostels in South Wales. Set right on the banks of the River Wye, the hostel is in the middle of an official Area of Outstanding Natural Beauty. This means it's not easy to get to, but for walkers, cyclists, and water babies, it's worth the trip.

Long ago, these feisty borderlands were a British hot potato. The ribbon of castles and fortresses that lines the north-south boundary between the two countries is a reminder of these turbulent days. Since time immemorial, the river has been an important waterway for the local mining industry, making this a bustling commercial area.

Nowadays, though, this green zone is almost entirely dedicated to pleasure cruising, mountain biking, forest walking, and the like. Tourist traffic is kept to a minimum, probably because the tremendous Royal Forest of Dean seems to swallow up visitors. With 27,000 acres of broadleafs and conifers, it provides a leafy canopy for its resident deer herds, and a prismatic profusion of flowers smother the forest floor in summer and autumn. Visitors flock here for the nature trails, heritage center, and the re-created cottages, and you can lose yourself in loads of secluded spots. With caving, mountain biking, and boat rentals nearby, this area is definitely for the outdoorsy hosteler; others would likely find it stifling. It's quiet in these parts. The closest big town, Ross-on-Wye (5^1/$_2$ miles away), has your basic necessities, although most people come to catch the view of nearby St. Mary's Church spire from the town's clifftop promontory.

Welsh Bicknor Youth Hostel

Welsh Bicknor Rectory
Near Goodrich
Ross-on-Wye, Herefordshire HR9 6JJ
Tel: 01594/860300. Fax: 01594/860300.

A Victorian rectory built around 1858, this hostel in the woods is still part of the parish of Welsh Bicknor, even though it left the fold 58 years ago. Formerly the rector's cottage, it sits tucked away on a 25-acre woodland with more than a quarter mile of private riverbank.

A peaceful atmosphere settles over the hostel and area—that is, when the school groups aren't filing in and out. Because of its prime location near the forest and river-related activities, this hostel gets a fair share of groups in addition to walkers, cyclists, and solo backpackers adventurous enough to make it out here.

The hostel is fairly well cared for. Out back is the Laundry Cottage: a self-contained annex down a path (300 meters away) with 14 beds, a common room, and washing facilities. The main building isn't as secluded, but it's cute enough, with a comfy common room and a sweet little dining room with leaves painted on the wall. The TV room, boasting views over the Wye Valley, generally elicits sighs of contentment, and the quiet room next door has a good nature library (including a teetering stack of *National Geographics*).

The grounds of the hostel, however, are what make Welsh Bicknor such a special place. Just outside the front door, furry and feathered friends abound. Rabbits, deer, and pheasants (which the wardens feed out of the back door of the hostel) wander around, and all sorts of birds can be spotted peeping out from the trees. It's a most pleasant spot to spend a few days.

Services

🚄 The closest train stations are Gloucester and Hereford (in England). From either one, take Stagecoach Red and White bus no. 34 to Ross-on-Wye. Change for Ross-Monmouth and alight at Goodrich. From the town center of Goodrich, follow the signs to the Youth Hostel, about 1^1/$_2$ miles uphill. Otherwise, from the no. 34, you can take the Ross-Coleford bus and alight at Lower Lydbrook. From there, take the footpath next to SCA Packaging and cross the river on the footbridge. Turn right on the footpath to get to the hostel; it's the only building in sight.

🚌 The closest major coach stations are also in Gloucester and Hereford; follow directions from the train station, given above.

🚗 Take the M50 to Ross-on-Wye; then pick up the A40 to Monmouth but exit at Goodrich Village. Then follow the signs to the hostel, about 1¹/₂ miles away. From **London,** take the M4 to Chepstow, then follow the A466 to Monmouth and then the A40 in the direction of Ross-on-Wye. Get off at Goodrich and follow signs over the hill to the hostel.

▦ Open Feb 15–Nov 30. Mar, Oct, Nov: weekends only. Hostel opening dates vary; call ahead to check. BABA.

🕐 Reception open 8–10am and 5–11pm. Curfew 11pm.

🛏 80 beds. 2-, 4-, 6-, 8-, and 10-bed rooms; family rooms available with daytime access (not en suite). 14-bed annex.

£ Members: adults £8; under 18 £5.35.

🍴 Standard self-catering kitchen facilities. Breakfast: 8am. Lunch: packed lunch; should be ordered by 10:30pm the night before. Dinner: 7pm. Homemade food, including vegetarian meals.

🍸 No table license.

🧳 No lockers.

⬚ Washers £1; dryers take 50p coins; drying room.

P Available.

🛍 Shop at hostel sells candy; canned goods; souvenirs.

🛋 TV lounge; quiet room.

🚬 In first-floor TV lounge.

♿ Not wheelchair accessible.

 See "Currency Exchange" under "The Basics" in Ross-on-Wye.

Cheap Eats Nearby

Courtfield Arms

Take a pleasant evening stroll to the only eatery within walking distance of the hostel. It serves traditional English pub fare, so brace your stomach muscles, digestive system, and artery walls. Main dishes are £4 to £5. Sandwiches cost £2 to £3.

Lower Lydbrook, Gloucestershire. Tel: 01594/860207. Cash only. From the hostel, walk down the road 1¹/₄ miles into Lower Lydbrook.

Wye Fry

Your typical lip-smacking, cholesterol-inducing fish-and-chips joint. Fish and chips are £3 to £4. The two-mile walk from the hostel will do you good.

Central Lydbrook. Tel: 01594/522502. Cash only. From the hostel, take the footpath 2 miles (by road it's 5 miles) into Central Lydbrook.

Experiences

The area right around Welsh Bicknor is nirvana for nature lovers and nautical types. The winding Wye is a dream for canoeing and kayaking. You can rent them at the nearby **Monmouth Canoe and Activity Centre,** paddle your way up to the hostel, and then return them when you're ready to leave. Instruction and river guides are available, and caving, abseiling, rock climbing, and mountain biking can all be organized from the center, eight miles from the hostel.

About $3^1/_2$ miles from the hostel, the **Royal Forest of Dean** spreads out over 27,000 acres. Originally a hunting ground for Norman kings, it later became an industrial center for timber, iron, coal, and stone. Thankfully someone with a kind heart (and a green thumb) decided to restore it to its original state. Discarded railway lines have been neatened up for biking and walking on flat trails. The forest also has a relatively interesting heritage center where a few restored buildings re-create the experience of the forest miner; charcoal burns are held in the summer and autumn. A profusion of forest trails spill out from here. (The hostel warden can tell you about them.)

Nearby, Symonds Yat is a locally famous old village with a rocky gorge on the edge of the Forest (also about $3^1/_2$ miles away from the hostel). You can go climbing, abseiling, caving, and canoeing at Symonds Yat right on the river.

The old iron mines at **Clearwell Caves** are open to visitors, and a museum recounts the lengthy history of iron and lead mining in the area. They're basically for show, but deep-level visits involving climbing and caving can be organized for groups.

Finally, no tour of the Welsh Borders would be complete without a castle tour. **Goodrich Castle** is a nice walk from the hostel, about five miles south of Ross-on-Wye. Towering over the countryside, it overlooks an ancient crossing of the Wye, with huge cylindrical towers, arches, a chapel, and a mazelike succession of small rooms and passageways. All are accessible on foot.

Monmouth Canoe and Activity Centre. Old Dixon Road. Monmouth. Tel: 01600/713461. Canadian canoes: full day £15; half day £13. Single kayaks: full day £8.50; half day £6.50. River instruction, abseiling, caving by arrangement.

Forest of Dean and Dean Heritage Centre. Soudley, Forest of Dean, Gloucestershire. Tel: 01594/822170. The Forest is open at all times. Heritage Centre open: Feb–Mar: daily 10am–5pm. Apr–Oct: daily 10am–6pm. Nov–Jan: Sat–Sun 10am–4pm. Last entry 45 minutes before closing time. Admission: adults £2.75; seniors £2.50; children £1.60. Most areas are wheelchair accessible.

Forest Adventure. Symonds Yat. Abseiling and canoeing and stuff. Tel: 01594/834661.

Clearwell Caves. Near Coleford, Royal Forest of Dean. Tel: 01594/832535. Open: Mar–Oct: daily 10am–5pm. Nov–Dec: Mon–Fri 2–6pm; Sat–Sun 10am–5pm.

Goodrich Castle. Near Ross–on–Wye. Tel: 01600/890538. Open: Apr–Sept: daily 10am–6pm. Oct–Mar: Tues–Sun 10am–4pm. Admission: adults £1.70; concessions £1.30; children 85p.

The Basics

Tourist Office: The nearest T.I.C. is in Ross-on-Wye, $5^1/_2$ miles away. Ross-on-Wye T.I.C. Edde Cross Street, Ross-on-Wye. Tel: 01989/562786. Open: Mon–Fri 9am–5:30pm; Sat 10am–4pm.

Post Office: The nearest is in Goodrich, $1^1/_2$ miles away. Jolly's of Goodrich. Goodrich. Tel: 01600/890135. Open: Mon–Fri 9am–5:30pm; Sat 9am–12:30pm.

Currency Exchange: Ross-on-Wye T.I.C. Edde Cross Street, Ross-on-Wye. Tel: 01989/562786. Open: Mon–Fri 9am–5:30pm; Sat 10am–4pm. Also in the Ross-on-Wye post office (see "Post Office" under "The Basics" in Ross-on-Wye).

Bike Rental: Pedalaway. Forest of Dean. They'll deliver to hostel. Tel: 01989/770357.

Telephone Code: 01594.

Getting There: It's not terrifically easy to get here; just be prepared for a 1¹/₂-mile walk if you're coming by public transport. The best bet for **train**-riders is to get to **Gloucester** (on the Bristol-Cardiff line), which is 19 miles from the hostel. From there, local buses (no. 61) will take you to Goodrich Village; walk from there. The same is true for long-distance **coaches: Gloucester** is a major thoroughfare, and local buses (no. 35) take you to within a mile of the hostel. By **car:** from **Cardiff,** take the M4 east, and at Chepstow switch for the A466 north. When you reach Monmouth, change for the A40 north, and follow signs for Welsh Bicknor and Ross-on-Wye. The hostel is 8 miles from Monmouth. From **London,** take the A40 to the M40. Pass Beaconsfield and High Wycombe; at Junction 8 (just before Oxford), exit onto the A40, and continue through Cheltenham and Gloucester, following signs to Ross-on-Wye. The hostel is 5¹/₂ miles south.

What's Next

The closest hostel, a mere eight miles south, offers the rare opportunity to stay overnight in an honest-to-goodness castle. **St. Briavel's Castle,** at the bottom of the Forest of Dean, will satisfy all your long-held fantasies about castles with stony walls, clanging bells, and dank hallways. The hostel keeps the mood lively with medieval banquets in summer. Music, revelry, a speech from the lord of the manor entertain you as snarling wenches serve you your grog and gruel. Farther south lies the Welsh capital city of **Cardiff,** a different experience entirely. The hostel is your usual midsize city affair. A bus ride from the center, it's a pleasant spot. The city itself, borne anew from the ashy doldrums of industrial decline, has a castle, folk museums, leafy parks, and a hopping cultural scene. If you head east toward England (via Gloucester), you won't be far from the Cotswolds.

ST. BRIAVEL'S CASTLE

About 45 miles northeast of Cardiff and wedged between the Forest of Dean and the Black Mountains of Wales, the village of St. Briavel's is known for one thing: its mammoth Norman castle. It just happens to be a Youth Hostel. In the early 1100s, the Earl of Hereford decided he needed a lookout post to protect the River Wye from Welsh invaders, so he rustled up a few lowly subjects and ordered the construction of a standard motte and bailey. It was built as a typical point-and-shoot fortress, but when King John (of Magna Carta fame) succeeded to the throne in 1199, he converted it into a hunting lodge to take advantage of the nearby forest.

From these origins, the small village of St. Briavel's grew; it has remained a quiet, uneventful little place, preferring to let the castle dominate the region. Thankfully, you don't have to hold a title to get in anymore—a Hostelling International card and a few pounds are enough to gain entrance. Inside, it's medieval to the max: The stone walls, gatehouse prison, and moat are all more or less intact, making it a fascinating piece of living history.

❋ St. Briavel's Castle Youth Hostel

The Castle, St. Briavel's
Lydney, Gloucestershire GL15 6RG
Tel: 01594/530272. Fax: 01594/530849.

At one time or another, Henry I, Henry II, Richard I, John, and Edward I all crossed the moat to spend at least a few nights apiece in this castle. The first thing you sense is that this is the authentic article. From the stone walkway to the elaborate, massive gates to the latches on the doors, there's no mistaking that this is a true historic treasure.

Aside from the carefully renovated rooms (and the installation of omnipresent hostel bunk beds), the castle remains largely unchanged. The centuries-old floors can sustain only soft shoes, and the stone walls send shivering hostelers to the log fires in King John's Room downstairs. You can stay in the old chapel, a hanging room, and a prison. A trap door in one bedroom leads you to a dank, musty dungeon. Another bedroom boasts medieval graffiti: frustrated prisoners took their gripes out on the castle walls, and their etchings are still visible if you know where to look. Yet another dormitory has a piscina left over from the days when it was used as a chapel.

Not surprisingly in a building with so much history, ghosts have been spotted: a crying baby, an old woman dressed in white, and a knight in shining armor who clanks down the halls. The old refectory remains intact, and on Saturday nights in summer a medieval banquet is thrown in lieu of the usual £4 set evening meal. Scrawny wenches (in costume) serve mead and mush to guests, and entertainment (courtesy of the warden) is also provided.

With background heating, the stone building gets chilly, so they throw a few logs into the fire the way they did in the Dark Ages. Nobody seems to mind—the crowd is a generally harmonious mix of backpackers and schoolchildren out for a memorable experience in the old castle.

Services

🚆 The nearest train station is Lydney (7 miles away) on the Gloucester-Chepstow line, but Chepstow is actually more convenient since bus no. 69 from Monmouth-Chepstow lets you off about 2 miles from the hostel. From there, follow the signs to St. Briavel's.

🚌 The closest bus station is Chepstow. Take Stagecoach Red & White no. 69 from Chepstow and alight at Bigsweir Bridge. From there it is a 2-mile walk to the hostel.

🚗 From the M4 at Chepstow, take the A466 north, past Tintern Abbey. After about 5 miles, turn right, following the signs to St. Briavel's village. From there, follow the signs to the hostel and look for the castle.

▦ Open Mar–Oct; closed some nights. In winter, the hostel is open to groups for overnight accommodations and medieval banquets; and it's open to individuals on selected days in Nov and Feb only. Call ahead to check. BABA.

🕗 Reception open 8–10am and 5–10pm. Curfew: 11pm.

🛏 70 beds. 5-, 6-, 8-, 9-, 10-, and 12-bed rooms.

£ Members: adults £8; under 18 £5.35.

🍴 Spartan self-catering kitchen facilities. Breakfast: 8:30am. Lunch: packed lunch; order by 9am. Dinner: 7pm; always a plate of the day. Medieval banquets during August weekends and for special groups.

Y Table license.

🧳 No lockers.

□ Drying room only.

P In front of hostel; ample and free of charge.

🛍 Shop at hostel open: 9–10am, 5–6pm, 8–8:30pm. Sells food, drinks, and souvenirs.

🛋 Three lounge areas, two with open fires.

🚬 In one lounge.

♿ Not wheelchair accessible.

💱 See "Currency Exchange" under "The Basics" in St. Briavel's.

Cheap Eats Nearby

The Crown

Cozy banquettes and a couple of fruit machines occupy this standard bar. A pool table will entertain you while you wait for the grub. Chili, steak-and-kidney pie, and cottage pie cost £4 to £5. Vegetarian lasagne is £5.10.

Pystol Lane, St. Briavel's. Tel: 01594/530205. Open: Mon–Fri 11am–2pm and 6–11pm; Sat 11am–2:30pm and 6–11pm; Sun 11am–2:30pm and 6–10:30pm. From the hostel, turn right and then left onto Pystol Lane. It's on the left; a 5-minute walk.

The George

A crackling log fire welcomes you, and you can study the coats of arms on the wall as they prepare your moussaka, hock of ham, or mushroom stroganoff. Main meals run £5.50 to £7. The garden out front with tables is nice for sunny days.

St. Briavel's. Tel: 01594/530228. Open: Mon–Sat noon–2:30pm and 6:30–11pm; Sun noon–2:30pm and 7–10:30pm. Cash only. From the hostel gate, turn right, and follow the street around to the right. It's straight ahead; a 5-minute walk.

Grocery Store: The nearest supermarket is Gateway in Chepstow; but the Youth Hostel sells food and grocery items for use in the self-catering kitchen.

Experiences

St. Briavel's Castle is an experience in and of itself. The warden offers tours, and there's a lot to see. The building is a medieval masterpiece but has many layers of history that predate the Middle Ages. It has been used as a fortress, a hunting lodge, a forest headquarters, an arms factory, a law court, a prison, a school, and a private home during the last 800 years.

The castle lies in the 27,000-acre **Royal Forest of Dean.** There are lots of walking paths and cycle routes, most notably Offa's Dyke Path, a long-distance route that runs from Chepstow in the south to Prestatyn on the northern coast. Water sports are available in the forest, which is also home to the **Dean Heritage Centre** (about five miles from the hostel), with exhibitions on local mining history.

Four miles away lie **Clearwell Caves,** where you can take a tour of the massive iron mines that have been hacked away by fortune hunters and penny laborers for centuries. The ruins of **Tintern Abbey,** built by the Cistercians in 1131, lie only about four miles away against the wooded slopes of the Wye Valley. This idyllic setting even inspired a few lines from Lakeland litterateur William Wordsworth.

St. Briavel's Castle. For tours, contact the hostel warden. 50p per person.

Forest of Dean and Dean Heritage Centre. Soudley, Forest of Dean, Gloucestershire. Tel: 01594/822170. The Forest is open at all times. Heritage Centre open: Feb–Mar: daily 10am–5pm. Apr–Oct: daily 10am–6pm. Nov–Jan: Sat–Sun 10am–4pm. Last entry 45 minutes before closing time. Admission: adults £2.75; seniors £2.50; children £1.60. Most areas are wheelchair accessible.

Clearwell Caves. Near Coleford, Royal Forest of Dean. Tel: 01594/832535. Open: Mar–Oct: daily 10am–5pm. Nov–Dec: Mon–Fri 2–6pm; Sat–Sun 10am–5pm.

Tintern Abbey. Tintern. Tel: 01291/689251. Admission: adults £3.

The Basics

Tourist Office: The nearest T.I.C. is in Coleford, 6 miles away. Coleford T.I.C. 27 Market Place, Royal Forest of Dean. Tel: 01594/836307. Open: Mon–Fri 10am–5:30pm; Sat 10am–4pm. The St. Briavel's Post Office also has some tourist information (see "Post Office" below).

Post Office: St. Briavel's Post Office, St. Briavels. Open: Mon–Fri 9am–5pm; Sat 9am–12:30pm. From the hostel, turn right and follow the road around the castle. It's on the road up to the left; a 5-minute walk.

Currency Exchange: The nearest banks are in Chepstow, 6 miles away and accessible via local buses.

Telephone Code: 01594.

Bike Rental: Pedalaway. Forest of Dean. They'll deliver to hostel. Tel: 01989/770357.

Getting There: St. Briavels is about 45 miles from **Cardiff.** By **train** from there, it's a short ride east on the Cardiff-Gloucester line; get off at **Chepstow.** From Chepstow, you can get local buses out to the hostel. For train times and fares, call 01452/425543. **Chepstow** is also the main stop for **buses** from either **Gloucester** or **Cardiff;** for information, call 01222/344751. By **car:** from **Cardiff,** take the M4 east to Chepstow, and switch at Junction 22 for the A466. Go about 2 miles north, and turn off to the A48. Once on the A48, look for signs to the B4228, following signs for St. Briavel's and Colefore. From Chepstow, it's about 6 miles to the hostel.

What's Next

A brief eight-mile walk through the forest takes you to an old rectory on the banks of the River Wye. The Welsh Bicknor Youth Hostel is in a secluded, woodsy setting near **Ross-on-Wye.** If you don't want to walk, canoes are available for rent in Monmouth, and you can paddle your way up. About 45 miles to the south-west lies **Cardiff,** a much-underrated city with a castle; leafy, luscious parks; a thriving arts scene; and gentle architecture. For those on public transport wishing to get up to Snowdonian from here, you're probably best off heading to Cardiff first.

NANT GWYNANT (BRYN GWYNANT)

Located in the heart of Snowdonia National Park, Nant Gwynant (167 miles north of Cardiff and 25 miles south of Bangor) seems little more than a tiny marking on Ordnance Survey map no. 115, grid reference 641513. The Bryn Gwynant Youth

Hostel trembles beneath the summit of Snowdon on the shores of Llyn Gwynant, a shimmering sheet of ice-blue mountain water. Tucked in the middle of a triangle created by the villages of Beddgelert, Betws-y-Coed, and Caernarfon, Nant Gwynant offers unsullied vistas of snow-capped peaks, endless evergreens, cascading waterfalls and the glassy lake.

By night, puffs of smoke emanating from stone chimneys and a few silent sheep are the only signs of life. By day, however, the mountain is alive with walkers, cyclists, and adventurers of all shapes and sizes eager to become one with this rugged wonderland. Bus Gwynedd rumbles through here only a few times per day on the weekdays, and on the weekends public transport is close to nonexistent, so bring extra socks and provisions and factor in a few days of lag time.

The National Park, covering 840 square miles in North Wales, is worth at least a few days. Aside from the natural landscape, there's an amazing abundance of things to do here. Steam and narrow-gauge railways, ancient Welsh villages, lake steamers, and some excellent mountain hostels offer much more than you might expect in this lonely corner of Britain. Bryn Gwynant is an excellent place to start; from here, you can work your way north to the other towns that dot this picture-perfect landscape.

Bryn Gwynant Youth Hostel

Nant Gwynant
Caernarfon, Gwynedd
North Wales LL55 4NP
Tel: 01766/890251. Fax: 01766/890479.

A Victorian mansion made of stone, the Bryn Gwynant hostel sits right on the A498 above the placid waters of Llyn Gwynant. Recently renovated, it resembles an elegant mountain inn.

Big, cushioned bay windows in the downstairs dining room overlook the lake. Almost all the bedrooms have amazing views, and groups of four are sometimes able to luck into staying in the Penthouse, a self-contained little house behind the main building with its own bathroom. Pine beds, hot showers, and comfy quilts set you up for a good night's sleep after the home-cooked meals, which include vegetarian curry, shepherd's pie, and other hearty fare. There's no TV here, so there's usually a festive mood in the lounge and around the pool table in the entrance hall. The lively BYOB (bring your own bottle) atmosphere wears on late into the night, since the closest pub is three miles down the road. There are also Diablo and juggling balls, which the warden Nick can show you how to use in his (rare) spare moment.

The sun sets late even in spring, so after dinner there's still enough time for a walk around the lake across the street—just beware of the marshy land near the water, and make sure you don't get stuck on the rocks when night falls. For late-evening walks, the road offers views that are just as picturesque.

The guests at the hostel, who are all here for walking, cycling, and scrambling up the mountains, are a mixed bag of adventurers. Groups studying the local landscape, couples on a weekend away, and solo hikers mix and mingle, making it a great place to share advice and stories and make arrangements to car pool to nearby mountains. The hostel is well stocked with information on the area: maps, guide-books, and general mountain advice are abundant, so you shouldn't need to trek to the closest tourist office (eight miles away in Llanberis) unless you want information about another area.

Services

🚆 The closest train stations are in Betwys-y-Coed and Porthmadog, 20 miles away; from there, Bus Gwynedd buses can link you to the hostel. From Porthmadog, take bus no. 97, and at Beddgelert switch to bus no. 95 to Nant Gwynant; the bus drops you off right at the hostel, which is right on A498.

From Betwys-y-Coed, get bus no. 19 to Penygrwyd and change to bus no. 95 to Nant Gwynant; the bus drops you off right at the hostel, which is right on the A498. Schedules and bus routes may vary, so it's a good idea to phone Bus Gwynedd (tel. 01286/679535) in advance to verify departure times.

🚌 The main bus service from Cardiff (bus no. 701 goes along the coast, while no. 702 shoots straight through mid Wales) takes you into Caernarfon. From there, catch Gwynedd bus no. 95 to the town of Nant Gwynant, and the bus drops you off right at the hostel. Schedules and routes may vary, so it's a good idea to phone Bus Gwynedd (tel. 01286/679535) in advance to verify departure times.

🚗 Take the A5 to the A4086 at Capel Curig. The hostel is right on the A498, 8 miles from the village of Capel Curig.

🗓 Open Mar–Oct. Closed Sun in Mar. Nov–Feb: the hostel is open for two months, which vary from year to year. Rent-a-hostel: from Nov–Mar; only in the coach house.

🕐 Reception open 7:15–10am and 5–11pm. Check in by 10:30pm. Curfew 11pm.

🛏 67 beds. 2-, 4-, 6-, 8-, and 10-bed rooms. Family rooms (some en suite) for three-, four-, and six-person groups available in the self-contained converted coach house out back, which has a kitchen/classroom and its own shower/bath.

£ Members: adults £8; under 18 £5.35.

🍴 Self-catering kitchen facilities. Breakfast: 8:15am. Lunch: packed lunch only; order by 10pm the night before. Dinner: 7pm.

✗ No table license.

💼 Luggage storage in some rooms in coach house.

◻ The staff will do laundry for a fee; drying room.

P Available.

🗋 Shop at hostel sells candy and canned goods.

🛋 One sitting room, no TV.

🎱 In reception area, around pool table.

♿ Wheelchair accessible.

💱 See "Currency Exchange" under "The Basics" in Nant Gwynant.

🔺 Bike shed; wet weather shelter.

Cheap Eats Nearby

Beddgelert Antiques & Tea Room (aka Beddgelert Bistro)

This place is an antique shop by day and country bistro by night. Upstairs, this little dollhouse is loaded with old armoires and heavy china, and downstairs it's an intimate dining room with stone walls and timber beams. At lunchtime, dishes include vegetable lasagne (£5.25), pine-nut risotto (£5.50), prawn salad (£4.95), and other delicacies. Dinner is pricier: leek-and-broccoli bake (£8.50), swordfish steak

(£9), among other dishes, but starters aren't too expensive. Garlic mushrooms, pâtés, and cheese are £3 to £4.

Waterloo House, Beddgelert. Tel: 01766/890543. Open: daily 9am–5:30pm and 7–9pm. Reservations accepted. Credit cards: VA, MC, EC, Access (evenings only). From the hostel, walk 3¹/₂ miles into the village of Beddgelert. It's on the right, by the bridge. It's at least a 1¹/₂-hour walk.

Lyn's Café

This small, friendly stone house is filled with books for your perusal and has a little fireplace with dried flowers. Breakfasts run £1.50 to £2.95. Homemade pasties and quiches are £3.25 to £4.50. Broccoli bake, lasagne, and trout with lemon are £5 to £6.50; milkshakes 90p.

Church Street, Beddgelert (3 ¹/₂ miles away). Tel: 01766/890374. Open: Easter–Oct: daily 8am–10pm. Nov: daily 11am–5pm. Dec–Jan: Sat–Sun 11am–5pm; Feb–Easter: daily 11am–5pm. Reservations accepted. Credit Cards: VA, MC, EC, AE. From the hostel, walk 3 ¹/₂ miles down the A498 into the village of Beddgelert. Cross the bridge and it's up Church Street on the left. It takes at least 1¹/₂ hours to walk.

Grocery Store: Nant Gwynant Stores. In Nant Gwynant, on the A498, next to the post office. Open: Easter–Oct: daily 8am–8pm. Nov–Easter: daily 9am–5:30pm.

Experiences

From the hostel, there are abundant woodland walks, dotted with meandering sheep. Probably the most popular walk is the Watkin Path, which takes you up **Mount Snowdon** (3,560 feet). There are a number of paths to take up the peak. From the gentle walk alongside the **Snowdon Mountain Railway** to the scramble along the knife edge of Crib Groch, it can be as easy or as challenging as you want. Nonmountaineers can take the railway up from Llanberis, but that involves going around the mountain via the road and then getting the rail.

Just outside the doorstep of the hostel, there are **paddleboats** available for rent on Llyn Gwynant. Cyclists should be prepared for rough terrain: There really are no formally established bike paths around here. Nearby, the Porthmadog-Caernarfon route is a decent one. It's part of the National Cycle Network's plan to convert disused railways into bike paths. There's a labyrinth of off-road bike routes branching out in all directions. Many of the staff at the hostel are cyclists and quite knowledgeable about the area; they can point you in the right direction. About five miles down the road is a **pony trekking** center in Beddgelert; one of the nicest ways to see the area is on the back of one of these gentle beasts, and the center offers guided tours as well.

For a not-so-strenuous way to enjoy the countryside, you can walk the relatively easy 3¹/₂ miles to the sugary sweet town of **Beddgelert,** a good spot for afternoon tea or an evening meal and a bit of local lore. One day, the medieval Prince Llywelyn found his baby daughter dead and his pup Gelert covered in blood. Assuming the dog was the murderer, Llywelyn killed Gelert, only to discover that his supposedly murderous mutt had been defending the kid against a vicious wolf. Wracked with guilt, Llewelyn dug a grave for the heroic pooch and named the town for him: Bedd (grave) gelert (Gelert). His grave is still here, by the river behind St. Mary's church in town.

On the way back to the hostel, you can stop off at an old **Sygun Copper Mine** that has been converted into a mini-tourist trap. It's nonetheless a worthwhile glimpse into local history. Other than that, ask at the hostel: Snowdonia has more than 90 peaks that top 1,900 feet, so you won't lack for things to do.

Snowdonia National Park Information Centre. Betwys-y-Coed. Tel: 01766/770274.

Snowdon Mountain Railway. Llanberis. Tel: 01286/870223. Open: Mid Mar–mid Apr: daily 9:30am–3:30pm. Mid-Apr to mid-Sept: Sun–Fri 9am–5pm; Sat 9am–3:30pm. Mid-Sept to Oct: daily 9:30am–3:30pm. $2^{1}/_{2}$-hour round trip.

Cycle routes. Ask at the hostel.

Paddleboats. Ask at the hostel; they can arrange rental.

Hafod y Lyn Stables. Near Nantmoor, about 6 miles from the hostel. Tel: 01766/890280.

Sygun Copper Mines. Beddgelert, Gwynedd. Tel: 01766/890595 or 890564. Open: Easter–Sept: Mon–Fri 10am–5pm; Sat 10am–4pm; Sun 11am–5pm. Oct–Nov: Mon–Sat 10:30am–4pm. Dec–Jan 11am–3:30pm. Feb–Mar: Mon–Sat 10:30am–4pm.

The Basics

Tourist Office: in Llanberis (about 8 miles away). Museum of the North. Tel: 01286/870765. Open: Easter–Sept: daily 10am–5:45pm. From the hostel, take the A498 to Pen-y-Passand then the B3279 into Llanberis.

Post Office: Inside Nant Gwynant Store (about 1 mile away). Tel: 01766/890227. The post office hours are limited: Mon–Thurs 10:30–11:30am. From the hostel, turn left and walk down the A498 in the direction of Beddgelert; it's on the left.

Currency Exchange: At the Post Office (see "Post Office" under "The Basics" in Nant Gwynant) or banks in Caernarfon.

Bike Rental: In Beddgelert. Beics Beddgelert Bikes. Haford Ruffydd Uchaf, Bedgelert Forest, Gwynedd. Tel: 01766/686434. £3 per hour; £14 per full day (8 hours).

Telephone Code: 01766.

Getting There: The only way to head up to Snowdonia from south Wales (and the prettiest, too) is via the TrawsCambria **bus** no. 701 goes west along the coast, stops at Aberystwth, then skirts Snowdonia before arriving in Caernarfon. If you are a student, you can command a nice discount, so tell the bus driver before paying. This is about a seven-hour bus ride, scenic and stomach-churning at the same time. Once in Caernarfon, change for the Gwynedd bus no. 95 and tell the driver you're headed for the Youth Hostel on Nant Gwynant, which is right on the main road, A498. For TrawsCambria information, call 01970/617951 or 01248/370295. For local bus info, call 01286/679535.

Those coming from **London, York, Chester,** and other points east can take a relatively easy **train** ride. Take the train to Betws-y-Coed (change at Conwy), which is only 12 miles from the hostel. You'll be able to connect to local buses from there, but call ahead for information. Those coming from **Cardiff** can take the train to Shrewsbury and then switch for the Heart of Wales line, getting off at Porthmadog,

12 miles from the hostel. Buses run from there as well. For train information, call 01492/585151. By **car,** take the A55 west from **Chester** to Bangor. From there, switch to the A5 south to Capel Curig. From Capel Curig, it is 8 miles west on the A4086; after about 5 miles, bear left onto the A498 to Nant Gwynant. From **Cardiff,** take the A470 north all the way into Snowdonia. At Betws-y-Coed, change to the A5 west, and at Capel Curig, turn onto the A4086; after about 5 miles, bear left onto the A498, which takes you to Nant Gwynant.

What's Next

Only seven miles from Nant Gwynant by mountain footpath is Snowdon Ranger, a quiet little hostel in **Rhyd Ddu** across from the peaceful Llyn Cwellyn and at the base of mighty Mount Snowdon. It's easily accessible from the Snowdon Mountain Railway and other local sights. The hostel at **Pen-y-Pass,** four miles northeast, is an idiosyncratic old mountain climbers' hotel and an excellent center for serious modern climbers. Located across from the mountain warden, the hostel rents climbing equipment and offers weekend courses in a small selection of mountain-related activities.

RHYD DDU (SNOWDON RANGER)

Rhyd Ddu isn't much of a village. In fact, with one grocery store and a telephone booth, it's even less of a village than Nant Gwynant (which has a post office and grocery store), where the Bryn Gwynant Youth Hostel is located. If you're looking for disco dancing and shopping malls, you probably shouldn't be amid 840 square miles of national park anyway. Unspoiled nature at its greenest is what attracts cyclists, walkers, and scramblers from all over Britain and the Continent here.

Rocky peaks, gurgling waterfalls, plunging cliffs, and glacial mountain lakes are the entertainment here. The Snowdon Ranger hostel sits right in the center of the action at the base of Mount Snowdon. At 3,560 feet, the mountain is the highest peak in Britain south of the Scottish Highlands and is often shrouded in mist, even on sunny days. As you meander through the footpaths leading up to it, you're likely to come across light railway lines, old copper mines, and maybe even a few baby lambs at play.

Outdoors enthusiasts have long hiked the mountains here, but the really wonderful thing about Snowdonia is that it isn't limited to experts. There are trails for walkers of all levels, a comprehensive bus service, a relatively well-trafficked road, and even a local steam railway that climbs Snowdon for you, so amateurs and pros alike can enjoy this natural wonder.

Snowdon Ranger Youth Hostel

Rhyd Ddu
Caernarfon, Gwynedd LL54 7YS
Tel: 01286/650391. Fax: 01286/650093

The Snowdon Ranger Youth Hostel, on the road between Beddgelert and Caernarfon, is an old mountain inn that became a hostel in 1967. It's a legend among seriously dedicated Snowdon walkers who value the peace and solitude of this lakeside lodge.

Unlike its rambunctious neighbor nine miles down the road at Nant Gwynant, this hostel is comparatively low key. The wardens, veteran mountain climbers themselves, have been running the show for more than 25 years and know the mountain well. They can point you toward footpaths of all levels. Kath is the resident chef, and more than a few hostelers choose this place because of her homey touch in the kitchen. Most of the meals are home cooked, and the menus vary depending on the season. Cawl cennin, a traditional Welsh soup, is a local specialty, but roast beef and Yorkshire pudding and dishes from other regions are served as well and often finished off with homemade rhubarb pie or black currant crumble.

The bedrooms on the top floor (usually reserved for women) have skylights with views of the Llyn Cwellyn across the way and provide comfy beds for a quiet night's sleep. When the temperature dips, the staff lights fires in the first-floor sitting room, the perfect place to write postcards or read a book. There's no TV here, but the guests, many of whom arrive after a long day's walk, don't seem to care. An evening walk by the lake to see the spectacular sunset or a jaunt down one of the footpaths seem to be the preferred evening activities.

Services

🚆 The closest train station is Porthmadog, 13 miles away. From there, take bus no. 97 to Caernarfon, then pick up Gwynedd bus no. 95. It passes right in front of the hostel, which is across Llyn (Lake) Cwellyn right on the A4085 highway road between Beddgelert and Caernarfon. Bus schedules tend to vary, so call ahead to verify departure times. From the Bangor train station, take bus no. 5A to Caernarfon. Then take bus no. 95 to the hostel.

🚌 Buses from Cardiff drop you off in Caernarfon; from there, take bus no. 95. Follow directions from the train, given above.

🚐 From Bangor, take the A487 into Caernarfon, then switch to the A4085, going in the direction of Bedgellert. The hostel is about 8 miles down the road on your left. Look for Llyn Cwellyn.

▦ Open Apr–Sept and on selected days in the off-season. Call in advance to check. BABA. Rent-a-hostel: during the winter months.

🕐 Reception open 8–10am and 5–11pm. Curfew 11pm.

🛏 67 beds. 2-, 3-, 4-, 5-, 6-, 7-, 8-, and 9-bed rooms. No family rooms per se, but they're willing to accommodate families with private rooms.

£ Members: adults £8; under 18 £5.35.

🍴 Standard self-catering kitchen facilities. Breakfast: 8:15am. Lunch: packed lunch only; order by 9pm the night before. Dinner: 7pm.

🍸 No table license.

🧳 No lockers; luggage can be stored in the drying room at your own risk.

▢ Drying room only.

P Available.

🛍 Shop at hostel sells guidebooks and maps of the area; candy, canned goods. They also sell from the kitchen for self-caterers.

🛋 Common area downstairs with fireplace and big maps of the area and a historical display; upstairs games room with Ping-Pong, pool, and video games.

☎ In reception area.

♿ Not wheelchair accessible.

💱 See "Currency Exchange" under "The Basics" in Rhyd Ddu.

Cheap Eats Nearby

See "Cheap Eats Nearby" under Nant Gwynant. To get to **Lyn's Café** from the hostel, walk five miles down the A4085 into the village of Beddgelert. Cross the bridge and it's up Church Street on the left. It's at least a two-hour walk. To reach **Beddgelert Antiques and Tea Room (aka Beddgelert Bistro)** from the hostel, walk five miles down the A4085 into the village of Beddgelert. It's on the right, by the bridge. The walk takes at least two hours. The nearest grocery store is in Nant Gwynant, on the A498, next to the post office.

Experiences

Situated at the foot of **Snowdon** mountain, the hostel is in an ideal spot to begin an ascent to the top. The path that begins right alongside the hostel is one of the easiest routes to the top and takes about 2 to $2^1/_2$ hours to complete. The return journey along the Rhyd Ddu road makes for a perfect, relaxing day's walk. A multitude of other paths fan out from here as well. The Pyg track is good for scramblers and those who don't mind a hair-raising edge or two; the Miner's track is better for 'fraidy cats.

To make the ascent as easy as possible, The **Snowdon Mountain Railway** runs up to the summit from nearby Llanberis. You can take a relaxing stroll through the valley behind the hostel to get to Llanberis and then hop on the railway. On the path to Llanberis, historians will be interested to see the remains of old rifle ranges from World War I. Other nearby routes include the Mountain of the Hawk (Moel Hebog) and Elephant Mountain (Mynydd Mawr), both within walking distance from the hostel.

A public footpath beginning at Llyn (lake) Cwellyn across the road from the hostel leads to nearby Drws-y-Coed, where there is a ruined copper mine and a small but beautiful lake with an island in the middle. The pebble beach on the shores of Llyn Cwellyn is great on a sunny day for picnicking and even dipping into the cold waters after a day's hike. For those hunting for castles, nearby **Caernarfon Castle** (eight miles away) has the dubious claim to fame of being the site where the gussied-up 11-year-old Prince Charles was officially invested as Wales's fearless leader in 1969.

Snowdonia National Park Information Centre. Betwys-y-Coed. Tel: 01766/770274.

Snowdon Mountain Railway. Llanberis. Tel: 01286/870223. Mid-Mar to mid-Apr: daily 9:30am–3:30pm. Mid-Apr to mid-Sept: Sun–Fri 9am–5pm; Sat 9am–3:30pm. Mid-Sept to Oct: daily 9:30am–3:30pm. $2^1/_2$-hour round trip.

Caernarfon Castle. Caernarfon. Tel: 01286/667617. Open: Apr–Oct: daily 9:30am–6:30pm. Nov–Mar: Mon–Sat 9:30am–4pm; Sun 2–4pm. Admission: adults £3.

The Basics

Tourist Office: The nearest T.I.C. is in Caernarfon, 8 miles away. Caernarfon T.I.C. Caernarfon, across from the castle. Tel: 01286/672232. Open: daily 10am–6pm. From the hostel, turn right and take the A4085 north into Caernarfon.

Post Office: The nearest Post Office is in Caernarfon, 8 miles away. Castle Square, Caernarfon. Tel: 01286/672116. Open: Mon–Fri 9:30am–5:30pm; Sat 9:30am–12:30pm. From the hostel, turn right and take the A4085 north into Caernarfon.

Currency Exchange: At the banks or post office in Caernarfon.

Telephone Code: 01286.

Bike Rental: The nearest place is in Beddgelert, 5 miles away. Beics Beddgelert Bikes. Hafod Ruffydd Uchaf, Beddgelert Forest, Gwynedd. Tel: 01766/86434.

Getting There: If you're coming from **London, York,** or **Leeds, trains** head into Bangor frequently, and from Bangor you can connect to the local buses, which take you to Caernarfon and then Snowdon Ranger. For train info call 01492/585151. For information on local bus times and routes: 01286/679537. From the south, **buses** are your best option: from **Cardiff,** TrawsCambria no. 701 winds its way up the coast (no. 702 goes inland) and then through the mountains to Caernarfon. At Caernarfon, change for Gwynedd bus no. 95, which takes you straight to the hostel. By **car,** take the A470 north from **Cardiff.** When you reach Ffestiniog, get on the A487 west; at Penrhyndeudfaeth, switch to the A4085 north the Beddgelert. The hostel is about 5 miles beyond the town.

What's Next

Those looking for a more intense mountain scene should head up to **Pen-y-Pass,** 13 miles away by road, 10 miles by footpath. At the head of the Llanberis Pass, it's a well-equipped hostel (ice axes and crampons available for rent); it was formerly a hotel frequented by some of Britain's more illustrious mountain climbers. Nine miles away in **Nant Gwynant** lies a hostel in a stone house by the shores of Llyn Gwynant. It's a lively little place, recently refurbished à la Victorian mountain chalet and has a pool table and juggling warden.

PEN-Y-PASS

At the head of Llanberis Pass, 1,168 feet above sea level, stands Pen-y-Pass. The only two human-made structures in sight are a Youth Hostel on one side of the road and a mountain rescue shack across the way. Thankfully, they don't interfere too much with the vista of the searing, craggy ridges of the Three Peaks surrounding this mountaintop retreat. That's the way the guests who descend on the Youth Hostel/mountain center all year long like it.

Most hostelers make it out here, 18 miles south of Bangor and 175 miles north of Cardiff, with one goal in mind: ascending Snowdon, the highest peak in England and Wales. There are many tracks up to the summit (3,560 feet), the most popular of which begin right outside the front door of the hostel. From easy to expert, there are paths for walkers of all levels and even a railway to help you ascend the peak.

Mountain climbing aside, there are some relatively interesting sights, including a power station, old copper mines, and a handful of steam railways that crisscross this National Park. All these activities center around the town of Llanberis five miles away, a friendly little mountaineer's mecca with a few good cafes, outdoor shops, and basic necessities.

The Pen-y-Pass hostel itself (which doubles as a mountain center) is likely your best resource on the mountain: stocked with maps, climbing gear, and advice, it boasts an extremely knowledgeable staff of devoted climbers who know the area inside and out. The manager is a member of the mountain rescue team, making this an excellent spot for anyone prepared for serious mountaineering.

Pen-y-Pass Youth Hostel

Pen-y-Pass, Nant Gwynant
Caernarfon, Gwynedd LL55 4NY
Tel: 01286/870428. Fax: 01286/872434.

The front entrance to the hostel says it all: "Ice picks for hire (£1.50)." Hiking boots hang over the mantelpiece, and the hostel contains the ice pick Geoffrey Winthrop-Young used to hack his way through Snowdonia and a Climber's Library where you can borrow books on the area. There's a long history of climbing in this former hotel: The Gorphwysfa Club, one of the oldest mountaineering clubs in Wales, held its very first meeting here. There's a casual, confident air to the place: *Real* mountaineers come here.

The two Victorian dining rooms add to the ambience with bric-a-brac, plants, and bay windows overlooking the mountains outside. The meals consist of traditional home cooking, and a proper roast is still served on Sundays. In the reception area, a wood-burning stove takes the chill out of the night air and a piano lurks in the corner. In addition, movies are available free and the hostel has a decent little video library.

Upstairs, the bedrooms are the usual dormitories, and showers get nonstop use. The hostel's annex, known as The Barn, looks like a transplanted Alpine ski lodge, with a skylight, minikitchen, and 1970s neon orange curtains in the rooms; it helps to diffuse the crowds.

The hostel accommodates a broad cross section of travelers: Australian and German backpackers during summer; families on weekends all year long; and the inevitable school groups in spring and summer. Things can tend to get hectic here, so call ahead.

Services

🚆 The closest train station is Bangor, 18 miles away, or Betws-y-Coed, which is open only seasonally. From Bangor, take Gwynedd bus no. 77 to Llanberis (a 30-minute ride), then take Gwynedd bus no. 19 to Pen-y-Pass (15 minutes). The bus drops you off right in front of the hostel. Bus schedules in this area tend to change frequently, so call ahead to check departure times. Bus Gwynedd Information Service tel: 01286/679535.

🚌 The closest major bus route is the TrawsCambria Cardiff-Bangor service (bus no. 701). It's not easy to get here. At Caernarfon, change for the Sherpa Bus (which runs once a day in winter, more frequently in summer), which cruises by a number of hostels in the area. It drops you right at the driveway of Pen-y-Pass hostel. Call the bus company ahead to check departure times (see from the train, above).

🚗 On the A4086 from Capel Curig, turn right at Pen-y-Gwyrd Hotel towards Llanberis. The hostel is on your right after one mile.

▦ Open Apr–Oct. Nov, Feb, Mar open Mon–Fri only. BABA .

🕐 Reception open 8:30–10am and 5–10:30pm; access to rooms is available from 1pm. Curfew 11pm.

🛏 100 beds. 2-, 3-, 4-, 5-, 6-, 7-, and 13-bed rooms available. Family rooms available with daytime access; one is en suite.

£ Members: adults £8.80; under 18 £5.95.

🍴 Standard self-catering kitchen facilities. Breakfast: 8:15am. Lunch: packed lunch only; order by the night before. Dinner: 7pm.

⟙ No table license. BYOB (bring your own bottle).

▐▌▌ No lockers.

◯ Drying room only.

P Across the road, at the National Park Car Park; hostelers get a permit from reception. 50p.

⬭ Shop at hostel sells candy; good stock of food; canned goods; maps and guidebooks of the area; T-shirts and posters of the local area. Hiking boots, rain jackets, and ice picks for rent (all £1.50 per day; £5 deposit).

▐▌▌ Sitting room by reception area; TV lounge/games room with pool table, Ping-Pong table, and foosball. Classroom with TV, video, overhead projectors mainly for groups.

⌇ In entrance hall only.

♿ Wheelchair accessible.

💱 See "Currency Exchange" under "The Basics" in Pen-y-Pass.

🔺 Bike shed; photography room/darkroom.

Cheap Eats Nearby

The Pen-y-Gurid Hotel

This place is legendary among visitors, mainly because the ceiling is inscribed with the names of the Mount Everest team, who stayed here when they were training in Snowdonia. A traditional hotel with a good local reputation, they serve hearty food: shepherd's pie, roast duck, steak-and-kidney pie (£6.50). They also have a midday hot-and-cold buffet for £3.50. Dinner is a five-course affair and pricey at £14.

Nant Gwynant. Tel: 01286/870211. Open: daily noon–2pm and 7:30–8pm (one seating for dinner). Reservations accepted. Cash only. Wheelchair accessible. From the hostel, turn left up the A4086 and it's about 1 mile on foot. On the left.

Pete's Eats

In Llanberis five miles away, this is a favorite among locals and tourists alike for a post-climb snack, huge mugs of coffee and tea, and a large bulletin board with notices for classes, courses, and mountain equipment for sale. It's very friendly and a good value. An especially nice breakfast includes muesli and banana £1.55; flapjacks 65p. For lunch, burgers and chips and other fried delights, including hazelnut-and-rice burgers £1.75.

High Street, Llanberis. Tel: 01286/870358. Open: Easter–Oct: Mon–Fri 9am–8pm; Sat–Sun 8am–8pm. Nov–Easter: Mon–Fri 9am–6:30pm; Sat–Sun 8am–8pm. From Pen-y-Pass, take bus no. 19 into Llanberis, a five-minute ride. Otherwise, it's a two-hour walk.

Grocery Store: Spar, in Llanberis. The Youth Hostel has a decent supply of food.

Experiences

One of the best things about staying at Pen-y-Pass is the comforting presence of the mountain ranger across the road. The general area offers much of the same activities as do the hostels at Bryn Gwynant and Snowdon Ranger, but here you're closer to the action. The wardens at **The Snowdonia National Park Wardens Centre** are probably the best sources of climbing advice, since they're the people who dispatch

RAF helicopters when unlucky souls lose their footing on these dangerous peaks. They regularly scoop people out of The Pinnacles, a rocky aerial climb on one side of Snowdon with a razor-sharp drop; even experienced climbers find this tricky. The park center offers competitive events as well as a lecture series.

Walking paths abound: The **Miner's** and **Pyg Tracks** up to Snowdon begin right in front of the hostel, and the hostel is also the starting and finishing point for **The Snowdon Horseshoe,** which is said to be the best ridge walk in these parts. Nearby Llanberis Pass, with its three cliffs, is excellent for rock climbers, but be careful: Don't go alone, and make sure you've got the right equipment.

For those seeking guidance, a good option is one of the weekend packages offered by the hostel's **Pen-y-Pass Mountain Centre.** Under the careful guidance of the hostel manager and big, bearded mountain man Harvey Lloyd, they offer weekend courses led by qualified instructors. Courses include Snowdonia Sunrise, Walking the High Ridges, Camera in Snowdonia, and others. For groups, the hostel can often devise an adventure weekend to suit specific wishes. For absolutely nonathletic pursuits, there are a handful of things to do. In Llanberis, five miles away, you can catch the **Snowdon Mountain Railway** or the **Llanberis Lake Railway** to take in the local scenery at your leisure.

Snowdonia National Park Warden's Centre. Pen-y-Pass. Tel: 01286/872555. Open: daily 9am–4:30pm.

Miner's Track and Pyg Track. Leaflets available at the hostel.

Pen-y-Pass Mountain Centre. Pen-y-Pass Youth Hostel. Tel: 01286/870428. Packages offered on selected weekends throughout the year. Prices £70–£125.

Snowdon Mountain Railway. Llanberis. Tel: 01286/870223. Mid-Mar to mid-Apr: daily 9:30am–3:30pm. Mid-Apr–mid-Sept: Sun–Fri 9am–5pm; Sat 9am–3:30pm. Mid-Sept–Oct: daily 9:30am–3:30pm. 2^1/$_2$-hour round trip.

Llanberis Lake Railway. Llanberis. Tel: 01286/870549. Mar–Apr: Mon–Thurs departures. May–June and Sept: Sun–Fri departures. July–Aug: daily departures.

The Basics

Tourist Office: The nearest T.I.C. is in Llanberis, 5 miles away. Llanberis T.I.C. High Street, Llanberis. Tel: 01286/870765. Open: daily 10am–6pm. Take bus no. 19 from the hostel into Llanberis, a 5-minute ride. The hostel is fully stocked with information, and the park wardens across the street also have information on Snowdonia. You don't really need to make the trek unless you want information for outside Snowdonia.

Post Office: The nearest post office is in Llanberis, 5 miles away. Llanberis Post Office. High Street, Llanberis. Tel: 01286/870201. Open: Mon–Tues 9am–5:30pm; Wed 9am–midnight; Thurs–Fri 9am–5:30pm; Sat 9am–midnight. Take bus no. 19 from the hostel into Llanberis, a 5-minute ride.

Currency Exchange: The closest place is in Llanberis, 5 miles away, at the Snowdon Mountain Railway Centre. Tel: 01286/870223. The Llanberis Post Office can exchange money, but it takes 3–4 days.

Telephone Code: 01286.

Bike Rental: in nearby Betwys-y-Coed (8 miles away). Beics Betws. Tel: 01690/ 710766.

Getting There: Buses are the only way to get up here from **Cardiff:** TrawsCambria no. 701 or 702 are your best options; they take a while to snake through the mountains (no. 701 goes along the coast and then the mountains), but there are no train links directly into Snowdonia from the south of Wales. TrawsCambria offers a good discount to students, so if you can produce an International Student Identification Card (ISIC), do so before paying the driver. For TrawsCambria information, call 01248/370295. For those coming from England, there are **train** connections from **London, York,** and **Chester** that connect to Bangor, which is 18 miles away; local buses can connect you to the hostel. For train information, call 01492/585151. By **car,** take the M6, M54, or A5, which gets you into Snowdonia. Turn left off the A5 at Capel Curig onto the A4086, which is 5 miles away; keep going up the hill, turn right at the Pen-y-Gwryd Hotel, and the hostel is 1 mile from there on your right.

What's Next

The Bryn Gwynant hostel, in **Nant Gwynant** on the shores of (lake) Llyn Gwynant, is a bit further removed from the mountain scene, but it is a dream house made of stone and has a lively atmosphere. Low-level walks around the lake complement the more rigorous mountain walks, and it's only about four miles from Pen-y-Pass, a nice morning's hike. Snowdon Ranger, in **Rhyd Ddu** on the other side of the mountain, is about 13 miles away by road and 10 miles by mountain path. On the shores of Llyn Cwellyn, this hostel seems almost like a bed-and-breakfast, from the hand-painted sign outside to the home-cooked meals inside. On sunny summer days, the rocky lakeside is a nice place to catch some rays.

CHESTER (ENGLAND)

The only city in England that's still entirely surrounded by Roman walls, Chester is one of the more attractive fortress towns lining the Welsh Borders. While on the map it may look like it's in no-man's-land, Chester is actually quite centrally located: 179 miles west of London, it's a hop from Liverpool (20 miles north), Manchester, Shrewsbury, and all North Wales. Because of its location, it was an important legionary fortress, and a cathedral was built here as well. The town is laid out in the traditional Roman grid pattern. During medieval times, windy streets worked their way into the cityscape.

The city is probably best known for its "rows," the shopping galleries that occupy both the ground and first-floor levels of the ancient buildings. With stone staircases leading up to airy balconies, this medieval mall of sorts now houses boutiques, jewelry shops, and cafes on its second level. Nobody really knows why the rows exist, but some speculate that during the Middle Ages there was so much Roman rubble the medieval folks just built on top.

Chester is also home to the oldest race course in Britain. Set on the banks of the River Dee (and sometimes in the River Dee, when the winters get cold), the race course hosts the annual Chester Races. Prince Charles usually stops by, making it one of the social scenes of the year. It's a natural amphitheater of sorts, surrounded by the area known as the Roodee, which has beautiful Victorian homes owned by Chester's privileged class.

Right across the river from the Roodee, the hostel is just as elegant as any of these houses. It's a bustling hostel in a bustling city. The city sees its fair share of tourists: School groups descend upon the hostel in spring and are replaced by backpackers in summer. It's the busiest city on the Welsh Borders and worth a couple of days, especially for those headed into the more remote hinterlands of North Wales or the Peak District.

Chester Youth Hostel

Hough Green House
40 Hough Green
Chester, Cheshire CH4 8JD
Tel: 01244/680056. Fax: 01244/681204.

A Victorian town house that has been redecorated in its original style, this hostel feels like the stately private home it was before the YHA took it over. A sweeping old-fashioned entrance hall with tile floors and fancy wall decorations lures you in. The staircase, with a 19th-century clock, would be just as appropriate supporting the rustling crinolines of a Victorian maid as it is welcoming bedraggled hostelers.

The sitting rooms have nice big picture windows and are decorated with period wallpaper and Victorian-motif furniture, but there's a spanking-clean 20th-century polish to everything. The ceiling moldings are intricately plastered, and the walls have soothing landscape paintings. The bedrooms upstairs are also brand-new, and some of them have rare private bathrooms—reason alone to stay here. The other baths aren't shabby either. Check out the view from the second-floor baths: To the east, you can see as far as Liverpool on a clear day, and in the other direction, you can make out Northeast Wales.

In the back yard, a garden, lawn, and scattered cypress trees create a nice resting spot, especially comforting to the many cyclists who stop here on their way up to John O'Groats. Your fellow bunkmates are likely to include backpackers, walkers, cyclists, and school groups: The usual crowd stops by this slightly unusual hostel.

🚆 From the train station, take any bus into the city center. Then from behind the library (look for the clock tower), take bus no. 7 or 16 from Stand 4 to the hostel. Tell the driver to drop you off at the hostel. It's directly in front of you.

🚌 From the bus station, turn right onto George Street, then left onto Northgate Street, and look for the sign "Bus Exchange—local" behind the library. From there, follow directions from the train, given above.

🚗 Avoid the city center if possible. If you are coming by motorway, take the M6 to the M56, and then go onto the M53 towards Chester. Stay on the M53 and it becomes the A55 (all the time disregarding signs to Chester). Stay on the A55 until the junction with the A483; then follow the signs to Chester until the sign to A5104, which is the road where the hostel is located. Turn right, and the hostel is a quarter mile down on the right-hand side. Follow the signs.

🗓 Open first Fri in Jan to first Sun in Dec. IBN and BABA.

🕐 Reception open 7–10am and 3–10:30pm. Doors locked at 11pm, but there's a security code.

🛏 130 beds. 2-, 4-, 6-, 8-, 10-, and 12-bed rooms. Family rooms en suite available.

£ Members: adults £8.80; under 18 £5.95.

Services

¶¶ Self-catering kitchen facilities. Breakfast: 7:30–8:30am. Lunch: packed lunch only; order by 9pm the night before. Dinner: 6–7:30pm. Main menu is call order, and there are dishes of the day.

✗ No table license.

▥ Individual lockers with keys free of charge (but with a returnable deposit).

⬚ Washers (£1.20), dryers (take 20p coins) in a drying room.

P Available; free of charge.

⬚ Shop at hostel sells candy, souvenirs.

▦ TV lounge; small adjacent sitting room that's off-limits to groups; games room downstairs with pool table.

⬚ In basement and entrance hall only.

♿ Not wheelchair accessible.

⬚ See "Currency Exchange" under "The Basics" in Chester.

▲ Classroom with TV, video, overhead projector; Bike shed.

Cheap Eats Nearby

Telford's Warehouse

This old place was once, yes, a warehouse, and an old crane sits in the center of the spacious bar area as a reminder of its past. It's very popular; the hostel staff says hands-down it's the coolest place in town. In addition to food, they offer live bands, from folk to world music and Sunday jazz lunches overlooking the River Dee. Cover charges (£3 to £8) are waived if you eat here. Bar food available. Fare includes vegetarian pastas (£4.50 to £4.95); chicken balti (£4.95); and steak-and-Guinness pie (£4.95).

Tower Wharf, Chester. Tel: 01244/390090. Bar open: Mon–Tues 11am–11pm; Wed–Sat 11–12:30am. Sun 11am–3:30pm and 7–10:30pm. Restaurant open: daily noon–3pm and 6–9:30pm.

Vincent's Caribbean

This little cavelike place has straw hats on the old brick walls. Vincent tempts his patrons with specials such as pepper pot soup, spiced duck breast, and seafood dishes. Lunch specials are £3 to £4. Dinner entrées cost from £7 to £10, but you can get away with ordering a few appetizers (£3 to £6). Many exotic and tantalizing fruit drinks are offered.

58 Lower Bridge St., Chester. Tel: 01244/310854. Open: Mon–Sat noon–2:30pm and 6pm onward. Credit cards: VA, MC, Access. Reservations accepted. From the hostel, turn left onto Howe Street, right onto Dingle, cross the bridge, and head straight up Lower Bridge Street. It's a 15-minute walk. This place is on your left, amid loads of other restaurants.

Grocery Store: Marks and Spencer, Foregate Street. Open: Mon–Wed 9am–5:30pm; Thurs 9am–8pm; Fri 9am–7pm; Sat 8:30am–6pm; Sun 11am–5pm.

Experiences

Different people come to Chester for different things. Many come here for the **shopping.** Chester boasts the best High Street in all England for its shop-to-square-acreage ratio. It's packed solid with quaint local shops, jewelers, boutiques, and multinational chains like Laura Ashley and a Disney store. All the stores are located in Chester's beautiful medieval buildings.

Others come to Chester to study the local history, which is said to represent "England in miniature," since so many significant eras reached their peak here.

There are a few **tours** that are inexpensive and good for getting acquainted with the city. For those on their own, the **city walls** are a great place to start. They stretch for two miles, but the main sights focus around the compact city center.

The **Chester Cathedral** has an unusual history. It was a Saxon church in the 10th century, a Benedictine abbey in the 11th century, and a proper cathedral ever since. With some intricately carved "misericords" of biblical stories, cloistered gardens where you can hear tinkling water, and original monastic quarters, it's worth a wander. There are also some nice bike paths through the city and some lovely Cheshire villages beyond the city walls.

For evening entertainment, Chester has loads of live music, from folk bands at **Telford's Warehouse** to Brahms recitals at St. John's Church. *What's On in Chester*, available from the tourist office, lists local musical events.

Summertime livens up with **festivals** and other events, starting in May with the Chester Races, the oldest horse racing event in England. The Chester Regatta sails by in June, and music and fringe festivals follow in July. A regular event in summer is the town crier's public proclamations: Every day (except Sunday and Monday) at noon and 2pm, he screams out his announcements at the Market Cross. Audience participation is welcome.

City tours. Past Finder Walking Tours. Tel: 01244/324324, ext. 2445. Tours depart from the tourist office daily at 10:45am. Adults £2.25; concessions £1.75. The Ghost Hunter Trail Tours. Tel: 01244/324324. May–Oct: Thurs–Sat. Tours last 1½ hours and depart from the tourist office at 7:30pm. Adults £2.25; concessions £1.75.

Chester Cathedral. Tel: 01244/324756. Open: daily 7am–6:30pm. Admission: free.

Telford's Warehouse. Tower Wharf, Chester. Tel: 01244/390090. Bar open: Mon–Tues 11am–11pm; Wed–Sat 11–12:30am. Sun 11am–3:30pm and 7–10:30pm. Restaurant open: daily noon–3pm and 6–9:30pm.

Festivals. Contact the Chester T.I.C. Town Hall, Northgate Street, Chester. Tel: 01244/318356. Open: Mon–Sat 9am–7:30pm; Sun 11am–4pm.

The Basics

Tourist Office: Chester T.I.C. Town Hall, Northgate Street, Chester. Tel: 01244/318356. Open: Mon–Sat 9am–7:30pm; Sun 11am–4pm. From the hostel, turn left, and then left again on Howe Street. Go up Dingle, cross the bridge, and turn left into town. Go up Lower Bridge Street, then Bridge Street, and curve around the clock to Northgate Street. It's on your left. There's also a branch at the train station. Tel: 01244/351609. Open: Mon–Sat 10am–6pm; Sun 11am–6pm.

Post Office: 2 St. John St. Tel: 01244/348315. Open: Mon–Fri 9am–5:30pm; Sat 9am–7pm.

Currency Exchange: At the post office on St. John Street. Also at Thomas Cook, 10 Bridge St. Tel: 01244/349687. Open: Mon–Tues 9am–5:30pm; Wed 10am 5:30pm; Thurs–Sat 9am–5:30pm. American Express, 23 St. Werburgh St. Tel: 01244/311145. Open: May–Sept: Mon–Fri 9am–6pm; Sat 9am–5pm; Sun 10am 6pm. Oct–Apr: Mon–Fri 9am–5:30pm; Sat 9am–5pm.

Telephone Code: 01244.

Bike Rental: Chester Cycle Hire. Tel: 01244/312253. £5 per day; they deliver to the hostel.

Getting There: Chester is exceptionally accessible to public transport and highways. From **London, Manchester, Liverpool, Cardiff,** and **Holyhead,** Chester is easily reachable by **train.** For schedule information, call 0151/709 9696. National Express and Crosville Cymru **buses** travel to **Cardiff, London,** and other major cities from the bus station on Rivacre Center. For information, call 01244/381515. En route to **Snowdonia, Bangor, Llandudno,** and **Llangollen,** Crosville Cymru buses leave from the bus exchange behind the town hall. For local bus information, call 01233/602666 or 01492/596969. By **car,** Chester is reachable via the M56-M53 from **Liverpool** and **Manchester.** From **London,** take the M1 through Milton Keynes, passing Northampton and switching to the M6 at Junction 19. From there, take the M6 north past Newcastle-Under-Lyme to Junction 18. From there, head west on the A454, following signs for Chester. From North Wales, take the A55 east from Holyhead, Bangor, Llandudno Junction, and Colwyn Bay.

What's Next

Most people who come here don't tend to make Chester part of a local itinerary; more likely, they shoot off to Edinburgh and London from here. Nevertheless, there are some nearby gems that are well worth the detour. Four buses a day head out to **Llangollen,** 22 miles away in the Vale of Clwyd in northern Wales. With a 12th-century fortress and tranquil ancient Welsh villages nearby, it's a beautiful spot set on a rushing river. The rambling mansion-turned-Youth-Hostel (also a YHA activity center) has a relaxed, friendly staff running the show. Heading directly north and west will take you to **Bangor,** an unremarkable town except for its position as the northern point of entry into Snowdonia, Wales's national park and national treasure. Heading south takes you directly into **Cardiff,** which has emerged from the soot of the nearby coal mines to become a lively university town and proud capital city. With good arts and music action, a couple of interesting local museums, and an unbelievably ostentatious castle, it's one of Britain's most underrated cities.

LLANGOLLEN

Even if it weren't the site of one of the YHA's two activity centers, where total klutzes come for (slightly pricey) weekend courses in all sorts of outdoor pursuits, Llangollen would still be worth at least a couple of days. Sitting at the far end of the Dee Valley on the Welsh-English border, this town is sandwiched between sloping hills and set right on top of a rushing river. In early July, the International Eisteddfod draws choirs, folk singers, dancers, and actors the world over to compete in its merry festival that has the town bulging at the seams. In calmer months, there's still a lot to see and do: Beautiful bike routes follow the canal up and down the Llangollen Valley; boat rides and white-water rafting are on offer in the River Dee; and a smattering of historical buildings round out the sights.

Despite its proximity to the English border, the town is decidedly Welsh in character. Only 23 miles from Chester and 195 miles northwest of London, Llangollen and its country lanes and active nightlife (13 pubs alone in this town with two main streets!) make a nice introduction to Wales. About $1^1/_2$ miles outside of the town center, the Youth Hostel is a rambling old mansion in a woodsy, hilly setting. A laid-back bunch of youthful mountaineers run the activity center.

❋ Llangollen Youth Hostel & Activity Centre

Tyndwr Hall
Tyndwr Road, Llangollen
Clwyd, LL20 8AR
Tel: 01978/860330 or 01978/861750. Fax: 01978/861709.

This rambling Victorian house, called Tyndwr, is as full of history as its stained-glass windows, elaborate fireplaces, and dark-wood paneling suggest. The red-velvet furniture, tile floors, and labyrinthine halls upstairs are remnants of what was surely a stately mansion in the 1800s.

The grandeur of the current decor has faded, thanks to the children who scamper through the place in spring and autumn. The classrooms, outdoor activity center, and large bedrooms naturally attract large school groups to this countryside hostel, lending it the feeling of a huge old summer house. Luckily, though, the quarters aren't too cramped, so there's some room to spread out. School parties tend to peter out by summertime and are replaced by independent hostelers and festival-goers.

Check out the vibes in the members' kitchen: This is where the gentlemen of the manor used to retire to play billiards after their evening meal. You may want to buy your own food and cook it here because the food served is standard and not home cooked. The formerly grand bedrooms upstairs have fallen victim to the subdivide-and-conquer philosophy of hostel dormitory planning, but they retain an air of elegance. Most have high ceilings, and some even have old fireplaces.

🚆 The closest train stations are Chirk or Ruabon (both 5 miles away). From Ruabon, take the Bryn Melyn bus or Crosville Cymru bus into Llangollen. The bus drops you off right in the center of Llangollen town, and the hostel is 1^1/$_2$ miles away. Before reaching the Tourist Information Centre on your right, hang a left down Bridge Street then left again on Church Street and left onto Queen Street. After about half a mile, you'll reach a fork in the road. Bear right; the hostel is half a mile up the road. A slight uphill walk, it takes about 35 minutes from town.

🚌 The bus drops you off right in the center of Llangollen town; hostel is 1^1/$_2$ miles away. Follow directions from the train station, given above.

🚗 From the A539 (Manchester and Chester), cross the bridge and go straight up Castle Street to the traffic lights. Turn left onto Regent Street, which turns into Queen Street. Pass the fire station on your left, and then bear right onto Birch Hill. The hostel is about half a mile from this crossroads.

▦ Open Apr–Oct, but opening times vary from year to year. Call ahead. IBN and BABA.

🕐 Reception open 8:30am–11pm. Strict curfew 11pm.

🛏 120 beds. 6-, 14-, and 20-bed rooms in the main building. In the coach house annex, 8-, 10-, and 20-bed rooms.

£ Members: adults £8; under 18 £5.35

🍴 Standard self-catering kitchen facilities. Breakfast: 8–9:30am. Lunch: packed lunch only; order by 10pm the night before. Dinner: 6–7pm.

🍸 Table license.

Services

📦 Hall lockers; keys available at reception. 50p (£2 deposit).

🔲 Washers and dryers (tokens available at reception); drying room.

P Out front; ample and free of charge.

🛍 Shop at hostel sells candy, canned goods, souvenirs.

🛋 Reception area; lounge (no TV cable).

🚬 In lounge only.

♿ Not wheelchair accessible.

💱 See "Currency Exchange" under "The Basics" in Llangollen.

🔺 Bike shed; three classrooms with TV, VCR, overhead and slide projectors; darkroom; well-organized activity center for outdoor sports.

Cheap Eats Nearby

Maxine's Café & Books

Enjoy breakfast, lunch, dinner, and some Robert Heinlein to top it all off. Downstairs, it's an airy lunch spot-cum-gaming parlor, and upstairs is the biggest selection of sci-fi books this side of a Star Trek convention. Great for browsing, but don't get your big English breakfast (sausage, egg, and chips £3.75) on the merchandise. Sandwiches from £1.85; quiches £3.75; tea cakes and treats from 65p.

17 Castle St., Llangollen. Tel: 01978/861963. Open: May–Sept: daily 9am–9pm. Oct–Apr: daily 9am–5pm. Credit cards: VA, MC, AE, Access. Reservations accepted for large groups. From the hostel, walk straight down the road to Regent Street, turn right on Castle Street, and it's the big yellow place on your right. About 1¹/₂ miles from the hostel; a 35-minute walk.

Sylhet Restaurant

This is your standard Indian restaurant: pink tablecloths; color-coordinated wallpaper; and the latest imported Indian lager, Lall Tafan. Madras curries are (£4.50 to £6.75); vegetable balti £7.50; good selection of chef's specials. Party room upstairs has bay windows overlooking the vale of Llangollen. Takeout is available.

Regent Street, Llangollen. Tel: 01978/861877. Open: daily 6pm–midnight. Credit cards: VA, MC, Access, Delta. From the hostel, walk down the street onto Queen Street, then Regent Street. It's on your left as you walk toward the town center; a 20-minute walk.

Grocery Store: Spar. Castle Street. Open: daily 8am–10pm.

Experiences

There are lots of things to do in Llangollen. There's the ruins of an old castle, **Castell Dinas Bran.** The **Valle Crucis Abbey** is nearby. You can also visit a Victorian house with formal gardens and viney footpaths. Did you know you can climb here? Everyone's doing it: bricklayers on their days off, bartenders, insurance salesmen. Everyone. You can, too, under the helpful guidance of the activity instructors at the hostel **activity center,** where courses in rock climbing, mountain biking, abseiling, caving, paragliding, and other death-defying weekend pursuits are on offer.

If you're on your own, though, one great way to get up the valley is to **rent a bike** from the hostel. There are lots of challenging bike routes up and down the sloping hills, but there are also some easy, flat trails. For a great view of the Vale of

Llangollen (sheep included), take a right after the bridge, and ride down about a mile toward Trevor. When you reach the pub, cross the bridge over the canal, which leads you to a grassy ridge where you can survey the valley. The real beauty of the ride (panoramic scenery notwithstanding) is that it's almost 100% flat so even the laziest person can do this easily and thereby brag that he or she had biked through the Welsh mountains. Follow the track straight back into Llangollen town alongside the boats cruising down the canal.

When you get back to town, you can take a **horse-drawn boat ride** up the canal. The ride takes you to nearby Berwyn, where the local steam train terminates. If you take your bike in the other direction up Castle Street and turn right, after about half a mile you'll come to **The River Wild,** a combination cafe/canoe rental shop along the River Dee. Lessons and canoe rentals come with all necessary equipment.

For those who can't get enough of Victorian history, 1 mile from the hostel is **Plas Newydd,** the former Victorian home and now museum of the legendary grand dames of Llangollen, a pair of Irish expatriates who entertained the likes of Walter Scott and Wordsworth in their house and gardens, which are now open for public view.

If you're in town on a Wednesday night, head over to Prince of Wales pub, where Wrexham's, the local brew, is served up amid the strains of live music. The mood at this popular local hangout is friendly, just like the town. Since 1947, Llangollen has hosted the **International Eisteddfod,** a festival in early July that brings more than 75,000 visitors to town. With church music, folk singing, dancing, and other performances, it's probably the merriest time of year here—just make sure there's room at the hostel before you come.

Castell Dinas Bran. About 2 miles outside of Llangollen, 1,000 feet up to the summit of the Hill of Bran. Ask at hostel reception for footpath map.

Valle Crucis Abbey. On the B5103, Llangollen. Tel: 01978/860326. Open: Mar–Oct: daily 9:30am–6:30pm. Nov–Feb: Mon–Sat 9:30am–4pm; Sun 2–4pm. Admission: adults £1; children 60p.

Bike rental. Ask at the hostel.

Llangollen Activity Centre. Llangollen Youth Hostel. Tel: 01978/860330. Courses change depending on the season; prices vary: two nights from £79; four nights from £159.

Horse-drawn boats. Llangollen Wharf. Tel: 01978/850702. Easter–Oct. Frequent daily departures. 45-minute boat trip: adults £2.50; children £1.50.

The River Wild. J. J. Canoeing. Mile End Mill, Berwyn Road, Llangollen. Tel: 01978/860763. Kayak rental: full day £12; half day £8. Inflatable three-seater: full day £20; half day £14. Instruction: £12 per person per hour. Full-day instruction from £31. Weekend courses from £59. Canoe slalom, mountain biking, and rock climbing courses available.

Plas Newydd. Parade Street, Llangollen (1 mile away). Tel: 01978/861523. Open: Apr–Oct: Mon–Sat 10am–5pm. Admission: adults £1.70; children 75p.

Llangollen International Musical Eisteddfod Office. Llangollen, Clwyd, Wales. LL20 8NG. Tel: 01978/860236. Ticket prices and performance times vary.

The Basics

Tourist Office: Llangollen T.I.C. Castle Street, Llangollen. Tel: 01978/860828. Open: Apr–Oct: daily 10am–6pm. Nov–Mar: Thurs–Tues 9:30am–5:30pm. From the hostel, walk toward the town and turn left onto Queen Street. Continue onto Regent Street, and when you reach Castle Street turn right. It's about two blocks ahead on the left; a 30-minute walk.

Post Office: Castle Street, Llangollen. Tel. 01978/860230. Open: Mon–Fri 9am–5:30pm; Sat 9am–1pm. From the hostel, a 30-minute walk. Head toward the town and turn left onto Queen Street. Continue onto Regent Street, and when you reach Castle Street turn right. It's on the right.

Currency Exchange: Llangollen Post Office, Castle Street, Llangollen. Tel: 01978/860230. Open: Mon–Fri 9am–5:30pm; Sat 9am–1pm.

Telephone Code: 01978.

Bike Rental: At the hostel. £7.50 per half day; £14 per full day; helmets provided.

Getting There: The two large cities nearest Llangollen are Chester to the north and Shrewsbury to the east. From **Chester,** Llangollen town (1¹/₂ miles from the hostel) is reachable only by **bus.** Crosville Cymru coaches go from Chester into Wrexham, where you change for local buses. Crosville Cymru also services the Snowdonia area and has buses from **Bangor** and **Llandudno** that head into Wrexham as well. For Crosville Cymru information, call 01248/370295 or 01492/596969. **Train** links are decent as well; the closest stations are Ruabon and Chirk (each 6 miles away) on the Chester-Shrewsbury route. From there, local buses can take you into Wrexham, where you can switch for Llangollen. For train information, call 01743/364041. By **car** from **Shrewsbury,** take the A5 north. When you reach Ruabon, turn onto the A539 west to Llangollen, which is another 6 miles. From **Chester,** take the A483 to Ruabon and switch there for the A539 west to Llangollen, another 6 miles.

What's Next

Chester, about 23 miles away in England, is a nice change of pace; it's an easy ride on the train from Ruabon or Chirk. The city, surrounded by medieval walls, has a 900-year-old cathedral, as well as some pleasant cafés, boutiques, and museums tucked in its "rows," unique two-story shopping arcades. **Manchester,** only about an hour further on the train, is an industrial city with an excellent music scene, cutting-edge arts, and a luxury hostel alongside the city's historic canal. If you go in the other direction toward Bangor and Llandudno, you can get bus and highway connections into Snowdonia National Park, where a circuit of Youth Hostels, all relatively close to one another, dots the 840 square miles of mountain passes, craggy peaks, sheer drops, and icy pools of water.

5

THE BEST HOSTELS IN SCOTLAND

Edinburgh & the East

From the broom-smothered hills along the Borders to the celebrated cities of Edinburgh and Stirling to the shockingly blue Grampian and Cairngorm mountain ranges, central Scotland has been long fought over for its strategic location. The visitor here is awarded with ever-changing natural landscapes and a mother lode of monuments, castles, and museums.

Stretching from Berwick-upon-Tweed in the east to Galashiels in the west, the Borders have historically been Britain's hot potato. Henry VIII of England fueled the fiery rivalry between Scotland and England when he tried to forge an alliance between his sickly son Edward and bouncing baby Mary, Queen of Scots, in the mid-1500s. When his efforts were flatly rejected, he ordered his merciless armies to sack, slash, and set aflame everything they could, including the capital city of Edinburgh. Today, the ruins of four abbeys amid the peaceful rolling hills stand as dramatic reminders of these bitter raids. The hostel in Melrose is an excellent base from which to check out the entire area, which birthed the Scottish national treasure Sir Walter Scott, author of *Ivanhoe* and *Rob Roy*.

Edinburgh, Scotland's splendid capital, boasts medieval buildings along its cobblestoned streets; a spectacular hilltop castle and historic Royal Mile; oodles of museums, churches, and watering holes; and a great green park. The city overflows with revelers all year long. In August, the town explodes during its annual arts festival, when the streets roil with merrymakers, jugglers, musicians, and all sorts of performers in a round-the-clock frenzy. The two hostels in the capital are usually packed solid.

The quieter city of Stirling lies 36 miles up the M9. A castle and university (as well as a first-class hostel) play host to a huge student population all year long. It makes an especially worthwhile stop for fans of braveheart William Wallace: A monument and museum commemorate his contributions to Scottish independence, most notably at nearby Stirling Bridge, where he led a famous battle in 1297.

To the north, the unremarkable city of Perth makes a good overnight stay en route to the seaside university town of St. Andrews, known the world over as the birthplace of golf. Traveling north on the M9 from there takes you into the beginning of the Scottish Highlands. In the ski center of Aviemore, you'll get your first taste of countryside hosteling in the cold blue hills and barren landscape for which Scotland is famous. The heather-covered moorland of the Grampians gives way to the solid granite of the Cairngorm range. Mountain climbers, hill walkers, and cyclists can all do a good deal of hamstring busting in these parts, where the lonely roads wind around the wind-whipped hills.

All of Scotland is easily accessible via the Glasgow/Edinburgh-Inverness train line, which links to England via Newcastle and connects as far north as Thurso and

Wick on Scotland's northern coast. Where trains don't dare to go, coaches, local buses, and postbuses do, making this region a snap to explore using public transport. The same is true for cars—the motorways are easy to get on and off, and road signs are excellent. The Haggis Backpackers bus storms through here, taking scenic side roads to almost all the hostels on their funhouse-on-wheels. The hostels are all within walking distance of the bus and train stops and all are open during the daytime.

MELROSE

This sweet little town (pop. 2,276) lies beneath the Eildon Hills on the banks of the River Tweed. Nestled smack in the middle of the 1,800 square miles comprising the hilly, castle-ridden Scottish Borders, Melrose is 37 miles southeast of Edinburgh, 73 miles southeast of Glasgow, about 75 miles north of Newcastle, and nothing like any of them.

The town is known for two things: an eponymous 12th-century abbey and Abbotsford, the stately home of Scotland's favorite son and author, Walter Scott. Originally the site of a Roman fort, Melrose guarded the banks of the River Tweed against unwanted intruders from all directions. These days, though, the only folks you'll have to fend off are the bookworms and Scottish history buffs crawling over Abbotsford in summer and the map-toting walkers stopping here as they make their way across the Southern Upland Way, a long-distance walking route that passes through Melrose.

The hostel itself is right in the town and makes a great base for exploring the Borders area. Castles, abbeys, and other ancient monuments remain from scrappy Scotland's long fight for its sovereignty. You'll need some kind of transportation to reach many of the attractions, but Melrose is worth a stop. It makes a nice introduction to Scotland, and the rambling Youth Hostel is especially welcoming for those looking for rest on their way to, or recovering from, Edinburgh, Glasgow, and Newcastle.

Melrose Youth Hostel

Priorwood
Melrose
Roxburghshire TD6 9EF
Tel: 01896/822521.

Wannabe lords and ladies won't be disappointed at this hillside manor. Once the stately home of a prominent Scottish solicitor, the Georgian mansion boasts all the comforts of modern hosteling (carpeted stairs, good heating, TV in the common room) without abandoning its 18th-century charms.

Scarlett O'Hara would've felt right at home pining over Ashley from the huge picture window on the landing of the grand staircase overlooking Melrose Abbey and grounds below. A formal entrance hall, old fireplaces, and eye-popping moldings evoke memories of yesteryear, and the common room also commands a spectacular view of the lawn below and the abbey.

As in most hostels, you're likely to be sharing your visions of grandeur with a group of runny-nosed schoolchildren, but thankfully there's room for everyone.

The enormous lawn is big enough to accommodate a ball game or two, and the TV room/classroom downstairs swallows up the crowds at night. When the kids have disappeared, you can resume your reverie in the common room by immersing yourself in the reading material, which includes an extensive set of Mills and Boon romance novels.

The self-catering kitchen and corresponding dining room are ample, with the latter overlooking the lawn and abbey. Melrose is also one of the few Scottish hostels that offers meal service, and the managers pride themselves on the healthful, hearty menu they offer in a separate downstairs dining room.

Services

The closest train station is in Edinburgh, 37 miles away; from there, take bus no. 95 to Galashiels (hourly service) and then the no. 59, 60, 61, 62, 65, 66, 67, or 68 to Melrose (frequent service). The bus leaves you at the Market Square. From there, walk up the main street past Walters Supermarket at the corner. Turn left onto the lane between the fish monger's and the Ship Inn; the hostel is at the end of lane/car park. Look for the little gate signposted "Youth Hostel."

The bus leaves you at Market Square. From there, follow directions from the train, given above.

Going north from Carlisle on the A7, follow signs to Edinburgh and Galashiels. When you reach the traffic circle just before Galashiels, turn right and follow signs to Melrose (3 miles away). Pass the first exit sign to Melrose and stay on the motorway until the next (east) exit. From there, follow the signs into Melrose and turn right at Priorwood. Look for "Youth Hostel" signpost on the left side of the road.

Open year-round. BABA.

Reception open 7–11:45pm. Curfew 11:45pm.

86 beds. 4-, 6-, 8-, and 14-bed rooms.

Members: adults £6.95; under 18 £5.85.

Meals served Easter–Sept 30 only. Self-catering kitchen facilities. Breakfast: 8:30am. Lunch: packed lunch for groups only; order in advance. Dinner: 7pm.

Lockers.

Washer, dryer, and drying room.

P Ample and free of charge.

Shop at hostel sells candy, canned goods, souvenirs.

Common area overlooking lawn and abbey; TV lounge downstairs.

In downstairs common room only.

Not wheelchair accessible. Ground-floor rooms available but no washrooms for people with disabilities.

See "Currency Exchange" under "The Basics" in Melrose.

Bike shed.

Cheap Eats Nearby

Marmion's Brasserie
We're not in England anymore, Toto: Candlesticks on the tables are lovingly adorned with little tartan bows, and the menu in this airy high-ceilinged dining room boasts some mouth-watering/stomach-churning (you decide) Scottish dishes. Black pudding (£2.50) is not for the faint of heart. Simpler fare includes croissants and jacket potatoes with a variety of fillings (£2.50 to £3.50), as well as daily pasta and vegetarian dishes (£4 to £5).

Bucchleuch Street, Melrose. Tel: 01896/822245. Open: Mon–Sat 9am–10:30pm for light food and tea. Lunch from noon–2pm and dinner from 6:30–9:45pm. Credit cards (accepted for dinner only): VA, MC. Reservations recommended. From the hostel, a 5-minute walk: walk down the footpath and turn right onto Abbey Street then left onto Bucchleuch Street. It's on the left, across from the Post Office.

Pyemont & Company Tea & Coffee House

This Edwardian coffeehouse (which doubles as a gourmet shop) claims to be the only place in all Scotland that roasts its own coffee. The array of jolting brews blended in their 18th-century cellars includes Kenyan, Colombian, and Jamaican Blue Mountain. They also serve filling, elegantly prepared lunches and afternoon teas. Soup and roll are £1.75; sandwiches £2.75 to £3.75. Main meals might include chicken curry (£4.40), pasta with mushrooms (£4), and jacket potatoes (£3.75). Freshly baked sweets.

28 Market Square, Melrose. Tel: 01896/822223. Open: Mon–Sat 9am–5pm. Cash only. From the hostel, a 5-minute walk down the footpath onto Market Square. Turn left and it's on the corner across the street.

Grocery Store: Walters Supermarket, High Street, Melrose. Open: Mon–Sat 8am–10pm.

Experiences

The ambitious hosteler can cover Melrose (including Abbotsford) in a day. The town itself has two sights worth seeing: **Melrose Abbey** (which has a museum) and **Priorwood Garden,** both about five minutes from the hostel. The abbey was built by Cistercian monks in 1136 and is now mostly in ruins, save for some interesting stonework (look for the bagpiping pig on the roof). The heart of Robert the Bruce, Scotland's medieval freedom fighter and king, is rumored to be interred on abbey grounds. Right next door is Priorwood Garden, where you can stroll through an apple orchard, sniff your way through the flower beds, and walk or picnic in the secluded woodland area. There's also an herb garden, a gift shop, and even a demonstration hut where drying techniques are displayed.

Abbotsford, the stately home of Sir Walter Scott, lies on the banks of the River Tweed three miles outside Melrose. Once you get past the main road out of Melrose, it's a pleasant walk down a country lane (don't forget bug spray) to Abbotsford. Huge manicured lawns overlook the river. Inside the enormous stone "farmhouse" you can swoon over a mind-boggling display of armor, including a sword that once belonged to Rob Roy. A guided tour takes you through the impressive house and provides a detailed account of Scott's tumultuous life and times, making it well worth your £3, even if you read only the Cliff Notes to *Ivanhoe* in high school.

For those who prefer outdoor pursuits, Melrose is well situated in the lap of the broom-covered Eildon Hills, formed from volcanic rock. Legend has it that the devil himself split the mountain into three hills, all conveniently located behind the hostel. Traveling straight out of Melrose on the B6359, the **Eildon Walk** leads you to the peak, 422 meters above the Borders. If you do the walk, watch out for the prickly broom plants; they rank a close second behind midges as one of Scotland's natural hazards. Long-distance walkers can catch the **Southern Upland Way** (aka the Scottish Coast-to-Coast Walk) by following the River Tweed straight toward the Abbey and the pedestrian suspension bridge. Just beyond it lies the footpath.

Melrose Abbey and Museum. Abbey Street, Melrose. Tel: 01896/822562. Open: Apr–Sept: daily 9:30am–6:30pm. Oct–Mar: Mon–Sat 9:30am–4pm; Sun 2–4pm. Admission: adults £2.50, children £1, senior citizens £1.50.

Priorwood Garden. Abbey Street, Melrose. Tel: 01896/822493. Open: Apr, Nov–Dec: Mon–Sat 10am–5:30pm. May–Sept: Mon–Sat 10am–5:30pm; Sun 2–5:30pm.

Abbotsford. Melrose. Tel: 01896/822043. Open: Late Mar–Oct only: Mon–Sat 10am–5pm; Sun 2–5pm. Admission: adults £3, children £1.50. Discounts for groups. Access for people with disabilities. Located 3 miles west of Melrose on the B6360.

The Basics

Tourist Office: Melrose T.I.C. Abbey Street, Melrose. Tel: 01896/822555. Open: Apr–May and Oct: Mon–Sat 10am–5pm. June and Sept: Mon–Sat 10am–6pm; Sun 2–6pm. July–Aug: Mon–Sat 9:30am–6:30pm; Sun 10:30am–6:30pm. From the hostel, walk down the footpath through the Abbey Park and turn right onto Abbey Street. It's across the street, on your left.

Post Office: Melrose Post Office. Buccleuch Street, Melrose. Tel: 01896/822040. Open: Mon–Fri 9am–1pm and 2–5:30pm; Sat 9am–12:30pm.

Currency Exchange: George and Abbotsford Hotel. High Street, Melrose. Tel: 01896/822308. Open: 24 hours.

Telephone Code: 01896.

Bike Rental: None in Melrose. The closest place is in Selkirk, 10 miles away. Scottish Border Trails. Bowhill Estate, Selkirk. Tel: 01721/722934. £10 per day, not including value-added tax (VAT).

Getting There: Trains don't come to Melrose at all; the line was dismantled in the 1960s, and the closest stations are in Berwick or Edinburgh. Trains go into **Edinburgh** (30 miles away) from virtually anywhere; from there, local buses connect you to Melrose. National Express **coach** service (nos. 383 and 989) runs from **Edinburgh** to Newcastle twice daily. For National Express info, call 0131/452 8777. From other cities, head for **Galashiels,** 4 miles away; from there, Lowland Omnibus nos. 59, 60, 61, 62, 65, 66, 67, 68, and 96 go to Melrose. For Lowland bus info, call 01896/758484 or 01896/752237. By **car,** the A7 is the main north/south road that runs from **Edinburgh** and **Galashiels** in the north down to Carlisle (England) in the south. Once in Galashiels, take the exit and follow signs to Melrose, 3 miles away. From **Newcastle,** follow the A68 to Jedburgh; about 9 miles north of Jedburgh, turn left at the roundabout for Melrose.

What's Next

From Melrose, you can dart out in any number of directions, all radically different from one another. The cathedral, castle, and endless festivals of **Edinburgh** make it the most logical next stop for anyone traveling north; only 37 miles away, it's why most travelers come to Scotland. About 66 miles to the northwest is the "preservation village" of New Lanark, where Robert Owen launched the cooperative movement in Scotland. To the south, the no-nonsense university city of **Newcastle** is only about 75 miles away. It's not a bad stop for re-entry into England, decent music, nightlife, and boat connections to Scandinavia.

EDINBURGH (BRUNTSFIELD & EGLINTON)

Royal burgh, festival town, capital of Scotland, and home to more than 400,000 souls, Edinburgh is a bright, sunny spot on the often-dour British landscape. Who couldn't love this jewel of a city, especially if you're among the thousands pushing their way onto the Royal Mile through the drunken crowds during the August festival? Even in the "off season" (if there is one), Edinburgh is usually teeming with tourists, but the feeling is convivial.

The two most famous landmarks in this city, which was built on a solid core of volcanic rock, sit on hills created from this ancient geological phenomenon. To the west, towering above the entire city, is Edinburgh Castle, home of the Scottish crown jewels, 11th-century buildings, and the spectacular 18th-century parade ground known as the Esplanade. To the east, nestled in the green hills of Holyrood Park, is the Palace of Holyroodhouse, the official residence of the monarch in Scotland.

These sights split the city into two. The Old Town, centered around the Royal Mile, is bounded on the east by the Edinburgh Castle and on the west by the palace. The New Town, bounded by Princes Street Gardens on the other side of the castle, was built in the 18th century on a grid format, making it easier to navigate. Elegant neighborhoods lined with trees and grassy crescents make this part of town a mixture of the posh and the commercial; the main drag, Princes Street, is lined with every imaginable British chain.

The sights in Edinburgh can be overwhelming—a castle, a palace, excellent art museums, loads of theater, a never-ending nightlife, and an internationally renowned festival in summer. It's wise to dump your load at one of the hostels (lock everything up), grab a map, and start walking. There are buses aplenty here, but the city is best explored on foot. There's something for all tastes in this beautiful, bubbling city.

Edinburgh Bruntsfield Youth Hostel

7 Bruntsfield Crescent
Edinburgh EH10 4EZ
Tel: 0131/447 2994. Fax: 0131/452 8588.

Set on a quiet street south of the Old Town, the Bruntsfield Youth Hostel is run by a friendly, relaxed team. A mixture of Scotsmen and seasoned travelers from all over give this busy hostel a mood of international camaraderie, and the big friendly mutt, Jeddah, sniffs even the smelliest backpackers.

There are some decent lounges (usually crowded), a TV room, and ample self-catering facilities. While there's no meal service, there are restaurants in the neighborhood and the Old Town is only about a 20-minute walk away. This hostel, along with the one on Eglinton Crescent (see below), fills up fast, so it's wise to book your bed well in advance to ensure a space.

In 1995, there was a rash of robberies in the neighborhood, and the hostel was hit pretty badly: Backpacks, cameras, passports, and the like disappeared with alarming regularity. The hostel has since tightened up security, and there are now locks on all dormitory doors. As in all large cities, take special care of precious belongings. The bedrooms here are large and the beds creaky. Many hostelers I surveyed didn't seem to care a whit, though. The entrancing city seems to dispel the sometimes inconvenient and uncomfortable facets of hostel life.

Services

From Waverley station or Princes Street (from the side of the tourist office), take bus no. 11, 15, 16, or 17 to Bruntsfield Place (55p; exact change only). When you get off at Forbes Road, turn back on the street and then turn right onto Bruntsfield Terrace, keep the park on your left. The hostel is just up the block on your right; a 10-minute ride.

From the coach station on St. Andrew's Square, exit, turn left, and take bus no. 11, 15, 16, or 17 to Bruntsfield Place (55p; exact change only). When you get off, follow directions from the train, given above.

If you're coming from **Newcastle and points south,** take the city bypass, the A720, and then turn right onto A702, which takes you into Bruntsfield Place. From there, turn right onto Whitehouse Loan and right again onto Bruntsfield Crescent. The hostel is on your left. From **Glasgow,** take the A720 (Edinburgh city bypass) and turn left onto the A702, which takes you into Bruntsfield Place. Turn right onto Bruntsfield Crescent.

Open Feb–Dec. IBN and FABA.

Reception open 7am–11:15pm. Curfew 2am.

170 beds. 8-, 10-, 12-, 18-, and 24-bed rooms.

£ Members: adults £7.80; under 18 £6.40.

No meal service. Fully equipped self-catering kitchen facilities: microwave, oven, stove.

Coin-operated lockers.

Washers and dryers.

P Overnight parking only on the park side of the street. Parking nearby is free of charge (a 2-minute walk from the hostel).

Shop at hostel sells Slow Coach tickets; candy; canned goods.

TV room; common room.

Only in TV room or on steps outside.

Not wheelchair accessible.

See "Currency Exchange" under "The Basics" in Edinburgh.

Edinburgh Eglinton Youth Hostel

17/18 Eglinton Crescent
Edinburgh EH12 5DD
Tel: 0131/337 1120. Fax: 0131/313 2053.

This building has been a lawyer's home, a hotel, a Forces Club for the army during World War II, a private nursing home with its own operating room, and a morgue (this is where the present-day warden lives). The SYHA bought the building in 1965 and it's been a Youth Hostel ever since. About five years ago, it was renovated to comfortable modern standards, but it's still a grand old place.

The hostel serves breakfast (free) and evening meals (not free), and the decent self-catering kitchen has its own dining room. Comfortable sitting rooms and a separate TV room mean there's space to spread out, and you may need it: large groups are often attracted to the amenities here, so it can get a bit crowded. Like the Bruntsfield hostel (see above), this place is jam-packed in summer: Call as far ahead as possible to book your bed. The Haggis Backpackers bus, driven by fearless, cheery road warriors, begins its tour of Scotland here, bright and early in the morning.

Services

🚆 From any train coming in from the south, get off at **Haymarket** instead of Waverley (Haymarket is closer). From the station, turn left onto Glasgow Road and take the second right, which is Coates Terrace. When you reach the crescent at the top of Coates Terrace, bear left (not a sharp left) onto Eglinton Crescent, with the gardens to your right. The hostel is 10 meters ahead on your left; look for the Scottish flag.

If you have to get out at **Waverley,** walk onto Princes Street just outside the station, and take bus no. 3, 4, 12, 13, 22, 28, 31, or 33 (all westbound) to Palmerston Place. Walk up Palmerston Place toward St Mary's Cathedral. Walk past the cathedral and take the second left, which is Eglinton Crescent. The hostel is up the street (about 150 yards) on your right; a 5-minute walk.

🚌 From the coach station at St Andrews Square, take bus no. 3, 4, 12, 13, 22, 28, 31, or 33 to Palmerston Place. From there, follow directions from Waverley train station, given above.

🚗 From the **south,** the A1 comes from the east coast. The M6/A702 comes from the west coast (Manchester), the A68 from Newcastle, and the A7 from Hawick. Head for Princes Street, going in the direction of the west end of Princes Street. Go straight onto Shandwick Place and follow the one-way circuit (follow the signs) to Haymarket Railway Station. Drive past the railway station and take the second turn on the right, which is Coates Terrace. At the top of the road, bear left onto Eglinton Crescent (not a sharp left), with the gardens to your right. The hostel is just up on your left; look for the Scottish flag.

🎫 Open Jan–Nov. Opening dates may vary, so call ahead to check. IBN and BABA.

🕐 Reception open 7am–midnight. Curfew 2am.

🛏 172 beds. 3-, 4-, 6-, 8-, 10-, and 12-bed rooms.

£ Members: adults £10.45; under 18 £9. Prices include continental breakfast.

🍴 Self-catering kitchen facilities. Breakfast: 7–9:30am. Continental breakfast included in price: £1 extra for cooked breakfast. Lunch: packed lunch only; should be ordered by 5pm the night before. Dinner: 6:30–7:30pm.

🧳 Coin-operated lockers. All rooms have locks.

☑ Washers, dryers, and drying room.

P No parking. Parking on the other side of Eglinton Crescent costs £1.20 for two hours. Free street parking about $1/2$ mile away. No parking restrictions 5pm–8:30am.

🛍 Shop at hostel has candy and canned goods.

🛋 Bavarian room (quiet room); Ballantyne room (TV room); big hallway/reception area/entrance hall.

📺 In reception area, entrance hall, and TV room.

♿ Very limited access: toilets on ground floor but no wheelchair-accessible bedrooms.

💱 See "Currency Exchange" under "The Basics" in Edinbrugh.

🔺 Bike shed.

Cheap Eats Nearby

Café Byzantium

This cafe has a cool modern bar with a balcony overlooking the jewelry, record, and used-clothing shops in the gallery below. There's a notice board chock-full of local events. Very vegetarian. Vegetable or meat/chicken curries are £2.95 to £4.95; veggie buffet lunch £3.50; salads £3; sandwiches £1.50 to £2.

9 Victoria St., Edinburgh. Tel: 0131/220 2241. Open: Mon–Sat 10am–5:30pm; in August, until midnight. Cash only. From Waverley Station on Princes Street, cross the Waverley Bridge, turn onto Cockburn Street, and take a right on High Street. Turn left onto George IV Bridge and then right onto Victoria Street. It's on the left.

The Last Drop

A friendly pub with outside tables, this place is loaded with customers on sunny summer days. Inside, comfy banquettes look out onto the Grassmarket, where people were hanged in ye olde Edinburgh. Everything's homemade here: steak-and-Guinness pie (£4.95); broc-and-cheese pasta (£3.50); vegetarian Bolognese (£3.50); and the usual run of baked potatoes (£3 to £3.50) and baguettes. Students get a discount.

The Grassmarket, Edinburgh. Tel: 0131/225 4851. Open: daily 11am–6:30pm for food; until 9pm during festival season. Bar hours: daily 11am–1am. From Waverley Station on Princes Street, cross the Waverley Bridge and follow Cockburn Street. Then take a right on High Street. Turn left onto George IV Bridge, and then turn right onto Victoria Street. Follow Victoria Street to Grassmarket; it's on your right.

Netherbow Café

This cute stone-walled eatery has flowered tablecloths, potted sunflowers, and an outdoor patio. The friendly staff lets you linger. Breakfast is supreme: eggs, bacon, beans, tomatoes, toast, and coffee/tea only £2.75. Sandwiches are £2 to £4; thick, filling soups £1; bread extra. Quiches, burgers, veggie options are available as well. Students get a 10% discount.

43 High St., Edinburgh. Tel: 0131/556 9579. Open: Mon–Sat 9:30am–4:30pm; later on performance nights. In August, open until 10pm. Cash only. From Waverley Station on Princes Street, cross the Waverley Bridge and follow Cockburn Street to High Street. Turn right; it's on your right, next door to John Knox House.

Pierre Victoire

A friendly waitstaff serves up tasty cuisine in the very first branch of this successful French chain offering good values. Wine racks, wooden floors, and French accents create an unchainlike atmosphere. The three-course lunch (£4.90) always includes a vegetarian option. Menu rotates daily but may include game casserole or lemon chicken. Arrive early before they run out of fudge cake.

10 Victoria St., Edinburgh. Tel: 0131/225 1721. Open: Mon–Sat noon–3pm and 6–11pm. Reservations accepted. Credit cards: VA, MC, EC, Access, Switch. From Waverley Station on Princes Street, cross the Waverley Bridge, turn onto Cockburn Street, and take a right on High Street. Turn left onto George IV Bridge, and then right onto Victoria Street. It's on the right.

Grocery Store: Marks and Spencer, Princes Street. Open: Mon–Wed 9am–5:30pm; Thurs 9am–8pm; Fri 9am–7pm; Sat 8:30am–6pm; Sun noon–5pm.

Experiences

Edinburgh Castle, Scotland's most touristed spot, is well worth the admission to catch a glimpse of the Scottish Crown Jewels uncovered by Sir Walter Scott as well as the 11th-century chapel. The Castle Esplanade is especially packed during festival time in August, when the Military Tattoo takes place. Nightly performances by military bands and a fireworks display add to the incredible spectacle.

The Royal Mile, forming the backbone of the Old Town, is littered with sights. **The High Kirk of St. Giles,** Edinburgh's main church, is a requisite stop for history students and most visitors. The spire (dating from 1495) and the Thistle Chapel are especially beautiful. On the Lawnmarket stretch of the Royal Mile sits Lady Stairs House, home of **The Writer's Museum,** housing bits and bobs owned by Robert Louis Stevenson, Walter Scott, and Robert Burns. At the far end of the Royal Mile on Canongate is a cluster of museums: the **People's Museum;** the **Museum of Childhood;** and **Huntly House,** with local history exhibits and a headache-inducing collection of cutlery and tableware.

In the other direction are three museums, possibly Scotland's most impressive: the **National Gallery,** with its collection of old masters (Rembrandt, Raphael, Titian, Rubens); the **Scottish National Gallery of Modern Art** (Matisse, Monet, Picasso); and the **National Portrait Gallery** with pictures mostly of famous Scotsmen and Scotswomen. Those interested in the Protestant Reformation won't want to miss **John Knox House,** the home of Scotland's religious pioneer. His efforts resulted in the conversion of St. Giles into a Protestant house of worship.

A 45-minute walk up **Arthur's Seat** leads you in the other direction through **Holyrood Park** toward Holyrood Palace. The lookout over the Firth of Forth is spectacular, as is the view of the palace: It's well worth the hike.

Edinburgh is crammed with pubs, clubs, and lots of live music. The best thing to do is get a copy of *The List,* which covers goings-on by category. Victoria Street and the Grassmarket are popular stomping grounds.

A few words on the **Festival:** Held during the second half of August and the beginning of September, it's the world's largest arts festival. It's actually a bunch of different festivals running concurrently, including the Fringe (theater of all sorts); Jazz; Film; Edinburgh International Festival (classical concerts and drama); Book (every other year); the Military Tattoo; and a conglomeration of street players, jugglers, mimes, and every other kind of exhibition imaginable. For freebies, hang around the Mound by the Royal Mile. Beware of ticket scalpers during this especially busy time of year.

Edinburgh Castle. Castle Hill, Edinburgh. Tel: 0131/668 8800. Open: Apr–Sept: daily 9:30am–6pm. Oct–Mar: daily 9:30am–5pm. Admission: adults £5.50; children £1.50; senior citizens £3.50.

High Kirk of St. Giles. High Street, Royal Mile, Edinburgh. Tel 0131/225 9442. Open: summer: daily 9am–7pm. Winter: daily 9am–5pm. Donations requested.

The Writers Museum. 477 Lawnmarket, Edinburgh. Tel: 0131/529 4901. Open: Apr–Sept: Mon–Sat 10am–6pm. Oct–May: Mon–Sat 10am–5pm. Admission: free.

The People's Story Museum, The Museum of Childhood, and **Huntly House.** Royal Mile, Edinburgh. Tel: 0131/225 2424. All open: Mon–Sat 10am–6pm. Admission: free.

National Gallery of Scotland. The Mound, Edinburgh. Tel: 0131/556 8921. Open: Mon–Sat 10am–5pm; Sun 2–5pm. Admission: free.

Scottish National Gallery of Modern Art. Belford Road, Edinburgh. Tel: 0131/556 8921. Open: Mon–Sat 10am–5pm; Sun 2–5pm. Admission: free.

Scottish National Portrait Gallery. 1 Queen St., Edinburgh. Tel: 0131/556 8921. Open: Mon–Sat 10am–5pm; Sun 2–5pm. Admission: free.

John Knox House. 43/45 High St., Edinburgh. Tel: 0131/556 9579. Open: Mon–Sat 10am–4:30pm. Admission: adults £1.30; concessions £1; children 75p.

Edinburgh Festival Fringe Box Office. 180 High St., Edinburgh. Tel: 0131/226 5257 or 0131/226 5259.

Edinburgh International Festival Box Office. 21 Market St., Edinburgh. Tel: 0131/226 4001.

The Basics

Tourist Office: Edinburgh Tourist Board. Waverley Market, 3 Princes St. Tel: 0131/557 1700. Open: Apr: Mon–Sat 9am–6pm; Sun 11am–6pm. May–June: Mon–Sat 9am–7pm; Sun 11am–7pm. July–Aug: Mon–Sat 9am–8pm; Sun 10am–8pm. Sept: Mon–Sat 9am–7pm; Sun 11am–7pm. Oct: Mon–Sat 9am–6pm; Sun 11am–6pm; Nov–Mar: Mon–Sat 9am–6pm. **From Bruntsfield hostel:** Turn left on Bruntsfield Crescent and then right onto Bruntsfield Place. Follow it up Leven Street, Home Street, Earl Grey Street, and turn right on Bread Street. Cross Lady Lawson Street to Westport, Grassmarket through to George IV Bridge. Turn right on High Street, left on Cockburn Street, and cross the Waverley Bridge. At Princes Street, turn left. Tourist office is on your left; a 20-minute walk. **From Eglinton hostel:** Turn left onto Eglinton Crescent, right on Palmerston Place, and left to Shandwick Place. Follow Shandwick Place to Princes Street. Walk down Princes Street; just before the train station, it'll be on your right; a 15-minute walk.

Post Office: St. James's Centre. Tel: 0131/556 0478. Open: Mon–Fri 9am–5:30pm; Sat 9am–7pm. **From Bruntsfield hostel:** Turn left on Bruntsfield Crescent and then right onto Bruntsfield Place. Follow it up Leven Street, Home Street, Earl Grey Street, and turn right on Bread Street. Cross Lady Lawson Street to Westport, Grassmarket through to George IV Bridge. Turn right on High Street, left on Cockburn Street, and cross the Waverley Bridge. At Princes Street, turn right, then left onto Leith Street. The entrance to St. James's Centre is on your right. **From Eglinton:** Turn left onto Eglinton Crescent, right on Palmerston Place, and left to Shandwick Place. Follow Shandwick Place to Princes Street. Walk down Princes Street; two blocks past the train station, you'll reach Waterloo Place. Cross the road and turn left onto Leith Street. The entrance to St. James's Centre is on your left.

Currency Exchange: American Express. 139 Princes St., Edinburgh. Tel: 0131/225 7881. Open: Mon–Fri 9am–5:30pm; Sat 9am–4:30pm. Thomas Cook. 79a Princes St., Edinburgh. Tel: 0131/220 4039. Open: Mon–Sat 9am–5:30pm (Thurs 10am opening). Also: Thomas Cook. Waverley Steps (outside train station), Edinburgh. Tel: 0131/557 0905. Open: Mon–Sat 9am–9pm; Sun 10am–8pm.

Bike Rental: Central Cycle Hire. Lochrin Place, Edinburgh. Tel: 0131/228 6333. Full-day rental £10–£15.

Telephone Code: 0131.

Getting There: By **train**, Edinburgh is at the end of a main line service from **London, York, Newcastle, Glasgow,** and **Inverness** and is easily reachable from any of these cities. Service is frequent. For schedule information, call 0131/556 2451. **Coach** service is mainly via National Express/Scottish Citylink, which services **Edinburgh, Glasgow, Inverness,** and most major cities in Britain. For exact timetables, call 0990/505050. Traveline goes to **Aberdeen** and **Aviemore** in Scotland, **Newcastle,** and some other English cities. Call 0131/225 3858. If you're coming by **car**, from points south Edinburgh is reachable by the M6 from **Manchester** area; switch to the A702 in Abington; the route goes directly into Edinburgh. From **London,** the best route to take is the M1/A1 motorway going through Newcastle. From **Glasgow,** it's a straight zip across on the M8.

What's Next

Heading north from Edinburgh, there are a number of possible stops on the Edinburgh-Inverness road/rail line. Those on the tourist trail probably want to head straight for **Inverness,** where there's a decent hostel only a bus ride away from the famous, frightening Loch Ness. The city itself is pleasant enough; it's the gateway to the far north and only a train ride away from John O'Groats and the ferries out to the Orkney Islands. Otherwise, go west: The Kyle of Lochalsh leads you out to the misty island of **Skye** (222 miles northwest) famous for its red-and-black Cuilin Hills, fairy tales, and magnificent landscapes.

A straight car, train, or bus ride will take you to **Glasgow,** 46 miles away. It's less touristed and less expensive than Edinburgh but offers some excellent museums, first-class shopping, and a university. Loads of trendy restaurants, arts center, and pubs make this a lively, friendly city with less of the in-your-face tourism of Edinburgh.

STIRLING

Much of Scotland's history was lived out here. Agricola, the governor of the Roman province of Britain, decided to base his headquarters in Stirling in the first century. The castle that overlooks the city is evidence of the importance Stirling had in later years, given its strategic location at the very crossroads of Scotland. Many of the city's historic buildings are still intact, and some (especially the one housing the Youth Hostel) are interesting to explore.

Stirling's main attraction these days, however, is its excellent road and rail links to the rest of the country. The city is 36 miles up the Firth of Forth from Edinburgh, 26 miles to the east of Glasgow via a short hop on the Edinburgh-Inverness rail line. The town itself is rather lackluster. A modern shopping center lies in the middle of the city, and urban decay is unfortunately evident here. Other attractions include modern Stirling University, with its country-club campus and excellent arts center, the must-see Wallace Monument, and the quaint town Bridge of Allan.

As the home base for the Scottish Youth Hostels Association (SYHA), the hostel rules! A renovated former church situated on an ancient preaching green, the hostel itself is a local landmark just down the Castle hill and across from the old tollbooth (now an Indian restaurant). Castle-goers and Scottish historians won't want to miss Stirling. Others have been warned.

✸ Stirling Youth Hostel

St. John Street
Stirling FK8 1DU
Tel: 01786/473442. Fax: 01786/445715.

The Stirling Youth Hostel, in a listed building, is the jewel in the crown of the SYHA. Boasting an impressive history, it offers all the comforts not usually associated with hostels: sparkling bedrooms with private bathrooms, a shiny new dining room dishing up excellent meals, and a splendid view of King's Park and the Stirling Golf Course below. The hostel was renovated from its former incarnation as a church built by Reverend Ebenezer Erskine in 1740, when he broke away from the Church of Scotland (his tomb is in the front yard). Vandals set the place on fire in the 1980s, but the hosteling association rescued it from ruin.

In the busy summer, those unlucky enough not to secure a bed in the main luxury lodgings might be placed in the annex on Union Street, just up from the railway station and conveniently close to Tesco's. During the academic year, these apartments serve as student housing and resemble rental flats with full daytime access, a key to the front door and to the bedroom, and a communal kitchen. Both lodgings are booked through the main hostel building on St. John Street, and both receive high praise on the Scottish hosteling grapevine.

Walk straight out of the station up to Murray Place, the main street. Turn left onto Murray Place, then take a sharp right onto King Street. Walk about one block and bear left on Spittal Street, which turns into St. John Street. The hostel is on your left after about three blocks (slightly uphill); a 10-minute walk from the station.

Turn right out of the station, then bear left on the street in front of the railway station and left onto Murray Place. Follow directions from the train, given above.

From the A9, follow signs to Stirling. Head into the town center and continue past the first roundabout, passing the bus and railway stations. Turn left onto Station Road, then left onto Murray Place. Take the first right onto King Street, bearing left onto Spittal Street, which becomes St. John Street. The hostel is on your left.

Open year-round. IBN and FABA.

Reception open 7am–11:15am. Curfew 2am.

128 beds. 2-, 4-, and 5-bed rooms; all en suite with keys for daytime access.

£ Members: adults £10.45; under 18 £9. Prices include continental breakfast.

Meal service throughout the year. Self-catering kitchen facilities. Breakfast: 7:30–9am. Continental breakfast included; £1 extra for cooked breakfast. Lunch: Available for groups only. Dinner: 6–7pm.

Lockers; all rooms are locked.

Washers and dryers.

P Ample and free of charge.

Shop at hostel sells candy and canned goods.

TV room.

In reception area and TV lounge.

Wheelchair accessible.

See "Currency Exchange" under "The Basics" in Stirling.

Bike shed; conference room with overhead projector.

Services

Cheap Eats Nearby

Archy's Diner

A cheerful young waitstaff serves up Tex-Mex food from a little perch in the back of this friendly sombrero-and-cactus adorned restaurant. Fajitas (£6 to £8) are the best-sellers, but burgers (£3 to £4) and enchiladas (£5 to £6) are a bit cheaper and the portions enormous.

17 Barnton St., Stirling. Tel: 01786/452423. Open: Mon–Sat noon–3pm and 6–10pm; Sun 6–9pm. Reservations accepted Fri–Sat. Credit cards: AE, MC, VA, EC, Switch, Access. From the hostel, walk down St. John as it becomes Spittal Street and turn left onto Friars Street. Turn left onto Barnton Street and it's two blocks up on your left; a 10-minute walk.

Barnton Bar & Bistro

Load up on your favorite poisons in this popular watering hole, formerly the site of the local chemist. The Victorian decor includes etchings on the wall, a fancy old bar, and a dark little dining area. Live music on summer weekends. Burgers cost £3 to £4. Creative sandwiches are £2 to £3.50; finger-lickin' french toast £2.65.

3 ¹/₂ Barnton St., Stirling. Tel: 01786/461698. July–Sept: Mon–Sat 10:30am–8pm; Sun noon–8pm. Oct–June: Mon–Sat 10:30am–5pm; Sun noon–6:30pm. Bar open until midnight.

Grocery Store: Tesco. Wallace Street, Stirling. Open: Mon–Wed 8am–8pm; Thurs–Fri 8am–9pm; Sat 8am–8pm; Sun 9am–6pm.

Experiences

Mary, Queen of Scots, spent her ill-fated formative years in Stirling. Robert the Bruce defended the city. And James II murdered the earl of Douglas here and tossed his body out a window. Why not pop in yourself? **Stirling Castle** is the city's main attraction, and you can either huff and puff your way up or take a bus here to relive some of Scotland's history.

Across the Stirling Old Bridge and two miles out of town, **Stirling University** offers more contemporary delights, even though it has the highest suicide rate of any university town in the United Kingdom. The buildings are said to be modeled after a Swedish prison, but the grounds are pleasant, with lots of green space, sparkling artificial lakes, and a rolling golf course. The **MacRobert Centre** here is the heart of the arts scene in Stirling and hosts traveling shows as well as local and student artists. The two theaters (one experimental, one more traditional) provide year-round drama and live music. On your way back into Stirling, you can stop at the **Wallace Monument,** one of Stirling's must-see attractions. Holograms and a virtual-reality exhibition space bring history to computer-age travelers, and even locals say it's worth a visit.

Back in town, the **Albert Halls** hosts antique, record, and crafts fairs on selected weekends, as well as *ceildhs* (traditional Scottish dances with pipers and accordionists) twice a week in summer. For those on bikes, there's a good deal to see around Glen Devon, which is in Ochil Hills, and cyclists wind their way around Stirling. Twice a week during summer, you can catch the pipe bands that tune up in front of the hostel and then march up to the castle, where they play alongside traditional Highland dancers. Then they march back down to the hostel playing their pipes, providing good, free entertainment.

Stirling Castle. Upper Castle Hill, Stirling. Tel: 01786/450000. Open: Apr–Sept: daily 9:30am–6pm. Oct–Mar: daily 9:30am–5pm. Admission: adults £3.50; children £1; senior citizens £2.

MacRobert Arts Centre. University of Stirling, Stirling. Box office tel: 01786/461081. Box office open: Mon–Sat 11am–6pm and up to performance times. Films: adults £3.50; students and senior citizens £2.50.

National Wallace Monument. Abbey Craig, Causewayhead, Stirling. Tel: 01786/ 472140. Open: June and Sept: daily 10am–6pm. July–Aug: daily 9:30am–6:30pm. Oct and Mar–May: daily 10am–5pm. Nov and Feb: Sat–Sun 10am–4pm. Admission: adults £2.50; children and senior citizens £1.50.

The Albert Halls. Dumbarton Road, Stirling. Tel: 01786/473544. Admission: adults £5; students and senior citizens £3.50. Call for performance times.

The Basics

Tourist Office: Stirling T.I.C. 41 Dumbarton Rd., Stirling. Tel: 01786/475019. Open: Apr–May: Mon–Sat 9am–5pm. June: Mon–Sat 9am–6pm; Sun 10am–4pm. July–Aug: Mon–Sat 9am–7:30pm; Sun 9:30am–6:30pm. Sept: Mon–Sat 9am–7pm; Sun 10am–5pm. Oct–Mar: Mon–Sat 9am–5pm; Sun 10am–6pm. Currency exchange available. From the hostel, turn right onto St. John Street, and continue down Spittal Street. Turn right on Corn Exchange Road and then left onto Dumbarton Road. It's on your right; a 10-minute walk.

Post Office: Stirling Post Office. 84/86 Murray Place, Stirling. Tel: 01786/465392. Open: Mon–Fri 9am–5:30pm; Sat 9am–12:30pm. From the hostel, turn right onto St. John Street, continue down Spittal Street, and then turn left onto King Street. Bear right onto Friars Street, toward Murray Place. It's across the street.

Currency Exchange: Thomas Cook. 11/13 Murray Place, Stirling. Tel: 01786/ 464077. Open: Mon–Sat 9am–5:30pm (Thurs 10am opening).

Telephone Code: 01786.

Bike Rental: New Heights Cycle Hire. 26 Barnton St., Stirling. Tel: 01786/450809. Half day £6; full day £10.

Getting There: By **train**, Stirling is about a 40-minute ride from **Edinburgh** and **Glasgow** on the main line up to Inverness. For information, call 01786/464754. By **bus**, it's slightly longer. Midland Bluebird goes to **Glasgow** and **Edinburgh.** For information, call 01324/613777. Scottish Citylink covers all the rest of the connections, from eastern **Scotland (Perth, Aviemore)** to the west (**Fort William, Oban**). For information, call 0990/505050. By **car,** Stirling is an easy ride up the A80 M80 from **Glasgow** and the A90/M9 from **Edinburgh,** as well as the A9 from **Perth.**

What's Next

Stirling is just about equidistant (around 30 miles) from both **Glasgow** and **Edinburgh.** Glasgow offers postindustrial busy city life, while Edinburgh offers Scottish tradition. Peaceful, lakeside grandeur in the castlelike mansion of Loch Lomond is straight across to the west (33 miles). If you're headed north, **Perth** is quick hop en route to the Scottish Highlands.

PERTH

Perth is one of those towns that has the unfortunate fate of being near a lot of other interesting places. About 20 miles north sit the Grampian and the Cairngorn mountains, only 40 miles south are the bright lights of Edinburgh, and to the east lies the quaint seaside university town of St. Andrews. The town isn't really close enough to Edinburgh to be very exciting, yet it's not far enough north to be part of the misty, mysterious Highlands. Perth is right on the main Edinburgh-Inverness rail line, making it a good transport hub en route to Aviemore and Inverness to the north as well as Stirling and Glasgow to the south.

Just about every chain store in Britain is crammed into a few gridlike streets surrounding the main shopping center in town. Situated at the juncture of three rivers (the Tay, Earn, and Almond), Perth offers some nice riverside walks, all within 10 to 20 minutes from the hostel. Some formal gardens, a nice old church, a local art museum, a military museum, and a working watermill provide you with a day's worth of activities—but not too much more. At the end of May, the Perth Festival livens up the town a wee bit, offering (expensive) live music, drama, and opera during its two-week run.

The Youth Hostel is cut straight from the Old Scottish Hostel cloth. It's about a 15- to 20-minute uphill walk from town. The big, burly warden will trade war stories with any interested travelers.

Perth Youth Hostel

Glasgow Road
Perth PH2 0NS
Tel: 01738/623658.

Wake up to the cheerful (or annoying, depending on your mood) sound of bagpipes playing over the P.A. system in this rambling late 19th-century mansion. In a listed building, the hostel was built as the private home of the minister of St. John's Kirk. Hardly an ascetic monk, the minister made sure the house was quite grand. There are interesting ceiling moldings, nice picture windows with views of Perth, and lawns and gardens. A superstitious man, the minister planted ewe and holly trees in his gardens to ward off evil spirits and placed a false window on one side of the building as protection from unwelcome visitors.

The 10- and 12-bed dormitories and hall showers bespeak more of utilitarian accommodations than gracious manor life. The beds are no better than the usual saggy-spring variety. If you hit him in the right mood, warden Jim can cheer up sagging spirits with a few off-color jokes. Anything from Queen's "Bohemian Rhapsody" to Mozart's *Fifth Symphony* will blast as you eat your Rice Krispies in the self-catering kitchen.

Services

Go down Leonard Street, which is directly in front of the station. When you reach County Place, turn left and follow the road as it turns into York Place and then Glasgow Road. Follow Glasgow Road for about 5 minutes, and when you see the sign outside the Lovat Hotel, turn right. The hostel is at the end of the drive; a 15-minute walk.

The hostel is a 15-minute walk from the coach station. Cross Leonard Street and turn left onto Caledonian Road, then left again at York Place, which turns into Glasgow Road. Follow Glasgow Road for about 5 minutes, and when you see the sign outside the Lovat Hotel, turn right. The hostel is at the end of the drive.

From **Edinburgh,** exit the A9 at Junction 11. This brings you to Glasgow Road. Follow the road for 2 miles, and the hostel will come up on your left. From **Inverness and other points north,** exit the A9 at Junction 11, which leads you to Glasgow Road. Follow the road for 2 miles and the hostel will come up on your left.

▦ Feb 24–Oct 30 open full time. Nov–Feb 24 open Fri–Sat only. Open New Year's week. FABA.

◷ Reception open 7am–11:30pm. Curfew 11:30pm.

🛏 64 beds. 4-, 6-, 8-, 10-, and 12-bed rooms. Family rooms with daytime access available.

£ Members: adults £6.95; under 18 £5.85.

🍴 No meals served. Self-catering kitchen facilities.

🧳 Coin-operated lockers in entrance hall.

⊙ Coin-operated washers, dryers, and drying room.

P Ample and free of charge.

🗄 Shop at hostel sells candy and canned goods.

🛋 TV room and sitting room.

📺 In TV room only.

♿ Not wheelchair accessible.

💱 See "Currency Exchange" under "The Basics" in Perth.

▲ Bike shed; SYHA discount at local swimming pool and local shops.

Cheap Eats Nearby

La Bamba

Well-priced Mexican food is served in a sparklingly clean, sparsely furnished (three tables) green storefront right on High Street. Mexican flags and sombreros hang from the ceiling in front of the kitchen, where you can watch the chefs slap together quesadillas (£1.80 to £3), burritos (£2.70 to £3.70), and tacos (£1.90 to £2.20). Corona and Budweiser are £1.50; takeout available.

254 High St., Perth. Tel: 01738/639680. Open: Sun–Thurs 4–11pm; Fri–Sat 4pm–1am. Cash only. From the hostel, about a 20-minute walk: turn left on Glasgow Road and follow it through York Place and County Place. Turn left on South Methven Street, then take the first right onto High Street. It's on your right after one block.

Littlejohn's

English tearoom meets 1950s-style chain restaurant in this eatery with a laid-back atmosphere. A huge teapot sits in the back, and a papier-mâché waiter lurks near the front, ready to serve up pizzas (£3 to £4), sandwiches (£3 to £5), and a variety of Mexican dishes (£4 to £6). Vegetarian specials are offered.

24 St. John's St., Perth. Tel: 01738/639888. Open: Mon–Sat 10am–11pm; Sun noon–11pm. Credit cards: VA, MC, EC, Access. From the hostel, a 20-minute walk. Turn left onto Glasgow Road. Follow it through to York Place, County Place, and South Street. Turn left onto St. John's Place and it's just up on your right.

Grocery Store: Spar, Glasgow Road. Open: Mon–Sat 6:30am–10pm; Sun 7:30am–10pm. It's near the hostel and very basic. Marks and Spencer, High Street. Open: Mon–Wed 9:30am–5:30pm; Thurs 9am–7pm; Fri 9am–6pm; Sat 8:30am–6pm.

Experiences

Probably the most famous attraction in Perthshire is the home of the earls of Mansfield, also called Scone Palace, but most locals advise against paying the £6 admission. Perth does have a good deal of other activities that won't break your budget. The **Black Watch Regimental Museum,** housed in the Balhousie Castle, is worth the trip just to hear the kilt-clad ex-soldiers who often work here in their off-season. The museum details the 250-year history of the Black Watch Regiment with displays of armor, paintings, and tartans.

From the museum, you can take a walk through the floral gardens of the North Inch along the River Tay; the gardens make a nice picnic spot and Frisbee-tossing venue. The gardens take you to another freebie: the **Perth Museum and Art Gallery,** which displays a decent variety of rotating exhibitions from glass blowing to watercolors to local arts and crafts.

Perth has a couple of formal gardens, but for wider vistas and lusher foliage take a half-day walk across the River Tay at Queen's Bridge to Kinnoull Hill Woodland Park. It's a welcome respite from modern Perth and offers good views of north and south Perthshire. Farther afield is the seaside university town of **St. Andrews,** an excellent day trip (a 1¹/₂-hour bus ride; change at Dundee). Full of crumbling old buildings facing the Firth of Tay, it's best visited on Sunday in spring, when students strut about in their red-and-yellow robes and golfers tote their clubs to the many courses in the region.

Black Watch Regimental Museum. Balhousie Castle, Perth. Tel: 01738/621281. Open: May–Sept: Mon–Sat 10am–4:30pm; Oct–Apr: Mon–Fri 10am–3:30pm. Admission: free.

Perth Museum and Art Gallery. George Street, Perth. Tel: 01738/632488. Open: Mon–Sat 10am–5pm. Admission: free.

St. Andrews. For information contact St. Andrews Tourist Information Centre. 70 Market St., St. Andrews. Tel: 01334/72021. Open: Apr–May: Mon–Fri 9:30am–5pm; Sat 11am–5pm; Sun 2–5pm. June and Sept: Mon–Sat 9:30am–6pm; Sun 11am–5pm. July–Aug: Mon–Sat 9:30am–7pm; Sun 11am–5pm. Oct–Mar: Mon–Fri 9:30am–5pm; Sat 11am–5pm.

The Basics

Tourist Office: Perth Tourist Information Centre, 45 High St. Tel: 01738/638353. Open: Apr 10–June 25: Mon–Sat 9am–6pm; Sun noon–6pm; June 26–Sept 10: Mon–Sat 9am–8pm; Sun noon–6pm; Sept 11–Oct 29: Mon–Sat 9am–6pm; Sun noon–6pm; Oct 30–Apr 9: Mon–Sat 9am–5pm. From the hostel, turn left onto Glasgow Road and follow it through York Place and County Place. Turn left on Scott Street and then right on High Street. The office is past the Perth Theatre, a block up on your left.

Post Office: 109 South St. Tel: 01738/637424. Open: Mon–Fri 9am–5:30pm; Sat 9am–12:30pm.

Currency Exchange: Thomas Cook, 65 High St. Tel: 01738/635279. Open: Mon–Sat 9am–5:30pm (Thurs 10am opening). Also at the Post Office, 109 South St. Open: Mon–Fri 9am–5:30pm; Sat 9am–12:30pm.

Telephone Code: 01738.

Bike Rental: Climb and Axe, 71 South Methven St. Tel: 01738/636993. Mountain bikes £10 per day.

Getting There: By **train,** Perth is easily reached by the main line from Edinburgh-Inverness line, which has frequent service to Perth. For information, call 01738/37117 or 01738/46233. Scottish Citylink **coaches** come in regularly from

Edinburgh, Glasgow, Stirling, and **Inverness.** For schedule information, call the station at 017380/626848 or the national line at 0990/505050. By **car,** Perth is an easy hop up the M90 from **Edinburgh** and down the same A9 from **Inverness.** Connections to **Glasgow** are easy via the A9, switching to the M9 and onto the M80/A80 motorway.

What's Next

Inverness and the Highlands lie a bit farther along the road, but are easily reachable by train. If you're going south from Perth, **Stirling** and **Edinburgh** are logical stops for those in search of city life, universities, and the inevitable castles.

Inverness & the Far North

Rugged mountains, lonely glens, and the most famous loch in the country lie in Northern Scotland. The now tranquil Highlands have witnessed centuries of fierce clan battles and English invasions. When the English throne decided it needed meat for its hungry armies in the late 1700s, the monarch enacted the hideous Highland Clearances and summarily expelled Highland farm folk from their land. The English ruthlessly rounded up clansmen and burned their small stone cottages to the ground. Their captors shipped the Scotsmen off on rickety, scurvy-infested ships bound for North America in order to allow sheep to roam wild before being cut up and fed to the bloated ranks of the British army. Sheep still dot the desolate landscape.

This merciless display of English might has left an indelible mark on the region: Bagpipers bellow out laments of these tragic times, and Highlanders still consider themselves a breed apart from the rest of their countrymen. Nowadays, the Highlands remain a region of intrigue and mystery.

The industrial city of Inverness is the administrative center of the Highlands. A river snakes through the city, which serves as an excellent base for visits to nearby Loch Ness, home of the legendary monster. The hostel is far from Scotland's finest but offers a place to drop your pack before heading out to the few museums and riverside nooks.

About 60 miles west lies the peppy little port town of Ullapool, where trawlers haul in the seafood for which Scotland is famous. It offers a surprisingly active nightlife in its 10 pubs—a thankful homecoming for those braving the rugged coastal walks by day. The hostel, right on the waterfront, is maintained in ship-shape condition.

If you take the slippery, rocky footpath up the coast, you'll reach the tiny town of Achiltibuie, home to nothing more than the Achininvet hostel in a simple crofter's cottage and some spectacular coastal landscape. The hostel here is one of Scotland's most remote: It's a half-mile walk from the single-track road that winds through the lochs north of Ullapool.

Heading back east toward some semblance of civilization, the Carbisdale Castle Youth Hostel towers over the tiny village of Culrain, 20 miles north of Inverness on the Kyle of Sutherland. Once a wealthy dowager's palatial home, this is reckoned to be one of Scotland's most spectacular hostels. It boasts an art collection, monster-size sitting rooms, and ghostly apparitions, and it's conveniently situated a quarter of a mile from the train stop.

The north of Scotland provides a healthy challenge for those on public transport, but it's by no means impossible. The towns here are reachable via local buses and postbuses, but allow lots of extra time, since service is often limited. Those hoping to thumb their way through here should be prepared for long roadside waits: This is the most thinly populated region in Scotland, and there's very little highway action. Trains only go directly north from Inverness, so Carbisdale Castle is the only major hostel near a station. Drivers should hone their skills before braving the roads. They're winding, dangerous, and mostly single track (with sections for passing). Cars tend to creep cautiously down them. The reward for the brave hearted, however, is some of the most unspoiled, dramatic landscape in the country: craggy promontories hanging over midnight-blue waters, sheep scattered across barren hills and byways, and the occasional stone cottage.

INVERNESS

Inverness suffers from many of the same woes that befall teenage boys: It's awkward, overgrown, and in some places pretty greasy. The industrial and administrative capital of northern Scotland, the city is trying hard to outgrow its image as the unattractive kid brother of Scotland's more popular cities and countryside tourist spots.

The inevitable results of modernization are in full force: McDonald's and Burger King rank among the busiest places on the High Street. Many people pass through here for only a day or two on their way to the Western Isles or northern Scotland and miss out on some little-known treasures. While industrial parks are scattered along the highway as you come into the city and the Loch Ness tourist traps continue to heave with camera-toting visitors, inside Inverness beats the heart of a sophisticated, eclectic, and relatively amiable metropolis. A rushing river with swaying suspension bridges and leafy walking paths, a handful of first-rate art galleries and museums, a good local theater, cathedrals, and even a castle provide at least a couple of days' amusements.

This is the largest city in northern Scotland, and if you're moving farther north or into the lochs, this is the place to get money and provisions to last you through long stays in more remote locales. Most hostelers use the city as a gateway to the Highlands and Western Isles. The city continues on its way nonetheless, rather oblivious to the transient Ness-sters.

Inverness Youth Hostel

1 Old Edinburgh Rd.
Inverness
Inverness-shire IV2 3HFTel: 01463/231771.

From its photo in the SYHA directory, the red-and-white Inverness Youth Hostel looks like a grand mansion. Once you're inside, however, the word *barracks* will spring to mind. Run-down halls and creepy bedrooms lurk behind the cheerful tartan entrance hall. Downstairs, an ample, if dank, self-catering kitchen leads into an antiseptic dining room. If you look up from the lived-in decor, however, you'll notice attractive, commanding views of the gardens and the city beyond.

The house may not be in the shape it once was, but it does have charm. It was built in 1843 by Joseph Mitchell, the engineer who supervised and built the railway lines in Scotland last century. He carved out enough room for a wee walled garden, now outfitted with picnic tables. From there, you can look over the river Ness toward the Caledonian canal. The hostel has the usual sliced-and-diced interior with a maze of stairways that lead up to the dormitories and a security code to keep out intruders. On the other hand, the price is hard to beat—and who hangs out inside, anyway?

🚆 Exit the station, turn left, and walk down Academy Street to Marks and Spencer. Turn right onto Inglis Street, then bear left down High Street. When you reach McDonald's, turn left up Castle Street. The hostel is three blocks past the castle on your left at the corner of Old Edinburgh Road; a 10-minute walk.

🚌 Follow directions from the train station, given above.

🚗 From all roads into Inverness, follow signs for the city center and then tourist information center. When you reach McDonald's, turn right up Castle Street and go through the first set of traffic lights. The hostel is on the first road to the left; it's on the corner. Look for the sign.

🎫 Open year-round. IBN and FABA.

🕐 Reception open 7am–11:30pm. Curfew 2am.

🛏 126 beds. 6-, 8-, 10-, 12-, 16-, 18-, and 20-bed rooms.

£ Members: adults £7.80; under 18 £6.40.

🍴 No meals served. Self-catering kitchen facilities.

💼 Coin-operated lockers.

🔘 Washers, dryers, and drying room.

P Limited and free of charge.

🗄 Shop at hostel sells candy and canned goods.

🛋 TV lounge; one common room.

☎ In common room only.

♿ Not wheelchair accessible.

💱 See "Currency Exchange" under "The Basics" in Inverness.

🔺 Bike shed.

Cheap Eats Nearby

The Copper Kettle
This slightly artificial country kitchen has little boughs of holly hanging in welcome. The price is right and the portions are good. All main dishes are served with chips and salad. Dish of the day is £3; steak pie £3.85; burgers £1.50 to £2.50; sandwiches £1.70 to £2.75.

50 Baron Taylor St., Inverness. Tel: 01463/233307. Open: Mon–Sat 10am–10pm. Cash only. From the hostel, turn right down Castle Street, then left onto High Street and left again onto Mealmarket Close. The restaurant is at the end of the street, on the corner of Baron Taylor Street. It's upstairs.

The River Café & Restaurant
This elegant lunch spot overlooking the River Ness has New Age music and a natural therapy center upstairs. About 60% of the menu is thoughtfully prepared vegetarian and vegan dishes. A bulletin board lists local goings-on. Dishes include pastas (£4 to £5); omelets (£3 to £4); baguette sandwiches (£2.75 to £3).

10 Bank St., Inverness. Tel: 01463/714884. Open: Jan–Oct: Mon–Sat 10am–10pm. Nov–Dec: Mon–Sat 10am–8pm. Credit cards: VA, MC, EC, Access. From the hostel, a 10-minute walk. Turn right

down Castle Street. When you reach McDonald's, turn left, and when you reach the river turn right (don't cross the bridge). It's two blocks farther on the right.

Grocery Store: Safeway. Rose Street, near the train and bus stations. Open: Mon–Wed, 8am–8pm; Thurs–Fri 8am–9pm; Sat 8am–8pm; Sun 9am–6pm.

Experiences

There's no way around it: **Loch Ness** pulls in any traveler who has made it all the way up here. Glistening and mysterious, 22-mile-long Loch Ness is a 700-foot-deep land-locked freshwater lake; it's the largest body of fresh water in Europe. Due to glaciation during the Pleistocene Age, it's a good deal deeper than the North Sea and much of the Atlantic.

As for the monster, nobody knows for sure. The legend has persisted since A.D. 565, when St. Columba reputedly fended off the briny beast as she nibbled on a villager. Two exhibitions offer holograms, video tours, and historical tableaux, but the preferred tour (if any) is the **Official Loch Ness Monster Exhibition,** 14 miles from Inverness in the village of Drumnadrochit. You can also take to your own tour around the massive lake.

The ruins of **Urquhart Castle,** one of the largest in Scotland, sits on the lochs not far from Inverness. Even the most castle-weary travelers recommend a visit here. Back up toward Inverness, there are some exceptionally pretty paths around the river Ness for walking or cycling into the nearby parks and Ness Isles.

Right along the river, just blocks from the Youth Hostel, are a few museums worth a visit. **Highland Printmakers Workshop and Gallery** on Bank Street features contemporary prints by local artists, and **Balnain House,** on the other side of the river, presents a popular interactive exhibition as well as a live music program. Just behind the tourist office is the **Inverness Museum and Art Gallery,** which has a good variety of events, from textile demonstrations to Archeological Treasures of the Highlands to Wartime Scotland as well as a permanent collection.

The Official Loch Ness Monster Exhibition. Drumnadrochit, Inverness-shire. Tel: 01456/450573. Open: daily 9am–6pm.

Urquhart Castle. Loch Ness, Inverness-shire. Tel: 01456/450255. Open: Apr–Sept: daily 9:30am–6:30pm. Oct–Mar: Mon–Sat 9:30am–4:30pm; Sun 11:30am–4:30pm.

Bus service to Loch Ness and Urquhart Castle. Inverness Traction. Tel: 01463/239292.

Highland Printmakers Workshop and Gallery. 20 Bank St., Inverness. Tel: 01463/712240. Open: Tues–Sun 10am–5pm.

Balnain House. 40 Huntly St., Inverness. Tel: 01463/715757. Open: July–Aug: daily 10am–5pm. Sept–June: Tues–Sun 10am–5pm.

Inverness Museum and Art Gallery. Castle Wynd, Inverness. Tel: 01463/237114. Open: Mon–Sat 9am–5pm. Admission: free.

The Basics

Tourist Office: Inverness T.I.C. Castle Wynd, Inverness. Tel: 01463/234353. Open: Jan–Apr: Mon–Fri 9am–5pm; Sat 10am–4pm. May–June: Mon–Sat 9am–5pm; Sun 10am–4pm. July–mid-Sept: Mon–Sat 9am–8:30pm; Sun 9:30am–6pm. Mid-Sept–Oct: Mon–Sat 9am–6pm; Sun 10am–5pm. Oct–Dec: Mon–Fri

9am–5pm; Sat 10am–4pm. From the hostel, turn right down Castle Street. When you reach McDonald's, turn left, and it's on your left; a 5-minute walk.

Post Office: Inverness Post Office. 14–16 Queensgate, Inverness. Tel: 01463/234111. Open: Mon–Fri 9am–5:30pm; Sat 9am–12:30pm. From the hostel, turn right onto Castle Street. When you reach McDonald's, turn right onto High Street. Turn left at Burger King onto Inglis Street and then the second left onto Queensgate. It's on your left.

Currency Exchange: Alba Travel (American Express Travel Service). 43 Church St., Inverness. Tel: 01463/239188. Open: Mon–Fri 9am–5:30pm; Sat 10am–2pm. Currency exchange also at T.I.C. (see "Tourist Office" under "The Basics" in Inverness) and train station.

Telephone Code: 01463.

Bike Rental: Thornton's. 23 Castle St., Inverness. Tel: 01463/222810. Open: Mon–Sat 9am–5:30pm. Rentals from £6.

Getting There: Inverness is no problem by **train;** it's the northern transportation hub in Scotland and lies at the end of the Edinburgh-Glasgow line. Service is frequent (4 per day). Catch connections north to **Thurso** and **Wick** as well as **Kyle of Lochalsh** for Skye and Western Scotland. For train information, call 01463/245039 or 01463/242124. By **coach,** Scottish Citylink covers most major routes from cities to the south. For information, call 0990/505050. For connections to the north and west (including **Culrain** and **Achininver**), call Inverness Traction at 01463/239292. For buses to **Ullapool,** call Rapsons Coaches at 01463/233371. For those coming by **car,** Inverness is at the northern end of the A9, which connects to **Perth** (via the M90 to Edinburgh) and **Stirling** (via the M80 toward Glasgow).

What's Next

Where you go from Inverness depends on what you're looking for: The lively fishing village of **Ullapool** and its waterfront hostel lie only 60 miles to the northwest. From there, you can take day trips to the Outer Hebridean isles of Harris and Lewis. Farther north on the Inverness-Thurso train line lies **Culrain,** home to the legendary Carbisdale Castle Youth Hostel—the Taj Mahal of the Scottish hostels, with art collections, gigantic sitting rooms, expansive grounds, and ghostly apparitions. To the west, it's no problem to reach the mystical and legendary island of **Skye** (100 miles away). There's direct bus service to Kyleakin from Inverness; stay there or switch buses to Broadford, 8 miles farther up the coast.

ULLAPOOL

You wouldn't expect to find much 235 miles northwest of Edinburgh and 59 miles from Inverness, but the little port town of Ullapool, on the shores of Loch Broom, bristles with commerce and activity. Its roots date from Viking times, but much of its ancient history remains a mystery because of the constantly shifting shoreline. The town began booming in 1788, when the British Fishery Society anchored here to take advantage of the abundant waters, which still provide lip-smacking fish for much of Scotland. During summer, shellfish (prawns, crabs, scallops) are brought ashore, and in winter mackerels sustain the fishermen here. There's enough seafood to go around, especially in the excellent—and inexpensive—restaurants on the waterfront.

Despite the town's small size, there are 10 pubs (many offering music) and a friendly, casual nightlife. Trips to the Outer Hebridean isles of Harris and Lewis are available from a number of enterprising sailors, and for landlubbers there's a local museum and leisure center to keep busy. The Youth Hostel, sitting right on the waterfront, has picture-postcard views of the harbor and the briny beyond.

Ullapool Youth Hostel

Shore Street
Ullapool
Ross-shire IV26 2UJ
Tel: 01854/612254.

The warden, Chrissy, runs a tight ship here. Pubs beckon, but she makes sure her visitors are tucked in by midnight. You won't mind having to turn in early when you wake up to the sight of lovely Loch Broom, and if you're lucky you may catch an early-morning seal or two frolicking in the foamy waters. The showers here are nice and warm, providing wonderful relief from a day on the water or in the hills.

Though slightly rigid when it comes to the rules, the staff is fairly knowledge-able and can point you in the right direction for whatever you choose to do. (Ask about the death-defying 12-mile "walk" to the hostel at Achiltibuie.) The hostel's main virtue is its location, right in the center of town by the pubs, the pier, and all the seafaring action. It makes a perfect base for those who want a taste of Scotland's northwest without having to rough it too much.

Services

The closest major train station is Inverness, 55 miles away. From there, take the Scottish Citylink Ullapool bus from the coach station at Inverness. The bus drops you off at the pier. From there, turn around and walk back up Shore Street, with the shops on your left. The hostel is about 300 yards up on the left, past the row of shops.

Buses come into Ullapool from Inverness and Strathpeffer. The bus drops you off at the pier. From there, follow directions from the train, given above.

The A835 from Strathpeffer and the east takes you directly into the town via the main waterfront street, Shore Street. Go past the petrol station, and when you reach the Ferry Boat Inn, the hostel is just up on your left.

Open Mar 15–Oct. Opening dates can vary, so call ahead to check. Rent-a-hostel: during closed period. FABA.

Reception open 7:30am–10:30pm. Curfew 11:45pm.

72 beds. 4-, 6-, 8-, and 10-bed rooms.

£ Members: adults £6.95; under 18 £5.85.

No meals served. Self-catering kitchen facilities.

Lockers.

Washer, dryer, and drying room.

P No parking. Limited street parking. There's a free car park about a 5-minute walk from the hostel.

Shop at hostel sells candy and canned goods and rents walking maps.

TV/smoking room; common room (off dining room).

In common room only.

Not wheelchair accessible.

See "Currency Exchange" under "The Basics" in Ullapool.

Bike shed.

Cheap Eats Nearby

The Ceilidh Place

Rather incongruous in a town whose mascot could easily be a fried fish, this whole foods cafeteria is slightly more upscale than many restaurants here, but it's worth the trip. There's a piano in the atrium; well-worn bulletin boards are stocked with local information. Sandwiches are £1.75 to £2. Main courses include nut roast (£2.25), broccoli-and-Stilton tart (£4.25), and vegetarian curry (£3.95).

14 West Argyle St., Ullapool. Tel: 01854/612103. Open: daily 9:30am–6pm. Credit cards: AE, VA, MC, Access, Switch. From the hostel, a 10-minute walk. Turn right onto Shore Street and right again onto Quay Street. Turn left on Argyle Street and it's two blocks ahead on the right.

The Ferry Boat Inn

A comfortable bar with beer steins and an intriguing collection of paper currency on the wall. Soups are £1.50; salad with roll £3.75; bar meals £3 to £5. The restaurant serves evening meals for £8 to £9. There's a good selection of beer. Live music is performed on Thursday nights.

Shore Street, Ullapool. Tel: 01854/612366. Open: daily noon–2:30pm and 6–9pm. Credit cards: VA, MC, EC, DC, Switch, Access. From the hostel, turn left and it's three doors down the street.

Grocery Store: Presto. Shore Street, Ullapool. Open: Mon–Wed 8:30am–7:30pm; Thurs–Fri 8:30am–8pm; Sat 8:30am–6pm.

Experiences

Three tour operators, all with stands on the pier, offer **boat trips** out to the uninhabited Summer Isles, where sheep are hauled out every summer for grazing. The scenery is spectacular: cliffs, crags, and barren landscapes. Puffins, porpoises, and guillemots reside on these islands, and you can also spot seals hanging out on the rocks. If it's in the stars, you may be able to witness the Northern Lights, visible only under certain atmospheric conditions in spring and autumn. Boat trips out to Lewis Island (with connections to Harris) include a bus tour to inspect the ancient Callanish Standing Stones.

Ullapool is an excellent spot for **hill walking.** The best-known route is the Rock Path to Achiltibuie; it's only for those brave souls who can endure the 12 lonely miles of cliff walks. The path takes you under the ridge of Ben More Coigach and is a slippery, craggy challenge even for pros. An easier route goes up the Ullapool Hill path toward Loch Achall; the daylong hike takes you high enough to get good views of the village and Loch Broom.

Back in town, the **Ullapool Bookshop and Museum** is something of a local landmark, displaying a motley assortment of "treasures," including a lock of Napoleon's hair, bullets from Fort Ticonderoga, and some eye-popping examples of local taxidermy. It's free, and most visitors here wander through at some point during their stay.

Islander Nature Cruises to Summer Isles. Shore Street, Ullapool. Tel: 01854/ 612200. Morning, afternoon, and evening cruises.

Summer Queen to Summer Isles. Shore Street, Ullapool. Tel: 01854/612472. Three-hour tours: adults £12; children £8; seniors and students £10. Two-hour tours: adults £6; children £4; students and seniors £5.

Caledonian MacBrayne Hebridean and Clyde Ferries. Ullapool Pier, Ullapool. Tel: 01854/612358. Day trip: adults £17.75; children £8.90. Boat and coach tour: adults £19.75; children £9.90.

Ullapool Bookshop and Museum. Quay Street, Ullapool. Tel: 01854/612356. Open: daily 9am–10pm. Admission: free.

The Basics

Tourist Office: Ullapool T.I.C. 6 Argyle St., Ullapool. Tel: 01854/612135. Open: Apr: Mon–Fri 9am–1pm and 2–5pm; Sat 10am–1pm and 2–5pm. May: Mon–Fri 9am–6pm; Sat 10am–1pm and 2–5pm; Sun 1–5pm. June: Mon–Fri 9am–6pm; Sat 10am–1pm and 2–6pm; Sun 1–6pm. July–Aug: Mon–Sat 9am–7pm; Sun 1–6pm. Sept: Mon–Fri 9am–6pm; Sat 10am–1pm and 2–6pm; Sun 1–6pm. Oct: Mon–Fri 9am–1pm and 2–5:30pm; Sat 10am–1pm and 2–5pm. Nov: Mon–Fri 1–5pm; Sat 10am–1pm and 2–4pm. From the hostel, turn right on Shore Street then right on Quay Street and right onto Argyle Street. It's on your left; a 5- to 10-minute walk.

Post Office: Ullapool Post Office. 4 West Argyle St., Ullapool. Tel: 01854/612228. Open: Mon–Fri 9am–1pm and 2–5pm; Sat 9am–12:30pm. From the hostel, turn right onto Shore Street, right on Quay Street, then left onto West Argyle Street. It's on your right.

Currency Exchange: Westering Home (local shop). 28 Argyle St., Ullapool. Tel: 01854/612374. Open: Mon–Sat 9am–10pm; Sun 9am–6pm.

Telephone Code: 01854.

Bike Rental: Ullapool Mountain Bike Hire. 11 Pulteney St., Ullapool. Tel: 01854/612260. Open: Mon–Sat 9am–6pm. Full day £10; half day £6. Deposit required.

Getting There: There's a **train** station in nearby **Garve** (30 miles away) that's on the Inverness-Kyle of Lochalsh route, but it's quicker and easier to get here by coach or car. **Coaches** come in from **Inverness** twice daily (except Sundays) via Strathpeffer to service the ferryboats going out to the outer Hebrides. For information, call Inverness Traction at 01463/239292. By **car,** it's a 59-mile drive from **Inverness**. Take the A9 north to Tore. At Tore, switch to the A835, following signs for Tarvie, Braemore, and Ullapool.

What's Next

About 25 miles north of Ullapool down single-track roads along cliffs and lochs lies the tiny village of **Achiltibuie,** where a simple stone croft house sits on the banks of Badentarbat Bay across from the Summer Isles. The landscape is forbidding and the area thinly populated (hitchhikers are in for long spells on the roadside), but it's perfect for solitude and quiet contemplation of the awesome natural loch and rock formations. Otherwise, take the bus back to **Inverness.** From there, the Carbisdale Castle Youth Hostel in **Culrain** is an easy hop by train and an awesome, regal place to write home about.

ACHILTIBUIE (ACHININVER)

The drive (or postbus ride) here is a 25-mile stretch north of Ullapool along a single-track road off the A835. Skirting Loch Broom and winding around Loch

Badagyle and the towering, craggy Stag Pollaidh, you're likely to catch a glimpse of an eagle, a deer or two, and some incredible peaks, valleys, and untouched waters—if you dare to take your eyes off the twisty roads. This is a lonely corner of Scotland: Spectacular scenery notwithstanding, it's only for the most intrepid.

Aside from a store, a post office, and a hothouse with an enormous indoor garden, there's not much in the tiny town of Achiltibuie. The Youth Hostel, a little stone croft house that holds 20 beds, looks out onto the water from its isolated perch at the far end of the loch. Naturalists, bird watchers, hill walkers, and travelers who want to take on the terrain and retreat from civilization come to this forgotten land for simplicity, contemplation, and silence. Visitors should get their tourist information food and supplies in Ullapool (25 miles away) before coming here: The only store in the village is 2¹/₂ miles from the hostel and its stock is limited at best.

Achininver Youth Hostel

Achiltibuie
Ullapool IV26 2YL
Tel: 01854/622254

Set on the shores of Loch Broom, the lonely little 20-bed Achininver Hostel overlooks the Summer Isles. You'll have to dodge sheep and lambs as you drive past the tiny village of Achiltibuie to get here. From the two-car car park, you take a half-mile walk to a rickety bridge en route to this little hut.

This hostel is the essence of simplicity. Hot showers are a new feature, and even phone service can be erratic. If worldly amenities aren't a concern, however, you won't be disappointed—Achininver is simple hosteling at its very best. With three rooms of spanking-new varnished pine, this former croft house hasn't forgotten its 19th-century roots. Outdoor bathrooms, a stone wall with a coal-burning stove, and a few sturdy wooden tables with chairs and benches take you back to the hosteling days of yore. The two well-insulated bedrooms with soft tartan blankets offer unbelievable views of the craggy hills protecting Loch Broom.

The gurgling waterfall behind the hostel is the only noise here at night, and guests seem to like it that way. Achininver tends to draw the hardiest of hard-core hostelers. Lots of hill walkers, geology buffs, and bird watchers enjoy the rugged peaks by day and the sound of silence at night.

🚆 Inverness is the closest train station (60 miles away). From there, take the bus to Ullapool, then switch for the Spa Coaches local service (twice daily) to Achiltibuie. The bus leaves you at the hostel car park. Turn right at the sign pointing you to the hostel, one-half mile down the track and over the scary footbridge.

🚌 The bus from Ullapool and Strathpeffer leaves you at the hostel car park. From there, follow above directions from the train.

🚗 From Ullapool and the south, take the A835 to the junction at Drumrunie. There, turn left onto the single-track road and go 8 miles, following signs to Achiltibuie. After 8 miles, you'll reach another junction. Turn left again and follow the road for 3 miles through Achiltibuie. It's another 3 miles to the hostel car park, which will come up on your left. From there, it's half-mile walk along a footpath and over a footbridge to the hostel.

▦ Open May 15–Oct 1. Rent-a-hostel: during closed period.

Services

⏰ Reception open 7am–10:30am and 5–11pm.

🛏 20 beds. One 4-bed room and two 8-bed rooms.

£ Members: adults £4; under 18 £3.30.

🍴 No meals served. Self-catering kitchen facilities.

💼 No lockers.

⚪ Drying room only.

P Limited parking half a mile up the road.

🛍 No shop at hostel.

🍽 One common room/dining room.

🚭 Not allowed.

♿ Not wheelchair accessible.

💱 See "Currency Exchange" under "The Basics" in Achiltibuie.

🔺 Bike shed.

Cheap Eats Nearby

The Lily Pond Café at the Hydroponicum

This airy greenhouse and indoor garden offers a beautiful atrium where you can feast on their house-grown strawberries and thoughtfully prepared food beside a sparkling indoor pool. Soups and sandwiches are £1.50 to £2; chicken-and-mushroom pie £3.50; vegetarian dishes such as lentil bake £3.

Achiltibuie. Tel: 01854/622202. Open: daily 10am–6pm. From the hostel, walk up the dirt track to the main road and turn left; it's 2 miles away.

The Summer Isles Bar

It's a two-mile walk up the road from the hostel to this elegant hotel with a limited bar menu. Munch your sandwiches (from £2.50) at the tiny wooden bar or go into the dining room for a slightly pricey but decent lunch (£6 to £15). Dinner is quite expensive, so you may want to stock up for later.

Achiltibuie. Tel: 01854/822240. Open: Mon–Sat noon–11pm; Sun noon–2:30pm and 6–11pm. Cash only. From the hostel, walk up the dirt track to the main road and turn left; it's 2 long miles away.

Grocery Store: Achiltibuie Stores, Achiltibuie. Tel: 01854/622256. Open: Mon–Sat 8:30am–5:30pm.

Experiences

Despite its remote location, the crofting township of Achiltibuie does see some action during summer. The twenty-odd **Summer Isles** are right across the bay and boats meander up and down the waters. Hostelers can take advantage of the **cruise boats** that depart from Badentarbat Pier. There are excursions for cruising and deep-sea angling (rods available for rent). You're likely to see nesting birds, seals, dolphins, and maybe even a whale on the expeditions.

The **Inverpollie National Nature Reserve** (12 miles away by road, eight miles by footpath) is an excellent place for hill walking: Stag Pollaidh (2,009 feet) makes for an excellent, if strenuous, walk. The nature reserve also has eagles, buzzards, and deer wandering around its dramatically barren grounds. An equally challenging mountain closer to the Youth Hostel is Ben More Coigach (2,438 feet); it towers above Loch Broom and can involve some scrambling. Closer to home (two miles from the hostel) is the **Achiltibuie Hydroponicum,** where state-of-the-art gardeners grow a mind-boggling array of flowers, plants, fruits, and vegetables in their soil-free greenhouse.

Summer Isles Boat Cruises. Ian MacLeod, Achiltibuie Post Office, Achiltibuie. Tel: 01854/622200 or 01854/622315. Three-hour boat trip: adults £9; children £4.50. Three-hour deep-sea angling trip: adults £5.50. Fishing rod rental: £11. The pier is about 4 miles from the hostel.

Inverpolly National Nature Reserve. For information, contact The Secretary. Achiltibuie Tourist Association. P.O. Box No. 1, Achiltibuie.

The Achiltibuie Hydroponicum Limited. Achiltibuie. Tel: 01854/622202. Open: Easter–Oct only. Guided tours daily at 10am, noon, 2pm, and 5pm.

The Basics

Tourist Office: The closest is in Ullapool, 25 miles away; pick up your information here before heading out. Ullapool T.I.C. 6 Argyle Street, Ullapool. Tel: 01854/612135. Also, contact The Secretary, Achiltibuie Tourist Association, P.O. Box No. 1, Achiltibuie, Ullapool, Ross-shire.

Post Office: Achiltibuie Post Office. Achiltibuie. Tel: 01854/622200. Open: Mon–Wed, Fri 9am–midnight and 1–5:30pm; Thurs 9am–1pm; Sat 9am–12:30pm. From the hostel, walk up to the main road and turn left; a 2-mile walk.

Currency Exchange: The nearest exchange is in Ullapool, 25 miles away. Westering Home (local shop). 28 Argyle St., Ullapool. Tel: 01854/612374. Open: Mon–Sat 9am–10pm; Sun 9am–6pm. Also available at Ullapool T.I.C. (see "Tourist Office" under "The Basics" in Achiltibuie).

Telephone Code: 01854.

Bike Rental: The nearest place is in Ullapool, 25 miles away. Ullapool Mountain Bike Hire. 11 Pulteney St., Ullapool. Tel: 01854/612260. Open: Mon–Sat 9am–6pm. Day rental £10; half day £6. Deposit required.

Getting There: Achininver isn't easy to reach for those without a car. However, it's not impossible. **Coach** service from **Ullapool** is decent, but call ahead for schedules. Inverness Traction tel: 01463/239292. **Trains** are nonexistent.

Take care driving here by **car,** and allow for extra time: a large part of the ride is on single-track roads, which are best taken slowly. From **Inverness,** it's an 84-mile drive. Take the A9 heading north and switch to the A835 in the direction of Ullapool. Bypass Ullapool and keep heading north, following signs for Drumrunie. From there, turn off the A835, following signs for Badentarbat Bay and Achiltibuie. You'll pass the right side of Loch Lurgainn, then Loch Badagyle, and finally Loch Osgaig before turning left at the crossroads. From there, head for Badentarbat, then turn left again at the next crossroads, which is signed for Achiltibuie. The hostel is about five miles up the road, two miles past the post office in Achiltibuie.

What's Next

Heading back to civilization, 25 miles south of here lies the lively port town of **Ullapool,** with a bustling fishing community, waterfront hostel, and decent nightlife. It's a lively change from the dramatic isolation of Achininver. Fifty-two miles to the east is Carbisdale Castle in Culrain. The hostel here offers the polar opposite experience: set among vast acres of forest land, this gigantic mansion houses an art collection.

CULRAIN (CARBISDALE CASTLE)

Ask anyone—even Scotsmen—where the town of Culrain is and you're likely to get a quizzical look. But ask anyone where Carbisdale Castle is and you'll get a response. Hostelers from around the world don't seem to mind making the trek up to this tiny town, 42 miles north of Inverness on the Inverness-Thurso/Wick train line, to visit the legendary Carbisdale Castle Youth Hostel.

Sitting high atop the south bank of the Kyle of Sutherland, the hostel is the only place in Britain where hostelers can stay in a real-life castle for less than £10 a night. With its own art collection and a forest in its backyard, this is probably the most splendid and awe-inspiring property in the SYHA. The castle has seen a king, a prince, a duchess, and countless happy hostelers pass through its imposing gates, and it seems to get more popular all the time.

The town of Culrain has little more than a train station, so bring your provisions with you. The hostel itself is enough to keep most people feeling pampered, cultured, and genteel—at least for a few days.

❀ Carbisdale Castle Youth Hostel

Culrain
Sutherland IV24 3DP
Tel: 01549/421232.

Built by the Dowager Duchess of Sutherland in 1914, Carbisdale Castle is the happy result of a bitter family squabble that ensued after the duke's untimely death in 1892. When his inheritance was meted out (mostly to the duchess), the duke's family threw her out of the nearby county of Sutherland and agreed to build her a new home at Carbisdale Castle. In 1933, she sold it to a businessman who used it to provide refuge for King Haakon of Norway and the young crown prince during the Nazi occupation of Norway. In 1945 it was turned over to the SYHA, and it's still every bit as regal as its history would imply.

You can, and probably will, get lost in here—that's how big it is. The art collection includes Renaissance and Baroque paintings, statues, and even a tapestry. Monstrous wooden doors lead to common rooms with luxurious couches and regal chairs. You can choose the room that fits your mood: the flowered sitting room with velvet chaises and a picture window overlooking the hills and loch; the tartan-decorated reading room; the games room downstairs. The hostel provides a detailed list of the collection, and you could easily spend a day just gawking at the stuff.

The manager is a former captain in the merchant navy who led a ship in the Falklands Islands War and keeps the place in shipshape condition. He can tell you all about the ghostly apparitions spotted here. One is the Lady in White: With long blonde hair and about six feet tall, she comes around about six times a year in either a long white shift or a blue-silver ball gown. The manager, whose Gaelic ancestry has endowed him with the abilities of a seer, says that despite the ghosts, the vibes here are friendly. Judging by the hostelers that come here in droves, he's probably right.

Services

🚆 Exit the train station and turn right. Walk about 100 yards and you'll reach the stone entrance gates and the hostel sign. Go through the gates and up the driveway for one-quarter mile.

🚌 The closest bus stop is 4$^1/_2$ miles away in Ardgay. From there, walk 4$^1/_2$ miles up the road or, wait for the train to Culrain and walk one-quarter mile to the hostel.

🚗 From the A9, follow signs to Culrain. Before reaching the village, you will pass the railway station. From there, the hostel is one-quarter mile up the road; the entrance gates and sign are to your left.

🏢 Open Mar–Nov. IBN and BABA.

🕐 Reception open 7am–11:30pm. Curfew 2am, but you can't go out after midnight.

🛏 225 beds. 5-, 6-, 8-, 10-, 16-, 18-, and 20-bed rooms.

£ Members: adults £9.65; under 18 £8.25.

🍴 Meals served Easter–Sept. Two self-catering kitchens, each with dining facility. Breakfast: 7:30–8:30am. Lunch: not available. Dinner: 7pm.

🧳 Lockers.

▣ Washers, dryers, and drying room.

P Ample and free of charge.

🗋 Shop at hostel sells candy, canned goods.

🛋 TV lounge, common room, games room, quiet room. Two main galleries with paintings and sculptures.

☎ In TV room and reception area.

♿ Not wheelchair accessible.

💱 See "Currency Exchange" under "The Basics" in Culrain.

🔺 Bike shed.

Cheap Eats Nearby

Bridge Hotel

This dank little bar with stone walls and a few stools lies in the neighboring town of Bonar Bridge. Jacket potatoes with a variety of fillings run £3; sandwiches £1.50 to £3; battered haggis £3.95. Specials are on the chalkboard.

Dornoch Road, Bonar Bridge. Tel: 01863/766685. Open: daily noon–3pm and 5–9:30pm. Credit cards: VA, MC, Access. From the hostel, exit the front gates, turn right, and go 5 miles to the town of Ardgay. From there, turn left and it's 2 miles to the town of Bonar Bridge. Cross the bridge and it's to your right; a 10-minute car ride.

The Lady Ross

Your basic small-town luncheonette, this place also rents videos. The food is less than inspiring, but it's the only place within five miles of the hostel. Sandwiches are £1 to £1.50; deep-fried haddock is £1.85; hot entrées £3 to £5.

High Street, Ardgay. Tel: 01863/766315. Open: Mon–Sat 8:30am–9pm; Sun 10am–9pm. Cash only. From the hostel, exit the front gates and turn right. The restaurant is 5 miles down the road in the village of Ardgay, across from the only store in the area.

Grocery Store: Ardgay Shopping, Ardgay (5 miles away). Tel: 01863/766323.

Experiences

The **Castle** containing the hostel is an experience in itself. The art collection (open only to hostelers) is too huge to list here, but look for the solemn statue of Jael (from the book of Kings) clutching a spike and *Joseph with Potiphar's Wife* on the main staircase. Just outside the doorstep are some forest walks right on the hostel property, but most guests seem just as happy resting on the huge stone patio in back. The walks range from simple to strenuous and pass by hills and glens.

Farther afield, touristy **Falls of Shin Visitor Centre,** a $3^1/2$-mile walk away, has salmon jumping, forest walks, arts and crafts exhibits, and an impressive waterfall. Bear in mind that Culrain makes a great base for taking day trips farther north. **Wick,** a train ride away, has a cool **glassblowing factory** you can visit for free. A few miles farther along at **John O'Groats,** you can catch a ferry out to the desolate, sheep-ridden Orkney Islands.

Carbisdale Castle Art Collection. Ask for the leaflet at reception.

Falls of Shin Visitor Centre. Achany Glen, Lairg. Tel: 01549/402231.

Caithness Glass Visitor Centre. Airport Industrial Estate (near A9), Wick. Tel: 01955/602286. Open: Mon–Sat 9am–7pm. Glass making: Mon–Fri 9am–4:45pm. Admission: free.

John O'Groats Ferries. John O'Groats, Caithness. Tel: 01955/611353. Burwick day return: £20. Kirkwall day return: £22.

The Basics

Tourist Office: Carbisdale Castle has a well-stocked information section; the nearest T.I.C. is in Dornoch, about 20 miles away. Dornoch T.I.C. The Square, Dornoch. Tel: 01862/810400. From the hostel, take the A836 south to the A949, which takes you straight into Dornoch.

Post Office: Ardgay Post Office. High Street, Ardgay (5 miles away). Tel: 01863/766201. Open: Mon–Thurs 9am–1pm and 2:15–5:30pm; Fri 9am–1pm; Sat 9am–12:30pm. From the hostel, turn right and continue for 5 miles to the village of Ardgay. It's past the square and on the left: 10 minutes by car.

Currency Exchange: The nearest bank is in Bonar Bridge, 5 miles away. Bank of Scotland. Dornoch Road, Bonar Bridge. Tel: 01863/766203 or 01863/766777. Open: Mon 9:15am–2:30pm and 1:30–3:30pm; Thurs–Fri 9:15am–12:30pm and 1:30–4:45pm.

Telephone Code: 01549.

Bike Rental: Inverhouse Cycles. Tel: 01549/421213. Full-day rental £5. They deliver to the hostel.

Getting There: The **train** is by far the easiest way to get here: three per day leave Inverness station, and the ride is about $1^1/2$ hours, dropping you close to the hostel. For information, call Inverness at 0345/212282. **Coaches** are trickier: Some come out of Inverness but drop you at Ardgay, 5 miles away. Inverness Traction operates the service; call 01463/239292. By **car,** take the A9 (scenic views along the Cromarty Firth) to Tain, then follow signs for the A836, which takes you straight into Culrain.

What's Next

Many people use Carbisdale Castle as a launching pad for forays into the northern-most part of Scotland. There are Youth Hostels at **John O'Groats** (95 miles north) and on the **Orkney Islands.** Heading directly west leads you to the friendly fishing town of **Ullapool** (46 miles away), which has a Youth Hostel right on the water-front and offers ferryboat trips out to the Summer Isles. Going south leads you to **Inverness,** only 42 miles away, where you can take day trips to Loch Ness or just enjoy this city of art museums and leafy parks along the River Ness.

The West Highlands, Skye & Islay

The West Highlands of Scotland stretch from the Kyle of Lochalsh (82 miles south-west of Inverness) down to the port town of Oban on the west coast. Some of the highest peaks in Scotland are found in this region—from Ben Nevis (4,406 feet) just outside of Fort William to Ben Lomond (3,192 feet), towering over the banks of Loch Lomond farther south. Comprising staggering mountains, bustling ports, misty islands, and one of the most legendary train routes in Britain, the area is well worth the time and energy of mountain climbers, nature lovers, and water lovers.

Just miles from the Kyle of Lochalsh lies the luminous island of Skye, which claims two waterfront Youth Hostels and the magical Cuilin hills. Whirling clouds envelop walkers and cyclists drawn to the shadowy mystique of the hills.

Fort William and Oban are lively, if slightly overtrafficked, port towns sur-rounded by some breathtaking coastal scenery, especially appreciated by those trav-eling by train. The West Highland Line, starting up at Mallaig and working its way down the coast, takes you through viaducts and over bridges as you pass icy lochs, heather-covered moorland, and incredible corkscrew mountains.

Southwest of Oban lies the 32-mile-long island of Islay, with a wildlife reserve, sandy beaches, and friendly locals who are happy to help wandering travelers. Far-ther south are small villages hovering around the lochs in Argyll and Dumbartonshire.

Farther east, the 24-mile-long Loch Lomond boasts a hostel on either side. To the east is Rowardennan, lying in its own forest in the shadow of Ben Lomond. To the west, the Loch Lomond Youth Hostel boasts a luxurious mansion and sumptu-ous garden on its hilltop perch above the lake.

The entire west coast of Scotland is surprisingly accessible by train and bus, and reliable, frequent ferry service shuttles you to the islands. The coastal roads can be tricky, but the excellent inland roads lead you down Loch Lomond and through to Glasgow.

SKYE

This glowing, misty isle, 48 miles long, means "winged island" in Gaelic. Some would contest its designation as an island: Since October 1995, a bridge has con-nected it, for better or for worse, to the mainland. Only time will tell what kind of effect its connection to the mainland will have.

The powerful, incredibly varied scenery lends a heavenly aura to Skye. The barren landscape of the massive Cuilin Hills dominates central Skye, while to the west gurgles seal-filled Loch Dunvegan. The lush Sleat peninsula, warmed by the waters of the Gulf Stream, flourishes along the southern coast. Visitors come to experience the terrain on foot, bike, or bus tour, and the mysterious whims of Mother Nature don't seem to dampen their mood.

The very history of the island is shrouded in mystery, although it is known that visitors ranging from St. Columba to the Viking kings to Virginia Woolf have made their way onto these shores. Now that the bridge has been built, you can make it over here a lot easier than they did: It's a quick and painless hop from Kyle of Lochalsh.

Don't base your judgment of Skye on what you see in Kyleakin. The shuttle bus brings you right to this active little village, making it a convenient place to stay, but not much more. Aside from a few restaurants, a couple of hotels, and a hostel, there's not much here, and it's by no means representative of the rest of the island.

Hop on one of the tours here or rent a bike and head for the hills. When you return, share your spiritually uplifting experiences over a whisky at the King Haakon bar across from the hostel. You're likely to find Pat (the Kyleakin manager) there as well as the Haggis team; Scotsmen through and through, they know everything there is to know about the island and can point you to the abundant must-see sights.

Kyleakin Youth Hostel

Kyleakin, Isle of Skye
IV41 8PL
Tel: 01599/534585.

Despite the dreamy, spiritual quality of the island, the hostel has a decidedly different atmosphere. Because hostelers spill out by the busload, Kyleakin, housed in a former waterfront hotel, feels like a friendly college dorm.

The rooms are manageably sized (there are lots of quads), and some have water views; those on the other side of the building look out onto the hills or the churchyard next door. The mazelike building contains a small dining room. The huge members' kitchen has a separate dining area with a common room overlooking the water. Pat, the friendly no-nonsense manager, is a hill walker and can provide loads of information on the area.

Services

🚆 From the Kyle of Lochalsh train station, look for the Skyeways shuttle bus headed for Kyleakin, Skye. Alternatively, you can try to get on the Glasgow or Inverness coaches (nos. 916 and 917) that Scottish Citylink runs out to Skye; they stop at Kyle on their way to Kyleakin.

🚌 From the Kyleakin bus stop, walk across the road.

🚗 From the bridge, turn left and the hostel is just up on your right in the village of Kyleakin.

▦ Open year-round. IBN and FABA.

🕐 Reception open 7am–2am. Curfew 2am.

🛏 78 beds. 2-, 4-, and 6-bed rooms.

£ Members: adults £7.80; under 18 £6.40.

🍴 Meals served Easter–September only. Self-catering kitchen facilities with separate dining room. Breakfast: 8am. Lunch: not available. Dinner: 6pm.

🧳 Coin-operated lockers.

▢ Washer, dryer, and drying room.

🚬 In TV room only.

P Ample and free of charge.

♿ Not wheelchair accessible.

📓 Shop at hostel sells canned goods, confectionery; maps for rent.

💱 See "Currency Exchange" under "The Basics" in Skye.

📺 TV room; reception/lounge area; large common room.

▲ Bike shed.

Cheap Eats Nearby

Castle Moil Restaurant and King Haakon Bar

This friendly eatery, featuring a pool table, a decent jukebox, and a disc jockey on selected nights, is the main nightspot in Kyleakin. Pat, the Kyleakin hostel manager, loves it here. Bar meals are generous and filling. Burgers are £3 to £3.50; jacket potatoes £2 to £3; salads £5 to £8.

On the waterfront, Kyleakin. Tel: 01599/534164. Open: June–Oct 9am–9pm. Limited opening in winter. Cash only. From the hostel, turn right and it's on the left along the water; a 3-minute walk.

Pier Coffee House

They swear by the hot chocolate in this comfy cafe. Some tables look out onto the water. Sandwiches and burgers are £1.50 to £1.75. All-day breakfast of egg, bacon, toast, beans, and sausage is £3.30.

On the waterfront. Kyleakin. Tel: 01599/534641. Open: June–Aug only: daily 9:30am–7pm. Cash only. From the hostel, turn right and walk along the road toward the ferry terminal. It's on the left; a 3-minute walk.

Grocery Store: In Kyle of Lochalsh. Cameron Stores. Open: Mon–Fri 8:30am–1pm, 2–5:30pm, and 7–8pm; Sat 8:30am–1pm and 2–5:30pm.

Experiences

Because of Skye's size, the best way to see the misty isle is put yourself in the capable hands of guide Ted Badger, a transplanted Australian who fell in love with the place and never left. His daylong **bus tour** is well worth £12, and locals recommend his chatty, informative, and at times spiritual journey through the Cuilin Hills, past Portree, and around the northern part of Skye. There's time built in for wandering around, so you won't be stuck sitting on the bus all day. Most people leave his tours educated and exhausted. There are a few other local tours similar to his; ask at the hostel for Bob or Nick.

Those going solo can take a good day trip to **Dunvegan Castle,** seat of the MacLeod Clan. On the way there, you'll pass some of the beautiful hilly Cuilins. The castle is set on a rocky promontory overlooking Loch Dunvegan, and until 1748 the only entrance to this forbidding island fortress was by sea gate. Nowadays, you can enter and (for a price) take a look at the fairy flag. It's said to bring good luck to the family, which has seen fierce battles with its neighboring nemesis, the Clan MacDonald. Another excellent option is to rent a bicycle and explore the southern part of the island. Up in Uig, you can go **canoeing** and **windsurfing** in summer.

Tour of Skye. Book at hostel reception desk or call Ted Badger at 01599/534169.

Dunvegan Castle. Loch Dunvegan, Skye. Tel: 01470/22206. Open: Easter–Sept: Mon–Sat 10am–5:30pm; Sun 1–5:30pm.

Whitewave Activities. Idvigill, Uig, Skye. Tel: 01470/42414. Windsurfing, canoeing, and guided walks.

The Basics

Tourist Office: The nearest T.I.C. is either across the bay at Kyle of Lochalsh or in Broadford, 8 miles away. Kyle of Lochalsh T.I.C. Car Park, Kyle of Lochalsh. Tel: 01599/534276. Open: Apr–May and Oct: Mon–Sat 9:15am–7pm. June and Sept: Mon–Sat 9:15am–7pm. July–Aug: Mon–Sat 9:15am–7pm; Sun 12:30–4:30pm. The office is adjacent to the ferry terminal at Kyle of Lochalsh. Broadford T.I.C. Broadford, Skye. Tel: 01471/822463. Open: Apr–June and Oct: Mon–Sat 9am–5:30pm. July–Aug Mon–Sat 9am–7:30pm; Sun 12:30–4:30pm. From the Youth Hostel, take bus no. 700 to Broadford. It's on the main street.

Post Office: Kyleakin Post Office. Kyleakin. Tel: 01599/534523. Open: Mon–Tues 9am–1pm and 2–5:30pm; Wed 9am–1pm; Thurs–Fri 9am–1pm and 2–5:30pm.

Currency Exchange: The nearest place is in Kyle of Lochalsh, across the kyle. Kyle Hotel. Main Street, Kyle of Lochalsh. Tel: 01599/534204.

Telephone Code: 01599.

Bike Rental: Skye Bikes. The Pier, Kyleakin, Skye. Tel: 01599/534795. Rentals: £6.50–£10.

Getting There: There's excellent **train** service to Kyle of Lochalsh from **Inverness** (100 miles east), **Edinburgh** (176 miles southeast), and **Glasgow** (145 miles southeast). For train info, call 0345/212282. From **Kyle,** Skyeways operates a **shuttle bus** that goes over the bridge to Kyleakin. For info, call: 01599/534328. **Coaches** from **Inverness** and **Glasgow** heads straight out to Skye, stopping in Kyleakin, right in front of the hostel. Scottish Citylink information is at 0990/505050.

By **car** from **Inverness,** take the A82 past Loch Ness and switch to the A887 west at Invermoriston. Continue, following it as it turns into the A87, and Kyle of Lochalsh is at the end of the road. Cross the bridge and you're in Skye. From **Fort William and points south**, take the A82, which will lead to the A887 and A87 headed for Kyle.

What's Next

From Kyleakin, you have a few easy options. For those wanting to explore the mainland, it's a short ferry ride to Mallaig, where you can catch the West Highland train that passes through lonely lochs and craggy peaks as it winds its way toward **Fort William** and the Glen Nevis Youth Hostel, home of Ben Nevis, the highest peak in all of Scotland.

FORT WILLIAM (GLEN NEVIS)

Munro-seekers, the military, and mere mortals all come here for one thing: big, bad Ben Nevis. At 4,406 feet, it towers over the glen and hostel, which tremble in the shadow of its greatness. The highest peak in Scotland, it has endured the fierce tread of many courageous climbers and is looked upon by locals with a mixture of respect and fear. Every year, it claims at least a few victims of Scotland's mysterious weather patterns, which can change drastically within minutes, catching many unsuspecting climbers in its foggy clutches.

Three miles from the port town/mountain center/souvenir mecca of Fort William and sitting right in Ben's lap, the Glen Nevis Youth Hostel is heaven to the hordes who attempt to huff and puff their way up the mountain. Other than outdoor pursuits, though, the town of Fort William is something of a disappointment. In addition to Ben Nevis, the area is famous for the legendary train ride that runs up the West Highland coast to Mallaig. The town is all too happy to pander to the demanding tourists who pour off the *Flying Scotsman*. Souvenir shops with sweaters, tartans, and little Nessie dolls are everywhere.

Outside of Fort William, the area lives up to its reputation for challenging ridge walking, low-level forest walks, and ice climbing in winter. Famous for having been the center of commando training for Allied soldiers during World War II, the mountains here are still used for military training—a stern reminder of the dangers they pose for civilian climbers. In addition, the West Highland Way, Scotland's 95-mile footpath from Milngavie to Fort William, comes to its end here. The town is usually abuzz with outdoorsy types.

Glen Nevis Youth Hostel

Glen Nevis
Fort William
Inverness-shire PH33 6ST
Tel: 01397/702336.

One of the first hostels in Scotland, Glen Nevis was originally a simple bothy for walkers climbing Ben Nevis and the West Highland Way before the road was built around 1934 and 1935. In the 1940s, the original building was burnt down, and a group of Norwegians reconstructed it in Norwegian pine wood as a way of giving thanks to Fort William for the town's help in World War II.

It's not so hard to imagine the hostel as an army barracks, with the smell of sweaty socks and the sounds of pots and pans clanging in the kitchen. You'll be reminded that it's indeed a hostel when you hear the familiar shrill cries of schoolchildren away from Mum and Dad for the very first time. Glen Nevis is packed with school groups from early spring to June.

Despite the kids, the hostel does have a comforting, cozy feel. It's set against the breathtaking backdrop of Ben Nevis, which you can see straight out of the common room window. The wardens thoughtfully provide a route book for hostelers to sign before and after their hikes as a safety precaution. The mountains around here claim about 40 lives a year, so the hostel tries to look out for its own. The wardens show their concern in other ways, too: Lights out here is strictly observed, and the hostel warden makes sure people are tucked in at night and out of their beds by check-out time in the morning. Be on your best behavior and you'll be fine.

Services

🚆 The closest train station is in Fort William, 3 miles away. From there, turn left and walk up the road for 3 miles, keeping the river to your left. The hostel is just past the Glen Nevis Café. Alternatively, turn left out of the train station and wait at the bus stop for the Gaelicbus, which takes you straight to the hostel. This bus service is limited (4 per day) and runs only from Easter to October. Otherwise, a taxi will cost around £3.

🚌 The closest bus stop is in Fort William, 3 miles away, and is next to the train station. From the train station, follow directions from the train, given above. Alternatively, you can wait at the bus stop for the Gaelicbus, which takes you straight to the hostel. Check times and schedules: service is limited (4 per day) and runs only in spring and summer. Otherwise, a taxi will cost around £3.

🚗 From **Glasgow and the south,** take the A82 toward Loch Lomond and then follow signs to Crianlarich, Glencoe, and Fort William. Pass through the town of Fort William and turn right at the roundabout by the train station. Take the next left, pass the hospital and leisure center on your right, and follow the road for 3 miles, keeping the river to your left. The hostel is on the right, just past the Glen Nevis Café.

▦ Open Dec–Oct. IBN and BABA.

🕐 Reception open 7am–11:45pm. Curfew 2am.

🛏 127 beds. 2-, 3-, 4-, 8-, 14-, and 24-bed rooms.

£ Members: adults £7.80; under 18 £6.40.

🍴 No meals served. Self-catering kitchen.

🛄 Coin-operated lockers by the reception area.

⃞ Washers, dryers, and drying room.

P Ample and free of charge.

⃞ Shop at hostel sells candy, canned goods, fruit, bread.

🛋 Quiet room, TV room, games room (video games and pool table).

🚬 In TV room and reception area only.

♿ Wheelchair accessible. Ground-floor bedrooms but no bathrooms.

💱 See "Currency Exchange" under "The Basics" in Fort William (Glen Nevis).

🔔 Bike shed.

Cheap Eats Nearby

Glen Nevis Centre Café

"Walkers welcome!" declares this mountain climbers' rest stop, where postcards, climbing supplies, and tasty homemade food are available all day. Offerings include soup and roll £1.55; toasted sandwiches £1.50 to £2; and jacket potatoes £2.95. Elegant evening entrées include ratatouille (£5.95) and eggplant stuffed with mushrooms (£6.25).

Glen Nevis. Tel: 01397/703601. Open: daily 8am–9pm. From the hostel, turn left and it's right next door.

The Grog & Gruel

One of Fort William's many bars, this place features Orkney Dark Island Ale and a comfortable wood-paneled restaurant upstairs. Burgers run £4 to £5. Salads are £3 to £4. Mexican dishes range from £5 to £7.

66 High St., Fort William. Tel: 01397/705078. Open: Mon–Wed 11am–11:30pm; Thurs–Sat 11am–1am; Sun noon–midnight. Credit cards: VA, MC, EC, accepted in restaurant only. Exit the hostel, turn left, and walk the 3 miles into Fort William, or take the Gaelicbus. Walk down High Street for about three blocks; it's on the left.

Grocery Store: Safeway. Next to the train station, Fort William. Open: Mon–Thurs 8am–8pm; Fri 8am–9pm; Sat 8am–8pm; Sun 9am–6pm.

Experiences

Aside from the obvious mountain climb, there are masses of beautiful low-level **walks** in the area along the glen. With the mountain hovering above, the walks are particularly beautiful after a spell of rain. The climb to the top of **Ben Nevis** is only for the most experienced, well-equipped climbers (never go alone); weather has been known to go from Aegean to Arctic in a matter of minutes.

One very pretty walk starts at Fort William and runs behind the row of modern houses. Just beyond, you can catch the forest path and walk through part of the **West Highland Way.** The route takes you directly to the Lower Falls, about 3¹/₂ miles farther up the glen from the hostel. Another 6 miles farther on are the main waterfalls, the Steil Bridge and waterfall. Even the main road from town to hostel is pleasant, since it follows the path of the glen.

Nevis Range, 10 miles from the Youth Hostel on Aonach Mor, has a gondola that was built to access the upper slopes of this 4,000-foot mountain. In winter it's the local ski resort, and in summer it's worth a trip if you have an extra day to spare. They also have guided walks and bikes for rent. For the unathletic, **cruises** of all shapes and sizes are available down the pier in Fort William. The most popular are the Seal Island Cruises, which glide down Loch Linnhe, the island home of common and gray seals. From the water, you'll get some impressive views of Ben Nevis.

West Highland Way. Leaflet available from Fort William T.I.C.

Nevis Range. Torlundy, Fort William. Tel: 01397/705825. Open: Dec–mid-Nov: daily 10am–5pm. Gondola prices (return trip): adults £5.50; children £3.75; senior citizens £4.95; under 5 free. Guided walks: adults £3; children £2. Mountain bike rental: full day £12; half day £8.

Seal Island Cruises. Town pier, Fort William. Tel: 01397/705589. Apr–Oct only: four trips daily (1¹/₂ hours).

The Basics

Tourist Office: Fort William T.I.C. Cameron Square, Fort William. Tel: 01397/703781. Open: Jan–Apr: Mon–Thurs 10am–4pm; Fri 10am–5pm; Sat–Sun 10am–1pm. May: Mon–Sat 9am–5pm; Sun 11am–5pm. June: Mon–Sat 9am–7pm; Sun 9am–6pm. July–Sept: Mon–Sat 9am–8pm; Sun 9am–6pm. Oct–Nov: Mon–Sat 9am–5pm; Sun 11am–3pm. Dec: Mon–Thurs 10am–4pm; Fri 10am–5pm. From the hostel, turn left and go 3 miles into Fort William. Turn left onto High Street. After two blocks, turn left onto Cameron Square.

Post Office: Fort William Post Office. 5 High St., Fort William. Open: Mon–Fri 9am–5:30pm; Sat 9am–12:30pm. From the hostel, turn left and go 3 miles into Fort William. Turn left onto High Street. It's on your right at the end of the row of shops.

Currency Exchange: Fort William T.I.C. Cameron Square, Fort William. Also available at the Fort William Post Office. (See "Tourist Office" and "Post Office" under "The Basics" in Fort William.)

Telephone Code: 01397.

Bike Rental: Off Beat Bikes. High Street, Fort William. Tel: 01397/704008. Full day £12; half day £8.

Getting There: The **train** is reliable and comfortable. If you come down from Mallaig, you'll cross bridges and viaducts; snake through tunnels; whiz past moors, mountains, glens, and lochs on one of Scotland's most scenic railway rides. There are also good connections to **Glasgow, Edinburgh,** and **Stirling** from here. For schedule information, call 01397/703791. **Coaches** aren't too hard to catch, even though there's no major bus station. For coaches to **Inverness, Glasgow,** and **Loch Ness,** call Highland Omnibuses at 01397/702373. For coaches to **Mallaig, Kyle of Lochalsh,** and other points north, call Citylink/Skyeways at 0141/3329191. Those coming to Fort William by **car** should take the A82 north from **Glasgow.** From **Edinburgh,** take the M8 west to Glasgow and switch to the A82, and continue north until you see signs for Fort William. Glen Nevis is 3 miles from the town.

What's Next

Heading south, Oban is only 50 miles away. It's a pleasant little port town with a tower perched high above the city, overlooking the pier and bay beyond. It also has ferries that can take you out to the Isle of Mull and Islay (Wednesdays only). Heading north, Skye isn't too far away (87 miles north), and the misty isle is always worth the trip: barren mountain landscapes and a land shrouded in mystery. Vikings, Picts, Celts, and even Bonnie Prince Charlie form part of the historic fabric of the island, which has two excellent hostels. The bridge, inaugurated in 1995, makes it an easy trip by bus or by train (with connecting shuttle bus).

OBAN

Coliseum-like McCaig's tower guards the busy port town of Oban (95 miles northwest of Glasgow, 125 miles northwest of Edinburgh, and 50 miles south of Fort William). The Gaelic name means "little bay," but the development of steamboats and railways in Victorian times forever changed the bay's stature. Modern-day Oban rattles with tourist activity, from the hotels lining the esplanade to the bustling shopping district down by the pier.

If you don't mind dodging the crowds, the town can be quite pleasant. Ferries chug up and down the Firth of Lorn, shuttling passengers to the nearby islands of Mull, Staffa, and Iona. Rowboats, canoes, and motorboats are all available for rent. For landlubbers and whisky lovers, there's a local distillery, a weekly open-air market, and some good suntanning up at the tower, if the weather's right.

Oban is easily reached via rail and bus and is also a stop on the ever-popular Haggis tour. The friendly hostel is right on the esplanade overlooking the water. Blessedly away from the crowds in the town center, it's a five-minute walk.

Oban Youth Hostel

Esplanade
Oban
Argyll PA34 5AF
Tel: 01631/562025.

Sitting smack on the esplanade overlooking Oban Bay, the Oban Youth Hostel is a Georgian stone town house. It's at the end of a long lineup of other former homes that died and went to hotel heaven sometime after the Industrial Revolution. A five-minute walk (no hills) from the hectic town center, the area around the Youth Hostel is peaceful and quiet, perfect for serious sunset watching. There are even a few well-placed chairs in the grassy front yard.

The helpful staff here has put together a small leaflet listing the discounts available to Hostelling International members in Oban—restaurants, cruises, and some local sights. The informal and relaxed atmosphere helps dispel the gloom of the dining room, which has dreary wooden tables. You may not want to spend too much time inside anyway—this is one of the SYHA hostels with a 2am curfew, so lots of hostelers take advantage of it to prowl about the pubs in and around Oban.

🚆 Exit the station, turn right, and walk down the esplanade, keeping the water to your left. Continue for about three-fourths of a mile and the hostel is just past the Oban Bay Hotel on your right.

🚌 The bus stop is right next to the train station. Follow directions from the train, given above.

🚗 Turn off the A85 into the center of town. Follow the one-way traffic system, keeping the water to your left. Look for the sign to the Youth Hostel along the esplanade. It's just past the Catholic church on your right.

▦ Open Mar–Nov. IBN and FABA.

🕐 Reception open 7am–11:30pm. Curfew 2am.

🛏 114 beds. 4-, 6-, 10-, 13-, 14-, and 16-bed rooms. Annex with 4- and 6-bed rooms.

£ Members: adults £7.80; under 18 £6.40.

🍴 Breakfast for groups only. Self-catering kitchen.

🛄 Lockers.

🔲 Washers, dryers, and drying room.

P Limited; free of charge.

🏠 Shop at hostel sells candy and canned goods only.

🛋 TV lounge; games room with pool table and video games.

🚬 In common room only.

♿ Not wheelchair accessible.

💱 See "Currency Exchange" under "The Basics" in Oban.

▲ Bike shed.

Services

Cheap Eats Nearby

The Gallery Restaurant

This cheery yellow dining room has comfortable booths, soft banquettes, and a huge menu. Make a meal out of their high tea (served between 5:30 and 6:30pm; £4.95). Omelets are £5 to £6; soups £1.35; burgers £1.65 to £2.25. You'll find vegetarian meals aplenty.

Argyll Square, Oban. Tel: 01631/564641. Open: Jan–Oct: Mon–Sat 9am–4pm and 5–9:30pm. Open Sun evenings July–Aug. Nov: Mon–Sat 9am–4pm. Credit cards: VA, MC, EC, Access. From the hostel, turn left onto the Esplanade, left onto Stafford Street, and right on George Street. Continue through Argyll Square past the tourist office and cross the street; a 15-minute walk.

McTavish's Kitchens

A bar/cafeteria/restaurant that serves everything from sandwiches (£1.70) to Piper Heidsieck Brut (£30). The cafeteria is most economical and tasty. Every evening there's a Scottish show upstairs (8:30 to 10:30pm), and on weekends there's live music at their bar around the corner. Burgers cost £3 to £4. Main courses (steak pie, mac and cheese) come with potato and vegetable (£4 to £6). Bargain specials (£2 to £3) are on the blackboard.

34 George St., Oban. Tel: 01631/563064. Open: Easter–July: daily 8:30am–7pm. July–Sept: daily 8:30am–10pm. Sept–Easter: daily 8:30am–5pm. Closed Sun in Jan. Cash only. From the hostel, turn left down the esplanade until you reach Stafford Street (on the main square). Turn left on Stafford and right on George. It's on your left; a 10-minute walk.

Grocery Store: Tesco, behind the railway station. Open: Mon–Fri 8:30am–8pm; Sat 8am–8pm; Sun 10am–5pm.

Experiences

The day begins early in Oban. **Ferries** depart for the Isle of Mull (£4.80 round-trip) at 8am, leaving you ample time to see the two castles, rabbit farm, and distillery on the island. Or check out the sandy beaches, rocky cliffs, and pastoral crofting houses on the moors, then come back in the afternoon. Organized **tours** start out there and go to the smaller islands of Iona and Staffa. Iona has a restored abbey, and Staffa has the shining, spectacular Fingal's cave, which inspired Mendelssohn to compose *Fingal's Cave Overture*. **Rowboats, motorboats,** and **canoes** are also available for rent by the pier at Oban.

For less expensive pursuits, there's an open-air market on Fridays, with the usual junk mixed in with good bargains. **McCaigs Tower** dominates Oban's landscape and is only three quarters of a mile up some steep steps and a hill. From there, you can see out to Mull, Lismore, Kerrera, and the Morvern Peninsula, at its most beautiful when the sun is setting. Pulpit Hill is another spot perfect for a Kodak moment. To get there, walk in the direction just beyond the ferry terminal and follow the signposts; it's about $1^{1}/_{2}$ miles away and has the same views of the firth and islands. Best of all, there's no admission charge.

Isle of Mull ferries. Caledonian MacBrayne. Ferry Terminal, Oban. Tel: 01631/ 566688. Ferries run from 8am; last ferry back is at 7pm. Adult round-trip £4.80. Three Isles Excursion to Mull, Iona, Staffa. Gordon Grant Tours. Ferry Terminal, Oban. Tel: 01631/562842. Apr–June: Tues–Thurs, Sat 10am departure; Fri 8am departure. June–July: daily 10am departures, except Fri 8am departure. Sept: Tues–Thurs, Sat 10am departure; Fri 8am departure. Adults £22; children £11. Discount for HI members.

BorroBoats. Lighthouses Pier, Oban. Tel: 01631/563292. Open: daily 10am–6pm. Sailing dinghies £8–£9.50 per hour; £30–£37 per day. Rowboats £5 per hour; £18.50 per day.

The Basics

Tourist Office: Oban T.I.C. Argyll Square, Oban. Tel: 01631/563122. Open: Apr–June and Sept: Mon–Sat 9am–5:30pm; Sun 9am–4pm. July–Aug: Mon–Sat

9am–9pm; Sun 9am–5pm; Nov–Mar: Mon–Fri 9am–5:30pm. Ten-minute walk: from the hostel, turn left and walk up the esplanade. Turn left onto Stafford Street, right on George Street, and it's straight ahead.

Post Office: Oban Post Office. Esplanade, Oban. Tel: 01631/562430. Open: Mon–Fri 9am–1pm and 2–5:30pm; Sat 9am–1pm. From the hostel, turn left onto the esplanade and walk past the hotels. It's on your left.

Currency Exchange: A. T. Mays. 8 George St., Oban. Tel: 01631/566166. Open: Mon–Tues 9am–5:30pm; Wed 9:30am–5:30pm; Thurs–Fri 9am–5:30pm; Sat 9:30am–5pm.

Telephone Code: 01631.

Bike Rental: Oban Cycles. Craigard Road, Oban. Tel: 01631/566996. Open: daily 8am–6pm. Full-day rental £10; half day £5.

Getting There: Trains come into Oban from **Glasgow** and **Edinburgh;** service is good. For schedule information, call 01631/563083. **Coaches,** operated by Scottish Citylink, come and go to **Glasgow, Edinburgh, Loch Lomond,** and other destinations. Highland Scottish Omnibuses take you to **Inverness, Fort William,** and **Skye.** For information, contact the Oban and District Travel Shop, Queens Park Place, Oban. Tel: 01631/562856. There's no bus station in Oban. Those coming by **car** should take the A82 from Central Scotland; at Tyndrum, get on to the A85, following signs to Oban.

What's Next

Because of Oban's strategic location, you can get to lots of places either by rail or by ferry. On Wednesdays only, there's ferry service to Islay; the soothing four-hour ride passes the islands of Mull, Colonsay, and Jura before reaching the peaceful, friendly haven, where elegant vacation homes, wildlife refuges, and glorious sandy white beaches lie unspoiled by tourism.

ISLAY

Barely 30 miles long and 26 miles wide, Islay might be the only place in Britain where drivers regularly stop along the road to ask walkers if they need a lift. The population is only 3,500, so it's not surprising that most people wave to one another from their cars as they cruise along the beautiful beach road. Guests seem to adapt quite well to the easygoing island life and locals warmly welcome them.

The island is rich in Celtic heritage and there are lots of historical sights, but the gently curving white-sand beaches could tempt even the most dutiful museum-goer to the shore. Nonetheless, a local history museum, woolen mill, and eight distilleries provide at least a few rainy days' worth of activities. A nature reserve offers excellent bird watching, as does the nearby island of Jura (a 10-minute boat ride)—a wild and thinly populated island visited mainly by bird watchers and literary pilgrims en route to the hut where George Orwell wrote *1984*.

Anyone trying to squeeze Islay into a busy schedule will be disappointed: It deserves at least two or three days. Located about 12 miles off the mainland, it's accessible by ferry either from the mainland via Kennacraig, where ferries run twice daily, or via Oban, from which there's one crossing per week.

Islay Youth Hostel

Port Charlotte
Islay, Argyll PA48 7OX
Tel: 01496/850385.

Some say you can still smell the faint aroma of whisky at the Youth Hostel in Port Charlotte. Formerly the warehouse for a whisky distillery, this white building on the sandy shores of Loch Indaal houses the Youth Hostel upstairs and a Wildlife Centre downstairs, with displays, a library, a laboratory, and a lecture room. Hostelers have access to the center at a discounted price.

The hostel is sturdy and comfortable; since its renovation a few years back, it has remained squeaky clean and gleams like new. Despite the old stone warehouse walls, the common room is warm and welcoming, with comfortable couches and a TV with surprisingly good reception. The members' kitchen and dining room and the common room all have views across the saltwater loch that stretches out to the Irish Sea. It's a most relaxing place to have your morning coffee—unless there's a group of fidgety children clamoring for their morning muesli. The hostel gets a few school groups, but there isn't too much cause for concern: The manager is quite certain about how she likes her hostelers to behave. Everyone seems to coexist peacefully on this dreamy isle.

Services

🛳 The two ferry ports are Port Askaig (15 miles away) and Port Ellen (20 miles away). From the ports (if someone hasn't already offered you a ride), local buses run by Islay Coaches meet arriving ferries and head to Port Charlotte. Tell the bus driver you're going to the Youth Hostel; you may need to change buses at Bridgend. Buses don't meet the evening boat, so you can either call a taxi or catch a ride.

🚐 From **Port Askaig,** follow the only main road straight to Bridgend. From there, turn right to Port Charlotte, about 8 miles from Bridgend. From **Port Ellen,** take a left through the village, following signs to Bowmore, 10 miles away. When you get to Bowmore, drive through the town, following signs to Bridgend, about 2 miles away. At Bridgend, turn left, and this road will take you straight into Port Charlotte.

🎫 Open Feb 25–Oct. FABA.

🕐 Reception open Oct–Apr: 7–11am and 4–11:45pm. May–Sept: 7–10:30am and 5:30–11:45pm.

🛏 42 beds. 2-, 4-, 6-, and 8-bed rooms.

£ Adults £5.25; under 18 £4.30.

🍴 No meals served. Self-catering kitchen.

🧳 Lockers.

▢ Drying room only.

P Ample and free of charge.

🛍 Shop at hostel sells candy and canned goods.

📺 TV room.

🚬 In TV room only.

♿ Not wheelchair accessible.

💱 See "Currency Exchange" under "The Basics" in Islay.

🅰 Bike shed.

Cheap Eats Nearby

The Croft Kitchen

You'll find crafts in the cupboards, books on the bookshelf, and homemade food in this little country kitchen on the beach. You'll find fish dishes for £4 to £5; salads £4 to £5; a ploughman's lunch with Islay cheese for £3; sandwiches £ to £3; and daily specials.

Port Charlotte, Islay. Tel: 01496/850230. Open: Apr–Nov only: daily 9am–9pm. Cash only. Exit the hostel, turn right and it's a 2-minute walk; on your right.

The Lochindaal Hotel

This local pub has a pool table, dart board, and jukebox, so you can toss back one of the 250 malt whiskies to the strains of the "Bohemian Rhapsody." Food here is varied, including vegetable curry (£4.50); lasagne (£4.50); lentil bake (£4.50); and the standard sandwiches and fried fish.

Main Street, Port Charlotte. Tel: 01496/850202. Open: daily 12:30–2pm and 6–8:30pm. Cash only. From the hostel, turn left, walk up the main street, and it's on the right after about three blocks.

Grocery Store: Spar. Main Street, Port Charlotte.

Experiences

You could spend a week here just exploring the **beaches.** By Port Charlotte and Bridgend, there are sandy and peaceful beaches facing Loch Indaal. The west coast, from Lossit Bay to Machir Bay, doesn't permit swimming but does have some excellent cliffside walks. Tayvulin on Loch Gruinart at the north side of the island has the warmest waters for bathing and is good for collecting cockles and mussels in season. To the east, Claggan and Ardtalla have beautiful views out to Kintyre on the mainland.

The **Royal Society for the Protection of Birds Reserve,** which covers 4,000 acres near Loch Gruinart, protects 30,000 to 40,000 barnacle and white-fronted geese that flock here from Greenland in autumn. Other mammals, including hares, deer, bats, and seals, as well as a host of flowers and plants, are on view.

If you curve around the hostel from Port Charlotte, you'll reach Bridgend, where a tiny **woolen mill** weaves tartans for the likes of Liam Neeson (as the film character Rob Roy), Mel Gibson (in *Braveheart*), and many other discriminating customers. Gordon will give you a tour of the mill, which has been cranking out tartans for more than a century. Also at Bridgend is the Bridgend Bowling Green, where the local **bowling club** meets. For £1.50 you get playing time and balls, and they ask that you wear flat-soled shoes.

The tourist office can provide leaflets on the eight local **distilleries. Laphroaig** is the one that offers a free tour; it's located in Port Ellen, about 20 miles away. Right next door to the hostel is the **Islay Creamery,** which makes cheese that's sold all over the island. You'll find all that and more (ask at the hostel about pony trekking and boat trips) on 30 short miles.

Royal Society for the Protection of Birds Reserve. Loch Gruinart, Islay. Visitor center open: daily 10am–5pm. Admission: adults £1; children 50p.

Islay Woollen Mill. Bridgend, Islay. Tel: 01496/810563. Open: Mon–Sat 10am–5pm. In summer, also Sun 2–4pm. Admission: free.

Bridgend Bowling Club. Bridgend, Islay. Open: daily 2pm–dusk. £1.50 for as long as you want to play; pay the fee at the Bridgend Spar and Freezer Shop.

Laphroaig Distillery. Port Ellen, Islay. Tel: 01496/302418. Call ahead.

Islay Creamery. Port Charlotte, Islay. Tel: 01496/985229. Open: Mon–Fri 9am–4:30pm; Sat 9am–3pm.

The Basics

Tourist Office: The nearest T.I.C. is in Bowmore, 8 miles from Port Charlotte. Bowmore T.I.C. The Square. Bowmore, Islay. Tel: 01496/810254. Open: July–Sept: Mon–Sat 9:30am–6pm; Sun 2–5pm. Oct–June: Mon–Sat 9:30am–1pm and 2–5pm. From the hostel, turn right and walk 7 miles to Bowmore; otherwise take bus no. 451 to Bridgend and then the no. 450 or 452 to Port Charlotte.

Post Office: Port Charlotte Post Office. Main Street, Port Charlotte. Tel: 01496/850232. Open: Mon–Tues 9am–12:30pm and 1:30–5:30pm; Wed 9am–12:30pm; Thurs–Fri 9am–12:30pm and 1:30–5:30pm; Sat 9am–12:30pm. From the hostel, turn left; it's on your left after about a 5-minute walk.

Currency Exchange: Royal Bank of Scotland. Main Street. Bowmore, Islay. Tel: 01496/810555. Open: Mon–Fri 9:15am–4:45pm.

Telephone Code: 01496.

Bike Rental: Bowmore Post Office. Bowmore, Islay. Tel: 01496/810366. Full-day rental £6.

Getting There: The only way to get to Islay is by **ferry,** either from **Kennacraig** (2–3 per day; 2-hour ride) or Oban (once a week in summer only, 4-hour ride). Both carry cars and individual passengers. Information is available from Caledonian MacBrayne at 01496/302209. Kennacraig is about 100 miles west of Glasgow; Scottish Citylink and Western Buses have **coach** service leaving from Buchanan Bus Station twice daily. For information, call 0141/225 4826 or 0141/332 9191. Once on the island, buses are timed to meet the ferries and operated by Islay Coaches; schedule information is available at 01496/840273. If you're coming by **car,** get onto the A82 to the A83, following signs to Campbeltown. Kennacraig is about 4 miles past Tarbert, on the way to Campbeltown. From there, get on the Caledonian MacBrayne ferry.

What's Next

Ferry service from Islay can take you to **Oban;** it's a beautiful four-hour ride past Colonsay and Mull. At Oban, you can launch out on your own (rented) rowboat or hop on another CalMac ferry to Iona, Staffa, and Mull. If you're headed in the other direction (and have a strong stomach), take the ferry from Port Ellen to Kennacraig. There you can catch a bus to Claonig and another ferry out to **Arran Island,** which boasts Brodick Castle and gardens, a creamery, and 10 peaks over 2,000 feet. There are two Youth Hostels there.

ROWARDENNAN

Across the bonny banks of Loch Lomond from Inverbeg, beyond the pass of Balmaha, lies the "village" of Rowardennan. The sum total of civilization here consists of the Youth Hostel, the Rowardennan Hotel, and the campsite between them.

"Rowardennan" actually refers to the area of woodland to the east of Loch Lomond, about 42 miles north of Glasgow and 34 miles west of Stirling.

The area's biggest asset sits 3,192 feet above the hostel and the loch: venerable Ben Lomond. The 95-mile Highland Way from Glasgow to Fort William passes through here. Shorter woodland and loch side walks also abound, and the lower trails of Ben Lomond are gentle.

If you're not into hiking or nature, don't come here because there are no other attractions. Walkers don't seem to mind when the rain comes (which it does frequently), but if you're lucky enough to catch one of the three ferries over here, bring a sweater and long pants: The midges mean business in these parts. The closest town is Drymen, 14 miles away, so bring provisions with you if you come by public transportation.

Rowardennan Youth Hostel

Rowardennan
Glasgow G63 0AR
Tel: 01360/870259.

Set right beneath Ben Lomond and right on top of Loch Lomond, this hostel is doubly blessed. Azalea trees line the driveway, and as you approach the front door you'll notice a little lawn leading out to a tiny dock. The garden out back has a field just perfect for picnicking, Frisbee tossing, and general frolicking.

The National Trust watches over the Rowardennan Forest, so the woodlands around the hostel are well protected and unspoiled, and Ben Lomond is a short walk from the driveway. The hostel is also right on the path of the 95-mile West Highland Way (the hostel is usually reached on the second day of the hike), so its main clientele is walkers. Troops of schoolchildren also come here to take advantage of the hills and loch. There's enough room for everyone: The common room is calm and quiet and has bay windows overlooking the loch. The dining/TV room resembles an elementary-school lunchroom (the resemblance is further enhanced by the food), but there's a good self-catering kitchen.

Because of its remote location and ideal setting, this sturdy hostel is the SYHA's activity center. They offer all sorts of weekend and weeklong vacation deals at reasonable prices. "Breakaway holidays" are multiactivity vacations with archery, orienteering, canoeing/kayaking on Loch Lomond, hill walking, windsurfing, and occasionally mountain biking. Weeklong breaks begin at £149 and include accommodations, equipment, and full board. They can be booked in advance through the SYHA national office in Stirling.

The closest train station is Balloch (17 miles away). From there, you must take a bus to Balmaha and then walk 7 miles up the road to the hostel.

The closest bus stop is across Loch Lomond at Inverbeg. From there, walk down the footpath to the pier and take the ferry across the loch to Rowardennan (5 minutes). From the pier at Rowardennan,

walk to the dirt road and turn left; the hostel driveway is straight ahead after about 400 yards.

From **Glasgow,** head for Balloch on the A82; then take the A81 to Drymen. From **Stirling,** head for Drymen on the A81. Once you reach Drymen, take the B837 to Balmaha, and follow it to the end (about 7 miles from Balmaha). Note that the last

Services

portion of the road is unsuitable for coaches.

▦ Open Feb 25–Oct. Opening dates may vary slightly, so call ahead. FABA.

🕐 Reception open 7am–11:30pm. Curfew 11:30pm.

🛏 82 beds. 4-, 6-, and 8-bed rooms.

£ Members: adults £6.95; under 18 £5.85.

🍴 Meals served Easter–Sept. Self-catering kitchen facilities. Breakfast: 8am. Lunch: available for groups. Dinner: 7pm.

▯ Lockers in some rooms.

◎ Washer, dryer, and drying room.

P Ample and free of charge.

🛍 Shop at hostel sells canned goods, candy, and some groceries.

🛋 Common room; TV room.

📞 In reception area and TV room only.

♿ Wheelchair accessible.

💱 See "Currency Exchange" under "The Basics" in Rowardennan.

🔺 Bike shed.

Cheap Eats Nearby

The Sun Lounge at the Rowardennan Hotel

This is the only place for miles. An airy little room with cushioned banquettes, it looks out onto the hotel garden. The friendly staff seems to like Sinatra. Jacket potatoes run £2.65 to £2.95; poached Loch Lomond salmon is £5; hot dishes are £4 to £6. When meal hours are over, they serve sandwiches (£1 to £2) and scones.

Rowardennan. Tel: 01360/870273. Open: daily noon–2pm and 6–8pm. Bar open: daily 11am–11:30pm. Cash only. Wheelchair accessible. From the hostel, walk down the driveway past the campsite; about a 10-minute walk.

Grocery Store: At the hostel store, canned goods and microwaveable dinners available.

Experiences

Either the very active or the very sedentary will love it here; those who fall in between might feel otherwise. **Walking** is the main activity in Rowardennan, which is full of beautiful wooded paths and loch side routes. There's very little in the way of organized tours and guided walks, except for walks organized through the forest ranger.

Rental equipment for windsurfing or jet skiing (unless you're on one of the hostel's planned activity breaks) is scarce, but that doesn't stop hostelers from dipping into the loch or hiking up 3,192-foot Ben Lomond (bring insect repellent and watch out for the muddy path). If you bring a bike, you can catch the ferry to Inverbeg and walk up Glen Douglas, a valley that runs between Loch Lomond and Loch Long, about six miles away.

Ranger-guided walks. The National Trust for Scotland Ranger Service, Ardess Lodge, Rowardennan. Tel: 01360/870224. Full-day walks: adults £5; under 16 £2. Half-day walks: adults £2; under 16 50p.

The Basics

Tourist Office: Drymen T.I.C. and Library. The Square, Drymen (14 miles away). Tel: 01360/660751. From the hostel, it's a straight 8 miles on the dirt road out of the forest to Balmaha; from there, take the B837 the remaining 6 miles into Drymen.

Post Office: Drymen Post Office. 1 Stirling Rd., Drymen. Tel: 01360/660743. Open: Mon–Tues 9am–1pm and 2–5:30pm; Wed 9am–1pm; Thurs–Fri 9am–1pm and 2–5:30pm; Sat 9am–12:30pm. From the hostel, it's a straight 8 miles on the dirt road out of the forest to Balmaha; from there, take the B837 the remaining 6 miles into Drymen.

Currency Exchange: Royal Bank of Scotland. 52 Main St., Drymen. Tel: 01360/660260. Open: Mon–Fri 9am–4:30pm.

Telephone Code: 01360.

Bike Rental: Lomond Activities. Hope House, 64 Main St., Drymen. Tel: 01360/660066.

Getting There: The best way to get here for those coming by public transport is by **coach.** Scottish Citylink coaches from **Glasgow** to Fort William or Oban stop at **Inverbeg,** where you get off and take the *Frisky Jean,* a motorboat (maximum capacity 12), for a 5-minute ride across Loch Lomond to Rowardennan. The buses run regularly; for information, call Strathclyde Transport at 0141/2264826 or Scottish Citylink at 0990/505050. The ferry operates daily from May 15–Sept 31, and weekends only from Easter–May. There are three crossing times daily: 10:30am, 2:30pm, and 6:30pm. For ferry info, call: 01360/870273. By **car:** Those coming from the **north** have to take the A82 (which originates in Fort William) down the west side of Loch Lomond to Balloch and switch to the A811 going east to Drymen. From there, follow signs down the dirt road to Rowardennan, 14 miles north. From **Edinburgh,** take the M8 to Glasgow and the A82 north to Balloch; from there follow the above directions.

What's Next

Taking the ferry back over to Inverbeg and the bus 10 miles farther south will get you to the massive, regal mansion that's the **Loch Lomond** Youth Hostel, home of a British TV series. Green space aplenty, comfortable sitting rooms, and a ghost or two await. If you're ready for a jolt of reality, **Glasgow** is only 20 miles away. The city is not nearly as menacing as its gritty reputation would lead you to believe. In an elegant residential neighborhood, the luxurious Youth Hostel has marble bathrooms in every room, an ample TV and sitting room, as well as a friendly, helpful staff to get you going. The city offers shopping, museums, galleries, a university, and nighttime activities—bars with live music, foreign and alternative films, and a hopping club scene.

LOCH LOMOND

Loch Lomond, 24 miles long and 653 feet deep, is Scotland's largest loch, flanked by craggy mountains to the west and serene woodlands to the south. These days, it owes its fame to soap-opera fans across the land, who tune in weekly to watch the compelling saga *Take the High Road,* set in nearby Luss.

Gerard Manley Hopkins and William Wordsworth both mused about the area's beauty, as do the crowds of tourists that cram in here every summer to take cruises to the loch islands, rent rowboats, and climb the hills to reach the proverbial High Road. A lonely prisoner once wrote about the High Road in song as he yearned for the bonny banks of Loch Lomond, where he met his true love.

There's a lovin' feeling at the hostel, about 10 miles south of Inverbeg and two miles from Balloch, the nearest train station. A mansion resembling a castle is set on a hill overlooking the loch; it's another of those I-can't-believe-I'm-staying-in-a-hostel hostels, and most guests gawk for at least an hour or two at the grand salons, stained-glass windows, and fountain bubbling out front.

✳ Loch Lomond Youth Hostel

Arden
Alexandria, Dumbartonshire G83 8RB
Tel: 01389/850226.

Resembling a castle, the hostel is an 1866 mansion sitting atop a hill across the street from Loch Lomond. Rhododendrons line the driveway on the (uphill) walk to the front door, and fragrant flora grow in the gardens.

The interior looks like a film set in Victorian times. The focal point of the building is the central gallery, with a vaulted roof and frosted skylight that casts a glow on the upstairs balcony and sitting room below. The huge sitting room/conference room has an elaborate fireplace and a serious-looking oil painting; the TV room is more modern, though equally comfortable. Both rooms have dazzling views of the water, gardens, and big old Ben Lomond on the east side of the loch. Even the doorknobs are interesting. The staircases are decorated with classical sculptures in little niches. Photos of the cast of TV series *Take The High Road* are on display at reception. The photos come in handy, since the show is often filmed on the hostel grounds.

The young, friendly staff manages to keep the place in good, clean shape—not easy with the large flocks of schoolchildren that migrate here every spring. Graciously served meals are offered, and the self-catering kitchen has all the basic equipment. The bedrooms are standard and decent, but beware of dormitory 27: In the late 1800s, the daughter of the family that lived here had an affair with the stable hand. When the family found out, they locked her in the tower as punishment and eventually she committed suicide. While she was locked up, she did some carvings and paintings around the door and windows in the tower, now dormitory 27. Her ethereal figure has been sighted in period costume, drifting up and down the back stairs.

Services

🚆 The closest train station is in Balloch, 2 miles away. Exit and turn left. On the main street, turn left. Continue up the road, and at the Old Luss Road bear right at the fork (ignoring the Dead End sign). Follow that until the end, and when you reach the main road (A82) turn right and go down the hill for about 5 minutes. The hostel is just up on your left. Alternatively, a taxi costs about £2.50. Alexandria Coach Hire buses headed to Luss will drop you off on the road in front of the Youth Hostel, but service is infrequent.

🚌 Buses coming from Glasgow in the direction of Oban, Fort William, Campbeltown, and Skye all go past the hostel and will drop you at the end of the driveway. Follow the sign up the long driveway.

🚗 The hostel is situated on the A82, 2 miles north of Balloch, on the Glasgow-Crianlarich road. Follow signs for the Duck Bay Marina; the hostel is across the street and up the hill.

🎫 Open Mar–Oct. IBN and FABA.

🕐 Reception open 7am–11:30pm. Curfew 2am.

🛏 200 beds. 4-, 6-, 8-, 10-, and 12-bed rooms.

£ Members: adults £7.80; under 18 £6.40.

🍴 Meals served Easter–Oct. Self-catering kitchen facilities. Breakfast: 8am. Lunch: available for groups. Dinner: 6pm.

📦 Coin-operated lockers in reception area.

▣ Washer, dryer, and drying room.

P Ample and free of charge.

🛍 Shop at hostel sells candy, groceries, and some outdoor gear.

🛋 Upstairs gallery; conference/ common room; TV room; games room.

🚬 In upstairs gallery only.

♿ Not wheelchair accessible.

💱 See "Currency Exchange" under "The Basics" in Loch Lomond.

🔺 Bike shed.

Cheap Eats Nearby

The Balloch Hotel

You can sit at loch side picnic tables or traditional timber-beamed pub inside. It's best to fill up on a few starters such as stuffed tomatoes and other delicacies (£2 to £3). Main dishes might include anything from haggis to moussaka (£4 to £6). Fish and chips are £4.95.

Balloch Road, Balloch (2 miles from the hostel). Tel: 01389/752579. Open: daily noon–9:30pm. Credit cards: VA, MC, EC, Access. From the hostel, turn right onto the A82. On the left side of the road is a footpath, the Old Luss Road. Follow it for about 1 1/2 miles to the end. When you reach the filling station, turn left onto Balloch Road. Pass the train station, go over the bridge, and it's on your left; a 45-minute walk.

The Duck Bay Marina

Part of a hotel/marina complex, this restaurant is right across the street from the hostel, overlooking Loch Lomond. Good selection in a T.G.I. Friday's atmosphere. The salad bar is £4; fish and chips are £4 to £5.

Duck Bay, Loch Lomond. Tel: 01389/751234. Open: Mon–Sat noon–2:30pm and 6–10pm; Sun noon–5pm and 6–10pm. Bar meals: daily noon–7pm. Credit cards: VA, MC, EC, AE, Access. Wheelchair access. From the hostel, it takes 5 minutes: Walk down the driveway, turn left, and it's across the street.

Grocery Store: All'ours Newsmarket. Balloch Road, Balloch (2 miles away). Open: daily 6:30am–10pm.

Experiences

Tourist-hungry boat operators plaster the area with leaflets advertising their tantalizing **boat rides,** which travel to some of the islands in the loch but can be pricey. There are some easy **walks** up to Ben Bowie and Stoney Mullen behind the hostel; they only take about an hour and reward you with substantial loch views. Another nice place to while away an afternoon is right across the street and up the road from the hostel, where there's a picnic spot right on the loch.

A few miles north on the A82, the "conservation village" of **Luss** (aka Glendarroch on the TV series *Take the High Road*) is kept picture-perfect, with rose-covered cottages lining the narrow lanes. The town was originally built by local landowners to provide housing for workers at the local slate quarries and cotton mills. The town church has some of the oldest, moldiest graves in Scotland.

On the southern edge of the loch in the farming village of Gartocharn (four miles from the hostel), there are **pony trekking** and riding lessons. The neighboring village of Drymen makes a nice visit; it's a traditional village with a sweet little square.

Sweeney's Cruises. Loch Lomond, Balloch. Tel: 01389/752376.

Duncryne Equitation and Trekking Centre. Gartocharn, Loch Lomond. Tel: 01389/830425. 1-hour trek: £15. Lessons available. Call ahead.

The Basics

Tourist Office: Balloch T.I.C. Old Station Building, Balloch Road, Balloch (2 miles away). Tel: 01389/753533. Open: Apr–June: daily 10am–5pm. July–Aug: daily 9:30am–7:30pm. Sept: daily 10am–7pm. Oct: daily 10am–5pm. From the hostel, turn right and go down the A82 to Balloch, or walk to the footpath on the left side of the A82 (the loch side), which leads you to Old Luss Road. Walk straight until you reach the filling station; then turn left onto Balloch Road. The T.I.C. is about two blocks up on the left; a 45-minute walk.

Post Office: Balloch Post Office. Dalvait Road, Balloch (2 miles away). Tel: 01389/752583. Open: Mon–Tues 9am–1pm and 2–5:30pm; Wed 9am–12:30pm; Thurs–Fri 9am–1pm and 2–5:30pm; Sat 9am–12:30pm. From the hostel, turn right, and go down the A82 to Balloch, or walk to the footpath on the left side of the A82 (the loch side), which leads you to Old Luss Road. Walk straight until you reach the filling station; then turn left onto Balloch Road. Cross the bridge, and turn right onto Dalvait Road. It's on your left; a 45-minute walk.

Currency Exchange: Balloch T.I.C. See "Tourist Office" under "The Basics" in Loch Lomond.

Telephone Code: 01389.

Bike Rental: Tullichewan Caravan Park. Balloch. Tel: 01389/759475. Hefty deposit required. Also in Drymen (8 miles away). Lomond Activities. Hope House, 64 Main St. Tel: 01360/660066.

Getting There: The nearest **train** stop is **Balloch,** 2 miles away, which is on the Glasgow-Oban/Fort William line. Service is frequent; call 0141/284 2884 for information. Alexandria Buses (no. 305) run up to the hostel. Call 01389/750078 for info. By **coach,** Scottish Citylink runs past the hostel on its Oban and Fort William route; call 0990/505050 for info. By **car,** take the A82, following signs for Balloch. The hostel is 2 miles north, on the west side of Loch Lomond.

What's Next

Glasgow is a mere 19 miles from Loch Lomond, and all the joys and pains of big-city life can be had there. Busy streets, an active nightlife, museums, art galleries, as well as a contemporary arts center make it less forbidding than its reputation might have you believe. For those headed north, **Rowardennan** is only 10 miles up the A82 and a ferry ride (passengers only, summer service) across Loch Lomond. There's nothing but beautiful forest walks, the monstrous Ben Lomond, and a loch side hostel nestled between the water and the trees.

Glasgow & the Southwest

The area to the south of Loch Lomond and to the north of the English border roughly comprises Glasgow, the Strathclyde region, and the county of Dumfries and Galloway. Just off the west coast lies the small island of Arran.

Thanks to the wealthy tobacco barons and industrialists of the 1800s who happened to have great taste in architecture, Glasgow is a surprisingly lovely city. It saw its heyday in the late 19th century and then fell into the doldrums; urban decay and a lackluster economy contributed to its general decline in the 1960s. Lazarus-like, it rose from the ashes (and postindustrial soot) in the 1980s.

Now it's a cheerful, friendly city. Glasgow University and the Glasgow School of Art provide a trendy population of students to feed the many bars, music venues, hip restaurants, and cool clothing stores. The manageable load of tourists that come here are almost uniformly pleased by the free museums, active arts scene, elegant neighborhoods, and huge park that make the busy metropolis bearable. The Youth Hostel is equally extraordinary: It's a former luxury hotel.

Just miles away lies the historic town of New Lanark, where Robert Owen pioneered the cooperative movement. A factory man with a heart, he masterminded the idea of the modern industrial community. Plucking scores of souls from abject poverty, he gave them a livable wage, a safe community, and even a kindergarten in this mill town. The village of New Lanark remains almost unchanged from his day (although it's no longer operating as a mill). The hostel is smack in the middle of town, a gathering place for students of social history.

Lovers of Scottish literature make pilgrimages to the town of Ayr, one mile from Alloway, the birthplace of poet Robert Burns. The hostel in Ayr is a rambling old stone house on the windy beach looking out onto the isle of Arran. A ferry ride from the mainland, Arran has two castles, innumerable hilly walks, and some simple coastal towns lining its perimeter. The two hostels here, more like guest houses, are basic lodgings with cozy atmospheres.

This entire region is fairly well connected by trains and buses. For those coming from or going to England, there's direct service from Glasgow Central to Carlisle. From Glasgow to New Lanark and Ayr, there's reliable frequent service. To Arran, the car/passenger ferries are timed with the trains that pull in to Ardrossan Harbour. Once on the island, you'll find decent bus service (bring Dramamine) to get around. It can be tricky to drive in and around Glasgow, but outside the city the highways are decent and have helpful signs.

GLASGOW

Travelers on Scotland's tourist trail often snub Glasgow, preferring to herd, sheeplike, among the legions of camera-toting, festival-frenzied crowds in Edinburgh. Let them. Edinburgh's siphoning off of the tourist flow only makes this stylish, vibrant city less crowded, less expensive, and more fun to explore.

A far cry from its former image as Edinburgh's poor relation, Glasgow has polished itself off from its postindustrial decline and developed an identity all its own. The city is downright elegant, thanks to the mighty vision of master architect Charles Rennie Mackintosh. With an active contemporary arts scene, it's a hotbed of emerging artists: Museums, galleries, and workshops sprinkled around the city support their cause. The university neighborhood teems with trendy, kitschy restaurants and live-music venues as well as excellent alternative cinemas. The shopping area—with everything from haute couture to cheap chic—is a thankful blast of fresh air for those suffocating amid the piles of cut-rate Scottish woolen stores.

Outdoors types can even find things to do. Kelvingrove Park provides a green respite from the grit and grime of city life, and bike paths along the River Clyde can take you as far out of town as Loch Lomond. During summer, there's a grab bag of festivals ranging from the usual folk and jazz to software, Pakistani music, and gay pride. The incredibly elegant Youth Hostel, right by the park, is a converted luxury hotel. It boasts small dormitories, private bathrooms, and a knowledgeable staff ready to help you get to know this oft-overlooked gem of a city.

Glasgow Youth Hostel

7/8 Park Terrace
Glasgow G3 6BY
Tel: 0141/332 3004.

It's a slight hike from the train and bus stations to the hostel, which is in a tranquil, upscale neighborhood with software firms and young professionals on their lunch hours. Recently remodeled, the hostel sparkles.

The bedrooms in this former luxury hotel have their own marble bathrooms with brass fixtures, and the shower is a shoulder-soothing sensuous experience. The competent, friendly staff mans the reception area downstairs with efficient ease. You could play basketball in the gargantuan TV room, and the games room has a pool table, checkers, pinball, and even a little disco area. This means that when the hostel is bursting with large parties, there's room enough for everyone. A conference room and a common room overlooking the street are available.

The downstairs dining room is a departure from the otherwise Victorian decor: A postmodern fantasy of slate gray and red, it would work well on the starship *Enterprise*. They dish up breakfast (included in the overnight price) and evening meals as well. They haven't overlooked a thing here.

Services

There are two train stations in Glasgow. From **Glasgow Central** (where trains from England and southwest Scotland arrive), turn left up Gordon Street as you exit the station and take the first right onto Hope Street. Continue until you reach Sauchiehall Street and turn left. Walk up Sauchiehall Street for eight blocks until you reach Charing Cross intersection. Look for the brown monument with a clock and turn right, passing the Clydesdale Bank. Walk up Woodlands Road, past a short row of shops, and then turn left at the car showroom. Follow the signs to the hostel, which is on Park Terrace overlooking the park. It's a 20-minute walk. Alternately, take bus no. 44 or 59 to the first stop: Woodlands Road. Follow the signs to the hostel.

From **Queen Street Station** (where trains from Edinburgh and the north arrive), turn left onto Bath Street and follow it until you reach the Charing Cross intersection. Look for the brown monument with a clock and turn right, passing the Clydesdale Bank. Walk up Woodlands Road, past a short row of shops, and then turn left at the car showroom. Follow the signs to the hostel, which is on Park Terrace, overlooking the park. A 15- to 20-minute walk. Alternatively, take bus no. 11 from Cathedral Street to the first stop on Woodlands Road and follow the signs to the hostel. Note that bus no. 11 doesn't run on Sundays.

From the bus station, turn right onto Sauchiehall Street and follow the street for about 10 blocks until you reach the Charing Cross intersection. Look for the brown monument with the clock and turn right, passing the Clydesdale Bank. Walk up Woodlands Road, past a short row of shops, and then turn left at the car showroom. From there, follow the signs to the Youth Hostel. Alternatively, take bus no. 11 and get off at the first stop on Woodlands Road. Follow signs to the hostel.

🚌 Follow signs to Charing Cross. When you reach the intersection, go straight onto Woodlands Road, and turn left after the first set of lights on Woodlands Road. Turn onto Lynedoch Street and left at the Bank of Scotland and then right onto Woodlands Terrace. Continue up as it turns into Park Terrace. The hostel will appear on your right.

⊞ Open year-round. IBN and FABA.

🕐 Reception open 7am–11pm. Curfew 2am.

🛏 168 beds. 4-, 6-, 8-, and 10-bed rooms, all with bathrooms en suite. All rooms have keys.

£ Members: adults £10.45; under 18 £9. Prices include continental breakfast.

🍴 Meals served May–Sept. Self-catering kitchen facilities. Breakfast: 7–9am. Lunch: not available. Dinner: 6:30pm.

💼 Lockers.

◻ Washers, dryers, and a drying room.

P Unrestricted street parking in front of the hostel.

🗋 Shop at hostel sells candy, canned goods, phone cards, maps. Discount on bus tours of Glasgow (£3).

🛋 Common room; TV room; games room with pool table, jukebox.

🚬 In smoking room only.

♿ Not wheelchair accessible.

💱 See "Currency Exchange" under "The Basics" in Glasgow.

🔺 Bike shed; conference room.

Cheap Eats Nearby

The Bay Tree Vegetarian Café

"Eats without meats" proclaims the menu of this popular eatery, which also caters to vegans. Good music on the radio and mesmerizing art on the walls in a friendly, casual atmosphere. Dishes include salads £2 to £3.50; hummus with pita or oatcakes £2.40; baked potatoes £1.95 to £3.10. Daily specials are on the blackboard.

403 Great Western Rd., Glasgow. Tel: 0141/334 5898. Open: Mon–Sat 11am–9pm; Sun 10am–8pm. Credit cards: VA, MC, EC, Access. From the hostel, turn left and walk to Woodlands Road. Turn left on Woodlands Road, and before reaching the river, take a right, which leads you to Great Western Road. It's on the right, just past the U station.

The Granary

This whole foods restaurant has the spirit of a country inn. Order at the counter. Homemade dishes (mostly £3 to £5) may include lasagne, vegetarian chili, and vegetable bake; offerings change depending on the season and the fresh food available locally. All dishes come with a selection of two salads. Save room for devilishly decadent sweets.

82 Howard St., Glasgow. Tel: 0141/226 3770. Open: Mon–Sat 9:30am–6pm; Sun 11am–5pm. Cash only. Wheelchair access. From the hostel, walk to Woodlands Road then down Sauchiehall Street for about 9 blocks. Turn right on Renfield Street. Walk to the far end of St. Enoch Square (the mall to your left), turn left on Howard Street, and it's on your right; a 20-minute walk.

Grocery Store: Woodlands Road has several small grocery stores.

Experiences

Pull out a city map and plan your attack: There's a lot to see and do. The tourist office has a *Where to Go Free* guide, packed with information on museums, clubs, pubs, and restaurants. It's a good way to begin exploring Glasgow. In addition, the municipal council offers **city walks** that aren't outrageously priced and are of special interest to anyone compelled by Glasgow's famous architecture.

The city's **museums** are all free. The **Kelvingrove** and the **Burrell Collection** are probably the most celebrated and have a mixture of works by old masters and newer, more experimental installations. The **Hunterian Museum and Art Gallery,** part of the university, also has a mixed collection. Both Kelvingrove and Hunterian are on the grounds of Glasgow University in Kelvingrove Park, through which the River Clyde winds its way; it's a nice place for a breather. The university also offers lectures and talks free of charge; pick up info in the basement of the Hunterian.

Other museums worth a peek include St. Mungo's for religious art, the People's Palace, and the Museum of Transport. Down Sauchiehall Street lies the innovative, slightly self-conscious **Centre for Contemporary Art,** which houses exhibition space, hosts all sorts of performances and lectures, and even has a short list of children's activities in summertime. A **Buddhist Centre** resides across the street for those looking for urban serenity, and around the corner is the **Glasgow Film Theatre,** where independent, unusual, and foreign films are shown. The cafe inside is perfect for sagely discussing film theory and existential philosophy with the local intelligentsia.

If you go farther toward the center and turn right onto King Street, you'll find some excellent printmaking galleries/workshops that welcome wandering art lovers. For music and merrymaking, get a copy of *The List* (£1.50), an excellent guide detailing hot dance spots and music venues; otherwise, prowl the pubs in the student area around the far end of Sauchiehall Street (closer to the hostel).

Glasgow plays host to a parade of **festivals.** Mayfest, a tamer version of the Edinburgh Fringe, comes to town with unusual theater, experimental music, and other avant-garde events in various venues throughout the city. In early June there's a folk festival (Ravi Shankar played last year), followed by a jazz festival in early July. Pakistan Music Village blows into town with an explosion of bards, bands, and bhajis in a four-day music and eating extravaganza, and other, smaller events pop up throughout the year.

Glasgow City Walks. The $1^1/2$-hour walk begins at the tourist office, St. Vincent Place, Glasgow. Tel: 0141/204 4400. May–Sept only. Heart of Glasgow tour: Mon–Fri 6pm; Sun 10:30am. The Cathedral Walk: Wed, Sun 2:15pm. Tours: adults £2.50; concessions £1.50.

Art Gallery and Museum, Kelvingrove. Tel: 0141/221 9600. Open: Mon–Sat 10am–5pm; Sun 11am–5pm. Wheelchair access. Admission: free.

The Burrell Collection. 2060 Pollokshaws Rd., Glasgow. Tel: 0141/649 7151. Open: Mon–Sat 10am–5pm; Sun 2–5pm. Admission: free.

Hunterian Museum and Art Gallery. University of Glasgow, Glasgow. Tel: 0141/330 4221 or 0141/330 5431. Open: Mon–Sat 9:30am–5pm. Wheelchair access. Admission: free.

Centre for Contemporary Arts. 350 Sauchiehall St., Glasgow. Tel: 0141/332 0522. Galleries open: daily 11am–6pm (Thurs–Fri until 7pm). Admission: free. Box office open: Mon–Sat 10am–7pm, later on performance nights.

Glasgow Buddhist Centre. 329 Sauchiehall St., Glasgow. Tel: 0141/333 0524. Open: Mon–Fri 11:30am–5pm. Free public talks. Meditation courses, yoga classes, cultural evenings have price tags, but they're suggested donations.

Glasgow Film Theatre. 12 Rose St., Glasgow. Tel: 0141/332 6535. Evening shows, Mon–Fri: adults £4, concessions £3. Sat, all tickets £4. Matinees, Mon–Sat: adults £3; concessions £2. Double features: adults £4; concessions £3.

Festival information. Glasgow City Council. Tel: 0141/227 5887.

The Basics

Tourist Office: Glasgow T.I.C. 35 St. Vincent Place, Glasgow. Tel: 0141/204 4400. Open: Easter–May: Mon–Sat 9am–6pm; Sun 10am–6pm. June: Mon–Sat 9am–7pm; Sun 10am–6pm. Jul–Aug: Mon–Sat 9am–8pm; Sun 10am–6pm. Sept: Mon–Sat 9am–7pm; Sun 10am–6pm. Oct–Easter: Mon–Sat 9am–6pm. From the hostel, turn left and walk to Woodlands Road. Take bus no. 44 or 59 to St. Vincent Street. Turn left onto St. Vincent, and the T.I.C. is three blocks up on your left. Look for the flags. Otherwise, from Woodlands Road, walk down to Charing Cross intersection, cross, and go down Sauchiehall Street. When you get to the concert hall, turn right and the T.I.C. is just up on your left.

Currency Exchange: American Express. 115 Hope St., Glasgow. Tel: 0141/221 4366. Open: Mon–Fri 8:30am–5:30pm (Tues 9:30am opening); Sat 9am–midnight. Thomas Cook. 15/17 Gordon St. Tel: 0141/221 6614. Open: Mon–Sat 9am–5:30pm (Thurs 10am opening).

Telephone Code: 0141.

Bike Rental: Tortoise Cycle Centre. 1417 Dumbarton Rd. Scotstoun, Glasgow. Tel: 0141/958 1055.

Getting There: Glasgow has two **train** stations. Trains coming from the **southwest** (including the Stranraer ferry port) and England come into Glasgow Central. Trains from **Edinburgh** and **the north** go to Queen Street. For rail info, call 0141/204 2844. Scottish Citylink and numerous other **coaches** come into Buchanan Bus Station from all over. For bus info, call the Travel Centre at St. Enoch Square at 0141/226 4826; they have all bus information for Glasgow and the Strathclyde region (open: Mon–Sat 9:30am–5:30pm). By **car,** the M8 is the main motorway from **Edinburgh, Dundee,** and **the northeast.** The A77 works its way up to Glasgow from the **south.** The Glasgow **airport** can be reached at 0141/887 1111.

What's Next

Loch Lomond is only about 21 miles north of Glasgow via an easy 45-minute train ride. A palatial mansion disguised as a Youth Hostel sits high on a hill overlooking Scotland's longest loch, and it can make a nice base for those wishing to visit Glasgow by day and come home to countryside tranquility by night. In the other direction, the shrine to Robert Burns and seaside resort town of **Ayr** also has an impressive beach-side hostel not far from the wonder boy's birthplace and old haunts. It's also easily accessible by train, 36 miles south of Glasgow.

NEW LANARK

For students of social history, a pilgrimage to the village of New Lanark is a required stop on any tour of the Clyde valley in southern Scotland. Just 20 miles southeast of Glasgow, it was the birthplace of the cooperative movement.

Built around 1789, New Lanark was established by wealthy mill owners intent on exploiting the crashing waters of the Falls of Clyde. New Lanark grew to be the largest cotton mill in Scotland, and eventually 2,500 thankful souls escaped poverty to live and work in the village. Robert Owen, the son-in-law of the mill owner, came to the village in 1800. He planted the seeds of the Utopian social movement by creating and administering the self-sustained industrial community.

A village store brought quality goods to the workers at near cost, and the profits were reinvested in the village. As New Lanark grew, the world's first nursery school was established here (children under 10 were prohibited from working). The village became a model for cooperative communities around the world, including the town of New Harmony, Indiana. The mill stopped operating in 1968, but almost all the original buildings still stand. The Falls of Clyde still cascade, making New Lanark a popular destination for coaches—especially those carrying school groups. The entire village is a museum of sorts, allowing visitors to "experience" life as it was in the community's heyday.

The Youth Hostel is in the sandstone row houses once occupied by mill workers, and despite its gleaming modern interior it still offers a singular historic voyage. You should stop in the village of Lanark (where the train stops, about 1½ miles away) for provisions and information.

❀ New Lanark Youth Hostel

Wee Row
Rosedale Street
New Lanark ML11 9DJ
Tel: 01555/666710.

Redone last year, the hostel is spanking new and clean—it's almost at odds with the simplicity of the village. Plunked in the middle of Wee Row, a lineup of four tenement-style former workers' houses, the hostel has a gleaming interior and features small bedrooms and private bathrooms. If the mill workers could see it now! A continental breakfast is included in the price; evening meals are available as well, but you must book them before you arrive.

The TV lounge has cushioned booths, carpeted floors, and board games, and the reception desk boasts a small but growing library of travel guidebooks and literature. Expect to hear the pitter patter of little feet: The hostel's facilities and the village's attractions make it an obvious destination for school groups. Call ahead before taking the trip here.

Services

🚊 From the train station in Lanark, the hostel is 1½ miles. Take a left out of the station and pass the tourist office on your left. At the T junction, turn right and follow the signs for New Lanark. After a quarter of a mile, take a sharp left and New Lanark Hostel is about 1 mile down the road. There's limited bus service to New Lanark; ask at the tourist office. A taxi is about £1.50.

From the bus station in Lanark, the hostel is 1 $^1/_2$ miles. To walk, take a left out of the station, pass the tourist office on your left. Follow directions from the train, given above. Alternatively, take the bus from the railway station.

From the M74, the motorway to Glasgow, take Junction 13, and follow signs to Lanark and New Lanark. The hostel is in the center of New Lanark.

Open year-round. FABA.

Reception open 7am–11:30pm. Curfew 11:30pm.

64 beds. 4-bed rooms, all with bathrooms en suite.

£ Members: adults £8.80; under 18 £7.70. Prices include continental breakfast.

Meals served year-round. Self-catering kitchen. Breakfast: 8:30–9:30am; continental breakfast. Lunch: by special request. Dinner: 7pm (call ahead to check).

Room keys available on request.

Washer, dryer, and drying room.

P Ample and free of charge.

Shop at hostel sells candy and canned goods.

TV room, common room.

In common room only.

Not wheelchair accessible.

See "Currency Exchange" under "The Basics" in New Lanark.

Bike shed.

Cheap Eats Nearby

The Horse & Jockey

This is one of a number of comfortable pubs on Lanark's main drag. Up the tartan-covered stairs is a timber-beamed restaurant with an old copper fireplace. The locals swear by the food, which features jacket potatoes for £1.50 to £1.95 and a three-course lunch for £3.95. Daily specials include steak pie, fish and chips, and other classic British dishes.

56 High St., Lanark (1$^1/_2$ miles away). Tel: 01555/664825. Open: Mon–Sat 11:30am–2:30pm and 5–8:30pm. Cash only. From the hostel, head back up to Lanark. From the train station, turn right; it's about 5 minutes up High Street, on the left.

New Lanark Visitor Centre

Inside the village museum and up the spiral walkway sits this cheery cafeteria—the only eatery around. Study the wall covering that chronicles New Lanark history as you munch on the standard lunchroom grub. Sandwiches cost £1.50 to £2.25; quiche and salad are £3; soup and homemade bread £1.25. Daily specials run £3 to £3.50.

New Lanark Mill, level 3. New Lanark. Tel: 01555/665876. Open: daily 10am–5pm. Cash only. From the hostel, turn right, and go through the gate to the visitor center. The restaurant is up the walkway.

Grocery Store: Somerfield. Next to the train station in Lanark. Open: Mon–Thurs 8:30am–8pm; Fri 8:30am–9pm; Sat 8:30am–8pm; Sun 10am–5pm.

Experiences

If you've taken the trouble to come to **New Lanark,** you might as well follow the crowds and pay £3.45 for the passport ticket to check the place out. It's worth the money, if only for the eerie tour you get in the museum—a multimedia ride on an indoor chairlift. Hosted by the dulcet yet ghostly tones of "10-year-old mill girl Annie MacLeod," the tour takes you through her life in 20th-century comfort, complete with holograms and a host of other audiovisual effects. Ethereal Annie is the highlight of the package, but the ticket also gets you into the village store, Robert Owen's house, and a millworkers' house.

After visiting the museum, check out the **Falls of Clyde:** The waters cascading from Corra Linn are just a short walk away, and a wildlife exhibition indicates some nice walks through the 170-acre nature reserve. Badger watches make an entertaining evening activity during summer, and there are guided walks available. The nearby town of Biggar (about 10 miles away) has a host of museums, and the **Clydesdale Arts Network** occasionally holds poetry readings and other arts-related activities in the town hall.

New Lanark Visitor Centre. New Lanark. Tel: 01555/661345. Open: daily 11am–5pm. Passport ticket: adults £3.45; students and senior citizens £2.25; admission free for children under 3.

Falls of Clyde Visitor Centre. New Lanark. Tel: 01555/665262. Open: Easter–Oct: daily 11am–5pm. Oct–Easter: Sat–Sun 1–5pm. Admission: adults £1; children, students, and senior citizens 50p. Wildlife reserve open all year. Badger watches on summer evenings only.

Clydesdale Arts Network. Clydesdale District Council, Lanark Library, Lanark. Tel: 01555/661331. Call for leaflet; prices vary for activities.

The Basics

Tourist Office: Lanark T.I.C. Horsemarket, Lanark (1¹/₂ miles away). Tel: 01555/661661. Open: Apr–June: Mon–Sat 10am–5pm; Sun noon–5pm. July–Aug: Mon–Fri 9am–7pm; Sat 10am–6pm; Sun 11am–5pm. Sept–Nov: Mon–Sat 9am–4pm; Sun noon–5pm. From the hostel, take the bus or walk 1¹/₂ miles up the hill into Lanark; from the train station, turn left, and the T.I.C. is just ahead on the left.

Post Office: Lanark Post Office. 26/28 St. Leonard's St., Lanark (1¹/₂ miles away). Tel: 01555/662230. Open: Mon–Fri 9am–5:30pm; Sat 9am–12:30pm. From the hostel, take the bus or walk 1¹/₂ miles up the hill into Lanark; from the train station, turn right and it's 5 minutes down the street on your right.

Currency Exchange: A. T. Mays. 53 High St., Lanark. Tel: 01555/661417. Open: Mon–Fri 9am–5:30pm.

Telephone Code: 01599.

Bike Rental: William Withers and Co., Loch Garage. Hyndford Road, Lanark. Tel: 01555/665878.

Getting There: Lanark is 25 miles southeast of Glasgow and an easy ride from Glasgow Central. **Trains** leave five times daily (change at Motherwell). For information, call 0141/2042844. **Coaches** come in from a variety of places in southern Scotland and are operated by three different companies. Wilsons Nationwide tel: 01555/820249; Stokes tel: 01555/870344; Kelvin Central Buses tel: 01698/263575. From Lanark to New Lanark, catch local bus no. 35/40. By **car** from **Edinburgh,** take the A70 southeast following signs to Carstairs and Lanark. From **Glasgow,** take the A72 south straight to Lanark.

What's Next

After Lanark, it's an easy enough hop north to **Glasgow** for shopping, museum-going, and all the wonders of postindustrial city life: great pubs and clubs, a luxury hostel, and relatively few tourists. Otherwise, pass through Glasgow and head east to **Edinburgh.** Prepare to push your way through the camera-toting tourists on the Royal Mile and head up Princes Street to one of the two Youth Hostels. It's every woman for herself out there during festival time, but no visit to Scotland would be complete without a visit to the celebrated city. Heading west, the beach town of **Ayr,** 43 miles away, provides green space; calm, tree-lined streets; and invigorating sea breezes.

AYR

A beach resort for more than a century, Ayr was where wealthy Glaswegians once came to escape the soot and sweat of city life. It's just up the road from Alloway, the home town of Scotland's bawdy bard, Robert ("My Love Is Like a Red Red Rose") Burns. Most tourist activity in Ayrshire revolves around uncovering and landmarking every nook and cranny he ever touched: Hence a large percentage of visitors here are literary pilgrims.

Nowadays, Ayr's slightly faded elegance still manages to attract tourists for the beach, the Burns sites, and nearby Prestwick Airport, which offers the cheapest flights to Dublin. Ayr itself is an old market town and fishing port with a lively theatrical tradition: three theaters provide entertainment year-round. You can load up on performances the first week in June, when the Ayr Arts Festival comes to town. Summer is the nicest time to visit: The weather is balmy, and the wind dies down on the beach; on a clear day, you can see straight across to Arran and the Kintyre peninsula. The hostel, which stands guard at the beachfront, is a stone mansion with a Scottish flag flying at full mast.

Ayr Youth Hostel

Craigweil House
Craigweil Road
Ayr KA7 2XJ
Tel: 01292/262322.

This Victorian villa, built in the Scottish baronial style, was constructed in 1879 and became a hostel in 1968. Overlooking the esplanade on the west, the hostel offers excellent views of Arran and the Firth of Clyde; some lucky hostelers will wake up to this lovely seascape.

Fans of Scottish architecture will delight in knowing that this former residence was built by legendary Scottish architect John Murdoch. Two stories high (plus an attic), it's built of fitted rubble and has crow-stepped gables and an imperial conical tower. The common room, with a cabinet piano, an armoire, and huge picture windows, is a nice escape from the windy but lovely garden out front.

Many who stay here don't even notice the hostel's architecture, though, as they use Ayr for a fast overnight stop on the way to Ireland or Arran. School groups tend to descend on this seaside escape in May, but they disappear in summer. Generally, it's a relatively quiet place tucked away in a residential neighborhood about 10 minutes from the town.

Services

🚆 Exit the train station, turn left, and walk past the tourist office, toward the shore. Turn right down Parkhouse Street, then left onto Beresford Terrace, and left onto Bellevue Street. At the crescent, bear left onto Bellevue Crescent and left again onto Racecourse Road. Take the second right onto Blackburn Road, then follow the signs to the hostel, which is on Craigweil Road, the second turn on the right; a 20-minute walk. A taxi ride costs £1.50.

🚌 Exit onto Wellington Square, then follow Racecourse Road until you reach Blackburn Road. Follow signs to the hostel, which is on Craigweil Road, the second turn on the right; a 15-minute walk.

🚗 Follow signs to Ayr. When you reach the town, look for signs for the shorefront. From the Glasgow direction, take a left when you reach the shorefront, turn left off the small roundabout. Turn left onto Blackburn Road and left onto Craigweil Road. The hostel is on the left. If you're coming from Stranraer (Irish ferry), look for the hostel sign when you reach Racecourse Road.

▦ Open Feb 25–Nov 1. Opening dates may vary slightly; call ahead. FABA.

🕐 Reception open 7am–midnight. Curfew midnight.

🛏 86 beds. 4-, 6-, 10-, and 14-bed rooms.

£ Members: adults £6.95; under 18 £5.85.

🍴 Meals served Easter–Sept. Self-catering kitchen facilities. Breakfast: 8:30–9:30am. Lunch: for groups only. Dinner: 6:30pm (sometimes not available).

🧳 Lockers.

◻ Washers, dryer, and drying room.

P Ample and free of charge.

🛍 Shop at hostel sells candy and some groceries.

🛋 Sitting room.

🚬 In common room only.

♿ Not wheelchair accessible.

💱 See "Currency Exchange" under "The Basics" in Ayr.

🔺 Bike shed.

Cheap Eats Nearby

Footlights Bistro

Inside an old church that houses the local experimental theater, this friendly little cafe offers homemade food at surprisingly good prices. Pastas, stir-fries, and vegetarian meals run £2.50 to £4; sandwiches and toasties 80p to £2.

North Harbour Street, Ayr. Tel: 01292/288998. Open: Mon–Sat 10am–5pm; until 9pm on performance nights. Cash only. From the hostel, turn right onto Craigweil, left on Blackburn Road, and left onto Racecourse Road. At the fork, bear right onto Sandgate. Follow it to the river and cross the bridge; it's on your right; a 20-minute walk.

The Old Racecourse Hotel

You'll find comfortable banquettes, picture windows, and a beastly plant in the center of this dining room in the calm residential neighborhood by the hostel. Fare includes salads for £5 to £6; fish and chips £5 to £6. A two-course lunch costs £3.95. Takeout and delivery are available.

Racecourse Road, Ayr. Tel: 01292/262873. Open: Mon–Thurs noon–2:30pm and 5–9pm; Fri–Sat noon–2:30 and 5–10pm. Reservations accepted on weekends. Credit cards: VA, MC, EC, Access.

From the hostel, turn right down Craigweil, left on Blackburn Road, and right on Racecourse Road. It's three blocks down on the left; a 10-minute walk.

Grocery Store: Marks and Spencer. 82 High St., Ayr. Open: Mon–Tues 9:30am–5:30pm; Wed–Thurs 9am–5:30pm; Fri 9am–6pm; Sat 8:30am–6pm.

Experiences

The tumultuous, lusty life of poet Robert Burns can be relived only two miles down the road at **Alloway,** where a **museum** and a **heritage park** tell his story. A 10-mile beachfront walk will take you to **Culzean** (pronounced "killain") **Castle,** where Dwight Eisenhower masterminded intelligence operations during World War II; there's a small but interesting exhibition devoted to him, as well as a 560-acre park with a swan pond and deer park.

Closer to the hostel, the **Borderline Theatre** has a repertory company that puts on shows. During amateur night, local writers have a chance to use the stage to present their works in progress. The other theaters in the town offer more traditional Scottish performances as well as shows from London.

For more active pursuits, the Ayr hostel offers weekend and weeklong **cycling** packages that take you across the Firth of Clyde for some rigorous biking up the hills of Arran, Islay, and Jura islands. Bike paths abound in the immediate vicinity of Ayr, and the town itself is a pleasant place for a bike ride. A bowling green and garden area by the water make for decent suntanning if the winds die down and cloudy skies disappear, which they do every so often in this part of Scotland.

The Robert Burns National Heritage Park. Alloway. Tel: 01292/443700. Open: Sept–June: daily 9am–6pm. July–Aug: daily 9am–8pm.

Culzean Castle and Country Park. By Maybole. Tel: 01655/760274. Open: Apr–Oct: daily 10:30am–5:30pm. Nov–Apr: daily 9am–sunset. Country park and castle admission: adults £5.50; concessions £3. Country park only: adults £3; concessions £1.50.

The Borderline Theatre. North Harbour Street, Ayr. Tel: 01292/288998. Box office open: Mon–Fri 10am–5pm; Sat 10am–3:30pm; until 7:30pm on performance nights. Performances: £4.50–£6.50.

Bicycle vacations to Arran, Jura, and Islay. Contact the Ayr Youth Hostel or the SYHA National Office: 7 Glebe Crescent, Stirling. Tel: 01786/451181.

The Basics

Tourist Office: Ayr T.I.C. Burns House, Burns Statue Square, Ayr. Tel: 01292/262555. Open: Sept–Jun: Mon–Sat 9am–6pm; Sun 10am–6pm. Jul–Aug: Mon–Sat 9am–7pm; Sun 10am–7pm. From the hostel, turn right on Craigweil Road, left on Blackburn Road, and left on Racecourse Road. Bear right up Bellevue Crescent to Beresford Terrace. Follow it to the left until you reach Parkhouse Street. Turn right onto Parkhouse Street, and follow it around to the left. It's on your left; a 15-minute walk.

Post Office: Ayr Post Office. 65 Sandgate, Ayr. Tel: 01292/287264. Open: Mon–Fri 9am–5:30pm; Sat 9am–7pm. Exit the hostel, go right on Craigweil Road, left on Blackburn Road, and left down Racecourse Road into the town center. When you reach the fork, bear left onto Sandgate. It's on your right; a 15-minute walk.

Currency Exchange: Thomas Cook. 61 High St., Ayr. Tel: 01292/611633. Open: Mon–Sat 9am–5:30pm. Thurs 9:45am opening. American Express office: Premier Travel. 2c Boswell Park, Ayr. Tel: 01292/282822. Open: Mon–Fri 9am–5:30pm; Sat 9am–5pm.

Telephone Code: 01292.

Bike Rental: AMG Cycles. 55 Dalblair Rd., Ayr. Tel: 01292/287580. Weekend rate £12.50; weekly rate £15.

Getting There: Trains come to Ayr directly out of **Glasgow,** Central-Stranraer (the ferry port to Ireland and the Isle of Man). For information, call 0141/212282. Those coming by **coach** can get Stagecoach service from **Glasgow;** call 01292/264643. AA Buses run from **Prestwick Airport, Kilwinning,** and **Ardrossan** (the Arran ferry terminal); for information, call 01292/212282. By **car,** Ayr is reachable from **Glasgow** via the A77 south via Kilmarnock.

What's Next

Arran Island, only a short trip across the Firth of Clyde, is a tempting and easy trip from Ayr. Catch the train or bus to Ardrossan Harbour, a depressing town that happens to be the ferry port. On this peaceful island, a distillery, castles, and sandy beaches lie in wait. From Arran, you can do a little island hopping: Ferries run out to tiny Holy Island, the location of a new Buddhist sanctuary (the one in Dumfries was too close to the motorway), and a spot with a centuries-old history of spiritual serenity. There are two equally peaceful hostels on the island: one on **Whiting Bay,** the other on **Lochranza,** frequented by cyclists and climbers exploring the hills and valleys there.

Arran Island

Arran, the largest island in the Firth of Clyde, is a half-hour ferry ride from the grim town of Ardrossan and a five-minute boat ride from the Kintyre peninsula. Only 20 miles from tip to tip and 56 miles in circumference, it manages to pack quite a bit into such a small area. There are mountains, a couple of castles, a distillery, and pebbly beaches, along with a handful of sleepy firth-side villages.

It's quiet here, and there's an air of simplicity and serenity; perhaps the island owes its mellow mood to the Gulf Stream that passes through, which is the reason the seemingly incongruous palm trees grow here. City folks might not have much to do, but most visitors tend to be climbers and cyclists. If you don't fall into one of these categories, buses can shuttle you up and down the quiet coastal roads.

There are two hostels on Arran. One is at Lochranza, not far from Goat Fell, a 2,866-foot "hill" towering over the northern part of the island. The other, at Whiting Bay on the southeast shore, has pebbly beaches and gentler hills.

WHITING BAY

If you come to Arran on the ferry from Ardrossan to Brodick, you'll find Whiting Bay about eight miles south. It's a friendly little hamlet on the Firth of Clyde. People take advantage of the location to explore nearby Brodick, with its castle and gardens, as well as the island's south coast, dotted with wee villages and decent crafts shops.

Nearby, Holy Island beckons those hungry for spiritual nourishment. A Buddhist retreat is being built there, and ferries head out to the island in summer. Mild-mannered road warriors drive Stagecoach buses around the winding coastal roads here, so those not prone to car sickness can use Whiting Bay as a base to see the other parts of the island.

Whiting Bay Youth Hostel

Shore Road
Whiting Bay, Arran KA27 8QW
Tel: 01770/700339.

The hostel at Whiting Bay, a sturdy stone country house, receives a surprisingly broad cross section of travelers for such a remote hostel. Families come for the self-contained family room, and Buddhists come to get a look at the Holy Island project, still being built. Mountain bikers, climbers, and motorcyclists check out the island along with geologists, who study the unusual rock formations in the area.

The hostel is right across from the beach. The views from the bedrooms are dazzling, and since the hostel is right on the east coast the sunrises are glorious. The frothy waters of Whiting Bay, however, aren't glorious—they're usually too cold for bathing. The building is quite small, so guests tend to chat in the common room and the area around the reception. The warden is a veteran, and she keeps the place running like clockwork.

The closest train station is on the mainland in Ardrossan Harbour, where there's a ferry terminal. From there, the 30-minute ride to the island takes you to Brodick. From there, take Stagecoach's South Arran bus to Whiting Bay, and the hostel is right on the road.

The closest bus station is on the mainland in Ardrossan Harbour, where there's a ferry terminal. From there, the one-hour ride to the island takes you to Brodick. From there, take Stagecoach's South Arran bus to Whiting Bay, and the hostel is right on the road.

From the ferry port at Brodick, follow South Road for 8 miles. The hostel is at the south end of Whiting Bay village, across from the beach.

Open Feb 25–Oct. FABA.

Reception open 7am–10:30am and 5–11:45pm. Curfew 11:45pm.

48 beds. 4-, 6-, and 8-bed rooms. One self-contained family unit with 3 bedrooms, shower, toilet, kitchen, and dining area.

£ Members: adults £5.40; under 18 £4.40.

No meals served. Self-catering kitchen facilities.

Coin-operated lockers.

Drying room.

P Ample and free of charge.

Shop at hostel sells candy and canned goods.

Smokers' room overlooking the water; TV room.

In common room only.

Not wheelchair accessible.

See "Currency Exchange" under "The Basics" in Whiting Bay.

Bike shed.

Services

Cheap Eats Nearby

The Coffee Pot

Tree branches form an arched entranceway to this sweet cafe with excellent bay views. Menu items include Toasties for £1.60 to £1.95; salads £4 to £5; and jacket potatoes £2.50 to £4.50. Outdoor seating is on chairs fashioned from huge tree trunks.

Whiting Bay, Arran. Tel: 01770/700382. Open June–Sept: daily 10am–7pm. Oct–May: daily 10am–4pm. Cash only. From the hostel, a 5-minute walk: turn left and it's up the road on the left.

The Pantry

This elegant spot overlooking the bay serves home-cooked, thoughtfully prepared dishes as well as simpler fare. Service is solicitous. Sandwiches and baked potatoes are £2 to £3. Main dishes (£5 to £10) include lasagne, potato-and-leek bake, and other hot entrées. There's always a vegetarian dish.

Whiting Bay, Arran. Tel: 01770/700489. Open: Mar–Oct only: Sun–Thurs 10:30am–5:30pm and 6–7:30pm; Fri–Sat 10:30am–5:30pm and 6–8:30pm. Reservations accepted on weekends. Credit cards: VA, MC, EC, Access. From the hostel, turn left and walk about 10 minutes down the road. It's set back from the road; look for the sign to the left. Go up the stairs.

Grocery Store: Mother Goose. Open: Mon–Sat 8:30am–9:30pm; Sun 10am–9pm.

Experiences

The pebbly beach along Whiting Bay is great for gathering agates; it's a nice place to while away an afternoon or two. Scenic forest walks abound in **Glenashdale,** just to the west of the bay.

At the jetty on Whiting Bay or a few miles up the coast in Lamlash, there's a ferry service to **Holy Island,** where the Buddhist Monks from the Samye Lang Tibetan Centre live in isolation. They are currently building a comprehensive retreat, with a temple for contemplation, a heritage center, and a cloister for the monks to live during their three-year novitiate. Those interested in assisting them with the building work should contact them about longer stays.

Back on Whiting Bay **boat rental** is available, as well as fishing rods and bait. A bus ride up to Brodick brings you to **Brodick Castle,** with its regally decorated rooms, beautiful fragrant gardens, and even a little cafe.

Holy Island ferries. Whiting Bay Jetty, Whiting Bay. Tel: 01770/700382. Easter–Oct only. Departures at 10am, 11am, noon, 2pm, 4:30pm, 6pm. Lamlash Pier, Lamlash. Tel: 01770/600349. Departures at 10am, 11am, noon, 2pm, 5pm.

Holy Island Project. Contact Venerable Lama Yeshe Losal. Samye Ling Tibetan Centre. Eskdalemuir, Langholm, Dumfries and Galloway. DG13 0QL. Tel: 01387/373282.

Boat rental. Whiting Bay Hires. The jetty, Whiting Bay. Tel: 01770/700382. Open: daily 10am–6pm. July–Aug 6–9pm. 14-foot motor boats (capacity 4): 1 hour £7.50; 2 hours £12. Rods £1.50; bait £1.

Brodick Castle. Garden and Country Park. Brodick Castle, Arran. Tel 01770/302202. Castle open: Easter–Sept: daily 1–5pm. Apr and Oct: Sat–Sun 1–5pm. Garden and country park open: daily 9:30am–sunset. Admission: castle £2 (with HI card); gardens and country park £1.

The Basics

Tourist Office: Brodick T.I.C. The Pier, Brodick (8 miles away). Tel: 01770/302140. Open: Mar–Nov: Mon–Sat 9am–7:30pm; Sun 10am–5pm. Nov–Feb: Mon–Sat 9am–5pm. From the hostel, turn left and follow the road 8 miles north. Or catch bus no. 323 to Brodick.

Post Office: Whiting Bay Post Office, inside the Pillar Box (shop and video rental), Whiting Bay. Tel: 01770/700205. Open: Mon–Tues 9am–12:45pm and 2–5pm; Wed 9am–1pm; Thurs–Fri 9am–12:45 and 2–5pm; Sat 9am–12:45pm. From the hostel, turn left and walk up the path; it's on the left.

Currency Exchange: Brodick T.I.C. The Pier, Brodick (8 miles away). Tel: 01770/ 302140. Open: Mar–Nov: Mon–Sat 9am–7:30pm; Sun 10am–5pm. Nov–Feb: Mon–Sat 9am–5pm.

Telephone Code: 01770.

Bike Rental: Whiting Bay Hires. The jetty, Whiting Bay. Tel: 01770/700382. Full day £4.50.

Getting There: The only way to the island is by **ferry**, which runs from **Ardrossan Harbour** on the mainland. **Trains** run to Ardrossan Harbour from **Glasgow.** For schedule info, call 0141/204 2844. For **coaches** to Ardrossan, call the Travel Centre in Glasgow at 0141/226 4826. By **car,** take the A737 from **Glasgow** to Androssan Harbour. Caledonian MacBrayne runs the ferry, which accepts both passengers and cars. There are about six trips per weekday, fewer on Sundays. Call 01294/ 463470 for departure times. Local buses (see above) take you out to the hostel.

What's Next

A beautiful bus ride around the south coast of the island via the village of Blackwaterfoot takes you to **Lochranza** on the north side of the island. A golf course, wrecked castle, distillery, and mountain provide activities for a few days. If you're headed back to the mainland, the seaside town of **Ayr** is only a few stops farther along on the train. Scot-o-philes and literature students can check out the museums devoted to Robert Burns in nearby Alloway. Otherwise, it's a pretty standard seaside town, nice if the weather's agreeable; otherwise, it's windy and cold.

LOCHRANZA

The northernmost village on Arran, Lochranza is another quiet village with precious little to distract you from the spectacular hills and sandy nooks. A 15th-century castle sits in the bay as a lonely monument to the island's past. A nine-hole golf course, distillery, and mountain are enough to keep you busy for a few days.

It's an isolated little spot; get your business taken care of down in Brodick before coming here. The hostel is run by a friendly couple, and sheep wander aimlessly about the yard in front.

Lochranza Youth Hostel

Lochranza
Isle of Arran KA27 8HL
Tel: 01770/830631.

Formerly the Lochranza Hotel, this 19th-century building was turned into a Youth Hostel during World War II and served as a billet for soldiers during the war.

Nowadays, it's a cheery home away from home, with beautiful views of Loch Ranza from the plant-filled common room.

Hill walkers and mountain bikers tend to be the main clientele, so it's a rugged, robust air you breathe here. The friendly managers and their sons swear that sometimes you can see deer from the hostel, and if you come in October you can hear the male deer bellowing out during their mating season. The gravelly beach is right in front of the hostel, and from there you can catch a pastel sunset across Kilbrannan Sound out to the Mull of Kintyre.

Services

The closest train station is on the mainland at Ardrossan Harbour. From there, take the Caledonian MacBrayne ferry to Brodick on the isle of Arran. Stagecoach bus no. 324 meets the ferries to take you out to Lochranza. Or, post buses run between Brodick and Lochranza every day except Sunday.

The closest bus station is on the mainland at Ardrossan Harbour. From there, follow directions from the train, above.

From the ferry port at Brodick, you come to a junction. Turn right and follow signs to Lochranza, 14 miles away at the north tip of the island. The hostel is on your left in the village of Lochranza before the castle.

Open Mar–Oct. FABA.

Reception open 7–11:45pm. Curfew 11:45pm. Common room and public rooms are open during the day.

74 beds. 4-, 5-, 6-, 8-, and 12-bed rooms.

£ Members: adults £6.95; under 18 £5.85.

No meals served. Self-catering kitchen.

No lockers.

Washers, dryers, and drying room.

P Ample and free of charge.

Shop at hostel sells candy, groceries.

One common room.

In designated area only.

Not wheelchair accessible.

 See "Currency Exchange" under "The Basics" in Lochranza.

Bike shed.

Cheap Eats Nearby

Avaloch Centre Tea Rooms

This cheery, clean little cafe overlooks the water. Order at the counter. Soup (always vegetarian) is £1.50; sandwiches £1.30 to £1.75. Jacket potatoes cost £1.50 to £2.

The Pier, Lochranza. Tel: 01770/830217. Open: Mon–Thurs, Sat–Sun 8am–6pm. Fri noon–6pm. Cash only. From the hostel, turn left and walk about a half mile up the road. It's on your left.

The Lochranza Hotel

The comfortable pub in this hotel is the local watering hole; spend the afternoon watching rugby games on the TV as you nosh on the generous portions of steak pie and chili (£4 to £5) or hefty pizzas (£4). Chalkboard specials include vegetarian options.

Lochranza. Tel: 01770/830223. Open: daily noon–10pm. Credit cards: VA, MC, EC, Access. From the hostel, turn left and walk up the road for about 10 minutes. It's on the left.

Grocery Store: Lochranza Stores. Lochranza. Open: Mon–Thurs 8am–9pm; Fri–Sat 8am–6pm; Sun 10am–3pm and 5–6pm.

Experiences

Lochranza Castle, actually the ruins of a 13th-century hunting lodge, sits on the bay and is a nice place to start exploring. From there, loads of **walking paths** spread out: the cock of Arran, around the very top of the island, is a good four-hour walk over a hill (not a mountain), so it's not too difficult for inexperienced climbers. If offers excellent views of the main mountains of the island, as well as the neighboring islands of Bute and Cumbrae. About $4^1/_2$ miles south of Lochranza, you can begin the walk along Coirein Lochain, a small lake on the northeastern part of the island. It's actually a corrie, carved out of a glacier that created the loch. Some say Coirein Lochain, totally surrounded by mountains, is the nicest loch. The island's highest peak, **Goat Fell,** is between Lochranza and Brodick and is easily reachable from the hostel by bus. Right from the hostel, you can walk to the island's second highest peak, called the Castle.

At King's Cave, 18 miles from the hostel on the southwest part of the island, Scottish freedom fighter Robert the Bruce supposedly saw a little spider that kept falling down. This is where he's said to have coined the adage, "If at first you don't succeed, try try again." Closer to the Whiting Bay hostel, the King's Cave-Lochranza walking route is the flattest on the island. A flat fare of £2.50 gets you a rural day card good for an entire day's bus rides, so you can mix up walking with taking the bus. **Open-top bus tours** are available during summer.

Hutton's Unconformity, a pileup of centuries' worth of sedimentary, igneous, metamorphic rocks, are proof of the inconsistencies of current geological theories. Geologists can (and do) spend hour after hour examining the rocks. Lochranza is also good for bird watching, especially for golden eagles and red deer, and seals pop up out of the water. Lochranza also offers **golf:** A nine-hole course with clubs for rental is open days and evenings in the summertime. The upstart **Arran Distillery,** brand-new in 1995, offers tours.

Lochranza Castle. Key can be obtained at the Lochranza Stores/post office.

Stagecoach Open Top Bus Tours. The Pier, Brodick. Tel: 01770/302000. June–Oct only: daily, with hourly departures from 11am–6pm. Full-day tour: adults £6; children and senior citizens £4. Half-day tour: adults £4; children and senior citizens £2.50.

Lochranza 'Pay & Play' Golf Course. Lochranza. Tel: 01770/830273. Open: May–Oct: daily. Nine holes: adults £5; under 18 £2.50. Clubs available for rent.

Isle of Arran Distillers. Lochranza, Arran. Contact the Lochranza T.I.C. for information.

The Basics

Tourist Office: Lochranza T.I.C, The Pier, Lochranza. Tel: 01770/830320. Open: May–Oct only: Mon–Sat 9am–5pm. From the hostel, turn left and walk about $^1/_2$ mile down to the pier, which is on your left. It's in the hut. Alternatively, the tourist office in Brodick (8 miles away) is open all year long. Tel: 01770/302140.

Post Office: Lochranza Stores/Post Office. Lochranza. Tel: 01770/830641. Open: Mon–Sat 8:30am–6pm. From the hostel, turn left down the path, and the store is on the right.

Currency Exchange: Brodick T.I.C. The Pier, Brodick (8 miles away). Tel: 01770/302140. Open: Mar–Nov: Mon–Sat 9am–7:30pm; Sun 10am–5pm. Nov–Feb: Mon–Sat 9am–5pm.

Telephone Code: 01770.

Bike Rental: Mr. and Mrs. Kerr, Knockanrioch. Tel: 01770/830676. Three-speed bikes only. £4 per day. Two-hour minimum rental.

Getting There: The only way to the island is by **ferry.** If you can get yourself to **Claonig** on the Kintyre Peninsula, there's a summertime ferry service that runs straight to Lochranza, but Claonig is difficult to reach by public transport. The other ferry, which runs from **Ardrossan Harbour** on the mainland to Brodick on Arran, is easier to reach, and buses can shuttle you up to Lochranza. **Trains** run to **Ardrossan Harbour** from **Glasgow.** For schedule information, call 0141/204 2844. For **coaches** to **Ardrossan,** call the Travel Centre in Glasgow at 0141/226 4826. By **car,** take the A737 from **Glasgow.** Caledonian MacBrayne runs the ferry, which accepts both passengers and cars. There are about six trips per weekday, fewer on Sundays. Call 01294/463470 for departure times from Ardrossan. Local buses (see above) take you out to the hostel.

What's Next

Whiting Bay, with its pebbly beach and proximity to Holy Island, is only a short but stomach-wrenching bus ride away down to the south end of the island. The ride around the west coast of Arran is a beautiful coastal route and gives you an idea of the climbing possibilities on the island. Back on the mainland, **Ayr** isn't far (only a train ride from the ferry terminal at Ardrossan); the seaside town offers theater and sandy beaches. Nearby Alloway is the home of Robert Burns, Scottish national poet and lewd lyricist. From Ardrossan, **Glasgow** is close (31 miles away); it boasts excellent museums (mostly free of charge), chic boutiques, and more than 10,000 students scattered in its pubs, theaters, and trendy restaurants.

DIRECTORY OF HOSTELS

ENGLAND & WALES

Acomb. Main Street, Acomb, Hexham, Northumberland NE46 4PL. ☎ (1434) 602864.

Alfriston. Frog Firle, Alfriston, Polegate, East Sussex BN26 5TT. ☎ (1323) 870423. FAX (1323) 870615.

Alston. The Firs, Alston, Cumbria CA9 3RW. ☎ (1434) 381509. FAX (1434) 381509.

Ambleside. Waterhead, Ambleside, Cumbria LA22 0EU. ☎ (15394) 32304. FAX (15394) 34408.

Arnside. Oakfield Lodge, Redhills Road, Arnside, Carnforth, Lancashire LA5 0AT. ☎ (1524) 761781. FAX (1524) 762589.

Arundel. Warning Camp, Arundel, West Sussex BN18 9QY. ☎ (1903) 882204. FAX (1903) 882776.

Aysgarth Falls. Aysgarth, Leyburn, North Yorkshire DL8 3SR. ☎ (1969) 663260. FAX (1969) 663110.

Badby. Church Green, Badby, Daventry, Northamptonshire NN11 3AS. ☎/FAX (1327) 703883.

Bakewell. Fly Hill, Bakewell, Derbyshire DE45 1DN. ☎ (1629) 812313. FAX (1629) 812313.

Baldersdale. Blackton, Baldersdale, Barnard Castle, Co Durham DL12 9UP. ☎ (1833) 650629. FAX (1833) 650629.

Bangor. Tan-y-Bryn, Bangor, Gwynedd LL57 1PZ. ☎ (1248) 353516. FAX (1248) 371176.

Bassenthwaite. *See* Skiddaw House.

Bath. Bathwick Hill, Bath, Avon BA2 6JZ. ☎ (1225) 465674. FAX (1225) 482947.

Beer. Bovey Combe, Townsend, Beer, Seaton, Devon EX12 3LL. ☎ (1297) 20296. FAX (1297) 23690.

Bellever. Bellever, Postbridge, Yelverton, Devon PL20 6TU. ☎ (1822) 88227.

Bellingham. Woodburn Road, Bellingham, Hexham, Northumberland NE48 2ED. ☎ (1434) 220313.

Beverley. The Friary, Friar's Lane, Beverley, East Yorkshire HU17 0DF. ☎ (1482) 881751. FAX (1482) 881751.

Blackboys. Blackboys, Uckfield, East Sussex TN22 5HU. ☎ (1825) 890607. FAX (1825) 890104.

Black Sail. Black Sail Hut, Ennerdale, Cleator, Cumbria CA23 3AY.

Blaencaron. Blaencaron, Tregaron, Dyfed SY25 6HL. ☎ (1974) 298441.

Blaxhall. Heath Walk, Blaxhall, Woodbridge, Suffolk IP12 2EA. ☎ (1728) 688206.

Boggle Hole. Boggle Hole, Mill Beck, Fyling Thorpe, Whitby, North Yorkshire YO22 4UQ. ☎ (1947) 880352. FAX (1947) 880987.

Borrowdale (Longthwaite). Longthwaite, Borrowdale, Keswick, Cumbria CA12 5XE. ☎ (17687) 77257. FAX (17687) 77393.

Borth. Morlais, Borth, Dyfed SY24 5JS. ☎ (1970) 871498. FAX (1970) 871827.

Boscastle Harbour. Palace Stables, Boscastle, Cornwall PL35 0HD. ☎ (1840) 250287.

Boswinger. Boswinger, Gorran, St Austell, Cornwall PL26 6LL. ☎ (1726) 843234.

Bradenham. Village Hall, Bradenham, High Wycombe, Buckinghamshire HP14 4HF. ((1494) 562929. FAX (1494) 564743.

Bradwell Village. Manor Farm, Vicarage Rd, Bradwell, Milton Keynes, Buckinghamshire MK13 9AJ. ((1908) 310944. FAX (1908) 310944.

Brandon. Heath House, off Warren Close, Bury Rd, Brandon, Suffolk IP27 0BU. ((1842) 812075. FAX (1842) 812075.

Bretton. Nether Bretton, Derbyshire. ((114) 2884541.

Bridges Long Mynd. Ratlinghope, Shrewsbury SY5 0SP. ((1588) 650656. FAX (1588) 650656.

Bridport. West Rivers House, West Allington, Bridport, Dorset DT6 5BW. ((1308) 422655. FAX (1308) 425319.

Brighton. Patcham Place, London Rd. Brighton, Sussex BN1 8YD. ((1273) 556196. FAX (1273) 509366.

Bristol. International YHA. Hayman House. 14 Narrow Quay, Bristol BS1 4QA. ((117) 9221659. FAX (117) 9273789.

Broad Haven. Broad Haven, Haverfordwest, Dyfed SA62 3JH. ((1437) 781688. FAX (1437) 781100.

Broadstairs. Thistle Lodge, 3 Osborne Rd, Broadstairs, Isle-of-Thanet, Kent CT10 2AE. ((1843) 604121. FAX (1843) 604121.

Bryn Gwynant. Bryn Gwynant, Nant Gwynant, Caernarfon, Gwynedd LL55 4NP. ((1766) 890251. FAX (1766) 890479.

Bryn Poeth Uchaf. Hafod-y-Pant, Cynghordy, Llandovery, Dyfed SA20 0NB. ((1550) 750235.

Burley. Cottesmore House, Cott Lane, Burley, Ringwood, Hampshire BH24 4BB. ((1425) 403233. FAX (1425) 403233.

Buttermere. King George VI Memorial Hostel, Buttermere, Cockermouth, Cumbria CA13 9XA. ((17687) 70245. FAX (17687) 70231.

Buxton. Sherbrook Lodge, Harpur Hill Rd, Buxton, Derbyshire SK17 9NB. ((1298) 22287. FAX (1298) 22287.

Byrness. 7 Otterburn Green, Byrness, Newcastle-upon-Tyne, NE19 1TS. ((1830) 520424.

Cambridge. 97 Tenison Rd, Cambridge CB1 2DN. ((1223) 354601. FAX (1223) 312780.

Canterbury. 54 New Dover Rd, Canterbury, Kent CT1 3DT. ((1227) 462911. FAX (1227) 470752.

Capel Curig Youth Hostel. Plas Curig, Capel Curig, Betws-y-Coed, Gwynedd LL24 0EL. ((1690) 720225. FAX (1690) 720270.

Capel-y-Ffin. Capel-y-Ffin, Abergavenny, Gwent NP7 7NP. ((1873) 890650.

Cardiff. 2 Wedal Rd, Roath Park, Cardiff CF2 5PG. ((1222) 462303. FAX (1222) 464571.

Carlisle. Etterby House, Etterby, Carlisle, Cumbria CA3 9QS. (/FAX (1228) 23934.

Carrock Fell. High Row Cottage, Haltcliffe, Hesket Newmarket, Wigton, Cumbria CA7 8JT. ((16974) 78325.

Castle Hedingham. 7 Falcon Square, Castle Hedingham, Halstead, Essex CO9 3BU. ((1787) 460799. FAX (1787) 461302.

Castleton. Castleton Hall, Castleton, Sheffield S30 2WG. ((1433) 620235. FAX (1433) 621767.

Charlbury. The Laurels, The Slade, Charlbury, Oxfordshire OX7 3SJ. ((1608) 810202.

Cheddar. Hillfield, Cheddar, Somerset BS27 3HN. ((1934) 742494. FAX (1934) 744724.

Chester. Hough Green House, 40 Hough Green, Chester CH4 8JD. ((1244) 680056. FAX (1244) 681204.

Clun Mill. The Mill, Clun, Nr Craven Arms, Shropshire SY7 8NY. ((1588) 640582. FAX (1588) 640582.

Cockermouth. Double Mills, Cockermouth, Cumbria CA13 0DS. ((1900) 822561.

Colchester. East Bay House, 18 East Bay, Colchester, Essex CO1 2UE. ((1206) 867982. FAX (1206) 868628.

Coniston (Holly How). Holly How, Far End, Coniston, Cumbria LA21 8DD. ((15394) 41323. FAX (15394) 41803.

Coniston Coppermines. Coppermines House, Coniston, Cumbria LA21 8HP. ((15394) 41261.

Copt Oak. Copt Oak, Whitwick Rd, Markfield, Leicester LE67 9QB. ((1530) 242661.

Corris. Old School, Old Rd, Corris, Machynlleth, Powys SY20 9QT. ℂ (1654) 761686.

Coverack. Park Behan, School Hill, Coverack, Helston, Cornwall TR12 6SA. ℂ (1326) 280687.

Crowcombe Heathfield. Denzel House, Crowcombe Heathfield, Taunton, Somerset TA4 4BT. ℂ (1984) 667249. FAX (1984) 667249.

Crowden-in-Longdendale. Peak National Park Hostel, Crowden, Hadfield, Hyde, Cheshire SK14 7HZ. ℂ (1457) 852135. FAX (1457) 852135.

Cynwyd. The Old Mill, Cynwyd, Corwen, Clwyd LL21 0LW. ℂ (1490) 412814.

Dartington. Lownard, Dartington, Totnes, Devon TQ9 6JJ. ℂ (1803) 862303. FAX (1803) 862303.

Dentdale. Cowgill, Dent, Sedbergh, Cumbria LA10 5RN. ℂ (15396) 25251. FAX (15396) 25251.

Derwentwater. Barrow House, Borrowdale, Keswick, Cumbria CA12 5UR. ℂ (17687) 77246. FAX (17687) 77396.

Dimmingsdale. Little Ranger, Dimmingsdale, Oakamoor, Stoke-on-Trent, Staffordshire ST10 3AS. ℂ (1538) 702304.

Dolgoch. Tregaron, Dyfed SY25 6NR. ℂ Wales Regional Office (1222) 222122.

Dover. 306 London Rd, Dover, Kent CT17 0SY. ℂ (1304) 201314. FAX (1304) 202236.

Dufton. 'Redstones', Dufton, Appleby, Cumbria CA16 6DB. ℂ (17863) 51236. FAX (17683) 51236.

Duntisbourne Abbots. Duntisbourne Abbots, Cirencester, Glos GL7 7JN. ℂ (1285) 821682. FAX (1285) 821697.

Earby. Katherine Bruce Glasier Memorial Hostel, Glen Cottage, Birch Hall Lane, Earby, Colne, Lancashire BB8 6JX. ℂ (1282) 842349.

Eastbourne. East Dean Rd, Eastbourne, East Sussex BN20 8ES. ℂ (1323) 721081. FAX (1323) 721081.

Edale. Rowland Cote, Nether Booth, Edale, Derbyshire S30 2ZH. ℂ (1433) 670302. FAX (1433) 670243.

Edmundbyers. Low House, Edmundbyers, Consett, Co Durham DH8 9NL. ℂ (1207) 55651.

Ellingstring. Lilac Cottage, Ellingstring, Ripon, North Yorks HG4 4PW. ℂ (1677) 460216.

Elmscott. Hartland, Bideford, Devon EX39 6ES. ℂ/FAX (1237) 441367.

Elterwater. Elterwater, Ambleside, Cumbria LA22 9HX. ℂ (15394) 37245. FAX (15394) 37245.

Elton. Elton Old Hall, Main St, Elton, Matlock, Derbyshire DE4 2BW. ℂ (1629) 650394.

Ennerdale (Gillerthwaite). Cat Crag, Ennerdale, Cleator, Cumbria CA23 3AX. ℂ (1946) 861237.

Epping Forest. Wellington Hall, High Beach, Loughton, Essex IG10 4AG. ℂ/FAX (181) 5085161.

Eskdale. Boot, Holmrook, Cumbria CA19 1TH. ℂ/FAX (19467) 23219.

Exeter. 49 Countess Wear Rd, Exeter, Devon EX2 6LR. ℂ (1392) 873329. FAX (1392) 876939.

Exford. Exe Mead, Exford, Minehead, Somerset TA24 7PU. ℂ (164383) 1288. FAX (164383) 1650.

Eyam. Hawkhill Rd, Eyam, Sheffield S30 1QP. ℂ/FAX (1433) 630335.

Glascwm. The School, Glascwm, Llandrindod Wells, Powys LD1 5SE. ℂ (1982) 570415.

Golant. Penquite House, Golant, Fowey, Cornwall PL23 1LA. ℂ (1726) 833507. FAX (1726) 832947.

Gradbach Mill. Gradbach Mill, Gradbach, Quarnford, Buxton, Derbyshire SK17 0SU. ℂ (1260) 227625. FAX (1260) 227334.

GRASMERE (2 Hostels):

Grasmere—Butterlip How. Butterlip How, Grasmere, Ambleside, Cumbria LA22 9QG. ℂ (15394) 35316. FAX (15394) 35798.

Grasmere—Thorney How. Thorney How, Grasmere, Ambleside, Cumbria LA22 9QW. ℂ (15394) 35591. FAX (15394) 35866.

Great Yarmouth. 2 Sandown Rd, Great Yarmouth, Norfolk NR30 1EY. ℂ/FAX (1493) 843991.

Greenhead. Greenhead, Carlisle, Cumbria CA6 7HG. ℂ/FAX (16977) 47401.

Grinton. Grinton Lodge, Grinton, Richmond, North Yorkshire DL11 6HS. ℂ (1748) 884206. FAX (1748) 884876.

Hartington. Hartington Hall, Hartington, Buxton, Derbyshire SK17 0AT. ℂ (1298) 84223. FAX (1298) 84415.

Hastings. Guestling Hall, Rye Rd, Guestling, Hastings, East Sussex TN35 4LP. ℂ (1424) 812373. FAX (1424) 814273.

Hathersage. Castleton Rd, Hathersage, Sheffield S30 1AH. ℂ/FAX (1433) 650493.

Hawes. Lancaster Terrace, Hawes, North Yorkshire DL8 3LQ. ℂ/FAX (1969) 667368.

Hawkshead. Esthwaite Lodge, Hawkshead, Ambleside, Cumbria LA22 0QD. ℂ (15394) 36293. FAX (15394) 36720.

Haworth. Longlands Hall, Longlands Drive, Lees Lane, Haworth, Keighley, West Yorkshire BD22 8RT. ℂ (1535) 642234.

Helmsley. Carlton Lane, Helmsley, North Yorkshire YO6 5HB. ℂ/FAX (1439) 770433.

Helvellyn. Greenside, Glenridding, Penrith, Cumbria CA11 0QR. ℂ/FAX (17684) 82269.

High Close. *See* Langdale.

Hindhead. Devils Punchbowl, off Portsmouth Road, Thursley, Nr Godalming, Surrey GU8 6NS. ℂ (142) 8604285.

Holford. *See* Quantock Hills.

Holmbury St Mary. Radnor Lane, Holmbury St Mary, Dorking, Surrey RH5 6NW. ℂ (1306) 730777. FAX (1306) 730933.

Honister Hause. Honister Hause, Seatoller, Keswick, Cumbria CA12 5XN. ℂ (17687) 77267.

Hunstanton. 15 Avenue Rd, Hunstanton, Norfolk PE36 5BW. ℂ (1485) 532061. FAX (1485) 532632.

Idwal Cottage. Idwal Cottage, Nant Ffrancon, Bethesda, Bangor, Gwynedd LL57 3LZ. ℂ (1248) 600225. FAX (1248) 602952.

Ilam. Ilam Hall, Ashbourne, Derbyshire DE6 2AZ. ℂ (1335) 350212. FAX (1335) 350350.

Ilfracombe. Ashmour House, 1 Hillsborough Terrace, Ilfracombe, Devon EX34 9NR. ℂ (1271) 865337. FAX (1271) 862652.

Ingleton. Greta Tower, Ingleton, Carnforth, Lancashire LA6 3EG. ℂ (15242) 41444. FAX (15242) 41854.

Instow. Worlington House, New Rd, Instow, Bideford, Devon EX39 4LW. ℂ (1271) 860394. FAX (1271) 860055.

Ironbridge Gorge. Paradise, Coalbrookdale, Telford, Shropshire TF8 7NR. ℂ (1952) 433281. FAX (1952) 433166.

Ivinghoe. The Old Brewery House, Ivinghoe, Leighton Buzzard, Bedfordshire LU7 9EP. ℂ (1296) 668251. FAX (1296) 662903.

Jordans. Welders Lane, Jordans, Beaconsfield, Buckinghamshire HP9 2SN. ℂ (1494) 873135. FAX (1494) 875907.

Keld. Keld Lodge, Upper Swaledale, Keld, Richmond, North Yorkshire DL11 6LL. ℂ/FAX (1748) 886259.

Kemsing. Church Lane, Kensing, Sevenoaks, Kent TN15 6LU. ℂ (1732) 761341. FAX (1732) 763044.

Kendal. 118 Highgate, Kendal, Cumbria LA9 4HE. ℂ (1539) 724066. FAX (1539) 724906.

Keswick. Station Rd, Keswick, Cumbria CA12 5LH. ℂ (17687) 72484. FAX (17687) 74129.

Kettlewell. Whernside House, Kettlewell, Skipton, North Yorkshire BD23 5QU. ℂ (1756) 760232. FAX (1756) 760402.

Kings, Dolgellau. Kings, Penmaenpool, Dolgellau, Gwynedd LL40 1TB. ℂ (1341) 422392. FAX (1341) 422477.

King's Lynn. Thoresby College, College Lane, King's Lynn, Norfolk PE30 1JB. ℂ (1553) 772461. FAX (1553) 764312.

Kirk Yetholm. *See* Scotland.

Kirkby Stephen. Fletcher Hill, Market St, Kirkby Stephen, Cumbria CA17 4QQ. ℂ/FAX (17683) 71793.

Land's End. Letcha Vean, St Just, Penzance, Cornwall TR19 7NT. (7km N of Land's End) ℂ (1736) 788437. FAX (1736) 787337.

Langdale (High Close). High Close, Loughrigg, Ambleside, Cumbria LA22 9HJ. ℂ/FAX (15394) 37313.

Langdon Beck. Langdon Beck, Forest-in-Teesdale, Barnard Castle, Co Durham DL12 0XN. ℂ/FAX (1833) 622228.

Langsett. Langsett, Nr Penistone, Sheffield S30 5GY. ℂ (114) 2884541. Res. (c/o John & Elaine Whittington, 7 New Bailey, Crane Moor, Nr Sheffield S30 7AT. ℂ (114) 2884541.

Lincoln. 77 South Park, Lincoln LN5 8ES. ((1522) 522076. FAX (1522) 567424.

Linton. The Old Rectory, Linton-in-Craven, Skipton, North Yorkshire BD23 5HH. (/FAX (1756) 752400.

Litton Cheney. Litton Cheney, Dorchester, Dorset DT2 9AT. ((1308) 482340.

Llanbedr. Plas Newydd, Llanbedr, Gwynedd LL45 2LE. ((1341) 241287. FAX (1341) 241389.

Llanberis. Llwyn Celyn, Llanberis, Caernarfon, Gwynedd LL55 4SR. ((1286) 870280. FAX (1286) 870936.

Llanddeusant. The Old Red Lion, Llanddeusant, Llangadog, Dyfed SA19 6UL. ((1550) 740634, 740619.

Llangollen. Field Study & Activity Centre, Tyndwr Hall, Tyndwr Rd, Llangollen, Clwyd LL20 8AR. ((1978) 860330. FAX (1978) 861709.

Lledr Valley. Lledr House, Pont-y-Pant, Dolwyddelan, Gwynedd LL25 0DQ. ((1690) 750202.

Llwyn y Celyn. Llwyn y Celyn, Libanus, Brecon, Powys LD3 8NH. (/FAX (1874) 624261.

Llwynypia. Glyncornel Centre, Llwynypia, Rhondda, Mid Glamorgan CF40 2JF. ((1443) 430859. FAX (1443) 423415.

Lockton. The Old School, Lockton, Pickering, North Yorkshire YO18 7PY. ((1751) 460376.

LONDON (7 Hostels):

London—City of London. 36 Carter Lane, London EC4V 5AD. ((171) 236 4965. FAX (171) 236 7681.

London—Earls Court. 38 Bolton Gardens, London, SW5 0AQ. ((171) 373 7083. FAX (171) 835 2034.

London—Hampstead Heath. 4 Wellgarth Rd, Golders Green, London NW11 7HR. ((181) 458 9054/7196. FAX (181) 209 0546.

London—Highgate Village. 84 Highgate West Hill, Highgate, London N6 6LU. ((181) 340 1831. FAX (181) 341 0376.

London—Holland House. King George VI Memorial Hostel, Holland House, Holland Walk, Kensington, London W8 7QU. ((171) 937 0748. FAX (171) 376 0667.

London—Rotherhithe. Rotherhithe YH, Salter Rd, London SE16 1PP. ((171) 232 2114. FAX (171) 237 2919.

London—Oxford Street. 14 Noel St, London W1V 3PD. ((171) 734 1618. FAX (171) 734 1657.

Longthwaite. *See* Borrowdale.

Ludlow. Ludford Lodge, Ludford, Ludlow, Shropshire SY8 1PJ. ((1584) 872472. FAX (1584) 872095.

Lulworth Cove. School Lane, West Lulworth, Wareham, Dorset BH20 5SA. ((1929) 400564. FAX (1929) 400640.

Lynton. Lynbridge, Lynton, Devon EX35 6AZ. ((1598) 53237. FAX (1598) 53305.

Maeshafn. Holt Hostel, Maeshafn, Mold, Clwyd CH7 5LR. ((1352) 810320.

Malham. John Dower Memorial Hostel, Malham, Skipton, North Yorkshire BD23 4DE. ((1729) 830321. FAX (1729) 830551.

Malton. Derwent Bank, York Rd, Malton, North Yorkshire YO17 0AX. (/FAX (1653) 692077.

Malvern Hills. 18 Peachfield Rd, Malvern Wells, Malvern, Worcestershire WR14 4AP. ((1684) 569131. FAX (1684) 565205.

Manchester. Potato Wharf, Castlefield, Manchester M3. ((161) 839 9960. FAX (161) 835 2054.

Mankinholes. Mankinholes, Todmorden, Lancashire OL14 6HR. ((1706) 812340. FAX (1706) 812340.

Manorbier. Manorbier YH, Manorbier, Nr Tenby, Dyfed SA70 7TT. ((1834) 871803. FAX (1834) 871101.

Marloes Sands. Runwayskiln, Marloes, Haverfordwest, Dyfed SA62 3BH. ((1646) 636667.

Matlock. 40 Bank Rd, Matlock, Derbyshire DE4 3NF. ((1629) 582983. FAX (1629) 583484.

Maypool. Maypool House, Galmpton, Brixham, Devon TQ5 0ET. ((1803) 842444. FAX (1803) 845939.

Meerbrook. Old School, Meerbrook, Leek, Staffordshire ST13 8SJ. ((1629) 650394. Res. (c/o Mrs. I Carlile, Elton YH, Elton Old Hall, Main St, Elton, Matlock. ((1629) 650394.

Milton Keynes. *See* Bradwell Village.

Minehead. Alcombe Combe, Minehead, Somerset TA24 6EW. ((1643) 702595. FAX (1643) 703016.

Monmouth. Priory Street School, Priory St, Monmouth, Gwent NP5 3NX. ((1600) 715116.

Newport. Newport YH, Lower St Mary's St, Newport, Pewmbrokeshire, Dyfed SA42 0TS. ((1239) 820080. FAX (1239) 820080.

Newcastle upon Tyne. 107 Jesmond Rd, Newcastle upon Tyne NE2 1NJ. ((191) 281 2570. FAX (191) 281 8779.

Ninebanks. Orchard House, Mohope, Ninebanks, Hexham, Northumberland NE47 8DO. (/FAX (1434) 345288.

Norwich. 112 Turner Rd, Norwich NR2 4HB. ((1603) 627647. FAX (1603) 629075.

Once Brewed. Once Brewed, Military Rd, Bardon Mill, Hexham, Northumberland NE47 7AN. ((1434) 344360. FAX (1434) 344045.

Osmotherley. Cote Ghyll, Osmotherley, Northallerton, North Yorkshire DL6 3AH. ((1609) 883575. FAX (1609) 883715.

Oxford. 32 Jack Straw's Lane, Oxford OX3 0DW. ((1865) 62997. FAX (1865) 69402.

Patterdale. Goldrill House, Patterdale, Penrith, Cumbria CA11 0NW. ((17684) 82394. FAX (17684) 82034.

Pendennis Castle. Pendennis Castle, Falmouth, Cornwall TR11 4LP. ((1326) 311435. FAX (1326) 315473.

Pentlepoir. The Old School, Pentlepoir, Saundersfoot, Dyfed SA9 9BJ. ((1834) 812333.

Penycwm (Solva). Solva, Hafod Lodge, White House, Penycwm, Nr Solva, Haverfordwest, Dyfed SA61 6LA. (/FAX (1437) 720959.

Pen-y-Pass. Nant Gwynant, Caernarfon, Gwynedd LL55 4NY. ((1286) 870428. FAX (1286) 872434.

Penzance. Castle Horneck, Alverton, Penzance, Cornwall TR20 8TF. ((1736) 62666. FAX (1736) 62663.

Perranporth. Droskyn Point, Perranporth, Cornwall TR6 0DS. ((1872) 573812.

Plymouth. Belmont House, Belmont Place, Stoke, Plymouth PL3 4DW. ((1752) 562189. FAX (1752) 605360.

Poppit Sands. 'Sea View', Poppit, Cardigan, Dyfed SA43 3LP. ((1239) 612936.

Port Eynon. The Old Lifeboat House, Port Eynon, Swansea, West Glamorgan SA3 1NN. (/FAX (1792) 390706.

Portsmouth. Wymering Manor, Old Wymering Lane, Cosham, Portsmouth, Hampshire PO6 3NL. ((1705) 375661. FAX (1705) 214177.

Pwll Deri. Castell Mawr, Tref Asser, Goodwick, Dyfed SA64 0LR. ((1348) 891233.

Quantock Hills. Sevenacres, Holford, Bridgwater, Somerset TA5 1SQ. ((1278) 741224.

Ravenstor. Ravenstor, Millers Dale, Buxton, Derbyshire SK17 8SS. ((1298) 871826. FAX (1298) 871275.

Ridgeway. Ridgeway Centre, Courthill, Wantage, Oxfordshire OX12 9NE. ((12357) 60253. FAX (12357) 68865.

Rowen. Rhiw Farm, Rowen, Conwy, Gwynedd LL32 8YW. Res. (The Warden, Colwyn Bay YH).

Saffron Walden. 1 Myddlylton Place, Saffron Walden, Essex CB10 1BB. (/FAX (1799) 523117.

St Briavels Castle. The Castle, St Briavels, Lydney, Gloucestershire GL15 6RG. ((1594) 530272. FAX (1594) 530849.

St David's. Llaethdy, St David's, Haverfordwest, Dyfed SA62 6PR. ((1437) 720345. FAX (1437) 721831.

Salcombe. 'Overbecks', Sharpitor, Salcombe, Devon TQ8 8LW. (/FAX (154884) 2856.

Salisbury. Milford Hill House, Milford Hill, Salisbury, Wiltshire SP1 2QW. ((1722) 327572. FAX (1722) 330446.

Sandown. The Firs, Fitzroy St, Sandown, Isle of Wight PO36 8JH. ((1983) 402651. FAX (1983) 403565.

Scarborough. The White House, Burniston Rd, Scarborough, North Yorkshire YO13 0DA. ((1723) 361176. FAX (1723) 500054.

Sheringham. 1 Cremer's Drift, Sheringham, Norfolk NR26 8HX. (/FAX (1263) 823215.

Shining Cliff. Shining Cliff Woods, near Ambergate. ((1629) 650394. Res. (Mrs. I Carlile, Elton YH, Main St, Elton, Near Matlock, Derbyshire DE4 2BW).

Shrewsbury. The Woodlands, Abbey Foregate, Shrewsbury, Shropshire SY2 6LZ. ℂ (1743) 360179. FAX (1743) 357423. Res. Ironbridge Gorge YH. ℂ (1952) 433281.

Skiddaw House. Skiddaw House, YHA Bothy, Bassenthwaite, Cumbria. ℂ (16974) 78325.

Slaidburn. King's House, Slaidburn, Clitheroe, Lancashire BB7 3ER. ℂ (1200) 446656. Res. PO Box 11, Matlock, Derbyshire. ℂ (1629) 825850. FAX (1629) 824571.

Slimbridge. Shepherd's Patch, Slimbridge, Gloucestershire GL2 7BP. ℂ (1453) 890275. FAX (1453) 890625.

Snowdon Ranger. Snowdon Ranger, Rhyd Ddu, Caernarfon, Gwynedd LL54 7YS. ℂ (1286) 650391. FAX (1286) 650093.

Solva. *See* Penycwm.

Stainforth. Taitlands, Stainforth, Settle, North Yorkshire BD24 9PA. ℂ (1729) 823577. FAX (1729) 825404.

Steps Bridge. Steps Bridge, Dunsford, Exeter, Devon EX6 7EQ. ℂ/FAX (1647) 252435.

Stouthall. Stouthall Environmental Centre, Reynoldston, Gower, West Glamorgan SA3 1AP. ℂ (1792) 391086.

Stow-on-the-Wold. Stow-on-the-Wold, Cheltenham, Gloucestershire GL54 1AF. ℂ (1451) 830497. FAX (1451) 870102.

Stratford-upon-Avon. Hemmingford House, Alveston, Stratford-upon-Avon, Warwickshire CV37 7RG. ℂ (1789) 297093. FAX (1789) 205513.

Streatley-on-Thames. Hill House, Reading Rd, Streatley, Reading, Berks RG8 9JJ. ℂ (1491) 872278. FAX (1491) 873056.

Street. The Chalet, Ivythorn Hill, Street, Somerset BA16 0TZ. ℂ (1458) 442961. FAX (1458) 442738.

Swanage. Cluny, Cluny Crescent, Swanage, Dorset BH19 2BS. ℂ (1929) 422113. FAX (1929) 426327.

Tebay. The Old School, Tebay, Penrith, Cumbria CA10 3TP. ℂ (15396) 24286.

Telscombe. Bank Cottages, Telscombe, Lewes, East Sussex BN7 3HZ. ℂ (1273) 301357. Res. ℂ (1825) 890607.

Thirlmere. The Old School, Stanah Cross, Keswick, Cumbria CA12 4TQ. ℂ (17687) 73224.

Thixendale. The Village Hall, Thixendale, Malton, North Yorkshire YO17 9TG. ℂ (1377) 288238.

Thurlby. 16 High St, Thurlby, Bourne, Lincolnshire PE10 0EE. ℂ (1778) 425588.

Tintagel. Dunderhole Point, Tintagel, Cornwall PL34 0DW. ℂ (1840) 770334.

Totland Bay. Hurst Hill, Totland Bay, Isle of Wight PO39 0HD. ℂ (1983) 752165. FAX (1983) 756443.

Trevine. 11 Ffordd-yr-Afon, Trevine, Haverfordwest, Dyfed SA62 5AU. ℂ (1348) 831414.

Treyarnon Bay. Tregonnan, Treyarnon, Padstow, Cornwall PL28 8JR. ℂ (1841) 520322. FAX (1841) 520322.

Truleigh Hill. Tottington Barn, Truleigh Hill, Shoreham-by-Sea, West Sussex BN43 5FB. ℂ (1903) 813419. FAX (1903) 812016.

Tyncornel. Tyncornel, Llanddewi-Brefi, Tregaron, Dyfed SY25 6PH. Wales Regional Office ℂ (1222) 222122.

Ty'n-y-Caeau. Ty'n-y-Caeau, Groesffordd, Brecon, Powys LD3 7SW. ℂ (1874) 665270. FAX (1874) 665278.

Wastwater. Wasdale Hall, Wasdale, Seascale, Cumbria CA20 1ET. ℂ (19467) 26222. FAX (19467) 26056.

Welsh Bicknor. The Rectory, Welsh Bicknor, Nr Goodrich, Ross-on-Wye, Herefordshire HR9 6JJ. ℂ (1594) 860300. FAX (1594) 861276.

Whitby. East Cliff, Whitby, North Yorkshire YO22 4JT. ℂ/FAX (1947) 602878.

Wight, Isle of. *See* Sandown and Totland Bay.

Wilderhope Manor. The John Cadbury Memorial Hostel, Easthope, Much Wenlock, Shropshire TF13 6EG. ℂ (1694) 771363. FAX (1694) 771520.

Winchester. The City Mill, 1 Water Lane, Winchester, Hampshire SO23 0ER. ℂ (1962) 853723. FAX (1962) 855524.

Windermere. High Close, Bridge Lane, Troutbeck, Windermere, Cumbria LA23 1LA. ℂ (15394) 43543. FAX (15394) 47165.

Windsor. Edgeworth House, Mill Lane, Windsor, Berkshire SL4 5JE. ℂ (1753) 861710. FAX (1753) 832100.

Woody's Top. Woody's Top, Ruckland, near Louth, Lincs LN11 8RQ. ☎ (1722) 337494. FAX (1722) 414027.

Wooler. 30 Cheviot St, Wooler, Northumberland NE71 6LW. ☎ (1668) 281365. FAX (1668) 282368.

York. York International YH, Water End, Clifton, York. Yorkshire YO3 6LT. ☎ (1904) 653147. FAX (1904) 651230.

Youlgreave. Fountain Square, Youlgreave, Bakewell, Derbyshire DE4 1UR. ☎/FAX (1629) 636518.

Ystradfellte. Tai'r Heol, Ystradfellte, Aberdare, Mid Glamorgan CF44 9JF. ☎ (1639) 720301.

Ystumtuen. Glantuen, Ystumtuen, Aberystwyth, Dyfed SY23 3AE. ☎ (1970) 890693.

Supplementary Accommodations Outside the Assured Standards Scheme

Bala. Plas Rhiwaedog, Rhos-y-Gwaliau, Bala, Gwynedd LL23 7EU. ☎ (1678) 520215.

Colwyn Bay. Foxhill, Nant-y-Glyn, Colwyn Bay, Clwyd LL29 6AB. ☎ (1492) 530627. FAX (1492) 535518.

Rochester Capstone Farm, Capstone Rd, Chatham, Kent. ☎ (1722) 337494 South England Regional Office. FAX (1722) 414027.

Tanners Hatch. Tanners Hatch, Polesden Lacey, Dorking, Surrey RH5 6BE. ☎ (1372) 452528.

Wheathill Malthouse Farm, Wheathill Bridgnorth, Shropshire WV16 6QT. ☎ (1746) 787236.

Wheeldale. Wheeldale Lodge, Goathland, Whitby, North Yorkshire YO22 5AP. ☎ (1947) 896350.

SCOTLAND

Aberdeen. The King George VI Memorial Hostel, 8 Queen's Rd, Aberdeen AB1 6YT. ☎ (1224) 646988.

Achininver. Achininver, Achiltibuie, Ullapool, Ross-shire. ☎ (1854) 622254.

Achmelvich. Achmelvich, Recharn, Lairg, Sutherland IV27 4JB. ☎ (1571) 844480.

Ardgartan. Ardgartan, Arrochar, Dunbartonshire G83 7AR. ☎ (1301) 702362.

Armadale. Ardvasar, Sleat, Isle of Skye. ☎ (1471) 844260.

Aviemore. Aviemore, Inverness-shire, PH22 1PR. ☎ (1479) 810345.

Ayr. Craigweil Rd, Ayr KA7 2XJ. ☎ (1292) 262322.

Berneray. (North Uist Detached) Lochmaddy PA82.

Braemar. Corrie Feragie, Braemar, Aberdeenshire AB3 5YQ. ☎ (1339) 741659.

Broadford. Broadford, Isle of Skye IV49 9AA. ☎ (1471) 822442.

Broadmeadows. Old Broadmeadows, Yarrowford, Selkirk TD7 5LZ. ☎ (175076) 262.

Cannich. Cannich, Beauly, Inverness-shire IV4 7LT. ☎ (1456) 415244.

Carbisdale Castle. Carbisdale, Culrain, Ardgay, Ross-shire IV24 3DP. ☎ (1549) 421232.

Carn Dearg. Carn Dearg, Gairloch, Ross-shire IV21 2DJ. ☎ (1445) 712219.

Coldingham. The Mount, Coldingham, Eyemouth, Berwicks TD14 5PA. ☎ (1890) 771298.

Craig. Craig, Diabaig, Achnasheen, Ross-shire IV22 2HE.

Crianlarich. Crianlarich, Perthshire FK20 8QN. ☎ (1838) 300260.

Durness. Smoo, Durness, Lairg, Sutherland IV27 4QA. ☎ (1971) 511244.

Eday. London Bay, Eday, Orkney KW17 2AB. ☎ (18572) 622283.

EDINBURGH (2 Hostels):

Edinburgh—Bruntsfield. 7 Bruntsfield Crescent, Edinburgh EH10 4EZ. ☎ (131) 4472994.

Edinburgh—Eglinton. 18 Eglinton Crescent, Edinburgh EH1 25DD. ☎ (131) 3361120.

Falkland. Back Wynd, Falkland, Fife KY7 7BX. ☎ (1337) 857710.

Garenin. Garenin, Carloway, Isle of Lewis, PA86 9AL.

Glasgow. 7/8 Park Terrace, Glasgow G3 6BY. ☎ (141) 3323004.

Glen Affric. Allt Beithe, Glen Affric, Cannich, by Beauly, Inverness-shire IV4 7ND.

Glenbrittle. Glenbrittle, Isle of Skye IV47 8TA. ℂ (1478) 640278.

Glencoe. Glencoe, Ballachulish, Argyll PA39 4HX. ℂ (1855) 811219.

Glendevon. Glendevon, Dollar, Clackmannanshire FK14 7JY. ℂ (1259) 781206.

Glendoll. Glendoll, Clova, Kirriemuir, Angus DD8 4RD. ℂ (1575) 550236.

Glen Nevis. Glen Nevis, Fort William, Inverness-shire PH33 6ST. ℂ (1397) 702336.

Helmsdale. Helmsdale, Sutherland KW8 6JR. ℂ (1431) 821577.

Hoy. Hoy, Stromness, Orkney KW16 3NJ. ℂ (1856) 873535. Res. (County Youth Service, Education Office, Kirkwall, Orkney).

Inveraray. Inveraray, Argyllshire PA32 8XD. ℂ (1499) 2454.

Inverey. Inverey, by Braemar, Aberdeenshire AB3 5YB.

Inverness. 1 Old Edinburgh Rd, Inverness IV2 3HP. ℂ (1463) 231771.

Islay. Islay YH, Port Charlotte, Island of Islay PA48 7TX. ℂ (1496) 850385.

John o'Groats. Canisbay, Nr John o'Groats, Wick, Caithness KW1 4YH. ℂ (1955) 611424.

Kendoon. Kendoon, Dalry, Castle Douglas, Kircudbrightshire DG7 3UD.

Killin. Killin, Perthshire FK21 8TN. ℂ (1567) 820546.

Kirkwall. Old Scapa Rd, Kirkwall, Orkney KW15 1BB. ℂ (1856) 872243.

Kirk Yetholm. Kirk Yetholm, Kelso, Roxburghshire TD5 8PG. ℂ (1573) 420631.

Kyleakin. Kyleakin, Isle of Skye. ℂ (1599) 534585.

Lerwick. Lerwick YH, Islesburgh House, King Harald St, Lerwick, Shetland ZE1 0EQ. ℂ (1595) 692114.

Loch Lochy. South Laggan, Loch Lochy, Spean Bridge, Inverness-shire PH34 4EA. ℂ (1809) 501239.

Loch Lomond. Loch Lomond Arden, Alexandria, Dumbarronshire G83 8RB. ℂ (1389) 850226.

Lochmaddy. Ostram House, Lochmaddy, North Uist PA82 5AE. ℂ (1876) 500368.

Loch Morlich. Loch Morlich, Glenmore, Aviemore, Inverness-shire PH22 1QY. ℂ (1479) 861238.

Loch Ness. Loch Ness, Glenmoriston, Invernessshire IV3 6YD. ℂ (1320) 351274.

Loch Ossian. Loch Ossian, Corrour, Inverness-shire PH30 4AA. ℂ (1397) 732207.

Lochranza. Lochranza, Isle of Arran KA27 8HL. ℂ (1770) 830631.

Melrose. Priorwood, Melrose, Roxburghshire TD6 9EF. ℂ (1896) 822521.

Minnigaff. Minnigaff, Newton Stewart, Wigtownshire DG8 6PL. ℂ (1671) 402211.

New Lanark. New Lanark YH, Wee Row, Rosedale St, New Lanark ML11 9DJ. ℂ (1555) 666710.

Oban. Esplanade, Oban, Argyll PA34 5AF. ℂ (1631) 562025.

Papa Westray. Beltane House, Papa Westray, Orkney KW17 2BU. ℂ (1857) 644267.

Perth. 107 Glasgow Rd, Perth PH2 0NS. ℂ (1738) 623658.

Pitlochry. Braeknowe, Knockard Rd, Pitlochry PH16 5HJ. ℂ (1796) 472308.

Raasay. Creachan Cottage, Raasay, Kyle, Ross-shire IV40 8NT. ℂ (1478) 660240.

Rackwick. Rackwick Outdoor Centre, Hoy, Stromness, Orkney, KW16 3NJ. ℂ (1856) 873535.

Ratagan. Ratagan, Glenshiel, Kyle, Ross-shire IV40 8HT. ℂ (1599) 511243.

Rhenigidale, Rhenigidale, North Harris, PA85 3BD.

Rowardennan. Rowardennan by Drymen, Glasgow G63 0AR. ℂ (1360) 870259.

Snoot. Snoot, Roberton, Hawick, Roxburghshire TD9 7LY. ℂ (1450) 880259.

Stirling. St John Street, Stirling FK8 1DU. ℂ (1786) 473442.

Stockinish. Kyles, Stockinish, Tarbert, Harris PA85 3EN. ℂ (1859) 530373.

Strathpeffer. Strathpeffer, Ross-shire IV14 9BT. ℂ (1997) 421532.

Stromness. Stromness, Mainland, Orkney. ℂ (1856) 850589.

Tighnabruaich. Tighnabruaich, Argyll PA21 2BD. ℂ (1700) 811622.

Tobermory. Tobermory, Isle of Mull, Argyll PA75 6NU. ℂ (1688) 302481.

Tomintoul. Main St, Tomintoul, Ballindalloch, Banffshire AB3 9HA.

Tongue. Tongue, Lairg, Sutherland IV27 4XH. ℂ (1847) 611301.

Torridon. Torridon, Achnasheen, Ross-shire IV22 2EZ. ℂ (1445) 791284.

Uig. Uig, Isle of Skye IV51 9YD. ℂ (1470) 542211.

Ullapool. Shore St, Ullapool, Ross-shire IV26 2UJ. ℂ (1854) 612254.

Wanlockhead. Lotus Lodge, Wanlockhead, Biggar, Lanarkshire ML12 6UT. ℂ (1659) 74252.

Whiting Bay. Whiting Bay, Brodick, Isle of Arran KA27 8QW. ℂ (1770) 700339.

Supplementary Accommodation Outside the Assured Standards Scheme

Edinburgh-Central. Edinburgh Youth Hostel, 7 Roberston Close, Cowgate, Edinburgh EH1. Res. Edinburgh District Office, 161 Warrender Park Road, Edinburgh.

INDEX

M

N

O

P

Q

R

FROMMER'S COMPLETE TRAVEL GUIDES

(Comprehensive guides to sightseeing, dining, and accommodations, with selections in all price ranges from deluxe to budget)

Acapulco/Ixtapa/Taxco, 2nd Ed.
Alaska, 4th Ed.
Arizona '96
Australia, 4th Ed.
Austria, 6th Ed.
Bahamas '96
Belgium/Holland/Luxembourg, 4th Ed.
Bermuda '96
Budapest & the Best of Hungary, 1st Ed.
California '96
Canada, 9th Ed.
Caribbean '96
Carolinas/Georgia, 3rd Ed.
Colorado, 3rd Ed.
Costa Rica, 1st Ed.
Cruises '95-'96
Delaware/Maryland, 2nd Ed.
England '96
Florida '96
France '96
Germany '96
Greece, 1st Ed.
Honolulu/Waikiki/Oahu, 4th Ed.
Ireland, 1st Ed.
Italy '96
Jamaica/Barbados, 2nd Ed.
Japan, 3rd Ed.

Maui, 1st Ed.
Mexico '96
Montana/Wyoming, 1st Ed.
Nepal, 3rd Ed.
New England '96
New Mexico, 3rd Ed.
New York State '94-'95
Nova Scotia/New Brunswick/Prince Edward Island, 1st Ed.
Portugal, 14th Ed.
Prague & the Best of the Czech Republic, 1st Ed.
Puerto Rico '95-'96
Puerto Vallarta/Manzanillo/Guadalajara, 3rd Ed.
Scandinavia, 16th Ed.
Scotland, 3rd Ed.
South Pacific, 5th Ed.
Spain, 16th Ed.
Switzerland, 7th Ed.
Thailand, 2nd Ed.
U.S.A., 4th Ed.
Utah, 1st Ed.
Virgin Islands, 3rd Ed.
Virginia, 3rd Ed.
Washington/Oregon, 6th Ed.
Yucatan '95-'96

FROMMER'S FRUGAL TRAVELER'S GUIDES

(Dream vacations at down-to-earth prices)

Australia on $45 '95-'96
Berlin from $50, 3rd Ed.
Caribbean from $60, 1st Ed.
Costa Rica/Guatemala/Belize on $35, 3rd Ed.
Eastern Europe on $30, 5th Ed.
England from $50, 21st Ed.
Europe from $50 '96
Greece from $45, 6th Ed.
Hawaii from $60, 30th Ed.

Ireland from $45, 16th Ed.
Israel from $45, 16th Ed.
London from $60 '96
Mexico from $35 '96
New York on $70 '94-'95
New Zealand from $45, 6th Ed.
Paris from $65 '96
South America on $40, 16th Ed.
Washington, D.C. from $50 '96

FROMMER'S COMPLETE CITY GUIDES

(Comprehensive guides to sightseeing, dining, and accommodations in all price ranges)

Amsterdam, 8th Ed.
Athens, 10th Ed.
Atlanta & the Summer Olympic Games '96

Bangkok, 2nd Ed.
Berlin, 3rd Ed.
Boston '96

Chicago '96
Denver/Boulder/Colorado Springs, 2nd Ed.
Disney World/Orlando '96
Dublin, 2nd Ed.
Hong Kong, 4th Ed.
Las Vegas '96
London '96
Los Angeles '96
Madrid/Costa del Sol, 2nd Ed.
Mexico City, 1st Ed.
Miami '95-'96
Minneapolis/St. Paul, 4th Ed.
Montreal/Quebec City, 8th Ed.
Nashville/Memphis, 2nd Ed.
New Orleans '96
New York City '96

Paris '96
Philadelphia, 8th Ed.
Rome, 10th Ed.
St. Louis/Kansas City, 2nd Ed.
San Antonio/Austin, 1st Ed.
San Diego, 4th Ed.
San Francisco '96
Santa Fe/Taos/Albuquerque '96
Seattle/Portland, 4th Ed.
Sydney, 4th Ed.
Tampa/St. Petersburg, 3rd Ed.
Tokyo, 4th Ed.
Toronto, 3rd Ed.
Vancouver/Victoria, 3rd Ed.
Washington, D.C. '96

FROMMER'S FAMILY GUIDES

(Guides to family-friendly hotels, restaurants, activities, and attractions)

California with Kids
Los Angeles with Kids
New York City with Kids

San Francisco with Kids
Washington, D.C. with Kids

FROMMER'S WALKING TOURS

(Memorable strolls through colorful and historic neighborhoods, accompanied by detailed directions and maps)

Berlin
Chicago
England's Favorite Cities
London, 2nd Ed.
Montreal/Quebec City
New York, 2nd Ed.

Paris, 2nd Ed.
San Francisco, 2nd Ed.
Spain's Favorite Cities
Tokyo
Venice
Washington, D.C., 2nd Ed.

FROMMER'S AMERICA ON WHEELS

(Guides for travelers who are exploring the USA by car, featuring a brand-new rating system for accommodations and full-color road maps)

Arizona and New Mexico
California and Nevada

Florida
Mid-Atlantic

FROMMER'S SPECIAL-INTEREST TITLES

Arthur Frommer's Branson!
Arthur Frommer's New World of Travel, 5th Ed.
Frommer's America's 100 Best-Loved State Parks
Frommer's Caribbean Hideaways, 7th Ed.
Frommer's Complete Hostel Vacation Guide to England, Scotland & Wales

Frommer's National Park Guide, 29th Ed.
USA Sports Traveler's and TV Viewer's Golf Tournament Guide
USA Sports Minor League Baseball Book
USA Today Golf Atlas

FROMMER'S BEST BEACH VACATIONS

(The top places to sun, stroll, shop, stay, play, party, and swim, with each beach rated for beauty, swimming, sand, and amenities)

California
Carolinas/Georgia
Florida
Hawaii

Mid-Atlantic from New York to
Washington, D.C.
New England

FROMMER'S BED & BREAKFAST GUIDES

(Selective guides with four-color photos and full description of the best inns in each region)

California
Caribbean
Great American Cities
Hawaii
Mid-Atlantic

New England
Pacific Northwest
Rockies
Southeast States
Southwest

FROMMER'S IRREVERENT GUIDES

(Wickedly honest guides for sophisticated travelers and those who want to be)

Amsterdam
Chicago
London

Manhattan
New Orleans
San Francisco

FROMMER'S DRIVING TOURS

(Four-color photos and detailed maps outlining spectacular scenic driving routes)

Australia
Austria
Britain
Florida
France
Germany
Ireland

Italy
Scandinavia
Scotland
Spain
Switzerland
U.S.A.

FROMMER'S BORN TO SHOP

(The ultimate travel guides for discriminating shoppers from cut-rate to couture)

Great Britain
Hong Kong

London
New York

FROMMER'S FOOD LOVER'S COMPANIONS

(Lavishly illustrated guides to regional specialties, restaurants, gourmet shops, markets, local wines, and more)

France
Italy